AMERICA'S REGIONALIZED GARDEN BOOK

Horticultural Associates

Executive Producer:	Richard M. Ray
Contributing Authors:	Claire Barrett, John Ford, Alvin Horton, Michael MacCaskey, Robert L. Ticknor, Lance Walheim
Consultants:	Dodge Ely, Fred Galle, Ralph Miller, Carl A. Totemeier, Richard Turner, Joseph A. Witt
Photography:	Michael Landis
Art Director:	Richard Baker
Book Design:	Judith Hemmerich Hughes
Associate Editor:	Lance Walheim
Research Editor:	Randy Peterson
Copy Editors:	Gregory H. Boucher, Miriam Boucher
Production Editor:	Kathleen Parker
Book Production:	Lingke Moeis
Illustrations:	Charles Hoeppner, Roy Jones
Typography:	Linda Encinas
Additional Photography:	William Aplin, Pamela Harper, Susan A. Roth
Cover Photo:	William Aplin.

Acknowledgements: Gary Blum, Ireland Landscaping Inc., East Norwich, NY; Mrs. Alice Burlingame, Birmingham, MI; Harrison Chandler, Arcadia, CA; Mr. & Mrs. Robert Cheesewright, Pasadena, CA; Francis Ching, Los Angeles State and County Arboretum, Arcadia, CA; Tom Courtright, Orchard Nursery, LaFayette, CA; Dr. William and Christine Cress, Troy, MI; Mr. R. Roy Forster, Van Dusen Botanical Display Garden, Vancouver, B.C., Canada; Ann Gammond, The Atlanta Botanical Garden, Atlanta, GA; Jim Gibbons, Horticulturist, San Diego Wild Animal Park, Escondido, CA; Goldberg & Rodler, Huntington, NY; Alfred H. Goldner, Pontiac, MI; Green Bros. Landscaping, Inc., Smyra, GA; Mr. & Mrs. Howard Havens, Horticulturists, Ventura, CA; Mrs. Edith Henderson, Landscape Architect, Atlanta, GA; Eric Johnson, Landscape Architect, Palm Springs, CA; Gordon E. Jones, Planting Fields Arboretum, Oyster Bay, NY; Theodore Kalil, Horticulturist, Santa Barbara, CA; Chuck Kline, Horticulturist, Sea World, San Diego, CA; Bill Knerr and Robert Ward, Zoological Society of San Diego, San Diego, CA; Donn Lobb, New Orleans Parkway and Park Commission, New Orleans, LA; Long Vue Gardens, New Orleans, LA; Gary Martin, Landscape Innovations Inc., Melville, NY; Neel's Nursery, Palm Springs and Indio, CA; William Robinson, Japanese Garden Society of Oregon, Portland, OR; George Harman Scott, Horticulturist, Arcadia, CA; Nancy Davidson Short, Bellevue, WA; James A. Slezinski, Pontiac, MI; William M. Tomlinson, Tomlinson Select Nurseries, Brea, CA; Van Winden's Nursery, Napa, CA; Dave Whiting, Whitings Nursery, St. Helena, CA; Wildewood Gardens, Napa, CA

Contents

Top-Rated Plants for American Gardens

Visually interesting landscapes are created by combining plants with different textures, forms, and colors, in a naturalistic manner.

America's gardens and home landscapes are as varied as her geography and her people. Decorative groupings of drought-tolerant plants ornament the yards of southwestern gardens, and lush green shrubs and fragrant-flowered vines create stately settings for old southern homes. In New England, tall maples and oaks shade colonial-styled houses in summer and provide a burst of festive autumn colors each year. Flower gardens everywhere delight gardeners with cheerful colors from spring through fall.

So in love with their gardens are Americans, that city rooftops sprout full-grown trees in pots, and apartment balconies everywhere are bedecked with potted shrubs and vines to provide softening greenery and privacy. Planters and window boxes of gay annuals are tucked wherever there's a bit of space.

As different as gardens can be, the basic choices gardeners have to make are the same. Which plants will thrive in their climate; which plants suit their landscaping needs; which plants are most attractive; and how should they be cared for, are questions facing gardeners everywhere.

This book is designed to provide answers to all the home gardener's landscaping questions.

INSIDE THIS BOOK

Climate and regional plant choices: Selecting plants that grow well in your region is of primary importance to successful gardening. The following chapter discusses climate and has two very useful maps. The *new* USDA map shows the 11 cold hardiness regions and the other shows the 10 climate regions of North America. You'll also find information on planting dates for your region. A climate chart lists the regional adaptation of all the top-rated plants.

Top-Rated: Professional gardeners, horticulturists, and nurserymen throughout the United States and Canada selected the landscape plants described in this book. They judged these plants to be top-rated. Their choices are dependable, attractive, easy-to-grow, and readily available. In short, top-rated plants are the best trees, shrubs, vines, ground covers, and flowers for most home gardeners.

Many top-rated plants, such as little-leaf linden, English holly, and boxwood, are long-time garden favorites. Gardeners generations ago planted and raised plants identical to those we grow today. Other top-rated plants, however, are new arrivals to the garden. They were created by plant breeders and hybridizers for some special attributes.

The encyclopedia sections of this book describes all of the top-rated plants in detail. Their cultural needs are explained and landscaping suggestions are given with each entry.

Botanical names: All plants have Latin scientific, or botanical, names that are used throughout the world. Because these names are universal and because common names vary from person to person and from region to region, scientific names are used in this book. If you call a plant by its scientific name, there's no mistaking which plant you mean. The plant encyclopedia section is alphabetized by Latin name and so are the charts throughout the book.

To help you locate a plant that you know only by common name, look up the common name in the index. There common names are matched with their proper Latin name.

Landscaping: You'll find the chapter on landscaping gives you abundant practical information. The basic principles of landscaping, how to plant to achieve special effects, and ways to solve problems with plants, are all covered. Charts listing the best plants for many landscape uses make choosing the right plants for each situation easy.

Planting and care: Once you've selected the best plants for your landscape, protect your investment by caring for them properly. Correctly planted, pruned, watered, and fertilized, your top-rated landscape plants will serve you for years to come. The last chapter provides you with basic care and planting information as well as information on insects and diseases.

USING THIS BOOK

There are many ways you can use this book—simply leafing through it and selecting plants by their pictures is one way—but if you use all the sections together when choosing plants, the book becomes an efficient regional garden tool.

If you are looking for a particular plant to fill a specific landscape need, here's how to best use the book. For instance, if you live on Long Island in New York state and are looking for a medium-sized flowering tree with decorative fruits to shade a patio, here's what you might do.

Unless you already know it, determine which cold hardiness zone you live in by using the map on pages 6 and 7 in the climate chapter. Once you know your zone, (zone 7 in this case) you can turn immediately to the landscape use charts in Chapter

2, pages 38 to 57. Look over the lists of patio trees and spring-flowering trees, as well as the list of trees with berries, making note of the ones that appear on all these charts and that are recommended for Zone 7. You'll find the lists suggest several possibilities including crab apple, *Malus sp.,* hawthorn, *Crataegus sp.,* and dogwood, *Cornus sp.*

You'll next want to be sure these plants are also suited to your climate. Make note of the plant names on a scratch pad and look them each up in the regional adaptation charts on pages 8 to 21. You'll learn that all of these plants are recommended for the Northeast region.

Now it's time to look up the recommended flowering trees in the encyclopedia. Read the descriptions of each tree and study the pictures. Make note of the special attractions each one offers and any drawbacks of the plant.

After reading the descriptions, you'll know that if you decide on a crab apple, you'd best select one with small fruit or you'll have a cleanup problem on the patio. And a thornless variety of hawthorn is best in an area that is heavily used. You can choose the widely grown flowering dogwood, which blooms in early spring, or the Japanese dogwood, which blooms later in spring than most other flowering trees.

Selecting the best plants for your garden is easily accomplished when you use all the information this book has to offer. The climate maps, regional adaptation charts, landscape use charts, and the encyclopedia work together to help you choose suitable trees, shrubs, vines, flowers, and ground covers. And the photographs and landscape chapter will give you ideas about using the plants you select in attractive and effective ways.

Mock orange (*Philadelphus* sp.)

Clematis (*Clematis* sp.)

'Rosebud' (Gable Hybrid)

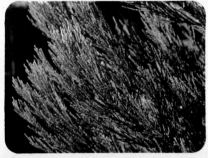
Giant sequoia (*Sequoiadendron* sp.)

Climate Adaptation of Top-Rated Plants

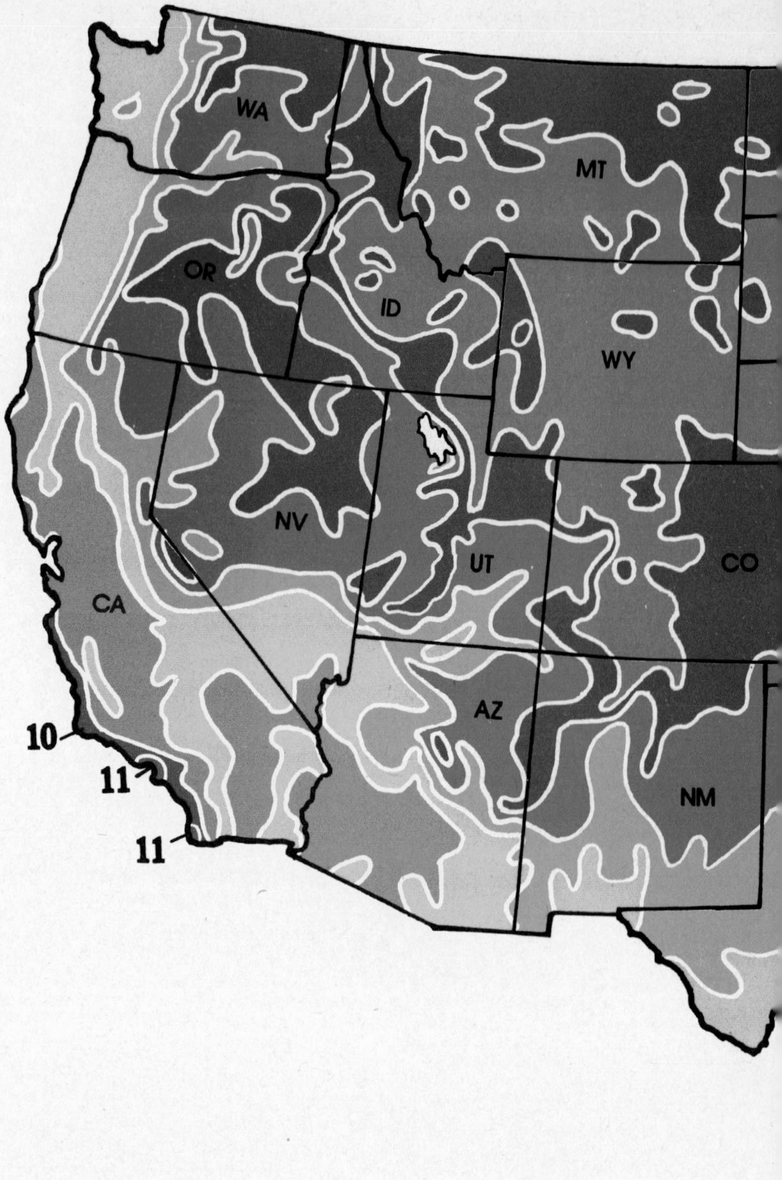

ABOUT THE NEW MAP

Henry M. Cathey
Director, U.S. National Arboretum

This map supersedes U.S. Department of Agriculture, "Plant Hardiness Map," which was published in 1960 and revised in 1965. It shows in detail the lowest temperatures that can be expected each year in the United States. These temperatures are referred to as "average annual minimum temperatures" and are based on the lowest temperatures recorded for each of the years 1974 to 1986 in the United States. The map shows 10 different zones, each of which represents an area of winter hardiness for the plants of our natural landscape. It also introduces zone 11 to represent areas that have average annual minimum temperatures above 40°F (4.4°C) and that are therefore essentially frost free.

The plant hardiness map shows the average low temperatures throughout the United States and Southern Canada. It divides North America into 11 zones with the average minimum temperature of each zone differing by 10 degrees Fahrenheit. All plants in this book are identified in the following charts and in the encyclopedia sections by the zones where they are considered to be top-rated.

As every gardener learns, cold hardiness is only one factor of a plant's adaptation. A plant's ability to do well in a certain location depends on unique combinations of soil type, wind, rainfall, length and time of cold, humidity, summer temperatures, and temperatures in relation to humidity. For example, American and European grape varieties are prone to disease problems in the southern United States because of high humidity. However, the native muscadine grape is widely used in southern states because it thrives in hot humid conditions.

Many plants require a certain amount of winter cold to flower

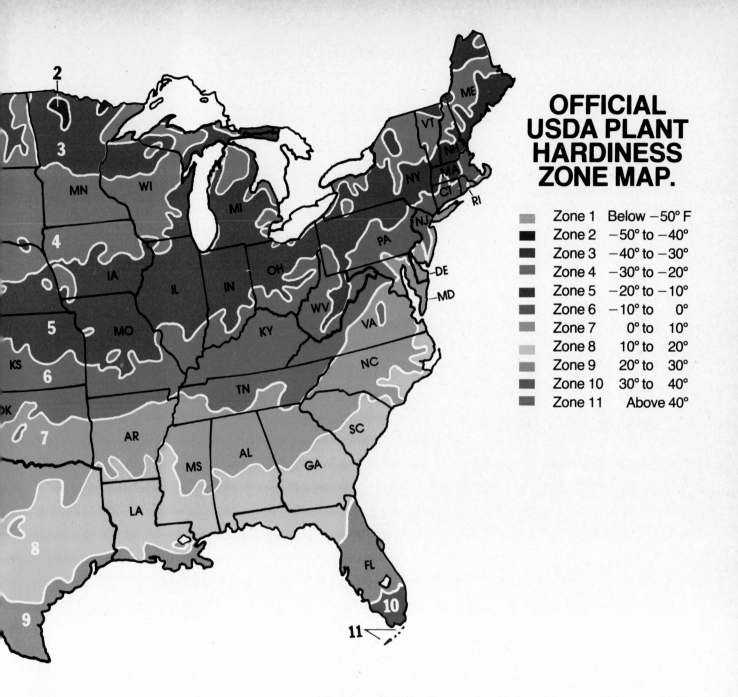

OFFICIAL USDA PLANT HARDINESS ZONE MAP.

	Zone 1	Below −50° F
	Zone 2	−50° to −40°
	Zone 3	−40° to −30°
	Zone 4	−30° to −20°
	Zone 5	−20° to −10°
	Zone 6	−10° to 0°
	Zone 7	0° to 10°
	Zone 8	10° to 20°
	Zone 9	20° to 30°
	Zone 10	30° to 40°
	Zone 11	Above 40°

and begin spring growth. Oriental flowering cherry trees bloom well in Washington D.C., the Northwest, and Northern California, but do not blossom as prolifically in Southern California or along the Gulf Coast where the winters are too warm to provide a sufficient cold period.

Note that in listing zone numbers, a plant's adaptation to warm climates as well as to cold climates is indicated. For instance, common lilac, *Syringa vulgaris*, is listed in Zones 3-8, while lauristinus, *Viburnum tinus*, is listed for Zones 7-10.

The USDA hardiness zone map does not take other climate factors into consideration. The map and charts on the following pages break down the United States and Canada into 10 climate regions. For a plant to be adapted to your area, it should be recommended for both your USDA hardiness zone and your climate region.

Bailey acacia (*Acacia baileyana*), for example, is recommended for USDA hardiness Zone 9, a zone including portions of the western and southern United States. Climates in these two portions of Zone

9 are remarkably different. Bailey acacia does well only in warm dry areas of the West.

USDA Zones 8 and 10 are particularly complex in the western United States. Many plants with a warm limit of Zone 8 in the East can also be grown in Zones 9 and 10 in the West. In these cases, it is best to follow regional recommendations given in the following charts.

Note: Plants adapted to Zone 10 are also adapted to *new* Zone 11. Plants shown adapted to Zone 11 only, are recommended specifically for Zone 11.

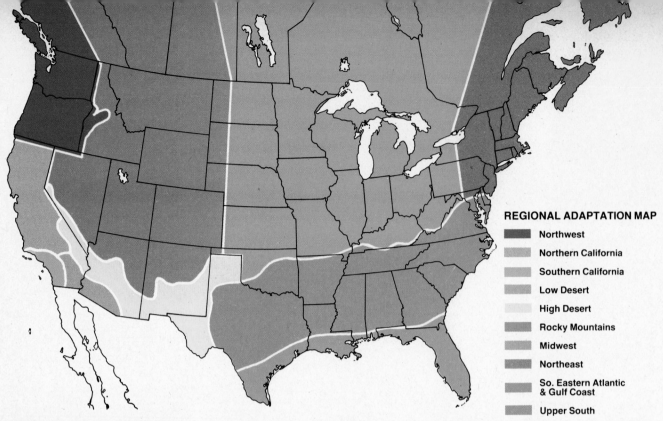

REGIONAL ADAPTATION MAP
- Northwest
- Northern California
- Southern California
- Low Desert
- High Desert
- Rocky Mountains
- Midwest
- Northeast
- So. Eastern Atlantic & Gulf Coast
- Upper South

SHRUBS and TREES

Note: Plants adapted to Zone 10 are also adapted to *new* Zone 11. Plants shown adapted to Zone 11 only, are recommended specifically for Zone 11.

PLANT NAME	ZONES	NORTHWEST	NORTHERN CALIFORNIA	SOUTHERN CALIFORNIA	LOW DESERT	HIGH DESERT	ROCKY MOUNTAINS	MIDWEST	NORTHEAST	SO. EASTERN ATLANTIC & GULF COAST	UPPER SOUTH
Abelia x grandiflora	6-10	■	■	■	■	■		■	■	■	■
Abies sp.	5-8	■	■				■	■	■		■
Acacia baileyana	9		■	■	■						
Acacia longifolia	7-10		■	■							
Acer campestre	5-8	■	■				■	■	■		■
Acer ginnala	3-8	■	■				■	■	■		■
Acer negundo	3-9	■	■	■	■	■	■	■	■	■	■
Acer palmatum	6-8	■	■	■			■	■	■		■
Acer platanoides	3-7	■	■				■	■	■		■
Acer rubrum	4-9	■	■				■	■	■		■
Acer saccharinum	4-9	■	■	■			■	■	■	■	■
Acer saccharum	4-8	■	■				■	■	■		■
Aesculus x carnea	5-9	■	■				■	■	■		■
Aesculus hippocastanum	4-8	■	■				■	■	■		■
Albizia julibrissin	7-10	■	■	■	■	■				■	■
Alnus cordata	6-10		■	■							
Alnus glutinosa	3-10	■	■			■		■	■		
Alnus rhombifolia	8-10	■	■	■							
Amelanchier sp.	4-8	■	■				■	■	■	■	■
Arbutus menziesii	6-9	■	■								
Arbutus unedo	7-10	■	■	■	■					■	■
Aucuba japonica	7-10	■	■	■	■	■				■	■
Azalea (See Rhododendron)											
Baccharis pilularis	8-10		■	■		■					
Bambusa	5-10	■	■	■	■	■	■	■	■	■	■

PLANT NAME	ZONES	NORTHWEST	NORTHERN CALIFORNIA	SOUTHERN CALIFORNIA	LOW DESERT	HIGH DESERT	ROCKY MOUNTAINS	MIDWEST	NORTHEAST	SO. EASTERN ATLANTIC & GULF COAST	UPPER SOUTH
Bauhinia variegata	9-10		■	■						■	
Berberis x chenaultii	6-9	■	■				■	■	■		■
Berberis darwinii	8-10	■	■							■	■
Berberis x gladwynensis 'William Penn'	5-8	■	■				■	■	■		■
Berberis julianae	6-8	■	■				■	■	■		■
Berberis x mentorensis	5-8	■	■				■	■	■		■
Berberis thunbergii	4-9	■	■				■	■	■		■
Berberis verruculosa	5-9	■	■				■	■	■		■
Betula nigra	5-9	■	■	■	■	■	■	■	■	■	■
Betula papyrifera	2-5						■	■	■		
Betula pendula	2-9	■	■	■		■	■	■	■		■
Brunfelsia pauciflora 'Floribunda'	8-10		■	■						■	
Buddleia davidii	5-10	■	■	■			■	■	■	■	■
Buxus sp.	5-10	■	■				■	■	■	■	■
Callistemon citrinus	8-10		■	■	■					■	■
Callistemon viminalis	8-10		■	■						■	■
Calluna vulgaris	4-7	■	■					■	■		
Calocedrus decurrens	6-10	■	■	■		■	■				■
Camellia sp.	7-10	■	■	■						■	■
Caragana arborescens	2-7	■	■	■	■	■	■	■	■		■
Carissa grandiflora	10			■	■					■	
Carpinus betulus	4-9	■	■					■	■	■	■
Carya illinoinsis	7-9	■	■	■	■	■				■	■
Cassia excelsa	10			■							
Catalpa sp.	5-10	■	■	■	■	■	■	■	■	■	■
Ceanothus sp.	8-10	■	■	■							
Cedrus atlantica	6-10	■	■	■		■			■	■	■
Cedrus deodara	7-10	■	■	■		■			■	■	■
Cedrus libani	7-10	■	■	■	■	■			■	■	■
Celtis australis	7-9		■	■	■				■	■	■
Celtis laevigata	5-9							■		■	■
Celtis occidentalis	4-8	■	■	■	■	■	■	■	■		■
Ceratonia siliqua	9-10		■	■						■	
Cercidiphyllum japonicum	4-9	■	■				■	■	■		■
Cercidium sp.	8-10			■	■	■					
Cercis canadensis	4-7	■	■				■	■	■		■
Cercis occidentalis	7-10	■	■	■	■	■					
Chaenomeles sp.	5-9	■	■		■	■	■	■	■		■
Chamaecyparis lawsoniana	6-9	■	■					■	■		■
Chamaecyparis obtusa	5-9	■	■					■	■		■
Chamaecyparis pisifera	5-9	■	■					■	■		■
Chamaecyparis thyoides 'Andelyensis'	5-9	■	■					■	■		■
Chimonanthus praecox	7-9	■	■								■
Chionanthus virginicus	5-9	■	■					■	■	■	■

Evergreen azaleas (*Rhododendron sp.*)

Mock orange (*Philadelphus* sp.)

Shrubs and Trees continued

PLANT NAME	ZONES	NORTHWEST	NORTHERN CALIFORNIA	SOUTHERN CALIFORNIA	LOW DESERT	HIGH DESERT	ROCKY MOUNTAINS	MIDWEST	NORTHEAST	SO. EASTERN ATLANTIC & GULF COAST	UPPER SOUTH
Choisya ternata	8-10	■	■	■	■					■	■
Chorisia speciosa	9-10		■	■							
Cinnamomum camphora	9-10		■	■	■					■	
Cistus x purpureus	8-10	■	■	■	■						
Citrus	9-10		■	■	■					■	
Cladrastis lutea	4-9	■	■				■	■	■		■
Cleyera japonica	8-10	■	■	■						■	■
Cocculus lauriflorius	8-10		■	■	■						
Convolvulus cneorum	7-10		■	■	■					■	■
Coprosma repens	9-10		■	■							
Cornus alba	2-8	■	■	■			■	■	■		■
Cornus florida	5-9	■	■	■				■	■	■	■
Cornus kousa	6-9	■	■	■				■	■		
Cornus mas	4-8	■					■	■	■		■
Cornus sericea	2-9	■	■	■			■	■	■		■
Cortaderia selloana	5-10	■	■	■	■	■		■	■	■	■
Cotinus coggygria	5-8	■	■	■	■		■	■	■	■	■
Cotoneaster adpressus praecox	5-10	■	■	■	■	■	■	■	■	■	■
Cotoneaster apiculatus	5-10	■	■	■	■	■	■	■	■	■	■
Cotoneaster buxifolius	7-10	■	■	■	■		■	■	■	■	■
Cotoneaster congestus	6-10	■	■	■	■		■	■	■	■	■
Cotoneaster dammeri	5-10	■	■	■	■		■	■	■	■	■
Cotoneaster divaricatus	5-10	■	■	■	■		■	■	■	■	■
Cotoneaster franchetii	5-9	■	■		■		■	■	■	■	■
Cotoneaster horizontalis	5-10	■	■	■			■	■	■	■	■
Cotoneaster lacteus	7-10	■	■	■	■					■	■
Cotoneaster salicifolius	6-10	■	■	■	■	■				■	■
Crataegus sp.	3-9	■	■			■	■	■	■	■	■
x Cupressocyparis leylandii	5-10	■	■	■	■			■	■	■	■
Cupressus arizonica	6-10	■	■	■	■	■				■	
Cupressus macrocarpa	7-10		■	■							
Cupressus sempervirens	7-10	■	■	■	■	■				■	■
Cytisus x praecox	6-9	■	■	■	■			■	■		■
Cytisus racemosus	7-10	■	■	■	■			■	■		■

PLANT NAME	ZONES	NORTHWEST	NORTHERN CALIFORNIA	SOUTHERN CALIFORNIA	LOW DESERT	HIGH DESERT	ROCKY MOUNTAINS	MIDWEST	NORTHEAST	SO. EASTERN ATLANTIC & GULF COAST	UPPER SOUTH
Cytisus scoparius	6-9	■	■	■				■	■		■
Daphne cneorum	5-9	■	■					■	■		■
Daphne odora	8-10	■	■	■						■	■
Deutzia gracilis	5-8	■	■				■	■	■		■
Dodonaea viscosa	8-10		■	■	■						
Elaeagnus angustifolia	2-10	■	■	■	■	■	■	■	■	■	■
Elaeagnus pungens	7-10	■	■	■	■					■	■
Enkianthus campanulatus	5-9	■	■					■	■		■
Erica sp.	4-8	■	■					■	■		■
Eriobotrya japonica	8-10	■	■	■	■	■				■	■
Erythrina caffra	9-10			■						■	
Erythrina coralloides	9-10			■	■					■	
Erythrina crista-galli	9-10		■	■						■	
Erythrina humeana	9-10			■	■					■	
Escallonia x exoniensis	7-10	■	■	■							
Eucalyptus sp.	7-10	■	■	■	■	■				■	
Eugenia uniflora	9-10			■						■	
Euonymus alata	3-9	■	■				■	■	■		■
Euonymus fortunei	4-8	■	■		■	■		■	■		■
Euonymus japonica	7-9	■	■		■	■				■	■
Euonymus kiautschovica 'Manhattan'	6-9	■	■	■	■	■		■	■	■	■
Fagus sylvatica	5-9	■	■	■			■	■	■		
Fatsia japonica	8-10		■	■						■	■
Feijoa sellowiana	8-10		■	■	■					■	■
Ficus benjamina	11			■	■					■	
Ficus elastica	9-10			■						■	
Ficus lyrata	11			■						■	
Ficus retusa	9-10		■	■						■	
Ficus rubiginosa	9-10			■						■	
Forsythia x intermedia	5-9	■	■			■	■	■	■		■
Franklinia alatamaha	6-8	■						■	■		■
Fraxinus americana	4-9	■	■			■	■	■	■	■	
Fraxinus excelsior 'Hessei'	4-9	■	■	■	■		■	■	■		■
Fraxinus holotricha 'Moraine'	5-8	■	■	■	■			■	■		■
Fraxinus latifolia	7-10	■	■	■	■	■					
Fraxinus ornus	6-8	■	■					■	■		■
Fraxinus oxycarpa	5-9	■	■	■				■	■		■
Fraxinus pennsylvanica	3-9	■					■	■	■		■
Fraxinus quadrangulata	3-9	■					■	■	■		■
Fraxinus uhdei	9-10		■	■	■						
Fraxinus velutina	6-10		■	■	■	■					
Fuchsia x hybrida	9-10	■	■	■						■	
Fuchsia magellanica	6-10	■	■	■			■	■	■	■	■
Gardenia jasminoides	8-10		■	■	■					■	■
Ginkgo biloba	4-9	■	■	■			■	■	■		■
Gleditsia triacanthos inermis	4-10	■	■	■	■	■	■	■	■		■

Shrubs and Trees continued

PLANT NAME	ZONES	NORTHWEST	NORTHERN CALIFORNIA	SOUTHERN CALIFORNIA	LOW DESERT	HIGH DESERT	ROCKY MOUNTAINS	MIDWEST	NORTHEAST	SO. EASTERN ATLANTIC & GULF COAST	UPPER SOUTH
Grevillea sp.	8-10		■	■	■						
Gymnocladus dioica	5-8	■	■	■	■	■	■	■	■		■
Halesia carolina	5-8	■	■					■	■		■
Hamamelis x intermedia	6-8	■	■					■	■		■
Hebe sp.	9-10		■	■						■	
Hibiscus rosa-sinensis	9-10		■	■	■					■	
Hibiscus syriacus	5-10	■	■			■	■	■	■	■	■
Hydrangea arborescens	5-9	■	■		■	■	■	■	■	■	■
Hydrangea macrophylla	6-10	■	■	■	■	■	■	■	■	■	■
Hydrangea paniculata	5-9	■	■			■	■	■	■	■	■
Hydrangea quercifolia	6-9	■	■			■	■	■	■	■	■
Hymenosporum flavum	9-10		■	■							
Hypericum sp.	5-10	■	■	■	■	■	■	■	■	■	■
Ilex x altaclarensis 'Wilsonii'	6-10	■	■	■	■	■				■	■
Ilex aquifolium	6-9	■	■	■					■	■	■
Ilex x aquipernyi	6-9	■	■	■					■	■	■
Ilex cornuta	6-10	■	■	■			■	■	■	■	■
Ilex crenata	5-10	■	■	■			■	■	■	■	■
Ilex glabra	3-8	■	■				■	■	■	■	■
Ilex x meserveae	4-8	■	■	■	■	■		■	■	■	■
Ilex opaca	6-9	■	■	■					■	■	■
Ilex verticillata	3-7	■	■				■	■	■		■
Ilex vomitoria	7-10		■	■	■					■	■
Jacaranda mimosifolia	9-10		■	■						■	
Juniperus sp.	2-10	■	■	■	■	■	■	■	■	■	■
Koelreuteria bipinnata	5-9		■	■	■	■	■	■	■	■	■
Koelreuteria paniculata	5-9	■	■	■	■	■	■	■	■	■	■
Kolkwitzia amabilis	5-8	■	■	■		■	■	■	■		■
Laburnum x watereri 'Vossii'	6-9	■	■	■			■	■	■		■
Lagerstroemia indica	7-9	■	■	■	■	■			■	■	■
Lantana sp.	9-10		■	■	■					■	■
Larix decidua	3-7	■	■				■	■	■		
Larix kaempferi	5-8	■	■				■	■	■		
Laurus nobilis	8-10	■	■	■	■					■	■
Leptospermum scoparium	9-10		■	■						■	
Leucothoe axillaris	6-9	■	■					■	■		■
Leucothoe fontanesiana	5-8	■	■					■	■		■
Ligustrum x ibolium 'Variegata'	5-10	■	■	■	■	■	■	■	■	■	■
Ligustrum japonicum	7-10	■	■	■	■	■			■	■	■
Ligustrum lucidum	8-9	■	■	■	■	■				■	■
Ligustrum ovalifolium	7-10	■	■	■	■	■				■	■
Ligustrum sinense 'Variegatum'	8-10									■	■
Ligustrum x vicaryi	4-10	■	■	■	■	■	■	■	■	■	■
Liquidambar styraciflua	5-9	■	■	■			■	■	■	■	■
Liriodendron tulipifera	5-9	■	■	■			■	■	■	■	■
Magnolia grandiflora	7-10	■	■	■		■				■	■
Magnolia x loebneri 'Merrill'	5-10	■	■	■				■	■		■
Magnolia quinquepeta 'Nigra'	5-10	■	■	■				■	■	■	■

PLANT NAME	ZONES	NORTHWEST	NORTHERN CALIFORNIA	SOUTHERN CALIFORNIA	LOW DESERT	HIGH DESERT	ROCKY MOUNTAINS	MIDWEST	NORTHEAST	SO. EASTERN ATLANTIC & GULF COAST	UPPER SOUTH
Magnolia x soulangiana	5-10	■	■	■				■	■	■	■
Magnolia stellata	5-10	■	■	■				■	■	■	■
Magnolia virginiana	6-10	■	■						■	■	■
Mahonia aquifolium	5-9	■	■	■	■	■	■	■	■	■	■
Mahonia bealei	5-10	■	■	■	■	■	■	■	■	■	■
Mahonia lomariifolia	8-10	■	■	■						■	■
Malus sp.	2-8	■	■	■		■	■	■			
Maytenus boaria	8-10		■	■						■	■
Melaleuca sp.	9-10		■	■						■	■
Melia azedarach	8-10		■	■	■	■					■
Metasequoia glyptostroboides	4-10	■	■	■			■	■	■	■	■
Morus alba	5-9	■	■	■	■	■	■	■	■	■	■
Murraya paniculata	9-11			■							
Myoporum laetum 'Carsonii'	8-10		■	■							
Myrica pensylvanica	3-10	■					■	■	■	■	■
Myrtus communis	9-10		■	■	■	■					
Nandina domestica	6-10	■	■	■	■	■			■	■	■
Nerium oleander	8-10		■	■	■	■				■	■
Nyssa sylvatica	5-9	■	■	■		■		■	■	■	■
Olea europaea	9-10		■	■	■						
Osmanthus heterophyllus	7-10	■	■	■					■	■	■
Ostrya virginiana	4-9	■						■	■	■	■
Oxydendrum arboreum	6-9	■	■					■	■	■	■
Palmae	8-10		■	■	■	■				■	■
Parkinsonia aculeata	8-10		■	■	■					■	■
Phellodendron amurense	4-8	■	■			■	■	■	■		■
Philadelphus coronarius	5-8	■	■		■	■	■	■	■		
Philadelphus x lemoinei	5-8	■	■		■	■	■	■	■		
Philadelphus x virginalis	4-8	■	■		■	■	■	■	■		
Photinia x fraseri	7-10	■	■	■	■	■				■	■
Picea abies	2-8	■	■				■	■	■		■
Picea glauca	2-5	■					■	■	■		
Picea omorika	5-8	■	■				■	■	■		■
Picea pungens	2-8	■	■				■	■	■		■
Pieris sp.	5-9	■	■				■	■	■		■
Pinus aristata	5-6	■	■			■	■	■	■		
Pinus bungeana	5-9	■	■		■	■	■	■	■		■
Pinus canariensis	9-10	■	■	■	■	■				■	
Pinus cembra	3-8	■	■				■	■	■		■
Pinus contorta	7-10	■	■						■	■	■
Pinus densiflora	5-9	■	■				■	■		■	■
Pinus halepensis	7-10	■	■	■	■	■			■	■	■
Pinus mugo	2-8	■	■	■	■	■	■	■	■	■	■
Pinus nigra	3-8	■	■	■	■	■	■	■	■		■
Pinus parviflora	5-8	■	■	■			■	■	■		■
Pinus patula	9-10	■	■	■						■	■
Pinus pinaster	7-10	■	■	■						■	■
Pinus pinea	7-10	■	■	■	■	■				■	■

Star magnolia (Magnolia stellata)

Weeping willow (Salix babylonica)

Shrubs and Trees continued

PLANT NAME	ZONES	NORTHWEST	NORTHERN CALIFORNIA	SOUTHERN CALIFORNIA	LOW DESERT	HIGH DESERT	ROCKY MOUNTAINS	MIDWEST	NORTHEAST	SO. EASTERN ATLANTIC & GULF COAST	UPPER SOUTH
Pinus radiata	7-10		■	■							
Pinus strobus	2-8	■	■				■	■	■		■
Pinus sylvestris	3-8	■	■				■	■	■		■
Pinus thunbergiana	5-9	■	■	■	■	■	■	■	■	■	■
Pistacia chinensis	7-10		■	■	■	■				■	■
Pittosporum tobira	8-10	■	■	■	■	■				■	■
Platanus x acerifolia 'Bloodgood'	5-10	■	■	■				■	■	■	■
Platycladus orientalis	6-10	■	■	■		■		■	■		■
Podocarpus gracilior	9-10		■	■	■					■	
Podocarpus macrophyllus	8-10	■	■	■	■					■	■
Populus alba	4-10	■	■	■	■	■	■	■	■		■
Populus angustifolia	3-10	■	■	■	■	■	■	■	■		■
Populus x canadensis	3-10	■	■	■	■	■	■	■	■	■	■
Populus deltoides 'Siouxland'	3-8	■	■	■	■	■	■	■	■		■
Populus fremontii	7-10		■	■	■	■	■				
Populus nigra 'Italica'	3-10	■	■	■	■	■	■	■	■	■	■
Populus tremuloides	2-8	■				■	■	■	■		■
Potentilla fruticosa	2-9	■	■	■	■	■	■	■	■	■	■
Prunus x blireiana	5-9	■	■	■	■	■	■	■	■		■
Prunus caroliniana	7-10		■	■						■	■
Prunus cerasifera 'Atropurpurea'	5-9	■	■	■			■	■	■		■
Prunus x cistena	2-9	■	■	■		■	■	■	■		■
Prunus laurocerasus	7-10	■	■					■	■	■	■
Prunus sargentii	5-7	■	■				■	■	■		■
Prunus serrulata	6-9	■	■						■		■
Prunus subhirtella	6-9	■	■						■		■
Prunus yedoensis	6-8	■	■	■					■		■
Pseudotsuga menziesii	4-9	■	■				■	■	■	■	■
Punica granatum	8-10		■	■	■	■				■	■
Pyracantha angustifolia	5-9	■	■	■	■	■	■	■	■		■
Pyracantha coccinea	5-9	■	■	■	■	■	■	■	■	■	■
Pyracantha 'Fiery Cascade'	6-9	■	■	■	■	■		■	■		■
Pyracantha fortuneana 'Graberi'	7-10	■	■	■	■	■				■	■

PLANT NAME	ZONES	NORTHWEST	NORTHERN CALIFORNIA	SOUTHERN CALIFORNIA	LOW DESERT	HIGH DESERT	ROCKY MOUNTAINS	MIDWEST	NORTHEAST	SO. EASTERN ATLANTIC & GULF COAST	UPPER SOUTH
Pyracantha koidzumii	7-10	■	■	■	■	■		■	■		■
Pyracantha 'Mohave'	6-9	■	■	■	■	■		■	■		■
Pyracantha 'Red Elf'	7-10	■	■	■	■			■	■		■
Pyracantha 'Teton'	6-9	■	■	■	■	■		■	■		■
Pyracantha 'Tiny Tim'	7-9	■	■	■		■		■	■		■
Pyracantha 'Watereri'	6-10	■	■	■	■	■		■	■	■	■
Pyrus calleryana 'Bradford'	5-9	■	■	■		■	■	■	■	■	■
Pyrus kawakami	9-10		■	■	■						
Quercus agrifolia	9-10		■	■							
Quercus alba	4-10					■		■	■	■	■
Quercus coccinea	4-9	■	■	■	■	■	■	■	■	■	■
Quercus ilex	9-10	■	■	■	■						
Quercus macrocarpa	4-10	■	■				■	■	■	■	■
Quercus palustris	5-9	■	■	■		■	■	■	■		■
Quercus phellos	6-10	■	■	■		■	■	■	■	■	■
Quercus robur	5-9	■	■	■			■	■	■		
Quercus rubra	4-10	■	■	■		■	■	■	■		■
Quercus virginiana	8-10	■	■	■	■	■				■	■
Raphiolepis indica	8-10	■	■	■	■	■				■	■
Rhamnus alaternus	7-10	■	■	■		■				■	■
Rhamnus frangula 'Columnaris Tallhedge'	3-8	■			■	■	■	■	■		■
Rhododendron Hybrids	4-10	■	■	■			■	■	■	■	■
Rhus typhina	3-8	■	■			■	■	■	■		
Robinia x ambigua 'Idahoensis'	5-10	■	■	■	■	■	■	■	■	■	■
Robinia pseudoacacia	3-9	■	■	■	■	■	■	■	■	■	■
Rosa Hybrids	5-10	■	■	■	■	■	■	■	■	■	■
Rosmarinus officinalis	7-10	■	■	■		■			■	■	■
Salix alba tristis	3-10	■	■	■	■	■	■	■	■	■	■
Salix babylonica	6-10	■	■	■	■	■	■	■	■	■	■
Salix discolor	3-10	■	■	■	■	■	■	■	■	■	■
Salix matsudana	5-10	■	■	■	■	■	■	■	■	■	■
Sarcococca hookerana humilis	7-10	■	■	■					■		■
Schinus sp.	9-10		■	■							
Sequoia sempervirens	7-10	■	■	■							
Sequoiadendron giganteum	6-10	■	■	■	■						
Skimmia japonica	6-8	■	■						■		■
Sophora japonica	5-8	■	■	■		■	■	■			■
Sorbus aucuparia	2-7	■	■				■	■	■		
Spartium junceum	7-10	■	■	■	■	■					
Spiraea x bumalda	3-9	■	■				■	■	■	■	■
Spiraea cantoniensis	6-9	■	■				■	■	■	■	■
Spiraea japonica	6-9	■	■				■	■	■	■	■
Spiraea nipponica tosaensis 'Snowmound'	4-9	■	■				■	■	■	■	■
Spiraea prunifolia	5-9	■	■				■	■	■	■	■
Spiraea x vanhouttei	5-9	■	■				■	■	■	■	■
Stewartia pseudocamellia	6-9	■	■					■	■		■

Shrubs and Trees Continued

PLANT NAME	ZONES	NORTHWEST	NORTHERN CALIFORNIA	SOUTHERN CALIFORNIA	LOW DESERT	HIGH DESERT	ROCKY MOUNTAINS	MIDWEST	NORTHEAST	SO. EASTERN ATLANTIC & GULF COAST	UPPER SOUTH
Styrax japonicus	6-9	■	■	■		■		■	■		■
Syringa x chinensis	4-7	■	■			■	■	■	■		■
Syringa vulgaris	3-8	■	■			■	■	■	■		■
Tamarix aphylla	7-10			■	■	■					
Taxodium distichum	5-10	■	■	■			■	■	■	■	■
Taxus baccata	6-9	■	■	■				■	■		■
Taxus cuspidata	5-9	■	■	■				■	■		■
Taxus x media	5-9	■	■	■				■	■		■
Ternstroemia gymnanthera	7-10	■	■	■	■					■	
Thuja occidentalis	3-9	■	■	■				■	■		■
Tilia americana	4-8	■	■			■	■	■	■		■
Tilia cordata	4-8	■	■			■	■	■	■		■
Tilia x euchlora	5-8	■	■			■	■	■	■		■
Tilia tomentosa	5-8	■	■	■		■	■	■	■		■
Tsuga canadensis	5-9	■	■					■	■		■
Tsuga caroliniana	5-7	■					■	■	■		■
Tsuga heterophylla	5-9	■	■				■	■	■		■
Ulmus parvifolia	5-9		■	■	■			■			■
Ulmus pumila	5-9	■	■	■	■	■	■	■	■	■	■
Viburnum x bodnantense	6-10	■	■	■						■	■
Viburnum x burkwoodii	5-10	■	■	■			■	■	■	■	■
Viburnum x carlcephalum	5-10	■	■	■			■	■	■	■	■
Viburnum carlesii	5-10	■	■	■			■	■	■	■	■
Viburnum davidii	7-10	■	■	■						■	■
Viburnum dentatum	3-8	■	■	■			■	■	■	■	■
Viburnum dilatatum	5-8	■	■					■	■		■
Viburnum japonicum	7-10	■	■	■						■	■
Viburnum macrocephalum	6-10	■	■	■			■	■	■	■	■
Viburnum odoratissimum	7-10	■	■	■						■	■
Viburnum opulus	3-10	■	■	■			■	■	■	■	■
Viburnum plicatum	4-9	■	■	■			■	■	■	■	■
Viburnum prunifolium	3-9	■	■	■			■	■	■	■	■
Viburnum rhytidophyllum	5-10	■	■	■			■	■	■	■	■
Viburnum rufidulum	5-10	■	■	■			■	■	■	■	■
Viburnum sargentii	6-10	■	■	■				■	■	■	■
Viburnum suspensum	9-10		■	■						■	■
Viburnum tinus	7-10	■	■	■	■					■	■
Viburnum trilobum	2-9	■	■				■	■	■	■	■
Weigela sp.	4-9	■	■			■	■	■	■		■
Xylosma congestum	8-10		■	■	■	■				■	■
Zelkova serrata	5-9	■	■	■	■	■			■	■	■

VINES and GROUND COVERS

PLANT NAME	ZONES	NORTHWEST	NORTHERN CALIFORNIA	SOUTHERN CALIFORNIA	LOW DESERT	HIGH DESERT	ROCKY MOUNTAINS	MIDWEST	NORTHEAST	SO. EASTERN ATLANTIC & GULF COAST	UPPER SOUTH
Actinidia chinensis	8-10	■	■	■						■	■
Aizoaceae sp.	8-10		■	■	■						
Ajuga reptans	4-10	■	■	■			■	■	■	■	■

Note: Plants adapted to Zone 10 are also adapted to *new* Zone 11. Plants shown adapted to Zone 11 only, are recommended specifically for Zone 11. PLANT NAME	ZONES	NORTHWEST	NORTHERN CALIFORNIA	SOUTHERN CALIFORNIA	LOW DESERT	HIGH DESERT	ROCKY MOUNTAINS	MIDWEST	NORTHEAST	SO. EASTERN ATLANTIC & GULF COAST	UPPER SOUTH
Antigonon leptopus	8-10			■	■					■	
Arctostaphylos uva-ursi	2-8	■	■	■			■	■	■		■
Arenaria verna	3-9	■	■	■			■	■	■		■
Baccharis pilularis	8-10		■	■	■	■					
Beaumontia grandiflora	11			■	■					■	
Bougainvillea sp.	9-10		■	■	■					■	
Campsis grandiflora	7-8		■	■	■	■					■
Campsis radicans	4-8	■	■	■	■	■	■	■	■		■
Campsis x tagliabuana 'Madame Galen'	4-8	■	■	■	■	■	■	■	■		■
Celastrus orbiculatus	5-9	■	■				■	■	■		■
Celastrus scandens	3-9	■	■				■	■	■		■
Chamaemelum nobile	7-10	■	■	■	■	■	■	■	■		■
Cistus x purpureus	8-10	■	■	■	■						
Clematis armandii	8-10	■	■	■	■					■	■
Clematis x jackmanii	5-10	■	■	■	■		■	■	■		■
Clematis texensis	4-10	■	■	■	■	■	■	■	■		■
Clytostoma callistegioides	9-10		■	■	■					■	
Convallaria majalis	3-9	■	■				■	■	■		■
Convolvulus cneorum	7-10		■	■	■					■	
Cotoneaster adpressus praecox	5-10	■	■	■	■	■	■	■	■		■
Cotoneaster buxifolius	7-10	■	■	■	■					■	■
Cotoneaster dammeri	5-10	■	■	■		■	■	■	■	■	■
Cotoneaster horizontalis	5-10	■	■	■	■	■	■	■	■	■	■
Cytisus x praecox	6-9	■	■	■	■			■	■		■
Cytisus racemosus	7-10	■	■	■	■			■	■		■
Cytisus scoparius	6-9	■	■	■				■	■		■
Distictis sp.	9-10		■	■						■	
Erica sp.	4-8	■	■	■				■	■		■
Euonymus fortunei	4-8	■	■		■	■	■	■	■		■
x Fatshedera lizei	9-10	■	■	■						■	
Festuca ovina glauca	5-10	■	■	■	■	■	■	■	■		■
Ficus pumila	9-10		■	■	■	■				■	■
Fragaria chiloensis	4-8	■	■	■	■	■	■	■	■		■
Gazania rigens	9-10		■	■						■	■
Gelsemium sempervirens	7-10		■	■	■					■	■
Hedera canariensis	8-10		■	■						■	■
Hedera helix	5-10	■	■	■	■	■	■	■	■	■	■
Hibbertia scandens	11			■						■	
Hosta sp.	3-9	■	■				■	■	■		■
Hydrangea anomala	5-9	■	■	■	■	■	■	■	■	■	■
Hypericum sp.	5-10	■	■	■	■	■	■	■	■	■	■
Jasminum nitidum	10		■	■						■	
Jasminum polyanthum	8-10		■	■	■					■	
Juniperus sp.	2-10	■	■	■	■	■	■	■	■	■	■
Lantana sp.	9-10		■	■	■					■	■
Liriope sp.	5-10		■	■	■			■	■	■	■

Rock cotoneaster *(Cotoneaster horizontalis)*

Star jasmine *(Trachelospermum jasminoides)*

Vines and Ground Covers continued

PLANT NAME	ZONES	NORTHWEST	NORTHERN CALIFORNIA	SOUTHERN CALIFORNIA	LOW DESERT	HIGH DESERT	ROCKY MOUNTAINS	MIDWEST	NORTHEAST	SO. EASTERN ATLANTIC & GULF COAST	UPPER SOUTH
Lonicera hildebrandiana	9-10		■	■						■	
Lonicera japonica	4-10	■	■	■	■	■	■	■	■	■	■
Lonicera sempervirens	4-10	■	■	■	■	■	■	■	■	■	■
Lonicera tatarica	3-9	■	■	■			■	■	■	■	■
Nandina domestica	6-10	■	■	■	■	■			■	■	■
Ophiopogon sp.	5-10		■	■	■			■		■	■
Osteospermum fruiticosum	9-10		■	■	■						
Pachysandra terminalis	4-9	■	■				■		■	■	■
Parthenocissus sp.	4-10	■	■	■	■	■	■	■	■	■	■
Passiflora x alatocaerulea	9-10		■	■						■	■
Passiflora caerulea	9-10	■	■	■						■	■
Passiflora edulis	9-10		■	■						■	
Polygonum aubertii	5-10	■	■	■	■	■	■	■	■	■	■
Pyracantha coccinea	5-9	■	■	■	■	■	■	■	■	■	■
Pyracantha koidzumii	7-10	■	■	■	■	■		■			■
Pyracantha 'Ruby Mound'	7-10	■	■	■	■	■		■			■
Rhoicissus capensis	10		■	■						■	
Sagina subulata	3-9	■	■	■			■	■	■		■
Sarcococca hookerana humilis	7-10	■	■	■					■		■
Sedum sp.	3-10	■	■	■	■		■	■	■	■	■
Tecomaria capensis	9-10		■	■	■					■	
Thymus sp.	3-10	■	■	■	■	■	■	■	■	■	■
Trachelospermum asiaticum	7-10	■	■	■	■	■				■	■
Trachelospermum jasminoides	8-10	■	■	■	■					■	■
Vinca sp.	5-10	■	■	■	■	■	■	■	■	■	■
Vitis labrusca	6-10	■	■	■			■	■	■		■
Vitis rotundifolia	8-10									■	■
Vitis vinifera	7-10	■	■	■		■					
Wisteria sp.	5-9	■	■	■	■	■	■	■	■	■	■

BULBS

Note: Plants adapted to Zone 10 are also adapted to *new* Zone 11. Plants shown adapted to Zone 11 only, are recommended specifically for Zone 11.

PLANT NAME	ZONES	NORTHWEST	NORTHERN CALIFORNIA	SOUTHERN CALIFORNIA	LOW DESERT	HIGH DESERT	ROCKY MOUNTAINS	MIDWEST	NORTHEAST	SO. EASTERN ATLANTIC & GULF COAST	UPPER SOUTH
Agapanthus sp.	9-10	■	■	■	■					■	
Allium giganteum	6-10	■	■	■	■	■			■	■	■
Allium moly	4-10	■	■	■	■	■	■	■	■	■	■
Allium neapolitanum	6-10	■	■	■	■	■			■	■	■
Allium ostrowskianum	4-10	■	■	■	■	■	■	■	■	■	■
Allium sphaerocephalum	4-10	■	■	■	■	■	■	■	■	■	■
Amaryllis belladonna	7-10	■	■	■	■	■				■	■
Anemone blanda	7-10	■	■	■			■*	■*	■*	■*	■*
Anemone coronaria	8-10	■	■	■	■	■*	■*	■*	■*	■*	■*
Anemone x hybrida	6-9	■	■	■	■	■	■*	■*	■*	■	■
Begonia x tuberhybrida	9-10	■*	■*	■*	■*	■*	■*	■*	■*	■*	■*
Caladium x hortulanum	11	■*	■	■	■	■*	■*	■*	■*	■	■*
Chionodoxa luciliae	3-8	■	■				■	■	■	■	■
Clivia miniata	10		■	■	■					■*	
Colchicum autumnale	5-10	■	■	■			■	■	■	■	■
Crocus sp.	3-10	■	■	■	■	■	■	■	■	■	■
Cyclamen sp.	5-10	■	■	■			■	■	■		■
Dahlia hybrids	9-10	■*	■	■	■	■*	■*	■*	■*	■	■
Eranthis hyemalis	4-8	■					■	■	■		
Freesia x hybrida	9-10	■	■	■	■					■	
Fritillaria imperialis	5-8	■	■				■	■	■		■
Fritillaria meleagris	4-8	■	■				■	■	■		■
Galanthus elwesii	4-9	■	■				■	■	■	■	■
Galanthus nivalis	3-8	■	■				■	■	■	■	■
Gladiolus hybrids	9-10	■*	■	■	■	■*	■*	■*	■*	■	■*
Hyacinthus orientalis	7-10	■	■	■					■	■	
Iris, Bearded	4-9	■	■	■	■	■	■	■	■	■	■
Iris cristata	6-10	■	■				■	■	■	■	■
Iris, Dutch	6-9	■	■	■	■		■	■	■	■	■
Iris kaempferi	5-9	■	■				■	■	■	■	■
Iris reticulata	5-9	■	■	■	■	■	■	■	■	■	■
Iris sibirica	3-9	■	■	■	■		■	■	■	■	■
Leucojum aestivum	5-10	■	■	■	■	■	■	■	■	■	■
Leucojum vernum	5-8	■	■				■	■	■		■
Lilium sp.	4-10	■	■	■	■		■	■	■	■	■
Muscari sp.	3-10	■	■	■	■	■	■	■	■	■	■
Narcissus sp.	5-10	■	■	■	■	■	■	■	■	■	■
Ranunculus sp.	8-10	■*	■*	■*	■*	■*	■*	■*	■*	■*	■*
Scilla sp.	3-10	■	■	■			■	■	■	■	■
Sparaxis sp.	10	■*	■	■	■	■	■*	■*	■*	■*	■*
Tulipa sp.	5-9	■	■	■*	■*	■	■	■	■	■*	■
Zantedeschia sp.	8-10	■	■	■	■*	■*	■*	■*	■*	■	■

*Should be dug after bloom, or needs special care in this zone. See encyclopedia text.

PERENNIALS

Note: Plants adapted to Zone 10 are also adapted to *new* Zone 11. Plants shown adapted to Zone 11 only, are recommended specifically for Zone 11.

PLANT NAME	ZONES	NORTHWEST	NORTHERN CALIFORNIA	SOUTHERN CALIFORNIA	LOW DESERT	HIGH DESERT	ROCKY MOUNTAINS	MIDWEST	NORTHEAST	SO. EASTERN ATLANTIC & GULF COAST	UPPER SOUTH
Achillea sp.	3-10	■	■	■	■	■	■	■	■	■	■
Alcea rosea	3-10	■	■	■	■	■	■	■	■	■	■
Anthemis tinctoria	3-9	■	■	■	■	■	■	■	■		■
Antirrhinum majus	8-10	■	■	■	■	A	A	A	A	■	■
Aquilegia x hybrida	3-9	■	■	■	■	■	■	■	■		■
Arctotis hybrids	9-10	A	■	■	■	A	A	A	A	■	A
Armeria maritima	3-9	■	■	■	■	■	■	■	■		■
Aster sp.	4-10	■	■	■	■	■	■	■	■	■	■
Astilbe x arendsii	4-9	■	■				■	■	■		■
Aurinia saxatilis	3-10	■	■	■		■	■	■	■	■	■
Begonia x semperflorens-cultorum	9-10	A	■	■	■	A	A	A	A	■	A
Bellis perennis	3-10	■	■	A	A	A	■	■	■	A	A
Bergenia cordifolia	2-10	■	■	■			■	■	■	■	■
Browallia speciosa	9-10	A	■	■	■	A	A	A	A	■	A
Campanula sp.	3-8	■	■	■			■	■	■	■	■
Catharanthus roseus	9-10	A	■	■	■	A	A	A	A	■	A
Centaurea cineraria	5-10	■	■	■	■	■	■	■	■	■	■
Cheiranthus cheiri	7-10	■	■				A	A	■	■	■
Chrysanthemum coccineum	2-10	■	■	■		■	■	■	■	■	■
Chrysanthemum frutescens	8-10	■	■	■	■	A	A	A	A	■	■
Chrysanthemum maximum	6-9	■	■	■	■	■	■	■	■	■	■
Chrysanthemum x morifolium	5-10	■	■	■		■	■	■	■	■	■
Chrysanthemum parthenium	4-9	■	■	■		■	■	■	■	■	■
Coreopsis grandiflora	5-10	■	■	■	■		■	■	■	■	■
Coreopsis lanceolata	3-10	■	■	■	■	■	■	■	■	■	■
Coreopsis verticillata	7-10		■	■	■	■		■	■	■	■
Cynoglossum amabile	7-10	■	■	■	■	A	A	A	A	■	■
Delphinium elatum	2-10	■	■	■			■	■	■	A	■
Dianthus sp.	2-10	■	■	■	■	■	■	■	■	A	■
Dicentra spectabilis	4-8	■	■	■			■	■	■	A	■
Digitalis purpurea	4-10	■	■	■	■	■	■	■	■	■	■
Echinacea purpurea	3-9	■	■	■	■	■	■	■	■		■
Felicia amelloides	8-10	A	■	■	■		A	A	A	■	A
Gaillardia x grandiflora	3-10	■	■	■	■	■	■	■	■	■	■
Gerbera jamesonii	8-10	■	■	■	■	A	A	A	A	■	■
Hemerocallis hybrids	3-10	■	■	■	■	■	■	■	■	■	■
Heuchera sanguinea	3-10	■	■	■	■	■	■	■	■	■	■
Hibiscus moscheutos	6-10	■	■	■	■		■	■	■	■	■
Iberis sempervirens	4-10	■	■	■	■	■	■	■	■	■	■
Lathyrus latifolius	4-10	■	■	■	■		■	■	■	■	■
Liatris spicata	3-10	■	■	■			■	■	■	■	■
Lobelia splendens	4-10	■	■	■			■	■	■	■	■

A = Grown as annual.

PLANT NAME	ZONES	NORTHWEST	NORTHERN CALIFORNIA	SOUTHERN CALIFORNIA	LOW DESERT	HIGH DESERT	ROCKY MOUNTAINS	MIDWEST	NORTHEAST	SO. EASTERN ATLANTIC & GULF COAST	UPPER SOUTH
Lobularia maritima	8-10	A	■	■	■	A	A	A	A	■	■
Lupinus 'Russell Hybrids'	3-9	■	■				■	■	■		■
Lychnis chalcedonica	3-9	■	■	■			■	■	■	■	■
Monarda didyma	4-10	■	■	■	■	■	■	■	■	■	■
Nicotiana alata	9-10	A	■	■	■	A	A	A	A	■	A
Nierembergia hippomanica	7-10	A	■	■	■	A	A	A	A	■	■
Paeonia hybrids	5-9	■					■	■	■	■	■
Papaver nudicaule	2-8	■	■	A	A	A	■	■	■	A	A
Papaver orientale	3-10	■	A				■	■	■	A	■
Pelargonium sp.	9-10	A	■	■	■	A	A	A	A	■	■
Penstemon gloxinioides	8-10	■	■	■	A	A	A	A	A	■	A
Petunia x hybrida	10	A	A	■	■	A	A	A	A	■	A
Phlox carolina	3-9	■	■	■		■	■	■	■	■	■
Phlox divaricata	3-9	■	■				■	■	■	■	■
Phlox nivalis	8-10	■	■							■	■
Phlox paniculata	3-9	■	■				■	■	■	■	■
Phlox stolonifera	3-9	■	■				■	■	■	■	■
Phlox subulata	3-9	■	■				■	■	■	■	■
Platycodon grandiflorus	3-9	■	■	■	■	■	■	■	■		■
Primula auricula	4-8	■	■				■	■	■		■
Primula denticulata	5-8	■	■				■	■	■		■
Primula japonica	5-8	■	■				■	■	■		■
Primula malacoides	8-10	A	■	■	■	A	A	A	A	A	■
Primula x polyantha	5-9	■	■	■	■	■	■	■	■	A	■
Primula sieboldii	5-9	■	■				■	■	■	A	■
Primula vulgaris	5-8	■	■				■	■	■		■
Rudbeckia hirta	4-10	■	■	■	■	■	■	■	■	■	■
Salvia azurea	6-10	■	■	■		■	■	■	■	■	■
Salvia farinacea	8-10	A	■	■	■	A	A	A	A	■	■
Salvia patens	8-10	A	■	■	■	A	A	A	A	■	■
Salvia pratensis	4-10	■	■	■	■	■	■	■	■	■	■
Salvia x superba	6-10	■	■	■		■	■	■	■	■	■
Sedum spectabile	3-10	■	■	■	■	■	■	■	■	■	■
Solidago hybrids	3-10	■	■	■	■		■	■	■	■	■
Tropaeolum majus	9-10	A	■	■	■	A	A	A	A	■	A
Verbena x hybrida	9-10	A	■	■	■	A	A	A	A	■	A
Veronica hybrids	4-10	■	■	■	■	■	■	■	■	■	■
Viola cornuta	8-10	A	■	■	A	A	A	A	A	A	■
Viola cucullata	6-10	■	■	■		■	■	■	■	A	■
Viola odorata	6-10	■	■	■		■	■	■	■	■	■
Viola sororia	6-10	■	■	■	■	■	■	■	■	A	■
Viola x wittrockiana	8-10	A	■	■	A	A	A	A	A	A	■

A = Grown as annual.

FROST DATES FOR ANNUALS

Since annual flowers are replanted every year, they can be grown almost anywhere unless some disease or pest is particularly hard to control. For this reason, annuals are not listed in the regional adaptation charts. They can all grow in USDA Zones 2-10. However, the best time to plant annuals differs in each of the hardiness zones.

Annuals are planted according to frost dates. If they are frost sensitive, they should be planted only after the average date of the last spring frost. If you plan to start seeds indoors and then transplant them outside after the threat of frost is over, they will usually be the perfect size if seed was sown indoors 6 to 8 weeks before the average last frost date, though certain annuals need longer; see encyclopedia entries. Most frost-tolerant annuals are planted as soon as the ground can be worked in spring.

To supplement the USDA map and the regional adaptation charts, the average first and last frost dates for major cities in each of the climate regions are listed below. Also included is the average length of the growing season, which is the number of days between the last frost in spring and the first frost in fall. By looking for your city, or one that is nearby, you can determine the best time to plant annuals. But keep in mind, these dates are only averages and actual last frosts may occur a week or so sooner or later. Keep a close eye on weather forecasts for frost predictions and be prepared to protect plants with plastic caps or covers.

Some annuals, such as pansies, violas, and fairy primrose, flower best in cool months of spring and fall. Others, such as zinnias, marigolds, and salvias, prefer the hottest months of summer. If you live in an area with a very short growing season, summers probably remain relatively cool and annuals that prefer mild weather can be grown the entire growing season. Many areas with very long growing seasons have mild winters, and cool-season annuals planted in fall provide color all winter long.

Frost dates are also helpful if you live in a cold climate and want to grow frost-sensitive plants. The average date of the last frost in spring tells you when it's safe to plant, and the average date of the first frost in fall lets you know when it's time to dig certain tender plants to store and protect them.

Frost dates can also aid you in predicting when a specific plant might bloom. A perennial or flowering shrub that blooms in midspring might flower in the first part of May in an area where the last spring frost occurs in mid-March. If the last spring frost isn't until the first of May, midspring probably isn't until six weeks later, or the middle of June.

FROST DATES AND LENGTH OF GROWING SEASON

NORTHWEST	Last Spring Frost	First Fall Frost	Average Number of Days of Growing Season
Bend, OR	June 8	Sept. 7	91
Centralia, WA	Apr. 27	Oct. 17	173
Boise, ID	Apr. 23	Oct. 17	177
Yakima, WA	Apr. 15	Oct. 22	190
Eugene, OR	Apr. 13	Nov. 4	205
Seattle, WA	Mar. 14	Nov. 24	255
Portland, OR	Mar. 6	Nov. 24	263

NORTHERN CALIFORNIA	Last Spring Frost	First Fall Frost	Average Number of Days of Growing Season
Santa Rosa, CA	Apr. 10	Nov. 3	207
Fresno, CA	Mar. 14	Nov. 19	250
Eureka, CA	Mar. 10	Nov. 18	253
Marysville, CA	Feb. 21	Nov. 21	273
Red Bluff, CA	Mar. 6	Dec. 5	274
San Jose, CA	Feb. 10	Jan. 6	299
Sacramento, CA	Feb. 6	Dec. 10	307
San Francisco, CA	Jan. 7	Dec. 29	359

SOUTHERN CALIFORNIA	Last Spring Frost	First Fall Frost	Average Number of Days of Growing Season
Riverside, CA	Mar. 6	Nov. 26	265
Bakersfield, CA	Feb. 21	Nov. 25	277
Pasadena, CA	Feb. 3	Dec. 13	313
Santa Barbara, CA	Jan. 22	Dec. 19	331
Los Angeles, CA	Jan. 3	Dec. 28	359
San Diego, CA	—	—	365

LOW DESERT	Last Spring Frost	First Fall Frost	Average Number of Days of Growing Season
Tucson, AZ	Mar. 19	Nov. 19	245
Phoenix, AZ	Feb. 5	Dec. 6	304
Palm Springs, CA	Jan. 18	Dec. 18	334

HIGH DESERT	Last Spring Frost	First Fall Frost	Average Number of Days of Growing Season
Reno, NV	May 8	Oct. 10	155
Las Vegas, NV	Mar. 16	Nov. 10	239
El Paso, TX	Mar. 26	Nov. 14	238

	Last Spring Frost	First Fall Frost	Average Number of Days of Growing Season
ROCKY MOUNTAINS			
Great Falls, MT	May 9	Sept. 25	139
Cheyenne, WY	May 14	Oct. 2	141
Ogden, UT	May 6	Oct. 8	155
Pocatello, ID	Apr. 28	Oct. 6	161
Denver, CO	Apr. 26	Oct. 14	171
Pueblo, CO	Apr. 23	Oct. 14	174
Sante Fe, NM	Apr. 24	Oct. 19	178
Salt Lake City, UT	Apr. 13	Oct. 22	192
Albuquerque, NM	Apr. 13	Oct. 28	198
MIDWEST			
Duluth, MN	May 22	Sept. 24	125
Bismarck, ND	May 11	Sept. 24	136
Huron, SD	May 4	Sept. 30	149
Rapid City, SD	May 7	Oct. 4	150
Sioux Falls, SD	May 5	Oct. 3	152
Marquette, MI	May 13	Oct. 19	159
Green Bay, WI	May 6	Oct. 13	161
Minneapolis/St. Paul, MN	Apr. 30	Oct. 13	166
Sioux City, IA	Apr. 27	Oct. 13	169
Des Moines, IA	Apr. 24	Oct. 16	169
Buffalo, NY	Apr. 30	Oct. 25	179
Fort Wayne, IN	Apr. 24	Oct. 20	179
Peoria, IL	Apr. 22	Oct. 20	181
Detroit, MI	Apr. 21	Oct. 20	182
Springfield, IL	Apr. 20	Oct. 23	186
Pittsburgh, PA	Apr. 20	Oct. 23	187
Milwaukee, WI	Apr. 20	Oct. 25	188
Omaha, NE	Apr. 14	Oct. 20	189
Grand Rapids, MI	Apr. 23	Oct. 30	190
Chicago, IL	Apr. 19	Oct. 28	192
Cincinnati, OH	Apr. 15	Oct. 25	192
Charleston, WV	Apr. 18	Oct. 28	193
Indianapolis, IN	Apr. 17	Oct. 27	193
Cleveland, OH	Apr. 21	Nov. 2	195
Columbus, OH	Apr. 17	Oct. 30	196
Lexington, KY	Apr. 13	Oct. 28	198
Topeka, KS	Apr. 9	Oct. 26	200
Springfield, MO	Apr. 12	Oct. 30	201
St. Louis, MO	Apr. 9	Nov. 1	206
Kansas City, MO	Apr. 6	Oct. 30	207
Charlottesville, VA	Apr. 11	Nov. 6	209
Wichita, KS	Apr. 5	Nov. 1	210
Evansville, IN	Apr. 2	Nov. 4	216
Louisville, KY	Apr. 1	Nov. 7	220
NORTHEAST			
Berlin, NH	May 29	Sept. 15	109
Caribou, ME	May 19	Sept. 21	116
St. Johnsbury, VT	May 22	Sept. 23	127
Concord, NH	May 11	Sept. 30	142

	Last Spring Frost	First Fall Frost	Average Number of Days of Growing Season
Burlington, VT	May 8	Oct. 3	148
Worcester, MA	May 7	Oct. 2	148
Bangor, ME	May 1	Oct. 4	156
Syracuse, NY	Apr. 30	Oct. 15	168
Portland, ME	Apr. 29	Oct. 15	169
Albany, NY	Apr. 27	Oct. 13	169
Bridgeport, CT	Apr. 26	Oct. 16	173
Scranton, PA	Apr. 24	Oct. 14	174
Hartford, CT	Apr. 22	Oct. 19	180
New Haven, CT	Apr. 15	Oct. 27	195
Providence, RI	Apr. 13	Oct. 27	197
Harrisburg, PA	Apr. 9	Oct. 30	204
Boston, MA	Apr. 5	Nov. 8	217
Trenton, NJ	Apr. 4	Nov. 8	218
Newark, NJ	Apr. 3	Nov. 8	219
New York City, NY	Apr. 7	Nov. 12	219
Atlantic City, NJ	Mar. 31	Nov. 11	225
Philadelphia, PA	Mar. 30	Nov. 17	232
SO. EASTERN ATLANTIC & GULF COAST			
Houston, TX	Mar. 14	Nov. 21	262
New Orleans, LA	Feb. 20	Dec. 9	292
Mobile, AL	Feb. 17	Dec. 12	298
Jacksonville, FL	Feb. 16	Dec. 16	313
Corpus Christi, TX	Jan. 26	Dec. 27	335
Tampa, FL	Jan. 10	Dec. 26	349
Miami, FL	—	—	365
UPPER SOUTH			
Roanoke, VA	Apr. 14	Oct. 26	195
Asheville, NC	Apr. 12	Oct. 24	195
Lubbock, TX	Apr. 1	Nov. 9	205
Richmond, VA	Mar. 29	Nov. 2	218
Knoxville, TN	Mar. 31	Nov. 6	220
Tulsa, OK	Mar. 25	Nov. 1	221
Oklahoma City, OK	Mar. 28	Nov. 7	224
Nashville, TN	Mar. 28	Nov. 7	224
Washington DC	Mar. 29	Nov. 9	225
Texarkana, AR	Mar. 21	Nov. 9	233
Raleigh, NC	Mar. 24	Nov. 16	237
Memphis, TN	Mar. 20	Nov. 12	237
Baltimore, MD	Mar. 26	Nov. 19	238
Birmingham, AL	Mar. 19	Nov. 14	241
Little Rock, AR	Mar. 17	Nov. 13	241
Atlanta, GA	Mar. 21	Nov. 18	242
Norfolk, VA	Mar. 19	Nov. 16	242
Dallas, TX	Mar. 18	Nov. 17	244
Columbia, SC	Mar. 14	Nov. 21	262
Shreveport, LA	Mar. 8	Nov. 15	262
Savannah, GA	Feb. 27	Nov. 29	275
Montgomery, AL	Feb. 27	Dec. 3	279
Charleston, SC	Feb. 19	Dec. 10	294

Landscaping Your Yard and Garden

There are no hard-and-fast rules when it comes to landscaping— taste is an individual matter—but most home gardeners find that some help in the way of general guidelines goes a long way toward creating an attractive, functional landscape. Success in landscaping depends upon selecting plants— trees, shrubs, vines, and ground covers—that fill a particular need, that are enjoyable to look at, and that can adapt to the conditions of their planting sites.

EVERGREEN AND DECIDUOUS

Evergreen and deciduous plants have different uses and create different visual effects. Deciding which kind you need where is the first step in selecting plants.

To many people, the term evergreen conjures up images of pines, firs, and junipers—the needled evergreens, or conifers. But conifers are only one kind of evergreen—the other kind is broad-leaved evergreens, plants with flat, leathery leaves. Both kinds provide year-round greenery.

Evergreen trees and shrubs, whether needle-leaved or broad-leaved, are important elements of every landscape. They remain green and unchanging throughout the year, giving the landscape a permanent structure that highlights the seasonal changes of deciduous flowering trees and shrubs. Some evergreen trees have showy flowers and fruits, but the evergreen foliage is of primary importance in the landscape.

Deciduous plants lose their leaves with the onset of cold weather, but they often do so in a blaze of red, gold, or yellow color.

At left: Evergreen shrubs and trees harmonize your home and garden year-round and provide a permanent background for seasonal color changes.

Grapefruit (*Citrus sp.*)

Fuchsia (*Fuchsia sp.*)

Variegated euonymus (*Euonymus sp.*)

Grape (*Vitis sp.*)

Fir trees *(Abies sp.)* and cedars *(Cedrus sp.)* are fine-textured evergreens good for large-scale plantings and adding skyline drama.

Azaleas and rhododendrons *(Rhododendron sp.)* are excellent for shaded sites. Curved planting lines are visually pleasing.

A stone walk contrasts handsomely with the medium-textured foliage of English ivy *(Hedera helix)* and aucuba *(Aucuba japonica).*

Deciduous plants are flowering plants and many have beautiful blossoms in spring or summer. Fall flowers are rarer. Colorful fruits and berries are another feature of many deciduous plants and these can add off-season interest during winter months.

SITE PLAN

A good way to go about designing your landscape is to do it first on paper by making a site or plot plan. A site plan is a sketch or diagram, drawn to scale, of your house and yard. It shows the locations of doors, windows, and rooms, as well as trees, shrubs, garden beds, and outdoor areas such as patios and walks.

Done properly, a site plan takes a good deal of time and observation. You should understand how the sun and wind patterns change with the seasons, since some areas of your property may be in full sun in winter but be shaded in summer. Noting the growing conditions of different areas of your yard will help you choose the trees and shrubs that will serve you best.

You can make an accurate site plan using graph paper and a copy of your survey. Record landscape

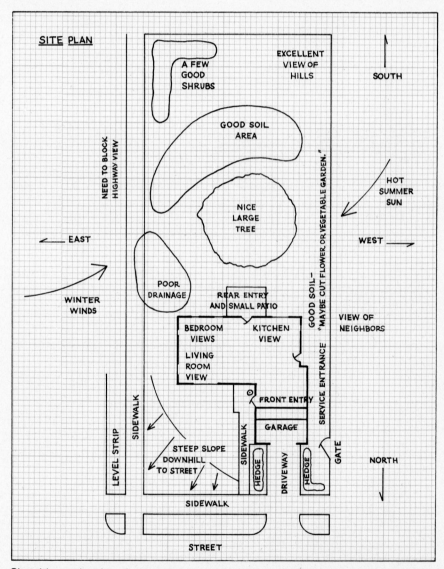

Sketching a site plan of your property, similar to the example shown above, helps you identify the landscape needs of your property. Once you note which views need to be blocked or preserved, where shade is needed, areas of poor soil or bad drainage, and paths of movement, you can begin to choose plants that meet your specific landscape requirements.

Using fine-textured needled evergreens together with broad-leaved plants creates visually interesting contrasts of form, texture, and color. Evergreen shrubs have been utilized here as hedging to frame the patio, screen the vegetable garden from view, and direct the eye to a pleasant, open vista. They also function as accent, transition, and background plants to display the pageantry of changing seasonal color.

features not noted on the survey, such as trees and garden plots, by carefully measuring their distances from the house. Mark trees and shrubs with circles indicating their branch spread at maturity. Draw a circle for a new tree on the plan where you wish to plant it. Before making a final decision, check to see where it will cast shade and if it will have enough room when mature.

When you have a good diagram of your property, you can place tracing paper over it and experiment with possible planting and landscaping ideas before you ever touch a shovel to the ground.

LANDSCAPE DESIGN BASICS

Trees, shrubs, and vines can cool and shade your house, provide you with privacy, and define the boundaries of your property, but most of all, they should create a visually appealing setting for your home. When thoughtfully positioned and combined into a design that uses colors, textures, and scale for best effect, landscape plants will make your home more attractive and more valuable.

The visual impact a plant makes depends upon its size and shape, the texture and color of its flowers, and the texture and color of its foliage. Plants are not static, and these attributes change throughout the growing season. Skillful garden designers consider all the seasonal changes when they select and locate any landscape plant.

Texture: Plants with small leaves and flowers or slender branches have a fine texture. Most needle-leaved evergreens are fine-textured, as are many deciduous plants. Some deciduous plants with big leaves become fine-textured in winter after their foliage drops and their twigs are bare.

Plants with big leaves and flowers or stout stems and trunks are bold-textured. Many broad-leaved evergreens are bold-textured, though some, such as Japanese holly, *Ilex crenata*, have small leaves and are fine-textured.

Fine-textured plants are more restful to look at. When seen from a distance they appear smaller and farther away than they really are. When used in small or enclosed areas they make the space seem larger. Bold-textured plants have the opposite effect. When viewed from a distance they appear closer and larger than they really are. Planted in quantity in a small space, they may seem overpowering.

Fine textures and bold textures can be combined to good effect, the contrasting textures creating visual excitement. Many garden designers group fine-textured shrubs at one end of the garden and bold-textured ones at the other end, so there is a visual progression from fine to bold textures. They also use larger groups of fine-textured plants, progressing toward smaller groups of bold-textured plants. This keeps the effect from becoming too busy.

If you want the planting area to seem larger, locate the fine-textured plants in the distance and the bold-textured ones nearby. Do just the reverse if you want a large area to seem more intimate.

It's usually better not to mix deciduous and evergreen trees or shrubs in a haphazard manner. Though in the summer they may have the same texture, in winter, the deciduous ones will be fine-textured and look visually weak mixed in with the evergreens. Plant the deciduous ones in groups among and in front of evergreen kinds.

The textures of your garden plants should be combined thoughtfully not only with each other, but also with the other physical elements in your landscape. House walls, garden structures, fences, and paving materials each has a texture that should be considered when you select plants. For instance, a small-leaved azalea looks more harmonious along a brick wall than a large-leaved hydrangea. The brick is bold and busy and blends with the small azalea leaves, but fights with the hydrangea foliage.

Color: Flowering trees, shrubs, vines, and even some ground covers provide dramatic displays of bright color when in bloom. Few landscape plants are constantly in bloom, yet a shrub border or foundation planting doesn't have to be boring just because there are no flowers. Color also comes from foliage, berries, bark, and buds.

The foliage of red-tip photinia (Photinia x fraseri) emerges a brilliant bronzy-red color, creating a vivid contrast to green shrubs.

Japanese skimmia (Skimmia japonica), a handsome evergreen shrub, has fragrant flowers and bright showy berries; is attractive year-round.

Wild lilac (Ceanothus) may attain a statuesque size and should be located where it will look in scale with other landscape elements.

A plant's longest-lasting color effect comes from its foliage. The leaves of evergreen and deciduous plants offer many shades of green—bright green, gray-green, blue-green, yellow-green, and dark green. Some plants have reddish-purple foliage and others are variegated with white, gold, or purple. These foliage colors can be combined to beautiful, subtle effect, so the colors are contrasted with each other and the plants are visually separated.

Many deciduous plants produce brilliant shows of color in fall when their foliage changes to fiery shades of yellow, red, and gold. The fall show is often accompanied by or followed by colorful berries and fruits. Berried branches offering eye-catching displays of red, black, blue, yellow, and gold are often showy right into winter. In the Northeast, snow-covered branches of glossy green holly leaves and clusters of red berries are a wintertime delight.

Considered alone, almost any flower has a beautiful color. But that beautiful color has to look good with the rest of the colors in the landscape. When choosing flowering plants, you'll be choosing from a full spectrum of colors including every hue and shade imaginable. When set side-by-side, many of these colors will clash. It's a good idea to select plants when they are in bloom, that way you can keep color mistakes to a minimum.

Flower colors of landscape plants should complement the colors of garden plants that will be in bloom at the same time. And they should also go with the color of your house or any other nearby landscape features. For instance, a white flowering dogwood may be lost when planted in front of a white frame house, but in the same spot, a pink flowering dogwood would shine. Violet-colored azaleas may look dark and dingy when planted in front of a red brick wall, but are stunning along a white house.

It is also a good plan to select trees, shrubs, and vines that bloom at different times of the season. The flowering season of all the top-rated plants included in this book are given in their descriptive entries and in the landscape charts. Most trees and shrubs bloom in spring, but you can select a balance of early, mid- and late spring-blooming plants for a long display. And wherever possible, include summer- and fall-blooming plants to provide color all during the growing season. You may wish to group the plants according to season so different parts of the garden are in bloom during different times. This gives the best show and avoids a polka-dot look.

When planting shrubs, it's also a good principle to arrange several shrubs all of the same color together. Clashing colors can be separated with white-flowered plants or with green foliage plants. This gives a more pleasing effect than a hodgepodge of random colors that each vies for attention.

Scale: The size and shape of your home and property largely dictates what scale your landscape plantings should have. Since trees are the largest, most dominant elements of the landscape, their size is of primary importance in achieving the correct scale for your home.

A large 2- or 3-story house needs several tall trees to frame it and blend the house into its setting. Small trees, lower than the house, are out of scale, and make the house look even more massive and imposing. A small house is made even more diminutive if tall trees tower over it. Medium-sized trees will give it a more substantial appearance and small, low trees will turn it into a quaint-looking tiny cottage.

When choosing permanent plants for your yard and garden, always keep their ultimate size in mind. Locate shrubs and trees where they have plenty of room to achieve their ultimate size without crowding your house or other plantings. And consider whether or not a plant will look in scale with its setting when it is full-grown. A small yard is more pleasant and feels more spacious if planted with numerous small-sized plants rather than with several massive ones.

Plant form and texture, primarily determined by leaf size and shape, and flower color can influence the apparent size of an area. Coarse texture, bold forms, hot colors, as shown above left, can make a garden seem smaller. Fine textures, delicate or simple forms, and cool colors, as illustrated above right, can make the same space seem larger. By selecting appropriate plants you can create an illusion of open space or warm intimacy in your garden.

Deciduous trees can help you conserve energy—in summer their shade blocks hot sun, keeping your house cool and reducing cooling costs; in winter their bare branches let sunlight through, warming your house and lowering heating costs. Spring or summer flowers and brilliantly colored autumn foliage may also be yours to enjoy.

Saucer magnolia trees *(Magnolia x soulangiana)* make graceful accent trees, providing summer shade and a fragrant spring flower show.

Monterey cypress *(Cupressus macrocarpa)* make excellent evergreen street trees in coastal climates.

TREES IN THE LANDSCAPE

Trees are the tallest, most dominant plants in the landscape. They frame your house and property, determining its scale and defining the boundaries of the skyline. Tall trees provide cooling shade, slow down strong winds, and act as noise buffers. Flowering trees are strikingly decorative when in bloom, holding their flower-laden branches against the sky.

Accent: A small ornamental tree can be arranged among low shrubs or beside an entryway or patio, where it acts as a focal point. Choose a tree with a long season of spring bloom, fall color, and showy berries for best effect.

Background: Evergreen trees with branches reaching down to the ground make an effective background for flowering trees and shrubs. Fine-textured trees are best.

Framing: Trees planted in the front of a house can frame the building and blend it into its setting. Locate trees to the sides of the front yard at an angle of 30° to 45° from the front door or center of the house. This positioning both frames your house and gives it an open, welcoming appearance.

Lawn tree: The best trees for gracing a lawn are ones that cast a light shade and have deep roots. Dense shade or shallow roots discourages grass from growing.

Screen: A row of evergreen trees planted closely together along your property line will give you privacy from the neighbors. Tall trees are needed to block views from upstairs windows.

Shade: Large deciduous trees are often called shade trees. Those with dense foliage cast heavy cooling shade in summer but allow warm winter sun through after leaves drop. Where shade is desired all winter, plant evergreen trees.

It requires forethought to locate trees so they cast shade where you want it. Since the angle of the sun changes during the year, a tree that casts its shadow where you want it in summer might not do so in winter. The farther a tree is away from your house, the taller it will have to be to shade it.

One way to decide where to locate a tree is to use a very tall pole and mark where it casts its shadow during the morning, at noon, and in the afternoon. When planting a deciduous tree, do this only in summer, but

Trees are dominant landscape elements that provide privacy and shade, define your property line, and blend your home into its garden setting. You can create the most visually dramatic and effective landscapes combining evergreen trees and deciduous flowering trees.

To landscape an entryway so that it appears attractive and welcoming in all seasons requires careful planning. Evergreen flowering shrubs are accents when in bloom and provide consistent greenery in other seasons. Container-grown plants can be changed to take advantage of seasonal flowers at their peak of beauty.

an evergreen tree requires both summer and winter observations.

Street trees: Trees lining a street give a neighborhood a homey feeling. Choose tall shade trees or small flowering trees, but be sure they can endure compacted soil, possible road salt, and exhaust, and that their branches do not interfere with traffic.

Skyline trees: Tall trees often have the sky as their background. They give your property more intimacy, are beautiful at sunset, and can frame views. The tops of tall trees planted in your backyard are visible from the front, effectively softening the lines of your house.

Windbreak: A row or grouping of tall evergreen trees planted on the north or windy sides of your house can slow cold winter winds and reduce your heating costs. In windy arid climates a windbreak can make outdoor living more pleasant. Wind will be slowed for a distance 25 times

the height of the windbreak. For best effect, locate the windbreak at a distance of 2 or 3 times the height of the mature trees.

SHRUBS IN THE LANDSCAPE

Because differences aren't always clear-cut, it's sometimes difficult to categorize a plant as either a shrub or a tree. Shrubs are plants with many trunks, while trees have a single main trunk. They are usually lower and fuller. Some tall shrubs can be pruned into single-trunked forms and used as small trees. Other landscape shrubs, most notably certain evergreens, are actually slow-growing or dwarf forms of trees.

Shrubs are useful for greenery and flowers at people-level. They soften the foundations of houses, define the boundaries of your property, provide privacy, and screen unattractive views. Hedges act as living fences, keeping children and pets inside your yard—or outside as the case may be.

Accent: Positioned where it is the dominant plant in a group of low shrubs, an especially colorful shrub is a focal point and a garden accent.

Barrier plant: Shrubs with thorns or very dense growth act as barriers, keeping people and animals from going where you don't want them.

Border planting: Shrubs are often planted along the edges of a yard, bordering it with flowers and foliage. Borders with curved contours rather than straight edges are most appealing. Arrange shrubs several deep if there is room, with the tallest ones in back and the lowest ones in front.

Container plants: Many shrubs thrive in tight quarters and make attractive accents when grown in a decorative container placed on a patio or beside a doorway.

Espalier: Espalier is the art of pruning and training plants into a pattern of lines in a flat plane. Often

Imagination and a cooperative fine-textured evergreen shrub, such as yew pine *(Podocarpus macrophyllus),* can produce fanciful topiaries.

Grapes *(Vitis sp.)* can quickly shade an arbor and reward you with a bounty of delectable fruits.

Aaron's-beard *(Hypericum calycinum)* forms a dense and colorful ground cover for steep slopes.

espaliers are made against a wall or an open trellis.

Foundation planting: Shrubs are traditionally used to decorate the front of a house and to conceal the house's foundation. Evergreen shrubs, whether flowering or non-flowering, are most suitable. Choose shrubs whose mature size will not block windows and walkways.

A traditional design places columnar shrubs at the house's corners and on either side of the door, and shrubs are pruned into regular shapes. This creates a more formal effect. For a less formal effect, try using shrubs pruned to retain their natural shapes and placing ones with horizontal branching patterns at the corners.

Hedge: Hedges make useful boundary markers, barriers, and privacy screens. For a *formal* hedge, shear into a neat shape. For an *informal* hedge, prune along natural lines.

Transition: A low bed of shrubs provides a visual transition and physical separation between parts of the yard, without blocking views.

Topiary: Plants pruned into fanciful or geometric shapes are called topiary. Fine-textured shrubs are best.

VINES IN THE LANDSCAPE

To grow upwards and off the ground, vines need to grab onto a support with their twining stems, coiling tendrils, or suctionlike holdfasts. Vines provide foliage and flowers where other kinds of plants cannot. They require minimal ground space, so they can scale a fence along a narrow side yard or provide a green backdrop behind a shallow flower bed.

Accent: An ornamental flowering vine growing on a lamppost, mailbox, or fence accents on otherwise dull structure.

Arbor cover: Grown on an overhead lattice-work structure, vines can be beautiful leafy bowers that provide shade and decoration.

Ground cover: Some vines will creep and root along the ground if they have no support to climb up. They can quickly dress up bare ground and provide erosion control.

Softening: Stark bare walls and fences, especially in narrow places, can be softened with green or flowering vines.

Trellis cover: Grown on a trellis, vines can act as narrow decorative walls to give privacy or divide parts of the garden.

GROUND COVERS IN THE LANDSCAPE

Low plants that spread thickly over the ground are called ground covers. They are usually plants whose stems run along the ground, rooting as they go. Some vines can also double as ground covers, and some shrubs have prostrate, or creeping, varieties that are excellent ground covers.

Accent: A bed of green or flowering ground cover located along a walkway or a patio provides a handsome textural contrast to lawn grass and a transition between lawn and paving.

Edging: Planted along the front of a flower bed or shrubbery border, a low ground cover provides a neat edging that accents the plantings.

Erosion control: On steep slopes and banks where soil erosion is a problem, ground covers will spread quickly and their roots will stabilize the soil.

Lawn replacement: Lawns demand a great deal of care. On large or small properties, ground covers can be used to replace expanses of lawn and require much less care, once they are established.

Shade garden: Where it's too shady for grass to grow, many kinds of shade-loving ground covers can be planted to dress up the area.

Many shrubs and garden flowers that are fussy about soil conditions can be grown successfully in raised planting beds or containers, where it is easy to amend the soil to satisfy their needs. Raised beds are also easy to work in, and position flowers at eye-level where they create an intimate, dazzling display.

Flower Gardens in the Landscape

Flowering annuals, perennials, and bulbs are the gardener's delight. The act of tending them and nurturing them into bloom is reward enough for many gardeners, but add to this armloads of cut flowers for indoor bouquets, sweet fragrances hanging in the evening air, and a constant show of changing colors, and you know why almost everyone has room for at least a small flower garden.

Annuals, perennials, and bulbs are *herbaceous plants*—that is, their stems are made of soft tissues rather than being made from hard wood and they have no permanent above-ground structure as do *woody plants* (trees and shrubs).

Annuals: Flowering annuals live for only one growing season and then they die. But during that time, annuals bloom profusely, often for several months. Some annuals, such as sweet peas and pansies, start and finish blooming early in the growing season while the weather is cool. In warm climates, cool-season annuals bloom from late fall through winter, putting on a welcome winter display. But most annuals bloom, and bloom constantly, from early summer into fall, some right up until frost. *Biennials* live for two years,

forming only leaves the first growing season and blooming and then dying the second.

The effort and expense of replanting annuals each year can reward you with a strikingly different garden each summer.

Perennials: Flowering perennials have a longer tenure in the garden than do annuals, blooming year after year and often living for 10 years or more. They usually die to the ground in late fall and resprout from their roots in spring. Some perennials die back at the end of the summer, but form a rosette of foliage that hugs the ground all winter. Other perennials, such as nasturtiums, are hardy only in mild climates and are killed by frost or extreme cold; in cold climates, these are grown as annuals.

Most perennials bloom for a week or two at the same time each year; some kinds bloom for as long as a month.

Bulbs: Gardeners call plants that have fleshy underground storage parts "bulbs," though botanists distinguish these bulbs further into "true bulbs," corms, rhizomes, and tubers. Bulbs usually bloom during or after a period of active growth, then flowers and foliage die to the ground. The plant lies dormant for the rest of the year. In areas with

warm winters, a few bulbs, such as Kaffir lily, are evergreen.

Because most kinds of bulbs make only a brief appearance, they present unique problems in the garden. The withering foliage of tulips for instance looks unsightly and leaves behind a bare spot that must be camouflaged. But on the other hand, when crocus is naturalized in a lawn, the bright flowers and grassy leaves often disappear before mowing is needed.

USING FLOWERS IN THE LANDSCAPE

Flowers can serve a wide variety of functions in the garden. Massed in flower beds or borders, they provide a vivid display of seasonal color; used in clumps between evergreen shrubs, they provide welcome color highlights. Flowers can soften harsh lines between ground and walls or fences during the growing season. In young gardens they can act as temporary fillers between small shrubs until the shrubs fill in.

But since annuals, perennials, and bulbs die to the ground at the end of the growing season, they do not provide year-round visual structure to your garden. They should be thought of as a seasonal addition of color and foliage and planted where their absence during part of the year will not be evident.

A Persian ranunculus *(Ranunculus asiaticus)* border provides an explosion of colorful blooms in late spring or early summer.

A garden of perennials rewards you with a long season of flower color, year after year, if planned carefully.

A curved bed of tulips *(Tulipa sp.)* highlights the spring season.

FLOWER BEDS AND BORDERS

Flowers are most often planted in beds and borders where they create their showiest and most dramatic effects. In the history of landscape design, beds and borders were strictly and separately defined. But today the distinctions are often blurred.

Borders: Borders are groupings of flowers backed up by a vertical landscape feature, traditionally shrubs or tall hedges, but also garages, houses, fences, or garden walls. They can be viewed—and entered by the gardener—from only one side. Lower flowers are planted in front and taller ones in back, so all can be seen.

The best backgrounds for setting off flowers are green vines or shrubbery, weathered or stained wood, wood painted white or dark neutral tones, and stone. Background brick and brightly colored walls call for flowers whose colors harmonize.

When you plan a border, consider size and proportion. Borders should not be narrow ribbons beneath towering walls—nor should they leave only a corridor of open space toward the center of your yard. And you must be able to reach every plant. Curved outlines rather than straight ones are most appealing.

It's best to make borders no deeper than about five feet. Stepping stones laid down to give you access to the interior of the garden can keep you from trampling plants and destroying soil structure, but they aren't adequate platforms from which to tend wide flower borders.

Perennial borders, unless they are quite large, usually have either a short season of intense blooming or a longer season of skimpy blooming. It takes careful planning to design a perennial border that is constantly in bloom, with a balanced mixture of spring-, summer-, and fall-blooming plants in a pleasing color scheme. A herbaceous border that includes annuals, perennials, and bulbs will have the longest and most colorful blooming season. The bulbs provide early spring interest and the annuals provide continuous color to offset the changing perennials show.

Herbaceous borders are usually lifeless in winter and may present an unattractive expanse of bare earth if located where they are highly visible. A happy solution to this problem is a mixed border, herbaceous and woody plants planted together. In winter, the evergreen shrubs and bare branches of the deciduous ones give substance, structure, and visual interest to the border.

Beds: In the traditional definition of the term, a flower "bed" has no backdrop such as a wall or hedge, but is meant to be visible—and accessible to the gardener—on all sides. A flower bed is used effectively to flank low, horizontal structures such as walkways, patios, or in some formal gardens, very low walls and hedges. Often they are situated beneath trees. Traditional types such as Victorian carpet beds add color and pattern but no vertical dimension to the garden.

Viewed from a patio, a flower bed can serve as a transition and make a beautiful foreground for your lawn. If situated between street and home, however, beds visually detract from the house by breaking up the welcoming expanse of lawn.

Island beds: An island bed is a cross between a border and a bed. It is situated as an island in a lawn and is meant to be seen from all sides, however plants are not kept low. Taller plants are located in the middle of the bed and lower ones along the edges. Island beds have better air circulation and are easier to care for than borders.

An island bed fits best into the design of a landscape if it flanks large structural lines such as a walkway or terrace, or if it follows a fold or contour of the land. The most attractive island beds are curving and asymmetrical. Least-successful ones have no connection with the framework of the landscape and limit open space.

Raised beds: Modern garden designs often include raised flower beds, bottomless planters that can

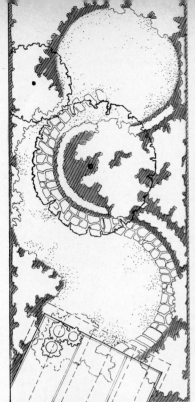

You can visually transform the size and shape of your yard by careful landscape planning. A small narrow lot will appear to be more spacious if you create movement toward the side property lines with a meandering pathway. Screening the farthest boundary seems to shorten the lot, giving the impression of a more pleasing proportion.

be small or extensive. Raised beds provide architectural interest as well as a location for growing flowers, breaking the monotony of a long wall or an empty expanse of ground or terrace. Their sides can be constructed to double as benches.

Raised beds are often problem solvers. Poor growing conditions such as poor drainage or heavy or alkaline soil can easily be made agreeable by simply constructing a raised bed filled with good soil over the troublesome spot. Elderly or handicapped gardeners find raised beds easier to tend since they require less stooping than ground-level gardens.

SPECIAL SITUATIONS

In planters: Planters and window boxes set flowers off as strong focal points for patios or entryways, creating a bold splash of color. Petunias that look sedate in the ground are dazzling in a window box. You can change the plants in most planters with the seasons, or you can move planters out of sight while flowers are clipped back and rejuvenated.

In a rock garden: Small, compact, low plants native to alpine regions or sunny, rocky slopes are often grouped together in a naturalistic planting called a rock garden. Rock gardens should be located in full sun and be built of rocks and gritty, fast-draining soil shaped into gentle mounds.

Under trees: Shady spots under trees can be beautified with shade-loving plants. Bulbs, which need good sunlight in spring to mature their foliage, can be planted beneath late-leafing deciduous trees. A grove of trees provides a naturalistic woodland setting for early bulbs, earliest annuals, and shade-loving annuals and perennials. Winter and spring sun and summer shade provide an ideal growing situation for these plants.

FLOWER GARDEN DESIGN BASICS

Formal or informal: Homes today are so informal that symmetrical, very formal landscaping looks out of place. The most successful gardens for typical modern-day houses

use gentle curves, rather than straight lines and right angles. The suggestion is not of disorder, but rather of the flexible and natural. Especially in small gardens, simplicity, restraint, and preservation of open areas are needed to create a restful setting.

If your house is formal and symmetrical, your property level, and trees regularly rather than randomly placed, your property would look elegant planted with a formal garden of symmetrically laid-out beds and borders and sheared hedges. Walls, walks, and borders could be laid out in straight lines and rectangles.

Visibility: Arrange flowers within beds and borders so small ones are visible in front of large ones, low ones in front of tall. Edging plants such as candytuft and sweet alyssum are appropriate in both formal and informal designs. Think in terms of creating foreground, midground, and background in a border, but let a few taller plants come forward here and there to keep the effect casual and natural, rather than rigid.

A mass planting or border of mixed bulbs creates a color spectacle during spring.

Mixed perennial borders offer gardeners a long season of exciting color and interesting combinations of flower texture and form.

Combinations of flower colors are limitless. Repeating drifts of the same colors create a harmonious garden.

Drifts: Natural-looking, gracefully spreading patches of a single kind of plant are called drifts. Flowers in most borders and island beds are best planted in small drifts of irregular, spreading, interlocking clumps and patches, rather than in rigid rows. This means grouping several plants of the same kind and color together.

Masses of color: Random splashes of color created by single plants or too small clumps placed among shrubs or out-of-bloom flowers can create a disappointing polka-dot effect. For most visually pleasing results, arrange sizable groups of plants all of the same color beside each other.

Geometric designs: Carpet beds (see page 34) use bands, arabesques, and rows—even entire beds—of a single variety of annual to create regular, geometric designs. The visual effect is dramatic and unsubtle. Plants should be planted in carefully spaced rows.

Single varieties of tulip, hyacinth, or bearded iris are often bedded alone or underplanted with a single filler such as forget-me-not, for a beautiful display in formal beds. Such beds are in bloom for a very short time however.

Succession of bloom: A flower garden that changes from spring through fall (and blooms even in winter in mild climates) is the most satisfying. Something new is always blooming or about to bloom, making the garden an exciting and dynamic scene. This succession of bloom is created by carefully selecting combinations of perennials and bulbs to provide an ongoing display of harmonious flower color from spring to fall. Annuals are often included to provide continuity. (See pages 54 to 57 for help in planning a garden that's never out of bloom.)

Flower shapes: Flowers should be combined with an eye towards creating a pleasing combination not just of textures but of flower shapes. Contrasting round, spiking, and irregular silhouettes creates dramatic visual impact. Too many spikes or daisy shapes grouped together would be monotonous. To create maximum visual appeal, you might, for example, set off the substantial round blooms of peony with the tall spikes of delphinium and the smaller globes of cornflower.

COLOR SCHEMES

You will be most satisfied with a garden color scheme that blends into the overall color scheme of your house and landscape. The same color principles that apply to shrubs, trees, vines, and ground covers apply to flowers in the garden.

Seasonal changes: Flower color schemes that shift seasonally are one of the great delights of gardening. Let your color scheme for any season center around closely related colors on the color wheel, or around a particular theme, such as red, white, and blue. Shifting colors provide variety and emphasize seasons. You might build your spring scheme around yellows to harmonize with new-greens; your summer scheme around rich reds, purples, and violets; your autumn scheme around the yellow-gold-bronze range to harmonize with fall foliage colors.

Colors for far and near: Warm, strong colors, the yellows, oranges, and reds, seem close to the viewer and carry well when viewed from a distance. Cool colors, the blues, purples, and violets, create a sense of distance and are weak when viewed from far away. Reds, yellows, and oranges in the foreground of a shallow garden, with the cool colors in the rear, create the illusion of greater depth. Warm colors can also make a distant bed seem closer.

Colors for moods: Cool colors are soothing and restful. Warm colors are lively and, if overused, often harsh and unrestful, especially in a small garden. Repeating clumps and drifts of the same color unifies the garden. You can use white flowers or gray foliage plantings to separate colors that do not combine harmoniously.

FINAL LANDSCAPE PLAN

This example of a complete landscape plan is one way the problems identified in the site plan on page 26 might be solved.

1. Dense planting of evergreen trees blocks the unwanted view, buffers highway noise, and provides privacy.

2. Ground cover planting provides low-maintenance erosion control on steep slope.

3. Evergreen hedges and small trees screen and define parking area.

4. A large deciduous flowering tree shades patio and house, creating a comfortable outdoor living area.

5. Low planting of shrubs and flowers frames attractive view.

6. Low hedge separates patio and lawn areas.

7. Annuals, perennials, bulbs, flowering shrubs, and small trees combine for a long season of garden color, providing a pleasant atmosphere for people using the patio or lawn.

8. Small flowering trees provide shade and make a visually pleasing front entrance.

9. Containers filled with flowering annuals provide color and break up expanse of a large patio.

10. Arbors create sheltered spots for shade-loving plants, provide a visual transition between house and yard, and prevent hot sun from entering house windows. They also provide support for flowering vines.

11. Flowering shrubs with a long season of color and an ability to withstand shearing serve multiple functions. They delineate and add color to the front entrance and conceal the house foundation without blocking the view from the front room window.

12. A curving island bed of annuals and bulbs brightens the front entrance and creates a colorful view from the front room window.

13. Flowering evergreen shrubs soften house corners.

14. Narrow evergreen shrubs block view of neighbor's home.

15. Raised bed full of flowering plants solves problem of poor soil and adds color to patio area.

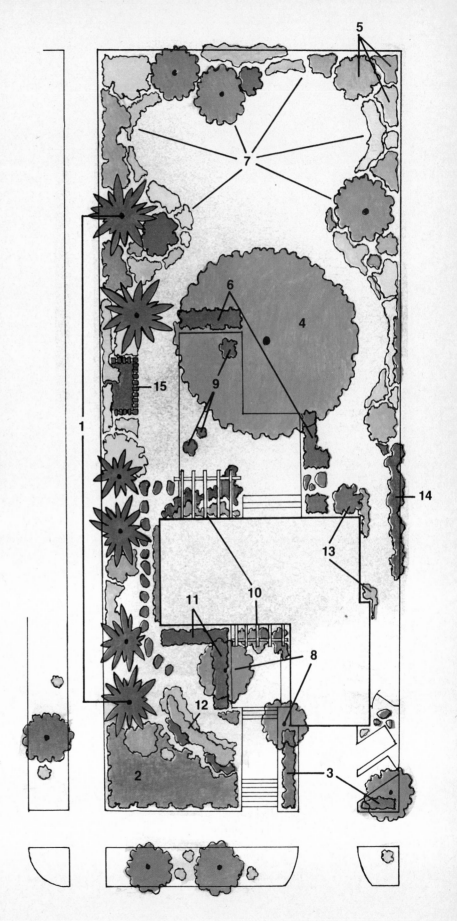

Spiraea *(Spiraea sp.)*

Landscape Use Lists

Climate Zones Note: In all lists, plants adapted to Zone 10 are also adapted to *new* Zone 11. Plants shown adapted to Zone 11 only, are recommended specifically for Zone 11.

Plants With Attractive Flowers

Here are flowering plants listed by season of bloom. Also included is blossom color. Use these lists to plan for a full season of color. See plant descriptions for exact blooming time.

Shrubs With Attractive Flowers

SPRING-FLOWERING

		Zones	
Acacia longifolia			
	Sydney Golden Wattle	7-10	Yellow
Brunfelsia pauciflora			
'Floribunda'	Yesterday-Today-and-Tomorrow	8-10	Purple, lavender, white
Callistemon citrinus			
	Lemon Bottlebrush	8-10	Red
Camellia sp.	Camellia	7-10	Red, pink, white
Caragana arborescens			
	Siberian Pea Shrub	2-7	Yellow
Carissa grandiflora			
	Natal Plum	10	White
Ceanothus sp.			
	California Lilac	8-10	Lavender, white
Chaenomeles sp.			
	Flowering Quince	5-9	Many colors
Chionanthus praecox			
	Wintersweet	7-9	Yellow
Cistus x purpureus			
	Orchid-Spot Rock Rose	8-10	Reddish-purple
Citrus sp.	Citrus	9-10	White
Cotoneaster sp.			
	Cotoneaster	5-10	White, pink
Cytisus sp.	Broom	6-10	Yellowish
Daphne odora			
	Winter Daphne	8-10	Pink
Deutzia gracilis			
	Slender Deutzia	5-8	White to pink
Enkianthus campanulatus			
	Enkianthus	5-9	Yellow
Erica sp.	Heath	4-8	White, pink

SPRING-FLOWERING (Continued)

		Zones	
Eugenia uniflora			
	Barbados Cherry	9-10	White
Feijoa sellowiana			
	Pineapple Guava	8-10	White with red
Forsythia x intermedia			
	Border Forsythia	5-9	Yellow
Grevillea 'Noell'			
	Noell Grevillea	8-10	Rosy-red and white
Kolkwitzia amabilis			
	Beautybush	5-8	Pink
Lantana sp.	Lantana	9-10	Many colors
Leptospermum scoparium			
	New Zealand Tea Tree	9-10	White, pink
Leucothoe sp.	Leucothoe	5-9	White
Ligustrum japonicum			
	Wax-Leaf Privet	7-10	White
Lonicera tatarica			
	Tatarian Honeysuckle	3-9	White, pink, red
Mahonia sp.	Oregon Grape	5-10	Yellow
Philadelphus sp.			
	Mock Orange	4-8	White
Photinia x fraseri			
	Red-Tip Photinia	7-10	White
Pieris sp.	Pieris	5-9	White, pink, red
Pittosporum tobira 'Wheeler's Dwarf'			
	Mock Orange	8-10	White
Prunus x cistena			
	Purple-Leaf Sand Cherry	2-9	White, pink
Pyracantha sp.	Firethorn	5-10	Creamy-white
Raphiolepis indica			
	Indian Hawthorn	8-10	White, pink, red
Rhododendron hybrids			
	Azalea, Rhododendron	4-10	Many colors
Rosa hybrids	Rose	5-10	Many colors
Rosmarinus officinalis			
	Rosemary	7-10	Light blue
Skimmia japonica			
	Skimmia	6-8	Yellowish-white
Spiraea sp.	Spiraea	3-9	White, pink, red
Syringa sp.	Lilac	3-8	Many colors
Trachelospermum sp.			
	Star Jasmine	7-10	White, yellow
Viburnum sp.	Viburnum	2-10	White
Weigela florida	Weigela	4-9	Pink, rose-red

WINTER-FLOWERING

		Zones	
Acacia longifolia			
	Sydney Golden Wattle	7-10	Yellow
Camellia sp.	Camellia	7-10	Red, pink, white
Carissa grandiflora			
	Natal Plum	10	White
Erica sp.	Heath	4-8	White, pink
Hamamelis x intermedia			
	Witch Hazel	6-8	Yellow
Lantana sp.	Lantana	9-10	Many colors
Raphiolepis indica			
	Indian Hawthorn	8-10	White, pink, red
Rosmarinus officinalis			
	Rosemary	7-10	Light blue
Viburnum tinus	Laurustinus	7-10	White

SUMMER-FLOWERING

		Zones	
Abelia x grandiflora			
	Glossy Abelia	6-10	White, pink
Brunfelsia pauciflora			
'Floribunda'	Yesterday-		
	Today-and-Tomorrow	8-10	Purple, lavender, white
Buddleia davidii			
	Butterfly Bush	5-10	Purple, lavender, white
Callistemon sp.	Bottlebrush	8-10	Red
Calluna vulgaris			
	Scotch Heather	4-7	White, purple
Carissa grandiflora			
	Natal Plum	10	White
Cistus x purpureus			
	Orchid-Spot Rock Rose	8-10	Lavender
Convolvulus cneorum			
	Bush Morning-Glory	7-10	White, pink
Enkianthus campanulatus			
	Enkianthus	5-9	Yellow
Erica sp.	Heath	4-8	White, pink
Escallonia exoniensis			
	Escallonia	7-10	White, rose
Fuchsia sp.	Fuchsia	6-10	Many colors
Gardenia jasminoides			
	Gardenia	8-10	White
Hebe sp.	Hebe	9-10	White, pink, purple
Hibiscus rosa-sinensis			
	Chinese Hibiscus	9-10	Many colors
Hibiscus syriacus			
	Rose-of-Sharon	5-10	White, pink, rose
Hydrangea sp.	Hydrangea	5-10	White, pink, blue
Hypericum sp.			
	St. John's-Wort	5-10	Yellow
Lagerstroemia indica			
	Crape Myrtle	7-9	Many colors
Lantana sp.	Lantana	9-10	Many colors
Ligustrum sp.	Privet	7-10	White
Lonicera tatarica			
	Tatarian Honeysuckle	3-9	White, pink, red
Murraya paniculata			
	Orange Jessamine	9	White
Myrtus communis			
	True Myrtle	9-10	White

SUMMER-FLOWERING (continued)

		Zones	
Nandina domestica			
	Heavenly Bamboo	6-10	Pinkish-white
Nerium oleander	Oleander	8-10	Many colors
Potentilla fruticosa			
	Shrubby Cinquefoil	2-9	White, yellow, red
Rosa hybrids	Rose	5-10	Many colors
Spartium junceum			
	Spanish Broom	7-10	Bright yellow
Spiraea sp.	Spiraea	3-9	White, pink, red
Trachelospermum jasminoides			
	Star Jasmine	8-10	White

FALL-FLOWERING

		Zones	
Abelia x grandiflora			
	Glossy Abelia	6-10	White, pink
Callistemon citrinus			
	Lemon Bottlebrush	8-10	Red
Calluna vulgaris			
	Scotch Heather	4-7	White, purple
Camellia sp.	Camellia	7-10	Red, pink, white
Carissa grandiflora			
	Natal Plum	10	White
Erica x darleyensis			
	Darley Heath	4-8	White, pink
Fatsia japonica			
	Japanese Aralia	8-10	Creamy-white
Fuchsia sp.	Fuchsia	6-10	Many colors
Hebe sp.	Hebe	9-10	White, pink, purple
Hydrangea sp.	Hydrangea	5-10	White, pink, red, blue
Lantana sp.	Lantana	9-10	Many colors
Murraya paniculata			
	Orange Jessamine	9	White
Nerium oleander	Oleander	8-10	Many colors
Potentilla fruticosa			
	Shrubby Cinquefoil	2-9	White, yellow
Raphiolepis indica			
	Indian Hawthorn	8-10	White, pink, red
Rosa hybrids	Rose	5-10	Many colors
Viburnum tinus	Laurustinus	7-10	White

Hydrangeas *(Hydrangea sp.)*

Shrubby cinquefoil *(Potentilla fruticosa)*

Vines with Attractive Flowers

SPRING-FLOWERING

		Zones	
Actinidia chinensis	Kiwi	8-10	White
Beaumontia grandiflora			
	Herald's-Trumpet	10	White
Bougainvillea sp.			
	Bougainvillea	9-10	Many colors
Clematis armandii			
	Evergreen Clematis	8-10	White
Clytostoma callistegioides			
	Violet Trumpet Vine	9-10	Purple
Distictis sp.	Trumpet Vine	9-10	Orange-red, violet
Gelsemium sempervirens			
	Carolina Yellow Jessamine	7-10	Yellow
Hibbertia scandens			
	Gold Guinea Plant	10	Yellow
Jasminum sp.	Jasmine	8-10	White, rose, purple
Passiflora sp.			
	Passion Vine	9-10	White, pink, purple
Rosa hybrids	Rose	5-10	Many colors
Trachelospermum sp.			
	Jasmine	7-10	Yellow, white
Wisteria sp.	Wisteria	5-9	Violet, blue, white

FALL-FLOWERING

		Zones	
Antigonon leptopus			
	Coral Vine	8-10	Pink
Clematis sp.	Clematis	4-10	Many colors
Clytostoma callistegioides			
	Violet Trumpet Vine	9-10	Purple
Distictis sp.	Trumpet Vine	9-10	Orange-red, violet
Hibbertia scandens			
	Gold Guinea Plant	10	Yellow
Passiflora sp.	Passionflower	9-10	White, red, lavender
Polygonum aubertii			
	Silver Lace Vine	5-10	White
Rosa hybrids	Climbing Rose	5-10	Many colors
Tecomaria capensis			
	Cape Honeysuckle	9-10	Reddish

SUMMER-FLOWERING

		Zones	
Antigonon leptopus			
	Coral Vine	8-10	Pink
Beaumontia grandiflora			
	Herald's-Trumpet	10	White
Bougainvillea sp.			
	Bougainvillea	9-10	Many colors
Campsis sp.			
	Trumpet Creeper	4-8	Orange, scarlet
Clematis x jackmanii			
	Jackman Clematis	5-10	Purple
Clematis texensis			
	Scarlet Clematis	4-10	Scarlet
Clytostoma callistegioides			
	Violet Trumpet Vine	9-10	Purple
Distictis laxiflora			
	Vanilla Trumpet Vine	9-10	Violet
Hibbertia scandens			
	Gold Guinea Plant	10	Yellow
Hydrangea anomala			
	Climbing Hydrangea	5-9	White
Jasminum sp.	Jasmine	8-10	White, rose, purple
Lonicera sp.	Honeysuckle	4-10	White, yellow, orange, scarlet
Passiflora sp.			
	Passion Vine	9-10	White, red, lavender
Polygonum aubertii			
	Silver Lace Vine	5-10	White
Rosa hybrids			
	Climbing Rose	5-10	Many colors
Tecomaria capensis			
	Cape Honeysuckle	9-10	Reddish
Trachelospermum sp.			
	Jasmine	7-10	Yellow, white

WINTER-FLOWERING

		Zones	
Gelsemium sempervirens			
	Carolina Yellow Jessamine	7-10	Yellow
Tecomaria capensis			
	Cape Honeysuckle	9-10	Reddish

Star jasmine (Trachelospermum jasminoides)

Evergreen clematis (Clematis armandii 'Apple Blossom')

Cape honeysuckle (Tecomaria capensis)

Trees with Attractive Flowers

SPRING-FLOWERING

	Zones	
Acacia baileyana		
Bailey Acacia	9	Yellow
Aesculus sp.		
Horse Chestnut	4-9	White, pink, red
Amelanchier sp.		
Serviceberry	4-8	White
Arbutus menziesii Madrone	6-9	White to pink
Bauhinia purpurea		
Purple Orchid Tree	9-10	Orchid-purple
Callistemon citrinus		
Lemon Bottlebrush	8-10	Red
Cercis sp. Redbud	4-10	Purplish-pink, white
Citrus sp. Citrus	9-10	White
Cornus florida Dogwood	2-9	White, pink, red
Cotinus coggygria		
Smoke Tree	5-8	Purple-gray, white
Crataegus sp. Hawthorn	3-9	White, pink, red
Erythrina sp. Coral Tree	9-10	Pink, red, orange
Fraxinus ornus		
Flowering Ash	6-8	White
Halesia carolina Silver-Bell	5-8	White
Jacaranda mimosifolia		
Jacaranda	9-10	Lavender-blue
Laburnum x watereri 'Vossii'		
Golden-Chain Tree	6-9	Yellow
Magnolia sp. Magnolia	5-10	White, purple
Malus sp.		
Flowering Crab Apple	2-8	White, pink, red
Parkinsonia aculeata		
Jerusalem Thorn	8-10	Yellow
Prunus sp. Flowering Fruit	2-10	White, pink
Pyrus sp. Pear	5-10	White
Robinia sp. Locust	3-10	White, rose-purple
Sorbus aucuparia		
European Mountain Ash	2-7	White

FALL-FLOWERING

	Zones	
Callistemon citrinus		
Lemon Bottlebrush	8-10	Red
Chorisia speciosa		
Floss-Silk Tree	9-10	Pink, red
Erythrina humeana		
Natal Coral Tree	9-10	Orange
Franklinia alatamaha		
Franklinia	6-8	White
Magnolia grandiflora		
Southern Magnolia	7-10	White
Melaleuca quinquenervia		
Cajeput Tree	9-10	Yellowish
Nerium oleander Oleander	8-10	Many colors

SUMMER-FLOWERING

	Zones	
Albizia julibrissin Silk Tree	7-10	Pink
Callistemon sp. Bottlebrush	8-10	Red
Cassia excelsa		
Crown of Gold Tree	10	Bright yellow
Catalpa sp. Catalpa	5-10	White
Chionanthus virginicus		
Fringe Tree	5-9	White

'Kwanzan' Japanese flowering cherry (*Prunus serrulata*)

SUMMER-FLOWERING (continued)

	Zones	
Cornus kousa		
Japanese Dogwood	6-9	Creamy-white
Erythrina crista-galli		
Cockspur Coral Tree	9-10	Pink, red
Eucalyptus sp. Eucalyptus	7-10	White, red
Franklinia alatamaha		
Franklin Tree	6-8	White
Hymenosporum flavum		
Sweetshade	9-10	Yellow
Jacaranda mimosifolia		
Jacaranda	9-10	Lavender-blue
Koelreuteria sp.		
Golden-Rain Tree	5-9	Yellow
Lagerstroemia indica		
Crape Myrtle	7-9	Many colors
Ligustrum sp. Privet	4-10	White
Magnolia grandiflora		
Southern Magnolia	7-10	White
Melaleuca sp. Melaleuca	9-10	White, yellow
Nerium oleander Oleander	8-10	Many colors
Oxydendrum arboreum		
Sourwood	6-9	White
Sophora japonica		
Japanese Pagoda Tree	5-8	Pale yellow
Stewartia pseudocamellia		
Japanese Stewartia	6-9	White
Styrax japonicus		
Japanese Snowbell	6-9	White

WINTER-FLOWERING

	Zones	
Acacia longifolia		
Sydney Golden Wattle	7-10	Yellow
Arbutus unedo		
Strawberry Tree	7-10	White, pink
Chorisia speciosa		
Floss-Silk Tree	9-10	Pink, red
Erythrina caffra Coral Tree	9-10	Red, orange
Pyrus kawakamii		
Evergreen Pear	9-10	White

Trailing ice plant *(Lampranthus spectabilis)*

Wild strawberry *(Fragaria chiloensis)*

Thyme *(Thymus sp.)*

Ground Covers with Attractive Flowers

SPRING-FLOWERING

		Zones	
Aizoaceae	Ice Plants	8-10	Many colors
Ajuga reptans	Carpet Bugle	4-10	Blue
Convallaria majalis	Lily-of-the-Valley	3-9	White
Fragaria chiloensis	Wild Strawberry	4-8	White, yellow
Gazania sp.	Gazania	9-10	Yellow, orange-red
Osteospermum fruticosum	Trailing African Daisy	9-10	White, purple
Sedum sp.	Sedum	3-10	Many colors
Vinca sp.	Periwinkle	5-10	Lavender-purple, white

SUMMER-FLOWERING

		Zones	
Aizoaceae	Ice Plants	8-10	Many colors
Ajuga reptans	Carpet Bugle	4-10	Blue
Arenaria sp.	Irish and Scotch Moss	3-9	White
Chamaemelum nobile	Roman Chamomile	7-10	Gold
Convallaria majalis	Lily-of-the-Valley	3-9	White
Gazania sp.	Gazania	9-10	Yellow, orange-red
Hosta sp.	Plantain Lily	3-9	White, lavender, purple
Liriope sp.	Lily Turf	5-10	White to lavender
Ophiopogon sp.	Mondo Grass	5-10	White to lavender
Osteospermum fruticosum	Trailing African Daisy	9-10	White, purple
Pachysandra terminalis	Japanese Spurge	4-9	White
Thymus sp.	Thyme	3-10	White, pink
Vinca sp.	Periwinkle	5-10	Lavender-purple, white

FALL-FLOWERING

		Zones	
Gazania sp.	Gazania	9-10	Yellow, orange-red
Osteospermum fruticosum	Trailing African Daisy	9-10	White, purple

WINTER-FLOWERING

		Zones	
Aizoaceae	Ice Plants	8-10	Many colors
Osteospermum fruticosum	Trailing African Daisy	9-10	White, purple

Floribunda rose 'Bahia' (*Rosa* hybrid)

Chinese jasmine (*Jasminum polyanthum*)

Wisteria (*Wisteria sp.*)

Plants with Fragrant Flowers

These plants please the nose as well as the eye. Some must be enjoyed up close, others will perfume an entire garden.

GROUND COVERS

		Zones
Convallaria majalis	Lily-of-the-Valley	3-9
Hosta sp.	Plantain Lily	3-9
Pachysandra terminalis	Japanese Spurge	4-9

SHRUBS

		Zones
Buddleia davidii	Butterfly Bush	5-10
Carissa grandiflora	Natal Plum	10
Citrus sp.	Citrus	9-10
Cleyera japonica	Japanese Cleyera	8-10
Cytisus sp.	Broom	6-10
Daphne odora	Winter Daphne	8-10
Elaeagnus pungens	Silverberry	7-10
Gardenia jasminoides	Gardenia	8-10
Hamamelis x intermedia	Witch Hazel	6-8
Osmanthus heterophyllus	Holly Olive	7-10
Philadelphus sp.	Mock Orange	4-8
Pittosporum tobira	Tobira	8-10
Rhododendron hybrids	Azalea, Rhododendron	4-10
Rosa hybrids	Rose	5-10
Sarcococca hookerana humilis	Sweet Box	7-10
Spartium junceum	Spanish Broom	7-10
Syringa vulgaris	Lilac	3-8
Trachelospermum sp.	Star Jasmine	7-10
Viburnum sp.	Viburnum	2-10

TREES

		Zones
Chionanthus virginicus	Fringe Tree	5-10
Citrus sp.	Citrus	9-10
Elaeagnus angustifolia	Russian Olive	2-10
Magnolia grandiflora	Southern Magnolia	7-10
Magnolia virginiana	Sweet Bay	6-10
Malus sp.	Flowering Crab Apple	2-8
Prunus sp.	Flowering Fruit	2-9
Robinia sp.	Locust	3-10
Sophora japonica	Japanese Pagoda Tree	5-8
Styrax japonicus	Japanese Snowbell	6-9
Tilia sp.	Linden	4-8

VINES

		Zones
Actinidia chinensis	Kiwi	8-10
Beaumontia grandiflora	Herald's-Trumpet	10
Clematis armandii	Evergreen Clematis	8-10
Distictis laxiflora	Vanilla Trumpet Vine	9-10
Gelsemium sempervirens	Carolina Yellow Jessamine	7-10
Jasminum sp.	Jasmine	8-10
Lonicera hildebrandiana	Giant Burmese Honeysuckle	9-10
Lonicera japonica	Japanese Honeysuckle	4-10
Passiflora x alatocaerulea	Hybrid Passionflower	9-10
Rosa hybrids	Climbing Rose	5-10
Trachelospermum sp.	Star Jasmine	7-10
Wisteria sp.	Wisteria	5-9

Vines for Arbor and Patio Cover

Using vines overhead for shade is a smart, attractive way to cool a sunny exposure. Dense vines can provide deep shade, while more open vines create a pleasing, dappled light. Choose a deciduous vine to let in the winter sun and screen the summer heat. A vine-covered arbor can also be used as a regal entryway, an invitation to the garden, or an accent for a special place.

		Zones
Actinidia chinensis	Kiwi	8-10
Antigonon leptopus	Coral Vine	8-10
Beaumontia grandiflora	Herald's-Trumpet	10
Bougainvillea sp.	Bougainvillea	9-10
Celastrus sp.	Bittersweet	3-9
Clematis sp.	Clematis	4-10
Distictis sp.	Trumpet Vine	9-10
Gelsemium sempervirens	Carolina Yellow Jessamine	7-10
Hedera helix	English Ivy	5-10
Hibbertia scandens	Gold Guinea Plant	10
Jasminum sp.	Jasmine	8-10
Lonicera sp.	Honeysuckle	4-10
Parthenocissus sp.	Boston Ivy, Virginia Creeper	4-10
Passiflora sp.	Passionflower	9-10
Polygonum aubertii	Silver Lace Vine	5-10
Rhoicissus capensis	Cape Grape	10
Rosa hybrids	Climbing Rose	5-10
Trachelospermum sp.	Star Jasmine	7-10
Vitis sp.	Grape	6-10
Wisteria sp.	Wisteria	5-9

Color in More than One Season

With any combination of colorful flowers, fruit, foliage, or bark, these plants are highlights for many months of the year.

GROUND COVERS		Zones
Ajuga reptans	Carpet Bugle	4-10
Convallaria majalis		
	Lily-of-the-Valley	3-9
Festuca ovina glauca		
	Blue Fescue	5-10
Fragaria chiloensis		
	Wild Strawberry	4-8
Hosta sp.	Plantain Lily	3-9
Pachysandra terminalis		
	Japanese Spurge	4-9
Sedum sp.	Sedum	3-10
Thymus sp.	Thyme	3-10

SHRUBS		Zones
Abelia x grandiflora		
	Glossy Abelia	6-10
Berberis sp.	Barberry	4-10
Callistemon citrinus		
	Lemon Bottlebrush	8-10
Carissa grandiflora	Natal Plum	10
Cornus sp.	Dogwood	2-9
Cotoneaster sp.	Cotoneaster	5-10
Enkianthus campanulatus		
	Enkianthus	5-9
Euonymus sp.	Euonymus	3-9
Hamamelis x intermedia		
	Witch Hazel	6-8
Hydrangea quercifolia		
	Oakleaf Hydrangea	6-9
Ilex sp.	Holly	3-10
Kolkwitzia amabilis		
	Beautybush	5-8
Lagerstroemia indica		
	Crape Myrtle	7-9
Leucothoe fontanesiana		
	Drooping Leucothoe	5-8
Mahonia sp.	Mahonia	5-10
Murraya paniculata		
	Orange Jessamine	9
Myrtus communis	True Myrtle	9-10
Nandina domestica		
	Heavenly Bamboo	6-10
Photinia x fraseri		
	Red-Tip Photinia	7-10
Pieris sp.	Pieris	5-9
Pittosporum tobira	Tobira	8-10
Pyracantha sp.	Firethorn	5-10
Raphiolepis indica		
	Indian Hawthorn	8-10
Rhododendron hybrids		
	Deciduous Azalea	5-8
Rosa hybrids	Rose	5-10
Sarcococca hookerana humilis		
	Sweet Box	7-10
Skimmia japonica	Skimmia	6-8
Spiraea sp.	Spiraea	3-9
Viburnum sp.	Viburnum	2-10

TREES		Zones
Amelanchier sp.	Serviceberry	4-8
Arbutus sp.	Arbutus	6-10
Betula sp.	Birch	2-9
Cercis sp.	Redbud	4-10
Citrus sp.	Citrus	9-10
Cornus sp.	Dogwood	2-9
Cotinus coggygria	Smoke Tree	5-8
Crataegus sp.	Hawthorn	3-9
Halesia carolina	Silver-Bell	5-8
Ilex sp.	Holly	3-10
Koelreuteria sp.		
	Golden-Rain Tree	5-9
Lagerstroemia indica		
	Crape Myrtle	7-9
Ligustrum sp.	Privet	4-10
Magnolia sp.	Magnolia	5-10
Malus sp.	Flowering Crab Apple	2-8
Ostrya virginiana		
	American Hop Hornbeam	4-9
Oxydendrum arboreum		
	Sourwood	6-9
Prunus sp.	Flowering Fruit	2-10
Pyrus calleryana 'Bradford'		
	Bradford Pear	5-9
Sophora japonica		
	Japanese Pagoda Tree	5-8
Sorbus aucuparia		
	European Mountain Ash	2-7
Stewartia pseudocamellia		
	Japanese Stewartia	6-9
Styrax japonicus		
	Japanese Snowbell	6-9

VINES		Zones
Actinidia chinensis	Kiwi	8-10
Antigonon leptopus	Coral Vine	8-10
Beaumontia grandiflora		
	Herald's-Trumpet	10
Bougainvillea sp.	Bougainvillea	9-10
Celastrus sp.	Bittersweet	3-9
Clematis sp.	Clematis	4-10
Clytostoma callistegioides		
	Violet Trumpet Vine	9-10
Distictis sp.	Trumpet Vine	9-10
Euonymus fortunei		
	Wintercreeper	4-8
Hedera helix 'Aureo-variegata'		
	Yellow-Variegated English Ivy	5-10
Hedera helix 'Gold Heart'		
	Gold Heart English Ivy	5-10
Hibbertia scandens		
	Gold Guinea Plant	10
Jasminum sp.	Jasmine	8-10
Lonicera sempervirens		
	Trumpet Honeysuckle	4-10
Parthenocissus sp.		
	Boston Ivy, Virginia Creeper	4-10
Passiflora edulis		
	Purple Granadilla	9-10
Polygonum aubertii		
	Silver Lace Vine	5-10
Rosa hybrids	Climbing Rose	5-10
Tecomaria capensis		
	Cape Honeysuckle	9-10
Vitis sp.	Grape	6-10

Smoke tree (Cotinus coggygria)

Firethorn (Pyracantha sp.)

Maple *(Acer sp.)*

Shamel ash *(Fraxinus uhdei)*

Colorful Fall Foliage

These plants provide a reliable source of autumn color. Their fall foliage is as spectacular as any flowers.

SHRUBS		Zones
Berberis x mentorensis		
	Mentor Barberry	5-8
Berberis thunbergii		
	Japanese Barberry	4-9
Cornus sp.	Dogwood	2-9
Cotinus coggygria	Smoke Tree	5-8
Cotoneaster divaricatus		
	Spreading Cotoneaster	5-10
Cotoneaster horizontalis		
	Rock Cotoneaster	5-10
Euonymus alata		
	Winged Euonymus	3-9
Hydrangea quercifolia		
	Oakleaf Hydrangea	6-9
Mahonia sp.	Oregon Grape	5-10
Nandina domestica		
	Heavenly Bamboo	6-10
Salix sp.	Willow	3-10
Spiraea sp.	Spiraea	3-9
Viburnum sp.	Viburnum	2-10

TREES		Zones
Acer sp.	Maple	3-9
Amelanchier sp.	Serviceberry	4-8
Betula pendula		
	European White Birch	2-9
Cercidiphyllum japonicum		
	Katsura Tree	4-9
Cercis sp.	Redbud	4-10
Cladrastis lutea		
	American Yellowwood	4-9
Cornus sp.	Dogwood	2-9
Crataegus sp.	Hawthorn	3-9
Fagus sylvatica		
	European Beech	5-9
Franklinia alatamaha		
	Franklin Tree	6-8
Fraxinus sp.	Ash	2-10

Ginkgo biloba		
	Maidenhair Tree	4-8
Gleditsia triacanthos inermis		
	Thornless Honey Locust	4-10
Gymnocladus dioica		
	Kentucky Coffee Tree	5-7
Halesia carolina	Silver-Bell	5-8
Koelreuteria bipinnata		
	Chinese Flame Tree	5-9
Lagerstroemia indica		
	Crape Myrtle	7-9
Larix sp.	Larch	3-8
Liquidambar sp.	Sweet Gum	5-9
Liriodendron tulipifera		
	Tulip Tree	5-9
Nyssa sylvatica	Sour Gum	5-9
Oxydendrum arboreum		
	Sourwood	6-9
Pistacia chinensis		
	Chinese Pistachio	7-10
Populus sp.	Poplar	2-10
Pyrus calleryana 'Bradford'		
	Bradford Pear	5-9
Quercus sp.	Oak	4-10
Rhus typhina	Staghorn Sumac	3-8
Salix sp.	Willow	3-10
Sophora japonica		
	Japanese Pagoda Tree	5-8
Sorbus aucuparia		
	European Mountain Ash	2-7
Stewartia pseudocamellia		
	Japanese Stewartia	6-9
Styrax japonicus		
	Japanese Snowbell	6-9
Taxodium distichum		
	Bald Cypress	5-10
Zelkova serrata		
	Saw-Leaf Zelkova	5-8

VINES		Zones
Celastrus sp.	Bittersweet	3-9
Parthenocissus sp.		
	Boston Ivy, Virginia Creeper	4-10
Vitis sp.	Grape	6-10

Trees to Garden Under

These trees have well-behaved roots and cast light enough shade to allow other plants to grow beneath them. Many are also excellent lawn trees.

		Zones
Albizia julibrissin	Silk Tree	7-10
Betula sp.	Birch	2-9
Celtis sp.	Hackberry	4-9
Cercis sp.	Redbud	4-10
Cornus sp.	Dogwood	4-9
Crataegus sp.	Hawthorn	3-9
Erythrina sp.	Coral Tree	9-10
Fraxinus sp.	Ash	2-10
Gleditsia triacanthos inermis		
	Thornless Honey Locust	4-10
Halesia carolina	Silver-Bell	5-8
Jacaranda mimosifolia		
	Jacaranda	9-10
Koelreuteria sp.		
	Golden-Rain Tree	5-9
Ligustrum sp.	Privet	7-9
Magnolia sp.	Magnolia	5-10
Ostrya virginiana		
	American Hop Hornbeam	4-9
Pinus sp.	Pine	2-10
Pistacia chinensis		
	Chinese Pistachio	7-10
Podocarpus sp.	Yew Pine	8-10
Prunus sp.	Flowering Fruit	5-9
Schinus terebinthifolius		
	Brazilian Pepper Tree	9-10
Sophora japonica		
	Japanese Pagoda Tree	5-8
Sorbus aucuparia		
	European Mountain Ash	2-7
Styrax japonicus		
	Japanese Snowbell	6-9
Xylosma congestum		
	Shiny Xylosma	8-9
Zelkova serrata		
	Japanese Zelkova	5-9

Natal plum *(Carissa grandiflora)*

English hawthorn *(Crataegus laevigata)*
Creeping fig *(Ficus pumila)*

Grow in Shade

Some plants grow best in shade. Others tolerate shade but grow best in full sun. Check a plant's full description to learn its best adaptation.

GROUND COVERS		Zones
Ajuga reptans	Carpet Bugle	4-10
Arenaria sp.		
	Irish and Scotch Moss	3-9
Chamaemelum nobile		
	Roman Chamomile	7-10
Convallaria majalis		
	Lily-of-the-Valley	3-9
Fragaria chiloensis		
	Wild Strawberry	4-8
Hosta sp.	Plantain Lily	3-9
Liriope sp.	Lily Turf	5-10
Ophiopogon sp.	Mondo Grass	5-10
Pachysandra terminalis		
	Japanese Spurge	4-9
Sedum sp.	Sedum	3-10
Vinca sp.	Periwinkle	5-10

SHRUBS		Zones
Buxus sp.	Boxwood	5-10
Camellia sp.	Camellia	7-10
Carissa grandiflora	Natal Plum	10
Chamaecyparis sp.		
	False Cypress	5-9
Cleyera japonica		
	Japanese Cleyera	8-10
Cocculus laurifolius		
	Laurel-Leaf Cocculus	8-10
Coprosma repens	Mirror Plant	9-10
Euonymus sp.	Euonymus	4-9
Gardenia jasminoides	Gardenia	8-10
Hydrangea sp.	Hydrangea	6-10
Ilex sp.	Holly	5-10
Leucothoe sp.	Leucothoe	5-9
Ligustrum japonicum		
	Japanese Privet	7-10
Mahonia sp.	Mahonia	5-10
Murraya paniculata		
	Orange Jessamine	9
Myrtus communis	True Myrtle	9-10
Nandina domestica		
	Heavenly Bamboo	6-10
Osmanthus heterophyllus		
	Holly Olive	7-10
Pieris sp.	Pieris	5-9
Pittosporum tobira	Tobira	8-10
Rhododendron hybrids		
	Azalea, Rhododendron	4-10
Sarcococca hookerana humilis		
	Sweet Box	7-10
Skimmia japonica		
	Japanese Skimmia	6-8
Taxus sp.	Yew	5-9
Viburnum sp.	Viburnum	7-10
Xylosma congestum		
	Shiny Xylosma	8-10

TREES, DECIDUOUS		Zones
Acer palmatum		
	Japanese Maple	6-8
Amelanchier sp.	Serviceberry	4-8
Cercis canadensis		
	Eastern Redbud	4-7
Chionanthus virginicus		
	Fringe Tree	5-9
Cornus sp.	Dogwood	2-9
Crataegus sp.	Hawthorn	3-9
Franklinia alatamaha		
	Franklin Tree	6-8
Oxydendrum arboreum		
	Sourwood	6-9
Styrax japonicus		
	Japanese Snowbell	6-9

TREES, EVERGREEN		Zones
Arbutus unedo		
	Strawberry Tree	7-10
Ficus sp.	Fig	9-10
Ilex sp.	Holly	3-10
Laurus nobilis	Grecian Laurel	8-10
Palmae	Palm	8-10
Podocarpus sp.	Yew Pine	8-10
Tsuga canadensis		
	Canadian Hemlock	5-9
Tsuga caroliniana		
	Carolina Hemlock	5-7

VINES		Zones
Actinidia chinensis	Kiwi	8-10
Celastrus sp.	Bittersweet	3-9
Clematis sp.	Clematis	4-10
Clytostoma callistegioides		
	Violet Trumpet Vine	9-10
Distictis sp.	Trumpet Vine	9-10
Euonymus fortunei		
	Wintercreeper	4-8
x Fatshedera lizei	Fatshedera	9-10
Ficus pumila	Creeping Fig	9-10
Gelsemium sempervirens		
	Carolina Yellow Jessamine	7-10
Hedera helix	English Ivy	5-10
Hibbertia scandens		
	Gold Guinea Plant	10
Hydrangea anomala		
	Climbing Hydrangea	5-9
Jasminum sp.	Jasmine	8-10
Lonicera sp.	Honeysuckle	4-10
Parthenocissus sp.		
	Boston Ivy, Virginia Creeper	4-10
Polygonum aubertii		
	Silver Lace Vine	5-10
Rhoicissus capensis		
	Cape Grape	10
Tecomaria capensis		
	Cape Honeysuckle	9-10
Trachelospermum sp.		
	Star Jasmine	7-10
Wisteria sp.	Wisteria	5-9

Ground Covers

HERBACEOUS

Herbaceous ground covers die back to the ground for the winter months, re-sprouting in the spring, so they provide cover only during the growing season.

		Zones
Aizoaceae	Ice Plants	8-10
Ajuga reptans	Carpet Bugle	4-10
Arenaria sp.		
	Irish and Scotch Moss	5-10
Chamaemelum nobile		
	Roman Chamomile	7-10
Convallaria majalis		
	Lily-of-the-Valley	3-9
Festuca ovina glauca		
	Blue Fescue	5-10
Fragaria chiloensis		
	Wild Strawberry	4-8
Gazania sp.	Gazania	9-10
Hosta sp.	Plantain Lily	3-9
Liriope sp.	Lily Turf	5-10
Ophiopogon sp.	Mondo Grass	5-10
Osteospermum fruticosum		
	Trailing African Daisy	9-10
Pachysandra terminalis		
	Japanese Spurge	4-9
Sedum sp.	Sedum	3-10
Thymus sp.	Thyme	3-10
Vinca sp.	Periwinkle	5-10

LOW SHRUBS

Low, spreading shrubs make excellent year-round ground covers. Check encyclopedia for suitable varieties.

		Zones
Abelia x grandiflora 'Prostrata'		
	Prostrate Glossy Abelia	6-10
Arctostaphylos uva-ursi		
	Kinnikinnick	2-8
Baccharis pilularis		
	Coyote Brush	8-10
Berberis thunbergii		
	Japanese Barberry	4-9
Calluna vulgaris		
	Scotch Heather	4-7
Camellia sasanqua		
	Sasanqua Camellia	7-10
Carissa grandiflora	Natal Plum	10
Ceanothus sp.	California Lilac	8-10
Cistus x purpureus		
	Orchid-Spot Rock Rose	8-10
Cotoneaster sp.	Cotoneaster	5-10
Erica x darleyensis		
	Darley Heath	4-8
Hebe sp.	Hebe	9-10
Hypericum calycinum		
	Aaron's-Beard	5-10
Juniperus sp.	Juniper	2-10
Lantana sp.	Lantana	9-10
Leucothoe fontanesiana		
	Drooping Leucothoe	5-8

Blue rug juniper *(Juniperus horizontalis 'Wiltonii')*

		Zones
Nandina domestica		
	Heavenly Bamboo	6-10
Pittosporum tobira 'Wheeler's Dwarf'		
	Tobira	8-10
Pyracantha sp.	Firethorn	5-10
Raphiolepis indica		
	Indian Hawthorn	8-10
Rosmarinus officinalis		
	Rosemary	7-10
Sarcococca hookerana humilis		
	Sweet Box	7-10
Taxus baccata 'Repandens'		
	Spreading English Yew	6-9

VINES

Vines left to sprawl on the ground root along their stems, covering the ground.

		Zones
Antigonon leptopus	Coral Vine	8-10
Bougainvillea sp.	Bougainvillea	9-10
Celastrus sp.	Bittersweet	3-9
Clematis sp.	Clematis	4-10
Euonymus fortunei		
	Wintercreeper	4-8
x Fatshedera lizei	Fatshedera	9-10
Gelsemiun sempervirens		
	Carolina Yellow Jessamine	7-10
Hedera helix	English Ivy	5-10
Hibbertia scandens		
	Gold Guinea Plant	10
Jasminum sp.	Jasmine	8-10
Lonicera japonica 'Halliana'		
	Hall's Honeysuckle	4-10
Parthenocissus sp.		
	Boston Ivy, Virginia Creeper	4-10
Passiflora caerulea		
	Blue Passionflower	9-10
Rhoicissus capensis		
	Cape Grape	10
Tecomaria capensis		
	Cape Honeysuckle	9-10
Trachelospermum sp.		
	Star Jasmine	7-10

Leyland cypress *(x Cupressocyparis leylandii)*

Evergreen Windbreaks

These are sturdy, dense-growing evergreen shrubs and trees that can stand up to frequent buffering by strong or gusty winds and still retain an attractive appearance.

		Zones
Cedrus deodara	Deodar Cedar	7-10
Ceratonia siliqua	Carob	9-10
Chamaecyparis lawsoniana		
	Lawson Cypress	6-9
x Cupressocyparis leylandii		
	Leyland Cypress	5-10
Cupressus sp.	Cypress	6-10
Dodonea viscosa	Hopbush	8-10
Elaeagnus pungens	Silverberry	7-10
Eucalyptus sp.	Eucalyptus	7-10
Juniperus (tree-types)	Juniper	3-10
Ligustrum japonicum		
	Japanese Privet	7-10
Myoporum laetum 'Carsonii'		
	Myoporum	8-10
Nerium oleander	Oleander	8-10
Picea sp.	Spruce	2-8
Pinus sp.	Pine	2-10
Pittosporum tobira	Tobira	8-10
Podocarpus sp.	Yew Pine	8-10
Prunus caroliniana		
	Carolina Cherry Laurel	7-10
Prunus laurocerasus		
	English Laurel	7-10
Pseudotsuga menziesii		
	Douglas Fir	4-9
Pyracantha sp.		
	Firethorn	5-10
Rhamnus alternus		
	Italian Buckthorn	7-10
Sequoia sempervirens		
	Coast Redwood	7-10
Taxus sp.	Yew	5-9
Thuja sp.	Arborvitae	3-9
Tsuga sp.	Hemlock	5-9

Yew pine (Podocarpus macrophyllus)

Crab apple (Malus sp.)

Evergreen pear (Pyrus kawakamii)

Hedges

These plants that can be used as hedges are grouped by the heights at which they can easily be maintained: 3 feet or lower, 6 feet or lower, and over 6 feet. Those marked with an asterisk * are best used as informal, unclipped hedges; others can be sheared.

Under 3 Feet		Zones
Berberis sp.	Barberry	4-10
Buxus sp.	Boxwood	5-10
Carissa grandiflora	Natal Plum	10
Chamaecyparis sp.		
	False Cypress	5-9
Coprosma repens	Mirror Plant	9-10
Cotoneaster sp.	Cotoneaster	5-10
Ilex sp.	Holly	3-10
Juniperus sp.	Juniper	2-10
Nandina domestica*		
	Heavenly Bamboo	6-10
Pittosporum tobira 'Wheeler's Dwarf'		
	Wheeler's Dwarf Tobira	8-10
Pyracantha sp.	Firethorn	5-10
Rosmarinus officinalis		
	Rosemary	7-10
Spiraea sp.*	Spiraea	3-9
Taxus sp.	Yew	5-9
Thuja occidentalis	Arborvitae	3-9
Viburnum sp.*	Viburnum	2-10

3 to 6 Feet		Zones
Berberis sp.	Barberry	4-10
Camellia sp.	Camellia	7-10
Chaenomeles sp.*		
	Flowering Quince	5-9
Chamaecyparis sp.		
	False Cypress	5-9
Citrus sp.	Citrus	9-10
Cotoneaster sp.	Cotoneaster	5-10
Elaeagnus pungens	Silverberry	7-10
Euonymus sp.	Euonymus	3-9
Ilex sp.	Holly	3-10
Juniperus sp.	Juniper	2-10
Ligustrum sp.	Privet	4-10
Lonicera tatarica		
	Tatarian Honeysuckle	3-9
Myrtus communis	True Myrtle	9-10
Nandina domestica*		
	Heavenly Bamboo	6-10
Photinia x fraseri		
	Red-Tip Photinia	7-10
Pinus mugo mugo*	Mugo Pine	2-8
Podocarpus sp.	Yew Pine	8-10
Pyracantha sp.	Firethorn	5-10
Rhamnus frangula 'Columnaris'		
	Tallhedge Buckthorn	3-8
Rosa hybrids*	Rose	5-10
Taxus sp.	Yew	5-9

3 to 6 Feet (continued)

Thuja occidentalis		
	American Arborvitae	3-9
Viburnum sp.*	Viburnum	2-10

6 to 12 Feet		Zones
Abelia x grandiflora		
	Glossy Abelia	6-10
Abies concolor*	White Fir	5-8
Acer campestre*	Hedge Maple	5-8
Acer ginnala*	Amur Maple	3-8
Berberis sp.	Barberry	4-10
Callistemon citrinus		
	Lemon Bottlebrush	8-10
Caragana arborescens		
	Siberian Pea Shrub	2-7
Carpinus betulus 'Fastigiata'		
	Upright European Hornbeam	4-9
Ceratonia siliqua	Carob	9-10
Cinnamomum camphora		
	Camphor Tree	9-10
Chamaecyparis sp.		
	False Cypress	5-9
Citrus sp.	Citrus	9-10
Cotoneaster sp.	Cotoneaster	5-10
Cupressus sp.	Cypress	6-10
Elaeagnus angustifolia		
	Russian Olive	2-10
Euonymus sp.	Euonymus	3-9
Feijoa sellowiana		
	Pineapple Guava	8-10
Ficus retusa nitida*	Laurel Fig	9-10
Forsythia x intermedia*		
	Border Forsythia	5-9
Ilex sp.	Holly	3-10
Juniperus sp.	Juniper	2-10
Laurus nobilis	Grecian Laurel	8-10
Ligustrum sp.	Privet	4-10
Murraya paniculata		
	Orange Jessamine	9
Nerium oleander*	Oleander	8-10
Photinia x fraseri		
	Red-Tip Photinia	7-10
Pinus radiata	Monterey Pine	7-10
Pinus thunbergiana		
	Japanese Black Pine	5-9
Prunus caroliniana		
	Carolina Cherry Laurel	7-10
Prunus laurocerasus		
	English Laurel	7-10
Pseudotsuga menziesii		
	Douglas Fir	4-9
Rhamnus frangula 'Columnaris'		
	Tallhedge Buckthorn	3-8
Sequoia sempervirens		
	Coast Redwood	7-10
Taxus sp.	Yew	5-9
Thuja occidentalis	Arborvitae	3-9
Tsuga sp.	Hemlock	5-9
Viburnum sp.*	Viburnum	2-10
Xylosma congestum		
	Shiny Xylosma	8-10

Espalier

These plants lend themselves to espalier. Espaliers are plants trained in a flat plane by tying branches to a wall or trellis, usually in geometric patterns.

SHRUBS

		Zones
Callistemon citrinus		
	Lemon Bottlebrush	8-10
Camellia sp.	Camellia	7-10
Carissa grandiflora	Natal Plum	10
Cocculus laurifolius		
	Laurel-Leaf Cocculus	8-10
Coprosma repens	Mirror Plant	9-10
Elaeagnus pungens		
	Silverberry	7-10
Euonymus fortunei (spreading types)		
	Wintercreeper	4-8
Gardenia jasminoides	Gardenia	8-10
Hibiscus rosa-sinensis		
	Chinese Hibiscus	9-10
Ilex sp.	Holly	6-10
Juniperus sp.	Juniper	2-10
Photinia fraseri		
	Red-Tip Photinia	7-10
Pyracantha sp.	Firethorn	5-10
Sarcococca hookerana humilis		
	Sweet Box	7-10
Taxus sp.	Yew	5-9
Viburnum sp.	Viburnum	2-10
Xylosma congestum		
	Shiny Xylosma	8-10

TREES

		Zones
Callistemon sp.	Bottlebrush	8-10
Citrus sp.	Citrus	9-10
Ficus benjamina	Weeping Fig	10
Feijoa sellowiana		
	Pineapple Guava	8-10
Ilex x altaclarensis 'Wilsonii'		
	Wilson Holly	6-10
Laburnum x watereri 'Vossii'		
	Golden-Chain Tree	6-9
Magnolia sp.	Magnolia	5-10
Malus sp.	Flowering Crab Apple	2-8
Podocarpus sp.	Yew Pine	8-10
Prunus sp.	Flowering Fruit	2-9
Pyrus sp.	Pear	5-10
Taxus cuspidata	Japanese Yew	6-9
Xylosma congestum		
	Shiny Xylosma	8-10

VINES

		Zones
Actinidia chinensis	Kiwi	8-10
Beaumontia grandiflora		
	Herald's-Trumpet	10
x Fatshedera lizei	Fatshedera	9-10
Hedera helix	English Ivy	5-10
Rosa hybrids	Climbing Rose	5-10
Vitis sp.	Grape	6-10

Weeping fig (*Ficus benjamina*)

Patio Trees

These relatively small trees fit neatly into areas of activity or limited space.

		Zones
Acer ginnala	Amur Maple	3-8
Acer palmatum		
	Japanese Maple	6-8
Amelanchier sp.	Serviceberry	4-8
Arbutus unedo	Strawberry Tree	7-10
Callistemon citrinus		
	Lemon Bottlebrush	8-10
Cercidiphyllum japonicum		
	Katsura Tree	4-9
Cercis sp.	Redbud	4-10
Chionanthus virginicus		
	Fringe Tree	5-9
Citrus sp.	Citrus	9-10
Cladrastis lutea		
	American Yellowwood	4-9
Cornus florida		
	Flowering Dogwood	5-9
Cornus kousa		
	Japanese Dogwood	6-9
Crataegus sp.	Hawthorn	3-9
Erythrina sp.	Coral Tree	9-10
Eucalyptus sp.	Eucalyptus	7-10
Ficus sp.	Fig	9-10
Halesia carolina	Silver-Bell	5-8
Hymenosporum flavum		
	Sweetshade	9-10
Koelreuteria sp.	Koelreuteria	5-9
Lagerstroemia indica		
	Crape Myrtle	7-9
Laurus nobilis	Grecian Laurel	8-10
Magnolia sp.	Magnolia	5-10
Malus sp.	Flowering Crab Apple	2-8
Nerium oleander	Oleander	8-10
Oxydendrum arboreum		
	Sourwood	6-9
Podocarpus gracilior		
	African Fern Pine	9-10
Prunus sp.	Flowering Fruit	5-10
Pyrus sp.	Pear	5-10
Schinus terebinthifolius		
	Brazilian Pepper Tree	9-10
Stewartia pseudocamellia		
	Japanese Stewartia	6-9
Styrax japonicus		
	Japanese Snowbell	6-9
Wisteria sp.	Wisteria	5-9
Xylosma congestum		
	Shiny Xylosma	8-10

Lombardy poplar (*Populus nigra* 'Italica')

Screens and Buffers

When planted close together these plants form a dense screen without being clipped. Use them to block unpleasant views, stifle noise, or create privacy.

		Zones
Abies concolor	White Fir	5-8
Acer campestre	Hedge Maple	5-8
Acer platanoides 'Columnare'		
	Pyramidal Norway Maple	3-7
Bambusa sp.	Bamboo	5-10
Berberis sp.	Barberry	4-10
Carpinus betulus 'Fastigiata'		
	Upright European Hornbeam	4-9
Cedrus deodara	Deodar Cedar	7-10
Ceratonia siliqua	Carob	9-10
Chamaecyparis lawsoniana		
	Lawson Cypress	6-9
x Cupressocyparis leylandii		
	Leyland Cypress	5-10
Cupressus sp.	Cypress	6-10
Elaeagnus angustifolia		
	Russian Olive	2-10
Eucalyptus sp.	Eucalyptus	7-10
Feijoa sellowiana		
	Pineapple Guava	8-10
Ficus retusa nitida		
	Indian Laurel Fig	9-10
Ilex sp.	Holly	3-10
Juniperus sp.	Juniper	3-10
Laurus nobilis	Grecian Laurel	8-10
Ligustrum sp.	Privet	4-10
Picea sp.	Spruce	2-8
Pinus sp.	Pine	2-10
Podocarpus sp.	Yew Pine	8-10
Populus sp.	Poplar	2-10
Prunus (evergreen species)		
	Flowering Fruit	7-10
Pseudotsuga menziesii		
	Douglas Fir	4-9
Rhamnus frangula 'Columnaris'		
	Tallhedge Buckthorn	3-8
Salix sp.	Willow	3-10
Sequoiadendron giganteum		
	Giant Sequoia	6-10
Sequoia sempervirens		
	Coast Redwood	7-10
Taxus sp.	Yew	5-9
Thuja sp.	Arborvitae	3-9
Tsuga sp.	Hemlock	5-9
Xylosma congestum		
	Shiny Xylosma	8-10

Algerian tangerine *(Citrus sp.)*

Bougainvillea *(Bougainvillea sp.)*
Pine *(Pinus sp.)*

Container Plants

These well-behaved plants are easily adapted to container-growing. Attractive over a long period, they are perfect companions for patio or porch. Many tall plants are excellent container subjects in their youthful years. Container-growing allows you to grow tender species in cold climates. Plants are easily moved to protected sites during cold weather.

SHRUBS

		Zones
Buxus sp.	Boxwood	5-10
Calluna vulgaris	Scotch Heather	4-7
Camellia sp.	Camellia	7-10
Carissa grandiflora	Natal Plum	10
Citrus sp.	Citrus	9-10
Cotoneaster sp.	Cotoneaster	5-10
Euonymus fortunei		
	Wintercreeper	5-8
Fatsia japonica	Fatsia	8-10
Fuchsia x hybrida		
	Common Fuchsia	9-10
Gardenia jasminoides	Gardenia	8-10
Hibiscus rosa-sinensis		
	Chinese Hibiscus	9-10
Hydrangea sp.	Hydrangea	6-10
Ilex sp. (dwarf varieties)	Holly	3-10
Juniperus sp. (dwarf varieties)		
	Juniper	2-10
Lagerstroemia indica		
	Crape Myrtle	7-9
Lantana sp.	Lantana	9-10
Leucothoe fontanesiana		
	Drooping Leucothoe	5-8
Ligustrum japonicum (dwarf varieties)		
	Japanese Privet	7-10
Mahonia sp.	Mahonia	5-10
Myrtus communis (dwarf varieties)		
	True Myrtle	9-10
Nandina domestica (dwarf varieties)		
	Heavenly Bamboo	6-10
Nerium oleander	Oleander	8-10
Photinia x fraseri		
	Red-Tip Photinia	7-10
Picea sp. (dwarf varieties)		
	Spruce	2-8
Pieris sp.	Pieris	5-9
Pinus sp. (dwarf varieties)	Pine	2-10
Pittosporum tobira	Tobira	8-10
Pyracantha (dwarf varieties)		
	Firethorn	5-10
Rhododendron (dwarf varieties)		
	Azalea, Rhododendron	4-10
Rosa hybrids	Rose	5-10
Rosmarinus officinalis (low varieties)		
	Rosemary	7-10
Skimmia japonica	Skimmia	6-8
Spiraea sp. (dwarf varieties)		
	Spiraea	3-9
Taxus sp. (dwarf varieties)	Yew	5-9
Thuja sp. (dwarf varieties)		
	Arborvitae	3-9
Viburnum sp. (dwarf varieties)		
	Viburnum	3-10

GROUND COVERS

		Zones
Chamaemelum nobile		
	Roman Chamomile	7-10
Gazania sp.	Gazania	9-10
Osteospermum fruticosum		
	Trailing African Daisy	9-10
Sedum sp.	Sedum	3-10
Thymus sp.	Thyme	3-10
Vinca sp.	Vinca	5-10

TREES

		Zones
Acer palmatum (dwarf varieties)		
	Japanese Maple	6-8
Cedrus sp.	Cedar	6-10
Chamaecyparis lawsoniana (dwarf varieties)		
	Lawson Cypress	6-9
Chamaecyparis obtusa (dwarf varieties)		
	Hinoki Cypress	5-9
Citrus sp.	Citrus	9-10
Eucalyptus sp.	Eucalyptus	7-10
Ficus sp.	Fig	9-10
Ilex sp. (dwarf varieties)	Holly	3-10
Juniperus sp. (dwarf varieties)		
	Juniper	2-10
Laurus nobilis	Grecian Laurel	8-10
Lagerstroemia indica		
	Crape Myrtle	7-9
Ligustrum japonicum (dwarf varieties)		
	Japanese Privet	7-10
Malus sp.	Flowering Crab Apple	2-8
Nerium oleander	Oleander	8-10
Picea sp. (dwarf varieties)		
	Spruce	2-8
Pinus sp. (dwarf varieties)	Pine	2-10
Podocarpus sp.	Yew Pine	8-10
Taxus sp. (dwarf varieties)	Yew	5-9
Thuja sp. (dwarf varieties)		
	Arborvitae	3-9
Tsuga canadensis 'Pendula'		
	Weeping Canadian Hemlock	5-9

VINES

		Zones
Bougainvillea sp.	Bougainvillea	9-10
Clematis sp.	Clematis	4-10
Euonymus fortunei		
	Wintercreeper	5-8
x *Fatshedera lizei*	Fatshedera	9-10
Ficus pumila	Creeping Fig	9-10
Gelsemium sempervirens		
	Carolina Yellow Jessamine	7-10
Hedera helix	English Ivy	5-10
Hibbertia scandens		
	Gold Guinea Plant	10
Jasminum sp.	Jasmine	8-10
Passiflora sp.	Passionflower	9-10
Rhoicissus capensis		
	Cape Grape	10
Rosa hybrids	Climbing Rose	5-10
Trachelospermum jasminoides		
	Star Jasmine	7-10
Wisteria sp.	Wisteria	5-9
Vitis sp.	Grape	6-10

Fast-Growing Plants

When a fast shade cover is desired or an unsightly view needs screening, these are the plants that can do the job quickly. They can give a young landscape a mature look in just a few years. However, be aware that many of these plants have bad habits associated with fast growth such as weak wood, invasive roots, and continued fast growth once they have reached the desired size.

GROUND COVERS

		Zones
Aizoaceae	Ice Plant	8-10
Ajuga reptans	Carpet Bugle	4-10
Chamaemelum nobile		
	Roman Chamomile	7-10
Fragaria chiloensis		
	Wild Strawberry	4-8
Osteospermum fruiticosum		
	Trailing African Daisy	9-10
Sedum sp.	Sedum	3-10
Vinca sp.	Periwinkle	5-10

SHRUBS

		Zones
Abelia x grandiflora		
	Glossy Abelia	6-10
Bambusa sp.	Bamboo	5-10
Baccharis pilularis		
	Coyote Brush	8-10
Berberis sp.	Barberry	4-10
Callistemon citrinus		
	Lemon Bottlebrush	8-10
Ceanothus sp.	California Lilac	8-10
Cistus x purpureus		
	Orchid-Spot Rock Rose	8-10
Coprosma repens	Mirror Plant	9-10
Cotoneaster dammeri		
	Bearberry Cotoneaster	5-10
Cytisus sp.	Broom	6-10
Dodonea viscosa	Hopbush	8-10
Elaeagnus sp.	Elaeagnus	2-10
Forsythia x intermedia		
	Border Forsythia	5-9
Hibiscus sp.	Hibiscus	5-10
Hydrangea sp.	Hydrangea	5-10
Hypericum calycinum		
	Aaron's-Beard	5-10
Lantana sp.	Lantana	9-10
Ligustrum japonicum		
	Japanese Privet	7-10
Myoporum laetum 'Carsonii'		
	Myoporum	8-10
Nerium oleander	Oleander	8-10
Philadelphus x virginalis		
	Virginalis Mock Orange	4-8
Prunus laurocerasus		
	English Laurel	7-10
Pyracantha sp.	Firethorn	5-10
Rosa hybrids	Rose	5-10
Weigela sp.	Weigela	4-9

TREES

		Zones
Acacia baileyana	Bailey Acacia	9
Acer saccharinum	Silver Maple	4-9
Albizia julibrissin	Silk Tree	7-10
Alnus sp.	Alder	3-10
Callistemon sp.	Bottlebrush	8-10
Catalpa sp.	Catalpa	5-10
Cedrus deodara	Deodar Cedar	7-10
x Cupressocyparis leylandii		
	Leyland Cypress	5-10
Cupressus arizonica		
	Arizona Cypress	6-10
Eucalyptus sp.	Eucalyptus	7-10
Fraxinus sp.	Ash	2-10
Gleditsia tricanthos inermis		
	Thornless Honey Locust	4-10
Grevillea sp.	Grevillea	8-10
Morus alba	White Mulberry	5-9
Nerium oleander	Oleander	8-10
Parkinsonia aculeata		
	Jerusalem Thorn	8-10
Pinus sp.	Pine	2-10
Populus sp.	Poplar	2-10
Robinia sp.	Locust	3-10
Salix sp.	Willow	3-10
Sequoia sempervirens		
	Coast Redwood	7-10
Sequoiadendron giganteum		
	Giant Sequoia	6-10
Ulmus sp.	Elm	5-9

VINES

		Zones
Actinidia chinensis	Kiwi	8-10
Antigonon leptopus	Coral Vine	8-10
Beaumontia grandiflora		
	Herald's-Trumpet	10
Bougainvillea sp.	Bougainvillea	9-10
Campsis sp.	Trumpet Creeper	4-8
Celastrus sp.	Bittersweet	3-9
Clematis sp.	Clematis	4-10
Clytostoma callistegioides		
	Violet Trumpet Vine	9-10
Distictis sp.	Trumpet Vine	9-10
Ficus pumila	Creeping Fig	9-10
Hedera helix	English Ivy	5-10
Hibbertia scandens		
	Gold Guinea Plant	10
Hydrangea anomala		
	Climbing Hydrangea	5-9
Jasminum polyanthum		
	Chinese Jasmine	8-10
Lonicera sp.	Honeysuckle	3-10
Parthenocissus sp.		
	Virginia Creeper, Boston Ivy	4-10
Passiflora sp.	Passionflower	9-10
Polygonum aubertii		
	Silver Lace Vine	5-10
Rosa hybrids	Climbing Rose	5-10
Tecomaria capensis		
	Cape Honeysuckle	9-10
Trachelospermum sp.		
	Star Jasmine	7-10
Vitis sp.	Grape	6-10
Wisteria sp.	Wisteria	5-9

Mock orange (Philadelphus sp.)

Cape honeysuckle (Tecomaria capensis)

Bougainvillea *(Bougainvillea sp.)*   Oleander *(Nerium oleander)*   Bailey acacia *(Acacia baileyana)*

Drought-Tolerant Plants

Once established these plants remain attractive with relatively little water. Occasional watering will bring them to their prime.

GROUND COVERS — Zones

Aizoaceae — Ice Plants — 8-10
Arctostaphylos uva-ursi — Kinnikinnick — 2-8
Gazania sp. — Gazania — 9-10
Osteospermum fruticosum — Trailing African Daisy — 9-10
Sedum sp. — Sedum — 3-10
Thymus sp. — Thyme — 3-10
Vinca sp. — Periwinkle — 5-10

Shrubs and vines marked with an asterisk * have varieties that can also be used as ground covers.

SHRUBS — Zones

Acacia longifolia — Sydney Golden Wattle — 7-10
*Baccharis pilularis** — Coyote Brush — 8-10
*Berberis sp.** — Barberry — 4-10
Callistemon sp. — Bottlebrush — 8-10
Caragana arborescens — Siberian Pea Shrub — 2-7
*Ceanothus sp.** — California Lilac — 8-10
Cistus x purpureus — Orchid-Spot Rock Rose — 8-10
Coprosma repens — Mirror Plant — 9-10
Cotoneaster sp. — Cotoneaster — 5-10
Cortaderia selloana — Pampas Grass — 5-10
*Cytisus sp.** — Broom — 6-10
Dodonaea viscosa — Hopbush — 8-10
Elaeagnus sp. — Elaeagnus — 2-10
Escallonia exoniensis — Escallonia — 7-10
*Hypericum calycinum** — Aaron's-Beard — 5-10
*Juniperus sp.** — Juniper — 2-10
Lagerstroemia indica — Crape Myrtle — 7-9
*Lantana sp.** — Lantana — 9-10
*Leptospermum scoparium** — Tea Tree — 9-10

Lonicera tatarica — Tatarian Honeysuckle — 3-9
*Mahonia sp.** — Mahonia — 5-10
Nerium oleander — Oleander — 8-10
Pittosporum tobira — Mock Orange — 8-10
Potentilla fruticosa — Shrubby Cinquefoil — 2-9
Prunus caroliniana — Carolina Cherry Laurel — 7-10
*Pyracantha sp.** — Firethorn — 5-10
Raphiolepis indica — Indian Hawthorn — 8-10
*Rosmarinus officinalis** — Rosemary — 7-10
Spartium junceum — Spanish Broom — 7-10
*Taxus sp.** — Yew — 5-9
Viburnum prunifolium — Black Haw — 3-9
Xylosma congestum — Shiny Xylosma — 8-10

TREES — Zones

Acacia baileyana — Bailey Acacia — 9
Acer campestre — Hedge Maple — 5-8
Albizia julibrissin — Silk Tree — 7-10
Arbutus sp. — Arbutus — 6-10
Callistemon citrinus — Lemon Bottlebrush — 8-10
Cedrus deodara — Deodar Cedar — 7-10
Celtis sp. — Hackberry — 5-9
Cercis occidentalis — Western Redbud — 7-10
Eucalyptus sp. — Eucalyptus — 7-10
Fraxinus sp. — Ash — 2-10
Juniperus sp. — Juniper — 2-10
Koelreuteria paniculata — Golden-Rain Tree — 5-9
Lagerstroemia indica — Crape Myrtle — 7-9

Ligustrum sp. — Privet — 4-10
Malus sp. — Flowering Crab Apple — 2-8
Melaleuca sp. — Melaleuca — 9-10
Nerium oleander — Oleander — 8-10
Olea europaea — Common Olive — 9-10
Parkinsonia aculeata — Jerusalem Thorn — 8-10
Pinus canariensis — Canary Island Pine — 9-10
Pinus halepensis — Aleppo Pine — 7-10
Rhus typhina — Staghorn Sumac — 3-8
Robinia sp. — Locust — 3-10
Schinus sp. — Pepper Tree — 9-10
Sequoiadendron giganteum — Giant Sequoia — 6-10
Sophora japonica — Japanese Pagoda Tree — 5-8
Tamarix aphylla — Athel Tree — 7-10
Taxus sp. — Yew — 5-9
Xylosma congestum — Shiny Xylosma — 8-10

VINES — Zones

Antigonon leptopus — Coral Vine — 8-10
*Bougainvillea sp.** — Bougainvillea — 9-10
Campsis sp. — Trumpet Creeper — 4-8
Ficus pumila — Creeping Fig — 9-10
*Gelsemium sempervirens** — Carolina Yellow Jessamine — 7-10
*Hedera helix** — English Ivy — 5-10
*Lonicera sp.** — Honeysuckle — 3-10
Parthenocissus sp. — Boston Ivy, Virginia Creeper — 4-10
Polygonum aubertii — Silver Lace Vine — 5-10
Tecomaria capensis — Cape Honeysuckle — 9-10
*Trachelospermum jasminoides** — Star Jasmine — 7-10
Vitis sp. — Grape — 6-10

Lemon bottlebrush (*Callistemon citrinus*)

Common olive (*Olea europaea*)

'Climbing Cecile Brunner' rose (*Rosa sp.*)

Heat-Resistant Plants for Hot Exposures

These plants are star performers in hot climates. Use heat-resistant plants in the desert as well as in hot southern or western exposures around any home. Be aware that many of these plants are not drought-tolerant and may need regular watering during dry spells.

GROUND COVERS

		Zones
Aizoaceae	Ice Plants	8-10
Festuca ovina glauca	Blue Fescue	5-10
Gazania sp.	Gazania	9-10
Sedum sp.	Sedum	3-10

Shrubs and vines marked with an asterisk * have varieties that can also be used as ground covers.

SHRUBS

		Zones
*Abelia x grandiflora**	Glossy Abelia	6-10
*Baccharis pilularis**	Coyote Brush	8-10
Callistemon sp.	Bottlebrush	8-10
*Ceanothus sp.**	California Lilac	8-10
Chaenomeles sp.	Flowering Quince	5-9
Citrus sp.	Citrus	9-10
Cistus x purpureus	Orchid-Spot Rock Rose	8-10
Coprosma repens	Mirror Plant	9-10
*Cotoneaster sp.**	Cotoneaster	5-10
Dodonaea viscosa	Hopbush	8-10
Elaeagnus pungens	Silverberry	7-10
Hibiscus rosa-sinensis	Chinese Hibiscus	9-10
*Juniperus sp.**	Juniper	3-10
Lagerstroemia indica	Crape Myrtle	7-9
*Lantana sp.**	Lantana	9-10
Ligustrum japonicum	Japanese Privet	7-10
Nerium oleander	Oleander	8-10
Photinia x fraseri	Red-Tip Photinia	7-10
Pittosporum tobira	Tobira	8-10
Prunus caroliniana	Carolina Cherry Laurel	7-10
*Pyracantha sp.**	Firethorn	5-10
Rosa hybrids	Rose	5-10
*Rosmarinus officinalis**	Rosemary	7-10
*Taxus sp.**	Yew	5-9
*Trachelospermum jasminoides**	Star Jasmine	7-10
Xylosma congestum	Shiny Xylosma	8-10

TREES

		Zones
Acacia baileyana	Bailey Acacia	9
Albizia julibrissin	Silk Tree	7-10
Callistemon citrinus	Lemon Bottlebrush	8-10
Cedrus atlantica	Atlas Cedar	6-10
Celtis sp.	Hackberry	4-9
Ceratonia siliqua	Carob	9-10
Cercis occidentalis	Western Redbud	7-10
Cinnamomum camphora	Camphor Tree	9-10
Citrus sp.	Citrus	9-10
Cupressus arizonica	Arizona Cypress	6-10
Cupressus sempervirens	Italian Cypress	7-10
Elaeagnus angustifolia	Russian Olive	2-10
Eucalyptus sp.	Eucalyptus	7-10
Fraxinus pennsylvanica	Green Ash	3-9
Fraxinus uhdei	Shamel Ash	9-10
Ilex x altaclarensis 'Wilsonii'	Wilson Holly	6-10
Juniperus sp.	Juniper	3-10
Koelreuteria paniculata	Golden-Rain Tree	5-9
Lagerstroemia indica	Crape Myrtle	7-9
Ligustrum sp.	Privet	4-10
Malus sp.	Flowering Crab Apple	2-8
Melaleuca sp.	Melaleuca	9-10
Nerium oleander	Oleander	8-10
Olea europaea	Common Olive	9-10
Parkinsonia aculeata	Jerusalem Thorn	8-10
Pinus halepensis	Aleppo Pine	7-10
Pinus thunbergiana	Japanese Black Pine	5-9
Robinia sp.	Locust	3-10
Xylosma congestum	Shiny Xylosma	8-10

VINES

		Zones
Antigonon leptopus	Coral Vine	8-10
Beaumontia grandiflora	Herald's-Trumpet	10
*Bougainvillea sp.**	Bougainvillea	9-10
Campsis sp.	Trumpet Creeper	4-8
Clytostoma callistegioides	Violet Trumpet Vine	9-10
*x Fatshedera lizei**	Fatshedera	9-10
Ficus pumila	Creeping Fig	9-10
*Gelsemium sempervirens**	Carolina Yellow Jessamine	7-10
*Hedera helix**	English Ivy	5-10
Hydrangea anomala	Climbing Hydrangea	5-9
*Jasminum sp.**	Jasmine	8-10
*Lonicera sp.**	Honeysuckle	4-10
Parthenocissus sp.	Boston Ivy, Virginia Creeper	4-10
*Passiflora sp.**	Passionflower	9-10
Polygonum aubertii	Silver Lace Vine	5-10
*Rosa hybrids**	Climbing Rose	5-10
Tecomaria capensis	Cape Honeysuckle	9-10
*Trachelospermum sp.**	Star Jasmine	7-10
Vitis sp.	Grape	6-10
Wisteria sp.	Wisteria	5-9

GARDEN FLOWER LANDSCAPE LIST

Note: Plants adapted to Zone 10 are also adapted to *new* Zone 11. Plants shown adapted to Zone 11 only, are recommended specifically for Zone 11.

Plant Name	Zones	Type of Plant	Height of Plant	Blooms in Spring	Blooms in Summer	Blooms in Fall	Full Sun	Partial Shade	Shade	Drought-Tolerant	Fragrant	White	Yellow	Orange	Pink	Red	Blue-Purple	Bicolors
Achillea sp. Yarrow	3-10	P	To 10 to 60 in.	■			■			■		■	■		■	■		
Agapanthus sp. Lily-of-the-Nile	9-10	B	To 15 to 48 in.		■							■					■	
Ageratum houstonianum Flossflower	2-10	A-w	To 5 to 10 in.	■	■	■	■					■			■		■	■
Alcea rosea Hollyhock	3-10	P	To 2 to 8 ft	■	■		■					■	■		■	■	■	
Allium sp. Ornamental Onion	4-10	B	6 in. to 5 ft	■	■		■				■	■			■	■	■	
Amaryllis belladonna Belladonna Lily	7-10	B	To 2 to 3 ft		■		■			■	■	■			■	■		
Anemone sp. Anemone	6-10	P/B	To 2 to 30 in.	■	■	■	■	■				■	■		■	■	■	■
Anthemis tinctoria Golden Marguerite	3-9	P	To 18 to 36 in.		■		■			■			■					
Antirrhinum majus Snapdragon	2-10	A	To 6 to 36 in.	■	■		■					■	■	■	■	■	■	■
Aquilegia x hybrida Columbine	3-9	P	To 18 to 36 in.	■	■	■		■				■	■	■	■	■	■	■
Arctotis hybrids African Daisy	2-10	A-w	To 10 to 12 in.		■		■			■		■	■	■	■	■		
Armeria maritima Sea Pink	3-9	P	To 12 in.	■	■		■	■				■			■	■	■	
Aster sp. Aster	4-10	P	To 6 in. to 6 ft		■	■	■					■			■	■	■	
Astilbe x arendsii False Spiraea	4-9	P	To 18 to 30 in.		■			■	■			■			■	■		
Aurinia saxatilis Basket-of-Gold	3-10	P	To 18 to 12 in.	■						■			■					
Begonia sp. Begonia	2-10	A-w B	To 4 to 20 in.	■	■	■	■	■				■	■		■	■		■
Bellis perennis English Daisy	3-10	A-c P	To 4 to 6 in.	■								■			■	■	■	■
Bergenia cordifolia Heartleaf Bergenia	2-10	P	To 12 to 18 in.	■			■	■	■	■		■			■			
Browallia sp. Browallia	2-10	A-w	To 8 to 14 in.		■	■		■	■								■	
Caladium x hortulanum Fancy-Leaved Caladium	11	B	To 12 to 24 in.	■	■	■		■	■			■			■	■		■
Calendula officinalis Calendula	2-10	A-c	To 12 to 18 in.	■	■	■							■	■				
Callistephus chinensis China Aster	2-10	A-w	To 8 to 36 in.		■	■						■			■	■	■	
Campanula sp. Bellflower	3-8	P	To 8 to 48 in.	■	■		■	■				■			■		■	
Catharanthus roseus Madagascar Periwinkle	2-10	A-w P	To 3 to 18 in.	■	■	■	■	■		■		■			■	■		■
Celosia cristata Cockscomb	2-10	A-w	To 4 to 36 in.		■	■								■	■	■		
Centaurea cineraria Dusty-Miller	5-10	A-w P	To 12 to 18 in.	■					■								■	
Centaurea cyanus Cornflower	2-10	A-w	To 12 to 36 in.	■		■					■					■	■	

Plant Name	Zones	Type of Plant	Height of Plant	Blooms in Spring	Blooms in Summer	Blooms in Fall	Full Sun	Partial Shade	Shade	Drought-Tolerant	Fragrant	White	Yellow	Orange	Pink	Red	Blue-Purple	Bicolors
Cheiranthus cheiri Wallflower	2-10	A-c	To 12 to 18 in.	■	■		■	■			■	■	■	■		■		■
Chionodoxa luciliae Glory-of-the-Snow	3-8	B	To 6 in.	■			■	■							■		■	■
Chrysanthemum sp. Chrysanthemum	2-10	P	To 5 to 48 in.	■	■	■	■	■				■	■	■	■	■	■	■
Cleome hasslerana Spider Flower	2-10	A-w	To 3 to 6ft		■	■	■								■			
Clivia miniata Kaffir Lily	10	B	To 24 in.	■				■	■			■		■	■	■		
Colchicum autumnale Autumn Crocus	5-10	B	To 6 in.			■	■	■				■			■		■	
Coleus x hybridus Coleus	2-10	A-w	To 6 to 12 in.	■	■			■						■	■	■		■
Coreopsis sp. Coreopsis	3-10	P	To 3 ft		■	■	■			■			■					
Cosmos sp. Cosmos	2-10	A-w	To 12 to 48 in.		■	■	■					■		■	■	■		
Crocus sp. Crocus	3-10	B	To 5 in.	*■		■	■	■			■	■	■				■	■
Cyclamen sp. Cyclamen	5-10	B	To 2 to 12 in.	■		■		■	■		■	■			■	■	■	■
Cynoglossum amabile Chinese Forget-Me-Not	2-10	A-c	To 18 to 24 in.	■	■		■					■			■		■	
Dahlia hybrids Dahlia	2-10	A-w P/B	To 10 to 60 in.		■	■	■					■	■	■	■	■	■	■
Delphinium elatum Delphinium	2-10	P	To 4 to 8 ft	■	■		■	■				■			■	■	■	■
Dianthus sp. & hybrids Carnation, Pink, Sweet William	2-10	A-c	To 3 to 22 in.	■	■	■	■				■	■		■	■	■	■	■
Dicentra spectabilis Bleeding-Heart	4-8	P	To 12 to 24 in.	■				■			■	■			■			
Digitalis purpurea Foxglove	4-10	P	To 2 to 5 ft	■	■			■	■			■	■		■	■	■	
Dimorphotheca sinuata Cape Marigold	2-10	A-c	To 6 to 12 in.	■			■					■		■				■
Echinacea purpurea Purple Coneflower	3-9	P	To 3 to 5 ft	■			■	■				■			■	■	■	
Eranthis hyemalis Winter Aconite	4-8	B	To 4 in.	*■			■	■	■				■					
Euphorbia marginata Snow-on-the-Mountain	2-10	A-w	To 12 to 18 in.		■		■	■		■		■						
Felicia amelloides Blue Marguerite	8-10	P	To 12 to 20 in.	■	■		■										■	
Freesia x hybrida Freesia	9-10	B	To 18 in.	■							■	■	■	■	■	■	■	■
Fritillaria sp. Fritillary	4-8	B	To 48 in.	■			■	■				■	■	■		■	■	■
Gaillardia x grandiflora Blanket Flower	3-10	P	To 12 to 36 in.		■	■	■			■			■	■		■		■
Galanthus sp. Snowdrop	3-9	B	To 4 to 12 in.	*			■	■				■						
Gerbera jamesonii Transvaal Daisy	8-10	A-w P	To 18 in.		■	■	■					■	■	■	■	■	■	

GARDEN FLOWER LANDSCAPE LIST (Continued)

Plant Name	Zones	Type of Plant	Height of Plant	Blooms in Spring	Blooms in Summer	Blooms in Fall	Full Sun	Partial Shade	Shade	Drought-Tolerant	Fragrant	White	Yellow	Orange	Pink	Red	Blue-Purple	Bicolors
Gladiolus x hortulanus Gladiolus	9-10	B	To 30 in. to 5 ft		■		■					■	■	■	■	■	■	
Gomphrena globosa Globe Amaranth	2-10	A-w	To 6 to 24 in.		■	■	■					■		■	■	■	■	
Helianthus annuus Sunflower	2-10	A-w	To 15 in. to 12 ft		■	■	■			■		■	■					
Helichrysum bracteatum Strawflower	2-10	A-w	To 12 to 36 in.		■	■	■			■		■		■	■	■		
Hemerocallis hybrids Daylily	3-10	P	To 1 to 7 ft	■	■	■	■	■	■	■	■		■	■	■	■		■
Heuchera sanguinea Coralbells	3-10	P	To 10 to 24 in.		■		■	■				■			■	■		
Hibiscus moscheutos Rose Mallow	6-10	P	To 5 to 8 ft		■	■	■					■			■	■		■
Hyacinthus orientalis Common Hyacinth	7-10	B	To 8 to 15 in.	■							■	■	■					
Iberis sp. Candytuft	2-10	A-c P	To 4 to 15 in.	■	■		■					■			■	■	■	
Impatiens wallerana Impatiens	2-10	A-w	To 8 to 20 in.	■	■	■		■	■			■		■	■	■		■
Ipomoea purpurea Morning-Glory	2-10	A-w	To 8 to 20 ft		■	■	■					■			■		■	■
Iris sp. Iris	3-10	B	To 8 to 48 in.	■	■	■	■	■		■	■	■	■		■	■	■	■
Lathyrus sp. Sweet Pea	2-10	A-c P	To 9 in. to 9 ft	■	■		■				■	■			■	■	■	
Leucojum sp. Snowflake	5-10	B	To 9 to 18 in.	■*			■	■				■						
Liatris spicata Blazing-Star	3-10	P	To 2 to 5 ft		■		■			■		■				■	■	
Lilium sp. Lily	4-10	B	To 1 to 8 ft		■		■	■			■	■	■	■	■	■		■
Lobelia sp. Lobelia	2-10	A-w P	To 48 in.	■	■	■	■	■				■			■	■	■	
Lobularia maritima Sweet Alyssum	2-10	A P	To 3 to 4 in.	■	■	■	■			■		■			■		■	
Lupinus 'Russel Hybrids' Russell Lupines	3-9	P	To 2 to 5 ft	■	■		■	■			■	■	■		■	■	■	■
Lychnis chalcedonica Maltese-Cross	3-9	P	To 18 to 36 in.		■		■					■		■	■	■		
Monarda didyma Bee Balm	4-10	P	To 2 to 3 ft		■		■	■			■	■			■	■	■	
Muscari sp. Grape Hyacinth	3-10	B	To 6 in. to 12 in.	■			■	■			■	■					■	
Myosotis sylvatica Forget-Me-Not	2-10	A-c	To 6 to 12 in.	■	■	■						■			■		■	
Narcissus sp. Daffodil	5-10	B	To 20 in.	■							■	■	■	■				■
Nicotiana alata Nicotiana	2-10	A-w	To 16 to 32 in.		■		■				■	■	■		■	■	■	
Nierembergia hippomanica Cupflower	2-10	A-w P	To 6 in.		■		■					■					■	
Paeonia hybrid Peony	5-9	P	To 2 to 4 ft	■			■	■			■	■	■		■	■		

GARDEN FLOWER LANDSCAPE LIST (Continued)

Plant Name	Zones	Type of Plant	Height of Plant	Blooms in Spring	Blooms in Summer	Blooms in Fall	Full Sun	Partial Shade	Shade	Drought-Tolerant	Fragrant	White	Yellow	Orange	Pink	Red	Blue-Purple	Bicolors
Papaver sp. Poppy	3-10	A-c P	To 1 to 4 ft	■	■		■	■			■	■	■	■	■	■		■
Pelargonium sp. Geranium	2-10	A P	To 10 to 36 in.	■	■	■	■	■			■	■		■	■	■		■
Penstemon gloxinioides Garden Penstemon	8-10	A-w P	To 18 to 24 in.		■		■	■		■					■	■	■	
Petunia x hybrida Petunia	2-10	A-w	To 12 to 14 in.	■	■		■	■			■	■	■		■	■	■	■
Phlox sp. Phlox	2-10	A-w P	To 6 to 48 in.	■	■		■	■		■	■	■			■	■	■	■
Platycodon grandiflorus Balloon Flower	3-9	P	To 18 to 30 in.		■		■	■				■			■		■	
Portulaca grandiflora Ross Moss	2-10	A-w	To 2 to 7 in.	■	■	■	■			■		■	■	■	■	■		
Primula sp. Primrose	2-10	A-c P	To 4 to 12 in.	■				■	■			■	■	■	■	■	■	■
Ranunculus asiaticus Persian Ranunculus	8-10	B	To 12 to 18 in.	■			■					■	■	■	■	■		
Rosa hybrids Rose	5-10	FS	To 3 to 10 ft	■	■	■	■				■	■	■	■	■	■	■	■
Rudbeckia hirta Black-eyed Susan	4-10	A-w P	To 36 in.	■	■	■	■			■			■	■		■		■
Salpiglossis sinuata Painted-Tongue	2-10	A	To 15 to 30 in.	■	■		■						■	■		■	■	■
Salvia sp. Sage	2-10	A-w P	To 2 to 5 ft		■		■			■		■			■	■	■	
Scilla sp. Scilla	3-10	B	To 20 in.	■			■	■				■			■		■	
Sedum spectabile Showy Stonecrop	3-10	P	To 18 to 24 in.	■	■	■	■			■		■			■	■		
Solidago hybrids Goldenrod	3-10	P	To 18 to 42 in.		■	■				■			■					
Sparaxis sp. Wandflower	10	B	To 12 to 18 in.	■			■			■		■	■	■		■	■	■
Tagetes hybrids Marigold	2-10	A-w	To 8 to 40 in.		■	■	■					■	■	■				■
Tropaeolum majus Nasturtium	2-10	A-c P	To 12 to 6 ft	■	■		■	■		■	■	■	■	■		■		
Tulipa sp. Tulip	5-9	B	To 3 to 30 in.	■			■					■	■	■	■	■	■	■
Verbena x hybrida Verbena	2-10	A-w P	To 6 to 30 in.	■	■	■	■			■		■	■	■	■	■	■	■
Veronica hybrids Speedwell	4-9	P	To 12 to 30 in.		■		■	■				■			■		■	
Viola sp. Viola	2-10	A-c P	To 5 to 12 in.	■			■	■	■		■	■	■	■	■	■	■	■
Zantedeschia sp. Calla Lily	8-10	B	To 4 ft.		■		■	■				■	■		■	■		■
Zinna hybrids Zinnia	2-10	A-w	To 4 to 36 in.		■	■	■					■	■	■	■	■	■	■

A - Annual; B - Bulb, Corm, Rhizome, or Tuber; P - Perennial
c - flowers best in cool weather.
w - flowers best in warm weather.
* Winter

Top-Rated Ornamental Landscape Plants

This encyclopedia includes trees, shrubs, vines, and ground covers—plants that form the permanent structure of your landscape. Flower garden plants are covered in a separate encyclopedia section beginning on page 218.

The plants included here were selected because of their outstanding growth performances and their reliability. Almost all of them are widely available in the climate zones where they are adapted—a few may be hard-to-find, but were listed because they were given special acclaim by our regional consultants.

Encyclopedia entries: Plant descriptions are arranged alphabetically by botanical name with the most widely used common names shown in dark type just below. If you only know a plant by it's common name, you can find its botanical name by looking in the index beginning on page 310.

Each encyclopedia entry includes the climate zones where the plant gives a top-rated growth performance. Ornamental characteristics of flowers, foliage, bark, and berries are discussed, and potential size and spread are given. Information on soil requirements, preferred planting sites, and care is included for each plant. If the genus includes many species or varieties, these are described in chart form for easier comparison and selection.

Climate Zones Note: Plants adapted to Zone 10 are also adapted to *new* Zone 11. Plants shown adapted to Zone 11 only, are recommended specifically for Zone 11.

At left: Using ground covers with different forms, textures, and colors produces a naturalistic, informal landscape that is easy to care for, once established.

Herald's-trumpet (*Beaumontia* sp.)

'Rainbow' bougainvillea (*Bougainvillea*)

Heavenly bamboo (*Nandina domestica*)

Golden-rain tree (*Koelreuteria* sp.)

Shiny green foliage that turns purple in fall and white or pink flowers that bloom all summer make glossy abelia *(Abelia x grandiflora)* a choice landscape plant.

White fir *(Abies concolor)*, with its fine-textured blue-green needles and tidy conical shape, is a very popular specimen tree.

Abelia x grandiflora
Glossy Abelia
Zones: 6-10. To 6 feet.
Deciduous or evergreen shrub.
Flowering.

Glossy abelia is the most popular and hardiest abelia. Evergreen in the South; deciduous in the North. Leaves are glossy green, turning bronze-purple in fall. Abundant small white or pink-tinged flowers bloom all summer until fall frost. Use this fine-textured shrub in borders or as a pruned or unpruned hedge.

Can be grown in Zone 5 on a well-protected site. Abelias flower more profusely in full sun but will grow in partial shade.

Several cultivars are available: 'Edward Goucher' is a compact shrub that bears lilac-pink flowers from early summer until fall frost; 'Prostrata', a prostrate form seldom exceeding 2 feet and somewhat more tender than the species, makes an excellent ground cover; 'Sherwoodii' is a dwarf cultivar that may reach 3 feet.

Abies
Fir
Evergreen trees.

Firs are large, needled evergreen trees native to the cool, moist areas of the Northern Hemisphere. They generally grow in high elevations and are not suitable for sites exposed to strong winds or areas with hot summers. Cylindrical cones are held upright on horizontally tiered branches.

Use firs as specimen or accent trees where their somewhat stiff, formal shape is appealing. Locate where they will have plenty of growing room.

Abies concolor
White Fir
Zones: 5-8. To 80-100 feet.
Evergreen tree.

White fir is the most widely adapted fir. It is able to tolerate warm climates but is at its best in cool, moist areas. Needles are bluish green, 1 to 3 inches long. Needs ample room to develop fully, but can be grown in containers.

Abies nordmanniana
Nordmann Fir
Zones: 5-8. To 65-100 feet.
Evergreen tree.

A very attractive evergreen with densely packed, 3/4- to 1-1/2-inch-long, deep green needles with silvery undersides. Can be grown in a container for several years as a living Christmas tree, but should have lots of room for development in open ground.

Acacia
Acacia
Evergreen trees and shrubs.
Flowering.

Acacia is a large genus of plants greatly appreciated in the dry climates of the West. Two species are top-rated.

Acacia baileyana
Bailey Acacia
Zone: 9. To 20-30 feet.
Evergreen tree. Flowering.

This fast-growing tree is widely planted in California. It is valued for its bright yellow, late winter flowers, drought tolerance, and ability to withstand neglect. Leaves are finely divided, fernlike. Prune lower limbs to obtain tree shape. Use in problem areas or where a quick effect is needed. Not a tree for small gardens.

Acacia longifolia
Sydney Golden Wattle
Zones: 7-10. To 18-20 feet.
Evergreen shrub.

This tall airy shrub blooms all summer long in the toughest climates. Yellow flowers are produced in 2- to 3-inch spikes. The bright green needlelike leaves are 3 to 6 inches long and give the plant a fine texture. A valuable screening shrub for dry climates or in coastal conditions. Often sold as *A. latifolia*.

Acer
Maple
Deciduous trees.

This large genus has over 200 species of mostly deciduous trees native to northern temperate regions. More than 125 varieties of maple are grown by nurseries in the United States, and forms suitable for nearly every landscape situation are readily available. They are widely used for lawn, park, and street plantings.

Maples come in many shapes and sizes. Their leaves, although usually green, can be red, yellow, dark purple, or variegated. Some have showy flowers and fruit, and many varieties have foliage that turns to brilliant scarlet, red, or yellow in fall.

Most species of maple are hardy in northern states and are adapted south to Zone 8. They grow beautifully in the Pacific Northwest, but are subject to leaf scorch in the hot dry climates of Southern California and the Southwest Desert.

Some species of maple are commercially important timber trees, producing wood used for the manufacture of furniture. Maple syrup and maple sugar are made from the sugar maple *(Acer saccharum)*.

Most maples have shallow root systems and require regular watering. Their root systems may be competitive with shrubs, lawns, and garden plants. Maples can be planted in either light or heavy soil if it is well-drained. However, good soil with ample organic matter will produce the most satisfactory growth. Most maples require full sun. Many species of maple are subject to aphid infestation.

Japanese maple *(Acer palmatum)* is highly ornamental as a lawn, patio, background, or specimen tree.

Acer

Botanical Name/Common Name	Zones	Size	Plant Description	Comments
Acer campestre Hedge Maple, English Maple	5-8	To 30 ft tall. Spreads to 25 ft.	Deciduous tree with rounded crown. Attractive corky bark. Leaves turn yellow in fall.	Often trained as a hedge. Tolerates drought and poor soil.
A. ginnala Amur Maple, Ginnala Maple	3-8	To 20 ft tall with equal spread.	Deciduous tree with upright habit, rounded head. Dense with twisted branching pattern. Fragrant flowers. Bright red fruit. Red fall foliage.	Can be grown as multistemmed shrub. Good patio tree.
A. negundo Box Elder, Ash-Leaved Maple	3-9	To 50-70 ft tall.	Deciduous tree with wide-spreading open crown. Grows rapidly. Compound leaves contain 3 to 5 leaflets. Wood is weak and splits easily in storms.	Withstands heat, drought, and cold. Useful as temporary screen or shelterbelt plantings.
A. palmatum Japanese Maple, Dwarf Japanese Maple, Cut-Leaf Maple	6-8	To 20 ft tall with equal spread. Dwarf forms 6-10 ft.	Deciduous tree grows in many forms, from a low mound to a broad, roundheaded tree. Leaves look like finely pointed fingers growing away from a small palm; or sometimes with no palm. Brilliant orange, yellow, or red fall color.	Excellent ornamental tree for entryways, as background or specimen plant, lawn or patio tree. Resistant to oak-root fungus. Grow in partial shade in hot summer areas.
A. p. 'Atropurpureum' Red Japanese Maple, Bloodleaf Maple	6-8	To 20 ft tall with equal spread. Dwarf forms 6-10 ft.	Red-purple leaves in spring and summer. Bright red full color.	
A. p. 'Bloodgood' Bloodgood Japanese Maple	6-8	To 20 ft tall with 15 ft spread.	Deciduous tree with brilliant red new foliage maturing to dark red.	Needs afternoon shade in hot, dry climates.
A. p. 'Burgundy Lace' Burgundy Lace Japanese Maple	6-8	To 20 ft tall with equal spread. Dwarf forms 6-10 ft.	Deciduous tree with finely serrated lacy red leaves. Bright green slender branches.	
A. p. 'Crimson Queen' Crimson Queen Japanese Maple	6-8	Dwarf form. To 6-8 ft tall.	Deciduous tree with finely divided leaves holding deep red color all season.	Good for entryways. Grows well in containers.
A. p. 'Dissectum' Lace-Leaf Japanese Maple	6-8	Dwarf form. To 6-10 ft tall.	Deciduous tree with pendulous branches. Light green finely divided leaves turn golden in fall.	Excellent for bonsai, containers, entryways.
A. p. 'Dissectum Atropurpureum' Red Lace-Leaf Japanese Maple, Cut-Leaf Green Maple, Thread-Leaf Maple	6-8	Dwarf form. To 6-10 ft tall.	Deciduous tree with weeping habit. Finely divided bright red leaves.	Prefers partial shade.
A. p. 'Oshio-beni'	6-8	Dwarf form. To 6-10 ft tall.	Deciduous tree. Graceful branching. Deeply cut orange-red leaves have finely toothed margins.	
A. platanoides Norway Maple	3-7	To 50 ft tall. Spreads to 75 ft.	Deciduous tree with dense foliage, rounded canopy. Good display of yellow flowers in early spring. Yellow-green in spring turns dark green in summer then golden in fall.	Casts heavy shade. Seedlings may create weed problem in gardens and shrub borders.
A. p. 'Cleveland' Cleveland Norway Maple	3-7	To 30 ft tall or more.	Deciduous tree with upright habit. Dark green foliage turns yellow in fall.	Fast grower.

Amur maple *(Acer ginnala)* is a graceful small specimen tree.

Norway maple *(Acer platanoides)* makes a good street tree.

Acer (continued)

Botanical Name/Common Name	Zones	Size	Plant Description	Comments
A. p. 'Columnare' **Pyramidal Norway Maple**	3-7	To 35 ft tall.	Deciduous tree with narrow upright habit. Dark green foliage forms dense canopy.	Good screening tree. Moderate growth rate.
A. p. 'Crimson King' **Crimson King Norway Maple**	3-7	To 35 ft tall.	Deciduous tree with upright oval habit. Red-purple leaves all summer.	Moderate growth rate.
A. p. 'Emerald Queen' **Emerald Queen Norway Maple**	3-7	To 50 ft tall.	Deciduous tree with upright habit. Good branching habit. Leathery, glossy green foliage turns bright yellow in fall.	Rapid growth rate.
A. p. 'Globosum' **Globe Norway Maple**	3-7	To 35 ft tall.	Deciduous tree with dense, spreading form, globe-shaped canopy.	Moderate growth rate.
A. p. 'Royal Red' **Royal Red Norway Maple**	3-7	To 50 ft tall. Spreads to 75 ft.	Similar to species. Somewhat hardier than 'Crimson King'. Crimson-purple leaves.	
A. p. 'Schwedleri' **Schwedleri Purple-Leaf Maple**	3-7	To 50 ft tall. Spreads to 75 ft.	Similar to species. Purplish-red spring foliage turns green by midsummer.	
A. p. 'Silver Variegated' **Silver-Variegated Norway Maple**	3-7	To 50 ft tall. Spreads to 75 ft.	Similar to species but slower-growing. Forms dense rounded canopy. Green leaves are edged with white.	
A. p. 'Summer Shade' **Summer Shade Norway Maple**	3-7	To 40 ft tall.	Deciduous tree with upright, spreading habit. Fine, dark green foliage.	Rapid grower.
A. rubrum **Red Maple, Swamp Maple,** **Soft Maple, Scarlet Maple**	4-9	To 50 ft tall or more. Spreads to 25 ft.	Deciduous tree with rounded-to-pyramidal canopy when mature. Red flowers in late winter or early spring. Red fruit (samaras) in late spring. Red twigs in winter. Leaves unfold red in spring, mature to green. Red fall color.	Fast grower.
A. r. 'Armstrong' **Armstrong Red Maple**	4-9	To 35 ft tall.	Deciduous tree with narrow columnar shape. Dark green leaves to scarlet and red in fall.	Good in tight planting sites. Moderate-to-fast growth.
A. r. 'Autumn Flame' **Autumn Flame Red Maple**	4-9	To 60 ft tall.	Deciduous tree forms shapely, dense, well-rounded head. Leaves smaller than species, turn brilliant scarlet in fall 2 weeks before species.	Moderate growth rate.
A. r. 'Gerling' **Gerling Red Maple**	4-9	To 30 ft tall.	Deciduous tree. Broad, pyramidal form.	Moderate-to-fast growth rate.
A. r. 'October Glory' **October Glory Red Maple**	4-9	To 50-60 ft tall.	Deciduous tree. Dark green foliage turns crimson in fall. Last maple to turn color in autumn.	Moderate growth rate.
A. r. 'Red Sunset' **Red Sunset Red Maple**	4-9	To 50 ft tall or more. Spreads to 25 ft.	Deciduous tree. Upright and spreading when young, becoming oval with age. Green leaves turn bright orange-red in fall.	Top-choice at Seacrest Arboretum for over 20 years.
A. r. 'Tilford' **Tilford Red Maple**	4-9	To 30 ft tall.	Deciduous tree. Tends to develop pyramidal rather than globe shape unless grown in the open.	Moderate-to-fast growth rate.
A. saccharinum **Silver Maple, White Maple** **Soft Maple, River Maple**	4-9	To 70-100 ft tall.	Deciduous tree. Fastest growing native maple. Develops spreading crown as wide as tall. Has weak wood and invasive roots.	Adapts to both wet and dry sites and a variety of soil conditions. Recommended for difficult sites only.
A. saccharum **Sugar Maple, Hard Maple,** **Rock Maple**	4-8	To 50 ft tall.	Deciduous tree of moderate growth rate. Upright spreading habit. Leaves are dark green above, light green beneath, have slightly rounded points. Fiery red and yellow fall color.	Source of maple syrup.
A. s. 'Bonfire' **Bonfire Sugar Maple**	4-8	To 50 ft tall or more.	Deciduous tree. Vigorous grower with upright habit, oval crown. Dark green foliage turns yellow and red in fall.	Can be grown where drought and dry summer winds cause leaf-scorch in common sugar maple.

Actinidia chinensis
Kiwi, Chinese Gooseberry, Yang-Tao
Zones: 8-10.
Deciduous vine. Flowering.

Kiwi, with its handsome large green leaves and fragrant flowers, has long been admired as an ornamental plant. It is well suited for covering fences, as an espalier against a wall, or for shading a patio. Kiwi has also gained appreciation in the United States as a valuable fruiting vine for home and orchard use.

When young stems and leaves first appear they are covered in bright red hairs. Leaves expand into 8-inch rounded hearts with woolly white hairs blanketing their undersides. Creamy flowers, 1-1/2 inches long, open in May, aging to a buff-yellow color. Female plants produce egg-shaped fruits that hang like ornaments from the vine. Brown and fuzzy on the outside, the flesh inside is succulent, lime-green, and dotted with edible black seeds. Kiwi fruits have a unique flavor all their own, described as tasting like a combination of banana, melon, strawberry, and gooseberry.

Kiwi is a vine for the West Coast and areas with similar climates. Mild spring and fall temperatures with hot summers are ideal. Vines are cold hardy when completely dormant but are subject to frost damage in fall and spring. To flower and set fruit, most varieties of kiwi must have between 600 and 800 hours of winter temperatures below 45°F.

Kiwi requires a well-drained soil but is not particular about soil type. However an iron deficiency may develop in alkaline soils. Provide plenty of water during the growing season to keep leaves lush. Feed with a nitrogen fertilizer before leaves emerge and after fruit sets.

Kiwi has vigorous branches that twine up to 30 feet and need a sturdy support. Pruning can either be for fruit production or to train as an ornamental vine. Flowers and fruit are produced on 1-year-old wood. Pruning cuts should be made to preserve flower buds, easily recognized by their large bulbous shape. In general, remove up to one-third of the previous year's growth for best fruiting.

Both male and female plants are required if fruit set is desired. Plants are labeled accordingly in the nursery. Several female varieties are available: 'Hayward' and 'Chico' are vigorous vines producing large oval fruit; 'Vincent' is similar but with a lower chilling requirement; 'Monty', 'Bruno', and 'Abbott' bear heavy crops of smaller, oblong fruit.

Aesculus
Horse Chestnut, Buckeye
Deciduous shrubs and trees. Flowering.

Thirteen species make up this genus of deciduous trees and shrubs native to east Asia, southeast Europe and North America. Several species have been selected as ornamentals for their large upright clusters of flowers, which may be red, pink, yellow, or white. Large leaves are divided into fanlike leaflets. Many species are subject to leaf scorch in hot, dry areas. Most horse chestnut trees cast dense shade.

Aesculus x carnea
Red Horse Chestnut
Zones: 5-9. To 40-70 feet.
Deciduous tree. Flowering.

This dramatic tree is pyramidal when young, forming a rounded crown when mature. Grows at a slow to moderate rate. Stunning red to pink flowers in spikes to 10 inches tall appear in late spring. Grows best in moist, well-drained soil in full sunlight. Originated as a chance cross between *A. pavia* and *A. hippocastanum*.

This species is sometimes planted as a street tree to replace *A. hippocastanum* but is losing favor because it also is a litter-producing tree that drops flowers, nuts, and large leaves. Plant as a specimen tree in parks, large gardens, campuses, and other open areas where litter will not be a problem.

Kiwi *(Actinidia chinensis)*, a vigorous twining vine that needs a sturdy support, performs multiple functions in the garden. It can cover a fence, form an attractive espalier, or provide shade for a patio. It perfumes the air with its fragrant flowers and can produce delicious fruit (shown below).

Red horse chestnut *(Aesculus x carnea)* is a handsome shade tree for open areas. In late spring it is covered with dramatic spikes of showy flowers (shown above right).

Common horse chestnut *(Aesculus hippocastanum)* tolerates city conditions. Showy white flowers in midspring produce shiny inedible nuts (shown above right).

A number of cultivars have been developed. 'Briottii' has large scarlet flowers. It is not hardy in Zone 5 except on sheltered sites. 'Rosea' has pink flowers.

Aesculus hippocastanum
Common Horse Chestnut
Zones: 4-8. To 50-75 feet.
Deciduous tree. Flowering.

This is an upright oval to round tree with a medium growth rate. In mid-spring, white flowers blotched with red and yellow open in large up-right showy spikes to 12 inches long. Produces shiny round nuts about an inch across. Native to the Balkans and brought to this country by the earliest settlers.

The horse chestnut is not as popular as it was a generation ago. It is a messy tree, dropping flowers, nuts, and leaves. Formerly considered a street tree, horse chestnut is now seldom planted for this purpose because of litter and pavement-breaking roots. Withstands city growing conditions and is tolerant of spray from deicing salts.

Grows best in moist, well-drained soil in full sunlight. Plant in parks and large open areas where litter will not be a problem. Some of its cultivars are favored. 'Alba' has pure white flowers; 'Baumannii' has double flowers and does not form nuts.

Horse chestnut is the famous chestnut of Paris. The nuts are poisonous, not edible.

Aizoaceae
Ice Plant Family
Zones: 8-10. To 2-15 inches.
Succulent ground covers.
Flowering.

This large family encompasses several genera of succulent creeping plants that make excellent ground covers in warm or arid climates. They are valued as drought-tolerant plants able to grow under adverse conditions in dry soil or in reach of salt spray. Many also bear beautiful colorful blossoms.

Members of the ice plant family *(Aizoaceae)* thrive in drought conditions in warm climates, adding color brilliance to difficult sites, when in bloom. White trailing ice plant *(Delosperma* 'Alba'), top left; rosea ice plant *(Drosanthemum floribundum),* top right; trailing ice plant *(Lampranthus spectabilis),* lower left; bush ice plant *(Lampranthus aurantiacus),* lower right.

Ice Plants

Botanical Name/Common Name	Zones	Size	Plant Description	Comments
Carpobrotus chilensis *(Mesembryanthemum aequilaterale)* **Pig's Face**	9-10	To 12-18 in.	Fast-growing with succulent, 2-in., 3-sided leaves. Rose-purple flowers in midsummer.	Good for stabilizing shifting sand. Do not overwater. Space 12 to 18 in. apart for a quick cover.
C. edulis *(Mesembryanthemum edule)* **Hottentot Fig**	9-10	To 12-18 in.	Fast-growing with succulent, 5-in., 3-sided, curved leaves. Light yellow to pale pink flowers in midsummer.	Fruit edible but not very tasty. Same uses and culture as *C. chilensis.*
Cephalophyllum 'Red Spike' *(Cylindrophyllum speciosum)* **Red Spike Ice Plant**	8-10	To 3-5 in.	Striking red leaves are small, spikelike. Cerise flowers in late winter and early spring.	Attracts bees. Space 6-12 in. apart for ground cover.
Delosperma 'Alba' **White Trailing Ice Plant**	9-10	To 6-7 in.	Fast-growing trailing stems root as they spread. Triangular leaves are 1 in. long. Small white flowers not very showy but attract bees.	Good slope stabilizer. Space 12 in. apart for quick cover.
Drosanthemum floribundum **Rosea Ice Plant**	9-10	To 6 in.	Leaves narrow and dense, crystalline texture. Wide-spreading stems. Bright pink flowers, late spring to early summer.	Best ice plant for erosion control on steep slopes. Will trail and spill over walls. Space 12 in. apart for ground cover.
D. hispidum	9-10	To 2 ft	Leaves similar to *D. floribundum* but has a more mounding habit. Purple flowers in late spring and early summer.	Does not bind soil as well as rosea ice plant. Space 12 in. apart for ground cover.
Lampranthus aurantiacus **Bush Ice Plant**	9-10	To 10-15 in.	Erect habit with gray-green, 1-in., 3-sided leaves. Flowers 1-1/2-2 in. wide, bright yellow or orange.	Brilliant colored flowers. Cut back for compact growth. Good in coastal climates. Space 8 in. apart for ground cover.
L. ficicaulis **Redondo Creeper**	9-10	To 3 in.	Slow-growing with small, fine-textured foliage. Small pink flowers in early spring.	Good small-scale ground cover. Space plants 12 in. apart.
L. productus **Purple Ice Plant**	9-10	To 15 in.	Upright habit with bronze-tipped, gray-green leaves. Bright purple flowers in late winter and spring.	Space plants 12-18 in. apart as a ground cover.
L. spectabilis **Trailing Ice Plant**	9-10	To 15 in.	Upright habit with gray-green leaves. Masses of red, purple, or pink flowers in spring.	Most spectacular blooming *Lampranthus.* An unbroken carpet of color at peak bloom. Space 12-18 in. apart for ground cover.

Mat-forming bugleweed *(Ajuga reptans)* is an effective quick-spreading ground cover for well-drained sites.

Wide-spreading silk trees *(Albizia julibrissin)* have feathery foliage that casts light shade. Flowers (shown below) are showy in mid- and late summer.

Ajuga reptans

Bugleweed, Carpet Bugle

Zones: 4-10. To 2-4 inches.
Herbaceous ground covers.
Flowering.

Making an ideal ground cover in areas where a lawn is not needed, bugleweed spread quickly, forming mats of oval leaves with prominent veins. Leaves are shiny dark green; varieties with purplish-green, bronze, or green and white leaf variegations are available. In spring, spikes of dainty flowers rise from the clumps. Blossoms are usually blue, but some kinds have pink or white flowers.

Use as a ground cover for large areas under trees, on slopes, and under shrubs in borders and beds. Beautiful in Oriental gardens.

Bugleweed spreads quickly by surface runners. Space plants 6 to 18 inches apart in light shade or partial shade. Foliage may mildew in too much shade in humid climates. Needs well-drained soil; root-rot is a problem in damp soil. Clip off faded flower spikes to improve appearance. May become invasive; use edging strips to prevent plants from invading lawn. Needs regular watering and fertilizing.

'Burgundy Lace' has purplish leaves edged with white and pink. 'Gaiety' has bronzy-purple leaves. 'Giant Bronze' has 9-inch flower spikes and bronze foliage. 'Giant Green' has wavy leaves with serrated edges; plants form small mounds. 'Pink Beauty' has pink flowers and green foliage. 'Purpurea', also called 'Atropurpurea', has large bronzy leaves variegated with cream and white. 'Variegata' has green leaves marked with soft yellow.

Albizia julibrissin

Silk Tree, Mimosa

Zones: 7-10. To 25-35 feet.
Deciduous tree. Flowering.

Pink flowers held above feathery foliage for two or more summer months highlight this wide-spreading, late-leafing tree. The light shade it casts provides an ideal environment for many low-growing plants and lawn grasses.

Silk tree, which is native from Iran to China, quickly forms multiple stems, developing a shape that is wider than tall with a flat top. The leaves are doubly compound with tiny leaflets that fold up on cool nights. The pink powder puff flowers, which consist of stamens rather than petals, open from July to September in northern areas and earlier in the South. Flowers bloom even on young trees. No fall foliage color develops. The flat 4- to 6-inch-long pods become brown and drop over a long period during fall and winter.

A tree for a sunny location, it will grow well in both poor and fertile soil as long as it is well drained. Silk tree tolerates considerable drought but grows best if kept moist. While most widely grown in mild climate areas, the botanical variety *rosea*, with bright pink flowers, grows well as far north as Boston (in Zone 6).

Mimosa wilt, which invades the root system, is serious in the South but is common in many other parts of the eastern United States. The first symptoms are yellow, wilted leaves, and tree death may follow within a year. There is no cure for this soil-borne fungus disease, but two cultivars, 'Charlotte' and 'Tryon', developed by the U.S. Department of Agriculture, are resistant to mimosa wilt and should be planted in problem areas.

Most silk trees are propagated by seed, so some variation in flower color and plant growth does occur. Flower color varies from almost white to dark pink.

Alnus

Alder

Deciduous trees.

This genus contains about 30 species of fast-growing trees and shrubs native to the Northern Hemisphere. They thrive in wet, poorly drained soils, adding lush greenery to the landscape in sites where few plants can survive. Alders are an excellent choice for planting along streams and creek beds where they control erosion effectively, but they have a vigorous, shallow root system that can clog pipes and strangle nearby plants.

Alnus cordata
Italian Alder, European Alder
Zones: 6-10. To 35-40 feet.
Deciduous tree.

Native to southern Italy and Corsica, Italian alder has an upright form while young, developing into a tree with a spread to 25 feet with age. Bright, lustrous green leaves are 4 inches long. They are egg-shaped but with rounded lobes at the base. Italian alder grows best in the warm Southwest. It grows rapidly, retains the best form, and requires the least soil moisture of all alders.

Alnus glutinosa
Black Alder
Zones: 3-10. To 50-70 feet.
Deciduous tree.

Black alder is native to Europe, western Asia, and Africa. It has an upright, irregular growth habit and large glossy green leaves. They are oblong but with narrowed or rounded ends. Black alder grows rapidly and is a good plant to provide quick screening or shade on wet sites with poor drainage.

Alnus rhombifolia
White Alder, California Alder, Sierra Alder
Zones: 8-10. To 50-90 feet.
Deciduous tree.

This tree is native to the northwestern regions of the United States and Canada where it is usually found growing on the banks of streams. White alder grows rapidly and has an upright, or spreading, irregular form. Branch tips have a weeping, graceful habit. The dark green leaves are coarsely edged and diamond-shaped. White alder grows

more rapidly than most alders and is very tolerant of heat and wind. Most valued as a tree to provide quick screening or shade. Tent caterpillars are a common problem.

Amelanchier
Serviceberry, Shadbush
Zones: 4-8. To 20-50 feet.
Deciduous tree. Flowering.

Any one of four species, *A. alnifolia*, *A. canadensis*, *A. x grandiflora*, or *A. laevis*, are sold in nurseries. They are native to woodlands in various parts of the United States and are often confused with each other. Graceful clusters of white flowers are borne on bare branches in spring. The new foliage unfolds grayish or reddish, depending on the species, before becoming bright green. Turns shades of red and yellow in fall. Red berries are edible, favored by birds and lovers of jam and preserves. Plant in full sun or half-shade.

Antigonon leptopus
Coral Vine, Queen's-Wreath
Zones: 8-10.
Deciduous vine. Flowering.

This vine is ideal for hot desert and warm, humid climates of the southern states, the Southwest, and California. Native to Mexico, the beautiful coral vine, also known as corallita, mountain rose, and rosa de Montaña, thrives in summer heat and poor soils. Grows rapidly from winter-dormant tubers to reach 20 to 40 feet by summer's end.

The branches are open, airy, and cascading. Leaves have a distinctive shape like a folded heart. Deep rose, pink, or occasionally white flowers held in long trailing sprays cover the branches in midsummer and fall. Branches often fold and curl back on themselves to clothe the vine with garlands of blooms. Flowers cut for indoor use are long-lasting. If temperatures remain warm, blossoms will hold on the vine well into fall.

Italian alder *(Alnus cordata)*

Serviceberry *(Amelanchier sp.)*

Strawberry tree *(Arbutus unedo)* tolerates tough sites. Bears tiny flowers fall into winter, bright fruit nearly year-round.

A tough, adaptable ground cover, kinnikinick *(Arctostaphylos uva-ursi)* bears flowers in spring, red berries in fall.

Coral vine clings by tendrils at the ends of flowering branches. Until these form, the vine will need to be tied to a support to encourage upright growth. The long, flowering sprays create a lovely effect hanging from an arbor or shading a patio. Coral vine can be trained to drape from the tops of eaves and garden walls. Use it on a fence or to screen a view and to provide a long-blooming accent in the landscape. Scrambling, slender branches will quickly cover bare soil in areas where a tough ground cover is needed.

Coral vine is a maintenance-free plant needing less attention than most vines. Keep coral vine green throughout summer with regular deep watering. It is drought-tolerant but without water may behave as a perennial, dying back to the ground in midsummer.

Prune in fall to thin branches and control growth. Coral vine may also be cut back to its base. Protect roots with mulch in Zone 8 where temperatures drop below 25°F.

Arbutus
Arbutus
Evergreen trees. Flowering.

These small to large trees provide color throughout the year. White to pinkish urn-shaped flowers, orange to red fruit, and colorful bark plus shiny evergreen leaves make arbutus a top choice for specimen use.

Arbutus menziesii
Madrone
Zones: 6-9. To 20-80 feet.
Evergreen tree.

Colorful, orange-brown smooth bark is the main attraction of this tree, native from British Columbia to California. Bark peels in thin sheets on small branches and trunk. When mature the trunk forms a dark, gray-brown bark. The tree forms a rounded, oval outline and grows at a slow to moderate rate. The glossy, dark green leaves are broad and oval, measuring 3 to 6 inches long. They last two years, then turn yellow, orange, or red before dropping in summer. Small urn-shaped flowers in terminal clusters, 3 to 9 inches tall and 6 inches wide, open in April or May. Orange or red fruits, 1/4 to 1/2 inch in diameter, are colorful from late summer into winter.

Madrone grows in sun or semishade. Soil should be acidic and well drained, but tree will tolerate drought and poor soils. May develop root rot if watered too frequently in the summer. Cool winter temperatures needed for normal growth.

Madrone is difficult to transplant, so should be moved when no more than 2 feet tall.

Arbutus unedo
Strawberry Tree
Zones: 7-10. To 10-35 feet.
Evergreen tree.

Strawberry tree, native to the Mediterranean region, is more tolerant of a wide range of soils and climatic conditions than is the madrone. Natural growth is multistemmed and shrubby. With pruning, a small tree with one or more trunks can be grown. A rounded crown, as broad as tall, develops at a slow to moderate rate. Red-brown bark cracks to reveal smooth, red inner bark. Leaves are dark, glossy green, 2 to 3 inches long, with a narrow, oval shape. Small, urn-shaped flowers, white to pinkish, appear in fall and winter while the previous year's 3/4-inch fruits are still providing yellow to red color. Fruit is edible but mealy and bland, and attracts birds.

Strawberry tree will grow in sun or semishade. Soil can be acidic or alkaline, and either dry or heavily watered, as long as it is well drained. Will grow at the seashore, or in the desert if shaded. Needs some protection when planted in Zone 7.

Arctostaphylos uva-ursi
Kinnikinick
Zones: 2-8. To 10 inches.
Evergreen shrubby ground cover.
Flowering.

This durable, low spreading shrub makes an excellent ground cover in coastal areas, where soil is sandy or dry and rocky, and in other problem areas. Plants grow less than a foot tall, but spread slowly to cover an area about 15 feet in diameter. Leaves are about an inch long, bright green, and are glossy and leathery. They take on an attractive reddish cast in winter. Pink urn-shaped flowers bloom in spring but are not particularly showy. Bright red berries ripen in fall and attract birds.

For a ground cover planting, space plants 3 feet apart and mulch heavily to keep down weeds since plants spread slowly. Plant in partial shade in well-drained, acid soil. Once established tolerates drought, but watering deeply once or twice in summer is recommended. Cut back old plants in spring to encourage renewed growth.

'Point Reyes' has dark, close-set leaves and is heat-tolerant. 'Radiant' has medium-green leaves and produces a heavy set of berries.

Arenaria verna
Irish Moss, Moss Sandwort, Scotch Moss
Zones: 3-9. To 1-3 inches. Herbaceous ground cover.

This mat-forming plant has diminutive dark green leaves and looks just like real moss. It is however much more durable and tolerates full sun in most climates. Tiny white flowers appear in summer. *Sagina subulata* is a very similar-looking plant with clusters of tiny flowers and it is also called Irish moss. Each has a bright yellow-green variety, 'Aurea', called Scotch moss.

Use both species of Irish moss as a pretty filler between stepping stones, or as a lawn substitute in small gardens. Makes a beautiful accent in Oriental gardens or woodland settings.

To plant, cut small plugs of Irish moss from a flat and place 6 inches apart in rich moist soil; the planting will quickly fill in. Where winters are mild, full sun to partial shade is fine.

Where winters are severe, some shade is best to prevent dehydration. Water regularly since roots are shallow. Fertilize lightly. Snails may be troublesome. Plants self-sow readily and can become weedy in tidy gardens.

Aucuba japonica
Japanese Aucuba, Japanese Laurel
Zones: 7-10. To 6-10 feet. Evergreen shrub.

Japanese aucuba has lush, large glossy leaves. It forms a neat rounded shrub and grows well in shade. Many cultivars have golden-yellow spots on the foliage. Scarlet berries are showy through fall and winter, but both male and female plants are required to set fruit.

Aucuba is adaptable to many growing conditions. It tolerates city pollution and is drought-hardy once established. Add organic matter to the planting hole to help create ideal growing conditions. Hot reflected sun will cause leaf burn. To maintain compact growth, prune branches to a leaf node.

Makes a good container plant useful for decorating a terrace or screening a view. Competes well with tree roots and often serves as a large filler under trees.

Azalea
Azalea
(See *Rhododendron sp.*)

Baccharis pilularis
Coyote Brush
Zones: 8-10. To 1-2 feet. Evergreen shrub.

This drought-tolerant West Coast native is an excellent ground cover for sunny locations in a variety of climates and soils. Grows densely with 1/2-inch toothed bright green leaves. Pruning once a year keeps it attractive. The low, compact 'Twin Peaks' makes an excellent ground cover.

Scotch moss (*Arenaria verna*) forms a ground-hugging lawn replacement. Petite white flowers add summer interest.

Tolerant of polluted air, Japanese aucuba (*Aucuba japonica*) adds lush evergreen foliage and a neat form to sunny or shady garden sites.

Where the climate is dry, coyote brush (*Baccharis pilularis*) is an excellent bright green ground cover.

Bambusa

Bamboo

Zones: 5-10. To 70 feet.
Evergreen shrubs.

These distinctive, fast-growing evergreen plants offer many different textures, growth habits, and landscape uses. The genus *Bambusa* includes many landscape plants, though similar bamboos (listed in the chart on pages 70 and 71) are in the genera *Arundinaria, Chimonobambusa, Phyllostachys, Sasa,* and *Semiarundinaria.*

Bamboos lend a tropical or Oriental appearance to the landscape and their stiff, erect stalks are familiar to most people. Leaves and habit vary among species however, offering a choice of garden effects. Some bamboos with long narrow leaves look fountainlike and soft-textured; others are distinctly upright and bold. Heights range from below 2 feet high to giants upwards of 25 feet.

Bamboos spread by running or clump-forming underground rhizomes. Running types spread rapidly over large areas and can create unwanted problems if not controlled. They are very effective as large screens or hedges. Running bamboos can be contained by underground barriers at least 18 inches deep. Clump bamboos are much more restrained and easier to control. These can be used in smaller areas for a graceful accent. Both types of bamboo can be grown in containers and used to add grace and distinction to patios and porches, or as portable screens. Low-growing species can be used as ground covers.

Bamboos will grow in most soils as long as there is adequate moisture. They tolerate drought but appearance suffers under dry conditions.

Alphonse Karr bamboo *(Bambusa glaucescens* 'Alphonse Karr') has golden stems.

Bamboo

Botanical Name/ Common Name	Cold Hardiness/ Zones	Size	Plant Description	Comments
Arundinaria humilis Pin-Stripe Bamboo	0°F 7-10	To 3 ft tall.	Evergreen. Running habit. Very slender, narrow, arching green stems. Leaf blades, to 6 in. long, have narrow white-yellow pinstripe.	Spreads rapidly. Use as ground cover; for erosion control.
A. pygmaea Dwarf Bamboo, Pygmy Bamboo	0°F 7-10	To 1-1/2 ft tall.	Evergreen. Running habit. Stems bright green, slender, somewhat flattened at top. Leaf blades to 5 in. long.	One of the smallest bamboos. Useful as ground cover, bank holder, or to control erosion.
A. simonii Simon Bamboo	0°F 7-10	To 25 ft tall.	Evergreen. Running habit. Hollow, somewhat arching stems. Grows vertically, spreads moderately. Leaf blades to 10 in. long.	Use for screens or hedges.
A. variegata Dwarf White-Stripe Bamboo, Dwarf White-Stem Bamboo	0°F 7-10	To 3 ft tall.	Evergreen. Running growth habit. Dwarf, spreads fast with vigorous rhizomes. Leaf blades, to 5 in. long, are striped with white.	Use as ground cover, or in containers.
Bambusa glaucescens Hedge Bamboo, Oriental Hedge Bamboo	15°F 8-10	To 10 ft tall.	Evergreen. Clump habit. Shrubby, stems green to yellow. Many branches with dense growth.	Use for screens, hedges, or in containers.
B. g. 'Alphonse Karr' Alphonse Karr Bamboo	15°F 8-10	To 35 ft tall.	Evergreen. Clump habit. New stems bright pinkish-yellow. Mature stems yellow, striped with green.	Use for screens, hedges, or in containers.
B. g. 'Golden Goddess' Golden Goddess Hedge Bamboo	15°F 8-10	To 10 ft tall.	Evergreen. Clump habit. Dense, arching growth. Golden-yellow leaves.	Use for screen or in containers. Tops require space to spread.
B. g. riviereorum Chinese Goddess Bamboo	15°F 8-10	To 6 ft tall.	Evergreen. Clump habit. Dwarf, with solid arching stems, delicate, lacy leaves.	Interesting silhouette. Use in containers or planter boxes.
B. oldhamii Oldham Bamboo, Giant Timber Bamboo	20°F 9-10	To 50 ft tall.	Evergreen. Clump habit. Many-branched, pale green stems. Open habit with dense foliage.	Use for large screens or as single plant for vertical effect.
B. ventricosa Buddha Bamboo, Buddha's Belly Bamboo	20°F 9-10	To 50 ft tall.	Evergreen. Clump habit. Straight, thick-walled stems. Leaf blades to 7 in. long. Can be very tall or short and thick, depending on culture.	When confined to pot or dry soil, stems thicken and swell; hence its name.

Dwarf bamboo *(Arundinaria pygmaea)* makes an unusual ground cover.

Black bamboo *(Phyllostachys nigra)* has lustrous black stems.

Botanical Name/ Common Name	Cold Hardiness/ Zones	Size	Plant Description	Comments
Chimonobambusa marmorea Marbled Bamboo	20°F 9-10	To 10 ft tall.	Evergreen. Running habit. Smooth stems have deciduous, purple-spotted sheaths. Mature stems almost black. Leaf blades 6 in. long.	Useful for hedges.
C. quadrangularis Square Bamboo, Square-Stem Bamboo	15°F 8-10	To 30 ft tall.	Evergreen. Running habit. Young slender stems rough, shaded dark green to purple. Square when old. Leaf blades 8 in. long.	Use for vertical effect.
Phyllostachys aurea Fish Pole Bamboo, Golden Bamboo	0°F 7-10	To 20 ft tall.	Evergreen. Running habit. Stiff, yellow densely foliated, erect stems. Leaf blades 4 in. long.	Use as screen, hedge, or in containers. Shoots edible in midspring.
P. aureosulcata Yellow-Groove Bamboo, Stake Bamboo	−20°F 5-10	To 30 ft tall.	Evergreen. Running habit. Slender stems green with yellow stripe when young.	Hardiest bamboo. Use as screen or hedge. Shoots edible in midspring.
P. bambusoides Giant Timber Bamboo, Japanese Timber Bamboo, Madake	0°F 7-10	To 70 ft tall.	Evergreen. Running habit. Stems glossy dark green. Leaf blades to 7 in. long.	Most important timber bamboo in the Orient. Shoots edible in late spring. Use for grove planting.
P. meyeri Meyer Bamboo	−4°F 6-10	To 30 ft tall.	Evergreen. Running habit. Straight green stems. Leaf blades 6 in. long.	Very hardy. Sometimes used for hedges. Shoots edible in midspring. Mature stems very strong.
P. nigra Black Bamboo	5°F 7-10	To 25 ft tall.	Evergreen. Running habit. Young stems green, maturing to brownish or purplish black. Leaf blades to 3-1/2 in. long.	Very ornamental. Use for screens or in containers. Shoots edible in midspring.
Sasa veitchii Kuma Bamboo Grass	0°F 8-10	To 3 ft tall.	Evergreen. Running habit. Narrow green stems. Dark green leaf blades, 8 in. long.	Spreads rapidly. Useful as ground cover. Leaf margins turn straw color in autumn.
Semiarundinaria fastuosa Narihira Bamboo, Seminole-Bread	−4°F 6-10	To 25 ft tall.	Evergreen. Running habit. Erect stems dark green becoming purplish. Leaf blades 7 in. long.	Very hardy. Grows slowly. Can be kept clumplike. Use for windbreak or hedge.

Purple orchid tree *(Bauhinia varie-gata)* is admired for its flowers.

Herald's trumpet *(Beaumontia grandiflora)* ornaments walls with flowers and foliage.

Red Japanese barberry *(Berberis thunbergii* 'Atropurpurea') has purple foliage in spring and summer.

Bauhinia variegata (B. purpurea)
Purple Orchid Tree

Zones: 9-10. To 20-35 feet.
Deciduous tree. Flowering.

This is a spectacular flowering tree for the mild winter climates of the Southwest and southern Florida. Produces a spectacular show of 2- to 3-inch purple flowers from midwinter to early spring. Usually grows as a multitrunk tree but can be trained to a single stem. Seed pods that follow blossoms are messy.

Beaumontia grandiflora
Herald's-Trumpet, Easter-Lily Vine

Zone: 11.

Evergreen vine. Flowering.

This vine from the Himalayan Mountains is a spectacular sight from spring to summer when it is festooned with lilylike blossoms. Growth is lush and strong with woody stems twining and arching to form a vine of grand proportions. It will reach 15 to 30 feet. Leaves are 6 to 9 inches, and have a bright, clean, glossy surface that adds a bold and tropical look to the landscape. Sweetly scented blossoms are white, tipped with pink, and have green veins on the throats. These funnel-shaped, 5-inch flowers are held in copious clusters at branch ends. Long, cylindrical pods follow in autumn.

Give herald's-trumpet full sun for maximum flowering. It will need shelter in areas with strong winds.

Herald's-trumpet makes a beautiful accent plant for large gardens. Use it to cover a fence or patio, espalier against a sunny wall, or train up a column for camouflage.

Herald's-trumpet has tuberous roots that need an unconstrained rooting zone. Plant in rich, composted soil that is deep and well-drained. For lush growth, give ample water and fertilizer in early spring before flowering. Plant in full sun.

Herald's-trumpet is a broad spreading vine that needs room to grow. Train the vine early and provide sturdy support for its heavy branches. Thin branches to reduce the mass of older vines. Flowers are produced on old wood. When pruning, in fall, retain some 1- to 3-year-old wood for good flower production the following year.

Berberis
Barberry

Zones: 4-10. To 10 feet.
Evergreen and deciduous shrubs.

There are nearly 500 species in this genus, native over a wide area of the world. Some species are deciduous, others evergreen, while some are evergreen in warmer areas and deciduous in the North. Most are thorny shrubs with yellow wood. Deciduous types usually have brightly colored red or orange foliage in autumn.

Grown as ornamentals for their small rounded leaves, barberries have yellow, or occasionally red, flowers and masses of yellow, red, or black berries. They have spiny stems and sometimes spiny leaves, making good barrier or hedge plants. Barberries withstand pruning or shearing and can easily be trained into an attractive formal or informal screen or hedge. Dwarf forms make excellent low hedges or border plantings.

Grow in full sun or light shade. Best growth is usually on moist, well-drained soils. The deciduous species can tolerate drier soils than the evergreen species.

Japanese barberry (Berberis thunbergii) offers showy red berries.

Warty barberry (Berberis verruculosa) has attractive yellow flowers in spring.

Darwin's barberry (Berberis darwinii) has spiny foliage.

Berberis

Botanical Name/Common Name	Zones	Size	Plant Description	Comments
Berberis x chenaultii Chenault Barberry	6-9	To 5 ft tall.	Evergreen. Arching branches accent long green leaves. Small yellow spring flowers. Red berries and red and orange foliage in fall.	Use for medium-size hedge. Tolerates partial shade.
B. darwinii Darwin's Barberry	8-10	To 8 ft tall.	Evergreen. Upright, arching branches. Small, shiny dark green dense foliage is hollylike and spiny. Orange flowers in spring followed by dark blue berries.	Good informal hedge or screen. Spreads by underground runners. Useful in natural plantings.
B. x gladwynensis 'William Penn' William Penn Barberry	5-8	To 2-3 ft tall.	Evergreen or deciduous. Broadly spreading dwarf. Leathery, rich green foliage on dense, arching branches. Profusion of bright yellow flowers in spring.	Good for low hedges, edging, mass plantings.
B. julianae Wintergreen Barberry	6-8	To 6-10 ft tall.	Evergreen or deciduous. Dense, upright, thorny habit. Dark, glossy green hollylike leaves with spiny stems. Small yellow flowers in spring followed by blue-black berries.	Good barrier or hedge plant.
B. j. 'Nana'	6-8	To 3-4 ft tall.	Evergreen or deciduous. Dwarf form.	Tolerates partial shade.
B. j. 'Pyramidalis'	6-8	To 3-4 ft tall.	Evergreen or deciduous. Dwarf used for its pyramidal shape.	Tolerates partial shade.
B. x mentorensis Mentor Barberry	5-8	To 7 ft tall.	Evergreen or deciduous. Stiff, upright branching habit. Thick, dark green spiny foliage. Small yellow flowers in late spring followed by dark red berries. Bright red fall foliage.	Makes an excellent hedge.
B. thunbergii Japanese Barberry	4-9	To 7 ft tall.	Deciduous. Dense, compact habit with spiny stems. Dark green leaves end in sharp points; turn red in fall. Yellow flowers with reddish tinge appear in spring; heavy crop of red berries in fall and winter.	Good choice for hedge or impenetrable thorny barrier.
B. t. 'Atropurpurea' Red-Leaf Japanese Barberry, Red Barberry	4-9	To 5 ft tall.	Deciduous. Similar to species but leaves are deep purplish-red in full sun (green in shade) throughout summer, turning deep amber with cool weather.	Use for hedge, barrier. Good contrast in shrub border.
B. t. 'Atropurpurea Nana' Crimson Pygmy Barberry	4-9	To 1-1/2 to 2 ft tall.	Deciduous. Low-growing, dwarf mounding form of red-leaf Japanese barberry. Deep purple-red leaves turn amber with cool weather.	Use for low hedge in rock garden, container. Good ground cover.
B. t. 'Aurea' Yellow Japanese Barberry	4-9	To 1-1/2 to 2 ft tall.	Deciduous. Slow-growing, similar in habit to crimson pygmy barberry, but has bright yellow foliage.	Excellent low hedge or border planting.
B. t. 'Kobold' Kobold Barberry	4-9	To 1-1/2 to 2 ft tall.	Deciduous. Dwarf. Similar in habit to crimson pygmy barberry, with a fuller, rounded form. Bright green foliage.	Use for low hedge.
B. t. 'Rose Glow' Rose Glow Barberry	4-9	To 3 ft tall.	Deciduous. Densely branched, compact growth. Similar in habit to red-leaf Japanese barberry. New growth variegated with light pink, turning dark rose-red at maturity. Outstanding fall color, holding longer than species.	Use for low hedge or barrier.
B. verruculosa Warty Barberry	5-9	To 3 ft tall.	Evergreen. Compact, spreading. Leaves spiny, dark green above, grayish white beneath; turn bronze in fall. Stems warty, spiny. Golden-yellow flowers followed by dark bluish-black fruit.	Good for border planting or low hedge. Tolerates partial shade.

European white birch *(Betula pendula)* is a beautiful shade tree with brilliant white bark and graceful weeping branches. Foliage turns vivid yellow in fall.

River birch *(Betula nigra)* is the only birch adapted to the South. It grows on both wet or dry sites, making a graceful shade tree with bright fall foliage.

Betula
Birch

Deciduous shrubs and trees.

This genus contains 50 to 60 species of deciduous trees and shrubs native to the north temperate zone. Some species grow in the Arctic in shrublike form. Best adapted to northern states, most birch species do not grow well in the South or in the hot, dry areas of the Southwest. Two species, river birch *(Betula nigra)* and European white birch *(Betula pendula)*, will succeed in warmer areas.

Birch species hybridize easily, so labels of nursery plants may be confusing. However, all birches make superb ornamental trees renowned for their graceful habit, colorful bark, and brilliant yellow fall foliage.

Most birch trees are short-lived. They are susceptible to aphid infestation and attack by bronze birch borers and birch leaf-miners. Some species are more resistant to insect pests than others. White-barked birch trees also attract vandals, who strip rings of bark from around tree trunks. The white bark does not grow back, and black "mourning bands" permanently commemorate the bark removal.

Betula nigra
River Birch, Black Birch, Red Birch

Zones: 5-9. To 70-90 feet.
Deciduous tree.

River birch thrives in wet soil, growing naturally beside creeks and in adjacent flatlands subject to frequent flooding. Young trees have shiny red bark. As they age the bark begins to peel and becomes pinkish-white and tattered in appearance. At maturity the trunk bark is scaly, turning to a dark, chocolatelike blackish-brown color.

When grown in open areas, river birch usually has a short trunk that may divide 15 or 20 feet above the ground and develops a rounded crown with softly drooping branches. It grows on both wet and dry sites and is the only birch recommended for planting in the low elevation areas of the South. The trees can be grown either with a single stem or as a multistemmed clump and are useful as shade trees, lawn trees, or as specimen plantings.

Bronze birch borer and birch leaf-miner usually are not serious problems for river birch. The variety 'Heritage' is pest-resistant. It is a vigorous tree with glossy foliage; develops a lighter bark color at an early age.

Betula papyrifera
Paper Birch, Canoe Birch, Eastern White Birch
Zones: 2-5. To 70-90 feet.
Deciduous tree.

Paper birch is grown for its attractive white bark, graceful habit, and bright yellow fall color. Young trees are conical or pyramidal; an oval crown develops as they reach maturity.

Paper birch trees have difficulty adapting in areas where the average temperature in July exceeds 70°F. South of the Great Lakes they grow only on cool sites at higher elevations or on steep northern and eastern slopes. Paper birch trees require full sunlight. If grown as lawn trees, care must be taken to avoid damaging their shallow roots with lawn mowers.

Paper birch is a short-lived tree maturing at 60 to 75 years of age. It is more resistant to bronze birch borer and birch leaf-miner than European white birch.

Betula pendula (B. alba, B. verrucosa)
European White Birch, White Birch
Zones: 2-9. To 60 feet.
Deciduous tree.

European white birch is pyramidal in shape when young, developing an oval crown as it matures. Trees have graceful drooping branches, handsome white bark, and foliage that turns to brilliant yellow in fall. It prefers moist, well-drained sandy or loam soils, and adapts better to the dry conditions found in California than other white birches.

The variety 'Dalecarlica', the cut-leaf weeping birch, has deeply lobed leaves and graceful weeping branches. It is less tolerant of dry climates than the species. Young's weeping birch (*B. pendula* 'Youngii') has a graceful weeping habit; requires careful staking to develop a tree form. Does not tolerate hot dry climates.

Bronze birch borer and birch leaf-miner can be serious problems unless controlled by regular pesticide applications.

Bougainvillea
Bougainvillea
Zones: 9-10.
Evergreen to partially deciduous vine. Flowering.

Of all the flowering vines in the California landscape, bougainvillea, with its spectacular flowers, is the most eye-catching. The colorful part of the bougainvillea flower is made up of 3 showy bracts that surround small white flowers. These bracts carpet the vine with vibrant color, in a spectrum from magenta, purple-pink, and crimson, to shades of bronze, orange, yellow, and white. In warm areas blooming is so prolific that color can last nearly year-round. When the vine is out of flower, the soft green, heart-shaped leaves create a dense foliage.

Bougainvillea has a wide range of garden uses, from ground covers to patio covers. Besides adding brilliant splashes of color in the landscape, they are used to shade, to beautify fences and walls, and to scramble over sunny slopes. Bougainvillea is a robust grower. If given something to twine around, strong branches can quickly cover the sides of houses. Vigor and shape will vary within the different cultivars. A few, such as 'Temple Fire', are shrubby vines for use as ground covers or container plants. Anticipate rapid growth with most vining types and allow plenty of room for spreading, unless pruned frequently.

The following are a few of the selections available for garden color:

'Afterglow' has abundant yellow-orange flowers; open growth. 'Barbara Karst' blooms early, and has light gold flowers. 'Cherry

A small grove of white-trunked birch (*Betula* sp.) forms a woodland setting.

European white birch (*Betula pendula*) is a breathtaking sight when dressed in its fall colors.

Under ideal growing conditions, bougainvillea (*Bougainvillea* sp.) provides vibrant color nearly year-round.

Blossom' has double flowers, shaded pink, with greenish-white centers. 'Jamaica White' is a moderate grower with white-green bracts and pale green veins. 'Lavender Queen' has numerous, large lavender flowers. 'Mrs. Butt' is an old-fashioned variety with crimson flowers; thrives in the hottest areas. 'Orange King' is frost-tender; has bronzy-orange bracts. 'San Diego Red' is one of the best for hardiness, good foliage, and prolonged bloom. This tall-growing vine has deep red flowers.

Bougainvillea is a tropical, frost-sensitive vine suitable for the hottest exposures.

Dry gardens in the West are the ideal setting for this vine. Water the plant to get it established and bring on new growth, then minimize watering for increased flowering. Bougainvilleas grow best in soils that are well drained but not too rich. Plant carefully because roots are easily damaged.

It takes a sturdy structure to hold bougainvillea's woody branches. Vines need to be tied to their support, otherwise, branches whip in the wind, shredding the soft leaves. Withstands heavy pruning. If cut to the base in spring or fall, the plant will return to bloom the next season.

Bougainvillea may be bothered by aphids, mealybugs, caterpillars, and scale.

Brunfelsia pauciflora 'Floribunda'
Yesterday-Today-and-Tomorrow
Zones: 8-10. To 10 feet.
Evergreen shrub. Flowering.

This colorful shrub is native to Brazil. The dark green leaves are 4 inches long and can be slightly twisted.

Tubular-shaped blossoms, borne in clusters, appear profusely from spring to summer. They open purple, turn lavender and then white, hence the common name. Should be pruned in spring to shape shrub and remove scraggly branches. Plant in a fertile, well-drained soil and protect from direct sunlight. Excellent in containers.

Yesterday-today-and-tomorrow *(Brunfelsia pauciflora* 'Floribunda'), an evergreen shrub, bears clusters of blossoms that open purple, turn lavender and then turn white.

Butterfly bush *(Buddleia davidii)* is irresistible to butterflies.

Buddleia davidii
Butterfly Bush, Summer Lilac

Zones: 5-10. To 6-10 feet.
Deciduous shrub. Flowering.

Butterfly bush is a wide-spreading leggy shrub with finely toothed narrow leaves about 10 inches long. It may be killed back to ground level by cold temperatures, and is often treated as a perennial and pruned nearly to its base in late winter or early spring. Although a plant late to start new growth in spring, when warm weather does arrive, butterfly bush grows vigorously and by midsummer 10-inch-long arching spikes of orange-eyed deep lavender, pink, blue, or white flowers will be borne on branch tips. Butterflies are lured to the fragrant blossoms.

Plant in well-drained soil in full sun or partial shade and water regularly. Heavy soils should be amended with organic matter. Butterfly bush makes a fine tall accent plant behind a perennial border. Spikes of blossoms make long-lasting cut flowers.

Spraying for sucking insects, such as spider mites, will control their damage but will also reduce the number of visiting butterflies.

Buxus
Boxwood, Box

Zones: 5-10. To 12 feet.
Evergreen shrubs.

The members of this genus of about 30 species of shrubs or small trees are grown for their fine-textured, tightly packed evergreen foliage. Leaves are usually small, oval, and lustrous deep green. Boxwoods respond so well to pruning and shearing that few plants can match them for formal hedges and topiary.

Because boxwoods are shallow-rooted, care should be taken not to damage their root systems. Planting too deep can smother roots; planting too high leads to roots drying out. Mulching with a loose material such as shredded bark is a good way to ensure planting success. However, too deep a mulch, over 4 to 6 inches, can also smother roots. Digging in the root area should be avoided. A moist site with good drainage is required for optimum growth.

Boxwoods grow in sunny or shady locations in mild winter areas. Under more severe conditions, such as in northern extremes of their range, they require a site protected from winds and winter sunshine.

Boxwoods (Buxus sp.) are fine-textured evergreen shrubs with many landscape functions; widely used as sheared hedges (shown above and below).

Buxus

Botanical Name/Common Name	Zones	Size	Plant Description	Comments
Buxus harlandii Harland Boxwood	5-10	To 18-20 in. tall.	Evergreen. Compact growth. Dainty, light green, narrow foliage.	Excellent for hedges. Responds well to shearing.
B. microphylla japonica Japanese Boxwood, Japanese Box	7-10	To 3 ft tall.	Evergreen. Compact growth. Leaves small, bright green.	Excellent for hedges, formal garden use. Responds to shearing. Tolerates shade.
B. m. j. 'Green Beauty' Green Beauty Japanese Boxwood	6-10	To 4-6 ft tall.	Evergreen. Hardier version of Japanese boxwood. Retains fine, dark green leaf color year-round.	Great for hedges.
B. m. koreana Korean Boxwood	5-10	To 3 ft tall.	Evergreen. Low-growing with small leaves. Hardy. Retains dark green foliage color.	The hardiest boxwood. Good choice for containers, low hedges.
B. m. 'Wintergreen' Wintergreen Boxwood	6-10	To 3 ft tall.	Evergreen. Improved variety. Holds its green color throughout winter.	Excellent for container-growing or hedges.
B. sempervirens English Boxwood, Common Boxwood, English Box	5-10	To 6-12 ft tall.	Evergreen. Slow-growing with compact habit. Dark green oval leaves.	Handsome lawn specimen, hedge, topiary. Responds to shearing. Tolerates shade.
B. s. 'Suffruticosa' Dwarf Boxwood, Edging Boxwood	6-9	To 2 ft tall.	Evergreen. Slow-growing, dense, with small leaves.	Ideal for border planting, hedge, container.

Lemon bottlebrush *(Callistemon citrinus)* normally grows as a multi-trunked shrub, but can be pruned as a tree.

Weeping bottlebrush *(Callistemon viminalis)* has weeping branches; can be trained as a shrub or a tree.

Callistemon
Bottlebrush

Evergreen shrubs or trees.
Flowering.

Callistemons are called bottle-brushes because the tightly-packed flowers, which are concentrated at the ends of the branches, are adorned with colorful stamens that resemble the bristles of a brush. These fast-growing Australian natives are used in sunny areas as a single plant specimen, as screens or informal hedges, or as an espalier on a wall or fence. Normally bushy plants, they can be pruned into the shape of a small tree.

Callistemon citrinus
Lemon Bottlebrush
Zones: 8-10. To 8-10 feet.
Evergreen shrub or tree. Flowering.

The lemon bottlebrush forms a tall shrub unless the lower limbs are removed. By pruning, it is possible to develop a 20-foot or taller, round-headed tree in 10 years. Narrow foliage can vary from 1 to 3 inches long and is copper-colored as it emerges, becoming bright green with maturity. Bright red flower clusters are 2 to 6 inches long with 1-inch-long stamens. Seed capsules are ovoid and remain on the plant for several years. Heaviest bloom is in the spring and summer but scattered flowering occurs throughout the year.

The common name of this species refers to the citrus odor emitted by the leaves when crushed. Much variability in leaf and flower cluster size occurs when this species is raised from seed. It is preferable to obtain plants grown by cuttings from select forms.

Lemon bottlebrush is drought-tolerant but grows best in a moist, well-drained soil. Alkaline and saline conditions are tolerated.

Callistemon viminalis
Weeping Bottlebrush
Zones: 8-10. To 20-30 feet.
Evergreen shrub or tree. Flowering.

With pruning and periodic thinning, this bottlebrush can be developed into an attractive weeping tree of about 30 feet high and half as wide. It is best as a multitrunk specimen. Without thinning, the tree loses its attractive appearance and becomes top-heavy.

The 6-inch-long light green leaves are clustered at the ends of the long drooping branches. The bright red flowers open primarily in spring and early summer, but scattered blooms occur throughout the year.

This species requires frequent watering and is not a good tree for hot, windy, or dry locations. The varieties 'McCaskill' and 'Red Cascade' are more vigorous, with very showy flowers.

Calluna vulgaris
Scotch Heather
Zones: 4-7. To 2-3 feet.
Evergreen shrub. Flowering.

Native from Iceland to Turkey and to North Africa, heather is eye-catching as a specimen in rock gardens and shrub borders, used as a ground cover or potted plant, and provides cut flowers, fresh or dried.

Usually grows 1 to 2 feet tall with tiny, scalelike, dense dark green leaves and spikes of small purplish-pink or white bell-shaped flowers, which open from July to September. However, growth characteristics are variable.

Calocedrus decurrens
California Incense Cedar
Zones: 6-10. To 85-100 feet.
Evergreen tree.

This handsome, stately conifer, native to California, is widely adapted and tolerates extremely cold winters and hot dry summers. It often lives several hundred years. Tree form is pyramidal to columnar. The upper branches are erect with broadly sweeping lower limbs. Scalelike foliage forms characteristic flat sprays. The deeply furrowed bark is cinnamon-red, adding colorful contrast. The entire plant is wonderfully aromatic.

California incense cedar is a tree for large spaces, adding rugged form and texture to the landscape. Its moderate growth and dense foliage make an effective wind screen or large hedge. These trees are tolerant of poor growing conditions, preferring neutral to acid soils that are deep and well-drained. Provide ample water regularly until well established.

Camellia
Camellia
Evergreen shrubs and trees.

This genus contains about 80 species of evergreen shrubs and small trees native to eastern and southeastern Asia. They are plants for warm areas and are not able to withstand subzero temperatures. Some are severely damaged by heavy frosts. Camellia is Alabama's state flower.

Camellias are grown for their showy, waxy flowers, which may be single or double, measure from 2 to 5 inches across, and come in a range of colors from white to pink to red. The leaves are glossy dark green and are attractive year-round.

Most camellias demand a moist but well-drained, slightly acid soil, rich in organic matter. Too much, or too little, water can cause problems and they suffer if planted too deeply. If the base of the trunk is covered by soil, plants will not thrive. Camellias benefit from a 2-inch-thick mulch that keeps roots cool and aids in controlling rapid changes of the moisture content of soil. These shrubs do well in light shade, blooming prolifically where other shrubs would flower only sparsely.

Camellias are often grown in containers in regions colder than their hardiness zone and can then be brought inside during cold weather. They are also grown in greenhouses.

Camellias are of special interest to many gardeners, and over 3,000 different cultivars have been selected.

Camellia japonica
Japanese Camellia
Zones: 7-10. To 15-45 feet.
Evergreen shrub. Flowering.

This is the most popular camellia, with over 2,000 named cultivars. Can be a large shrub or small tree. Leaves are thick, leathery, and dark green. Flowers are large, from 2 to 5 inches across, and are white, pink, red, or variegated. Blooming from October to April, they may be single or double. Size and color of flower may depend upon age of plant, weather, and site. All are beautiful specimen plants and make excellent screens or border plants.

Camellia sasanqua
Sasanqua Camellia
Zones: 7-10. To 15 feet.
Evergreen shrub. Flowering.

Flowers bloom just before *C. japonica* in autumn or early winter. Tolerates more sun than Japanese camellia. Its leaves are about 2 inches long. Over 75 cultivars have been selected with single, semidouble, and double blossoms in shades of white, pink, and red. Plant habit also varies. Low, spreading varieties are useful ground covers, espaliers, or container plants. Tall varieties are excellent specimen or entryway plants and can even be clipped as a hedge.

Campsis
Trumpet Creeper
Deciduous vines. Flowering.

Trumpet creepers are aggressive deciduous vines that bear spectacular flowers. They are suitable for large spaces.

Leaves are compound, having 7 to 11 leaflets with serrated margins. The vine is in peak form in midsummer when the showy blossoms appear. Terminal clusters hold 6 to 12 brilliant, 3-inch flowers shaped like funnels with wide, open mouths. Flowers, colored orange to scarlet, attract hummingbirds.

Varieties of Scotch heather *(Calluna vulgaris)* have different foliage colors and bloom times.

Camellias *(Camellia* sp.) are attractive evergreen shrubs much-loved for their wintertime flowers. Exquisite blossoms (shown below) are white, pink, or red.

Madame Galen trumpet creeper *(Campsis x tagliabuana* 'Madame Galen')

When pruned, Siberian pea shrub *(Caragana arborescens)* makes a neat accent tree.

Natal plum *(Carissa grandiflora)*

Trumpet creepers can grow up to 30 feet, with aerial rootlets attaching stems to rough surfaces. Grow these vines over large stone walls, as a filler against fences in expansive gardens, or up the trunks of tall trees. Roots send out suckers, spreading vines over large areas. These suckers should be removed if the vines threaten to become too invasive. Trumpet creepers can be pruned into a large hedge if trained at an early age. However these vigorous vines will need frequent pruning to maintain a compact form.

Trumpet creeper rootlets are not tenacious clingers. Young vines need support until clinging rootlets form. High winds can separate top-heavy branches from their support. This can be avoided by pruning to reduce the volume of branches, and by pinching growing tips to encourage growth at the base of branches.

Grow trumpet creepers in full sun. Plants are most attractive if given a rich soil and average water, but can withstand less desirable conditions.

Campsis grandiflora
Chinese Trumpet Creeper
Zones: 7-8.
Deciduous vine. Flowering.

Chinese trumpet creeper has large scarlet blossoms in midsummer. Leaflets grow 7 to 9 on a stem. Less cold hardy than other trumpet creepers but a good choice for smaller gardens because its growth is restrained.

Campsis radicans
Trumpet Creeper Vine
Zones: 4-8.
Deciduous vine. Flowering.

This native American vine grows vigorously to 40 feet. Leaves have 9 to 11 leaflets on a stem. Orange blossoms marked with red appear in mid-July. They are 3 inches long, with expanded lips. Five-inch-long capsules hang through winter. The vine dies to the ground where temperatures are freezing but tops regrow in spring. 'Flava' has yellow flowers.

Campsis x tagliabuana
'Madame Galen'
Madame Galen Trumpet Creeper
Zones: 4-8.
Deciduous vine. Flowering.

This is the top-rated hybrid of the two *Campsis* species. Salmon-red flowers are held in loose clusters. Reaches 25 to 30 feet high and has the cold hardiness of the trumpet creeper.

Caragana arborescens
Siberian Pea Shrub, Pea Tree
Zones: 2-7. To 15 feet.
Evergreen shrub. Flowering.

Native to Manchuria, this pea shrub was first brought to North America in the mid 1700's and it is extremely cold hardy. Its shape makes it very useful as an informal hedge or screen and it is used as a natural snow fence in cold windy regions.

Bright yellow flowers bloom in late spring, with pods forming in late summer. Flowers are like those found on peas, hence the common name pea shrub. Leaves are feathery and young twigs are yellow-green.

Grows best in well-drained sites with full sun or partial shade, but adapts to most soil conditions.

Carissa grandiflora
Natal Plum
Zone: 10. To 2-7 feet.
Evergreen shrub. Flowering.

Neat shiny leaves, dainty white flowers, and edible fruit make this shrub from South Africa a real asset to the landscape. Low-growing varieties are good ground covers, while taller varieties can be lightly pruned as a tall screen or heavily pruned as a low hedge. They are also used as specimen plants and will grow indoors as houseplants in good light conditions.

Varieties differ in growth habit from loose, open, upright forms to compact spreaders. Most have thorns. The oval leaves are 3 inches long, shiny, and deep green. Fragrant white flowers have 5 petals, are star-shaped, and measure 2 inches across. Blooms year-round. Red, plum-shaped fruits measure 1 to 2 inches around and vary in sweetness.

Natal plums are easy to grow and adapt to a variety of soils. They endure inland's summer heat, or coastal fog, growing both in sun or shade. Fruit quality and quantity will be less if grown in shade. Pruning to remove wild shoots may be needed.

Top-rated varieties include: 'Fancy', upright shrub to 6 feet high, flowers heavily and has large, tasty fruit; 'Green Carpet', a low-grower that reaches 1 to 1-1/2 feet high, spreads to 4 feet, and has small leaves; 'Ruby Point', upright, to 6 feet tall, with beautiful red-tipped foliage year-round.

Carpinus betulus
European Hornbeam
Zones: 4-9. To 40-60 feet.
Deciduous tree.

European hornbeam is considered one of the best trees for city plantings. It has dense growth and performs reliably even when grown in containers. When young, European hornbeam has a narrow upright growth habit that changes to a broad pyramidal shape with maturity. A low branching habit with many horizontal limbs and numerous fine twigs gives it an attractive silhouette. Dark green oval leaves are up to 5 inches long. Their fall color varies from bright yellow to yellowish brown, and dead brown leaves may persist on the trees until spring. The tree casts dense shade in summer and fairly heavy shade in winter months due to the persistent leaves and numerous twiggy branches.

European hornbeam will tolerate light shade but grows best in full sun; prefers a moist but well-drained soil. These trees withstand pruning and shearing and make an effective hedge or sculptured topiary.

The cultivar C. betulus 'Fastigiata', upright European hornbeam, differs from the species in growth habit. All branches angle upward and young trees form a dense columnar shape that changes to an upright oval form when mature. Leaves are 3-1/2 inches long and 1-1/2 inches wide. They emerge early in spring and turn a glowing yellow in fall. 'Fastigiata' is an excellent tree for use where space is restricted. It does not interfere with buildings or traffic when planted as a street tree. Fast-growing when young, it is a good choice when a dense screen is wanted quickly. Trees are not damaged by strong winds or ice.

European hornbeam has no major disease or insect pest problems.

Carya illinoensis
Pecan
Zones: 7-9. To 60-100 feet.
Deciduous tree.

The pecan is a stately, round-headed, relatively fast-growing tree. Leaves are divided into narrow leaflets and create a pleasant filtered shade. In areas of the South and West with long, hot summers, it also produces a bountiful harvest of edible nuts.

Pecans grow best and are most productive in Zones 8 and 9. Hardier strains, such as 'Starking's Hardy Giant', are occasionally seen as far north as Zone 6. However, they seldom set fruit and trees do not possess the character of those grown farther south.

Trees grow best in deep, well-drained soil with occasional deep watering during summer. They are subject to a number of pests; pecan scab is most troublesome in the South. Two varieties developed by Auburn University, 'Kaddo' and 'Chickasaw', are scab-resistant.

In the alkaline soils of the West, pecans are subject to zinc deficiency. Micronutrient sprays are most effective in controlling this problem.

Pecans require cross-pollination from another variety to set abundant crops, but most varieties will produce some nuts when planted alone. This is a distinct advantage since few homes can accommodate two of these large trees.

A valuable shade tree for urban use, European hornbeam (Carpinus betulus) has no disease or insect problems.

The pecan tree (Carya illinoensis) casts filtered shade; produces delicious nuts in areas with hot summer weather.

Crown-of-gold tree *(Cassia excelsa)* is a colorful shade tree for arid climates.

With showy flowers and bold dramatic foliage, Catalpa trees *(Catalpa* sp.) make excellent lawn trees for open spaces.

There are many varieties of pecan, most of which have a specific climate adaptation. 'Western Schley' and 'Wichita' are common varieties in the West. Disease-resistant varieties are the best choice for homeowners in the South. Check with your local nurseryman for pecan varieties best adapted to your area.

Cassia excelsa
Crown-of-Gold Tree
Zone: 10. To 25-30 feet.
Partially deciduous tree. Flowering.

This is a fast-growing tree for southern California and mild areas of the Southwest desert. Large clusters of bright yellow flowers are borne in late summer and fall. Leaves are divided into many small leaflets. Prune after flowering. Water infrequently but deeply during the growing season.

Catalpa
Catalpa
Deciduous or evergreen trees. Flowering.

This genus contains 13 species of deciduous, or rarely evergreen, trees native to North America and eastern Asia. Grown as ornamentals for their large clusters of showy flowers and dramatic foliage, catalpas offer flowers that are colored white, brownish pink, and yellow. Trees bloom in late spring or early summer. Most species will grow well in a wide range of soil types.

Catalpa bignonioides
**Common Catalpa,
Southern Catalpa**
Zones: 5-10. To 60 feet.
Deciduous tree. Flowering..

This broadly rounded, fast-growing tree has large heart-shaped leaves to 8 inches long with an unpleasant odor when bruised. Flowers in clusters to 10 inches long are white with 2 yellow stripes and brown spots. Mature trees, when in bloom, resemble a huge bouquet of flowers. Seed contained in long cylindrical pods gives the tree a local name of Indian bean tree.

A hardy tree able to withstand city smog and most other adverse conditions, common catalpa is native from Georgia to Florida and Mississippi but has proven hardy enough to plant farther north. In Zone 5 needs a sheltered site. Use as a lawn tree or as a specimen tree.

Cultivars include 'Aurea' with yellow leaves and 'Nana', a dwarf that is often grafted high to make umbrella-shaped trees with branches drooping to the ground.

Catalpa speciosa
**Northern Catalpa,
Western Catalpa**
Zones: 5-10. To 100 feet.
Deciduous tree. Flowering.

This is a pyramidal tree when young, becoming roundheaded as it matures. Leaves are up to 1 foot long and have less of an odor than the southern catalpa. Flowers are white with brown spots. The large clusters of flowers are very conspicuous and appear when most trees have finished flowering. The seeds are contained in long brown beanlike pods to 20 inches long. Fallen pods make a messy cleanup job in spring.

This catalpa is hardier than its southern counterpart—it originated in the Midwest and is native from Southern Indiana and Iowa south to Arkansas and Texas. It will withstand hot summers and dry soil, and is tolerant of city environments. Western catalpa grows too large for small properties and should be planted in large open areas.

The caterpillar of the catalpa moth feeds on this tree's leaves. This large worm is good fish bait, and normally only fishermen notice it feeding.

Ceanothus
California Lilac, Wild Lilac
Zones: 8-10. To 5-20 feet.
Evergreen shrub. Flowering.

The majority of the evergreen species are natives of California, where many improved varieties have been developed. Blue flowers, the rarest color for hardy shrubs, are the major attraction of wild lilac. They are sun-loving plants to use as ground and bank covers, for screening, or as specimens without irrigation.

Plant sizes vary from prostrate spreaders to rounded shrubs to small broad trees. Leaves are bright green. Flowers range from white to deep purple-blue and open from March to May depending on the variety. Once ceanothus is established, avoid summer watering, which will encourage root-rot diseases.

Cedrus
Cedar
Evergreen trees.

The true cedars are natives of mountainous areas of North Africa, Asia Minor and Asia. Best growth is made on well-drained, loamy soils in warm or mild climates. Young trees are conical or pyramidal. Needles are clustered on stout, lateral spurs. All cedars develop into excellent, large specimen trees if given ample space in which to grow. Not a tree for small gardens, although cedars can be kept dwarf if grown in containers. Upright cones on older trees are an added attraction.

Cedrus atlantica
Atlas Cedar
Zones: 6-10. To 60 feet and more.
Evergreen tree.

Growing in the Atlas Mountains of Algeria and Morocco, atlas cedar is one of the few conifers native to Africa. Has the potential of growing to be 120 feet in height with a crown spread nearly as wide, but usually attains only half that size. Fast-growing when young, becoming very slow-growing as it reaches maturity. Old trees are flat-topped with horizontally spreading branches and are very picturesque, rugged, and imposing. Bluish-green needles are less than 1 inch long. Although slight shade is tolerated, best development is in full sunlight. Atlas cedar is one of the few conifers that can thrive on alkaline soils.

A number of cultivars have been selected. Blue atlas cedar, cultivar 'Glauca', differs from the species mainly in the silvery-blue color of the foliage. Weeping blue atlas cedar, 'Glauca Pendula', has blue needles and drooping branches. If not trained to grow upright, it will become prostrate. It is often used as an espalier. Heights from 15 to 35 feet, with crown spreads to 50 feet, may be reached.

Cedrus deodara
Deodar Cedar
Zones: 7-10. To 70-80 feet.
Evergreen tree.

From the Himalayan Mountains, deodar cedar is the most tender of the three species. Grows rapidly to 70 or 80 feet, with crown spreads of 40 to 50 feet, in 40 to 50 years. Lower branches are pendulous. Older trees are wide-spreading and flat-topped. This is the most widely planted true cedar in the United States. Requires well-drained soil, sunny location. Hardy cultivars are 'Kashmir' and 'Kingsville'. 'Aurea' has yellow leaves while 'Pendula' has long, drooping branches.

Cedrus libani
Cedar-of-Lebanon
Zones: 7-10. To 70-80 feet.
Evergreen tree.

This cedar is conical when young but becomes flat-topped with age. Needles are usually bright green, but varieties with yellow-green, blue-green, or silvery needles are also sold, as is a form with weeping branches.

Regal and stately, blue atlas cedar (Cedrus atlantica 'Glauca') should be planted where it has growing room.

Deodar cedar (Cedrus deodara) has branches right to the ground, acting as an effective screen and windbreak.

A fast-spreading vine, American bittersweet *(Celastrus scandens)* has amber-colored autumn foliage and bright berries that stay dramatic after leaves fall.

Tolerant of adverse growing conditions, carob tree *(Ceratonia siliqua)* can be trained in tree form, grown as a shrub for screening, or clipped as a hedge.

Celastrus

Bittersweet

Deciduous vines. Flowering.

Both American and Oriental bittersweet are woody, twining deciduous vines best used in naturalistic landscapes. They are in their glory in fall, when leaves drop to expose scarlet-and-yellow berries that last through the season.

Bittersweet is a fast, vigorous grower, requiring little care. Avoid planting near small trees and shrubs because the twining vines will use them as supports, eventually smothering the plants with strong encircling stems. With careful pruning, vines make effective covers for an arbor, fence, or sturdy trellis. When used as a ground cover, branches circle around themselves forming a dense, mounded mat that is good over rocky banks and in open spaces.

Leaves are roundish and light green, changing to bright yellow before dropping in fall. Greenish-white flowers appear in late spring but are small and inconspicuous. Green fruits change to yellow-orange in fall, then burst open, revealing masses of beautiful scarlet berries. Before heavy frost, cut the ornamental branches for a lasting indoor decoration. Flowers occur on separate plants and both sexes are required for berry production. Plant male and female vines close together for best fruit set.

Bittersweet is an adaptable vine. Few vines can match its tolerance of cold winter temperatures and high winds found in the midwestern and northeastern states. It is less common in warm winter regions because fruiting is best with winter chill. Boggy, wet soils are not suitable. Bittersweet is drought-tolerant and grows well in poor, sandy soil.

Prune severely every year in early spring, before leaves appear. Flowers and fruit are produced on new wood. A harsh pruning will help contain twining stems.

Scale may be a problem on bittersweet. Watch for signs of infestation and treat with an appropriate control.

Celastrus orbiculatus
Oriental Bittersweet
Zones: 5-9.
Deciduous vine. Flowering.

Oriental bittersweet is a vigorous grower, spreading up to 40 feet. It is used to cover large areas. Very round leaves and lateral fruiting branches characterize this species.

Celastrus scandens
American Bittersweet
Zones: 3-9.
Deciduous vine. Flowering.

American bittersweet is a rapidly spreading vine with oval, light green, 4-inch leaves. It can be distinguished from Oriental bittersweet by the way its fruit is held in terminal clusters above the leaves. The plant is more contained than the Asian species, reaching 10 to 20 feet at maturity. This vine can be seen growing wild in its native range of eastern North America.

Celtis

Hackberry, Nettle Tree, Sugarberry

Evergreen or deciduous shrubs and trees.

This genus contains about 75 species of mostly deciduous trees and shrubs. Hackberries are widely adapted and tolerate extreme heat, drought, and poor soil. They are widely used in the landscape as shade trees and for street plantings.

Celtis australis
European Hackberry, Mediterranean Hackberry, Lote Tree, Honeyberry
Zones: 7-9. To 80 feet.
Evergreen tree.

When young, European hackberry has a more upright shape, and when mature a less spreading crown, than common hackberry or sugarberry. It is a valuable landscape tree for the hot, dry climates of the Southwest and is commonly used in highway plantings in areas that receive very little water.

Celtis laevigata
Sugarberry, Mississippi Hackberry
Zones: 5-9. To 60-80 feet.
Deciduous tree.

This species of hackberry is well adapted to the growing conditions found in the South, where it is used extensively as a street and shade tree. It develops a rounded to broadly rounded crown and tolerates strong winds, dry sites, and periodic flooding.

Sugarberry is resistant to witches' broom, an abnormal growth that often disfigures other hackberries.

Celtis occidentalis
Common Hackberry
Zones: 4-8. To 6-100 feet.
Deciduous tree.

Native to eastern United States, common hackberry has a round-topped crown and spreading, sometimes pendulous, branches. Bright green leaves have toothed edges. Immature bark is characterized by bumpy growths resembling warts.

Common hackberry tolerates dry sites, periodic flooding, and strong winds, but will not grow in soil with poor drainage or where the water table is always high. It has been widely and successfully used in shelterbelt plantings in the Great Plains, where it develops into a large shrub or small tree.

In parks and large open areas, common hackberry is frequently grown as a shade tree. It is subject to witches' broom.

Ceratonia siliqua
Carob, St. John's-Bread
Zones: 9-10. To 20-50 feet.
Evergreen tree. Flowering.

This species is a native to the eastern Mediterranean area. Called "St. John's-Bread" because the seeds and sweet pulp from the pods are supposed to be the "locusts and wild honey" St. John ate in the wilderness. Cultivated in its native area for the fruit pods, which are used for human and stock food. The pods, high in sugar content, are ground into a fine powder used as a substitute for chocolate.

Small red flowers form in short clusters in spring and are not showy. Trees are either male or female and flowers of the male trees have an unpleasant odor. Flattened, dark brown leathery pods ripen on the female trees in fall and may be a litter problem. Pods can be up to 12 inches long, but 6 to 8 inches is more usual.

Carob should be planted in a well-drained soil in full sun. Water infrequently but deeply, because root crown rot may be a problem if watered too frequently. Tolerates drought, polluted city air, poor and alkaline soils, and desert conditions. Young trees may need some winter protection but older trees are hardy to 18°F. Roots may crack paved surfaces. Carobs cast heavy shade.

Cercidiphyllum japonicum
Katsura Tree
Zones: 4-9. To 40-50 feet.
Deciduous tree.

When pruned to a single trunk, this formal-looking tree has a tall pyramidal shape that takes on a broader head with age. Leaves are heart-shaped and dense, creating a uniform-textured foliage. They emerge reddish purple and gradually change to dark green with silvery undersides. Fall color is orange or red.

Plant katsura tree in a site protected from dry winds and high temperatures. Water regularly. Use as a specimen or accent tree and for shade.

Cercidium
Palo Verde
Zones: 8-10. To 20 to 30 feet.
Deciduous trees. Flowering.

Palo verde is an unusual tree of the southwestern deserts. Its long, narrow leaf stalks, which stand out from smooth green branches, remain leafless most of the year, creating an open, airy effect. Small leaves, followed by a burst of yellow flowers that blanket the tree, appear with winter rains.

Katsura tree (*Cercidiphyllum japonicum*) is a widely adapted shade tree with changing foliage color.

A drought-tolerant desert denizen, palo verde (*Cercidium* sp.) is well-suited to naturalistic landscapes in arid climates.

Redbuds *(Cercis* sp.) bear colorful flowers in spring, provide shade in summer, and let sun shine through in winter.

Palo verde is especially attractive in desert gardens or near patios where its cool green branches cast a light shade. Though extremely drought-tolerant, deep watering once a month and a well-drained soil will increase its beauty.

Three species are grown, each distinquished by the color of its bark. Blue palo verde, *Cercidium floridum,* has bluish-green bark; Little-leaf palo verde, *Cercidium microphyllum,* has yellow-green bark, hairy leaves; and Sonoran palo verde, *Cercidium praecox,* has bright green bark, develops a wide-spreading crown.

Cercis
Redbud
Deciduous shrubs and trees. Flowering.

This genus contains 8 species of small deciduous trees or shrubs growing in warm areas of the Northern Hemisphere.

Cercis canadensis
Eastern Redbud, Redbud
Zones: 4-7. To 25-40 feet. Deciduous tree. Flowering.

This tree has a short trunk and spreading branches with a rounded crown when young, and becomes flat-topped in later life. The spread of the crown is often equal to the height of the tree. The tree is frequently multistemmed, dividing into several trunks close to the ground if it is not trained.

Dainty, pink to purplish-pink, pealike flowers, clustered along the twigs and branches, appear in early spring before the leaves. The heart-shaped leaves are reddish purple when first unfolding, soon becoming a dark green color that looks attractive all summer. An added plus is the yellow autumn foliage.

Redbud can be grown in full sun or light shade. In the wild it usually grows as an understory tree in hardwood forests, favoring the moist soils of valleys and slopes. It is not too fussy about soil pH and will grow in either acid or alkaline soils providing they are not too extreme,

Above left: Eastern redbud *(Cercis canadensis)* has small pealike flowers all along the branches. Above right: Flowering quince *(Chaenomeles* sp.) has beautiful flowers and sharp thorns.

but redbud dislikes wet soils with poor drainage. Best growth is made on deep, fertile, moist soils with good drainage.

Redbud has been used as an ornamental for many years in the United States. George Washington transplanted some from the woods into his garden at Mount Vernon. Redbuds are very effective as accent trees, set in group plantings, or planted in shrub borders. They are lovely naturalized in open woodlands, and they are excellent patio trees especially attractive against a light-colored background. The tree begins to bloom when quite young.

A number of cultivars and varieties have been selected. The variety *texensis* is adapted to Texas; *alba* has white flowers. Cultivars 'Wither's Pink Charm' and 'Pink Bud' have pure pink flowers and 'Oklahoma' has dark red flowers. These forms are slightly less cold hardy than the species.

Cercis occidentalis
Western Redbud
Zones: 7-10. To 10-18 feet.
Deciduous tree. Flowering.

Western redbud is a good tree for the dry areas of the western United States. It tolerates poor soils and drought. Smaller than eastern redbud, the plant usually grows in multitrunk form with a spread equal to its height. Small magenta spring flowers are followed by interesting seed pods that last on the branches after foliage turns yellow or red in fall, and drops.

Chaenomeles
Flowering Quince
Zones: 5-9. To 2-10 feet.
Deciduous shrubs. Flowering.

Plants commonly sold as flowering quince are a rather confusing group of species and hybrids in the genus *Chaenomeles*. Even the genus name has been changed from *Pyrus* to *Cydonia* and finally to *Chaenomeles*. Usually nursery plants are labeled simply as flowering quince with a cultivar name. They may be one of several species.

No matter which species you buy, all flowering quince offer brightly colored early spring flowers in shades of white, pink, orange, or red, borne on interestingly twisted, often thorned, bare branches. Flowering quince has a strong Oriental appearance when in full bloom. In fact, cut branches are often used in Oriental flower arrangements.

In the landscape flowering quince can be used as hedges, screens, or as colorful accent plants. Varieties vary from 2 feet to 10 feet high.

They are widely adapted, though they bloom best in areas subject to frequent winter frosts or prolonged cold weather. Plants tolerate a wide range of soil types and temperature extremes.

Chamaecyparis
False Cypress
Zones: 5-9. To 75 feet.
Evergreen shrubs and trees.

There are 6 species of evergreen trees, 3 from North America and 3 from Japan, in this genus. The species are large pyramidal or columnar trees. In their native habitat, all reach heights in excess of a hundred feet. In landscape situations, half this height is usually reached. Numerous dwarf cultivars are also available. All require full sun, adequate moisture, and good drainage for best growth. Sites exposed to drying winds should be avoided.

Leaves on juvenile plants are needlelike or awl-shaped, becoming scalelike in flat sprays on mature trees. The juvenile leaves are retained for varying periods of time depending upon the cultivar. Adult foliage strongly resembles some types of arborvitae. The Japanese species can withstand dryer atmospheric conditions; they are used in central and eastern United States. The western species grow better where there is more moisture in the air.

An old-fashioned plant, flowering quince (*Chaenomeles* sp.) blooms in early spring, even before forsythia.

False cypress (*Chamaecyparis* sp.) grow into tall and conical specimen trees. Use dwarf varieties as shrubs.

Dwarf false cypress (*Chamaecyparis* sp.) makes a useful border planting.

Thread-branch cypress (*Chamaecyparis pisifera* 'Filifera') has fine-textured weeping branches.

Lawson cypress (*Chamaecyparis lawsoniana*) makes a formal specimen or lawn tree.

Chamaecyparis

Botanical Name/Common Name	Zones	Size	Plant Description	Comments
Chamaecyparis lawsoniana Lawson Cypress, Port Orford Cedar	6-9	To 40-45 ft tall.	Evergreen. Forms narrow pyramid. Blue-green foliage on graceful drooping branches.	Effective tall screen or windbreak. Well adapted to dry western climates. Cultivars available in many colors, sizes, and shapes.
C. l. 'Allumii' Blue Lawson Cypress, Pyramidal Blue Cypress, Scarab Cypress	6-9	To 40-45 ft tall.	Evergreen. Same as species but narrower and more compact. Less graceful. Blue foliage.	Good for screen or specimen plantings.
C. l. 'Ellwoodii' Ellwood Cypress	6-9	To 6-10 ft tall.	Evergreen. Compact dwarf column with dense silver-blue foliage. Soft needlelike leaves.	Slow-growing. May grow taller with age.
C. l. 'Lutea' Golden Lawson Cypress	6-9	To 30-40 ft tall.	Evergreen. Same as species but new growth is yellow.	Sunburns in hot climates.
C. l. 'Stewartii' Stewart Golden Cypress	6-9	To 30-40 ft tall.	Evergreen. Slightly more narrow and upright than species. Yellow new growth.	Needs room to develop.
Chamaecyparis obtusa Hinoki Cypress	5-9	To 50-75 ft tall, spreads half as wide.	Evergreen. Irregular pyramidal shape. Dark green foliage in twisted sprays.	Has coarser texture and is more widely adapted than Lawson cypress. Dwarf cultivars most commonly grown.
C. o. 'Crippsii' Cripps Golden Cypress	5-9	To 25-30 ft tall, spreads almost half as wide.	Evergreen. Irregular pyramidal shape. Yellow foliage turns green as plant matures.	Takes pruning. Unique specimen. Good hedge or screen.
C. o. 'Gracilis' Slender Hinoki Cypress	5-9	To 20-25 ft tall, spreads to 4-5 ft.	Evergreen. Slightly weeping, compact tree with irregular branching pattern and shiny, dark green foliage.	Very slow-growing. Good in containers.
C. o. 'Nana' Dwarf Hinoki Cypress	5-9	To 3 ft tall, spreads to 2 ft.	Evergreen. Extremely slow-growing dwarf. Branches in compact layers. Dark green foliage.	Excellent miniature for bonsai, rock gardens, containers.
C. o. 'Nana Gracilis' Dwarf Hinoki Cypress	5-9	To 4-6 ft tall, spreads nearly half as wide.	Evergreen. Slow-growing dwarf. Stratified layers of dark green foliage.	Often sold as 'Nana'. Hardiest hinoki cultivar. Useful in Oriental or rock gardens. Distinctive accent or container plant.
C. pisifera Sawara Cypress	5-9	To 25-35 ft tall spreads 15-20 ft.	Evergreen. Pyramidal. Dark green foliage with lighter undersides.	Needs pruning to maintain dense habit. Cultivars vary greatly.
C. p. 'Cyanoviridis' Boulevard Cypress	5-9	To 5-8 ft tall, spreads half as wide.	Evergreen. Dwarf. Soft-textured foliage is silvery-green with a hint of blue.	Good accent shrub.
C. p. 'Filifera' Thread-Branch Cypress	5-9	To 6-8 ft tall, spreads 6 ft.	Evergreen. Dwarf. Weeping, threadlike, dark green foliage. Forms a neat mound when young, loses shape with age.	Distinctive accent plant. Often becomes larger.
C. p. 'Filifera Aurea' Golden Thread-Branch Cypress	5-9	To 6-8 ft tall, spreads to 6 ft.	Evergreen. Dwarf. Same as 'Filifera' but with golden-yellow foliage.	Useful for color contrast.
C. thyoides 'Andelyensis' White Cedar, Southern Swamp Cedar	5-9	To 3-6 ft tall, spreads half as wide.	Evergreen. Dwarf. Narrow pyramid with gray-green foliage.	Useful accent in Oriental gardens. Grows best in soggy, acid soils.

Chamaemelum nobile
Roman Chamomile

Zones: 7-10. To 12 inches.
Herbaceous ground cover.
Flowering.

Also called *Anthemis nobilis*, this herb makes a very pretty ground cover, and is also a favorite source for chamomile tea. (The other herbal chamomile is *Matricaria recutita*.) When mowed short, it grows low and hugs the ground and can be walked upon with no ill-effects. Use it where a high maintenance lawn is undesirable or between stepping stones in an herb or flower garden path.

Leaves are gray-green and finely divided, emitting an herbal fragrance when crushed or stepped on. Flowers bloom in summer and are little gold buttons or small daisies. If unmown, plants grow about a foot tall.

For a ground cover, space plants about 8 inches apart in well-drained soil in full sun or light shade. Clip once a week at first to promote dense growth, thereafter as needed. Water during dry weather.

Chimonanthus praecox
Wintersweet

Zones: 7-9. To 8-10 feet.
Deciduous shrub. Flowering.

An early-bloomer, wintersweet heralds spring along with forsythia and flowering quince. Fragrant, one-inch flowers are comprised of a row of yellow outer petals and a row of purplish-brown-striped inner petals. Flowers appear on bare branches before the willowlike leaves unfold. 'Grandiflorus' has larger leaves, deeper yellow flowers; 'Lutea' has pure yellow blossoms.

Plant wintersweet near walkways, windows, porches, or patios so its enticing fragrance can be enjoyed. Wintersweet grows 8 to 10 feet wide and 10 feet tall, with a bushy, open shape. It requires a sheltered, lightly shaded location and performs best when planted in deep, well-drained soil. Water regularly and fertilize in early spring. Prune after flowering to shape or thin.

Chionanthus virginicus
Fringe Tree

Zones: 5-9. To 30 feet.
Deciduous tree or shrub.
Flowering.

Fringe tree is a large, spreading, open shrub that can be trained into an attractive tree. It is native to, and most at home in, the Eastern United States from Pennsylvania south to Florida. It does not adapt well to the arid regions of the Southwest. Clusters of fragrant white flowers to 8 inches long appear in late spring or early summer. Blossoms are dainty, with narrow fringelike petals, hence the common name. Use in group plantings, as an accent, or as a transition tree. Needs full sun or partial shade and deep, well-drained, acid, loamy soil. Fringe tree tolerates city conditions.

Choisya ternata
Mexican Orange, Mock Orange

Zones: 8-10. To 4-8 feet.
Evergreen shrub. Flowering.

Mexican orange has glossy, spreading leaflets that are arranged in layered patterns, forming a charming informal shrub. When in bloom in spring the 1-inch-long white flowers perfume the garden with their delightful fragrance. This sweet scent, reminiscent of orange blossoms, accounts for the plant's common name.

Use Mexican orange as a tub plant on the terrace or patio, near pathways where its fragrance can be enjoyed, or as an informal foundation and border shrub. It is a good companion plant for azaleas, ternstromia, and other acid-loving plants.

Mexican orange needs well-drained organic soil. It grows best in areas without extreme summer heat. Plant in sun in cool summer areas or in partial shade in hot climates. Infrequent but deep watering promotes healthy growth and will reduce the incidence of sucking insects, root-rot, and salt burn.

Roman chamomile *(Chamaemelum nobile)* forms a foot-high ground cover that hugs the ground if mowed.

Fringe tree *(Chionanthus virginicus)* makes an unusual patio tree that bears copious clusters of dainty, fragrant white blooms in late spring.

An informal shrub with evergreen foliage, Mexican orange *(Choisya ternata)* blooms in spring, fills the garden with orange blossom fragrance.

From fall to winter in arid climates floss-silk tree *(Chorisia speciosa)* is crowned with bright reddish-pink blooms.

Camphor tree *(Cinnamomum camphora)* casts dense shade; keeps houses in sunny climates cool year-round.

Chorisia speciosa
Floss-Silk Tree
Zones: 9-10. To 35-50 feet.
Deciduous tree. Flowering.

Floss-silk tree has a textured trunk with odd conical-shaped thorns and bright green bark that ages to gray. When in bloom, from fall to winter, branch tops are crowned with festive flowers in shades of pink and red. The silky floss from the seed pods can be used as pillow stuffing.

Floss-silk tree establishes quickly then grows slowly to become a wide-canopied tree. It makes a distinctive specimen for large gardens and parkways where winter temperatures do not fall below 26° to 27°F.

Plant in well-drained soil and water deeply once a month until established. Keep dry just before flowering to encourage an abundant bloom.

'Los Angeles Beautiful' bears deep red flowers; the blossoms of 'Majestic Beauty' are pink.

Cinnamomum camphora
(Camphora officinalis)
Camphor Tree
Zones: 9-10. To 20-50 feet.
Evergreen tree. Flowering.

Camphor tree, native to warm areas of China and Japan, is the source of camphor used in medicines. It is also a top-rated landscape plant. Grown without pruning, a shrubby small tree with branches to the ground develops, which is useful for screening or as a windbreak. With shearing, a formal hedge of almost any height can be maintained. When the lower limbs are removed, camphor tree is useful as a shade or street tree.

This dense, roundheaded tree grows at a slow to moderate rate, becoming wider than tall. The heavy trunk and thick, upward-spreading branches are covered with dark brown bark that looks black when wet. Small plates, like those of some oaks, develop in mature bark. In spring, pink, bronze, or reddish new leaves contrast beautifully with the leathery, yellow-green mature leaves. Leaves are pointed, oval-shaped, 2-1/2 to 5 inches long, and 1/2 inch wide. A strong camphor odor is apparent if the leaves are bruised. Old leaves drop in March and are slow to decompose. Greenish-yellow flower clusters, which emerge in May or June, are slightly fragrant but not showy. Inconspicuous, glossy black, globe-shaped, toxic fruits are 3/8 inch in diameter.

Camphor trees do not transplant well and are best planted from small containers. Planting sites should be in full sun and well drained. Camphor trees grow best in areas of high summer heat where temperatures do not fall below 20°F in winter. Trees do not grow well in heavy, extremely alkaline soil. Heavy but infrequent watering will encourage deep rooting.

Growing other plants beneath a camphor tree may be difficult because of very dense shade and the vigorous, competitive surface root system. Thinning out branches in fall may enable grass to grow beneath a camphor tree.

Cistus x purpureus
Orchid-Spot Rock Rose
Zones: 8-10. To 3-4 feet.
Evergreen shrub. Flowering.

Orchid-spot rock rose is a fast-growing sun- and drought-tolerant hybrid between *C. lananiferus* and *C. villosus.* Use as a cover for dry banks, as a low divider, or for erosion control. A fire-resistant plant, it is recommended for planting in areas of fire hazard. It also withstands cold ocean winds and salt sprays.

Orchid-spot rock rose is a compact shrub growing to 4 feet tall and 4 feet wide. Leaves are rich green above and hairy gray beneath. Resembling a small single rose, the 3-inch flowers are lavender with maroon blotches at petal bases and have numerous yellow stamens. Flowering is continuous during June and July. Needs sun and well-drained soil.

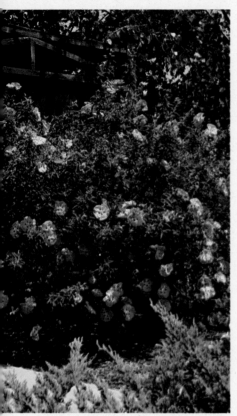

Orchid-spot rock rose *(Cistus x purpureus)* tolerates drought, ocean winds, and salt spray. Flowers prolifically in June and July.

Bright grapefruits *(Citrus* sp.) are highly visible against the shiny green foliage of this ornamental fruit tree.

Calamondins *(Citrus* sp.) are very attractive container trees suitable for growing indoors or out.

Citrus
Citrus

Zones: 9-10. To 30 feet.
Evergreen tree. Flowering.

Citrus trees provide colorful, edible fruit, fragrant white flowers, and evergreen foliage to shade or screen in warm climates. Size and habit of citrus trees varies with type. Lemons are the most vigorous and may grow 18 to 20 feet tall on standard rootstocks. 'Valencia' orange, grapefruits, pummelos, 'Dancy' tangerine, and navel oranges are also large trees. Some may grow 25 to 30 feet tall. Mandarins, blood oranges, and tangelos are usually smaller, less upright trees from 12 to 18 feet tall. Kumquats and kumquat hybrids are the smallest, reaching 8 to 12 feet. Varieties within groups can vary greatly. Trees on dwarf rootstocks will be 40 to 50 percent smaller than those grown on standard rootstocks.

Citrus grow best in full sun in fertile, well-drained soil. They require regular watering.

Top-rated citrus varieties are described in the chart on pages 92 and 93. They are recommended according to climate regions in which they are best adapted. However, even within these regions plant hardiness must also be considered. Limes are the most frost-sensitive top-rated citrus. They will usually be damaged if temperatures drop below freezing. Kumquats and kumquat hybrids are most hardy, able to withstand temperatures of 18° to 20°F. Between these extremes citrus are listed in order of increasing cold hardiness as follows: lemon, grapefruit, pummelo, tangelo, sweet orange, mandarin, and 'Meyer' lemon. However, hardiness is a difficult characteristic to predict as the length of cold and position of the tree in the landscape play important roles. Also, ripe fruit is often less

hardy than tree foliage. In colder areas, citrus grown on dwarf rootstock can be grown outdoors in tubs and brought inside before cold weather.

The chart of top-rated citrus varieties on the following pages lists ripening periods by early, (October to December); midseason, (December to January); and late, (after January). Local climate factors will influence ripening times. Many types of citrus can hold fruit on the tree after it ripens without loss of quality. In fact, the fruit of many varieties with good holding qualities actually get sweeter if they are left on the tree after initially becoming edible. Holding qualities are included in the chart of top-rated citrus.

Many mandarins and mandarin hybrids need a pollenizer for best fruit production. Another mandarin variety of similar adaptation can provide pollen.

Kumquat hybrids *(Citrus* sp.) are the most cold hardy citrus.

Valencia orange *(Citrus* sp.) is a large full tree suitable for landscape use.

Eureka lemon *(Citrus* sp.) is an attractive open-branched tree.

Citrus

Fruit/Variety Name	Florida & Gulf Coast	Low Desert	California	Season	Comments
GRAPEFRUIT					
'Duncan'	■			Midseason to late	Highly flavored but seedy variety grown in Florida and along the Gulf Coast. 'Ruby Red' is similar but with pink flesh. Fruit holds well on tree.
'Marsh Seedless'	■	■	■	Midseason to late	Widely grown for its seedless, deliciously flavored fruit. Fruit holds on tree long after ripening.
'Redblush'	■	■	■	Midseason to late	Same fruit qualities as 'Marsh Seedless' but develops pink rind and flesh color in hot climates.
KUMQUAT	■	■	■	Early	Smalls fruit with sweet rind and tart flesh are eaten whole. Trees small, compact. Small glossy leaves. Very hardy. Rank among the most ornamental citrus. 'Nagami' has oval fruits, best used in marmalades. 'Meiwa' has round fruits, best eaten fresh.
Calamondin Limequats Orangequats	■	■	■	Early	These hybrids combine the hardiness and beauty of kumquats with fruit quality of other citrus. Most are eaten whole. Group includes: orangequats, limequats, and the popular indoor-container plant, the calamondin.
LEMON					
'Eureka'		■	■	Early	Attractive ornamental tree. Bears flowers and fruit nearly year-round in cool climates. Supermarket-type lemon.
'Improved Meyer'	■	■	■	Early	Virus-free selection of the popular dooryard fruit tree. Not a true lemon, fruit slightly sweeter. Tree is small, very hardy, and ornamental. Flowers nearly year-round. Excellent in containers.
'Lisbon'		■	■	Early	Fruit similar to 'Eureka'. Attractive tree with light green foliage.
'Ponderosa'		■	■	Early	Not a true lemon. Fruits have lemonlike flavor, are large with thick rind. Good in containers or as hedge.
LIME					
Key or Mexican	■	■	■	Early	Aromatic, dark green fruits are also known as the bartender's or 'West Indian' lime. Small, thorny tree is very frost-sensitive. Requires long, hot summer. Best adapted to Florida.
'Rangpur'	■	■	■	Early	Not a true lime. Bears an abundance of orange fruits that hold on the tree nearly year-round. Can be used as a lime substitute. An attractive and hardy tree.
Tahitian or Persian	■	■	■	Early	Represented by the variety 'Bearss' in California. Larger, light green fruits turn yellow when ripe. Not as aromatic as Mexican lime but has good lime flavor and a more attractive tree habit. Frost-sensitive but does not require long hot summers. More widely adapted to Western gardens.

Fruit/Variety Name	Florida & Gulf Coast	Low Desert	California	Season	Comments
MANDARIN					
'Clementine'		■	■	Early	Develops best flavor in desert climates. Attractive weeping form. Sweet fruits hold well on tree. Needs pollinizer.
'Dancy'	■	■		Early	The traditional Christmas tangerine. Large tree. Fruit does not hold well on tree. Best flavor develops in Florida.
'Fairchild'		■	■	Midseason	Fruits small but delicious. Flavor best in hot climates. Holds fairly well on tree. Needs pollinizer.
'Kara'			■	Late	Best adapted to interior valleys of California. Sprightly flavor. Open habit. Fruit does not hold well on tree.
'Kinnow'		■	■	Midseason to late	Juicy, rich-flavored fruits hold well on tree. Attractive willowy habit. Excellent ornamental.
'Satsuma'	■		■	Early	Hardy variety especially popular in northern California. Low-growing, open tree. Mild-flavored fruits do not hold well on tree.
ORANGE, BLOOD					
'Sanguinelli'		■	■	Midseason	Most widely adapted blood orange. Attractive habit. Raspberry-flavored fruits hold well on tree. Unpredictable in Florida.
'Tarocco'			■	Midseason	Raspberry-flavored fruit. Open habit. Fruit does not hold well on tree. Grows best in moderate climates of California.
ORANGE, SOUR					
'Chinotto'	■	■	■	Early	Excellent ornamental. Compact tree with heavy bloom and abundant small fruits lasting on the tree almost year-round. Good in containers or as low hedge.
'Seville'	■	■	■	Early	The sour orange used in commercial marmalades. A fine ornamental often used as street trees or hedges in desert areas of the Southwest.
ORANGE, SWEET					
'Arizona Sweet'		■		Early to midseason	A group of oranges sold under one name in Arizona. May be 'Diller', 'Hamlin', 'Marrs', 'Pineapple', or 'Trovita'.
'Diller'	■	■		Early to midseason	Best adapted to desert regions. Sweet fruits make excellent juice. Holds well on tree.
'Hamlin'	■	■		Early	Sweet fruits excellent for juice. Fruits are small in desert climates. Holds well on tree.
'Marrs'	■	■		Early	Good juice orange. Small tree with sweet fruits. Hold well on tree.
'Pineapple'	■	■		Midseason	Rich flavored fruit with a delicate pineapple scent. Very popular in Florida. Does not hold well on tree.
'Parson Brown'	■			Early	Very popular Florida juice orange. Fruit rich and sweet but seedy. Holds fairly well on tree.
'Robertson' navel		■	■	Early	Related to 'Washington' navel. Bears at a young age, slightly earlier than parent. More heat resistant. Fruits hold well on tree and are easy to peel.
'Trovita'		■	■	Midseason	Seedling of 'Washington' navel but fruits do not have navels. More widely adapted than parent. Tends to bear well in alternate years. Fruits juicy. Holds well on tree.
'Valencia'	■	■	■	Late	The king of juice oranges. Widely adapted. Fruit can hang on tree for months after ripening.
'Washington' navel			■	Early	Easy-to-peel fruits are excellent for eating. Quality is poor in desert and coastal areas of the West. Will grow in the Northern Gulf Coast but other varieties are better suited. Fair holding quality.
PUMMELO	■	■	■	Midseason to late	Large grapefruitlike fruits lacking acidity. Best in hot climates. Excellent flavor. Flesh separates easily from inner membranes. Trees large and ornamental. 'Chandler' is a pink-fleshed variety. 'Reinking' has white flesh.
TANGELO					
'Lee'	■			Early	One of three Florida varieties developed from crosses of 'Dancy' mandarin and 'Orlando' tangelo. Others are 'Osceola' and 'Robinson'. 'Lee' has rich, sweet flavor. Others are more tart. Requires pollinizer. Holds fairly well on tree.
'Minneola'	■	■	■	Midseason	Attractive tree. Distinctively necked fruits hold well on tree. Rich, tart flavor develops best in hot climates.
'Orlando'	■	■	■	Midseason	Mildly sweet flavor develops best in hot climates. Fruit does not hold well on tree. Requires pollinizer.
TANGOR					
'Murcott'	■			Midseason to late	Very rich and sprightly flavor. Tree is frost-sensitive. Fruit holds well on tree.
'Temple'	■	■		Midseason	Rich, spicy flavor develops best in Florida. Frost-sensitive tree. Fruit does not hold well on tree.

American yellowwood *(Cladrastis lutea)* is an excellent shade tree. Fragrant white blooms are not borne every year.

Jackman clematis *(Clematis x jackmanii)* bears stunning blossoms for many weeks in summer.

Cladrastis lutea
American Yellowwood, Virgilia
Zones: 4-9. To 30-50 feet.
Deciduous tree. Flowering.

American yellowwood is one of our rarest native trees. It is seldom seen in the wild, but is widely used as an ornamental. Trees are wide-spreading with a rounded crown usually on a short trunk.

American yellowwood is very slow-growing and is a shy bloomer, especially if it isn't growing in the open where it receives full sunshine. It may not begin to blossom until 10 years or more after planting, but the wait will be worth it. The long, dangling clusters of fragrant, white, sweetpea-like flowers are reminiscent of wisteria and bloom in late spring to early summer. Trees may have a heavy bloom every second or third year.

Leaves are grass-green and divided into leathery leaflets that turn yellow in fall. Bark is smooth and gray, somewhat resembling beech tree bark. Trees have a tendency to branch close to the ground, forming narrow crotches between upright stems. These stems can split during storms.

Plant American yellowwood in full sun in a moist but well-drained soil. Withstands drought, heat, and extreme cold.

Use as a specimen tree or in group plantings in parks, cemeteries, and open spaces. It is also a good patio tree. Valued as a shade tree, when in full bloom it will become the center of attraction.

Clematis
Clematis
Deciduous and evergreen vines. Flowering.

Clematis are considered the "Queen of Climbers" because of their beautiful flowers and fine form. Both deciduous and evergreen species are available. A wide variety of colors and flower sizes has been developed, resulting in over 100 named cultivars. Flowers have many shapes, varying from large open saucers to dainty bells. Many shades of pink, purple, mauve, blue, lavender, and white blossoms are available and make long-lasting cut flowers. The feathery seed pods also are beautiful in arrangements.

Clematis forms slender, twisting stems that make well-mannered vines for use in large or small landscapes. Plant where flowers can be admired—beside a lamppost or a porch railing, or against a prominent wall or fence. If left to scramble, clematis forms a beautiful ground cover on banks. Indoor gardeners can successfully grow clematis in pots in sunny windows.

If a few simple rules for growing clematis are followed, you will be rewarded with healthy, vibrant plants. First, choose a variety suited to your climate zone with the form of flower you prefer. Then, plant the vine properly by preparing a deep planting hole that has been amended with ample organic matter for maximum aeration. Place the crown of the plant 2 to 3 inches deep and cover with soil. A layer of mulch will help keep roots cool and discourage weeds. Once the vine is set in place, young stems should be tied to supports. A light trellis is adequate to support twining stems. Stems of clematis are fragile and break easily. Tie them carefully.

Clematis grows best in neutral to slightly alkaline soils. Locate the vines where the foliage will be in full sun or light shade but where the roots will be cool and shaded. Such a location is needed to promote blooming. Clematis are shallow-rooted vines and will not disturb nearby plants.

Apply balanced fertilizer once a year during the growing season. Clematis thrive in a moist, well-drained soil, and need watering regularly.

Clematis armandii
Evergreen Clematis, Armand Clematis
Zones: 8-10.
Evergreen vine. Flowering.

Shiny, dark green foliage throughout the year makes this clematis a good background or accent plant. Leaves are 4 to 6 inches long, leathery and narrow, with 3 prominent veins. They are held in 3's on slender drooping stems. White fragrant blossoms, 1 to 2-1/2 inches wide, grace the vine in early spring. Long, plump seed pods follow in summer.

Evergreen clematis tolerates heat if given partial shade. Grow the vine in full sun in coastal locations. Prune soon after blooming because flowers are borne on old wood.

'Apple Blossom' is a light pink variety suitable for warm regions.

Clematis x jackmanii
Jackman Clematis
Zones: 5-10.
Evergreen or deciduous vine. Flowering.

Jackman clematis was the first large-flowered hybrid developed, and continues to be an all-time favorite. It is admired for its abundant, velvety, deep purple flowers that open flat and are 4 to 6 inches wide. They appear from July to October.

Flowers are produced on new wood. In early spring just before new growth begins, branches should be cut to within 2 feet, or 2 or 3 buds from the ground. Vines die to the ground in cold areas but regrow in spring.

Several varieties have come from this strain. 'Comtess de Bouchaud' is a silvery-pink-flowered form; 'Mme Edouard Andre' has purple-red blossoms; 'Perle d' Azur' is pale blue.

Clematis texensis
Scarlet Clematis
Zones: 4-10.
Deciduous vine. Flowering.

The showiest of our native clematis, scarlet clematis produces 1-inch, scarlet, bell-shaped flowers copiously from July to the first frost. Beautiful seed pods then become silvery plumes covering the plant. Glossy, thick leaves with 4 to 8 leaflets are an attractive feature. Scarlet clematis is a rapid-growing, compact vine that forms a lush mass suitable for low fences.

Protect the vine from strong winds. Flowers are produced on new wood, and plants should be pruned in early spring, before new growth begins.

These varieties offer a choice of flower color: 'Comtess de Onslow' bears scarlet-banded violet-purple blossoms; 'Duchess of Albany' bears pink flowers with brown centers; 'Etoile Rose' bears cerise-pink blooms with silver margins.

Cleyera japonica (Eurya ochnacea)
Japanese Cleyera
Zones: 8-10. To 15-18 feet.
Evergreen shrub. Flowering.

The leaves of this handsome foliage shrub are brownish red when new, turn to dark glossy green in summer, and change to reddish in winter. Small creamy-white flowers are followed by dark red berries.

Japanese cleyera is related to camellia and it shares their cultural requirements. Light shade, an acid, well-drained soil rich in organic matter, and regular water provide ideal growing conditions. Plants should also be sheltered from strong winds.

Clytostoma callistegioides
Violet Trumpet Vine
Zones: 9-10.
Evergreen vine. Flowering.

This tropical vine is a robust plant, growing to 40 feet high with a 15-to-20-foot spread. Long drooping branches hang gracefully from the vine and drape comfortably over tall fences or the eaves of buildings. When festooned with orchid-colored blossoms from midspring to fall, it creates a lovely, soft effect in the garden. Delicate 3-inch flowers are held in terminal clusters. They are an open trumpet shape, colored violet, and streaked with deep purple to their throats. Evergreen leaves are divided in pairs and are glossy, deep green with wavy leaf margins. Violet trumpet vine clings by tendrils to a wall or fence, but tendrils are not strong and the vines require securing to most surfaces.

The foliage, flowers and bright berries of Japanese cleyera *(Cleyera japonica)* adds changing color interest to the garden.

A vigorous evergreen, violet trumpet vine *(Clytostoma callistegioides)* drapes gracefully over walls or fences.

Laurel-leaf cocculus (*Cocculus lauri-folius*) makes a fine shade tree for a patio.

Lily-of-the-valley (*Convallaria majalis*)

Siberian dogwood (*Cornus alba* 'Siberica') is colorful in the winter landscape.

Adaptable to both sun and shade, this vine tolerates windy locations and is relatively pest-free. Nearly any garden soil, from clay to sandy texture, is acceptable. For best results provide good drainage and regular watering. Apply a balanced fertilizer in early spring.

Violet trumpet vine will need a strong support for its heavy mass of branches. Begin training the vine when young to direct growth.

Cocculus laurifolius
Laurel-Leaf Cocculus, Laurel-Leaf Snailseed
Zones: 8-10. To 10-25 feet.
Evergreen shrub or tree.

This foliage plant from the Himalayas has bright glossy green leaves. It can take several different forms. Without pruning, it becomes an arching multistemmed shrub, spreading as wide as tall, useful for a screen or background plant. Trained as a tree it develops an umbrella form. With pruning, it can be a low shrub or an espalier.

An adaptable plant, it will grow in sun or shade. Growth is more open with shading. It tolerates many soil types but must have a continuous supply of moisture to grow well.

Convallaria majalis
Lily-of-the-Valley
Zones: 3-9. To 8 inches.
Herbaceous ground cover.
Flowering.

In late spring, lily-of-the-valley sends up stalks of delicate, very fragrant bell-shaped white flowers. These are favorites for bridal bouquets and nosegays. The plants spread rapidly by underground runners, sending up pairs of handsome dark green leaves directly from the ground. The foliage dies back in fall, but the roots are very cold hardy and new leaves emerge in spring.

Use lily-of-the-valley to form a thick carpet in partially shaded gardens, beneath shrubs, in woodland settings, or in beds along the northern or eastern sides of the house. It can be invasive, so should be confined with edging strips if planted near lawns.

Plant clumps of underground stems, called pips, 1 to 2 feet apart; or individual pips 4 to 6 inches apart; 1 to 2 inches deep in rich soil in partial shade. Does best in eastern and northern gardens; finicky in mild-winter or arid regions. Keep soil fairly moist and fertilize regularly.

Varieties of the Excellenta strain have larger flowers. 'Rosea' has pink flowers. All parts of lily-of-the-valley are poisonous if eaten.

Convolvulus cneorum
Bush Morning-Glory
Zones: 7-10. To 4 feet.
Evergreen shrub. Flowering.

Native to southern Europe, bush morning-glory is a rapid-growing, evergreen shrub that grows as wide as it is tall. Leaves are very smooth, silvery-gray, and oval, measuring 2 inches long. Flowers are white or pinkish, with yellow throats. While the flowers are only about 1/2 inch across, they are valued for their persistence, blooming from late spring to early fall.

Plant in full sun and well-drained soil. Excellent used in a rock garden, or as a bank cover. Some pruning may be required because of rapid growth. If plant becomes too leggy, prune severely. It will soon return to a neat, compact form.

Coprosma repens (C. baueri)
Mirror Plant, Taupata
Zones: 9-10. To 10-25 feet.
Evergreen shrub.

This is a lovely foliage plant whose dark to light green leaves have extremely glossy surfaces. It is native to the warm coastal regions of New Zealand, where plant height varies from prostrate in exposed areas to a small tree when sheltered. Use as a hedge, screen, or tall ground cover. Plant in partial shade and water regularly. A good coastal plant.

Cornus
Dogwood

Zones: 2-9. To 30 feet.
Deciduous shrubs and trees.
Flowering.

There are 40 to 45 species in this genus of mostly deciduous shrubs and small trees. Most dogwoods require a fertile, slightly acid, moist but well-drained soil and grow best shaded from hot afternoon sun. While dogwoods are grown primarily for their spectacular spring floral display, many also have colorful fruit. They are also useful small patio or shade trees. Shrubby forms with colorful branches are unmatched for striking winter effects.

Above left: Flowering dogwood *(Cornus florida)* blooms for several weeks in mid-spring. Above right: Japanese dogwood *(Cornus kousa)* has excellent fall color.

Cornus

Botanical Name/ Common Name	Zones	Size	Flower Description	Plant Description	Comments
Cornus alba Tatarian Dogwood, Red-Bark Dogwood	2-8	To 10 ft tall with equal spread.	Flat clusters of yellowish flowers borne in spring. Not particularly showy.	Deciduous shrub. Fast-growing, wide-spreading with upright or creeping stems. Grown for its thicket of deep red stems.	Excellent in winter landscape.
C. a. 'Argenteo-marginata' Cream-Edge Dogwood	3-8	To 5-8 ft tall.	Same as species.	Deciduous shrub. Bright red stems. Green leaves edged with cream.	Foliage makes pretty contrast in summer. Stems showy in winter.
C. a. 'Sibirica' Sibirian Dogwood	2-8	To 8-10 ft tall.	Same as species.	Deciduous shrub. Bright red bark and porcelain-blue fruit.	Colorful stems and fruit. showy in winter.
C. florida Flowering Dogwood, Eastern Dogwood	5-9	To 20-40 ft tall.	Clusters of greenish flowers surrounded by 4 showy white bracts. Blooms in May.	Deciduous tree. Wide-spreading. Leaves turn crimson-red in early fall. Showy red berries late summer into fall.	Long blooming season. Picturesque silhouette in winter. Excellent patio or shade tree.
C. f. 'Cherokee Chief' Red Flowering Dogwood	6-9	To 20-30 ft tall.	Bracts deep rose-red.	Same as species.	Very popular.
C. f. 'Cherokee Princess' Pink Flowering Dogwood	6-9	To 20-30 ft tall.	Very light pink bracts.	Same as species.	
C. f. 'First Lady' Variegated Dogwood	6-9	To 20-30 ft tall.	Light pink bracts.	Deciduous tree. Leaves variegated creamy-white with green.	Unique leaf variegation. Attractive all summer.
C. f. 'Rubra' Pink Flowering Dogwood	6-9	To 20-30 ft tall.	Bright pink to rose bracts.	Same as species.	Combines well with white flowering dogwoods.
C. kousa Japanese Dogwood, Kousa Dogwood	6-9	To 10-20 ft tall.	White, pointed flower bracts, open later than *C. florida*.	Deciduous shrub or tree. Vase-shaped with distinctive upright branching. Edible, bright red bumpy fruits.	Blooms later than other dogwoods. Extends spring blooming season.
C. k. chinensis Chinese Kousa Dogwood	6-9	To 10-12 ft tall.	Long-lasting and profuse huge white bracts up to 5 to 6 in. across.	Same as species but with larger leaves.	Withstands heat better than species.
C. k. 'Summer Stars'	6-9	To 10-20 ft tall.	Large, long-lasting white bracts surround small pink flowers.	Similar to species.	Tolerates summer heat.
C. mas Cornelian Cherry	4-8	To 25 ft tall or more.	Clusters of small flowers cover twigs with yellow mist in early spring.	Deciduous shrub or tree. Grows rapidly. Open, spreading habit. Bright red edible fruit.	Valued because one of the first plants to bloom in spring.
C. sericea (C. stolonifera) Red-Osier Dogwood	2-9	To 10 ft tall.	Small white flowers.	Deciduous shrub. Spreads by underground runners. Brilliant red branches. Bright red fall foliage.	Beautiful in winter landscape. Grows in moist or dry soils. Will stabilize banks.
C. s. 'Flaviramea' Yellow-Twig Dogwood	2-9	To 10 ft tall.	Small white flowers.	Same as species but with vivid yellow bark.	Striking in winter landscape.

Rapid-growing pampas grass (*Cortaderia selloana*) withstands heat and drought, makes a durable windbreak.

Some varieties of smoke tree (*Cotinus coggygria*) have purple foliage in spring and summer; all have bright foliage in autumn.

The misty plumes of smoke tree (*Cotinus coggygria*) bloom in midsummer, accounting for its common name.

Cortaderia selloana (C. argentea)
Pampas Grass

Zones: 5-10. To 10-20 feet.
Evergreen shrub. Flowering.

This giant ornamental grass, native to South America, adds interesting form and texture to a shrub border or foundation planting. Pampas grass is a very rapid grower, reaching a height of 8 feet or more in one season. In warm climates it can reach a height of 20 feet every year. In Zone 8-10, foliage is evergreen. In colder areas, dies to the ground each fall.

Each long, strap-shaped, dark to medium green leaf is about 1/2 inch wide, tapering to a point. They can reach a length of 5 to 7 feet. Leaves rise from the plant base and then arch to the ground, giving the plant a fountainlike appearance. They have very sharp edges. The large, silvery-white flower plumes can be up to 2 feet long. They are very showy and dramatic, standing gracefully above the foliage in summer and early fall. The flower plumes of 'Rosea' are rosy-pink. Plumes are handsome when used in arrangements.

Plant pampas grass in full sun in any average soil in areas where there is ample room. Tolerates heat, drought and is one of the toughest windbreaks. In cold regions dead foliage turns straw-colored and is attractive most of the winter. Cut it off at about 18 inches above ground level in early spring. If a large area is covered with pampas grass and pruning is not feasible, plants can be burned to the ground periodically. Once established, these aggressive plants are very difficult to eradicate.

Pampas grass is easily propagated by divisions. Striking plumes are only produced on female plants so divisions should be taken only from those plants.

Cotinus coggygria
Smoke Tree

Zones: 5-8. To 20-25 feet.
Deciduous tree or shrub.
Flowering.

This interesting plant gets its common name because it appears smoke-covered in midsummer when in bloom. Plumelike flower clusters develop fuzzy purple hairs as they dry. Some varieties have white "smoke". Leaves are distinctly oval and bluish green, often turning red, yellow, or purple before they drop in fall. Varieties such as 'Velvet Smoke', 'Velvet Cloak', and 'Royal Purple' have purple foliage during the entire growing season.

Smoke tree grows best in full sun and well-drained soil. It withstands poor, rocky soils, and drought. Plant among other shrubs or trees as an accent or in masses. Prune lightly to remove dead wood and to keep the plant shapely.

Cotoneaster

Cotoneaster

Zones: 5-10. To 10 feet.
Evergreen and deciduous shrubs.
Flowering.

Cotoneasters are popular and adaptable shrubs, ranging in size from creeping ground covers to tall arching shrubs. There are both evergreen and deciduous species. All are dense, twiggy plants covered with small oval leaves. Dainty white to pinkish flowers line the branches in spring and are attractive but not showy. Long-lasting red berries in fall and winter are the outstanding feature. Berry production will be heavier in dry soil than in a fertile, well-watered garden. Growth is best in full sun although some will grow in partial shade. Use for ground covers and erosion control and as foreground plants in shrub borders or foundation plantings.

Fireblight, caused by a bacteria, can be a problem with cotoneaster.

Cranberry cotoneaster *(Cotoneaster apiculatus)* is covered with berries in fall and winter.

Rock cotoneaster *(Cotoneaster horizontalis)* is effective spreading over a retaining wall.

Cotoneaster

Botanical Name/Common Name	Zones	Size	Plant Description	Comments
Cotoneaster adpressus praecox Early Cotoneaster	5-10	To 2 ft tall. Spreads to 6 ft.	Deciduous shrub. Leaves small, round, shiny dark green with wavy edges, turn brilliant red in fall. Small pink flowers in spring are followed by heavy crop of red berries.	Use for ground cover, on banks, in rock gardens. Exceptionally resistant to fireblight.
C. apiculatus Cranberry Cotoneaster	5-10	To 4 ft tall. Spreads wider than tall.	Deciduous shrub. Leaves small, shiny green above, gray beneath. Flowers in spring are pinkish white, followed by cranberry-sized red berries persisting into winter.	Use as hedge or background plant.
C. a. 'Nanus' Dwarf Cranberry Cotoneaster	5-10	To 1-1/2 to 2 ft tall.	Dwarf shrub similar to species but evergreen in mild climates.	Well-suited for rock gardens, mound plantings, low hedges, containers.
C. buxifolius (C. glaucophyllus) Gray-Leafed Cotoneaster	7-10	To 1-2 ft tall. Spreads 4-6 ft.	Semievergreen shrub. Branches arching. Leaves oval, gray-green above, white or tan fuzz beneath. Flowers in dense clusters. Berries bright red along branches.	Frequently mislabeled in nurseries. Good for rock gardens, bank covers. Excellent for dry areas.
C. congestus 'Likiang'	6-10	To 3 ft tall.	Evergreen shrub. Compact, low-spreading habit with arching branches. Leaves small, dense, dark green. White flowers in early spring. Small red berries in fall.	Grows well in arid climates. Good for rock gardens, containers.
C. dammeri Bearberry Cotoneaster	5-10	To 6-12 in. tall. Spreads to 10 ft.	Evergreen shrub. Prostrate growth habit. Leaves 1 in., oval, bright green above, pale beneath. Flowers white, fairly showy. Brilliant red berries in fall.	Forms dense mat; ground cover. Excellent cascading effect over a wall and among rocks. Will grow in partial shade.
C. d. 'Coral Beauty' Coral Beauty Cotoneaster	5-10	To 6-12 in. tall. Spreads to 10 ft.	Evergreen shrub. Similar to species. Leaves small, rich green. Profusion of brilliant coral-colored berries in fall.	Good choice for rock gardens, containers. Trailing growth habit.
C. d. 'Lowfast'	5-10	To 6-12 in. tall. Spreads to 10 ft.	Evergreen shrub. Similar to species. Leaves glossy. White flowers 1/2 in. across. Showy berries are brilliant red.	Grows fast. Excellent ground cover. Good for containers.

Bearberry cotoneaster *(Cotoneaster dammeri)* hugs the ground, making a good lawn replacement.

Berries of cotoneasters *(Cotoneaster* sp.) persist through winter.

Spreading cotoneaster *(Cotoneaster divaricatus)* makes an excellent hedge.

Cotoneaster (continued)

Botanical Name/Common Name	Zones	Size	Plant Description	Comments
C. d. 'Moon Creeper'	5-10	To 6-12 in. tall. Spreads to 10 ft.	Evergreen shrub. Similar to species but lower-growing than most. Forms an even-topped cover.	Less tendency to mound-up where original clumps were planted.
C. d. 'Royal Beauty'	5-10	To 6-12 in. tall. Spreads to 10 ft.	Evergreen shrub. Similar to species. Deep coral-red berries formed early; contrast well with rich, glossy foliage.	Excellent low hedge, vigorous ground cover, or plant to cascade over wall.
C. divaricatus **Spreading Cotoneaster**	5-10	To 6 ft tall. Spreads 4-8 ft.	Deciduous shrub. Branches spreading. Shiny green leaves turn showy orange in fall. Bright pink flowers. Bright red berries hold into winter after leaf-drop.	Good choice for hedge or screen.
C. franchetii **Franchet Cotoneaster**	5-9	To 10 ft or more tall with equal spread.	Evergreen shrub. Fountainlike, arching growth habit. Leaves thick, oval, glossy above, downy beneath. Flowers small, pink. Berries in clusters, orange-red.	Grows to 5 ft tall in poor soil with little summer water. Shearing not recommended.
C. horizontalis **Rock Cotoneaster**	5-10	To 3 ft tall. Spreads to 15 ft.	Deciduous shrub. Small, round, dark leaves, glossy green above, pale beneath, turn reddish orange in fall before dropping. Pink flowers in spring. Berries shiny, bright red.	Berries so plentiful, deciduous habit goes unnoticed in winter. Use as low traffic barrier, bank cover, in containers.
C. lacteus (C. parneyi) **Parney Cotoneaster, Red Clusterberry**	7-10	To 8 ft tall. Spreads to 6 ft.	Evergreen shrub. Graceful, arching branches. Leaves large, leathery, deep green. Showy white flowers in spring. Berries in clusters, bright red, hold well into winter.	Use for espalier, screen, formal hedge, in containers. Grows well in arid climates.
C. salicifolius **Willow-Leaf Cotoneaster**	6-10	To 15 ft tall, with equal spread.	Semievergreen to evergreen shrub or tree. Branches arching. Leaves narrow, long, dark green above, grayish beneath. White flowers in clusters followed by bright red berries.	Use as multistemmed small tree, large screen or background. Good in shade.
C. s. 'Herbstfeuer' (C. s. 'Autumn Fire')	6-10	To 6 in. tall. Spreads to 8 ft.	Evergreen shrub. Similar to species.	Excellent ground cover for sun or shade.
C. s. 'Repens' (C. s. 'Repandens')	6-10	To 2-3 ft. Spreads to 8 ft.	Semievergreen shrub. Similar to species.	Very versatile; use as ground cover, on banks, or in hanging basket.

Crataegus
Hawthorn
Zones: 3-9. To 30-35 feet.
Deciduous trees. Flowering.

A large genus of mostly deciduous plants, *Crataegus* contains more named species than any other native genus—more than 1,100 have been described. With few exceptions they are dense and twiggy, armed with thorns up to 3 inches long. Tree forms vary from 15 to 35 feet tall. They are used for their ornamental white, pink, or red blooms in spring and for the red to orange fruit that ripens in late summer or early fall. The berries often remain on the trees all winter. Leaves are glossy green on most species and many have brilliant red to orange fall coloration. During winter their wide-spreading branches make a picturesque silhouette.

Hawthorns should not be used where thorns are objectionable or dangerous to passersby. Because pruning is tolerated these trees can be developed into trespass-proof hedges. They also make beautiful specimen trees on lawns, around buildings, and as screens.

Thornless, or essentially thornless, cultivars such as Ohio pioneer dotted hawthorn *(C. punctata* 'Ohio Pioneer') and thornless cockspur hawthorn *(C. crus-galli inermis)* have been selected. Care should be exercised to plant types that are resistant to fireblight, a disease that can be devastating in some areas of the country.

Hawthorns are tough plants able to withstand the adverse growing conditions of a city. They are difficult to transplant but once established they are long-lived. Although best growth is made in rich loamy soils, they can grow almost equally well on slightly acid or slightly alkaline soils and can survive on poor soils. Sunny locations are a must for maximum development of flowers and fruit. To avoid excessive growth, hawthorns should be grown on sites that are on the dry side.

English hawthorn *(Crataegus laevigata)* is highly ornamental, featuring late spring blossoms, red fall foliage, and persistent red berries. Blossoms shown below.

Masses of flowers adorn English hawthorn (*Crataegus laevigata*).

Washington thorn (*Crataegus phaenopyrum*) has clusters of showy berries and long, fierce thorns.

Crataegus

Botanical Name/Common Name	Zones	Size	Plant Description	Comments
Crataegus crus-galli **Cockspur, Cockspur Thorn**	5-9	To 18-25 ft tall. Wide-spreading.	Deciduous tree. White flowers. Long-lasting red fruit. Glossy green leaves orange and red in fall. Many stiff 3-inch thorns.	Tough. Able to withstand climate extremes and heavy pruning C. c. inermis is a nearly thornless cultivar.
C. laevigata (Crataegus oxycantha) **English Hawthorn, White Thorn, Quick-Set Thorn**	5-8	To 18-25 ft tall. Nearly as wide.	Deciduous tree. Species quite variable with white, pink, or red flowers. Unreliable fruit and fall color. Very thorny.	Susceptible to disease in hot, humid eastern climates. Cultivars more commonly grown.
C. l. 'Crimson Cloud'	5-8	To 18-25 ft tall. Nearly as wide.	Deciduous tree. Crimson flowers with white centers followed by bright red fruits. Very thorny.	The best and most disease-resistant for eastern climates.
C. l. 'Paul's Scarlet'	5-8	To 18-25 ft tall. Nearly as wide.	Deciduous tree. Rosy-red double flowers. Does not set fruit. Thorny.	Dense crown.
C. l. 'Superba Princeton'	5-8	To 14-16 ft tall.	Deciduous tree. Exceptionally large, single, bright red flowers with star-shaped white centers. Glossy red fruit. Thorny.	Resistant to leaf-spot disease. Good for eastern climates.
C. x lavallei **Lavalle Hawthorn**	5-8	To 20 ft tall. Spreads 12-15 ft.	Deciduous tree. White flowers. Long-lasting orange-red berries. Glossy green leaves turn bronzy-red in fall. Sparse 2-inch thorns.	Attractive form. More open-branching and erect than other hawthorns.
C. monogyna 'Stricta'	4-8	To 35 ft tall. Forms narrow column 8-10 ft wide.	Deciduous tree. White flowers. Clusters of small red berries are inconspicuous. Few 1-inch thorns.	Makes a good tall hedge or screen.
C. x mordenensis 'Toba'	3-8	To 12-15 ft tall.	Deciduous tree. Double blossoms open white, fade to rose-pink. Few berries. Dark green foliage. Interesting twisted trunk.	One of the finest hawthorns. Exceptionally hardy and disease-resistant.
C. phaenopyrum **Washington Thorn**	5-9	To 30 ft tall.	Deciduous tree. Columnar when young, eventually roundheaded. Abundant white flowers. Heavy set of red fruit. Glossy green leaves turn orange to scarlet in fall. Long fierce thorns.	One of the best hawthorns in form, flower, fruit, and fall color. Resists fireblight.
C. viridis 'Winter King'	4-8	To 30-35 ft tall.	Deciduous tree. Rounded top at maturity. Waxy white flowers. Long-lasting red fruit. Glossy green leaves and green stems. Fair yellow fall color. Many 1-1/2-inch thorns.	Abundant bright red fruit and green branches display dramatically in winter.

x Cupressocyparis leylandii
Leyland Cypress
Zones: 5-10. To 90-100 feet.
Evergreen tree.

This is a naturally occuring, inter-generic hybrid between Monterey cypress (*Cupressus macrocarpa*) and Alaska false cypress (*Chamaecyparis nootkatensis*).

Leyland cypress has a broad, co-lumnar shape with compact, up-right branches. The ultimate size is somewhat variable. Some selections can grow to be 90 to 100 feet tall. Others can reach 30 feet in ten years.

Leyland cypress is very adaptable and will grow on most soils with adequate drainage. Fast-growing, it will provide a tall screen in short order. Withstands heavy pruning, and can be developed into a hedge very rapidly. Set trees 3 to 5 feet apart for hedge plantings. Group plantings can also be effective.

Many cultivars have been selected and named. 'Leighton Green' is a narrow columnar form, strongly resembling its parent Alaska false cypress. Foliage is yellow-green. 'Castlewellan' is similar to Leyland cypress, but the color of the new foliage is a bright yellow. 'Silverdust' Leyland cypress is a cultivar with creamy-white variegated foliage. Tree growth is compact. Does not require as much clipping to form a hedge or screen as some of the other forms. 'Green Spire' develops into a very dense, narrow, columnar tree that frequently becomes multi-stemmed. Foliage is bright green.

Cupressus
Cypress
Evergreen shrubs and trees.

There are about 22 species of tall, aromatic evergreen trees and a few shrubs, most of which are subtropical, in this genus. Cypress are native from western United States to Mexico, and the Mediterranean region to China.

Cupressus arizonica
Arizona Cypress
Zones: 6-10. To 40-50 feet.
Evergreen tree.

A native species originally growing in Arizona, New Mexico and northern Mexico, Arizona cypress is now grown from Virginia to Arkansas, and in the South and West. Young trees have a narrow, pyramidal crown. Foliage is light green. Bark on the trunk and larger branches is reddish brown, separating into long strips. Branches become horizontal as the tree reaches maturity.

Arizona cypress is fast-growing and ideal for windbreaks and tall screens. It is useful as a specimen tree.

A number of varieties and cultivars exist but many are not generally available. The cultivar 'Gareei' has silvery blue-green foliage. 'Watersii' has a narrow compact crown. 'Pyramidalis' is compact and pyramidal.

Cupressus macrocarpa
Monterey Cypress
Zones: 7-10. To 40-60 feet.
Evergreen tree.

Conical when young, Monterey cypress becomes broad-topped, losing lower branches with age. This picturesque tree was almost extinct when discovered growing wild over 2 square miles on Monterey Peninsula, California, and the island of Guadalupe.

Withstands salt-laden air. Best cypress for seaside plantings, where it develops a unique, windswept form. Use as a windbreak or clipped hedge. The cultivar 'Donard Gold' is a tight-branching form with golden branch tips. It should also be planted near the coast. Other cultivars with yellow leaves and shoots are 'Golden Pillar' and 'Lutea'.

Monterey cypress is subject to a destructive canker disease, and is being replaced by Leyland cypress, which is much hardier, in some landscape situations.

Fast-growing and adaptable, Leyland cypress *(x Cupressocyparis leylandii)* forms a dense hedge or tall screen.

Monterey cypress *(Cupressus macrocarpa)* has fine-textured aromatic foliage and bears attractive clusters of cones (shown below). Prefers coastal climates.

Italian cypress *(Cupressus sempervirens)* provides a dramatic formal accent with its towering slender form.

An evergreen shrub of many virtues, broom *(Cytisus racemosus)* tolerates drought and infertile soils.

Cupressus sempervirens
Italian Cypress
Zones: 7-10. To 80-90 feet.
Evergreen tree.

Native to southern Europe and western Asia, Italian cypress is commonly grown in California, the Southeast, and the Gulf States. Trees grown from seed can be quite variable in growth habit. Two general forms grown are an upright type with tight, upward-reaching branches, and one with horizontal, wide-spreading branches and a flat-topped shape when mature. Foliage is dark green, becoming so dark with maturity it appears black. Cones are among the largest of the true cypress, often growing to 1 to 1-1/2 inches in diameter.

Italian cypress grows best on dry, deep, sandy loams in sheltered sites. Upright forms can be used in formal gardens and along driveways. Trees will become quite large and are not adapted to small gardens. Pruning or shearing may be required to keep the trees symmetrical and dense.

A number of cultivars have been selected over the years. 'Glauca' is columnar with dense, bluish-green foliage. 'Stricta', a narrow, upright compact tree, is the form used in Italian gardens. 'Horizontalis' has horizontal branches, forming a wide head that becomes flat-topped with age.

Cytisus
Broom
Deciduous and evergreen shrubs.
Flowering.

Broom is a common name that actually refers to many plants in three different genera: *Cytisus*, *Genista*, and *Spartium*. They are often confused and mislabeled, because all have pea-shaped flowers that are often sweetly fragrant. The erect branches of broom were cut and used to make brooms, centuries ago, accounting for their common name. Brooms are vigorous plants with a tendency to spread into areas where they are not wanted.

Some *Cytisus* species are evergreen, others are deciduous. However, the distinction makes little difference, since most have bright green stems that have an evergreen appearance whether they have leaves on them or not.

Brooms are easy to grow in well-drained soils, tolerating hot sun, wind, and seashore conditions. Nitrogen-fixing bacteria on the roots make broom adaptable to infertile soils. For best appearance, water occasionally. Too moist or rich soils will cause rank growth and reduced flowering. Lightly prune after flowering to maintain form and remove seed pods.

Cytisus x praecox
Warminster Broom
Zones: 6-9. To 3-5 feet.
Deciduous shrub. Flowering.

A real showstopper in early spring when covered with light yellow blossoms. Dense green stems give an evergreen effect in winter. Useful as an unpruned hedge or screen.

Cytisus racemosus (Genista racemosa)
Broom
Zones: 7-10. To 6-8 feet.
Evergreen shrub. Flowering.

This broom is drought-tolerant, making it an excellent shrub for a rocky slope, a dry shrub border, or a sunny rock garden. Many-branched, upright-growing, spreads nearly as wide as tall. Green stems hold silky, evergreen leaflets. In late spring, fragrant, pealike flowers appear in loose terminal sprays, providing a bright, sunny show.

Cytisus scoparius
Scotch Broom
Zones: 6-9. To 10 feet.
Evergreen shrub. Flowering.

This broom is familar in the Pacific Northwest where it has naturalized with tenacious vigor. Its golden-yellow flowers grace slopes, hillsides, and open lots in spring and early summer.

A number of varieties that behave better than the species have been developed. 'Andreanus' has blossoms colored burnt-red and yellow.

'Burkwoodii' has reddish-rose flowers. 'California' has rose-colored flowers touched with white. 'San Francisco' and 'Stanford' have red blooms. 'Lord Lambourne' has crimson-and-cream flowers. These varieties grow slightly lower, and are more compact than the species. Use for screens, shrub borders, or on slopes.

Daphne
Daphne

Evergreen shrubs.
Flowering.

This genus contains about 50 species of flowering deciduous and evergreen shrubs native to Europe and Asia. Flowers are usually fragrant and may be white, purple, lilac, or sometimes yellowish-green or yellow.

Garland Flower, Garland Daphne
Daphne cneorum

Zones: 5-9. To 6 inches.
Evergreen shrub. Flowering.

Garland flower is a popular low-growing plant in spite of its relatively exacting growth requirements. Moist soil and good drainage are essential. If you live where fog or a cloud cover is common, plant in full sun. Elsewhere plant in partial shade.

Garland flower will attain a height of 6 inches, occasionally slightly more, and will spread between 2 to 3 feet. Dark green leaves are 1 inch long. Fragrant rose-pink flowers are borne in clusters in spring. It is an excellent container plant.

Winter Daphne
Daphne odora

Zones: 8-10. To 4-6 feet.
Evergreen shrub. Flowering.

Of all the daphnes, and there are about 50 species, this is the most unforgettable. Its alluring, sweet scent fills the air in early spring. Deep rose to light pink blossoms are borne at the ends of branches in small rounded clusters. A handsome shrub with glossy, 3-inch-long leaves and a compact, upright habit, growing slowly to 4 to 6 feet. It makes a desirable specimen in partly shaded gardens, and is a good low plant for a border, foundation, or accent.

Needs an aerated, well-drained soil to prevent root-rot. Prepare planting hole with ample soil amendments for increased aeration. Plant high to avoid standing water around the crown. Avoid fertilizers that will over-acidify soil, but adjust alkaline soils to a more neutral pH. Water sparingly during summer months. Keep roots barely damp and covered with mulch, for a cool soil. Needs pruning very infrequently and has few pest problems, making this lovely plant easy to care for. Mature plants are unpredictable and may die for no apparent reason.

'Marginata', a somewhat hardier form, has yellow-edged leaves. 'Rubra' has deep red flowers, and 'Alba' bears pure white blossoms.

Slender Deutzia
Deutzia gracilis

Zones: 5-8. To 3-6 feet.
Deciduous shrub. Flowering.

Slender deutzia is a time-tested garden favorite grown for its abundant showy blossoms that cover its branches in spring. Flowers are usually white, but one hybrid offers shades of pink and rose. Not highly ornamental when out of bloom, this pest-free shrub should be planted where it will blend into a flowering shrub border.

Prune annually after flowering. Thin oldest branches and remove winter die-back in early spring.

Deutzia is an adaptable shrub and is easy to grow in almost any garden soil. Plant in full sun or partial shade and provide average water.

Two hybrids of slender deutzia are also useful shrubs. *Deutzia x lemoinei* has abundant white blossoms on erect branches 5 to 7 feet tall. *Deutzia x rosea* is compact, with 3- to 4-foot-long branches. Flowers are available in several shades of pink.

Garland flower *(Daphne cneorum)*, a low-growing evergreen shrub, is capped with fragrant flowers in spring.

Winter daphne *(Daphne odora)* adds evergreen beauty to shady gardens.

Slender deutzia *(Deutzia gracilis)* is easy to grow and pest-free. Blossom-covered branches are dazzling in spring.

Blood-red trumpet vine *(Distictis buccinatoria)* can cover posts and fences with year-round greenery.

The maroon-hued foliage of purple hopseed bush *(Dodonaea viscosa 'Purpurea')* adds visual landscape interest.

Distictis
Trumpet Vine
Evergreen vines. Flowering.

Glorious, trumpet-shaped flowers for several months are ample reward for anyone who grows either of these two top-rated vines.

Robust growers, climbing 20 to 30 feet by clinging tendrils, trumpet vines make excellent screens, arbors, or flowering wall covers. Grow in full sun near the coast or in a protected, shady location inland. Both vines are easy to grow and relatively pest-free. They thrive in most soils with good drainage if watered regularly. The evergreen foliage can be damaged by temperatures below 24°F. Give vines protection in colder, inland areas.

Distictis buccinatoria
Blood-Red Trumpet Vine ·
Zones: 9-10.
Evergreen vine. Flowering.

This trumpet vine is spectacular when its long, yellow-throated, crimson flowers are in bloom. Blossoms, which are held out from the foliage, fade to rose-red before dropping, and will color the garden from May to early fall. Where the weather remains warm they often bloom almost continuously. Heavy masses of lustrous green leaves make an attractive display year-round. Oval 2-inch leaves are held on twining branches ending with a 3-parted clinging tendril. When grown on a fence or arbor, provide strong support for the vigorous branches. Prune heavily after blossoms drop to control the plant's shape and size. Left unpruned, plants grow billowy and top-heavy.

Of the two top-rated trumpet vines, this species is the best choice for inland areas. It tolerates more intense heat and colder temperatures.

Distictis laxiflora
Vanilla Trumpet Vine
Zones: 9-10.
Evergreen vine. Flowering.

Several months of the year, this enchanting vine fills the air with the delicious fragrance of vanilla. The 3-inch-long trumpet flowers open purple, fading to orchid and white before dropping. They are held in terminal clusters on slender stems during warm months. In some areas they bloom for up to 8 months. Dark green leaves are oblong in shape and the last tendril of the growing shoot is unbranched, distinguishing it from the 3-parted tendril of blood-red trumpet vine.

Vanilla trumpet vine is a superb grower but never becomes rampant. Requires only light pruning to maintain its neat appearance. Use as a light screen for fences, against a wall, or on an arbor or pergola. Makes a wonderful patio plant, where its prolonged bloom and fragrant flowers can be enjoyed up close.

Dodonaea viscosa
Hopbush,
Hopseed Bush
Zones: 8-10. To 10-15 feet.
Evergreen shrub. Flowering.

This large fast-growing, multi-stemmed shrub has flaking bark and spreads almost as wide as tall. Leaves are willowlike. The flowers are not showy but female plants have attractive creamy or pinkish winged fruit in late summer. It is planted for hedges, informal screens, espaliers, or as a small tree. *D. viscosa* 'Purpurea', purple hopseed bush, is a purple-leaved form that is best in full sun and cool climates.

Elaeagnus
Elaeagnus
Deciduous and evergreen shrubs or trees.

Elaeagnus are rapid-growing deciduous and evergreen shrubs or small trees. They become very dense and make valuable screen or hedge plants. They are very tolerant of salt sprays, heat, winds, and drought. Most species have attractive foliage. The leaves of deciduous varieties are silver-gray while the leaves of evergreen forms are often covered with silver to brown reflective dots that sparkle in the sunlight. Yellow to white flowers are usually fragrant, but are small and inconspicuous. The fruit that follows is edible on some plants and can be dark red to yellow.

Elaeagnus angustifolia
Russian Olive, Silver Berry, Oleaster

Zones: 2-10. To 20-25 feet.
Deciduous tree. Flowering.

Russian olive is a fast-growing plant that can be trained as either a large shrub or a small tree. Both fruits and flowers are small and inconspicuous. Grayish-green to silver, 2- to 3-inch-long leaves add unique color to the landscape. This unusual foliage is Russian olive's main attraction. Interesting dark brown shredding bark covers the crooked, irregular trunk and branches, adding visual interest during the winter and early spring.

Russian olive is a rugged plant that can withstand adverse conditions such as road salt spray, heat, drought, and poor soil. It will not perform well in areas with mild winters and cool, moist summers. Excellent for use in land reclamation or erosion control, Russian olive also makes a good screen or hedge and can be trained as a colorful, rugged espalier.

Elaeagnus pungens
Silverberry

Zones: 7-10. To 6-15 feet.
Evergreen shrub. Flowering.

The most striking feature of silverberry is its silver-dotted leaves that reflect sunlight, creating a flashy effect in the landscape. It is a very fast-growing and adaptable shrub that can be clipped for a hedge or espalier and makes an effective barrier or screen. In a container silverberry withstands reflected heat and wind.

Oval leaves, 2 to 4 inches long, are grayish green above and silver below with silvery-brown dots on both surfaces. Fragrant flowers in fall are not showy but the red berries that follow, which are covered with silver scales, are eye-catching. Cultivars with variegated leaves provide even greater color interest.

'Maculata' has a yellow blotch in the center of the leaf. 'Tricolor' has yellow and pinkish-white leaf margins. 'Variegata' has yellowish-white margins.

Silverberries grow in soil that can be either slightly acid or alkaline. They tolerate both seashore and desert conditions. Established plants will tolerate drought.

Enkianthus campanulatus
Enkianthus

Zones: 5-9. To 15-20 feet.
Deciduous shrub. Flowering.

Enkianthus bears clusters of small bell-shaped flowers in midspring that are yellow marked with red. The plant has an interesting layered branching pattern with leaves arranged in whorls. The foliage turns vivid red in fall.

Enkianthus grows best in light shade and moist, well-drained acid soil rich in organic matter. Makes a fine specimen shrub for entryway or patio use.

Erica
Heath

Evergreen shrubs or trees.
Flowering.

The heaths are a large genus of plants closely related to Scotch heather, Calluna vulgaris. They share a need for acid soils, have small scalelike or needlelike leaves, and tiny tubular, bell-shaped flowers borne in late winter to early spring. Heaths are versatile landscape plants with a wide range of growth habits. Some are low-growing ground covers, others are tall and erect and make excellent hedges and screens.

Silver-foliaged russian olive (Elaeagnus angustifolia) makes a beautiful accent tree.

Silverberry (Elaeagnus pungens) has silver-dotted leaves that reflect light.

Enkianthus (Enkianthus campanulatus), the tall plant in the background, has vivid red fall color.

Low-growing and widely adapted, spring heath *(Erica carnea)* makes a fine-textured colorful ground cover.

Loquat *(Eriobotrya japonica)* is a handsome evergreen shade tree. Its colorful fruits (shown below) are very tasty.

Erica carnea
Spring Heath
Zones: 4-8. To 6-8 inches.
Evergreen shrub. Flowering.

This low, spreading plant has up-reaching branches. Leaves are green and needlelike. Rose-colored flowers appear in late winter or early spring depending on climate. Grows best in full sun in cool climates, light shade in hot areas. Trim lightly to keep the plant neat. Makes a colorful ground cover. There are many varieties. 'Ruby Glow' remains small, spreading, and compact, growing to 8 inches; foliage is dark green, flowers deep red. 'Springwood' is also low growing, with white flowers, and light green leaves; an excellent, fast-growing variety. 'Winter Beauty' has pink flowers on a very low plant.

Erica x darleyensis
Darley Heath
Zones: 4-8. To 1-2 feet.
Evergreen shrub. Flowering.

Winter flowers from November to April make this a most rewarding landscape plant. A hybrid between *E. mediterranea* and *E. carnea*, it is one of the most satisfactory heaths for use as a ground cover. It is also used as a low shrub for foreground plantings, a specimen in rock gardens, or as an edging or dwarf hedge.

Plants in the open will grow 1 foot tall and 3 feet wide. Planted closely as a ground cover, they can reach up to 2 feet tall. Small pink or white urn-shaped flowers in 2-inch-long spikes add a cheery note to the drab winter landscape. The Darley heath is one of the rare heaths and heathers that tolerate alkaline soil.

Eriobotrya japonica
Loquat
Zones: 8-10. To 15-30 feet.
Evergreen tree. Flowering.

The loquat is a striking plant with bold-textured leaves and the bonus of colorful, edible fruit. A native of China and south central Japan, fruit doesn't set in frosty areas but it is still worth growing for the striking foliage.

Loquat can be grown in sunny or shaded locations. It withstands pruning and can be grown as a trimmed hedge or even espaliered on a fence or trellis. Pruning also thins out the crown so the shade cast is less dense.

In sunny locations a dense, rounded crown, as wide as high, develops. In the shade the plant will be upright and slender. New branches are woolly. Sharply toothed, thick leaves are 6 to 12 inches long and 2 to 4 inches wide. Prominent veins show in the dark green upper surface and the lower surface is covered with a rust-colored wool. Dull white, 1/2-inch-wide flowers are borne in 3- to 6-inch woolly clusters in autumn. They have a pleasant vanillalike fragrance. Round- to pear-shaped fruit, 1 to 2 inches long, ripen in clusters from March to June in areas without much winter frost.

Most trees sold in nurseries are seedlings with fruit, of variable quality. Many have large seeds and a bland flavor. For quality fruit, one of the named cultivars should be planted. These include 'Mac-Beth', with extra-large golden fruit, creamy flesh, and good flavor; 'Gold Nugget', with orange skin and flesh, grows well near the seashore; and 'Champagne', with yellow skin and white flesh, does well in warmer areas.

Thinning fruit to avoid limbs breaking and to increase fruit size may be necessary if a heavy crop sets. Prune to let more light into the center of the tree to increase fruit set.

Loquats should be planted in well-drained soil. They tolerate some drought when established but grow better with irrigation. It is possible to grow a plant in a container for several years.

Fireblight is occasionally a problem with loquats. Red spider and mealybugs are the principal insect problems.

Erythrina
Coral Tree

Deciduous shrubs or trees.
Flowering.

These thorny deciduous trees and shrubs (some almost evergreen) are grown for their brilliant flowers, which often develop on bare branches. Leaves are divided into 3 leaflets. The strong trunk and branch structure give a sculptured appearance with or without leaves. They do best in full sun in well-drained soils but need watering in the dry season.

Erythrina caffra
Kaffirboom Coral Tree

Zones: 9-10. To 25-40 feet.
Deciduous tree. Flowering.

This South African native is renowned for its spectacular flowers that appear on bare branches during the winter. A fast-growing tree with stout, irregular branches, it grows wider than tall. All the young growth is thorny (even the stems of the dark green leaves have thorns), but old limbs usually are not. Leaves drop in January. New leaves develop in March, forming a dense leafy canopy.

Large clusters of 2-inch, deep orange to bright vermillion, tubular flowers bloom during February. The red seeds contained in the 4-inch, semiwoody seed pods that follow flowering are poisonous to animals and people. This species is excellent for planting in seaside locations, where few flowering trees perform well.

Erythrina coralloides
Naked Coral Tree

Zones: 9-10. To 25-30 feet.
Deciduous tree. Flowering.

Grown for its striking branch structure and fiery red flowers. Blossoms cluster like pinecones at the tips of the bare, twisted stems from March until May. A good shade tree, it grows about as wide as it is tall, but can be controlled by pruning.

Erythrina crista-galli
Cockspur Coral Tree

Zones: 9-10. To 15-20 feet.
Deciduous tree. Flowering.

A small multistemmed tree that becomes as wide as it is tall in frost-free areas. Prized for its birdlike pinkish-red flowers, which are produced in repeated flushes from spring to fall after the leaves develop.

Erythrina humeana
Natal Coral Tree

Zones: 9-10. To 20-30 feet.
Usually deciduous, but sometimes semievergreen, tree. Flowering.

Flowering starts when the tree is only 3 feet tall. Bright orange flowers appear continuously from late August to late November and are held well above the dark green foliage.

Coral trees *(Erythrina* sp.) flower prolifically; blossoms often appear before foliage on bare irregular branches. Striking as shade trees.

Escallonia x exoniensis
Escallonia

Zones: 7-10. To 7-10 feet.
Evergreen shrub. Flowering.

Escallonia is an excellent evergreen shrub with rose-tinted flowers that bloom over a long season from late spring to fall and nearly year-round in warm winter areas. It serves as an attractive screening hedge or windbreak. A fast grower that responds well to trimming, escallonia has small, neat, lustrous green leaves.

Escallonia is a particularly useful shrub in sunny areas near the seashore because it tolerates winds and salt air. Plant in a partly shaded location in hot inland areas. Most soils are suitable for escallonia, except the most alkaline. Partially drought-tolerant, this shrub looks its best if given good drainage and regular watering. Flowering will be reduced by heavy pruning.

'Fradesii' is an excellent compact grower, 5 to 6 feet tall, that flowers prolifically nearly year-round.

This compact form of escallonia *(Escallonia x exoniensis* 'Fradesii') bears rosy-pink blossoms nearly year-round.

Eucalyptus

Eucalyptus, Gum

Zones: 7-10. To 100 feet.
Evergreen shrubs or trees.
Flowering.

Eucalyptus are vigorous-growing trees and shrubs native to Australia. They provide evergreen foliage, light shade, wind protection, and attractive bark. Some have colorful flowers. Most eucalyptus are drought-tolerant, but the growth rate of new plants will be increased with some irrigation. A mulch to keep down weeds and reduce evaporation will also increase growth of young trees. Good drainage is essential. Eucalyptus are free of insect pests and resistant to foliage disease because they were imported in seed form from Australia, leaving their problem pests behind.

Scarlet-flowering gum *(Eucalyptus ficifolia)*

Fuchsia gum *(Eucalyptus forrestiana)*

Nichol's willow-leaved peppermint *(Eucalyptus nicholii)*

Dwarf white ironbark *(Eucalyptus leucoxylon)*

Eucalyptus

Botanical Name/ Common Name	Cold Hardi- ness/ Zones	Size	Plant Description	Comments
Eucalyptus camaldulensis Red Gum, River Red Gum	10°-15°F 8-10	To 80-120 ft tall.	Evergreen tree. Spreading crown, weeping branches. Bark smooth, dark gray, peeling. Leaves long and narrow.	Takes desert heat, cold. Many small seed capsules.
E. cinerea Silver-Dollar Tree, Dollar-Leaf Eucalyptus	15°-18°F 8-10	To 20-50 ft tall.	Evergreen tree. Irregular habit. Bark white, furrowed. Leaves round, silvery-blue.	Grown mainly for cut foliage. Takes wind. Seed capsules small.
E. citriodora Lemon-Scented Gum, Lemon Gum	24°-28°F 9-10	To 50-100 ft tall.	Evergreen tree. Tall, slender, fast-growing with high branches. Bark smooth, spotted white to pinkish. Leaves long, narrow, pointed, lemon-scented.	Very ornamental. Used for walkways, grove plantings.
E. cornuta Yate Tree	20°-25°F 9-10	To 30-60 ft tall.	Evergreen tree. Large, spreading crown. Bark furrowed, rough, dark. Leaves lance-shaped.	Good shade tree, takes wind. Summer flowers 3-in. fuzzy clusters, greenish yellow. Seed capsules with small horns in clusters.
E. ficifolia Red-Flowering Gum, Scarlet-Flowering Gum	25°-30°F 9-10	To 30-60 ft tall.	Evergreen tree. Roundheaded. Bark furrowed, dark. Leaves leathery, dark green.	Very showy clusters of 1-1/2-in. scarlet flowers cover tree in summer. Large seed capsules. Grows well in coastal areas.
E. forrestiana Fuchsia Gum	20°-25°F 9-10	To 12 ft tall.	Evergreen shrub or small tree. Bark smooth, gray-brown. Branches reddish. Leaves narrow, 2-1/2 in. long.	Flower bases red, fuchsia-like, long-lasting when cut. Good small garden and patio tree. Grows well in coastal and dry areas.
E. globulus 'Compacta' Dwarf Tasmanian Blue Gum, Bushy Blue Gum	15°-22°F 8-10	To 60 ft tall.	Evergreen tree. Shrublike with compact dense habit, many branches. Bark smooth, shedding. Leaves very long, sickle-shaped.	Can be sheared low. Good for low windbreaks even in coastal areas. Seed capsules large, messy.
E. gunnii Cider Gum	5°-10°F 7-10	To 40-75 ft tall.	Evergreen tree. Strong, vigorous, tall grower. Bark smooth, greenish-white. Leaves small, blue-gray.	Good for shade, windbreak or screening. Bell-shaped seed capsules in clusters.
E. lehmannii Bushy Yate, Lehmann's Gum	25°-30°F 9-10	To 20-30 ft tall.	Evergreen shrub or tree. Multistemmed, wide-spreading. Bark smooth, gray-brown, peeling. Leaves dense, short, blunt, light green tinged red.	Huge clusters of bottle-green flowers in summer. Good for screening in coastal areas.

Lemon-scented gum *(Eucalyptus citriodora)* makes a dramatic skyline tree.

Red-flowering gum *(Eucalyptus ficifolia)* has a very round head; makes a year-round shade tree.

Botanical Name/ Common Name	Cold Hardi- ness/ Zones	Size	Plant Description	Comments
E. leucoxylon 'Rosea' Dwarf White Ironbark	15°-20°F 8-10	To 20 ft tall.	Evergreen shrub or tree. Bark mottled white and blue-gray. Leaves narrow, gray-green.	Pink to red flowers. Excellent ornamental. Takes heat, wind. Wood used for railroad ties, telephone poles.
E. microtheca Flooded Box	5°-10°F 7-10	To 30 ft tall.	Evergreen tree. Bushy, with rounded top. Bark white, wrinkled, and cracked. Attractive sickle-shaped blue-green leaves.	Solid-structured tree for windbreaks in dry areas.
E. nicholii Nichol's Willow-Leaved Peppermint Gum	10°-15°F 8-10	To 40 ft tall.	Evergreen tree. Graceful with soft, willowy appearance, spreading crown. Bark brown, persistent. Leaves light green, tinged purple, peppermint-scented when crushed.	Good garden tree. Small seed capsules in round clusters.
E. niphophila Snow Gum	5°-10°F 7-10	To 20 ft tall.	Evergreen shrub or tree. Wide-spreading with smooth white shedding bark. Leaves showy, silvery-blue, curved and narrow to 4 in. long.	Creamy-white flower clusters. One of the hardiest of eucalyptus. Drought-tolerant.
E. polyanthemos Silver-Dollar Gum, Silver-Dollar Tree, Red Box	15°-20°F 8-10	To 20-60 ft tall.	Evergreen tree. Often multistemmed with low branches. Bark mottled, shedding, rough, brown or gray. Leaves oval, grayish-blue.	Creamy-white flower clusters. Very adaptable. Seed capsules have 1/2-in. diameter.
E. rudis Desert Gum, Swamp Gum	10°-15°F 8-10	To 30-50 ft tall.	Evergreen tree. Spreading to weeping habit with rough, persistent gray bark. Leaves broad or narrow, lance-shaped, gray-green.	Takes desert heat and wind. Good shade tree.
E. sideroxylon Red Ironbark, Pink Ironbark	10°-15°F 8-10	To 20-80 ft tall.	Evergreen tree. Variable structure. Bark rough, persistent, dark red or black. Leaves lance-shaped, blue-green.	Light pink to red flower clusters. Very ornamental. Use as street tree or for screening.
E. spathulata Swamp Mallee, Narrow-Leaved Gimlet	20°-25°F 9-10	To 6-20 ft tall.	Evergreen shrub or tree. Multistemmed habit. Bark smooth, red. Leaves lance-shaped, to 3 in. long.	Use for low hedge. Tolerates poor drainage.
E. torquata Coral Gum	25°-30°F 9-10	To 15-25 ft tall.	Evergreen tree. Narrow, slender with slightly drooping branches. Bark rough, flaky, brown on trunk; smooth and gray above. Light green to golden-green leaves are long and narrow.	Grown for its coral-red and yellow blossoms, shaped like Japanese lanterns. Blooms intermittently year-round.
E. viminalis Manna Gum, White Gum, Ribbon Gum	10°-15°F 8-10	Grows rapidly to 150 ft tall.	Evergreen tree. Open habit, weeping branches. Bark white to yellowish-white, shedding. Leaves willowlike, 4-6 in. long, pale green.	Makes interesting silhouette as skyline tree. Seed capsules small, pea-shaped.

Eucalyptus **111**

Eugenia uniflora (see page 114)

Euonymus
Euonymus
Zones: 3-9. To 12 feet.
Evergreen or deciduous shrubs
and vines.

This diverse genus offers a variety of useful plants with handsome glossy foliage. Serviceable and easily grown, they reach mature size in 8 to 10 years. Though their flowers are insignificant, some varieties have such brightly variegated leaves that few plants can match them for year-round garden color. Mature plants may have bright orange fruit in fall and winter.

Euonymus can be used a variety of ways in the landscape depending on the particular habit of the variety or species being grown. Most are shrubby plants that respond beautifully to shearing. They make excellent hedges or trimmed borders. Varieties with variegated foliage are colorful accent plants. Some euonymus are sprawling, vinelike plants that are superb used as ground covers and also make attractive espaliers.

Euonymus are adaptable to a broad range of garden conditions, growing well in all but the wettest soils. They are heat-tolerant in sun or shade and are a fine choice for seashore and city gardens.

Mildew may be a problem in moist, shaded locations. Sucking insect pests, especially scale, may also be troublesome.

Purple-leaf euonymus *(Euonymus fortunei* 'Colorata') has purple foliage in fall and winter, green leaves in summer.

Euonymus

Botanical Name/Common Name	Zones	Size	Plant Description	Comments
Euonymus alata Winged Spindle Tree, Winged Euonymus, Winged Burning Bush	3-9	To 10-12 ft tall with equal spread.	Deciduous shrub or small tree. Slow-growing. Twigs develop ornamental corky wings. Fall foliage bright red when grown in sun; pink in shade. Orange-red fruit.	Excellent for small multi-stemmed tree or large informal hedge.
E. a. 'Compacta' Dwarf Winged Euonymus, Dwarf Flame Euonymus, Burning Bush	3-9	To 6 ft tall.	Deciduous dwarf form. Slow-growing, compact. Fall color lively scarlet. Bright red fruit attracts birds.	Ideal screen, hedge, or lawn specimen. Brilliant color in fall.
E. fortunei 'Carrierei'	4-8	Trailing to 20 ft.	Evergreen vining shrub. Climbs if supported. Lustrous, dark green leaves. Orange fruit.	Excellent ground cover.
E. f. 'Colorata' Purple-Leaf Euonymus	4-8	To 4 ft tall.	Evergreen low-mounding shrub with dark green, glossy foliage. Turns plum color in fall.	Excellent ground cover. Can be pruned as low hedge or border.
E. f. 'Emerald Gaiety'	5-8	To 4 ft tall.	Evergreen shrub with dense mounding habit and erect branches. Rounded, deep, rich green leaves with white margins.	Useful for border, accent plant, or vinelike effect against walls, fences.
E. f. 'Emerald 'n Gold'	5-8	To 3 ft tall.	Evergreen shrub with compact, tight branching, mounded form. Dark, glossy-green leaves have bold yellow edges.	Good accent plant for any landscape.
E. f. 'Emerald Surprise'	5-8	To 3 ft tall.	Similar to 'Emerald 'n Gold' but faster-growing, stronger, with larger, more colorful leaves mottled green, gold, creamy-white.	
E. f. 'Golden Prince'	5-8	To 1-2 ft tall.	Evergreen shrub. Vigorous. New foliage tipped gold. Mature leaves solid green.	Hardiest of variegated euonymus varieties. Use in containers or as low hedge.
E. f. 'Gracilis'	5-8	Semi-trailing.	Evergreen vinelike shrub grows low and dense, bushy. Variegated green-and-white leaves turn pinkish in winter.	Fine ground cover. Easily shaped as container plant.
E. f. 'Greenland'	5-8	To 4 ft tall.	Evergreen low-spreading shrub. Erect-branching. Oval, lustrous green leaves will not discolor in cold winters. Bright orange berries in fall.	Versatile landscape plant, due to bushy, creeping, or climbing form.
E. f. 'Pauli'	5-8	Vinelike.	Evergreen shrub. Low-growing. Dense branching habit. Small, glossy, dark green leaves.	Useful ground cover.
E. f. 'Sarcoxie'	5-8	To 3 ft tall.	Evergreen shrub. Small, low-spreading. Dark metallic-green round leaves with creamy-white margins.	Good hedge or border.
E. f. 'Silver Queen'	5-8	To 3-4 ft tall.	Evergreen shrub. Small, low-spreading habit. Dark, metallic-green leaves are round with creamy-white margins.	Many garden uses.

Winged euonymus *(Euonymus alata)* turns scarlet in autumn.

Wintercreeper *(Euonymus fortunei)* makes an ornamental cover for walls and fences.

Gracilis euonymus *(Euonymus fortunei* 'Gracilis') forms a bright mound of variegated foliage.

Botanical Name/Common Name	Zones	Size	Plant Description	Comments
E. f. 'Sunspot'	5-8	To 3-4 ft tall with equal spread.	Evergreen shrub with mounding form. Rich green leaves have yellow spot in center. Yellow-colored stems.	Showy for accent or hedges.
E. f. vegata **Big-Leaf Winter Creeper**	5-8	Vinelike.	Evergreen shrub with upright branches. Strong-growing. Round, 1-in. glossy green leaves. Orange-red bittersweetlike berries in late summer, fall.	Unequaled as hardy evergreen wall or fence cover.
E. japonica **Evergreen Euonymus,** **Japanese Spindle Tree,** **Japanese Euonymus**	7-9	To 8 ft tall.	Evergreen shrub. Dense, compact. Shiny, dark green leaves hold into winter.	Good hedge or specimen plant. All varieties respond well to trimming, shaping.
E. j. 'Aureo-marginata' **Golden Euonymus**	7-9	To 8-10 ft tall.	Evergreen shrub. Densely branched, upright. Fast grower. Golden margins on dark green leaves.	Good accent plant.
E. j. 'Aureo-variegata' **Gold-Spot Euonymus,** **Golden-Center Euonymus**	7-9	To 10 ft tall.	Evergreen shrub. Dense, compact, upright. Yellow-blotched leaves have well-defined dark green margins.	Use for sheared hedge or tall border.
E. j. 'Golden Queen'	7-9	To 8 ft tall.	Evergreen shrub. Upright habit. Large, glossy green leaves have rich yellow edges.	Very showy in landscape. Good accent plant.
E. j. 'Grandiflora' **Big-Leaf Euonymus**	6-9	To 8-10 ft tall.	Evergreen shrub. Grows rapidly. Upright. Compact branching habit. Large, shiny, dark green leaves.	Can be sheared.
E. j. 'Microphylla' **Boxleaf Euonymus**	7-9	To 1-2 ft tall.	Evergreen shrub. Dwarf with erect branches. Tiny, narrow, shiny dark green leaves are closely arranged.	Outstanding dwarf shrub for edging and small areas.
E. j. 'President Gauthier'	6-9	To 8 ft tall.	Evergreen shrub. Upright habit. Large, showy green leaves have cream-colored margins.	Control height by pruning. Good contrast in landscape.
E. j. 'Silver King'	7-9	To 8-10 ft tall.	Evergreen shrub. Upright habit. Large, leathery, glossy green leaves with silvery-white margins.	Showy hedge, accent, or background shrub.
E. j. 'Silver Queen'	7-9	To 8-10 ft tall.	Evergreen shrub. Large leaves have dark green centers and creamy-white margins.	Excellent ornamental shrub. Use in containers, as hedge or border.
E. j. 'Variegata' **Variegated Boxleaf Euonymus**	6-9	To 2 ft tall.	Evergreen shrub. Slow-growing dwarf with dense erect stems. Waxy, dark green leaves, tightly arranged on branches, have gleaming white margins.	Good for borders, hedges.
E. kiautschovica 'Manhattan' **(E. patens)**	6-9	To 9 ft tall.	Evergreen shrub. Upright, bushy. Dark glossy green, serrated leaves. Small fruits open to show bright red seeds.	Good as sheared hedge, espalier.

Weeping beech *(Fagus sylvatica* 'Pendula') has attractive foliage on weeping branches; makes a fine specimen tree.

The bold foliage of Fatshedera *(x Fatshedera lizei)* looks dramatic silhouetted against a wooden fence.

Eugenia uniflora
Barbados Cherry, Surinam Cherry, Pitanga
Zones: 9-10. To 10-25 feet.
Evergreen shrub. Flowering.

Barbados cherry is a year-round delight with fragrant spring flowers that bloom intermittently through summer, edible fruit, and bronzy-green foliage that turns red with winter cold. The scented white blossoms are a ball of showy stamens 1/2 inch across. Fruit resembles ornamental Chinese lanterns and changes from yellow to deep red when ripe. It is juicy and deliciously spicy in jams and salads.

This compact slow-growing shrub withstands clipping. If unpruned it averages 6 to 8 feet with equal spread. Display Barbados cherries in pots near the patio or use for a neat clipped hedge. The plant will look its best if given partial shade in hot climates. Needs well-drained soil.

Fagus sylvatica
European Beech
Zones: 5-9. To 50-80 feet.
Deciduous tree.

A mature European beech has a mammoth short trunk covered with very smooth gray bark and wide-spreading branches that sweep to the ground. Leaves are dark glossy green and toothed, though forms with cut-leaves and dark purple summer foliage are popular.

European beeches are ornamental throughout the year. When bare of leaves in the winter, their majestic silhouette is shown to advantage. Though they are late to leaf out in spring, the new foliage is often copper-colored, especially in the purple-leaved forms. In fall foliage turns reddish-brown and leaves may cling to the branches well into winter. The tiny triangular nuts are edible.

Because of their thick foliage, low branches, and fibrous surface roots, beeches discourage grass from growing beneath their boughs. Try a shredded bark mulch to dress up

the ground. Prune away any sprouts that arise from the base or roots. Grows in most garden soils. Use as a specimen plant on a large property. Provide plenty of room to mature. A type of woolly aphid may trouble the bark or leaves.

Several varieties are popular. 'Asplenifolia', the fern-leaf beech, has narrow finely divided dark green leaves resembling a fern. 'Fastigiata' ('Dawyckii', 'Pyramidalis') is narrowly columnar, broadening with age; has green leaves. 'Pendula', weeping beech, has weeping branches, dark green leaves. 'Purpurea Pendula', weeping copper beech, has dark purple leaves. 'Riversii', River's purple beech, bears reddish young leaves that gradually turn dark purple and retain that color until fall; has a wide upright form. 'Rohanii' grows slowly and has purple, deeply cut leaves. 'Roseo-marginata' has purple leaves edged with pink.

x Fatshedera lizei
Fatshedera, Botanical-Wonder
Zones: 9-10.
Evergreen vine. Flowering.

Fatshedera is known as a botanical-wonder because of its unusual origin. In 1911, Lize Freres raised this plant by crossing plants from 2 different genera—*Fatsia japonica*, Japanese aralia, and *Hedera helix*, English ivy. Their names were combined to make *Fatshedera*.

The characteristics of both parents are reflected in the hybrid's growth and habit. It forms a semi-erect shrub, sending out long, rope-like branches bearing large, shiny, evergreen leaves. Long trailing stems need to be supported if they are to climb. If the growing tips are pinched back, the plant takes on a shrubby look similar to aralia.

Long spikes of greenish-white flowers appear in fall but it is the luxuriant foliage that makes fatshedera such a desirable specimen plant for use both in the garden and indoors. Large-lobed leaves with pointed ends are 5 to 9 inches in length and width and are rich glossy green. 'Variegata' has white-bordered leaves, providing added visual interest.

Use this decorative plant in a poolside setting or shaded entryway. When trained on a fence or placed against a wall, it makes an attractive background for flowers and shrubs. Use on a trellis, for an espalier, or as a screen. Young stems are flexible and easy to train. Branches need to be tied securely, but not tightly, to their support.

Fatshedera tolerates deep shade to full sun in cool coastal regions. Otherwise, needs protection from dry winds and hot sun. Provide a rich, well-drained soil and plenty of moisture.

Fatsia japonica
Japanese Aralia
Zones: 8-10. To 5-10 feet.
Evergreen shrub. Flowering.

Japanese aralia is a shade plant with a bold tropical appearance. Its leaves are broad 9- to 15-inch open fans with deeply cut oval lobes held flat on long stalks. In fall, rounded clusters of creamy-white flowers appear above the foliage. Plant in a shaded shrub border or beside an entryway. Makes a good houseplant.

Nearly any garden soil is suitable for growing Japanese aralia, though organic matter should be added when planting. Water freely where summers are warm. 'Variegata', has creamy-white leaf margins and needs more shade.

Feijoa sellowiana
Pineapple Guava
Zones: 8-10. To 20-25 feet.
Evergreen tree.

Considered the hardiest of subtropical fruit trees, pineapple guava is native from southern Brazil to Uraguay and parts of Argentina and Paraguay. Tolerating extensive pruning, it serves many landscape uses such as hedges, screens, or espaliers. By removing lower limbs, it can be developed into a small tree.

Growth habit without pruning is open and shrublike with many stems. Grows rapidly. Late spring is the best time to prune.

Oval leaves are glossy green above, and white-felted, with prominent veins, beneath. Measure 2 to 3 inches long and 1 inch wide. Spectacular, 1-inch-wide flowers have 4 thick edible petals that are white and slightly fuzzy on the outside and purplish on the inside. In the center is a large tuft of crimson stamens. Flowers are borne in May or June.

Fruit ripening takes 4-1/2 to 5 months in warm areas, 5 to 7 months in cool climates. Egg-shaped fruits are from 1 to 4 inches long, grayish green, and often blushed with red. Fruit grown in coastal areas is more flavorful than that from hot inland areas. Fruits fall from the tree when mature. If picked too early, full flavor does not develop.

Growth is best in good loam soil. Will grow in clay soils but does not do as well in light sandy soils unless watered frequently. Drought-tolerant, though growth is better in all soils if irrigated. Grows best in areas without high humidity where temperatures are cool part of the year. Will grow in partial shade, but needs full sun for fruit production.

Seedlings usually fruit in 3 to 5 years. Grafted plants often set fruit in 2 years. Not all plants will set fruit without cross-pollination. More than one plant must be planted for fruit production unless the self-fruitful cultivars, 'Coolidgei' and 'Pineapple Gem', are used.

Festuca ovina glauca
Blue Fescue
Zones: 5-10. To 4-10 inches.
Herbaceous ground cover.
Flowering.

This striking ornamental grass forms tufted mounds of slender silver-blue leaves capped in summer with small feathery flowers. Its appealing texture and unusual color make blue fescue an eye-catching ground cover.

Space small plants from flats 6 to 12 inches apart in well-drained soil in full sun or light shade. Divide clumps every 2 or 3 years, or clip to the ground in spring to renew growth. Mulch to keep out weeds.

Japanese aralia *(Fatsia japonica)* adds lush evergreen background foliage to the shade garden.

Versatile pineapple guava *(Feijoa sellowiana)* can be grown as an evergreen hedge or tree. Bears flavorful fruits.

The tufted mounds of blue fescue *(Festuca ovina glauca)* create a fine-textured ground cover.

Ficus

Fig

Zones: 9-10. To 50-60 feet.
Evergreen trees, shrubs, and vines.

This genus includes mostly evergreen trees, shrubs, and vines suitable for subtropical and tropical landscapes. They are common sights in most warm winter areas of the Southern and Western United States. Many of them make decorative houseplants. All have milky sap and evergreen species have simple, alternate leaves. The edible fig, *Ficus carica*, is a deciduous representative of the genus.

It has large deeply lobed leaves that have a dramatic tropical appearance but the trees are grown primarily for their sweet-tasting fruit. Figs are frost-sensitive, but most can be grown in well-lighted, interior locations in cold winter areas.

Above left: Rubber plant *(Ficus elastica)* has bold evergreen leaves. Above right: Indian laurel fig *(Ficus retusa nitida)* can be used as a formal privacy screen.

Ficus

Botanical Name/Common Name	Zones	Size	Plant Description	Comments
Ficus benjamina **Weeping Fig,** **Weeping Chinese Banyan**	11	To 15-50 ft tall.	Evergreen tree with graceful, irregular, broad-spreading outline. Thin, shiny dark green leaves have wavy edges. To 5 in. long. New growth light green.	Very popular houseplant. Keep soil evenly moist. Goes into shock from sudden environmental changes.
F. elastica 'Decora' **Broad-Leaved Indian Rubber Plant**	9-10	To 15-40 ft tall.	Evergreen tree. Usually with single trunk, stiffly upright habit. Bold, dark green leaves 8-12 in. long and 4-6 in. wide unfold from pink sheath.	Bold outdoor tree. Foolproof houseplant with bigger and brighter leaves than species. Takes low light. Let dry out between waterings.
F. e. 'Rubra'	9-10	To 15-40 ft tall.	Same as 'Decora' except new growth reddish. Mature leaves green have red edges.	Excellent houseplant. Distinctive in landscape in mild climates.
F. e. 'Robusta'	9-10	To 15 ft tall.	Same as 'Decora' except slower growing. Darker green leaf color.	Excellent houseplant. Distinctive in landscape in mild climates.
F. lyrata **Fiddle-Leaf Fig**	11	To 15-20 ft tall.	Evergreen tree. Stiffly upright with huge, fiddle-shaped, glossy deep green leaves with prominent veins. To 15 in. long, 10 in. wide.	Bold form. Pinch young plants to develop branching.
F. pumila **Creeping Fig, Climbing Fig**	9-10	Unlimited spread.	Evergreen vine clings readily to most surfaces. Can spread almost indefinitely. Leathery, dull green leaves.	Grows best in partial shade. Forms dense mat over support. Good for small space areas.
F. retusa **Indian Laurel Fig**	9-10	To 25-30 ft tall.	Evergreen tree with dense, roundheaded crown. Long weeping branches. Shiny dark green leaves with blunt tips. Closely spaced, 2-4 in. long. Pinkish-green new growth.	Widely used as street tree in mild areas of California. Good in containers. Subject to thrips.
F. r. nitida **Laurel Fig,** **Indian Laurel Fig**	9-10	To 25-30 ft tall.	Sames as species but denser foliage on upright branches. Glossier green leaves have pointed tip. New growth light green.	Responds well to shearing as a hedge or topiary. Subject to thrips.
F. rubiginosa **Port Jackson Fig, Rusty Fig,** **Little-Leaf Fig**	9-10	To 30-60 ft tall.	Evergreen tree with massive, broad-spreading crown. Thick, leathery, oval leaves to 5 in. long, deep green on top, usually with rust-colored hairs on undersides.	Branches covered with rusty hairs. Tolerates heat, drought, and coastal conditions. *F. r.* 'Florida' has lighter-colored leaves.

Early-blooming border forsythia *(Forsythia x intermedia)* heralds spring with a brilliant show of yellow blossoms.

Wild strawberry *(Fragaria chiloensis)* spreads quickly, forms a dense mat of dark green foliage brightened by flowers in spring.

Franklin tree *(Franklinia alatamaha)* blooms in late summer and fall and is prized as a specimen tree.

Forsythia x intermedia
Border Forsythia
Zones: 5-9. To 9 feet.
Deciduous shrub. Flowering.

Forsythias are among the earliest-blooming deciduous shrubs. In early spring they clothe their bare branches with beautiful clear yellow blossoms. Plants are upright-growing, developing arching canes. They have a spread of 10 to 12 feet, and make handsome specimen plants. They are widely used as a clipped or unclipped hedge, in shrub borders, and in mass or group plantings. Forsythias tolerate a wide range of conditions and have long lives.

Many cultivars have been selected with qualities superior to the parent. 'Lynwood', or 'Lynwood Gold', is a cultivar of Irish origin. It is upright-growing, spreading as wide as it is tall. Branches are covered with golden-yellow blossoms. 'Spring Glory' was introduced in 1942; flowers are rich yellow, borne on upright or spreading branches. 'Spectabilis' is a fast-growing plant

with dense, arching branches covered with large deep yellow flowers. Good as an informal hedge. 'Beatrix Farrand' has large, golden, 2-inch flowers with orange markings on the throat.

Fragaria chiloensis
Wild Strawberry
Zones: 4-8. To 6-12 inches.
Herbaceous ground cover.
Flowering.

This beautiful trailing plant with its clusters of dark green scallop-edged leaves and perky white spring flowers is a wild version of the edible strawberry. Its small red fruits are rather tasteless and appeal more to birds than to people.

Wild strawberry spreads rapidly by surface runners so should be used where neatness isn't important. Plant along the edge of a woodland garden and beneath shrubs or trees where its dense mat will dress up the ground. Foliage remains year-round and turns reddish in cold weather. Withstands occasional light foot traffic.

Space plants from flats and bare-root plants 6 to 12 inches apart in light, fertile soil. Grows in full sun along the coast; in hot inland areas provide some shade. Fertilize and water regularly. Mow off old foliage in spring to encourage vigorous new growth.

'Hybrid Number 25' is a larger more vigorous plant and produces tasty fruit.

Franklinia alatamaha
Franklin Tree
Zones: 6-8. To 20-30 feet.
Deciduous shrub or tree.
Flowering.

This small pyramidal tree or shrub is a choice native American tree that is now extinct in the wild. It is notable for its white flowers with yellow centers that appear in late summer and fall. Plant in moist, acid, well-drained soil with ample organic matter, in partial shade or sun. Best in protected sites. Leaves turn orange to red in fall with best coloration in full sun. Use as a specimen tree.

Fraxinus

Ash

Zones: 2-10. To 70 feet.
Deciduous trees.

This genus is comprised of sturdy, medium-sized and large trees, most of which tolerate hot summers and cold winters and a variety of soil types. The leaves of most species are divided into leaflets and cast moderate to dense shade. Most ash make good lawn, shade, and street trees. Best growth is in full sun in fertile, well-drained soils with good moisture.

Oyster-shell scale and ash borers may be troublesome and anthracnose may be a problem in areas with cool wet springs. Seedlings from the female trees can become weed and litter problems. Consequently, most named selections are males.

Flowering ash *(Fraxinus ornus)* has fluffy clusters of fragrant flowers on a round-headed tree.

Fraxinus

Botanical Name/Common Name	Zones	Size	Plant Description	Comments
Fraxinus americana **White Ash**	4-9	To 80 ft tall.	Deciduous tree. Upright, oval canopy. Leaves bright green in summer, turning yellow, orange and purple in fall.	Good lawn tree. Poor in hot, dry climates. Seedlings pose a weed problem.
F. a. 'Autumn Applause' **Autumn Applause White Ash**	4-9	To 80 ft tall.	Same as species, but holds brilliant purple and mahogany fall colors longer than other cultivars.	Seedless.
F. a. 'Autumn Purple' **Autumn Purple White Ash**	4-9	To 80 ft tall.	Same as species, but leaves have better substance, finer texture. Rich purple or mahogany fall color.	Seedless.
F. a. 'Champaign County' **Champaign County White Ash**	4-9	To 80 ft tall.	Same as species, but more vigorous with denser crown. Heavy trunk, robust branching.	Seedless.
F. a. 'Rose Hill' **Rose Hill White Ash**	4-9	To 60-70 ft tall.	Deciduous tree. Faster growing than species. Straight, upright, with strong lateral branches. Leaves dark green in summer; turn bronze-red in fall.	More pyramidal than species.
F. excelsior 'Hessei' **Hesse European Ash**	4-9	To 30-50 ft tall.	Deciduous tree. Roundheaded. Undivided leaves with serrated edges, leathery, glossy dark green; fall while still green.	Excellent street tree.
F. holotricha 'Moraine' **Moraine Ash**	5-8	To 30-35 ft tall.	Deciduous tree. Broad, upright crown. Elegant and graceful. Leaves light textured, small, olive-green, turn attractive yellow in fall.	Good, symmetrical street or lawn tree.
F. latifolia **Oregon Ash**	7-10	To 40-80 ft tall.	Deciduous tree. Rounded head. Leaves long, oval, light green. Withstands winter flooding.	Female and male flowers on different trees. Native to Pacific Northwest.
F. ornus **Flowering Ash,** **Manna Ash**	6-8	To 40 ft tall.	Deciduous tree. Broad, rounded head. Smooth bark. Leaves, shiny green, turn soft lavender or yellow in fall. Flowers, unlike most ashes, appear in fluffy white or greenish-white clusters; have spicy fragrance.	Messy seed clusters follow flowers.
F. oxycarpa 'Flame' **Claret Ash**	5-9	To 30-40 ft tall.	Deciduous tree. Roundheaded to upright. Leaves small, glossy, dark green; turn wine-red in fall.	Good choice for lawn, park or street tree. Seedless.
F. o. 'Raywood' **Raywood Ash, Claret Ash**	5-9	To 25-40 ft tall.	Similar to *F. o.* 'Flame'.	Same uses as 'Flame'.
F. pennsylvanica **Green Ash, Red Ash**	3-9	To 50 ft tall.	Deciduous tree. Pyramidal when young, becoming roundheaded with age, forming dense, oval crown. Bright green leaves turn yellow in fall.	Widely adapted. Drought-tolerant. Female and male flowers appear on different trees.

Green ash *(Fraxinus pennsylvanica)* is a widely adapted fast-growing shade tree.

Modesto ash *(Fraxinus velutina glabra)* lines this street with warm fall color.

Botanical Name/Common Name	Zones	Size	Plant Description	Comments
F. p. 'Fan West' Fan West Ash	8-10	To 40 ft tall.	Deciduous tree. Seedless cross of Texas green ash and Arizona ash. Good limb structure. Leaves light olive-green.	Good street or park tree for hot climates. Takes desert heat, wind.
F. p. 'Kimberly'	3-9	To 30 ft tall.	Similar to species with smaller leaves. Clear yellow autumn color.	Stems have yellowish tint. Large, black buds.
F. p. 'Marshall' Marshall Seedless Green Ash	3-9	To 60 ft tall.	Similar to species. Dark, glossy green leaves. Turn bright lemon-yellow in fall. Casts heavier shade than most ashes.	Seedless. Considered best green ash variety available.
F. p. 'Patmore' Patmore Ash	2-9	To 50 ft tall.	Deciduous tree. Erect trunk, well-spaced branches. Leaves glossy, more serrated than species. Yellow fall color.	Seedless. Extremely hardy, useful in prairie climates.
F. p. 'Summit' Summit Ash	3-9	To 50-60 ft tall.	Deciduous tree. Upright with strong central leader, oval crown. Leaves narrow, pointed. Yellow fall color.	Very neat and symmetrical.
F. quadrangulata Blue Ash	3-9	To 60 ft tall.	Deciduous tree. Young branches square, four-winged. Oval, dark green leaves with serrated edges; pointed at tips. Turn yellow and purple in fall.	Valuable timber tree. Dye derived from inner bark.
F. uhdei Shamel Ash, Evergreen Ash	9-10	To 50-60 ft tall.	Deciduous to semievergreen in mild climates. Rapid-growing, narrow, becoming spreading with age. Serrated, dark green leaves persist through warm winters.	Shallow-rooted, avoid planting near concrete.
F. u. 'Majestic Beauty'	9-10	To 50-60 ft tall.	Similar to species. Evergreen in mild climates. Branches strong. Leaves large, dark green.	Popular in Southwest.
F. u. 'Tomlinson' Tomlinson's Ash	9-10	To 50-60 ft tall.	Deciduous tree, evergreen in mild climates. Pyramid-shaped. Leaves dense, serrated, deep green.	Magnificent shade tree for park, patio, or containers.
F. velutina Velvet Ash, Arizona Ash	6-10	To 50 ft tall.	Deciduous tree. Upright branching, round-topped. Bright green leaves turn bright yellow in fall.	Susceptible to anthracnose.
F. v. glabra Modesto Ash	6-10	To 50 ft tall.	Deciduous tree. Faster growing than species. Light green leaves turn bright yellow in fall.	Weak limbs. Susceptible to many insects and diseases. Roots break pavement.
F. v. 'Rio Grande' Fan-Tex Ash	8-10	To 50 ft tall.	Similar to Modesto ash, with darker green leaves.	Good desert tree. Better adapted to hot, dry, windy areas than Modesto ash.

The flowers of fuchsia (*Fuchsia* sp.) have a graceful shape and come in many color combinations.

The fragrant blossoms of gardenia (*Gardenia jasminoides*) scent the garden from spring to autumn frost. Handsome as an evergreen screen or hedge.

Fuchsia
Fuchsia

Evergreen or deciduous shrubs. Flowering.

Fuchsias have long been admired for their fine foliage and elegant flowers that grace the garden from early summer to first frost. Hummingbirds are attracted to the brightly colored blossoms.

The basic conditions fuchsias require for healthy growth are: good drainage, a rich, moist soil, humid air, and partial shade. Misting foliage and mulching the soil will help create the cool, moist conditions fuchsias enjoy. Under these conditions, fuchsias have a reduced incidence of disease and insect problems, with an additional reward of lush leaves and abundant flowers. The Gulf Coast and especially coastal California are ideal climates for fuchsias.

Both shrubby and trailing fuchsias have been hybridized to create a vast assortment of flower forms in multiple colors ranging from white to pink, red, and purple.

Fuchsia x hybrida
Common Fuchsia

Zones: 9-10. To 2-12 feet.
Evergreen or deciduous shrub. Flowering.

This fuchsia has many types of glamorous flowers. They can be single or double, measure less than an inch long to over 4 inches long, and have a narrow and tubular or bulbous and flaring shape. Plants are available in either a trailing form suitable for hanging baskets, or as an upright shrub. Erect types make lovely garden shrubs, container plants for patios, and espaliers. Hang trailing plants where they can be admired up close.

This fuchsia remains evergreen in frost-free regions. Elsewhere it is deciduous or treated as an annual.

Spray, if necessary, to control insect pests such as whitefly, spider mites, and aphids. In early spring, cut back stems of the previous year's growth leaving 2 buds. Can

be tip-pruned when actively growing to encourage dense foliage. Container-grown plants also benefit from yearly root pruning.

Fuchsia magellanica
Hardy Fuchsia

Zones: 6-10. To 3-12 feet.
Evergreen or deciduous shrub. Flowering.

Hardy fuchsia is a widely adapted shrub displaying an abundance of colorful, slender blossoms with bright red sepals and blue inner petals. In Zones 6 to 8, hardy fuchsia acts like a perennial, with its top dying back at the first hard frost. Growth is renewed each year, keeping the plants about 3 feet tall. Hardy fuchsia remains evergreen where winters are mild, and can reach a height of 8 to 12 feet.

Use hardy fuchsia for a long-blooming accent plant or screening hedge. Provide a well-drained, rich soil and plenty of moisture.

Gardenia jasminoides
Gardenia

Zones: 8-10. To 1-8 feet.
Evergreen shrub. Flowering.

These small to medium-sized shrubs from China are renowned for the memorable fragrance of their blossoms. The incredibly aromatic white flowers measure 1 to 5 inches across. Dark green, thick, shiny oval leaves are 2 to 4 inches long and are opposite or in 3's on stems.

Growth habit varies from low and spreading to upright and open, depending on the variety. Some varieties make excellent hedges and screens. Others are suitable for containers or espaliers. All make stunning specimens.

Gardenias grow best in shade. In cool climates they can take full sun, but generally the warmer the climate, the more shade they need. They prefer a well-drained, acid soil with ample organic matter. Good growth and flowering require summer warmth, ample water, and frequent light applications of an acid fertilizer. Prune to remove straggly branches and old flowers.

'Mystery' has large 4- to 5-inch flowers, borne May to July, and is relatively open-branched, growing to 6 to 8 feet. 'Radicans' grows 6 to 12 inches tall and 2 to 3 feet wide. It has small leaves and 1-inch flowers in late spring. 'Veitchii' is a compact, upright 3- to 4-1/2-foot plant with many 1-1/2-inch flowers blooming from May to November.

Gazania rigens
Gazania, Clumping Gazania, Trailing Gazania, Treasure Flower
Zones: 9-10. To 6 inches.
Herbaceous ground cover.
Flowering.

Ground-hugging gray-green leaves and dazzling daisy-like flowers make gazania a distinctive ground cover in mild climates. Flowers appear throughout the year, most prolifically in May or June.

Clumping gazania forms dense clusters of toothed grayish foliage. Flowers are up to 5 inches across on 10-inch stems. May be yellow, copper, red, orange, pink, or white, solid-colored or striped.

Trailing gazania, *G. rigens leucolaena*, has yellow, orange, or gold flowers that measure 2 or 3 inches across and are held on 6-inch stalks. The plant sends out long trailing stems that root along the ground. Leaves are grayish, smooth-edged, and have silky hairs.

Favorite clumping kinds are: 'Aztec Queen' with yellow flowers and bronze midribs in leaves; 'Burgundy' with wine-colored flowers; 'Copper King' with very large, bright orange-and-brown flowers; 'Fiesta Red' with deep red blossoms; 'Moonglow' with double yellow flowers; and 'Royal Gold' with double gold flowers.

Top-rated trailing kinds are: 'Sun Burst' with deep orange blossoms shading outwards to light orange; 'Sun Gold' with deep yellow flowers and compact growth; 'Sunrise Yellow' with large, clear yellow flowers.

Use gazanias to edge a walkway or shrubbery border, or as a ground cover in a large planting area. Trailing gazania is excellent on steep slopes.

Grow in any well-drained soil in full sun. Space clumping gazania plants 1 foot apart. Mow foliage in late winter every few years to rejuvenate. Though drought- and heat-tolerant, occasional watering is beneficial. Fertilize lightly in spring and summer.

Gelsemium sempervirens
Carolina Yellow Jessamine
Zones: 7-10.
Evergreen vine. Flowering

This vine, native from Virginia to Texas, is the state flower of South Carolina. In early spring, its fragrant, bright yellow blossoms appear, filling the air with fragrance. An open, cascading vine, Carolina yellow jessamine is a welcome addition in any garden.

Carolina yellow jessamine has a moderate growth rate; the slender, reddish-brown stems climb by twisting, eventually reaching 20 feet. Long branches cascade from a wall or drape over a fence and bear glossy lance-shaped leaves 1 to 4 inches long. Funnel-shaped flowers cover the vine from spring into summer in Zones 7 and 8; nearly year-round in Zones 9 and 10. During the peak of bloom, it is blanketed with yellow flowers.

An adaptable vine, Carolina yellow jessamine can serve as an evergreen screen or patio shade, or a ground cover on banks.

Carolina yellow jessamine tolerates both full sun and partial shade and adapts to a wide range of soil types. In a windy location, the branches swing gracefully in the breeze.

Aztec queen gazania (*Gazania rigens* 'Aztec Queen')

Moonglow gazania (*Gazania rigens* 'Moonglow')

Carolina yellow jessamine (*Gelsemium sempervirens*)

Sunny blossoms in spring and an adaptable habit make Carolina yellow jessamine *(Gelsemium sempervirens)* a popular trellis cover.

With an unusual silhouette and lacy leaves that turn golden in fall, maidenhair tree *(Ginkgo biloba)* is a very attractive specimen tree.

Carolina yellow jessamine is restrained in its growth, making pruning an easy chore. Tie young stems to a sturdy support. Pruning should be done in fall once the vine matures; cut back side shoots and prune to desired shape. If the vine becomes top-heavy, cut back severely to renew growth and thin out branches. Keep the vine pruned to 3 feet if grown as a ground cover. A heavy pruning will also reduce the mass and encourage new branches. A mild fertilizer can be applied in early spring and after flowering.

Carolina yellow jessamine is reportedly a poisonous plant. No parts of it should be eaten.

Ginkgo biloba
Maidenhair Tree
Zones: 4-9. To 60-100 feet.
Deciduous tree.

Maidenhair tree has survived unchanged through the eons since the age of the dinosaurs, some 200 million years ago. It was unknown as a living plant until it was discovered growing in the gardens of Buddhist temples in Japan and China in 1690. Scientists believed this tree was extinct outside of these gardens until it was found growing wild in Cheki-ang Province, China, in 1914.

Maidenhair trees are now widely cultivated as city and street trees. They have no pests and diseases and tolerate compacted soil, though they are sensitive to air pollution.

Their picturesque silhouette and the unusual shape of their leaves sets them apart from other more commonly grown shade trees. Young trees are conical and become more spreading with age. Branches are heavy and have short leaf-bearing spurs rather than twigs, so the trees have an open airy look. Leaves are small and fan-shaped with scalloped edges, giving the foliage a 'lacy look. They turn clear golden-yellow in fall.

Only male trees should be planted, since female trees bear cherry-like fruits in autumn that have an extremely offensive odor when they ripen and fall to the ground.

Plant in full sun and give plenty of room to spread. Any garden soil is acceptable, though a deep, sandy loam is preferred. May grow slowly the first few years after transplanting.

The upright-growing cultivar 'Sentry' is a good choice for street plantings. On large lawns the broad spreading male cultivar 'Autumn Gold' is excellent.

Gleditsia triacanthos inermis
Thornless Honey Locust
Zones: 4-10. To 60-90 feet
Deciduous tree.

The thornless honey locust has all the fine attributes of the honey locust, but neither of its major drawbacks. Lacking both dangerous thorns and messy, unattractive seed pods, the thornless honey locust makes a desirable tree to shade a garden or patio.

Leaves are fine-textured and fernlike, casting a light filtered shade that is cooling but still allows lawn and garden plants to flourish. The leaves are late to leaf out in spring and drop early in fall after changing to light yellow. The leaves break apart when they drop, requiring very little raking. Most cultivars of the thornless honey locust do not produce seed pods, though the inconspicuous spring flowers are highly fragrant and attract honeybees.

Honey locusts are fast-growing, but have strong limbs that are not damaged by wind, ice, and snow. They do well in city conditions, tolerating air pollution and highway salts, though the roots of mature trees can damage sidewalks. There are few serious pests, though mimosa webworm can be troublesome in the South.

Several cultivars of the thornless honey locust are available. 'Moraine' grows to about 60 feet with a dense rounded head and has no seed pods. 'Rubylace' has wine-red leaves in spring that change to green by

midsummer; no seed pods are produced; grows to 60 feet tall. 'Sunburst' leafs out in spring with golden-yellow foliage, which turns green during the summer; grows to 60 feet; looks best contrasted against a dark background.

Grevillea
Grevillea
Evergreen trees and shrubs.

The plants in this genus are valued for their fine-textured foliage, fast growth rate, ability to thrive in poor soils, and tolerance of high temperatures and drought. They are most valuable in California. Two species are top-rated.

Grevillea 'Noell'
Noell Grevillea
Zones: 8-10. To 3-4 feet.
Evergreen shrub. Flowering.

Until it blooms, this compact hybrid grevillea resembles a juniper. It grows 4 feet tall and 4 feet wide. The narrow 1-inch-long leaves are glossy green. Clusters of rose-red and white flowers open over a long period in spring. Does poorly in wet soils. Plant in full sun.

Grevillea robusta
Silk Oak
Evergreen tree. Flowering.
Zones: 8-10. To 50-60 feet.

This fast-growing pyramidal tree serves well where a quick effect is needed or where few other trees will grow because of poor, dry soils and heat. Extremely brittle wood and leaves that drop continuously rule it out in most other situations.

Yellowish-green leaves with silvery undersides are deeply divided and fernlike. Large orangish-yellow comblike flowers are borne in spring, often turning an unattractive black as they dry.

Silk oak is useful as a quick screen or hedge and can be grown indoors as a houseplant.

Sunburst thornless honey locust (Gleditsia triacanthos inermis 'Sunburst')

Noell grevillea (Grevillea 'Noell')

Silk oak (Grevillea robusta)

Silver-bell *(Halesia carolina)* blooms in spring.

Witch hazel *(Hamamelis x intermedia)* is a bold-textured shrub. Feathery flowers bloom in late winter on bare branches.

Hebe *(Hebe elliptica)* forms a neat, dense evergreen hedge, brightened with fragrant blue flowers in spring.

Gymnocladus dioica
Kentucky Coffee Tree,

Zones: 5-8. To 70-90 feet.
Deciduous tree.

Kentucky coffee tree has a narrow crown when young, becoming open, spreading, and rounded as the tree ages. It has a tendency to fork low, developing a short trunk with heavy branches. Huge, doubly compound leaves cast a light filtered shade, permitting grass to grow underneath. Flowers are inconspicuous. Leathery seedpods, borne only on female trees, may be 6 to 10 inches long and the seeds may be used as a coffee substitute—hence the common name Kentucky coffee tree. There will often be 2 or 3 years between heavy flowering, so profuse pods are not formed every year.

In its native growing region the local name, stump tree, is an apt description of the tree when leafless, because its large branches and stubby twigs are prominently shown.

Kentucky coffee tree makes its best growth on rich bottomlands but will grow on a wide range of soils and sites. Once established it tolerates a range of adverse conditions, including excessive heat, cold, and drought. It will not grow in shade.

Kentucky coffee tree is best suited for large open areas such as parks, large lawns, and golf courses. The rugged branching pattern makes it especially effective when used as a skyline tree. Kentucky coffee tree is relatively pest-free.

Halesia carolina
Silver-Bell

Zones: 5-8. To 30-40 feet.
Deciduous tree. Flowering.

Silver-bell is pyramidal in youth, becoming a roundheaded tree or shrub. Petite (1/2-inch), white, bell-shaped flowers hang in graceful clusters in spring as the leaves appear. Oval, finely toothed leaves turn yellow in fall. Plant in rich, moist, well-drained acid soil in sun or partial shade. Use as a lawn

tree or an accent in woodland borders. A similar species, *H. monticola*, grows to 100 feet.

Hamamelis x intermedia
Witch Hazel

Zones: 6-8. To 15-18 feet.
Deciduous shrub. Flowering.

This plant actually represents a group of hybrid witch hazels that are a pure delight in late winter when their bare branches are covered with delicate, wonderfully fragrant, yellow or coppery flowers. They are the showiest blossoms, though not the most fragrant, of the witch hazel family. Leaves are large and rounded, with a bold texture. The variety 'Jelena' has coppery-colored flowers blended with red; fall foliage is orange and red. It has a more spreading habit than the variety 'Magic Fire', which has similar flowers. There are many yellow-flowered varieties.

Plant witch hazels in full sun or partial shade. Should be watered regularly and grown in soil that is rich in organic matter. Use them where their fragrance can be enjoyed, such as in an entryway or near windows. They can also be used as screens or trained into small trees. Flowers are best displayed against a dark background.

Hebe
Hebe

Evergreen shrubs. Flowering.

These evergreen shrubs are popular plants in the mild areas of California and the South. Most are native to New Zealand. They are valued for their neat foliage and their red-to-blue, late-blooming flowers. Closely related to *Veronica*, they are often mislabeled as such.

Hebe grows best in cool climates in full sun, with a moist, but well-drained soil. In warmer climates, plant in partial shade. They are useful in windy coastal conditions. Use in shrub borders, as low hedges, or as specimen plants.

Hebe elliptica
Hebe
Zones: 9-10. To 5-6 feet.
Evergreen shrub. Flowering.

This densely branched shrub has small, 1-inch, green leaves. Fragrant blue flowers are borne in 1- to 2-inch clusters in summer.

Hebe menziesii
Hebe
Zones: 9-10. To 5 feet.
Evergreen shrub. Flowering.

With a more spreading habit than most hebes, this species can be used as a tall ground cover. Has neat, tightly packed, lustrous green foliage and bears white flower clusters in summer.

In addition to the above species, the following hybrids are top-rated: 'Autumn Glory', a tight, mounding plant with a neat habit, to 2-feet high; purplish-blue flowers. 'Coed' has attractive, dark green foliage densely packed on reddish stems, to 3 feet high; bears pinkish-purple flowers. 'Reevesii' has attractive foliage mottled reddish purple and green; purplish-red flowers in summer.

Hedera
Ivy
Evergreen vines.

Historically, ivy is a prominent plant. These vines have been glorified in legends, graced the world's most famed gardens, and inspired artists and poets for centuries.

Ivy exhibits an interesting phenomenon—leaf shape and plant habit can change unpredictably. Ivy changes from its *juvenile state*, the form most often planted, to an *arborescent* or *mature state*. In the mature state, leaves are generally squarish and unlobed on non-clinging, bushy branches. These branches produce inconspicuous flowers and fruits.

The change from juvenile to mature form can occur when an upright, clinging branch grows beyond its support. Pruning prevents mature branches from forming.

Ivy is relatively easy to grow. Once established, vines can be maintained with occasional pruning and pest control programs. A neutral-to-alkaline, well-drained, moist soil is the ideal growing medium. However, a wide range of soil types is tolerated. Space plants 12 to 18 inches apart for use as a ground cover. Ivy makes its fastest, most lush growth if given adequate moisture.

Ivy's tolerance of full sun or the deepest shade contributes to its usefulness in the landscape. Partial shade is needed however in the hot desert to prevent sunburn and in the coldest climates to prevent winterkill of leaves.

Ivy can withstand considerable pruning to direct its growth and control volume. Shear edges 2 to 3 times a year for a neat appearance along walkways and fences. Mowing of ground covers in early spring will reduce the mass and encourage new growth.

Hedera canariensis
Algerian Ivy
Zones: 8-10.
Evergreen vine.

Algerian ivy, used primarily as a vining ground cover, has large, 5- to 7-inch leaves with distinctive red stems. Less drought-tolerant and cold hardy than English ivy. The variety 'Variegata' has leaves edged in white.

Hedera helix
English Ivy
Zones: 5-10.
Evergreen vine.

English ivy is a dependable, hardy, evergreen vine whose use in the landscape is limited only by one's imagination. As an upright vine, the aerial rootlets cling to the sides of buildings, creating a blanket of greenery. The plant's rootlets are tenacious and can pull paint off wood, or chip fragments from bricks when removed. On a fence, the plant can become hedgelike, forming a thick mass of leaves. As a trailing plant it forms a neat, lush ground cover. It grows vigorously by sidewalks or in median

English ivy *(Hedera helix)* is unsurpassed as a lush evergreen ground cover for sunny or shady areas; an easily trained vine to espalier on garden or house walls.

A fast-growing evergreen vine, gold guinea plant *(Hibbertia scandens)* softens posts and fences with its flowers from spring through fall.

Tropical hibiscus *(Hibiscus rosa-sinensis)* is a multipurpose landscape plant with brightly colored summer flowers.

strips, and is easily contained. Branching, rooting stems prevent hillside erosion.

For the more adventurous gardener, English ivy can be manipulated into fanciful shapes. It works well as a topiary form, espaliered into intricate wall patterns, or garlanded over windows and entryways. Indoors and out, English ivy is a handsome plant for hanging baskets and trellis-work.

Typically, English ivy leaves are 2 to 4 inches in length and width with a glossy, leathery green surface. The 5 lobes are wedge-shaped and veins are defined by their pale color. Variations on this theme have been developed by careful selection of desired characteristics. You can find ruffled edges, fans, heart shapes, bird's feet, tricolors, and every type of variegation. Varieties with interesting leaf form and variegation make striking accents.

The following are the most popular varieties of English ivy used in the landscape. They are just a few of the numerous forms that are grown.

'Aureo-variegata' has beautiful yellow-variegated foliage. 'Baltica' is one of the hardiest varieties for Zone 4; has whiter veins and smaller leaves than its parent. 'Bulgaria' is cold hardy in Zone 5 and somewhat drought-tolerant. '238th Street', discovered on this street in New York City, is one of the most cold hardy with heart-shaped leaves; not subject to sunburn. 'Digitata' is a 5- to 7-lobed variety. 'Fluffy Ruffles' has small leaves with wavy margins; good in small spaces. 'Gold Heart' has large yellow center markings on smooth leaves. 'Minima' is a small-leaved, lobed form. 'Conglomerata' is an interesting form with 1-1/2-inch leaves, ranked in two's on upright stems; slow-growing, good for small gardens or containers. 'Irish Laces' long, pointed 'birdsfoot' lobes make it attractive for topiary. 'California Fan' has graceful, broad leaves with short lobes, and is a compact grower. The variety 'Arborescens' is a shrubby type selected from mature branches.

Hibbertia scandens
Gold Guinea Plant
Zone: 11.
Evergreen vine. Flowering.

Gold guinea vine is a luxuriant, twining plant from Australia. It is a handsome vine with clean dense foliage year-round. Slender, reddish-brown stems carry it to 15 feet to form a tall shrubby vine. Left unsupported, the dense branches make a tidy ground cover.

Bright yellow flowers, which account for its name, adorn the plant from late spring to early fall, making it an excellent accent plant. The five-petaled blossoms look like small wild roses and are especially attractive against the glossy dark green leaves. Flowers are lightly scented with a musky odor. Leaves have winged stem attachments and their undersides are covered with fine silky hairs.

Gold guinea plant is a rapid grower. It is an excellent choice for a partly shaded patio, an entryway, or a fence. Its neat form makes it a good choice for small spaces or container growing, but it will need pruning to restrain its growth. It also performs nicely as a ground cover if partly shaded.

Gold guinea plant will thrive if given ample water and protected from hot, reflected sun. Light frost may burn the leaves but damage is only temporary. If exposed to drying winds or dry soil, the plant may be vulnerable to insect infestations. Otherwise it is relatively pest-free.

Prune to reduce top growth in early spring before flowering or in fall after blossoms fade.

Hibiscus
Hibiscus
Deciduous or evergreen shrubs. Flowering.

A large family of plants containing over 200 species of evergreen and deciduous trees, shrubs, and herbs. Two quite different species are top-rated.

Hibiscus rosa-sinensis
Hibiscus, Chinese Hibiscus, Tropical Hibiscus
Zones: 9-10. To 4-15 feet.
Evergreen shrub. Flowering.

Chinese hibiscus are beautiful plants with spectacular, vividly colored, tropical-looking flowers that bloom in summer. In mild climates they are versatile landscape plants. In cold climates, they can be planted in containers and moved to protected areas, or indoors, in winter. They add a tropical touch to patios and porches in summer.

There are many landscape uses for these plants in frost-free climates. They can be used as screen plants, container plants, espaliers, or specimen shrubs and small trees.

Growth habit varies from dense and compact to loose and open. In tropical areas, they can reach 30 feet tall. Glossy, pointed, oval leaves differ in size and texture depending upon the variety. Large flowers, 4 to 8 inches wide, may be single or double with smooth or ruffled petals. Colors range from white to red, and yellow to orange, with many multicolor blends. Many varieties are grown.

Good soil drainage is essential. If your soil does not drain well, plant hibiscus in raised beds or containers. Flowering is best in full sun except in hot inland areas where afternoon shade is preferred. Protect plants from strong winds. Warm temperatures are required for flower production. Water thoroughly and frequently. Fertilize plants monthly from April through August. Container plants need feeding twice a month.

Pinch and remove irregular branches to develop good branch structure on young plants. Remove 1/3 of the old wood on mature plants in early spring to encourage vigorous growth.

Protection from overhanging roofs or evergreen trees helps plants survive light frost. Where the temperature drops below 30°F, grow hibiscus in containers and move to a well-lighted, indoor area for winter.

Hibiscus syriacus
Rose-of-Sharon, Shrub Althaea
Zones: 5-10. To 8-12 feet.
Deciduous shrub. Flowering.

Rose-of-Sharon is a longtime favorite that has been grown for centuries in Europe and the United States. Two valued characteristics are its late summer blooming season and its adaptability to eastern coastal conditions. The shrub has a tall vase-shape suitable for a screen or unpruned hedge, or a specimen or accent plant.

Leaves are green with toothed margins, sometimes lobed. Flowers come in single, semidouble, and double forms, in white and pink, red, and purple shades. They are usually 2 to 4 inches across. Single-type flowers are the largest. Single flowers and some semidouble flowers are followed by unattractive seed pods. Many varieties are grown.

Plant in full sun or partial shade. Likes heat and will take some drought. Grows best with regular watering. Prune to encourage compact shape. Heavy pruning also encourages larger flower size.

Hosta
Hosta
See page 129.

Hydrangea
Hydrangea
Deciduous or evergreen shrubs and vines. Flowering.

This genus includes 23 species of erect or climbing, deciduous or evergreen shrubs native to east Asia, and North and South America. Flowers are borne in clusters and, depending upon the species, may be white, pink, lavender, or blue and appear in mid- or late summer.

A rich, porous, consistently moist, well-drained soil is required. Hydrangeas bloom freely in full sun in cool areas but are best in partial shade, protected from hot afternoon sun. For best flowering, prune to remove old stems, and thin young stems.

Adaptable and widely used as an informal hedge or screen, rose-of-Sharon *(Hibiscus syriacus)* blooms profusely late in summer.

Big-leaf hydrangea *(Hydrangea macrophylla)* produces dramatic blue or pink blossoms in midsummer.

Hills-of-snow *(Hydrangea arborescens)*, an excellent accent shrub, bears balls of cream-white flowers in summer.

Oakleaf hydrangea *(Hydrangea quercifolia)* has showy flowers in late spring. Leaves turn red in autum.

Climbing hydrangea *(Hydrangea anomala)* can cling to any surface; bears showy flower clusters in late spring.

Hydrangea anomala
Climbing Hydrangea
Zones: 5-9.
Deciduous vine. Flowering.

This vine produces dramatic blossoms and grows on a grand scale, covering tall buildings with its bold foliage and sturdy stems. It can cling to any supporting surface with its aerial rootlets and frequently climbs over 50 feet high. Although its growth rate is slow at the start, climbing hydrangea becomes a dense, vigorous grower once established.

This vine is in its full glory by late spring when clusters of showy white blossoms cover the plant with lacy caps. They are prominently displayed, held away from the foliage on stems 1 to 3 feet long. Flower clusters are flat, open, and 6 to 8 inches across.

Large, bright green, lustrous leaves appear in spring. Their heart shape and fine-toothed edges make them particularly handsome.

This decorative vine should be used on large surfaces in scale with the size of its flowers and leaves. Place it against big expanses of masonry walls, on a tall chimney, or as a climber in a large tree. Climbing hydrangea is best supported on an indestructible surface because rootlets can damage wood structures. If unsupported, the vine becomes a rambling creeping shrub.

Prune climbing hydrangea to maintain its symmetry and reduce mass. Heavy pruning in winter or early spring will restrain its robust nature.

Hydrangea arborescens
Smooth Hydrangea, Hills-of-Snow
Zones: 5-9. To 3-5 feet.
Deciduous shrub. Flowering.

Native to the eastern United States, this species forms a rounded bush and has balls of cream-white flowers in midsummer. Weak stems are often weighed to the ground by the heavy flower heads. The cultivar 'Annabelle' has huge, 10-inch, snow-white flower heads.

'Grandiflora', a common cultivar, is known as hills-of-snow; blooms heavily for several months beginning in early summer.

Hydrangea macrophylla
Big-Leaf Hydrangea
Zones: 6-10. To 6-10 feet.
Deciduous shrub. Flowering.

This large rounded shrub has bold-textured shiny leaves with toothed edges. Large ball-like flower clusters bloom in mid- and late summer. Soil pH influences flower color. Acid soils produce blue flowers; pink or red blooms result from alkaline soils. If you desire pink flowers, add garden lime to the soil. If blue flowers are desired, add a tablespoon of aluminum sulfate.

A long list of varieties are available, many of which were developed for greenhouse forcing. 'Tricolor' has foliage variegated with light green and creamy-white.

Hydrangea paniculata
Panicle Hydrangea, Peegee Hydrangea
Zones: 5-9. To 20 feet.
Deciduous or evergreen shrub or tree. Flowering.

This large shrub or small tree can be used as a specimen or hedge plant. It spreads as wide as it is tall. The cultivar 'Grandiflora', the peegee hydrangea, is usually grown. It is a vigorous plant valued for its long-lasting, large, pyramidal clusters of white flowers, which fade to rosy-brown. Blooms after hills-of-snow and big-leaf hydrangea.

Hydrangea quercifolia
Oakleaf Hydrangea
Zones: 6-9. To 6 feet.
Deciduous shrub. Flowering.

This species has large, attractive lobed leaves to 8 inches long, resembling those of an oak. They turn bronzy-red in fall. Large, cone-shaped clusters of white flowers are showy in late spring. Can be pruned heavily each year to maintain a lower height. Takes a bit more sun than other hydrangeas.

Hosta
Hosta, Funkia, Plantain Lily

Herbaceous ground covers.
Flowering.

Many species and varieties of this large genus of the lily family are garden favorites. They are pretty planted in groups in a flower bed, as an edging, or a ground cover naturalized in shady areas where they form lush bold-textured foliage. Hostas are also distinctive container plants for shaded patios, porches, and balconies.

Hostas grow as clumps of leathery leaves that can be many shapes and sizes and many shades of green, including white- and gold-variegated forms. Spikes of purple, lavender, or white flowers appear in late summer or early fall although hostas are grown primarily for their foliage.

Grows best in rich, moist soil in light, partial, or full shade, though poor soil is tolerated. Space 1 to 2 feet apart depending upon mature size. Divide crowded clumps in spring. Clip off faded flower stalks. Slugs and snails can damage foliage in some regions. Regular watering and fertilizing produces best plants. An organic mulch such as peat moss or compost adds a clean, finished look to new plantings.

Blue-leafed plantain lily *(Hosta sieboldiana)* contrasts with fine-textured plants.

Above left: Blunt plantain lily *(Hosta decorata)* is brightly variegated. Above right: Fragrant plantain lily *(Hosta plantaginea)* is noted for flowers and foliage.

Hosta

Botanical Name/ Common Name	Zones	Flower Description	Plant Description	Comments
Hosta decorata (H. 'Thomas Hogg') Blunt Plantain Lily	6-9	Purple flowers in profusion from mid to late summer.	Neat 2 ft mounds. Oval, slightly blunt leaves are 6 in. long, rich green edged white.	Often labeled 'Thomas Hogg'.
H.d. 'Honeybells'	6-9	Lavender-lilac streaked with blue on 3-1/2 ft spikes. Fragrant.	Same as species.	Showiest flowers of any hosta; smell like gardenia.
H. lancifolia (H. japonica) Narrow-leafed Plantain Lily	3-9	Pale lavender blooms on 2-ft stalks in late summer.	6-in. high clumps of slender, waxy, dark green leaves.	Variegated forms are sometimes available.
H. plantaginea (H. subcordata) Fragrant Plantain Lily	4-9	Fragrant white flowers on 2-ft stems, late summer or fall.	1 to 1-1/2 ft high and twice as wide with rounded bright green leaves.	
H. sieboldiana Blue-leafed Plantain Lily	3-9	White flowers in midsummer are nearly hidden by the leaves.	15-in. high and twice as wide. Bold, heavily ribbed, bluish-green leaves.	Most dramatic foliage of all hostas.
H. undulata (H. lancifolia) Wavy-leafed Plantain Lily	3-9	Pale lavender blooms on 18-in. stems in midsummer.	6-8 in. tall leaves are green with silvery white variegation and wavy margins. Fast-spreading.	One of the most popular hostas. Tolerates more sun than other species.

Hidcote hypericum (*Hypericum* 'Hidcote') forms a low shrub brightened with yellow flowers all summer.

Burford holly (*Ilex cornuta* 'Burfordii') makes an elegant evergreen specimen tree; also used as a privacy hedge.

Hymenosporum flavum

Sweetshade

Zones: 9-10. To 20-40 feet.
Evergreen tree. Flowering.

This slender, open-growing small tree from Australia makes an excellent accent plant in sun or light shade. Shiny dark green leaves are 2 to 6 inches long and 1 to 2 inches wide. Golden-yellow flowers smell like orange blossoms and open April to September. Ideal planting sites are well-drained and not subject to coastal winds.

Hypericum

St. John's-Wort

Evergreen or semievergreen shrubs. Flowering.

This large genus is comprised primarily of herbaceous perennials. Two forms are top-rated shrubs.

Hypericum calycinum

**Aaron's-Beard,
Creeping St. John's-Wort**

Zones: 5-10. To 12 inches.
Evergreen or semideciduous shrub. Flowering.

This low, spreading plant is valued as a tenacious ground cover for sun or shade. Green leaves are 4 inches long. Bright yellow flowers measure 3 inches across and are borne throughout the summer. Aaron's-beard will form a dense ground cover in the toughest situations. It spreads by underground stems and is so vigorous it often grows into areas where it is not wanted, unless it is contained.

Space plants 12 to 18 inches apart for a quick cover. Mow to the ground every second or third winter to keep its growth lush.

Hypericum 'Hidcote'

Hidcote Hypericum

Zones: 5-10. To 4 feet.
Evergreen shrub. Flowering.

This shrubby hypericum is useful as a hedge or for massed plantings. Has an arching shape. It is semideciduous in cold winter areas, and may be partially killed to the ground in northern extremes of its growing region, remaining about 2 feet high. Leaves have a blue-green tint. Yellow flowers, 3 inches across, are borne throughout the summer.

Ilex

Holly

Zones: 3-10. To 45 feet.
Evergreen and deciduous shrubs or trees.

Versatile, choice landscape plants, hollies are available in a variety of leaf shapes, textures, and growth habits. Though the common image of a holly is a large plant with shiny thorny leaves and red berries in the winter, there are also small hollies with spineless leaves, and hollies with yellow, orange, or black berries. Hollies can be used as single specimens in foundation and border plantings or as screens or hedges. Dwarf forms make good tall ground covers or container plants.

Most holly plants are either male or female and usually both sexes must be planted near each other for berries to set on female plants. A few exceptional varieties set berries without pollenization but most of these berries are small and don't last long. One male plant, with cooperation from bees, can ensure berries on up to 30 female plants of the same species.

Hollies are generally easy plants to grow if provided with moist, well-drained soil and full sun. Some species prefer soil slightly on the acid side. Deciduous hollies are most tolerant of harsh conditions. In cold winter areas make sure plants have sufficient moisture before the soil freezes. This will minimize the chance of winter damage. Protection from strong winter winds and direct sun also helps. Many hollies are harmed by cultivation around their roots. Use a mulch for weed control.

Most hollies do not do well in hot, dry desert climates. However there are two exceptions: Burford holly, *Ilex cornuta* 'Burfordii', and yaupon, *Ilex vomitoria*. Each will perform satisfactorily if grown in partial shade and protected from strong winds. Strongly alkaline soils may cause chlorosis.

Christmas holly (*Ilex aquifolium*) has gleaming red berries.

Smallest leaves are *Ilex crenata* 'Convexa'; medium-sized are *I. crenata* 'Rotundifolia'; largest are *I. cornuta* 'Rotunda'.

Foliage of *Ilex* 'Nellie R. Stevens' has few spines.

Ilex

Botanical Name/Common Name	Zones	Size	Plant Description	Comments
Ilex x altaclarensis 'Wilsonii' Wilson Holly	6-10	To 6-8 ft tall as shrub. To 45 ft tall as tree.	Evergreen shrub or tree. Attractive glossy green spiny foliage. Abundant bright red berries.	Excellent for warm climates. Use for clipped hedge, screen, windbreak, espalier, specimen.
I. aquifolium Christmas Holly, English Holly	6-9	To 35-40 ft tall.	Evergreen tree. Slow-growing with spiny green foliage. Numerous bright red berries.	Needs protection in hot, dry areas. Control height by shearing. Resists oak-root fungus; subject to leaf miners.
I. a. 'Argenteo-marginata' Silver-Variegated English Holly	6-9	To 35-40 ft tall.	Evergreen tree of vigorous habit. Leaves edged silvery-white. Bright red berries.	Excellent accent plant.
I. a. 'Balkans'	6-9	To 35-40 ft tall.	Evergreen tree. Slow-growing with smooth, dark green leaves. Deep red berries on female plants.	Hardiest of English hollies.
I. a. 'Boulder Creek'	6-9	To 35-40 ft tall.	Evergreen tree. Slow-growing with large, glossy black-green leaves. Brilliant red berries.	
I. a. 'Sadies Delux' Green English Holly	6-9	To 35-40 ft tall.	Evergreen tree. Slow-growing with bright green leaves. Brilliant red berries.	Sets fruit early.
I. a. 'Silver Queen' Silver Queen English Holly	6-9	To 35-40 ft tall.	Evergreen tree. Leaves have silvery edges. Red berries.	Good accent plant.
I. a. 'Variegata' Variegated English Holly	6-9	To 35-40 ft tall.	Evergreen tree of vigorous habit. Dark green leaves with creamy margins.	Good accent plant.
I. x aquipernyi 'San Jose' San Jose Holly	6-9	To 10-14 ft tall.	Evergreen shrub or tree with compact, pyramidal shape. Deep bluish-green leaves. Bright red berries.	
I. x a. 'Brilliant'	6-9	To 10 or more ft tall.	Evergreen shrub with dense conical habit. Generally thornless. Heavy producer or bright red berries, without male pollinator.	Resists oak-root fungus.
I. cornuta Chinese Holly	6-10	To 2-10 ft tall. Spreads 5-7 ft.	Evergreen shrub with rounded, upright form. Medium green glossy leaves with 4-5 spines. Large, bright red berries; varying amounts set without male pollinator.	Use as hedge or in mass plantings. Protect from sun in desert regions.
I. c. 'Berries Jubilee' Berries Jubilee Chinese Holly	6-10	To 2-3 ft tall. Spreads 3-4 ft.	Evergreen shrub with dwarf, compact, mounding habit. Leaves larger, spinier than *I.c.* 'Burfordii'. Superb display of large cardinal-red berries.	Good dwarf selection for container growing.
I. c. 'Burfordii' Burford Holly	6-10	To 10-14 ft tall. Spreads 6-8 ft.	Evergreen shrub or tree. Large, dense, globe habit. Dark green leaves with single spine at tip. Fruits heavily. Self-fruitful.	Good for hedge, espalier, specimen, or multistem small tree. Tolerates salt spray.
I. c. 'Carissa' Carissa Chinese Holly	6-10	To 2 ft tall. Spreads to 3 ft.	Evergreen shrub with dense spreading dwarf mounding form. Leaves smaller than *I.c.* 'Rotunda'.	Good as low hedge or in containers.
I. c. 'Dazzler'	6-10	To 8-12 ft tall.	Evergreen shrub with upright, compact habit. Dazzling display of large, bright red berries.	One of the heaviest fruiting Chinese hollies.
I. c. 'Emily Bruner' Emily Bruner Chinese Holly	6-10	To 6-20 ft tall.	Evergreen shrub or tree of vigorous habit. Bright red berries.	
I. c. 'Rotunda' Dwarf Chinese Holly	6-10	To 2-3 ft tall. Spreads 3-4 ft.	Evergreen shrub with low, mounded form. Attractive, glossy, spiny, green foliage. No fruit.	Has formal compact habit. Makes good hedge, foundation.
I. c. 'Willowleaf' Willowleaf Chinese Holly	6-10	To 8-12 ft tall.	Evergreen shrub or tree. Dense, spreading. Long narrow, spiny dark green leaves. Dark red berries.	Unique, narrow-foliage form.
I. crenata 'Buxifolia' Box Leaf Japanese Holly	6-10	To 6-8 ft tall.	Evergreen shrub forms compact pyramid. Small, dark green leaves resemble boxwood.	Good upright Japanese holly. Keeps form with light shearing.
I. c. 'Compacta' Compact Japanese Holly	6-10	To 3-5 ft tall.	Evergreen shrub with dense-branching, compact habit. Glossy, green foliage.	Tolerates city pollution. Good as hedge or very small tree.
I. c. 'Convexa' Convexa Japanese Holly	6-10	To 4-6 ft tall. Spreads 3-5 ft.	Evergreen shrub with rounded, dense shape. Very glossy leaves, small, cupped downward. Small black berries.	Can maintain compactness with light shearing. Possible substitute for boxwood.

Dwarf Chinese holly (Ilex cornuta 'Rotunda')

Foster's American holly (Ilex opaca 'Foster No. 2') has glossier leaves than the species.

Winterberry (Ilex verticillata) is a deciduous holly.

Ilex (continued)

Botanical Name/Common Name	Zones	Size	Plant Description	Comments
I. c. 'Green Island' Green Island Japanese Holly	6-10	To 2 ft tall.	Evergreen shrub with low-spreading habit. Dense branching. Small green leaves.	Excellent low-growing holly.
I. c. 'Green Luster' Green Luster Japanese Holly	5-10	To 4-6 ft tall.	Evergreen shrub with broad, spreading oval habit. Shiny small green leaves. Small black berries.	Hardier than other Japanese hollies. Use for hedging.
I. c. 'Helleri' Heller's Japanese Holly	6-10	To 2-4 ft tall. Spreads to 2 ft.	Evergreen shrub with dwarf mounding, low-spreading form. Small, dark green leaves.	Most popular dwarf Japanese holly. Perfect for low border, containers.
I. c. 'Hetzii' Hetz Japanese Holly	5-10	To 3-6 ft tall.	Evergreen shrub forms rounded mound. Vigorous. Similar to I.c. 'Convexa'.	Hardier than most Japanese hollies.
I. c. 'Microphylla' Little Leaf Japanese Holly	6-10	To 4-6 ft tall.	Evergreen shrub with upright habit. Small leaves.	Good upright Japanese holly. Can be trained as small tree.
I. c. 'Rotundifolia' Round Leaf Japanese Holly	6-10	To 6-8 ft tall.	Evergreen shrub with upright, rounded habit. Glossy, dark green foliage.	Tolerant of city pollution. Takes little care once established.
I. glabra Inkberry, Gallberry, Winterberry	3-8	To 6-8 ft tall.	Evergreen shrub of loose, upright habit. Light green leaves, 1-2 in. long. Small black berries.	Most hardy evergreen holly. I. g. 'Compacta' is 3-5 ft tall.
I. x meserveae 'Blue Angel'	5-8	To 6 ft tall. Spreads to 4 ft.	Evergreen shrub. Slow-growing, compact upright. Glossy, blue-green foliage has crinkled look. Turns deep blue in winter.	Grown for abundant scarlet berries.
I. x m. 'Blue Stallion'	5-8	To 12-15 ft tall. Spreads to 8 ft.	Evergreen shrub of vigorous habit. Pyramidal. Leaves not very spiny.	Use in high-traffic areas. Good pollinator.
I. x m. 'China Girl'	5-8	To 8 ft tall with equal spread.	Similar to I. x m. 'China Boy'. Heavy berry crop.	Takes shearing. One of the best berry sets of any holly. 'China Boy' is very similar and is the pollinator.
I. x 'Nellie R. Stevens' Nellie R. Stevens Holly	7-8	To 10-15 ft tall.	Evergreen shrub with pyramidal form can be trained as a tree. Shiny dark green foliage. Heavy berry set.	Hybrid of English and Chinese hollies.
I. opaca American Holly	6-9	To 15-50 ft tall. Spreads 10-20 ft.	Evergreen tree of pyramidal to conical habit. Horizontal branching. Spiny, dark green foliage. Shallow-rooted. Good berry crop although not as heavy as English holly.	Good for topiary, as specimen, screen, or tall hedge. Needs male planted within 90 ft. Susceptible to leaf miner.
I. o. 'Foster No. 2' (I. x attenuata) Foster's American Holly	6-9	To 30-50 ft tall.	Evergreen tree with pyramidal form. Slow-growing. Spiny, glossy green leaves. Bright red berries.	
I. o. 'Greenlace' Greenlace American Holly	6-9	To 45 ft tall.	Evergreen tree of open branching habit. Leathery, hard foliage.	
I. o. 'Jersey Knight' Male American Holly	6-9	To 30-50 ft tall.	Evergreen tree with pyramidal form. Rich green foliage.	Excellent pollinator.
I. o. 'Savannah'	7-9	To 30-50 ft tall.	Evergreen tree of upright, compact pyramidal habit. Produces many dark red berries.	
I. o. 'Wyetta'	6-9	To 30-50 ft tall.	Evergreen tree forms dense pyramid. Superior, shiny, heavily spined, dark green foliage displays large crop of large red berries to best advantage.	
I. verticillata Winterberry	3-7	To 9-10 ft tall.	Deciduous shrub. Bears profuse bright scarlet berries that hold into winter. Leaves lack spines.	Berries of I.v. 'Christmas Cheer' are even more persistent.
I. vomitoria Yaupon Holly	7-10	To 15-20 ft tall. Spreads to 6-12 ft.	Evergreen shrub or tree of upright, irregular habit. Small, narrow, gray-green leaves. Small, translucent red berries set without pollination.	Very versatile. Adapts to adverse conditions including alkaline soils.
I. v. 'Nana' Dwarf Yaupon Holly	7-10	To 18 in. high. Spreads to 3 ft.	Evergreen shrub. Dwarf, compact, dense. Fine gray-green foliage.	Excellent low border, specimen, or accent plant. Tolerates drought once established.

Jacaranda *(Jacaranda mimosifolia)* makes a graceful street tree, blooming in spring or summer.

In warm climates, angel-wing jasmine *(Jasminum polyanthum)* makes an easy-to-care-for ground cover or climbing vine.

Jacaranda mimosifolia

Jacaranda

Zones: 9-10. To 25-40 feet.
Deciduous to semievergreen tree.
Flowering.

This spectacular tree from Argentina and Brazil is grown in subtropical areas for its fernlike foliage·and large blue flowers.

Jacaranda is open growing with a shape varying from upright with a thick trunk, to irregular with several trunks. Width of the tree is 2/3 to 3/4 its height. The fernlike leaves, up to 18 inches long, are finely divided, each having 18 to 48 oblong leaflets 1/4 to 1/3 inch long. Jacaranda's leaves fall in February to March and new leaves may develop quickly, or the tree may stay bare until flowering time.

Flowering is usually in spring, but can be anytime between April and September. The slightly fragrant, showy blue flowers are arranged in 8-inch-tall, loose clusters of 40 to 90 tubular flowers, each 2 inches long and 1-1/2 inches wide. Woody, oval seed capsules, 1 to 2 inches across and 3/8 inch thick, are decorative in arrangements.

Young plants are damaged below 25°F but often grow back after freezing, forming multistemmed plants. Jacarandas grow best in acid, sandy soils, but will grow in other soils. Regular irrigation is necessary to maintain balanced growth. Jacaranda does not flower well when exposed to cool ocean breezes and is best planted in warmer areas sheltered from strong winds.

When viewed from above, as from a hillside house or a high deck, jacaranda is at its most spectacular, but is also very attractive viewed from ground level. As street trees, jacarandas should be planted 40 feet apart. Staking and pruning may be necessary to develop the desired form for this use.

Jasminum

Jasmine

Evergreen vines. Flowering.

True jasmines are unmistakeable when the sweet fragrance of their blooms fills the air. They have a graceful, neat habit with leathery green leaves. The evergreen foliage makes a fine backdrop for the plentiful and long-lasting flowers.

Jasmines are versatile landscape plants in warm climates; elsewhere grow them in a greenhouse. Support the twining stems by providing something secure for them to wrap around such as a post or a fence, or drape them over an entryway. Both species grow well as luxuriant ground covers in part shade or full sun. They grow best in moist, well-drained soil and are easy to care for and relatively pest-free.

Jasminum nitidum
Angel-Wing Jasmine
Zone: 10.
Evergreen vine. Flowering.

Angel-wing jasmine blooms in late spring and summer in the southern states and California. It flowers most abundantly where temperatures remain warm throughout its long growing period. Desert climates are ideal. The vine is considered semideciduous where temperatures drop below 32°F, but roots will survive at temperatures to 25°F.

When in bloom this jasmine is covered with highly fragrant blossoms that look like pinwheels. Flowers are white above and purple on the underside, measure 1 to 1-1/2 inches long, and are held in clusters of 3 on slender stalks. Leathery-textured foliage is an attractive background for the abundant flowers. The leaves are distinguished by their somewhat glossy surface and 3-inch-long, oval shape.

Angel-wing jasmine grows at a moderate rate to 10 to 20 feet. Unsupported, the plant forms a shrubby ground cover.

Jasminum polyanthum
Chinese Jasmine
Zones: 8-10.
Evergreen vine. Flowering.

Chinese jasmine is a vigorously growing vine reaching 20 feet. The plant is characterized by its finely divided leaves with 5 to 7 lance-shaped leaflets, which have a delicate, fine-textured appearance. Starlike blossoms will scent the garden for several months. In warm areas flowering begins in February and extends into summer. Flowers are white with rose-pink on the outside. They are held in dense clusters on side branches.

Juniperus
Juniper

Zones: 2-10. To 5 inches - 45 feet. Evergreen shrubs, trees, and ground covers.

Junipers form a large genus of evergreen trees or shrubs containing about 70 species. They produce two kinds of foliage—juvenile and adult. Young plants form sharp, short needlelike leaves that clasp the stems. As the plant matures, its new growth produces scalelike foliage that hugs the twigs. Juvenile foliage may continue to be formed on some plants for years. Other forms never produce adult foliage. The color of juniper foliage varies greatly, ranging from all shades of green through blue and gray and even yellow. Some needles have white undersides.

Junipers can be found for most landscape situations. There are prostrate forms that hug the ground at a height of less than 12 inches but spread up to 10 feet. They are perfect for ground covers and edgings. Others are shrubs that fit into foundation plantings, shrub borders, group plantings, and low hedges. Some species grow into sizable trees useful as specimen plants, screens, or tall hedges. The great diversity of foliage color and texture among junipers also adds to their landscape versatility.

Junipers may be pruned lightly to keep their shape symmetrical or sheared heavily for formal hedges or topiary. Many varieties have interesting, contorted branching habits that lend themselves beautifully to the ancient art of bonsai.

Junipers will grow almost anywhere in the United States. They grow in acid or alkaline soils and tolerate hot, dry climates. Best growth is made on dry, sandy, or gravelly soils. Sites must be well drained. A sunny location is best, though in hot areas light shade is acceptable. Plants growing in dense shade or on poorly drained sites are subject to root rot.

Juniper blight, frequently a problem in eastern states, is characterized by browning of branch tips. It is encouraged by moist conditions common when plants are watered by overhead sprinklers. Cedar-apple rust, a gall-producing disease that infects junipers and apples, is troublesome on junipers in some areas. Disease-resistant varieties are noted in the chart.

Juniperus

Botanical Name/Common Name	Zones	Size	Plant Description	Comments
COLUMNAR TREE FORMS				
***Juniperus chinensis* 'Blue Point'** Tear-Drop Juniper	4-9	To 8 ft tall.	Dense, formal pyramid. Blue-green foliage. Tolerates heat and poor soil.	Needs little or no shearing.
J. c. 'Hetzii Columnaris' (J.c. 'Fairview') Green Columnar Juniper	4-9	To 12-15 ft tall.	Rapid-growing. Pointed pyramid. Bright green foliage.	
J. c. 'Keteleeri' Keteleer Juniper	5-9	To 10-20 ft tall.	Vigorous, broad pyramid. Bright green foliage. Ascending branches.	
J. c. 'Robust Green' Robust Green Juniper	5-9	To 20 ft tall.	Informal pyramid. Unique tufted branching gives a rugged, informal appearance. Intense green foliage. Slow-growing.	Good in small landscapes.
J. c. 'Spartan' Spartan Juniper	5-9	To 15-20 ft tall.	Dense, compact, formal habit. Rich green foliage. Rapid-growing.	Good for hedges or screens.
J. c. 'Wintergreen' Wintergreen Juniper	5-9	To 20 ft tall.	Dense-branching with formal pyramidal shape. Deep green foliage.	
J. excelsa 'Stricta' Chinese Blue Column Juniper	4-9	To 12-15 ft tall.	Narrow pyramid. Sharp-pointed blue-green foliage.	
J. scopulorum 'Blue Heaven' Blue Heaven Juniper	3-9	To 20 ft tall.	Neat pyramidal form. Striking blue foliage.	Fine accent plant.
J. s. 'Cologreen' Cologreen Juniper	3-9	To 20 ft tall.	Compact pyramidal form. Bright green foliage.	
J. s. 'Cupressifolia Erecta'	3-9	To 25 ft tall.	Good, tall dense pyramid. Rich green foliage with silvery-blue undertones.	
J. s. 'Gray Gleam' Gray Gleam Juniper	3-9	To 10-20 ft tall.	Slow-growing. Very dense, columnar. Bright blue-gray foliage.	Excellent foliage color.
J. s. 'Moffetii' Moffet Juniper	4-9	To 20 ft tall.	Very dense pyramidal form. Blue-green foliage.	Excellent accent plant.
J. s. 'Pathfinder' Pathfinder Juniper	4-9	To 20 ft tall.	Rapid-growing. Broad column with age. Showy blue-green foliage.	Good in dry areas.
J. s. 'Sutherland' Sutherland Juniper	4-9	To 20 ft tall.	Broad pyramidal habit. Silver-green foliage.	Best form when lightly sheared.
J. s. 'Welchii' Welch Juniper	3-9	To 20 ft tall.	Narrow pyramid. Young foliage silvery-green. Mature foliage turns brighter green.	
J. s. 'Wichita Blue' Wichita Blue Juniper	4-9	To 20 ft tall.	Broad, full pyramid. Superb bright blue foliage holds color all year long.	
J. virginiana 'Burkii' Burk Eastern Red Cedar	3-9	To 10-20 ft tall.	Dense, narrow pyramid. Steel-blue foliage, has purplish cast in winter.	One of the bluest junipers.

Eastern red cedar (*Juniperus virginiana*) is an American native tree.

This columnar-shaped Rocky Mountain juniper (*Juniperus scopulorum*) adds vertical interest to foundation plantings.

Hollywood juniper (*Juniperus chinensis* 'Torulosa') is an eye-catching accent tree.

Botanical Name/Common Name	Zones	Size	Plant Description	Comments
J. v. 'Canaertii' Canaert Upright Juniper	3-9	To 20 ft tall.	Compact dense pyramid. Dark green foliage is tufted at branch ends.	Resistant to cedar apple rust. Produces abundance of blue berrylike cones.
J. v. 'Cupressifolia' (J.v. 'Hillspire') Hillspire Juniper	3-9	To 20 ft tall.	Formal, loosely branched pyramid. Dark green foliage.	
J. v. 'Manhattan Blue' Manhattan Blue Juniper	3-9	To 10-15 ft tall.	Compact pyramid. Bluish-green foliage.	Excellent accent plant.
J. v. 'Skyrocket' Skyrocket Juniper	3-9	To 10-20 ft tall.	One of the narrowest uprights. Rapid-growing. Tight branches with silvery-blue foliage.	Good accent for small space.

TREES

Botanical Name/Common Name	Zones	Size	Plant Description	Comments
Juniperus chinensis 'Torulosa' (J.c. 'Kaizuka') Hollywood Juniper	6-10	To 15 ft tall.	Large shrub or small tree with upright twisted branching. Rich green foliage. Irregular growth habit striking and unusual.	Excellent large accent plant. Can be espaliered.
J. scopulorum Rocky Mountain Juniper	4-10	To 35-50 ft tall.	Narrow pyramidal form. Reddish-brown bark. Blue-gray foliage.	Best tree juniper for hot, dry areas. Good screen or windbreak.
J. virginiana Eastern Red Cedar	3-10	To 40-45 ft tall. (To 90 ft where native.)	Pyramidal form. Slow-growing. Bright green foliage turns pinkish in cold winter climates.	Tolerates any condition except hot dry winds. Good windbreak or screen. Susceptible to apple cedar rust.

GROUND COVERS

Botanical Name/Common Name	Zones	Size	Plant Description	Comments
Juniperus chinensis 'San Jose' San Jose Creeping Juniper	4-9	To 1-2 ft tall. Spreads 6 ft or more.	Compact with irregular, husky branches.	Good in tub, trained as bonsai, or as ground cover.
J. c. sargentii Sargent Juniper	4-9	To 2-1/2 ft tall. Spreads 7-12 ft.	Creeping juniper. Moderately fast-growing. Holds green color in winter.	Resistant to juniper blight. Good for rock gardens, bonsai, or espalier.
J. c. sargentii 'Glauca' Blue Sargent Juniper	4-9	To 2-1/2 ft tall. Spreads 7-12 ft.	Attractive blue-green foliage.	Excellent ground cover.
J. c. sargentii 'Viridis' Green Sargent Juniper	4-9	To 2-1/2 ft tall. Spreads 7-12 ft.	Bright, light green foliage.	
J. c. 'Sea Spray' Sea Spray Juniper	4-9	To 12-15 in. high. Spreads 6-7 ft.	Dense with soft texture. Moderately fast-growing. Blue-green foliage.	Well adapted to hot and dry climates. Dense ground cover.
J. conferta Shore Juniper	6-9	To 1-2 ft tall. Spreads 8-10 ft.	Handsome weeping variety. Bluish-green foliage. Thrives in poor sandy soil and seaside conditions.	*J.c.* 'Emerald Sea' has bluer foliage; *J.c.* 'Blue Pacific' is bluer and more heat-tolerant.
J. horizontalis 'Bar Harbor' Bar Harbor Juniper	3-10	To 1 ft high. Spreads to 10 ft.	Silvery-blue foliage turns deep plum color in winter.	Fine ground cover, good on slopes, in rock gardens.

Gold coast juniper *(Juniperus chinensis aurea* 'Gold Coast') is a slow-growing, ground-hugging plant.

Shore juniper *(Juniperus conferta)* spreads rapidly.

Juniperus (continued)

Botanical Name/Common Name	Zones	Size	Plant Description	Comments
J. h. 'Blue Chip' Blue Chip Juniper	4-10	To 1 ft high. Spreads to 5 ft.	Low-mounding form. Silvery-blue foliage.	Superior ground cover. *J.h.* 'Blue Horizon' has same characteristics.
J. h. 'Emerald Spreader' Emerald Spreader Juniper	4-10	To 6-12 in. high. Spreads to 6 ft.	Very low-growing with feathery, emerald-green foliage.	Does not mound like other varieties
J. h. 'Hughes' Hughes Juniper	4-10	To 2-3 ft tall. Spreads 6-8 ft.	Graceful, low variety. Bluish-green foliage with silvery-blue new growth.	Use as an accent plant.
J. h. 'Plumosa Compacta' Compact Andorra Juniper	2-10	To 1-2 ft tall. Spreads to 10 ft.	Upright, plumelike branches. Grayish-green foliage turns unique plum color in winter.	Can be espaliered. *J. h.* 'Youngstown' is denser.
J. h. 'Prince of Wales' Prince of Wales Juniper	3-10	To 8 in. high. Spreads 8-10 ft.	Forms dense, plush carpet. Bright green foliage has tinge of purple in winter.	Cascades over walls or ledges. Beautiful ground cover.
J. h. 'Turquoise Spreader' Turquoise Spreading Juniper	4-10	To 6-12 in. high. Spreads 6 ft.	Similar to 'Emerald Spreader' with denser foliage having bluish cast.	
J. h. 'Webberi' Webber Juniper	4-10	To 1 ft high. Spreads 6-8 ft.	Dense, compact. Center does not thin. Bluish-green foliage with purplish cast in fall.	
J. h. 'Wiltonii' Blue Rug Juniper, Wilton Carpet Juniper	4-10	To 5 in. high. Spreads to 10 ft.	Excellent dense habit. Foliage is intense silver-blue, forming an attractive carpet of blue.	One of the most popular ground cover varieties.
J. h. 'Yukon Belle' Yukon Belle Juniper	2-10	To 6 in. high. Spreads to 10 ft.	Bright silvery-blue foliage.	Best ground cover choice in cold climates.
J. procumbens 'Nana' *(J. chinensis procumbens* 'Nana') Dwarf Japanese Garden Juniper	4-10	To 1 ft high. Spreads 4-5 ft.	Dense, low-spreader. Lush blue-green foliage.	One of the best juniper ground covers. Use in bonsai.
J. p. 'Variegata' Variegated Japanese Garden Juniper	6-10	To 2-3 ft tall. Spreads 8-10 ft.	Handsome gray-green foliage accented with patches of creamy-white.	
J. sabina 'Arcadia' Arcadia Juniper	3-9	To 18 in. high. Spreads to 4 ft.	Bright green, lacy foliage.	Resistant to juniper blight. Fine mass border, accent, or foundation plant.
J. s. 'Blue Danube' Blue Danube Juniper	3-9	To 1-1/2 ft high. Spreads 5-10 ft.	Slightly erect branches with handsome blue-green foliage.	
J. s. 'Broadmoor' Broadmoor Juniper	3-9	To 1 ft high. Spreads to 4 ft.	Attractive dense, low-mounding habit. Unusual green foliage.	Resistant to juniper blight. Adapts well to coastal climates.
J. s. 'Buffalo'	3-9	To 1 ft high. Spreads to 8 ft.	Lower-growing than tam juniper. Feathery, soft branches with bright green foliage.	Resistant to juniper blight. Very hardy.
J. s. 'Scandia' Scandia Juniper	3-9	To 12-18 in. high. Spreads to 8 ft.	Graceful variety with wide spread. Rich, dark green foliage.	Resistant to juniper blight.
J. s. 'Tamariscifolia' Tam Juniper	3-9	To 2 ft tall. Spreads 10-20 ft.	Dense-branching. Tends to mound. Bright green foliage.	Susceptible to juniper blight. Popular as ground cover or bank cover.
J. s. 'Tamariscifolia No Blight' No-Blight Tam Juniper	3-9	To 2 ft tall. Spreads 10-20 ft.	Exceptionally hardy. Blue-green foliage.	Disease-resistant.
J. virginiana 'Silver Spreader' Silver Spreader Juniper	4-9	To 18 in. high. Spreads 6-8 ft.	Silvery-blue foliage.	Good choice for colorful ground cover.

SHRUBS

Botanical Name/Common Name	Zones	Size	Plant Description	Comments
Juniperus chinensis 'Armstrongii' Armstrong Juniper	4-9	To 4 ft tall with equal spread.	Handsome, medium-sized conifer with soft, gray-green foliage. Has bird's-nest-like growth habit.	Available in globe form.
J. c. 'Blaauw' Blaauw Juniper	4-9	To 4 ft tall. Spreads to 3 ft.	Dense, vase-shaped shrub. Rich blue-green foliage.	Good for small sites.
J. c. 'Blue Vase' Texas Star Juniper	4-9	To 4 ft tall with equal spread.	Dense, upright spreading. Steel-blue foliage.	Good border plant. Takes shearing.

Bar harbor juniper (*Juniperus horizontalis* 'Bar Harbor') hugs the ground, making a good edging.

Golden pfitzer juniper (*Juniperus chinensis* 'Pfitzerana Aurea'), shown left, Pfitzer juniper (*Juniperus chinensis* 'Pfitzerana'), shown right.

Emerald spreader juniper (*Juniperus horizontalis* 'Emerald Spreader') grows low; does not mound.

Botanical Name/Common Name	Zones	Size	Plant Description	Comments
J. c. 'Fruitlandii' Fruitland Juniper	4-9	To 3 ft tall. Spreads to 6 ft.	Vigorous. Compact, dense bright green foliage.	Improved selection of *J.c.* 'Pfitzerana Compacta'.
J. c. 'Gold Coast' Gold Coast Juniper	4-9	To 4 ft tall with equal spread.	Graceful, spreading with compact branches. Golden-tipped foliage. Moderate growth rate.	Needs little shearing. One of the best golden junipers.
J. c. 'Hetzii' Hetz Blue Juniper	4-9	To 15 ft tall with equal spread.	Rapid grower. Upright spreading branches. Frosty blue-green foliage. Spreads in all directions.	
J. c. 'Maney' Maney Juniper	3-9	To 15 ft tall with equal spread.	Semi-erect, upswept branches. Blue-green foliage.	Good screen.
J. c. 'Mint Julep' Mint Julep Juniper	4-9	To 12 ft tall. Spreads to 6 ft.	Low arching, fountainlike branches. Brilliant mint-green foliage. Neat compact form.	
J. c. 'Pfitzerana' Pfitzer Juniper	4-9	To 5-6 ft tall. Spreads 15-20 ft.	Grows better in shade than other junipers. Spreading branches, feathery, gray-green, sharp-needled foliage.	Stands severe trimming. Excellent medium-sized, spreading screen or hedge.
J. c. 'Pfitzerana Aurea' Golden Pfitzer Juniper	4-9	To 4 ft tall. Spreads to 12 ft.	Golden-tipped foliage on spreading branches turns yellowish-green during winter.	
J. c. 'Pfitzerana Compacta' Compact Pfitzer Juniper	4-9	To 2 ft tall. Spreads to 6 ft.	Compact, dense, spreading branches. Grayish-green foliage results from white undersides of new foliage.	
J. c. 'Pfitzerana Compacta Mordigan' Mordigan Pfitzer Juniper	4-9	To 2 ft tall. Spreads to 4 ft.	Very dense, low-growing. Gray-green foliage.	Good choice for compact, low-maintenance spreader.
J. c. 'Pfitzerana Glauca' Blue Pfitzer Juniper	4-9	To 5-6 ft tall. Spreads 10-15 ft.	More dense than pfitzer. Rapid-growing. Spreading, arching branches. Silvery-blue foliage turns purplish blue in winter.	Easily trained in various forms.
J. c. 'Old Gold' Golden Armstrong Juniper	4-9	To 2 ft tall. Spreads to 5 ft.	Compact form with bright golden foliage.	Excellent low foundation plant or hedge. Adds color in landscape.
J. c. 'Plumosa' Plume Chinese Juniper	4-9	To 2 ft tall. Spreads to 5 ft.	Broad, spreading shrub. Horizontal branches are plume-shaped. Dark green foliage.	
J. c. 'Plumosa Aurea' Golden Plume Chinese Juniper	4-9	To 3-4 ft tall. Spreads to 3 ft.	Upright, arching branches. Bright yellow new growth. Bronzy-gold in winter.	Branches denser than 'Plumosa'.
J. c. 'Sea Green' Sea Green Juniper	4-9	To 4 ft tall. Spreads to 6-7 ft.	Fountainlike arching branches. Outstanding deep sea-green foliage.	More compact and slower-grower than pfitzer juniper.
J. communis 'Depressa' Pasture Juniper, Oldfield Juniper, Canadian Juniper	4-9	To 4 ft tall with equal spread.	Broad-spreading low shrub with branches rising from prominent base. Gray-green foliage.	*J.c.* 'Depressa Aurea' has yellow new shoots.
J. scopulorum 'Tabletop' Tabletop Blue Juniper	3-9	To 6 ft tall. Spreads to 8 ft.	Flat-topped, spreading. Very hardy. Rich, silver-blue foliage.	Good specimen or accent plant.
J. squamata 'Blue Star' Blue Star Juniper	5-9	To 2 ft tall. Spreads to 5 ft.	Slow-growing, compact. Striking silvery-blue foliage.	Good for rock gardens, bonsai, or espalier.

The spreading branches of Chinese flame tree (Koelreuteria bipinnata) cast welcome shade.

Yellow blossoms adorn golden-rain trees (Koelreuteria paniculata) in summer.

The yellow blossoms of golden-chain tree (Laburnum x waterii 'Vossii') are an unusual sight in spring when most trees are blooming in pinks and whites.

Koelreuteria
Koelreuteria

Deciduous trees. Flowering.

These medium-sized, deciduous trees are grown for their large clusters of yellow flowers, showy seedpods, and large divided leaves. They are deep-rooted and are excellent for use as street, shade, or patio trees.

Chinese Flame Tree
Koelreuteria bipinnata

Zones: 5-9. To 20-40 feet.
Deciduous tree. Flowering.

This wide-spreading native of China grows at a slow to moderate rate, eventually becoming flat-topped. The compound leaves measure up to 2 feet long and nearly as wide and have many oval, medium green leaflets that turn yellow before dropping in late fall. Large clusters of bright yellow flowers with purple-spotted bases are held above the foliage in summer. Two-inch-long, triangular, papery capsules, colored orange, red, or salmon, add interest during summer and fall.

Chinese flame tree grows in most soils that are well drained, but needs some irrigation. Staking and pruning are needed to develop a high head.

Golden-Rain Tree
Koelreuteria paniculata

Zones: 5-9. To 20-35 feet.
Deciduous tree. Flowering.

A native of Korea and China, golden-rain tree is more cold hardy than *K. bipinnata,* but the wood is weak and limbs may break during snow and ice storms. Grows at a moderate rate in an open pattern, spreading as wide as it is tall. Leaves are up to 18 inches long with 12 to 18 deeply cut, bright green leaflets. Yellow fall leaf color is not outstanding. Loose, triangular flower clusters with masses of small flowers open in July and August. Flower color varies from pale yellow-green to deep yellow. Bright green, inflated papery seed pods, which become tan or brown when mature,

follow the flowers. They resemble Chinese paper lanterns.

Grows best in fertile, well-drained, moist soil in full sun, but adapts well to poorer and drier soils. Tolerates air pollution, drought, heat, wind, and alkaline soil.

Large trees do not transplant well because of their deep root systems. Many seedlings develop near the tree, causing a weed problem. The fungus necteria canker, identified by coral-colored spots on dead wood, is the only troublesome disease.

Beautybush
Kolkwitzia amabilis

Zones: 5-8. To 7-8 feet.
Deciduous shrub. Flowering.

This upright shrub bears arching or pendulous branches that bend to the ground. Small light pink flowers with yellow throats cover the branches in early spring. Trunk and twigs have attractive peeling bark.

Grows well in dry, poor soil and in sun or shade. Relatively free of insect and disease problems. Do not prune—allow branches to cascade. Use as a specimen plant or as a screen.

Golden-Chain Tree
Laburnum x watereri 'Vossii'

Zones: 6-9. To 25-30 feet.
Deciduous tree. Flowering.

'Vossii' is a superior form of golden-chain tree that occurs naturally in Europe. Like all laburnums, it is grown chiefly for its showy yellow flowers that hang in clusters resembling wisteria blossoms. The species *L. x watereri* is a hybrid between *L. alpinum* and *L. anagyroides.* Its flowers are larger and deeper yellow than either parent, and its flower clusters are longer, up to 20 inches. All plant parts of laburnum, especially the seeds, are poisonous. However, seed often does not set on 'Vossii', so it is less likely to be a hazard than the species.

Golden-chain tree is best planted in an area where its spring bloom can be appreciated, but where it blends into the landscape the rest of the year, since it is an unassuming tree when not in bloom. Laburnum is not bothered by any pests other than mites.

Grow in moist soil in full sun or partial shade. Protect from strong winds.

Lagerstroemia indica
Crape Myrtle
Zones: 7-9. To 10-30 feet.
Deciduous shrub or tree.
Flowering.

The profusion of colorful flowers for several summer months makes this one of the best small flowering trees for patio, specimen, or street tree use. Native to China, crape myrtle is grown throughout the world in warm temperate areas. Normally a small tree, shrub types useful for espaliers, foundation plantings, shrub borders, and hedges have been bred.

A vase shape develops if pruned to several stems, while a round head forms if pruned to a single stem. The outstanding gray or light brown bark peels in patches revealing a pink inner bark, which adds interest all year long if the lower branches are removed. The glossy, dark green leaves are 1/2 inch long and 3/4 to 1-1/4 inches wide. Fall color depends on the climate and variety but leaves can turn yellow, orange, or brilliant red. Clusters of ruffled flowers, 6 to 15 inches tall, are crinkled like crepe paper and open from July to September. Individual flowers are up to 1-1/2 inches across and have 5 to 8 petals. Colors are white, pink, rose, red, lavender, and purple. A variety with white-edged petals, called 'Peppermint Lace', is a recent development.

Many selections are available trained in tree or shrub form. White varieties are: 'White', 'Glendora White'. Pinks: 'Pink Ruffles', 'Rosea'. Rose-pink flowers bordered with white: 'Peppermint Lace'. Reds: 'Durant Red', 'Watermelon Red'. Purples: 'Majestic Orchid',

'Select Purple'. The 'Petite' series is shrubby, with plants growing 5 to 7 feet tall in a full color range. 'Crape Myrtlettes', an even smaller-growing group, is raised from seed.

Crape myrtle should be planted in full sun and grows well in a wide variety of soils. A drought-resistant plant, it should be watered infrequently but thoroughly. Chlorosis may develop in alkaline soils but can be corrected by the application of iron. Mildew can be a serious problem in humid or cool areas. It can be controlled by fungicides. A group of mildew-tolerant varieties, with the names of Indian tribes, has been developed at the U.S. National Arboretum. Varieties in different flower colors and with colorful bark are available.

Lantana
Lantana
Deciduous or evergreen shrubs.
Flowering.

There are over 155 species of lantana native to North and South America and parts of Europe. They are sun-loving plants highly valued for their abundant flowers that bloom for many months of the year. In frost-free areas plants remain evergreen. In colder climates they can be treated as annuals or half-hardy perennials. These fast-growing shrubs tolerate heat, drought, and poor soils, making them problem-solvers in many tough landscape situations. Lantanas make a colorful display draped over a raised planter, in a hanging basket, or used on a bank to help stabilize soil. Shrub types can be used as a low hedge or in foundation plantings.

Lantanas are easy-care shrubs, requiring a minimum of watering and fertilizing. Occasional heavy pruning in early spring or fall will help keep the plant neat and free of woody growth. Watch for signs of mealybugs and whiteflies.

Numerous hybrids between the two common species of lantana are available, offering a wide selection of flower colors and plant forms.

Crape myrtle *(Lagerstroemia indica)* adds late-summer color as a street tree planting.

Easy-to-care-for bush lantana *(Lantana camara)* can solve many tough landscape problems. Blooms year-round in mild winter climates.

In warm climates bush lantana (Lantana camara) makes a fine mass planting capped with bright blossoms all year.

European larch (Larix decidua) grows soft feathery new needles in spring.

Grecian laurel (Laurus nobilis) is a versatile plant that can be used effectively as a formal plant in a container, or as a clipped or unclipped hedge or small tree.

Lantana camara
Bush Lantana
Zones: 9-10. To 4-6 feet.
Evergreen shrub. Flowering.

This robust shrub has pungent, prickly leaves. Flowers appear from spring to late fall, or year-round where winter weather stays warm. Flat-topped, 2-inch flower clusters cover the plant with yellow blossoms that become red as they age.

Lantana montevidensis (L. sellowiana)
Trailing Lantana
Zones: 9-10. To 1 foot.
Evergreen shrub. Flowering.

Decorated most of the year with a profusion of lavender flowers, trailing lantana is a low-growing shrub with weak stems that spread 3 feet or more.

Larix
Larch
Deciduous trees.

This unusual genus contains 10 species of coniferous trees native to the colder parts of the Northern Hemisphere. Larch have soft short needlelike leaves, but unlike other conifers, which are evergreen, larch drop their leaves in fall. Needles are arranged spirally on terminal shoots and clustered around spur shoots, giving the tree a feathery texture.

A number of larch species are important timber trees. Several are used as ornamentals but are rarely seen in nurseries. Like many deciduous hardwoods, larch trees are suitable for planting on western and southern sides of buildings where they provide shade during summer and let warming sun through during winter.

Larix decidua
European Larch
Zones: 3-7. To 70-100 feet.
Deciduous tree.

Young trees of this species tend to be tall and erect with a single trunk and horizontal branches with drooping branchlets. The crown widens and becomes more rounded with age. In spring, the bright green foliage is one of the earliest to appear. It becomes dark green during summer and turns bright yellow in fall.

Plant European larch in deep, fertile, well-drained soil and full sun. Water regularly. Does not tolerate city pollution or drought.

European larch trees may live 700 years. Growth rates are moderately fast. A seventy-six-year-old larch in the Secrest Arboretum at Wooster, Ohio, measured 100 feet tall with a trunk diameter of 23 inches.

Grown as a specimen tree, European larch is suited for open lawns with room for ample development. It can also be mass-planted for screen plantings.

Larix kaempferi
Japanese Larch
Zones: 5-8. To 20-60 feet.
Deciduous tree.

This larch is very similar to the European larch but with a wider spread and blue-green foliage that turns bright orange-yellow in autumn.

Laurus nobilis
Grecian Laurel, Sweet Bay
Zones: 8-10. To 20-40 feet.
Evergreen tree.

Grecian laurel has been cultivated since antiquity in its native Mediterranean region. Wreaths to crown Greek and Roman heroes were woven from its leaves. And its leaves are the bay leaves widely used as an herb for cooking. Many other trees known as laurels are so named because they have leaves of similar shape.

A slender, conical plant when young, it grows slowly into a broad, dense pyramid. A height of 15 to 20 feet in 20 years, or 25 feet in 30 years, is normal. Ascending but somewhat spreading branches will remain to the ground unless pruned.

Usually multistemmed, a single trunk can be developed by pruning. Smooth gray trunk bark is revealed when lower branches are removed.

Stiff, dull green leaves are 2-1/2 to 4 inches long and 3/4 to 1-3/4 inches wide and have a distinctive aroma when crushed. Creamy-yellow to greenish-white flower clusters open March to April in leaf axils. They are not showy. Followed by 1/2-inch oval berries that turn from dark green to deep purple or black. Birds eat the berries.

Very adaptable, Grecian laurel can be grown as a small tree or used as a clipped or unclipped screen or hedge. One of the best choices for a formally trimmed container plant and often used this way for an architectural accent.

'Angustifolia', the willow leaf bay, is a variety with long, narrow pale green leathery leaves having wavy edges. It is considered to be slightly more cold hardy; most Grecian laurels are damaged at 15°F.

Grows best in full sun, needing partial shade in hot climates. Grecian laurel will grow in most soils if they are well drained. Considerable abuse and neglect are tolerated without damage. It even grows well in city pollution.

Grecian laurel is subject to scale insects.

Tea Tree, New Zealand Tea Tree
Leptospermum scoparium

Zones: 9-10. To 1-10 feet.
Evergreen shrub or tree. Flowering.

Graceful and soft-textured, tea tree is available in a variety of useful cultivars that range in size from low ground covers to large shrubs or small trees. Leaves are very narrow, needlelike, only about 1/2 inch long and can be used to make tea, hence the common name. Striking flowers in a range of colors from white to red, with blooming time from early spring to early summer, can be found.

Grows best on a well-drained site. Can be planted on a sandy site and used to reclaim a coastal or beach area. Full sun is required. Very little pruning is needed. If any cuts are made, do not prune heavily back to bare wood.

Varieties include: 'Flore Plenum', compact plant producing double, pink flowers from late winter to early spring. 'Horizontalis', a creeping form to 1 foot high, bearing single, pink flowers in spring. 'Ruby Glow', an upright form to 6 feet, bears deep red double flowers in spring. 'Snow White' grows 2 to 4 feet high and bears white flowers in early spring.

Leucothoe
Leucothoe, Fetterbush
Evergreen shrubs. Flowering.

This genus contains about 50 species of evergreen and deciduous shrubs native to North and South America and Asia. They require moist, well-drained, slightly acid soil rich in organic matter, and will grow in sun or shade. Use in foundation plantings, mass plantings on banks, and as ground covers.

Leucothoe axillaris
Coast Leucothoe
Zones: 6-9. To 6 feet.
Evergreen shrub. Flowering.

This evergreen grows naturally in damp woods, swampy thickets, and along stream banks in the Coastal Plain. Bears white flowers in spring. 'Scarletta', a hybrid of *L. axillaris* and *L. fontanesiana*, grows compactly to 2 feet and has bright red new growth.

Leucothoe fontanesiana
Drooping Leucothoe
Zones: 5-8. To 6 feet.
Evergreen shrub. Flowering.

Drooping leucothoe features long, arching stems heavy with dark green leaves to 7 inches long. Evergreen in the South and semievergreen in the North. Stems are used as cut sprigs by florists. Bears pendulous clusters of white waxy flowers in spring. Leaves turn bronze in fall. Spreads by underground stems. Can be kept pruned to 18 inches and used as a ground cover. 'Girard's Rainbow' has red stems and green leaves marked by yellow.

Leucothoe *(Leucothoe fontanesiana)*

When in bloom, tea tree *(Leptospermum scoparium* 'Ruby Glow') is ablaze with red flowers.

Ligustrum
Privet

Zones: 4-10. To 30 feet.
Deciduous or evergreen shrubs and trees. Flowering.

Privets are easily propagated and grow rapidly, making them one of the least expensive hedge plants.

White or cream-colored flowers appear in clusters at stem tips in summer. Some are fragrant; others have an unpleasant aroma. Berries are black or dark blue.

Tough plants, privets can withstand heavy pruning or shearing, which makes them ideal for hedges. Do best in sunny locations but can tolerate shade and city environments. Adapt to a wide range of soils. Dry sites are acceptable although best growth is on moist, fertile soils.

Although a major landscape use for privet is for hedges and screens, they are also effective in foundation, border, and background plantings.

Wax-leaf privet *(Ligustrum japonicum)* makes a shapely small tree, above left; or a dense hedge, above right. Bears fragrant white flowers in spring and summer.

Ligustrum

Botanical Name/Common Name	Zones	Size	Plant Description	Comments
Ligustrum x ibolium 'Variegata' **Variegated Ibolium Privet**	5-10	To 15 ft tall.	Semideciduous shrub. Bright green leaves with creamy-yellow margins.	Hybrid of *L. ovalifolium* and *L. obtusifolium.*
L. japonicum **Wax-Leaf Privet,** **Japanese Privet**	7-10	To 10 ft tall.	Evergreen shrub or small tree. Roundish leaves to 4 in. long. Glossy dark green on top, near white beneath. Fragrant white flowers in spring and summer.	Use for tall drought-tolerant hedge. Train as small tree. Use for topiary.
L. j. rotundifolium **Curly-Leaf Privet**	7-10	To 10 ft tall.	Evergreen shrub. Deep green round, crinkly leaves.	Tolerates shade. Slower growing than most privets.
L. j. 'Silver Star'	7-10	To 10 ft tall.	Evergreen shrub. Grows slowly. Compact branching habit. Deep green leaves have silvery-cream edges.	Excellent for hedges, screens, topiary.
L. j. 'Texanum'	7-10	To 8 ft tall.	Evergreen shrub. Compact branching habit. Heavy-textured, glossy deep green leaves. Profusion of white flowers in spring.	Takes shearing. Good for trained forms. Fine windbreak.
L. lucidum **Glossy Privet,** **Chinese Privet**	8-9	To 30 ft tall.	Evergreen tree. Pointed, glossy green leaves to 6 in. long. Large feathery clusters of small creamy-white, fragrant flowers borne all summer.	Tolerates salt air. Can be pruned as shrub for hedges, screens, topiary. Good container plant.
L. l. 'Repandum'	8-9	To 20 ft tall.	Same as species but with more upright habit, darker leaves, flowers in small clusters.	
L. l. 'Variegatum' **Variegated Glossy Privet**	8-9	To 20 ft tall.	Same as species but leaves white-margined.	
L. ovalifolium **California Privet**	7-10	To 10 ft tall.	Semideciduous shrub. Evergreen in mild climates. Dark green oval leaves 2-1/2 in. long.	Takes shearing. Tolerates heat. Popular California hedge plant.
L. sinense 'Variegatum' **Variegated Chinese Privet**	8-10	To 10-12 ft tall.	Evergreen shrub. Thin erect stems. Small, oval green leaves with creamy-white edges.	Train into small clipped hedge.
L. x vicaryi **Vicary Golden Privet,** **Vicary Privet**	4-10	To 4-6 ft tall.	Deciduous shrub. Evergreen in mild climates. Erect branches. Bright golden leaves.	Best color in full sun. Good hedge, background, or specimen plant. Slower growing than most privets.

Liquidambar styraciflua

American Sweet Gum, Sweet Gum, Red Gum

Zones: 5-9. To 60-80 feet.
Deciduous tree.

An upright grower when young, American sweet gum becomes broad-crowned with age. Branches are ridged and strongly horizontal. Lustrous green leaves with 5 to 7 lobes are star-shaped and 3 to 5 inches long. Leaf color in fall ranges from dark red to yellow and is reliable even in mild climates. Round, spiny fruits can be messy in late fall or spring.

Sweet Gum makes a good street tree in residential areas, but should not be planted near sidewalks since surface roots can break pavement. Tolerates damp soil, but grows best in moist, rich, well-drained soil.

Many varieties are available with consistently good fall color. These selections include: 'Burgundy', with burgundy fall color; 'Palo Alto', a uniform grower with orange-red to bright red fall color; 'Moraine', uniform in habit with red fall color; 'Festival', narrow and upright with fall foliage a mixture of red, yellow, and green.

Liriodendron tulipifera

Yellow Poplar, Tulip Tree

Zones: 5-9. To 80-100 feet.
Deciduous tree. Flowering.

The tallest native hardwood in the eastern United States, yellow poplars in forests reach heights of 200 feet with 12-foot trunk diameters. Trees develop a long straight trunk with a narrow crown that becomes spreading with age. Yellow-green leaves are lyre-shaped and 5 to 6 inches long and wide. Leaves turn yellow in autumn.

When 10 to 12 years old, trees begin to bear tulip-shaped flowers. The greenish-yellow flowers, with orange stripes at the bases, appear after the leaves have developed. Flowers, from 1-1/2 to 2 inches long, are borne high in the tree and are inconspicuous unless one looks for them. As much as a teaspoonful of nectar is produced in a flower, and when in bloom, trees are alive with honeybees. The clean-looking, furrowed bark resembles that of a true poplar, accounting for one of the common names.

Yellow poplar needs lots of growing room. Used in open areas, such as parks, golf courses, large properties, and on spacious lawns, it makes an ideal shade, specimen, background, or skyline tree. Plant the cultivar 'Fastigiatum', a small upright tree reaching 35 feet, on small-sized properties.

Tulip trees should not be planted near parking areas or patios, since drip of nectar and honeydew from aphids and other sucking insects can mar the finish of parked cars or paved surfaces. A deep, wide-spreading root system may interfere with water and sewer lines if planted too close. The wood is somewhat brittle, and occasionally branches break off during ice and wind storms, making it unwise to plant this tree close to buildings or utility lines.

A fast-growing tree on good sites, in northern areas the tulip tree may increase in height up to 3 feet a year when young, then slows down, averaging a foot a year when 60 years old. In southern mountains its growth rate may reach half again this average. Natural growth is best in the deep, rich, moist, but well-drained, loamy soils found in the coves of the southern mountains. Prefers a slightly acid soil. Requires a good supply of moisture, becoming somewhat stunted on dry sites. Should be planted in full sun.

Liriope

Lilyturf

Evergreen or semievergreen
ground covers. Flowering.

These clump-forming plants have tufts of grass-like foliage and pretty flowers that resemble grape hyacinths. They bloom in late summer or early fall. Because lilyturf is fine-textured it is effective as a ground cover in large areas where bold-textured plants would be too busy looking.

American sweet gum *(Liquidamber styraciflua)* produces reliable fall color in all climates.

In open areas, tulip trees *(Liriodendron tulipifera)* make good shade, specimen, or background trees.

Big blue lilyturf *(Liriope muscari)* forms carpets of grassy foliage, making a low-maintenance ground cover.

Giant Burmese honeysuckle *(Lonicera hildebrandiana)* is a beautiful vine for ornamenting walls and trellises.

Does best in light, fertile soil in partial shade. Full sun is acceptable in cool, coastal areas. Cut back foliage in early spring to increase vigor. Fertilize lightly after cutting back. Water during dry spells. Slugs are occasional problems.

Liriope muscari
Big Blue Lilyturf
Zones: 7-10. To 24 inches. Evergreen or semievergreen ground cover. Flowering.

Stalks of deep lavender flowers appear on 2-foot-tall spikes nestled among the leaves in early fall. Has a somewhat coarser texture than creeping lilyturf. Space plants 12 to 18 inches apart.

'Gold Band' has leaves striped with golden-yellow. 'Lilac Beauty' is low-growing with deep violet flowers. 'Majestic' produces numerous stalks of deep violet flowers. 'Silvery Sunproof' tolerates full sun, flowers heavily, and has gold-bordered young leaves that mature to white-bordered. 'Variegata' grows 12 to 18 inches tall with yellow-edged leaves that mature to solid green, and 12-inch spikes of violet flowers.

Liriope spicata
Creeping Lilyturf
Zones: 5-10. To 6-10 inches. Evergreen or semievergreen ground cover. Flowering.

Foliage is fine-textured; remains evergreen in mild climates, but becomes ragged-looking where winters are cold. Flowers are pale lavender or white and appear on stalks that stand above the foliage in late summer.

Space 6 to 8 inches apart; spreads quickly by underground runners to fill in open areas. Pull weeds regularly until growth is dense.

Lonicera
Honeysuckle
Evergreen or deciduous shrubs and vines.

Honeysuckles can be found in historic gardens, growing wild in open and wooded areas, and in our modern landscapes. Most kinds have sweetly scented flowers that can fill the air with a heady fragrance on warm summer days. Hummingbirds are attracted to the nectar in honeysuckle flowers and many other birds feed on the berries.

Honeysuckle vines are rampant growers that need to be kept pruned or given room to roam. One type or another is adapted to almost every climate. They can be grown in a wide variety of soils and are relatively pest-free.

Lonicera hildebrandiana
Giant Burmese Honeysuckle
Zones: 9-10. Evergreen vine. Flowering.

This vigorous vine is the largest of the honeysuckles, its twining, rope-like branches reaching lengths of 40 to 80 feet. Glistening, dark green leaves, 4 to 6 inches long, make an attractive background for the slender, tubular flowers. In summer, fragrant, 7-inch blossoms open creamy-white, fading to shades of yellow then gold before dropping. Small, dark green, berrylike fruits may appear in fall after the blooming season.

A big, fast-growing vine, this honeysuckle needs a large area to spread, and the strong woody growth needs a sturdy support. Plant it to drape from tops of walls or grow along the eaves of a house. Espaliered against a fence, its large leaves and lovely flowers show to good advantage. Its fast growth and deep-rooting habit make it a very useful ground cover on slopes.

Giant Burmese honeysuckle grows in a wide range of soils. Soil should be kept evenly moist throughout the year. Occasional fertilizing keeps the vine looking healthy. Plant in full sun if near the coast or in partial shade in hot, inland areas. Prune the vine to remove or thin out old branches after blooms have faded.

Lonicera japonica
Japanese Honeysuckle
Zones: 4-10. Evergreen or semideciduous vine. Flowering.

Japanese honeysuckle is a heavily branched, rampant, climbing vine or ground cover best used in large gardens. Twining stems will quickly reach 15 to 30 feet. Leaves are evergreen in warm climates, semievergreen in cold climates. It is drought- and heat-tolerant, adapting to a wide range of climates. Sweetly scented flowers appear throughout the summer and attract bees. The flower buds are tinged purple and open white, aging to pale yellow. They are borne in pairs at the bases of the leaves, appearing as long, thin tubes with curled-back lips. Oval-shaped leaves are dark green, turning bronze with the onset of winter.

Japanese honeysuckle is a problem-solver for areas where other plants won't grow. It is not particular as to soil type and can be grown in poorly drained soils or on steep slopes. In some areas it is even considered a weed. In sun or shade, simply give it room to spread, or prune severely to control its growth. Provide a support for it to twine around and it will grow upwards, or leave unsupported and stems will root to help stabilize slopes and prevent erosion. It grows rapidly and will quickly cover a fence where a fragrant screen is desired.

Care for Japanese honeysuckle is primarily limited to controlling shape and size. Prune in fall or early spring. It responds well to both light and heavy pruning.

Three varieties are top-rated. 'Halliana', Hall's honeysuckle, has white flowers and green leaves and is the most vigorous and commonly grown variety. 'Gold-Net Honeysuckle' has distinctive yellow-marbled leaves, making it a good accent plant for the garden. It is less cold hardy and slower in growth rate than Hall's honeysuckle. 'Purple Japanese Honeysuckle' has a form similar to Hall's honeysuckle. Long flowers are tinged reddish purple, and leaves have purple undersides.

Lonicera sempervirens
Trumpet Honeysuckle
Zones: 4-10.
Evergreen or semideciduous vine. Flowering.

Native to the eastern United States, this evergreen to semideciduous vine is well adapted to a broad range of climate zones. Trumpet honeysuckle makes a handsome, twining vine with an open form and coral to red flowers throughout the summer. Narrow, tubular blossoms in showy clusters are held at the ends of branches. They are not fragrant. Scarlet-colored berries follow flowers in fall. Distinctive, broadly oval leaves have pale blue-green undersides and are joined to the stem at their bases.

This rampant-growing vine becomes shrubby if unsupported, making it a suitable ground cover for slopes and large areas. Used on a fence or trellis it forms an attractive screen. Provide sturdy support for the branches. Thin and cut back stems in early spring or after blooming. Pruning will control the size of the vine and encourage new branches.

Like other honeysuckles, this vine is easy to grow and will tolerate sunny or shady exposures. It is adaptable to a wide variety of soils, preferring moist conditions for best growth. Watch for aphids on new growth.

If a yellow-flowered vine is what your garden needs, try the variety 'Sulphurea'. 'Superba' boasts bright, scarlet-colored flower clusters.

Lonicera tatarica
Tatarian Honeysuckle
Zones: 3-9. To 8-10 feet.
Deciduous shrub. Flowering.

This is one of the hardiest and most reliable flowering shrubs for cold climates. Forms a many-branched, dense shrub with deep green leaves. Small, pink or white, very fragrant flowers appear in late spring and early summer and are followed by yellow or red berries. Makes an effective screen or informal hedge. Grows in most soils and is pest-free. Grow in full sun or partial shade.

'Alba' is a white-flowering form. 'Rosea' has pink flowers with deeper colored outsides. 'Zabelii' has dark red flowers.

Tatarian honeysuckle *(Lonicera tatarica)* is a very cold-hardy shrub with fragrant flowers borne from spring into summer.

Japanese honeysuckle *(Lonicera japonica)*

Magnolia
Magnolia
Zones: 5-10. To 60 feet.
Evergreen or deciduous shrubs or trees. Flowering.

This large genus has over 85 species native to warm temperate and tropical regions in North America and Asia. Evergreen species are not hardy in the North. Valued for their large flowers, some species bear among the largest of tree flowers. Blooms may be up to a foot in diameter. Flowers are fragrant in many species and colors may be white, yellow, red, or purplish red.

Fruits are often quite conspicuous and shaped like cucumbers. Ripe seeds, attached to long silken threads, are released and hang for several days before falling to the ground. The leaves are large, coarse and stiff.

Most magnolias do best in fertile, well-drained loamy soils that hold ample moisture. Some thrive in peaty soils if they are well aerated. Mixing peat or compost in the backfill when planting is recommended. A compost mulch spread beneath the branches is beneficial when applied in spring and fall. Magnolias should not be transplanted after they become established, because injury to large roots can be very damaging.

Large-growing magnolias should be planted at least 40 feet from other trees or buildings to allow room for full plant development. Magnolias with large leaves are not suitable for windy sites, because winds can whip the leaves about, tearing and shredding them until they become unsightly.

Pruning must be done during the growing season, because dormant trees do not heal their wounds easily. If possible, confine pruning to young plants and small branches. Wounds made by removing large branches do not heal well and decay can set in.

Star magnolia *(Magnolia stellata)* makes an early-blooming accent tree.

Magnolia

Botanical Name/ Common Name	Zones	Size	Flower Description	Plant Description	Comments
Magnolia grandiflora Southern Magnolia, Bull Bay	7-10	To 80-100 ft tall.	Huge, fragrant, cup-shaped white blossoms for several months in summer.	Evergreen tree matures to pyramidal form. Large, thick, glossy green leaves.	Legendary in the South. Can be espaliered. Interesting fruit.
M. g. 'Majestic Beauty' Majestic Beauty Magnolia	7-10	To 20 ft or more tall.	Cup-shaped, fragrant white flowers to 12 in. across.	Evergreen tree with compact branching habit. Vigorous growth. Pyramidal form. Very large glossy, deep green leaves.	Spectacular shade or street tree.
M. g. 'Russet' Russet Magnolia	7-10	To 30-40 ft tall.	Fragrant white flowers to 10 in. across.	Evergreen tree. Compact branching form. Small, dense, narrow leaves have russet-brown undersides.	
M. g. 'Saint Mary' St. Mary Magnolia	7-10	To 20 ft or more tall.	Blooms early. Many huge, cup-shaped white flowers.	Evergreen tree with compact form. Slow-growing. Leaves bright green above, showy bronze beneath.	Excellent small garden, patio and street tree.
M. g. 'Samuel Sommer' Samuel Sommer Magnolia	7-10	To 30-40 ft tall.	Highly fragrant white flowers to 14 in. across.	Evergreen tree with glossy deep green leaves 10 in. or more long.	Finest *M. grandiflora* cultivar. Good patio or street tree.
M. x loebneri 'Merrill' Merrill's Magnolia	5-10	To 20-30 ft tall.	Fragrant white, multi-petalled, starlike blossoms. Similar to star magnolia, but larger.	Deciduous tree with dense, pyramidal upright form. Fast-growing. Rich green foliage.	Blooms at an early age.
M. quinquepeta 'Nigra' Purple Lily Magnolia	5-10	To 10 ft tall.	Lilylike blossoms. Dark purple outside, whitish purple inside; 5 in. or more across.	Deciduous shrub or tree with compact habit. Fast-growing. Branches start close to ground; 6-in.-long leaves have pale undersides.	Excellent for lawn tree. Long, spectacular blooming season.
M. x soulangiana Saucer Magnolia, Chinese Magnolia, Tulip Tree	5-10	To 20-25 ft tall.	Purplish-pink buds before leaves open to creamy-white saucer-shaped flowers 6 in. across.	Deciduous shrubs or trees. Multi-trunked with broad growth habit.	

Above: Saucer magnolia *(Magnolia x soulangiana)* offers showy spring flowers and summer shade. Blossoms at right, top: Star magnolia *(Magnolia stellata)*, center: Saucer magnolia *(Magnolia x soulangiana)*, bottom: Southern magnolia *(Magnolia grandiflora)*.

Botanical Name/ Common Name	Zones	Size	Flower Description	Plant Description	Comments
M. x s. 'Burgundy'	5-10	To 20-25 ft tall.	Large deep purple flowers also have the inside of petals colored deep purple in the center and halfway out fading to white at petal tips.	Deciduous shrubs or trees. Multi-trunked with broad growth habit.	Beautiful lawn or small garden tree.
M. x s. 'Superba'	5-10	To 20-25 ft tall.	Large flowers with petals a deep pink on the outside, white on the inside.	Deciduous shrubs or trees. Multi-trunked with broad growth habit.	Good for lawns, small gardens, patios.
M. stellata Star Magnolia	5-10	To 10 ft tall.	Fragrant, white, many-petalled blossoms before leaves in early spring.	Deciduous shrub or multitrunked tree with rounded habit. Dense branching. Dark green foliage.	Bronzy-yellow fall color. Good small garden, or patio tree.
M. s. 'Rosea'	5-10	To 10 ft tall.	Pink buds. Blossoms similar to species.	Same as species.	Mix with white-flowered star magnolias in close plantings.
M. s. 'Royal Star'	5-10	To 10 ft tall.	Large, fragrant, double, white blossoms.	Same as species.	Blooms later than species. Good choice where late freezes occur.
M. virginiana (M. glauca) Sweet Bay	6-10	To 20-60 ft tall.	Waxy, deliciously scented, creamy-white flowers. Late spring.	Deciduous shrub or tree (evergreen in mild climates); 5-in.-long oval leaves green above, white beneath.	Good shade tree. Tolerant of wet soils. Red fruits in fall.

Oregon grape *(Mahonia aquifolium)* has glossy, bold-textured, spiny-edged evergreen leaves. Bright yellow flowers in spring, below left, are followed by showy blue berries, below right.

Mahonia
Mahonia
Evergreen shrubs. Flowering.

These are evergreen shrubs with bold-textured, shiny, compound leaves with spiny margins. Clusters or spikes of yellow flowers in spring are followed by blue-black berries that are relished by birds. Taller species are useful as textural contrast plants, while lower-growing species are good ground covers or low barrier plants.

Mahonia aquifolium
Oregon Grape
Zones: 5-9. To 2-6 feet.
Evergreen shrub. Flowering.

Upright stems grow from spreading underground stems, forming large patches in its native British Columbia to Northern California. A good plant wherever low masses of evergreen foliage are needed. Leaves are 4 to 10 inches long with 5 to 9 spiny-margined oval leaflets 1 to 2-1/2 inches long. The upper surface is glossy or dull depending on the variety. New growth is often coppery. Winter foliage turns maroon, especially in cold winter areas. 'Compacta' makes a tidy, uniform 2-foot-high planting.

Grows in sun or shade in cool areas. Best in shade in warm areas. Tolerates acid or slightly alkaline soils. Prune to the ground to thicken the stand.

Mahonia bealei
Leatherleaf Mahonia
Zones: 5-10. To 10-12 feet.
Evergreen shrub. Flowering.

The strong vertical stems and horizontal 12- to 16-inch-long compound leaves of this Chinese native make a striking contrast to other plants in the landscape. There are 7 to 15 thick, leathery leaflets 2 to 4-1/2 inches long, with 2 to 5 large spines on each side. The leaves are dull bluish green on top, and gray-green below.

Leatherleaf mahonia is a shade plant except in cool coastal areas where it can be grown in full sun. Soil should be moist and contain plenty of organic matter.

Mahonia lomariifolia
Chinese Holly-Grape
Zones: 8-10. To 6-10 feet.
Evergreen shrub. Flowering.

This is a dramatic plant with long, deeply divided, dark green leaves that have spines. They are arranged horizontally around upright stems and may be more than 24 inches long.

An excellent accent plant for entryways, patios, or container growing. Best in partial shade. Prune to induce branching.

Malus
Flowering Crab Apple
Zones: 2-8. To 35 feet.
Deciduous tree. Flowering.

This genus contains 30 species of deciduous, many-branched trees native to the North Temperate Zone. Both apples and crab apples are included and are distinguished by the size of the fruits. An apple has fruits over 2 inches in diameter, while crab apples have fruits less than 2 inches in diameter.

Crab apples are one of the most ornamental groups of flowering trees. They are grown for their masses of fragrant spring flowers, which range in color from white, pink, red to purplish red. Many have outstanding displays of red, yellow, or orange fruit in late summer or early fall that hang on after leaves drop. Over 600 hybrids, varieties, and cultivars have been named. Trees come in a variety of shapes and sizes and fit into many landscape situations. Use crab apples as specimen or accent trees in the lawn or garden. Plant fruitless varieties to screen a patio, line a driveway, or for an espalier.

Crab apples vary in height from shrub-like plants such as sargent crab apple, which seldom exceeds 6 to 8 feet, to tall trees like Jack crab apple, which may be 40 feet high. A weeping form is 'White Cascade'. 'Velvet Pillar' is a new upright-growing form. Nurseries are also now offering crab apples grafted to dwarfing rootstocks. Look for rootstocks such as *M. floribunda*, 'Hopa', *M. ioensis*, 'Klehm's Improved

Bechtel', 'Liset', 'Radiant', 'Red Splendour', 'Snowdrift', and 'Spring Snow' and 'MM106'.

Types bearing small fruits should be chosen because birds will usually eat the fruit, eliminating the ground litter of larger, uneaten apples. If you wish to grow a dual-purpose crab apple and use the apples for cooking or making jelly, plant one of the large-fruited crab apples, such as 'Centennial'. They have palatable fruit that can be eaten fresh, or made into jelly or apple sauce. If you do not wish to have fruiting trees, some cultivars, such as 'Spring Snow', flower abundantly but do not set fruit. Double-flowering varieties are also usually fruitless.

Best growth is made in sandy loam or silty clay soils, but the trees are not choosey and will grow in many soils as long as they are well drained. Do not plant in excessively moist areas. To obtain maximum flowering and fruit set, plant in full sun. Crab apples require average fertility. Excessive fertilization can cause succulent growth that is susceptible to disease.

Some crab apples are quite susceptible to a number of diseases including apple scab and fireblight. Some old time favorites, such as 'Almey', 'Flame', 'Eleyi', and 'Hopa', are so susceptible to disease that more resistant cultivars are replacing them. Still, these are some of the better eating varieties and you may wish to grow them and use control measures.

Apple scab, a fungus that attacks foliage and fruits, can cause heavy leaf defoliation by midsummer. Fireblight bacteria infects trees through wounds, and is carried by insects to the blossoms. In areas where fireblight or apple scab can be problems, select resistant trees. The incidence of disease also varies by climate. For instance, scab is not a problem in dry summer climates. Fireblight can kill entire branches or even the entire tree. Gypsy moth and tent caterpillar are often severe problems. Variety descriptions in the chart on the following pages include comments on outstanding susceptibility or disease resistance.

The fragrant blossoms of flowering crab apples *(Malus* sp.) scent the garden and make a lovely display along a path or driveway in spring.

Flowering crab apple varieties *(Malus* sp.) offer exquisite blossoms in a choice of colors from white, pink, red, to purplish.

Snowdrift crab apple (*Malus* 'Snowdrift') has a neat round head.

Many varieties of flowering crab apples (*Malus* sp.) have colorful fruits in late summer or early fall that persist after leaves drop.

Malus

Botanical Name/ Common Name	Zones	Size	Flower Description	Plant Description	Comments
Malus 'Almey' Almey Crab Apple	4-8	To 15 ft tall. Spreads 15-20 ft.	Rose-pink to pale lavender. Large, single, 1-1/2 to 1-3/4 in. Petals nearly white at base.	Deciduous tree. Moderate growth. Upright, spreading. Becomes rounded with age. 3/4 to 7/8-in. dark red fruits.	Susceptible to apple scab. Fruit makes good jelly.
M. 'American Beauty' American Beauty Crab Apple	4-8	To 30 ft tall. Spreads 18 ft.	Clear red. Large, double.	Deciduous tree. Moderate growth. Small red fruits. Sparse.	Cross between *M.* 'Almey' and *M.* 'Katherine'.
M. x atrosanguinea Carmen Crab Apple	5-8	To 20 ft tall with equal spread.	Red, single, 1-1/4 in.	Deciduous tree. Moderate growth. Forms broad rounded tree or moundlike shrub if unpruned. Yellow fruits turn brown.	An old favorite. Disease-resistant.
M. 'Dolgo' Dolgo Crab Apple	2-8	To 35 ft tall with equal spread.	White, single.	Deciduous tree. Vigorous growth. Spreading branches. Bright red 1-in. fruits.	Very hardy. Disease-resistant.
M. 'Oekonomierat Echtermeyer' Echtermeyer Crab Apple, Weeping Crab Apple	4-8	To 15 ft tall with variable spread.	Purplish-red, fade to rose-pink. Single, 1-1/2 in.	Deciduous tree. Moderate growth. Weeping form; shape by pruning. 1 to 1-1/4-in. fruits, showy in fall.	
M. floribunda Japanese Flowering Crab Apple	4-8	To 20-25 ft tall; spreads as wide.	Deep pink to red buds. Open to pink then fade to white. Single, 1 to 1-1/2 in.	Deciduous tree. Moderate growth. Densely branched. More horizontal than rounded. Yellow-and-red 3/8 in. fruits not showy.	Blooms profusely.
M. 'Hopa' Hopa Crab Apple	4-8	To 20 ft tall with equal spread.	Fragrant. Rose-red with white star in center. 1 to 1-1/2 in. Single.	Deciduous tree. Fast grower. Upright when young, broadens with age. Profuse 3/4 to 1-in. orange-red fruits.	Susceptible to apple scab. Fruit makes good jelly.
M. hupehensis Tea Crab Apple	5-8	To 15 ft tall. Spreads to 20 ft.	Deep pink buds. Open pink then fade to white. Single, 1-1/2 in.	Deciduous tree. Moderate growth. Open habit with Y-shaped branching. Small yellow-and-red fruits.	Disease-resistant.
M. ioensis 'Klehm's Improved Bechtel'	4-8	To 25 ft tall. Spreads to 20 ft.	Fragrant. Pink. Large double. Blooms late season.	Deciduous tree. Moderate growth. Vase-shaped. Sparse, inconspicuous 1-in. green fruits.	Disease-resistant.
M. 'Katherine'	5-8	To 20 ft tall with equal spread.	Double, 2 in. Deep pink buds open to pink, fade to white.	Deciduous tree. Moderate growth. Loose, open shape. Small fruits, yellow with red tinge.	Flowers profusely. Disease-resistant.
M. 'Liset'	4-8	To 15-20 ft tall. Spreads to 12 ft.	Dark crimson buds open to pink and red. Single, 1/2 to 1 in.	Deciduous tree. Moderate growth. Upright or columnar. 1/2 to 1 in. dark crimson fruits.	Disease-resistant. Fruit not showy.

Botanical Name/ Common Name	Zones	Size	Flower Description	Plant Description	Comments
M. 'Mary Potter'	4-8	To 12-15 ft tall. Spreads to 10 ft.	Single, 1 in. Pink buds open to white.	Deciduous tree. Moderate growth. Horizontal and low-spreading. Red fruits, 1/2 in.	Susceptible to fireblight.
M. 'Pink Perfection'	3-8	To 20 ft tall with equal spread.	Red buds open to pink, fade with age. 2 to 2-1/4 in., double.	Deciduous tree. Moderate growth. Rounded form. Insignificant yellow fruits.	Very hardy.
M. 'Profusion'	4-8	To 15 ft tall. Spreads to 12 ft.	Red to purplish red with white eye. Single.	Deciduous tree. Moderate growth. Rounded, shrubby form. Glossy small fruits; 1/2 in., blood-red.	Profuse flowers very showy.
M. 'Radiant'	4-8	To 25-30 ft tall; spreads as wide.	Deep red buds open to deep pink. Single.	Deciduous tree. Fast grower. Broad, medium-sized. 1/2-in., bright red fruits shows color early.	Disease-resistant. Minnesota introduction.
M. 'Red Jade'	4-8	To 15-20 ft tall; spreads as wide.	Single, 1-1/2 in., white.	Deciduous tree. Moderate growth. Elegant spreading shape. Graceful weeping branches. Egg-shaped, small bright red fruits.	Blooms profusely. Fruits showy in fall and winter.
M. 'Red Silver'	4-8	To 20-30 ft tall. Spreads to 15 ft.	Single, 1-1/2 in. China-rose to deep red.	Deciduous tree. Fast grower. Branch tips tend to droop gracefully. Purplish-red, 3/4-in. fruits.	Susceptible to apple scab. Fruit makes good jelly.
M. 'Robinson'	4-8	To 25 ft tall with equal spread.	Crimson buds open to deep pink. Single.	Deciduous tree. Fast grower. Upright, spreading with age. Dark red glossy fruits, 3/8 in., hold well.	Disease-resistant. Fruit hidden by foliage.
M. 'Royal Ruby'	5-8	To 15-20 ft tall. Spreads to 20 ft.	Dark red, double, cup-shaped, 2 in.	Deciduous tree. Fast grower. Narrow upright form. Seldom produces fruit.	Disease-resistant. One of the largest, double-flowering crab apples.
M. 'Royalty'	4-8	To 15 ft tall with equal spread.	Single, purple.	Deciduous tree. Moderate growth. Dense, mounding crown. Fruits dark red, 3/4 in. Leaves are dark purplish red all summer.	Resistant to fireblight.
M. sargentii Sargent Crab Apple	5-8	To 6-8 ft tall. Spreads 8-14 ft.	Fragrant, single, 1/2 in. Pure white.	Deciduous tree. Slow grower. Dense, shrubby with lacy branches. Abundant fruits, dark red, 1/4 to 1/3 in.	Disease-resistant. Blooms profusely.
M. x scheideckeri Scheidecker Crab Apple	4-8	To 20 ft tall. Spreads to 15 ft.	Pink, semidouble, 1-1/2 in.	Deciduous tree. Moderate growth. Dense, upright. 1/2-in. yellow to orange fruit.	Susceptible to apple scab. Takes shaping.
M. 'Selkirk'	5-8	To 20 ft tall with equal spread.	Deep purplish-pink, 1 to 1-1/2 in.	Deciduous tree. Moderate growth. Upright, spreading to vase-shape with age. Very glossy bright red 3/4-in. fruits.	Disease-resistant.
M. 'Snowcloud'	4-8	To 20 ft tall. Spreads to 12 ft.	Pink buds open white. Double.	Deciduous tree. Moderate growth. Narrow, upright. Sparse, insignificant yellow fruits.	Flowers glistening white when fully open.
M. 'Snowdrift'	4-8	To 20-25 ft tall. Spreads to 20 ft.	Red buds open white. Single. Blooms late.	Deciduous tree. Moderate to vigorous growth. Dense, rounded, and uniform as street tree. Fruits less than 1/2 in., orange-red.	Susceptible to fireblight.
M. 'Spring Snow'	4-8	To 20 ft tall. Spreads to 15 ft.	Pure white, fragrant, single.	Deciduous tree. Moderate growth. Rounded form. Nearly sterile, seldom fruits.	Good patio tree.
M. 'Van Eseltine'	5-8	To 18-20 ft tall. Spreads 8-10 ft.	Deep rose-red buds fade to pale pink. Double, 2 in.	Deciduous tree. Moderate growth. Upright, becoming vase-shaped. 3/4-in. angular fruit are yellow with red-brown or carmine cheeks.	Fruit is not showy.
M. 'Weeping Candied Apple'	4-8	To 16 ft tall. Spreads to 10 ft.	Purplish-pink, large, single.	Deciduous tree. Fairly rapid growth. Branches horizontal to pendulous. Cherry-red 1/2-in. fruits.	Disease-resistant.
M. 'White Angel'	4-8	To 15-20 ft tall; spreads as wide.	Pink buds open to white. Single.	Deciduous tree. Moderate growth. Rounded form. Fruits 1/2 in., scarlet-red.	Susceptible to fireblight.
M. 'Velvet Pillar'	4-8	To 10-12 ft tall. Spreads to 8 ft.	Purple to red. Double.	Deciduous tree. Moderate growth. Dense, upright. Can be grown as narrow tree or compact shrub. Sparse, small, glossy red fruit.	Disease-resistant. Use for hedge or screen.
M. x zumi calocarpa Redbud Crab Apple	4-8	To 25 ft tall. Spreads to 15 ft.	Fragrant. Pink buds open white to pinkish. Single, 1-1/4 in.	Deciduous tree. Moderate growth. Dense, pyramidal form. Branches tend to droop. Glossy bright red 1/2-in. fruits.	Susceptible to fireblight.

The fine-textured foliage and weeping branches of mayten tree (Maytenus boaria) resemble weeping willow.

Flaxleaf paperbark (Melaleuca linariifolia) bears delicate white flowers in summer.

Flowers of Chinaberry (Melia azedarach) tip the branches in spring.

Maytenus boaria
Mayten Tree
Zones: 8-10. To 20-30 feet.
Evergreen tree.

One of the most picturesque and graceful of all evergreen trees, mayten's broad crown and pendulous branches are reminiscent of weeping willow. However, its growth habit is more contained, and its roots less invasive, making it highly desirable in the landscape.

Mayten is an excellent lawn and street tree. Place near a patio for light shade. Train as a multiple or single-trunked tree. Growth is moderate if regularly fed and watered.

Best suited to a well-drained soil, and once established, the tree can tolerate drought conditions. Mayten resists most insect pests and oak root fungus. Prune when young to establish an open framework of branches. Small leaves make this a low-maintenance tree.

Melaleuca
Melaleuca
Evergreen trees. Flowering.

Native to Australia, these evergreen trees and shrubs are grown for their showy flower clusters and tolerance to drought conditions. New growth develops from tips of flower clusters, resulting in the stems being surrounded by decorative, persistent seed capsules. Trees can be used as specimen or street trees, or as trimmed hedges.

Melaleuca linariifolia
Flaxleaf Paperbark
Zones: 9-10. To 20-30 feet.
Evergreen tree. Flowering.

Tree growth is rapid, open, and willowy when young, but becomes umbrella-shaped and dense with age. Bark is white and spongy on young trees, but becomes light brown, papery, and peeling on older limbs and trunks. The stiff, needlelike, bright bluish-green leaves are 1-1 4 inches long. Fluffy white flowers bloom in 1- to 2-inch spikes at the ends of the slender branchlets. When in full bloom in summer the tree appears to be covered with snow.

Melaleuca quinquenervia
(M. leucadendra)
Cajeput Tree
Zones: 9-10. To 20-40 feet.
Evergreen tree. Flowering.

This is a favorite tree for windbreaks and specimen use. Grows rapidly, forming an oval to rounded, open crown and weeping branch tips. Thick, spongy, light brown to whitish bark peels in papery layers. The stiff, narrowly oval, pale green leaves are 2 to 4 inches long and 3 8 to 3 4 inch wide. Yellowish-white, bottlebrush-like flower spikes, 2 to 4 inches long, appear from June to October. Plants with pink or purplish flowers are occasionally seen. Grows best in sun and average soil, but tolerates poor drainage, drought, wind, salt spray, and grass fires. In moist soil areas, seedlings grow readily, quickly becoming problem weeds.

Melia azedarach
Chinaberry, Pride-of-India, Bead Tree
Zones: 8-10. To 40 feet.
Deciduous tree. Flowering.

Chinaberry is a fast-growing, dense shade tree that flourishes in the South and West where high heat, drought, and infertile soil discourage most other shade trees. It is so valuable for shade that its undesirable characteristics are only minor nuisances compared to its advantages.

This densely branched, round-headed tree has deep green compound leaves, divided into 5- to 8-inch-long leaflets. In spring, long clusters of fragrant lilac-colored flowers bloom at its branch tips. Small yellow berries ripen in autumn and hang onto the tree into winter. Inside the berries are small, hard pits that are used for rosary beads—hence the common name bead tree. Berries germinate easily and cause a weed problem in gardens and shrubbery borders.

The berries are eaten by birds, who suffer no ill-effects, but they are poisonous to people and to domestic animals. Fortunately, the berries are so sour that children are unlikely to eat enough of them to be poisoned.

Chinaberry grows rapidly and will quickly produce welcome shade and spring flowers. Like many fast-growing trees, however, it is short-lived and has weak wood that can be damaged in storms.

Tolerates poor soil, dry sites, and acid or alkaline soil, though does best in moist, sandy loam. Usually killed by temperatures below 0°F. Needs full sun.

The cultivar 'Umbraculifera', the Texas umbrella tree, is a shorter, more dense tree with an upright crown. It grows to about 30 feet and its radiating branches and drooping foliage give it an even, mounded shade reminiscent of an umbrella.

Metasequoia glyptostroboides
Dawn Redwood
Zones: 4-10. To 75-85 feet.
Deciduous tree.

A living fossil thought to have disappeared millions of years ago, dawn redwood was discovered growing in China, and introduced to the United States about 30 years ago. Until that discovery, it was known only in fossil records.

The dawn redwood is similar to the coast redwood, the redwood native to California, however it is a deciduous tree, dropping its needles in fall. The new spring foliage is bright green and soft to the touch. It turns yellow-green to bronze in fall before dropping. Trees are tall and conical, becoming pyramidal with age. Bark is reddish brown and loosens in large narrow strips. The trunk base swells with age and forms many flattened butts similar in appearance to bald cypress.

A fast grower, dawn redwood can increase by 4 feet in height each growing season if grown under favorable conditions. Needs a moist,

Given plenty of room to spread, dawn redwood *(Metasequoia glyptostroboides)* makes an excellent specimen tree. New spring foliage, shown below, is bright green and delicate. It turns yellow-green to bronze before dropping in autumn.

Fruitless varieties of white mulberry (*Morus alba*) are widely used shade trees in the Southwest where they tolerate adverse conditions other trees cannot endure.

Myoporum (*Myoporum laetum* 'Carsonii') provides privacy in difficult coastal sites.

sunny site with well-drained soil high in organic matter. Does not tolerate hot or dry locations.

Dawn redwood should be planted where there is plenty of room for it to mature. Makes a good specimen tree or grove planting on large properties. Can be grown in a large tub or planter where its growth rate will be curtailed.

Morus alba
White Mulberry, Silkworm Mulberry
Zones: 5-9. To 40 feet.
Deciduous tree.

This tree is top-rated in the Southwest, where it grows rapidly and provides cooling shade under conditions that other shade trees cannot tolerate. Elsewhere, it is usually not recommended because there are more attractive and less messy trees to choose from.

Leaves have various shapes, having few to many lobes, and cloak the round-topped tree densely from spring through fall. Inconspicuous flowers appear in late spring and by midsummer are followed by raspberry-shaped fruits that may be white, violet, or purple. Fruits are messy and can stain pavement, but they can be gathered and made into delicious jelly, though they are not tasty when eaten fresh. Birds are very fond of the fruits.

White mulberry grows on any kind of soil, and does well on poor dry sites and on rocky slopes, so is useful for solving difficult landscape problems. It is fast-growing and has weak wood. Careful pruning while young, and avoiding heading back large branches, will encourage stronger branching.

Fruitless varieties, which are male trees that do not set fruit, are less messy and are usually grown in the Southwest. Their pollen however can cause allergies. 'Mapleleaf', also called 'Stribling', is fruitless though not quite as cold hardy as the species, growing to Zone 6. 'Fan San', 'Kingman', and 'Cutleaf' are other fruitless varieties.

Murraya paniculata
Orange Jessamine
Zones: 9-11. To 5-15 feet.
Evergreen shrub. Flowering.

White flowers with a jasmine-like fragrance and deep green divided leaves on gracefully arching stems make orange jessamine a top-rated shrub. Blooms from late summer into fall. Grows best in filtered shade and with regular watering and fertilizing. Can be pruned as a hedge.

Myoporum laetum 'Carsonii'
Myoporum
Zones: 8-10. To 15-20 feet.
Evergreen shrub. Flowering.

This fast-growing shrub is greatly appreciated in coastal areas. Features shiny dark green leaves, small white flowers that are not particularly showy, and reddish-purple fruit. If watered regularly, will stand up to blowing sand, wind, and salty air. Grows best in full sun.

Myrica pensylvanica
Bayberry, Candleberry
Zones: 3-10. To 6 feet.
Deciduous or evergreen shrub.

Bayberry is native to the Atlantic Coast from Maryland to New Foundland, where it can be found growing very close to the ocean's salt spray. Because it is salt-tolerant, it can also be planted near roads where salt is used to control ice.

Leaves of bayberry are glossy green and aromatic. They are evergreen in mild climates, dropping off without changing color in late fall in cold climates. They were used by the Colonists to make a gray-green dye. The abundant waxy gray berries that line the stems of female plants all winter were also useful to the Colonists. They melted the berries into candles. The wonderfully fragrant berries are still used for scenting candles.

Bayberry grows well in dry, infertile, or sandy soils. Needs full sun. Withstands heavy pruning and can be kept compact for a hedge or screen. Plant both male and female plants near each other to ensure berry formation.

Myrtus communis
True Myrtle
Zones: 9-10. To 5-10 feet.
Evergreen shrub. Flowering.

A top-rated hedge plant with small lustrous green leaves, fragrant white flowers, and purplish-black fruit. Grows best in a well-drained soil in shade or hot sun. Tolerates drought. There are several varieties. 'Compacta' is extremely dense with small leaves. 'Microphylla' has small overlapping leaves.

Nandina domestica
Heavenly Bamboo
Zones: 6-10. To 3-8 feet.
Evergreen shrub. Flowering.

Nandina is a many-faceted shrub used to create a mood, spot of color, or interesting textural effect. Slender vertical stems, 3 to 8 feet high, hold open, delicate foliage. The effect suggests bamboo, although they are not related. Nandina is often used for an Oriental feeling in gardens. New leaves are tinted a bronzy-pink, later soft green, and with winter's cold change to dramatic shades of crimson and purple. Nandina's white flower clusters appear in July, followed by bright red berries that last for several months.

Heavenly bamboo is considered one of the most versatile shrubs for sun or shade, suitable for planting in narrow spaces, containers, borders, and at foundations. Plant shrubs in groupings for cross-pollination and more berry production.

Does well in crowded conditions and accepts almost any soil, although alkaline conditions can cause the shrub to become chlorotic due to iron deficiency. Resistant to oak root fungus and free of pests, nandina is also fairly drought-tolerant once established. In areas where temperatures reach below 0°F, treat it as a herbaceous perennial. Leaves

Bayberry *(Myrica pensylvanica)* tolerates salt spray and infertile and sandy soils. Glossy aromatic leaves are evergreen in mild climates.

The leaves of heavenly bamboo *(Nandina domestica)* change from bronzy pink to a soft green, finally becoming crimson and purple in winter.

Oleanders *(Nerium oleander)* normally grow as tall shrubs, but may be trained into a tree form.

The fall foliage of black gum *(Nyssa sylvatica)* ranges in color from scarlet to yellow.

are deciduous at 10°F. Remove all weak shoots to increase density.

'Alba' is a white-berried variety. 'Nana' grows to only 12 to 18 inches high. 'Compacta' is also restrained, but reaches 4 to 5 feet.

Nerium oleander
Oleander
Zones: 8-10. To 8-20 feet.
Evergreen shrub or tree. Flowering.

Oleander flourishes in hot, dry interior areas and also will grow in coastal locations. It is very adaptable and has one of the longest flowering seasons of any tree. Brilliant, waxy flowers from 1-1/2 to 3 inches wide are borne in clusters at twig or branch tips from May or June to September. Varieties with single or double flowers in white, yellow, salmon, pink, and red are available. Some varieties have fragrant blooms.

Oleanders usually develop a broad, bulky form at a moderate to fast rate, and are often used for hedges and screens. A small single- or multiple-trunked tree, with branches starting at 7 or 8 feet, can be developed by pruning. 'Sister Agnes', which has single white flowers, grows to 20 feet, and would be a good choice for use as a tree.

Thick, glossy dark green leaves, 3 to 6 inches long and 3/4 to 1 inch wide, are usually in whorls of three. Forms with leaves to 12 inches long and ones with golden-variegated leaves are sometimes available.

Oleanders are not particular about soil and withstand considerable drought, poor drainage, and relatively high salt levels. They also take heat and strong light, including reflected heat from paving, and tolerate wind, air pollution, and salt spray.

Growth is best in full sun in moist, well-drained soil. In shade or in cool locations, few flowers develop and growth is weak and leggy. Water infrequently in late summer and fall so growth hardens before cold weather begins. Prune in early spring to control size and form. Cut off stem tips that have flowered to

increase branching. Pull, don't cut, suckers, which occur at the base of the plant, to prevent bushiness.

Pest problems of oleander include yellow oleander aphids, scale insects, and bacterial gall. One spray in the spring usually controls aphids. Bacterial gall causes deformed flowers and warty, split stems. It is best controlled by pruning diseased branches well below the infected area.

All parts of oleander are poisonous to people and livestock. Don't use the wood for barbeque skewers. Also, smoke from burning plant parts can cause severe irritation.

Nyssa sylvatica
Black Gum, Sour Gum, Tupelo, Pepperidge
Zones: 5-9. To 30-50 feet.
Deciduous tree.

The native growing region of black gum extends from southern Canada and eastern United States to southern and central Mexico. On native sites it may reach 75 to 80 feet in height. It is prized for its brilliant fall foliage with colors including scarlet, orange, and yellow. Color is reliable even in mild climates.

Black gum has a slow to medium growth rate. It is upright when young and develops into a broad pyramid with interesting irregularities. Tree bark is narrowly fissured with age, has a reddish tinge, and is textured like alligator skin. The oval leaves are shiny dark green above and waxy gray beneath. They are 2 to 3 inches long, and have pointed tips. Deep red bark on young long twigs adds color to the landscape in winter and early spring. Flowers are small and not showy. The dark blue fruit are the size and shape of an olive and are edible. Berries have a pleasant acid taste that is attractive to birds.

Black gum grows well in average soil and climate conditions and will tolerate wet, swampy, and acidic sites. Should be transplanted when fairly young. After trunk reaches 3 to 4 inches in diameter, black gum will transplant poorly.

Olea europaea
Common Olive
Zones: 9-10. To 25-30 feet.
Evergreen tree.

Cultivated in the eastern Mediterranean area since ancient times, fruiting olive trees over 1,000 years old are known. Trees planted in California by the Spanish missionaries in the 1700's are still producing. Besides being grown for fruit, olive trees make striking, gray-green-foliaged landscape specimens.

A dense, rounded tree develops in poor soil with little water. Under better conditions, growth is irregular and more open. In both situations height and width are similar, but young trees with good growing conditions develop height quickly, then fill out slowly. Low branching is normal. Most trees are multi-trunked.

Bark is smooth and gray when young, becoming rough and dark brown on old trees. Willowlike leaves, 1-1/2 to 3 inches long, are gray-green on the upper surface and silver beneath. The fragrant, tiny yellow-white flowers are wind-pollinated. They appear on two-year-old branches during April and May. Glossy fruits, 1/2 to 1-1/2 inches long, ripen in fall after changing from green to purple and finally to black and wrinkled. They are inedible without special processing.

Three varieties are most commonly planted in the landscape. 'Fruitless', used only for landscaping, may produce some fruit. 'Manzanillo' is a low-growing, spreading, large-fruited variety used both commercially and for landscaping. 'Mission' is taller, more compact, and hardier, and is used for both purposes.

Olives are hardy to 15°F. They should be planted in full sun and well-drained soil. Faster growth occurs on moist, fertile soil but a more attractive, contorted shape develops on poor, dry, shallow, or alkaline soils. Grows well in hot, dry conditions as well as cool, moist coastal regions of California. Fruiting is not reliable in warm, humid areas of the southern United States.

Fruits stain any surface on which they fall. Nonfruiting varieties, picking, or hormone sprays can be used to reduce fruit set.

Ophiopogon
Mondo Grass, Lilyturf
Evergreen ground cover.
Flowering.

These grassy-leaved plants are similar in appearance, use, and culture to *Liriope sp.*, except that they are not as cold hardy. Stalks of white, lavender, or purple flowers are hidden among the leaves and though pretty, are not particularly showy.

Use as a ground cover in large areas or as an edging for drives and walks. Best in sandy loam in sun or shade. Fertilize lightly in spring and cut back if plants are ragged. Water during dry spells.

Ophiopogon jaburan
White Lilyturf
Zones: 6-10. To 24-36 inches.
Evergreen ground cover.
Flowering.

Flowers are white or pale lilac. Leaves may be green, but several white- or gold-striped varieties are available. White lilyturf is sometimes labeled in nurseries as *Liriope*.

Ophiopogon japonicus
Mondo Grass, Dwarf Lilyturf
Zones: 6-10. To 8-10 inches.
Evergreen ground cover.
Flowering.

Leaves of this popular ground cover are very narrow and low, creating a uniform carpet of green. Light purple flowers in late summer are partially hidden by the foliage. Space plants 6 to 8 inches apart.

Osmanthus heterophyllus
Holly Olive
Zones: 7-10. To 10 feet.
Evergreen shrub. Flowering.

Osmanthus has long been a garden favorite, admired for its spiny-edged lustrous green foliage and shapely form. Inconspicuous, yet highly fragrant clusters of small creamy-white flowers appear in

Common olives *(Olea europaea)* make interesting specimen trees. Their fruit is edible only after processing.

Mondo grass *(Ophiopogon japonicus)* makes a good formal flower bed edging.

Variegated holly olive *(Osmanthus heterophyllus* 'Variegatus') is a widely used pest-free evergreen.

Trailing african daisy *(Osteospermum fruticosum)* makes a colorful, durable ground cover. Flowers, in a choice of vivid colors, bloom throughout the year. Use in mass plantings, shown below left; or as an informal border, shown below right.

early fall. Bluish-black berries follow.

Holly olive is an easy-to-grow pest-free plant adaptable to almost any garden soil. Grows in partial shade or full sun. Shapely as an untrimmed or clipped hedge, holly olive is an excellent choice for an informal screen or in foundation or border plantings.

'Gulftide' is an excellent well-branched variety with a compact form growing to 5 to 8 feet. 'Purpureus' adds color to the garden with dark purple young leaves that remain tinted through the summer. 'Rotundifolius' makes a handsome slow-growing shrub to 5 feet. Its leaves are rounded rather than holly-like. 'Variegatus' will add sparkle to shaded areas with its white-margined leaves. Grows slowly to form a dense 5-foot shrub.

Osteospermum fruticosum
Trailing African Daisy
Zones: 9-10. To 6-12 inches.
Evergreen ground cover.
Flowering.

This durable, easy-care plant makes an excellent ground cover in hot, dry climates. It spreads quickly, forming dense clumps of light green leaves. Blooms throughout the year, though most heavily in spring and fall. Flowers are daisy-like, and usually colored purple, burgundy, or white, sometimes yellow or rusty-brown.

Use African daisies in mass plantings or as an edging. Looks handsome grown along the top of a retaining wall where its stems drape over the wall.

'African Queen' has purple flowers. 'Hybrid White' is white with dark centers. 'Burgundy' has dark wine-colored flowers. 'Sunshine' is ivory on top with bold yellow and white stripes on the petal undersides.

Set plants 1 to 2 feet apart in any well-drained soil in full sun. Fall planting is best. Requires little care. Drought- and heat-tolerant, but best to water deeply once or twice during the summer. Mow in spring every few years to encourage new growth.

Ostrya virginiana
American Hop Hornbeam

Zones: 4-9. To 30-50 feet. Deciduous tree.

This roundheaded, native tree is seldom planted but is often found hiding in the woods under the shelter of larger trees. It is an attractive, neatly shaped tree and deserves wider cultivation.

The leaves resemble those of birch, to which it is related. In fall they turn bright yellow. The trunk bark has an unusual, interesting appearance and is quite shredded and shaggy. Inconspicuous flowers produce clusters of seedpods that resemble hops.

American hop hornbeam prefers a moist medium loam soil that is neutral to slightly acid. It tolerates dry sites. Grows in shade or sun. Makes an attractive specimen tree on small properties. It does not tolerate heavy air pollution, and is difficult to transplant.

Oxydendrum arboreum
Sourwood, Sorrel Tree

Zones: 6-9. To 15-25 feet. Deciduous tree. Flowering.

A choice narrow, pyramidal tree, sourwood bears creamy-white bell-shaped flowers in drooping, 10-inch-long clusters in midsummer. Ornamental brown seedpods follow flowering. Rich green summer foliage turns to orange and red in fall. Tree grows slowly to 25 feet; may eventually reach 50 feet. Growth is best in cool summer areas of Zones 6 to 8. Needs moist, acid, well-drained soil, and full sun.

Pachysandra terminalis
Pachysandra, Japanese Spurge

Zones: 4-9. To 6-10 inches. Evergreen ground cover. Flowering.

Pachysandra is one of the star ground covers. It is both durable and beautiful. The dark green foliage is arranged in whorls around short upright stems. Underground stems quickly spread the plant, creating a dense uniform cover. Fluffy creamy-white flowers bloom in summer and are often followed by white berries.

Use pachysandra in large areas where a lawn is too much trouble or cannot grow. It is also elegant in small areas such as edging a walk or driveway or beneath shrubs.

Space plants from flats about 6 to 12 inches apart in early spring. Does best in light shade in rich, acid soil. Tolerates deep shade beneath trees. In too much sun, plants will be yellow-green. Fertilize lightly in spring. Water during dry spells.

'Green Carpet' is slightly lower and brighter green. 'Silver Edge' and 'Variegata' have white leaf edges; brighten up shady spots.

Palmae
Palm Family

Zones: 8-10. To 60 feet. Evergreen trees.

Palms are a varied group of plants that encompasses a great number of genera and species belonging to the family *Palmae*. Their bold features and tropical appearance make them invaluable landscape plants. They can be small plants, ideal for growing in containers, or statuesque specimens with towering trunks. Their leaves can be round and fan-like or long, narrow, feathery plumes. Some have colorful fruit.

In the landscape, palms lend a tropical feeling wherever they are used—around swimming pools, along avenues, in groups, or as specimens.

Palms grow best in fertile, well-drained soil with regular watering. They are easy to grow and easy to transplant. Even large specimens can be moved with relative ease. Palms get off to the best start when ample organic matter is added to the planting hole. Some grow best in shade, others prefer full sun. Many palms are frost-sensitive, while others tolerate light frost. Young plants are especially sensitive to cold. As trees mature, dead leaves should be removed from the lower portion of the canopy to keep the trunk clean.

Sourwood *(Oxydendrum arboreum)* is an excellent lawn tree, offering summer flowers and brilliant fall foliage.

Dense foliage, shown below, makes adaptable pachysandra *(Pachysandra terminalis)* a valuable ground cover.

Sago palm *(Cycas revoluta)* grows low and full.

Trunks of pygmy date palm *(Phoenix roebelenii)* are studded with woody leaf bases.

Palms

Botanical Name/ Common Name	Zones	Size	Native to	Plant Description	Comments
Archontophoenix cunninghamiana *(Seaforthia elegans)* **Australian King Palm**	9-10	To 30 ft tall or more.	Queensland, New South Wales	Small with single, slender, ringed trunk. Plumelike fronds are bright green. Bright red fruits hang on in warm months.	Good tub or patio tree. Quite fast-growing in hot climates. Not for windy sites. Hardy to 28°F.
Arecastrum romanzoffianum *(Cocos plumosa)* **Queen Palm**	9-10	To 40 ft tall or more.	Southern Brazil to Argentina	Rapid-growing with straight single trunk. Long, dark green, plumelike fronds. Orange fruits are decorative; ripen in cool months.	Handsome background plants. Good in groups or as accent trees. Sun or shade. Hardy to 25°F.
Brahea armata *(Erythea armata)* **Blue Fan Palm**	8-10	To 30 ft tall or more.	Baja, California	Slow-growing with single trunk. Fan-shaped fronds are waxy silver-blue, arch gracefully. Yellow fruits on long spikes.	Bold arresting specimen. Tolerates drought, heat, wind. Best in full sun. Hardy to 18°F.
B. edulis *(Erythea edulis)* **Guadalupe Palm**	8-10	To 20 ft tall or more.	Guadalupe Islands, Mexico	Slow-growing with strong, heavy trunk. Bright green fan-shaped leaves drop, leaving clean trunk. Fruits black when ripe.	Excellent palm for background use in the desert or near the coast. Best in full sun. Hardy to 20°F.
Butia capitata *(Cocos australis)* **South American Jelly Palm**	8-10	To 15-20 ft tall.	Brazil to Argentina	Heavy, stocky trunk. Exceptionally long, graceful recurving plume-type leaves are bluish green. Orange fruits in clusters in summer.	Use freestanding or in palm groups. Needs ample space. Full sun or light shade. Hardiest plume-type palm, to 15°F.
Chamaedorea elegans *(Neanthe bella)* **Parlor Palm**	9-10	To 8-10 ft tall.	Mexico, Guatemala	Dwarf, usually single-trunked. Pale green plume-type leaves. Small black fruits.	Requires some shade. Useful as patio specimen in tubs. Popular indoor plant. Frost-sensitive.
C. erumpens **Bamboo Palm**	8-10	To 10 ft tall.	British Honduras, Guatemala	Slender, green, bamboolike trunks in clumps. Feathery fronds with slender stems. Small black fruits.	Full shade. Frost-sensitive. Popular indoor plant.
Chamaerops humilis **European Fan Palm**	8-10	To 10-12 ft tall.	Only palm native to Europe	Slow-growing with multiple trunks. Fan-type fronds are gray-green, quite showy. Red-and-yellow fruits.	Takes heat, wind and full sun. Use as lawn or patio tree, or in tubs. Stands more cold than most palms. Hardy to 6°F.
Chrysalidocarpus lutescens *(Areca lutescens)* **Areca Palm, Butterfly Palm, Cane Palm, Yellow Palm**	10	To 10-15 ft tall.	Madagascar	Slow-growing with clump habit. Smooth, ringed, bamboolike trunks. Yellow-green feathery leaves. Violet-black fruits.	Grow in containers indoors or outdoors in sheltered spot. Frost-sensitive.

Above: Senegal date palm *(Phoenix reclinata)* often forms clumps. Top right: Mexican fan palm *(Washingtonia robusta)* has giant fan-shaped leaves. Bottom right: Windmill palms *(Trachycarpus fortunei)* have single trunks.

Botanical Name/ Common Name	Zones	Size	Native to	Plant Description	Comments
Cycas revoluta Sago Palm	9-10	To 6-8 ft tall.	Southern Japan, Ryukyu Islands	Very slow-growing with stout un-branching trunk. Dark green, feathery leaves to 4 ft long. Red seed.	A cycad, not a true palm. Rugged and hardy. Good choice for container growing on patio. Likes partial shade. Hardy to 15°F.
Dioon edule Chestnut Dioon	9-10	To 3-6 ft tall.	Mexico, Central America	Dwarf with cylindrical trunk 6-10 in. wide. Feathery leaves in a rosette, dark green and stiff at maturity. Edible seeds.	Excellent tropical effect when freestanding. Best in light shade. Hardy to 25°F.
Howea forsterana Sentry Palm, Kentia Palm	10	To 60 ft tall.	Lord Howe Islands, Australia	Slow-growing with single smooth trunk. Plumelike leaves are arching, dark green. Fruits yellow-green.	Traditional parlor palm. Smaller growth in containers. Use as lawn specimen. Best in light shade. Frost-sensitive.
Phoenix canariensis Canary Island Date Palm	8-10	To 30-50 ft tall.	Canary Islands	Sturdy, thick trunk. Yellow-green feathery fronds have thorny stems. Bright orange-yellow fruits.	Requires space but can be grown in container for years. Majestic, cascading effect. Full sun or light shade. Hardy to 20°F.
P. reclinata Senegal Date Palm	9-10	To 35 ft tall.	Tropical Africa	Clump-forming with slender trunks. Heavy crown of green-colored feathery fronds with thorny stems. Bright orange fruits.	Useful for large screens because of attractive clustering habit. Full sun. Hardy to 28°F.
P. roebelenii Pygmy Date Palm	10	To 6-10 ft tall.	Laos	Slow-growing dwarf with tendency to grow in clumps. Plumelike leaves with thorny stems. Black fruits.	Elegant pot plant for patio or indoors. Prefers moisture and shade. Frost-sensitive.
Trachycarpus fortunei (Chamaerops excelsa) Windmill Palm	8-10	To 25 ft tall.	Northern Burma, Central & Eastern China	Slow-growing with single slender trunk. Gray-green fan-type leaves. Fruits the size of peas.	Excellent accent shrub for borders. Full sun or light shade. Hardy to 10°F.
Washingtonia robusta Mexican Fan Palm, Washington Palm	8-10	To 60 ft tall.	Arid regions of Colorado, California, Southwest Arizona	Rapid-growing, straight trunk clothed with shag of old hanging leaves. Palm-type fronds are medium green, many gray threads. Stems have thorns. Black fruits.	Excellent for row planting on streets, along driveways. Tolerates drought and poor soil. Hardy to 20°F. *W. filifera* has a stalkier trunk, but is less common.

Jerusalem thorn *(Parkinsonia aculeata)* is a tree for difficult sites in the arid Southwest.

Tenacious and hardy, Boston ivy *(Parthenocissus tricuspidata)* clings tightly to walls and fences. Foliage, shown below, turns brilliant hues in fall.

Parkinsonia aculeata

Jerusalem Thorn

Zones: 8-10. To 25-30 feet.
Deciduous tree. Flowering.

Jerusalem thorn is valuable only in the arid Southwest where it provides light shade and yellow spring flowers in areas where few other trees will grow. Leaves are divided into many tiny leaflets and arranged sparsely on the greenish-yellow, thorned branches. They drop quickly during drought or cold. Withstands alkaline soil, heat, and drought.

Parthenocissus

Virginia Creeper, Boston Ivy

Deciduous vines.

Few vines can equal the dramatic fall color of Virginia creeper and Boston ivy, two top-rated vines of the grape family. Their leaves turn brilliant shades of red and gold, creating a dazzling autumn show. The vines climb with flat adhesive discs, borne at the ends of branching tendrils.

Use these vines to decorate sides of buildings or slopes where they can spread to cover large expanses. They are best on brick or stucco walls since they can damage shingles. Adaptable to a wide range of soils and climate zones, Virginia creeper and Boston ivy are popular vines for landscape use.

Parthenocissus quinquefolia
Virginia Creeper
Zones: 4-10.
Deciduous vine.

Virginia creeper is readily identified by its leaflets, which are arranged like fingers of a hand. There are 5 to a leaf, measuring 2 to 6 inches in length. They have coarsely toothed margins. When leaves appear in early spring, they are tinged purple, turning dark green as they mature, and then changing to shades of scarlet in the fall. Bluish-black berries on red stalks remain until winter when they drop to the ground or are eaten by birds.

Virginia creeper needs a rough surface to adhere to because its tendrils are less clinging than those of Boston ivy. Long drooping branches hang gracefully away from the vine. Use Virginia creeper to cover a trellis or fence, or the side of a building.

This vine can grow in almost any garden setting, withstanding freezing temperatures or high summer heat, and it is drought-tolerant. It will grow in a wide range of soil types but a well-drained, loamy, moist soil is preferred. Grows well in sun or shade.

When planting new vines, place them close to their support and space about 2 to 4 feet apart for adequate coverage. Cut back stems in early stages of growth to induce branching. Guide branches up their support during the first year. Once established, the vine may be pruned in early spring to direct growth or keep it in bounds. Watch for any leaf damage by Japanese beetles or leafhoppers. Mildew may be a problem in damp sites.

Two varieties of Virginia creeper are top-rated. Their smaller leaves create a softer effect when planted against a wall. 'Engelmannii', Engelmann creeper, forms a dense cover with small leathery leaves. 'Saint-Paulii', St. Paul's creeper, is a more tenacious clinger with rounder leaflets.

Parthenocissus tricuspidata
Boston Ivy
Zones: 4-10.
Deciduous vine.

There is no mistaking this vine when it displays its dramatic fall color, although at other times of the year it is sometimes confused with English ivy. In early fall the foliage changes to fiery shades of scarlet and yellow. An interesting meshwork of branches and persistent dark blue berries are left exposed after the leaves drop. Spring leaves are purplish when they first appear, maturing into large, green, 3-lobed leaves. They will eventually reach 8 inches in width. Individual leaves are held on long stems. They stand out from the branches and flutter gracefully in the breeze.

Boston ivy branches more and is a more tenacious climber than Virginia creeper. It will give good coverage over large expanses of wall. The vine branches from the base, spreading in all directions over its support. It is one of the best vines for city environments, tolerating dust and exhaust fumes. Use it to soften the appearance of exposed walls, especially those of city buildings or as a fence or ground cover.

Growing requirements for Boston ivy are similar to those of Virginia creeper.

The variety 'Lowii', Low's creeper, has deeply lobed 1-1/2-inch leaves on shorter stalks. Its growth is restrained, making it suitable for smaller areas. 'Veitchii', Veitch's creeper, has small, dainty leaves.

Passiflora
Passionflower
Evergreen vines. Flowering.

Passionflower vines are native to South America, where they grow as tall clinging vines. In the United States they are grown primarily for their unique flowers, which bloom from spring through fall, and are used as a dense screening cover. In warmer climates, large edible fruits may be produced.

Some varieties will reach 40 feet, climbing with clinging corkscrew-like tendrils. Numerous branches, thickly covered with large, deeply lobed leaves, are quite ornamental.

Passionflower vines require a large area in which to grow. They are often used for cascading wall covers or shading on patios. Rooting branches can be effective as a stabilizing ground cover on banks. In cold climates it's an exotic vine for growing in the greenhouse.

Passionflower grows in a variety of soil types. Regular watering and fertilizing produces best growth. Place in the sunniest spot in the garden. Where temperatures are cool, the plant should be held against a south- or west-facing wall to take advantage of reflected heat.

Passionflower is a vigorous grower and will need a sturdy framework for support. It usually requires heavy pruning each year to remove old branches and control the rampant growth. Remove stems at their origin to open up the vine.

Passiflora x alatocaerulea
Hybrid Passionflower
Zones: 9-10.
Evergreen or semievergreen vine. Flowering.

This hybridized vine is the most popular of the passionflowers because of its large flowers and pest resistance.

Three-inch-long leaves have 3 lance-shaped lobes with smooth margins. Long-lasting, fragrant flowers have white sepals and pink petals with green undersides that form a star-shaped outer ring. The showy filaments or corona are tipped white with blue centers and purple bases. No fruit forms.

Passiflora caerulea
Blue Passionflower
Zones: 9-10.
Evergreen or semievergreen vine. Flowering.

Blue passionflower is one of the most vigorous species. Its slender, intertwining stems grow to 40 feet. Leaves are deeply divided, have narrow lobes, and are smaller than those of the hybrid passionflower. Blossoms are 3 to 4 inches across and have white to pale pink sepals and petals. The corona is deep purple at the base, tipped white.

Two cultivars are available: 'Constance' has lovely, pure white flowers and 'Grandiflora' boasts 5- to 6-inch blossoms.

Passiflora edulis
Purple Granadilla, Passion Fruit
Zones: 9-10.
Semievergreen vine. Flowering.

Purple granadilla is a woody climber grown mainly for its exotic, edible fruit. The vine can cover a large area to form a thick screen. Dark green, shiny foliage completely covers the vine to its full height of 30 feet. Leaves can be

Purple granadilla *(Passiflora edulis)* quickly forms a thick screen over wide areas. Exotic flowers, shown below, appear from June to September and produce edible fruits in spring and fall.

The perfumed flowers of mock orange (*Philadelphus* sp.) bring fragrance and color to the garden in late spring and early summer. Some varieties have highly attractive double flowers, shown below.

identified by their 3-parted lobes with coarsely toothed margins. White flowers marked with purple, borne from June to September, are 2 to 3 inches across.

Fruits form in spring and fall. They are 2 to 3 inches long and egg-shaped, with a hard, dark purple rind when ripe. A long, warm growing season improves fruit quality. Vines bear fruit in their second year. Prune back branches to encourage flowering and control the size.

Phellodendron amurense
Amur Cork Tree
Zones: 4-8. To 30-50 feet.
Deciduous tree.

Native to China and Japan, amur cork tree develops massive wide-spreading branches and thick corky bark on older specimens. The outline of young trees is vase-shaped, becoming rounded as the tree matures. Open-growing, the tree casts filtered shade, permiting grass and other plants to grow beneath it.

Leaves are 12 to 16 inches long with 5 to 13 dark green glossy leaflets 3 to 4 inches long. Leaves emerge in midseason but drop early after developing yellow fall color. Female trees bear clusters of 1/4-inch black berries which can stain concrete.

Needs full sun. Grows in most soil types, including alkaline. Transplants well even when larger. Growth rate is average to fast. Withstands city conditions including some drought, and is a good lawn or park tree.

Philadelphus
Mock Orange
Deciduous shrubs. Flowering.

Mock oranges are admired for their perfumed white flowers that have the sweet fragrance of orange blossoms. They bloom in late spring or early summer, after the majority of spring flowering shrubs have faded, making them valuable landscape plants. Shrubs are vase-shaped with spreading or drooping branches.

Mock oranges are tough, durable plants, and although not too particular, grow best in a well-drained, loamy soil with lots of organic matter. They are easily grown, with few problems, if located in full sun or light shade. Partial shade is required in the hottest areas. Prune after flowering if necessary. Blossoms are produced on 1-year-old wood.

Mock oranges are used as specimen plants, in mass plantings, and in shrub borders. Lower-growing types make useful hedges or dividers.

Philadelphus coronarius
Sweet Mock Orange
Zones: 5-8. To 12 feet.
Deciduous shrub. Flowering.

This old-fashioned plant has been brightening gardens for centuries. It should have intensely sweet-scented flowers, but inferior plants are sometimes sold. Purchase blooming plants with good fragrance. It tends to become leggy in confined spaces, or when planted too close to buildings, so give it room to develop. Will grow as wide as it is tall. The cultivar 'Nanus' grows to 4 feet high.

Philadelphus x lemoinei
Lemoine Mock Orange
Zones: 5-8. To 5-6 feet.
Deciduous shrub. Flowering.

This hybrid mock orange has very fragrant flowers to 1-1/2 inches across. The cultivar 'Enchantment' has erect branches with free-flowering, double, white blossoms that are only lightly fragrant. 'Innocence', growing to 8 feet tall, has wonderfully fragrant flowers, 1 to 2 inches across.

Philadelphus x virginalis
Virginalis Mock Orange
Zones: 4-8. To 6-8 feet.
Deciduous shrub. Flowering.

Produces masses of large, semidouble, fragrant white blooms that are often used for cut flowers. Fast-growing, this mock orange likes full sun and open situations. Tolerates coastal conditions in the eastern United States. The cultivar 'Virginal' blooms all summer and has 2-inch, semidouble, white flowers. 'Minnesota Snowflake' has large, double, fragrant flowers and is hardy to −30°F.

Photinia x fraseri
Red-Tip Photinia
Zones: 7-10. To 10-12 feet.
Evergreen shrub. Flowering.

The bright, bronzy-red new leaves of photinia can equal any flowering shrub for a colorful display in early spring. Large, flat-headed clusters of white flowers follow in March and April, with subsequent red berries, which attract birds, continuing to add visual interest. The lustrous, heat-tolerant foliage is useful as an attractive background for other plants. Photinia is a large-scale screening shrub growing moderately fast to 10 feet high and spreading somewhat wider. It responds well to pruning for a neat shape or formal hedge. Young plants may be trained as attractive small trees.

Photinia readily accepts high heat and sun if watered regularly, or drier conditions in partial shade. Provide a well-drained soil rich in organic matter. Aphids and scale are occasional problems. Photinia is also susceptible to fireblight.

Picea
Spruce
Zones: 2-8. To 100 feet.
Evergreen shrubs and trees.

Picea is one of the largest and most important genera of conifers, containing mostly large conical-shaped trees growing in the cool, temperate regions of the Northern Hemisphere. In the southern United States, growing areas are confined to high elevations.

Needles are usually stiff and dark green. They are retained 6 to 8 years, unless affected by drought, making a dense foliage. Cones are pendulous, adding interest to the trees. Most species have a single trunk and mature at 100 feet or more. Not for small properties, unless you plan on removing them when they outgrow allotted space. You can also select one of the slow-growing or dwarf varieties. Use spruce for windbreaks, shelterbelts, in group plantings, or background plantings on large properties.

Spruces grow on most kinds of soil, providing there is good drainage and ample moisture. *P. omorika*

Red-tip photinia (*Photinia x fraseri*) makes a colorful hedge with its bronzy-red new foliage. White flowers, shown below, bloom in spring and are followed by red berries.

Spruce (*Picea* sp.), shown below, are normally tall trees; dwarf forms are useful as foundation and rock garden plants.

Blossoms of lily-of-the-valley shrub *(Pieris japonica),* shown below, are often showy for as long as a month and begin blooming in very early spring.

and *P. pungens* are more tolerant of dry or poor soils than other species. They are damaged by deicing salt and should not be planted where run-off or drifting spray caused by traffic could be a problem. Prune spruce by lightly shearing in early spring to control size, if desired.

(See chart on next page.)

Pieris
Andromeda, Pieris
Evergreen shrubs. Flowering.

Pieris are ornamental plants grown for their foliage and clusters of white or pink flowers in spring. They can be used as specimens in groupings with other evergreen plants, as well as in naturalistic plantings. Do not crowd, but allow shrubs room for development.

A moist, acid, well-drained soil is required. Grows best in partial shade. Light shade afforded by tall scattered trees is ideal. Some sun for short periods aids flower formation.

Pieris floribunda
Fetterbush, Mountain Andromeda
Zones: 5-9. To 6 feet.
Evergreen shrub. Flowering.

This dense shrub is the hardiest of the pieris. Bears upright pyramidal clusters of white flowers in early spring. Glossy green leaves are long ovals with toothed edges.

'Karenoma' is a fast-growing compact shrub with snow-white flowers in early spring.

Pieris japonica
Andromeda, Japanese Pieris, Lily-of-the-Valley Shrub
Zones: 5-9. To 9-10 feet.
Evergreen shrub. Flowering.

An upright-growing shrub with stiff, spreading branches, Japanese pieris bears pendulous clusters of white flowers very early in spring. New growth is bronze, changing to dark green as leaves develop. Dislikes strong winds and grows best on protected sites in Zone 5. Many cultivars have been selected.

Colorado blue spruce (*Picea pungens* 'Glauca') has a symmetrical shape and blue needles.

Bird's nest spruce (*Picea abies* 'Nidiformis') forms a dense mound, striking in a rock garden.

(*Picea abies* 'Pendula') will cascade over a retaining wall.

Picea

Botanical Name/Common Name	Zones	Size	Plant Description	Comments
Picea abies **Norway Spruce**	2-8	To 90-100 ft tall.	Evergreen tree with pyramidal crown, drooping branches. Becomes more open and picturesque with age. Dark green needles. Large cones to 6 in. long.	Most widely adapted spruce. Grows best in cool, moist climates. Needs regular watering. Makes good windbreak.
P. a. 'Clanbrasiliana'	2-8	To 6 ft tall. Spreads to 10 ft.	Evergreen shrub with globular shape. Grows slowly. Very dense branches.	
P. a. 'Nidiformis' **Bird's Nest Spruce**	3-7	To 4-6 ft tall. Spreads to 5-7 ft.	Evergreen shrub. Forms a compact, nestlike mound. Rich dark green foliage.	A good accent plant.
P. a. 'Pendula'	3-7	To 18 in. tall. Spreads to 10 ft.	Evergreen shrub with strongly weeping branches. Dark green foliage. Can be grown as 8 to 10-ft-tall weeping tree if staked.	If grown prostrate, drapes over walls or sides of container. A dramatic accent plant if trained upright.
P. a. 'Pygmaea'	3-7	To 2 ft tall. Spreads to 3 ft.	Evergreen shrub forms a dense spreading mound. Dark green foliage.	Use as accent plant or filler wherever a small spot of greenery is needed.
P. glauca **White Spruce**	2-5	To 70-80 ft tall.	Evergreen tree with conical shape, drooping branchlets, bluish-green needles.	Endures severe heat and cold.
P. g. albertiana **Alberta Spruce**	2-5	To 7 ft tall.	Dwarf evergreen tree with narrow conical shape, very tiny soft grass-green needles.	Grows slowly. Good in containers.
P. g. 'Conica' **Dwarf Alberta Spruce, Dwarf White Spruce**	2-5	To 8-10 ft tall.	Evergreen tree with compact pyramidal shape. Slow-growing. New growth soft green. Has grayish tinge with maturity.	Good formal accent or living Christmas tree. Protect from dry winds.
P. g. 'Densata' **Black Hills Spruce**	2-5	To 25-35 ft tall.	Evergreen tree with bluish-green needles. Forms dense compact pyramid.	Makes a good screen. Grows well in containers.
P. omorika **Serbian Spruce**	5-8	To 75-100 ft tall.	Evergreen tree forms a narrow cone. Short drooping branches curve up at tips. Needles whitish above; dark green below.	Very graceful. Takes less room than most spruce. Needs protection from cold winter wind.
P. pungens **Colorado Spruce, Colorado Blue Spruce**	2-8	To 80-100 ft tall.	Evergreen tree. Broad pyramidal habit. Horizontal branches, regularly spaced. Slow grower. Needles usually bluish-green.	Seedlings vary in needle color. Foliage color of varieties is more predictable.
P. p. 'Glauca' **Colorado Blue Spruce**	3-7	To 80-100 ft tall.	Same as species but with reliable steel-blue-colored foliage.	Good accent plant.
P. p. 'Hoopsii'	2-8	To 80-100 ft tall.	Same as species. The bluest-colored foliage of all Colorado spruce.	Good accent plant.
P. p. 'Koster' **Koster Blue Spruce**	3-7	To 80-100 ft tall.	Same as species. Has slightly irregular growth pattern. Reliable blue color. Deeper blue than 'Glauca'.	Good accent plant.
P. p. 'Moerheimii' **Moerheim Blue Spruce**	3-7	To 80-100 ft tall.	Similar to species with denser foliage and symmetrical habit. Good blue-gray color.	Good accent plant. Grows very slowly.

Pinus
Pine

Zones: 2-10. To 120 feet.
Evergreen shrubs or trees.

This large genus contains 90 species of usually tall coniferous trees. A few species are naturally dwarf and compact, and many shrubby and dwarf cultivars have been selected from other species.

Pines are native to the Northern Hemisphere with different species growing from the cold northern latitudes to the tropics. Many species are planted as ornamentals. Most are best suited to large areas as a single specimen or silhouette tree; some make useful windbreaks and shelterbelts. Planted in groves they create a serene woodland effect. Many dwarf varieties are ideal for containers.

Leaves are needlelike, usually borne in clusters of 2 to 5, rarely 1. Their length contributes to the character and texture of the tree. Those with long needles, such as *Pinus canariensis*, the Canary Island pine, are soft textured with an almost weeping appearance. Shorter needles result in a coarser texture. Many pines develop a twisted, contorted habit with age that adds greatly to their landscape appeal.

Most pines grow best in full sun and well-drained soil. Many are drought tolerant. Applications of fertilizers are usually not necessary. Pines are subject to a number of pests, including aphids, scale, mites, and rust fungus. However, if trees are well adapted to the area you live in and receive reasonable care, pests are rarely troublesome.

Mugo pines *(Pinus mugo)* form dense compact mounds.

Pinus

Botanical Name/Common Name	Zones	Size	Plant Description	Comments
Pinus aristata Bristlecone Pine, Hickory Pine	5-6	To 12-15 ft tall.	Evergreen tree with irregular twisted form. Very slow-growing. Short, stout needles in clusters of 5, held 20-30 years. Bushy appearance at branch tips.	Good pine for container-growing. Use in landscape when irregular form is desired.
P. bungeana Lacebark Pine	5-9	To 80 ft tall.	Evergreen tree. Slow-growing. Forms pyramidal to round-topped tree. Long, stiff needles in clusters of 3. Mottled gray-green and cream bark. Often multistemmed.	Has shrubby picturesque shape. Sensitive to salt.
P. canariensis Canary Island Pine	9-10	To 90 ft tall.	Evergreen tree. Grows rapidly. Pyramidal when young, becoming rounded with age. Foot-long, soft needles in clusters of 3. High branching.	Use for evergreen windbreak. Drought-tolerant. Good for street tree. Grows well in California and Deep South.
P. cembra Swiss Stone Pine, Russian Cedar	3-8	To 70 ft tall where native. To 15-25 ft tall in landscape.	Evergreen tree forms tight pyramid. Very slow grower. Long, dark green needles in clusters of 5. Formal habit.	Good pine for small gardens. Handsome in landscape.
P. contorta Shore Pine, Beach Pine	7-10	To 30 ft tall.	Evergreen tree with irregular form. Dense dark green needles held in clusters of 2.	Adds interesting landscape texture. Good in containers and most planting sites, except hot and dry.
P. densiflora Japanese Red Pine	5-9	To 90-100 ft tall.	Evergreen tree. Conical when young. Flat-topped with age. Short needles in clusters of 2. Interesting orange-red, scaling bark.	Picturesque tree for informal gardens.
P. d. 'Umbraculifera' Tanyosho, Japanese Umbrella Pine	5-9	To 12-20 ft tall.	Evergreen tree with broad, umbrellalike form. Attractive red bark.	Good in Japanese and rock gardens. Grows well in containers.
P. halepensis Aleppo Pine, Jerusalem Pine	7-10	To 30-50 ft tall.	Evergreen tree with medium-length needles in clusters of 2, rarely 3. Open crown can appear shrubby. Very fast grower.	Good windbreak. Suitable for hot, dry areas; seaside or desert. *P. h. eldarica* is similar and especially well adapted to the desert.
P. mugo Mugo Pine, Mountain Pine, Swiss Mountain Pine	2-8	To 4-6 ft tall.	Evergreen shrub with neat, compact, symmetrical form. Short, stout needles in clusters of 2.	Very popular and widely adapted. Good for container-growing, rock gardens, or bonsai. Dwarf varieties available.
P. nigra Austrian Pine, Black Pine	3-8	To 60-120 ft tall.	Evergreen tree. Conical when young. Loses lower branches, becoming umbrella-shaped when mature. Long, stiff needles in clusters of 2.	Tolerates acidic to alkaline soils, and drift from deicing salts.

White pine *(Pinus strobus)* makes a soft-textured screen.

Japanese black pine *(Pinus thunbergiana)* has long, stiff needles.

Botanical Name/Common Name	Zones	Size	Plant Description	Comments
P. parviflora **Japanese White Pine**	5-8	To 20-50 ft tall.	Evergreen tree. Forms picturesque, broadly pyramidal, irregular form. Short bluish-green needles in tufted clusters of 5.	Very wide-spreading. Often grown in containers. Good for bonsai.
P. patula **Mexican Yellow Pine,** **Jelecote Pine**	9-10	To 40-80 ft tall.	Evergreen tree with loose, open pyramidal crown of tiered branches. Rapid grower. Foot-long needles held in drooping clusters of 3. Casts light shade. Has interesting silhouette.	Unusual weeping foliage. Good for coastal areas of the Pacific Northwest and Southern California.
P. pinaster **Cluster Pine, Maritime Pine**	7-10	To 60-90 ft tall.	Evergreen tree. Conical with spreading branches. Long needles held in clusters of 2. Thrives on well-drained sandy soils.	Good for stabilizing sand dunes, general seaside planting. Does not like clay soils.
P. pinea **Italian Stone Pine,** **Umbrella Pine**	7-10	To 30-75 ft tall.	Evergreen tree with distinctive form. Globular, bushy when young. Flat-topped umbrella shape when mature. Long needles in clusters of 2.	Edible seeds. Withstands heat and drought. Grown in California and Pacific Northwest. Good coastal tree.
P. radiata **Monterey Pine**	7-10	To 80-100 ft tall.	Evergreen tree. Rapid grower. Conical when young. Rounded, nearly flat crown when mature. Long, bright green needles in clusters of 3.	Good for windy seashore conditions. Sensitive to smog. Intolerant of high heat. Cultivar 'Majestic Beauty' tolerates smog.
P. strobus **White Pine,** **Eastern White Pine**	2-8	To 100-150 ft tall.	Evergreen tree. Rounded or pyramidal shape at maturity. Long, thin needles in clusters of 5. Soft-textured in the landscape.	Intolerant of high heat, low humidity. Common in the Southwest. Susceptible to white pine blister rust.
P. s. 'Fastigiata'	2-8	To 100-150 ft tall.	Evergreen tree with a narrow columnar form.	
P. s. 'Nana'	2-8	To 3-7 ft tall.	Dwarf evergreen tree with a wide bushy shape.	Slow-growing.
P. sylvestris **Scots Pine, Scotch Pine**	3-8	To 70-100 ft tall.	Evergreen tree. Conical when young. Variable shape at maturity. Twisted, bluish-green needles in clusters of 2. Orange-red trunk bark.	Good windbreak, shade, specimen, or Christmas tree. Tolerates some drought. Not for desert regions. 'Fastigiata' forms column.
P. thunbergiana **Japanese Black Pine**	5-9	To 60-90 ft tall.	Evergreen tree. Broad pyramidal crown becomes irregular with age. Fast-growing. Long needles in clusters of 2.	Best pine for northeastern seashore. Tolerates salt spray. Can be pruned or trained for bonsai. 'Oculus-draconis' has needles striped with 2 yellow bands.

As a screening plant for mild climates, variegated tobira (Pittosporum tobira 'Variegata') is unsurpassed.

Bloodgood London plane tree (Platanus x acerifolia 'Bloodgood') is disease-resistant.

Pistacia chinensis
Chinese Pistachio, Chinese Pistache
Zones: 7-10. To 60 feet.
Deciduous tree.

Chinese pistachio was first introduced to the United States in 1921. It casts a diffused, filtered shade, and has reliable fall color even in warm climates, making it very popular as a lawn, street, patio tree, and as a background specimen.

Chinese pistachio has a broadly rounded crown, a short trunk and interestingly twisted branches. Trees 60 feet tall can have a crown spread of 50 feet. Spring flowers are inconspicuous and male and female flowers are borne on separate trees. Dense clusters of small red fruits on female trees are attractive in autumn.

Deeply divided leaves, up to a foot in length, have a pink tinge when they first appear in spring, soon turning bright green. In fall leaves become brilliant red, orange, or yellow. 'Keith Davey', a male variety, has fine form and consistently brilliant scarlet fall color.

Normally a dry-climate tree, best and most rapid growth is produced on a deep rich soil with good drainage. Will tolerate a variety of sites including moderately alkaline soil if well-drained. Drought conditions are acceptable once the tree becomes established.

Young trees may be straggly and lopsided. Corrective pruning may be required to train it to become the dense shapely tree that is characteristic of mature trees. Some young trees may also have to be staked for a few years until a satisfactory crown has developed.

Pittosporum tobira
Mock Orange, Tobira
Zones: 8-10. To 6-15 feet.
Evergreen shrub. Flowering.

Lustrous leaves, fragrant flowers, and low maintenance are responsible for the popularity of tobira. It is an excellent foundation, specimen, low hedge, or screening plant. Grows well in containers.

Tobira is a medium-sized shrub of vigorous growth and broad, upright habit with heavy branches. Leaves are leathery and glossy dark green. They are spaced so close together on the stems they appear to be in whorls, giving the plant a very solid appearance.

Creamy-white, five-petaled flowers have the scent of orange blossoms, accounting for the common name mock orange. They are about 1 inch across and are produced in 2- to 3-inch clusters at the branch tips in spring. Petals yellow with age. Small pear-shaped seed capsules split in fall revealing orange seeds.

Plant in sun or semishade. Fairly drought-resistant, but appearance is enhanced with moderate watering. Feed once a year in spring with a nitrogen fertilizer to produce greener, larger leaves. Not as tolerant to shearing as some other pittosporums. Head back and thin out to control growth. Aphids and scale are major insect problems.

'Variegata' has attractive gray-green leaves, edged with white; reaches an ultimate height of only 5 feet. 'Wheeler's Dwarf' is a 1- to 2-foot mounding plant with dense, whorled foliage; fragrant flowers are the same as on the larger-growing type; good foreground, border, or hedge plant.

Platanus x acerifolia 'Bloodgood'
Bloodgood London Plane Tree, Sycamore
Zones: 5-10. To 80-120 feet.
Deciduous tree.

Bloodgood London plane tree is a member of the sycamore family, which includes several widely planted species of deciduous trees. A hybrid between the American plane tree, *Platanus occidentalis*, and the Oriental plane tree, *P. orientalis*, this variety is top-rated above all others because of its resistance to the foliage disease anthracnose, which seriously disfigures many species of *Platanus*. It is also one of the few large trees that flourishes under polluted city conditions.

Bloodgood London plane tree has attractive flaking bark, casts good shade, and is long-lived. It is a very useful street, lawn, or shade tree.

This fast-growing pyramidal tree has a massive trunk and thick limbs covered with light gray bark. It peels in large patches, revealing a smooth yellowish underbark. Dense shade is cast by the 3- to 5-lobed, light green, maple-shaped leaves that measure up to 10 inches across. Fall color is a yellowish or orangish brown. If an early frost kills the leaves, they persist into winter. Ball-like, 1-1/2-inch fuzzy brown fruits hang in pairs on long stems and remain into winter.

Grows well in full sun or light shade. Prefers a moist well-drained soil, but most soils, including acid or alkaline, are tolerated. Some chlorosis and leaf burn may develop in desert areas.

Platycladus orientalis
Oriental Arborvitae
(See *Thuja*)

Podocarpus
Yew Pine
Evergreen trees and shrubs.

Yew pine is native to the Southern Hemisphere and the Orient. Closely related to yew, *Taxus sp.*, yew pines also have fleshy, berrylike fruits. They are used as street and lawn trees, and for many of the same purposes as yews: clipped hedges, topiaries, tub plants, and specimen plants. Often planted as shrubs in mild-climate gardens, where they later grow into trees.

Podocarpus gracilior
African Fern Pine
Zones: 9-10. To 50-60 feet.
Evergreen tree.

This is a slow-growing native of East Africa. Variable habit and form depend on the age and propagation method. Plants grown by cuttings from mature trees are limber and slow to develop upright stems; they have gray or blue-green leaves, 1 to 2 inches long. Seedling plants are more upright; branches are less

pendulous; needles are dark, glossy green up to 4 inches long.

Staking is often necessary to hold up the heavy top while the trunk is gaining strength. African fern pines are useful around patios and entryways, and can be used for hedges, espaliers, and even hanging baskets.

Podocarpus macrophyllus
Yew Pine
Zones: 8-10. To 50-60 feet.
Evergreen tree.

A native of Japan and China, yew pine is one of the hardiest species and tolerant of heat and drought. It has a narrow, erect growth habit with short horizontal branches and drooping branchlets. Reaches a height of 8 to 12 feet in 10 years. Makes a good street or lawn tree if thinned and staked. Plant to frame an entryway or use as a privacy screen. The variety *maki* is even slower growing than the species and is excellent in containers.

Flattened leaves are glossy, bright to dark green, 3 to 4 inches long and 1/4 to 1/2 inch wide with pointed ends. Purplish, 1/2-inch-long fruits are not showy.

Yew pine grows in most soils but does best in a moist loam. Chlorosis may develop in alkaline or heavy, wet soils. In cool areas, it grows best in full sun or light shade. Grow in shade and protect from wind in hot climates. Usually pest-free.

Polygonum aubertii
Silver Lace Vine
Zones: 5-10.
Evergreen or deciduous vine.
Flowering.

This profusely blooming vine is named for its billowy, small flowers that blanket the tops of its branches. Silver lace vine, also called fleece flower in some regions, blooms from late summer to midfall when most other plants have finished flowering. Greenish-white blossoms are held in dense, upright clusters above the stems. Distinctive, arrow-shaped leaves, 1-1/2 to 2 inches long, have wavy margins and glossy surfaces. New leaves appear pale

Yew pines *(Podocarpus macrophyllus)* are versatile evergreens used for clipped hedges, specimen plants, and street and lawn trees.

Silver lace vine *(Polygonum aubertii)* quickly covers a fence or arbor and is frosted with delicate greenish-white blossoms in late summer and fall.

A good shade tree for problems sites, white poplar *(Populus alba)* grows in wet or dry soils, tolerates city pollution.

Lombardy poplar *(Populus nigra* 'Italica'), with its columnar shape, is a fast-growing tree for accent or windbreak.

green with red tips. Grows rapidly to 15 to 30 feet and makes a quick cover for a fence or arbor. The vine is deciduous in cold winter areas and evergreen in mild climates.

Silver lace vine is an excellent accent plant for use in tough growing conditions. Thrives in heavy or sandy soils and requires only occasional fertilizing. The vine is partially drought-tolerant. In cold climates, the top of the plant may die to the ground in winter, but hardy roots will send up new shoots in spring.

Silver lace vine takes full sun in most areas, partial shade in areas with hot summers. Newly established plants will need branches tied to a support for early training.

When a light fence cover is desired, silver lace vine makes a splendid choice. Stems twine quickly over their support. Creates a lovely effect on a pergola or as a patio cover. At its best shown cascading over tops of walls. In bloom, the frothy flowers look like white foam.

Populus
Poplar, Cottonwood, Aspen
Deciduous trees.

Poplars are fast-growing, short-lived trees valued where quick effects are needed. They are excellent trees for areas with cold winters and hot summers, such as the Great Plains, but they also grow well in milder climates, where they are used as shade trees and tall screens.

Aggressive surface roots grow toward moisture sources including drain pipes, so planting locations must be chosen carefully. Poplars have weak wood and are subject to wind and snow damage. As a group, they are bothered by stem canker diseases and borers, which cause dieback. Although a trunk may die, it is usually replaced by numerous root suckers, so trees are rarely lost. Numerous suckers from the roots can be a problem in gardens. Poplars are generally used where more trouble-free trees won't grow.

Populus alba
White Poplar, Silver-Leaved Poplar, Abele
Zones: 4-10. To 40-70 feet.
Deciduous tree.

The contrast between the dark green upper surface and the woolly white under surface of the leaves is the outstanding feature of this Eurasian species. It grows well in exposed locations, both on the coast and inland, on wet or dry soils, and is tolerant of city pollution.

Most young trees have a broad oval shape with smooth, light gray bark on the younger branches. Older bark is dark gray. Leaves vary from triangular to maple-shaped with 3 to 5 lobes. Foliage turns yellow in fall.

Bolle's poplar, *P. alba* 'Pyramidalis', is a fast-growing slender pyramidal tree with upright branches. Leaves are maplelike with 3 to 5 lobes. Fall color is deep red, unusual for a poplar.

Populus angustifolia
Narrow-Leaved Cottonwood
Zones: 3-10. To 40-60 feet.
Deciduous tree.

Small narrow leaves to 5 inches long and 1-1/2 inches wide distinguish this small pyramidal tree. It is native along streams from Arizona to Saskatchawan at elevations up to 8,000 feet and is also drought-tolerant. It grows in hot desert climates without irrigation, where few other trees survive.

Populus x canadensis
Canadian Poplar, Carolina Poplar
Zones: 3-10. To 40-150 feet.
Deciduous tree.

This hybrid group is believed to be from crosses between *Populus deltoides* from America and *Populus nigra* from Europe. Canadian poplar is a vigorous tree with triangular leaves to 4 inches long. It is widely used as a specimen, screen, and shelterbelt planting in areas where longer-lived trees won't grow.

Populus deltoides
Cottonwood
Zones: 3-8. To 70-90 feet.
Deciduous tree.

Cottonwood is a roundheaded fast-growing tree suitable for a shade tree in the Midwest. Male trees should be planted since female trees produce a messy cottony mass of seeds. Susceptible to rust fungus.

The variety 'Siouxland', a rust-resistant tree, was introduced by the South Dakota Plant Pathology Department. It has dark green, triangular leaves 4 to 6 inches long and wide. They develop a golden color in fall. Useful as a shade or shelter-belt tree in climates with cold winters and hot summers.

Populus fremontii
**Western Cottonwood,
Fremont Cottonwood**
Zones: 7-10. To 40-60 feet.
Deciduous tree.

This fast-growing, wide-spreading, medium-to-large tree is native from western Texas to California. Trunk diameters may reach 5 to 6 feet. Yellow-green leaves are thick and triangular, and shorter than their 2- to 4-inch width. Only male trees should be planted to avoid the messy, cottony seeds. Tolerates dry conditions and will grow in extremely arid desert regions of the West where few other trees survive.

Populus nigra 'Italica'
Lombardy Poplar
Zones: 3-10. To 4-100 feet.
Deciduous tree.

Lombardy poplar is a tightly columnar form of *P. nigra*, native to Europe and western Asia. It is used as a dramatic accent tree and for windbreaks. Looks especially attractive against the sides of tall buildings.

A fast-growing male tree, it is densely covered with 4-inch-wide triangular leaves. Fall foliage is brilliant yellow. Many suckers grow from the crown and roots.

Populus tremuloides
**Quaking Aspen, Trembling Aspen,
Quiverleaf**
Zones: 2-8. To 60-80 feet.
Deciduous tree.

Quaking aspen is one of the most widely distributed native trees in North America, ranging from Alaska to Mexico and across the continent. Usually found at high elevations in areas with good soil moisture.

Quaking aspen is a fast-growing slender-trunked tree with white to light green bark. At its best in natural landscaping. Small 1- to 2-1/2-inch rounded leaves have long slender flexible stems and the leaves flutter in the slightest breeze. Foliage turns bright yellow in fall. Suckers from the roots frequently develop, forming groves of trees.

Potentilla fruticosa
Shrubby Cinquefoil
Zones: 2-9. To 4 feet.
Deciduous shrub. Flowering.

This many-branched, spreading shrub produces large numbers of bright yellow flowers throughout the summer, making it a prized garden shrub. Native from Labrador to Alaska, where it survives temperatures to −50°F, shrubby cinquefoil is also native to the Rocky Mountains at elevations over 11,000 feet and to Europe and Asia.

Shrubby cinquefoil withstands heat, drought, and poor soils. Best growth and fuller, more abundant bloom is produced on plants growing in moist but well-drained soils in full sunlight. Plants on excessively dry sites grow more slowly.

Many cultivars have been developed for garden use, with new forms being offered almost every year. Popular varieties include: 'Abbotswood' with white flowers; 'Katherine Dykes' with early yellow blossoms; 'Klondike', low-growing, with yellow blooms; 'Moonlight' with yellowish-white flowers; 'Mount Everest' with white flowers; and 'Red Ace', a profusely blooming variety, with red flowers.

Quaking aspen *(Populus tremuloides)* grows quickly and is best in natural landscapes since it tends to send up shoots from the roots, forming groves.

Shrubby cinquefoil *(Potentilla fruticosa)* is a compact shrub useful for borders and accents. Produces small yellow flowers throughout summer.

Flowering fruit trees *(Prunus* sp.) comprise a large genus with a wide range of blossom colors and landscape uses.

English laurel *(Prunus laurocerasus)* quickly forms an evergreen hedge or shrub. Fragrant white flowers are showy in late spring.

Prunus
Flowering Fruit, Prunus

Evergreen or deciduous trees or shrubs. Flowering.

Many beautiful and useful ornamental trees and shrubs and many of the most popular tree fruits, such as almond, apricot, cherry, nectarine, peach, plum, and prune, are included in this large genus. Selections have been made in all these groups for forms with superior flowers, but flowering cherries and plums are the most widely planted. They are described in the chart.

Evergreen species of *Prunus* are often used for screens, clipped hedges, and specimen trees. Deciduous types require a winter cold period for the flowers and leaves to develop normally. All grow best in well-drained soils and may fail in clay soils. Descriptions of top-rated evergreen species follow.

Prunus caroliniana
Carolina Cherry Laurel
Zones: 7-10. To 20-40 feet.
Evergreen tree or shrub. Flowering.

A large shrub or small tree, this species is top-rated as a large screen or clipped hedge. It can also be trained as a dense, broad-topped, single- or multiple-trunked tree.

Small, cream-white flowers in 1-inch spikes open between February and April. Black fruits, 1/2 inch or less in diameter, tend to persist if the birds don't eat them. Falling fruits and flowers can be messy on paved areas. Growth rate is moderate to rapid. Leaves are medium to dark glossy green, 2 to 4 inches long, and have smooth edges. New growth is bronze-colored.

Carolina cherry laurel grows well in average soil, but may show salt burn and chlorosis in alkaline soil. It is adapted to warm climates such as its native North Carolina to Texas region. Although growth is best in coastal areas, it can take full sun and high heat. Pruning is needed to achieve the desired tree shape. Problems include scale insects and the disease fireblight.

Prunus laurocerasus
English Laurel
Zones: 7-10. To 5-30 feet.
Evergreen tree or shrub. Flowering.

This rapid-growing shrub can easily reach 30 feet tall and as wide in mild climates. In cold areas growth will be curtailed. Makes a very effective screen or clipped hedge although the fast growth calls for frequent clipping. Prune for tree shape.

Glossy dark green, oval leaves are 3 to 7 inches long. Small, fragrant white flowers stand above the foliage in long clusters. They are followed by small black fruits. Has invasive roots.

Takes full sun in cool climates. Grow in partial shade in hot areas. 'Otto Luyken' is a low-growing variety.

Prunus

Botanical Name/ Common Name	Zones	Size	Flower Description	Plant Description	Comments
Prunus x blireiana Blireiana Plum, Flowering Plum	5-9	To 25 ft tall with equal spread.	Fragrant, pink, semidouble, 1 in. across. Early.	Deciduous tree has dense rounded form, slender branches. Leaves tinged purple, turning greenish bronze by summer.	Fruit sparse or none.
P. cerasifera 'Atropurpurea' (P. pissardii) Purple-Leaf Plum, Pissard Plum	5-9	To 30 ft tall. Spreads to 20-25 ft.	White to pink, 1 in. across, short-lived, early.	Deciduous tree has vase shape when young, becomes dense and rounded with age. Leaves, to 2-1/2 in., open coppery-red, turn wine-red then to greenish-bronze in summer. Color holds until leaves drop.	Abundant red, edible fruits, 1 in. around.
P. c. 'Hollywood' Hollywood Flowering Plum	5-9	To 40 ft tall. Spreads to 25 ft.	Whitish-pink, single, early.	Deciduous tree with upright habit. Leaves green above, deep red on undersides.	Tasty 2-in. fruits in early summer. Hybrid between purple-leaf plum and 'Duarte' Japanese plum.
P. c. 'Krauter Vesuvius' Krauter Vesuvius Flowering Plum	5-9	To 18 ft tall. Spreads to 12 ft.	Light pink, early.	Deciduous tree with upright rounded habit. Large purple-black leaves.	Darkest leaves of flowering plums. Seldom fruits.
P. c. 'Newport' Newport Flowering Plum	5-9	To 25 ft tall. Spreads to 20 ft.	Light pink, small, single.	Deciduous tree. Leaves open purple, turn bronzy-green.	Very hardy. Fruits sparse.
P. c. 'Thundercloud' Thundercloud Flowering Plum	5-9	To 25 ft tall with equal spread.	Pink to white, single, early.	Deciduous tree with rounded ball-shape. Leaves deep coppery-purple through growing season.	Red fruit. Produced occasionally. Good patio tree.
P. x cistena Purple-Leaf Sand Cherry, Dwarf Red-Leaf Plum	2-9	To 10 ft tall.	White to pink, single, small, early.	Deciduous shrub with dense branches. Can be trained as single-trunk tree. Leaves, to 2-1/2 in. long, open crimson, stay bronze-red throughout summer.	Small, edible, blackish-purple fruits.
P. sargentii Sargent Cherry, North Japanese Hill Cherry	5-7	To 40 ft tall or more.	Pale pink, single, 1-1/2 in. Midseason in clusters of 2 to 6.	Deciduous tree. Upright with rounded crown. Spreading branches. Leaves, 2 to 4 inch long, have serrated edges. Turn orange-red in fall.	Good for street tree plantings. Very small fruits.
P. serrulata 'Amanogawa' Amanogawa Cherry	6-9	To 25 ft tall. Spreads to 10 ft.	Deep pink, double, 2-1/2 in. Midseason.	Deciduous tree with narrow, columnar habit. Young leaves, tinged yellowish, turn green in summer, then yellow and red in fall.	Narrowest, most upright flowering cherry. Very small fruits.
P. s. 'Kwanzan' Kwanzan Cherry	6-9	To 35 ft tall with equal spread.	Deep pink, double, 2-1/2 in. across. Midseason.	Deciduous tree with high-branching habit. New leaves reddish copper, turn yellow and red in fall.	Most hardy ornamental flowering cherry.
P. s. 'Shirofugen' Shirofugen Cherry	6-9	To 40 ft tall with equal spread.	Pink buds open to white, fade to pink. Double, 2-1/2 in. across.	Deciduous tree with wide-spreading crown. Horizontal branches. Young leaves deep crimson-bronze.	Last to flower.
P. s. 'Shirotae' Mount Fuji Cherry	6-9	To 20 ft tall, spreads wider than high.	Fragrant, white, semi-double, 2-1/2 in. across, early.	Deciduous tree with horizontal branching, flattop. Young leaves pale green, fringed, mature to dark green.	Among the loveliest white flowering Japanese cherries. Use as screen or buffer.
P. subhirtella 'Ukon'	6-9	To 30 ft tall with equal spread.	Unusual pale yellow, semidouble.	Deciduous tree with irregular, open growth habit. New growth bronzy; compliments bloom. Leaves turn orange-red in fall.	Needs careful pruning and pinching to develop full habit.
P. s. 'Autumnalis' Autumn-Flowering Higan Cherry	6-9	To 25 ft tall or more with equal spread.	Pink buds open almost white with pink stamens. Almond-scented, semi-double, 3/4 in. Blooms autumn and early spring.	Deciduous tree with spreading, often slightly pendulous branches.	Blooms twice a year. Excellent patio tree.
P. s. 'Pendula' Single Weeping Cherry	6-9	To 12 ft tall with equal spread.	Pale pink, single, small, midseason.	Deciduous small tree with arching spreading branches, pendulous branchlets.	Often grafted at 5 ft or higher on upright rootstock. Good tree for patios.
P. s. 'Yae-Shidare-Higan' Double Weeping Cherry	6-9	To 12 ft tall with equal spread.	Light pink, double.	Same as P. s. 'Pendula'.	Same as P. s. 'Pendula'.
P. yedoensis Japanese Flowering Cherry, Potomac Cherry, Yoshino Cherry	6-8	To 40 ft tall with equal spread.	Fragrant, white to pink, single, early.	Deciduous tree with open, spreading habit. Rounded to flat-topped. Dark green, serrated leaves, 4 in. long.	Prominently displayed in Washington, D.C. Small, shiny black, bitter fruit.
P. y. 'Akebono' Akebono Cherry	6-8	To 25 ft tall with equal spread.	Similar to species but shell-pink, early.	Similar to species.	Most popular flowering cherry in Japan.

The stately Douglas fir *(Pseudotsuga menziesii)* is a beautiful specimen tree that can also be clipped as a hedge.

Pomegranate trees *(Punica granatum)* have red flowers and bronzy-green new leaves that turn yellow in fall. Some varieties have edible fruit.

Pseudotsuga menziesii

Douglas Fir

Zones: 4-9. To 50-200 feet.
Evergreen tree.

One of the world's most important timber trees, this symmetrical, cone-shaped species is native from British Columbia to California along the coast, and from British Columbia into Mexico in the interior mountains. Grows at sea level in the cool, humid coastal part of its range, but only in the mountains in the interior and southern part of its range.

Typical form for a tree growing in the open is a tall symmetrical cone shape. Limbs at the top of the tree may angle upward, in the middle are horizontal, and at the base are drooping.

In spring, shiny reddish-brown, sharply pointed buds open, exposing bright green needles that contrast nicely with the dark green, older needles. Soft, 1- to 1-1/2-inch-long needles are densely spaced all around the stems and persist up to 8 years. A three-pointed bract, projecting from each scale of the slender, 3- to 4-inch, light brown cones, immediately identifies the cone as coming from a Douglas fir. Cones mature each season on trees at least 10 years old and over 15 feet tall.

Growth is best on a moist, but well-drained, acid soil in full sunlight. Trees do not grow, or grow poorly, in alkaline or waterlogged soils, or in those with an impervious layer near the surface.

Christmas trees, specimen plants, windbreaks, and hedges are some of the landscape uses of Douglas fir. Shearing should be done before new growth has hardened. New shoots do not grow from old wood if severely pruned.

Punica granatum

Pomegranate

Zones: 8-10. To 10-15 feet.
Deciduous tree or large shrub.
Flowering.

Pomegranate provides a full season of beauty. Its leaves emerge a bronzy-green, becoming a clean, shiny light green in summer and bright yellow in fall. In mid- to late spring it produces large, bright orange red, carnationlike blossoms. Fruiting varieties, such as 'Wonderful', follow bloom with bright red edible fruit.

Pomegranates grow best in hot summer climates and full sun. Plants tolerate drought but for fruit production should receive constant moisture.

Pomegranates are colorful espaliers or container plants. 'Nana', the dwarf pomegranate, rarely exceeds 3 feet high and it is ideal for containers. It bears single orange flowers. Other varieties are available with either single or double flowers. Double forms produce few or no fruits.

Pyracantha

Firethorn

Zones: 5-10. To 15 feet.
Evergreen shrub. Flowering.

Six species of thorny, usually evergreen shrubs of this genus, native to southeastern Europe and Asia, are grown as ornamentals. They are used as specimen plants, in barrier hedges, and as espaliers. When trained as espaliers they can grow twice the height they achieve as a shrub. Some forms can be pruned into single-stemmed small trees.

Flat clusters of petite flowers make a pretty display in spring. The real color show begins in late summer or early autumn when the large clusters of berries turn red to orange. They persist into winter.

Firethorns thrive in a wide variety of well-drained soils. A sunny location is preferred. Although most species are evergreen, leaves may be winter-killed in cold northern climates.

In some areas some pyracantha varieties are subject to fireblight, a disease that kills branches. They can also be susceptible to apple scab, which blackens fruit and can defoliate the shrub. Select one of the recently developed disease-resistant hybrids such as: 'Fiery Cascade', 'Mohave', 'Rutgers', and 'Teton'.

Firethorns (*Pyracantha* sp.) may be shrubby or vining; all feature lacy clusters of white flowers in spring and a spectacular show of red or orange berries in fall and winter.

Pyracantha

Botanical Name/Common Name	Zones	Size	Plant Description	Comments
Pyracantha angustifolia 'Gnome' Gnome Firethorn	5-9	To 3-6 ft tall.	Evergreen shrub with compact, spreading form, dense branching pattern. Orange berries. Very hardy.	Use for low hedge.
P. coccinea 'Government Red' Government Red Firethorn	7-9	To 12 ft tall.	Evergreen shrub with upright growth form. Bright red berries.	Forms an impenetrable barrier.
P. c. 'Kasan' Kasan Firethorn	5-9	To 8-10 ft tall.	Evergreen shrub. Bright orange-red berries. Upright and spreading. Compact branching habit.	Use for screen, espalier.
P. c. 'Lalandei' Lalande Firethorn	5-9	To 8-10 ft tall.	Evergreen shrub with spiny growth. Orange-red berries. Very hardy. Resistant to fireblight.	Use as hedge or espalier.
P. c. 'Pauciflora'	5-9	To 4 ft tall with equal spread.	Evergreen shrub with low, compact growth. Orange berries.	Use as hedge, barrier, espalier.
P. c. 'Rutgers' Rutgers Firethorn	5-9	To 2-3 ft tall.	Evergreen shrub. Orange berries. Low-growing. Completely free of scab and fireblight. Introduced by Rutgers University.	Use as ground cover.
P. c. 'Wyattii' Wyatt Firethorn	6-9	To 8-10 ft tall.	Evergreen shrub. Orange-red berries. Upright growing form.	Makes an excellent hedge.
P. 'Fiery Cascade' Fiery Cascade Firethorn	6-9	To 8 ft tall. Spreads to 9 ft.	Evergreen shrub. Early orange berries turn red. Grows upright with multiple stems. Completely free of scab and fireblight. Introduced by Rutgers University.	Hardiest red-berried pyracantha. Good hedge.
P. fortuneana 'Graberi' Graber Firethorn	7-10	To 15 ft tall. Spreads to 10 ft.	Evergreen shrub. Scarlet berries. Grows upright. Has huge clusters of berries.	Use as informal hedge, screen, barrier.
P. koidzumii 'Santa Cruz' Santa Cruz Firethorn	7-10	To 3 ft tall.	Evergreen shrub with prostrate form. Red berries.	Use as ground cover or for bank planting.
P. k. 'Victory' Victory Firethorn	7-10	To 10 ft tall. Spreads to 8 ft.	Evergreen shrub bears heavy clusters of large red berries that color late.	Use as screen or informal shape.
P. k. 'Walderi Prostrata' Walder Firethorn	7-10	To 1-1/2 to 2 ft tall. Spreads 4-5 ft.	Evergreen shrub. Bright red berries. Similar to *P. k.* 'Santa Cruz' but lower growing.	Use as ground cover.
P. 'Mohave' Mohave Firethorn	6-9	To 12 ft tall with equal spread.	Evergreen shrub with upright, dense growth habit. Bright orange-red berries. Introduced by National Arboretum.	Use for screen or tall hedge. Disease-resistant.
P. 'Red Elf' Red Elf Firethorn	7-10	To 1-2 ft tall.	Evergreen shrub with compact, dwarf, mounding habit. Closely intertwining branches. Red berries.	Excellent as small hedge or container plant.
P. 'Ruby Mound' Ruby Mound Firethorn	7-10	To 2-1/2 ft tall. Spreads to 10 ft.	Evergreen shrub. Bright red berries. Abundance of long, graceful, intertwining branches create a bold mounding habit.	Use for ground cover.
P. 'Teton' Teton Firethorn	6-9	To 15 ft tall.	Evergreen shrub with narrow, vertical growth habit. Yellowish-orange berries. Semievergreen in cold climates. Resists scab and fireblight. National Arboretum introduction.	Good for unpruned narrow hedge or screen.
P. 'Tiny Tim' Tiny Tim Firethorn	7-9	To 3 ft tall.	Evergreen shrub. Cinnamon-red berries. Nearly thornless.	Makes eye-catching border, mound plant, or patio planter.
P. 'Watereri' Waterer Firethorn	6-10	To 8 ft tall with equal spread.	Evergreen shrub. Fire engine-red berries. Upright form, nearly thornless. Popular in Pacific Northwest.	Use as hedge or screen.

Bradford callery pear *(Pyrus calleryana 'Bradford')* is attractive during all seasons. Spring-borne blossoms, shown below.

Southern live oak *(Quercus virginiana)*, is an expansive evergreen tree for the Deep South.

Pyrus
Pear
Deciduous or evergreen trees.

There are 20 species of deciduous or semievergreen, small to medium-sized trees in this genus. They originated in Europe, Asia, and North Africa. Most pears that have been selected for cultivation are grown for their fruit and have heavy displays of flowers in the spring. The few selected as ornamentals usually have small inconspicuous fruits.

One of the pests most damaging to pears is fireblight. It can destroy sections of a tree, or even the entire tree. A few ornamentals, such as the callery pear, are resistant to fireblight. Callery pear has been used in breeding work to develop pears with resistance to fireblight. In areas where this disease is a problem, fireblight-resistant pears should be selected.

Pyrus calleryana 'Bradford'
Bradford Callery Pear
Zones: 5-9. To 40-50 feet.
Deciduous tree. Flowering.

This is a popular flowering tree in the eastern United States. It has a conical crown when young that becomes rounded or oval as the tree ages. It is covered with masses of white flowers in the spring and glossy dark green leaves in summer. One of the last trees to color in fall, Bradford pear becomes yellow to bronzy-red or purple, and the leaves often remain for two weeks or longer before falling. Russet-brown fruits are 1/2 inch or less around and are inconspicuous.

This tough tree will tolerate city pollution. Can be used as a street tree, lawn tree, and specimen or patio tree. Often grown on islands in parking lots. Adaptable to many different soils, but should be planted in full sun. Unlike the species, it is thornless.

Other cultivars of Callery pear are 'Aristocrat' with dark green, wavy-edged leaves and 'Faureri', dwarf Korean callery pear, a small tree to 25 feet that is good on windy, exposed sites where breakage would occur on larger trees.

Pyrus kawakamii
Evergreen Pear
Zones: 9-10. To 30 feet.
Evergreen to partially deciduous tree. Flowering.

Normally a spreading shrub, evergreen pear is easily trained into a small tree. Glossy light green leaves are a year-round feature in most areas. Fragrant masses of white flowers in spring. Use as a patio or park tree, or grow in containers. Full sun or light shade and average moisture are required for good growth. A popular plant in California. Evergreen in warm areas, becoming partially deciduous in cold climates.

Quercus
Oak
Zones: 4-10. To 100 feet.
Deciduous and evergreen trees.

Oaks are large, stately, long-lived trees, many of which have striking fall color. Deciduous oaks are divided into two groups—red (or black) and white. Red oaks have leaves with pointed lobes and are usually pyramidal in outline. White oaks have round-lobed leaves and have heavier limbs, giving rounded outlines to the trees.

Oaks are good garden trees. They have deep noncompetitive root systems and their wide-spreading limbs cast moderate shade, permitting other plants and grass to grow beneath them. Mature native oaks of the arid West require special attention when there is construction or landscaping in their vicinity. They may develop root diseases if there are plants beneath them that require summer watering. Soil compaction caused by construction equipment operating beneath their canopy or changes in soil levels within their root zone can also cause quick decline or death of large oaks.

Oaks do not propagate readily except by seed, so some variation between individual trees occurs. Top-rated oaks are described in the chart on the next page. Many other native species can be grown from acorns and make excellent landscape trees.

California live oak *(Quercus agrifolia)* is an evergreen oak for western states.

The new foliage of English oak *(Quercus robur)* is a fresh spring green, matures to dark green.

Red oak *(Quercus rubra)* is one of the best oaks for fall color.

Quercus

Botanical Name/Common Name	Zones	Size	Plant Description	Comments
Quercus agrifolia California Live Oak, Coast Live Oak	9-10	To 20-100 ft tall with equal spread.	Evergreen tree. Slow-growing with broad, rounded crown. Deep green, hollylike leaves have prickly edges. Needs well-drained soil.	Good shade tree. Established trees are drought-tolerant. Native to California.
Quercus alba White Oak, American White Oak	4-10	To 80-100 ft tall. Spreads to 50-80 ft.	Deciduous tree with wide-spreading crown. Horizontal branches become contorted with age. Deep green leaves turn purplish red in fall, may hang into winter. Slow grower.	Difficult to transplant. Native to eastern United States.
Quercus coccinea Scarlet Oak	4-9	To 60-75 ft tall. Spreads to 40-50 ft.	Deciduous tree. Fast-growing with broad pyramidal crown. Open habit. Deeply lobed leaves are bright green, turn scarlet in fall.	Large trees are difficult to transplant. One of best oaks for fall color. Native to eastern United States.
Quercus ilex Holly Oak	9-10	To 40-70 ft tall with equal spread.	Evergreen tree. Moderate growth. Forms dense, rounded crown. Dark green leaves, either smooth-edged or toothed, have silvery undersides.	Good street or lawn tree. Will grow in coastal conditions. Mediterranean native.
Quercus macrocarpa Burr Oak, Mossy-Cup Oak	4-10	To 60-100 ft tall. Spreads half as wide.	Deciduous tree. Moderate- to fast-growing. High-branching. Shiny green leaves with deeply cut lobes have whitish undersides. Reddish fall color not outstanding.	Common name derived from burred acorns. Native to eastern United States.
Quercus palustris Pin Oak	5-9	To 40-80 ft tall. Spreads at least half as wide.	Deciduous tree. Moderate to fast growth rate. Has pyramidal shape, usually with 1 central trunk. Glossy dark green leaves with deeply cut, pointed lobes turn red in fall, then turn brown and hang on branches into winter.	Grows well on dry or wet sites. Native to eastern United States.
Quercus phellos Willow Oak	6-10	To 50-80 ft tall. Spreads to 30-40 ft.	Deciduous tree. Moderate growth rate. Has pyramidal shape. Long, narrow, willowlike leaves turn dull yellow in fall, hang into winter.	Most graceful of the oaks. Native to eastern United States.
Quercus robur English Oak, Truffle Oak	5-9	To 40-80 ft tall. with equal spread.	Deciduous tree. Moderate growth rate. Spreading, open crown. Dark green leaves with rounded lobes drop late in fall. No color change.	'Fastigiata' has narrow, upright habit. Native to Asia, Africa and Europe.
Quercus rubra Red Oak, Northern Red Oak, Eastern Red Oak	4-10	To 60-80 ft tall. and nearly as wide.	Deciduous tree. Fast-growing. Pyramidal when young, becoming broad, spreading and round-headed. Bright green leaves with pointed lobes turn red in fall.	Good street or shade tree. Native to eastern United States.
Quercus virginiana Southern Live Oak	8-10	To 60 ft tall. Spreads to twice as wide.	Evergreen tree. Moderate to fast grower. Massive spreading branches. Smooth-edged, dark green leaves with whitish undersides are partially deciduous in cold areas.	Thrives in moist, deep soil. Native to southern United States.

Indian hawthorn *(Raphiolepis indica)* makes a showy hedge that blooms twice a year—from midwinter through spring and again in fall.

The dense, white-rimmed, glossy green leaves of Italian buckthorn *(Rhamnus alaternus* 'Argenteo-Variegata') makes this plant useful as a bright background shrub or hedge.

Raphiolepis indica
Indian Hawthorn
Zones: 8-10. To 2-5 feet.
Evergreen shrub. Flowering.

Neat evergreen foliage, pretty blossoms, and colorful berries give Indian hawthorn a top-rated reputation as a ground cover, informal hedge, colorful accent, and a foundation shrub. Its restrained growth and heat tolerance also make it useful for growing in large containers or raised planters.

Handsome, leathery foliage is often bronzy or red when young, changing to deep green. From midwinter through spring, and again in fall, a profusion of flowers appears. Varieties are available with white, pink, or deep rose-red blossoms, in growth forms from low and compact to tall and upright. Bluish-black berries are held through winter.

Indian hawthorn is adaptable to a wide range of soils. Fairly drought-tolerant, it does best with regular watering. In full sun, it will bloom prolifically but is quite suitable for partly shaded locations. Pinch back growing tips after flowering for dense, sturdy shrubs, or thin occasionally for a more open form. Leaf spot, aphids, and fireblight are occasional problems.

The variety 'Apple Blossom' has white-and-pink blossoms. 'Bill Evans' grows quickly to 5 to 7 feet, and has pink flowers and heavy-textured foliage. 'Coates Crimson' has crimson-pink flowers on a 2- to 4-foot plant. 'Rosea Dwarf' has a dense, compact habit from 2 to 4 feet high with light pink flowers. 'Snow White' bears white flowers on a 4-foot plant.

Rhamnus
Buckthorn
Evergreen and deciduous trees and shrubs.

These small trees and shrubs are related to horse chestnuts. They are grown for their fine texture, red foliage, and colorful fruit.

Rhamnus alaternus
Italian Buckthorn
Zones: 7-10. To 15-20 feet.
Evergreen shrub or tree.

Italian buckthorn has finely textured glossy green foliage, and is useful as a dense background for flowering shrubs or as a sheared screening hedge. Maximum height of 20 feet is reached in just a few years. Italian buckthorn is easily pruned lower or into a small tree. Near the coast or in hot inland valleys, this fast-growing plant will resist pests, damage from high winds, and tolerate drought. The selection 'Argenteo-variegata' has white-margined leaves.

Rhamnus frangula 'Columnaris Tallhedge'
Tallhedge Buckthorn
Zones: 3-8. To 8-12 feet.
Deciduous shrub.

This ideal hedge plant forms a narrow 4-foot-wide, 12-foot-tall shrub that may be pruned as low as 4 feet. It grows quickly into a neat, slender form requiring less pruning than many other shrubs. To plant as a screen, space 2-1/2 feet apart and cut back one-half their height to promote new branches and even growth.

Leaves are glossy green. The attractive berries are cream, turn pink to red, then black. They are showy against the foliage in summer.

Adaptable and dependable, tallhedge buckthorn is tolerant of a wide range of growing conditions.

Rhododendron
Azalea, Rhododendron
Evergreen and deciduous shrubs.
Flowering.

There are over 900 species and more than 10,000 named varieties of azaleas and rhododendrons in the genus *Rhododendron*, which includes all the plants once placed in the genus *Azalea*. They are native to many parts of the world, including North America.

Most people think of azaleas as low-growing, compact plants that cover themselves with bright-colored blossoms in late winter or early spring. Rhododendrons are thought of as taller plants with heavier foliage and large clusters of blossoms. Botanists have found the distinctions a bit more complex but for a gardener's purpose those distinctions are adequate.

Azalea flowers may be single, semidouble, double, or hose-in-hose. Double blossoms result from stamens becoming petal-like. Hose-in-hose flowers are formed when the sepals (the green "leaves" at the bases of the flowers) become petal-like. Hose-in-hose flowers may be single, double, and semidouble. Rhododendron flowers are single or more commonly in large clusters called trusses. Trusses may be described as "loose", "conical", "ball-shaped", or with other words that describe their overall appearance.

Flowering time varies from climate to climate and year to year. In the Northeast, early means April, midseason mean May, and late is late May or early June. In warmer climates the seasons are 2 to 4 weeks earlier; in colder climates they are 2 to 3 weeks later.

Rhododendrons and azaleas require a fertile acid soil (pH 4.5 to 5.5) that drains rapidly. Water-logging for only a few hours may be fatal. If drainage is questionable, plant in either raised beds or mounds. Add organic matter such as peat moss, ground bark, or compost to heavy soils to improve drainage. A soil mix of 50 percent peat moss or ground bark, or 50 percent sand and 50 percent garden loam is ideal as backfill or to fill containers and raised beds.

These shrubs are surface-rooted and therefore enjoy a mulch of organic matter such as fir bark or wood chips to protect the feeder roots that live at, or just below, the soil surface. Physically delicate, these roots are easily damaged by extremes of temperatures or water supply, or by shallow hoeing. Mulch protects the roots and is also important because as it decays mulch helps maintain soil acidity and releases small amounts of essential mineral nutrients to the soil.

Most azaleas and rhododendrons prefer very light shade cast from high tree branches. An eastern exposure with full morning sun or an unshaded northern exposure are also good. Plants will grow in heavier shade, but will not flower as well. Southern and western exposures are generally too hot and sunny, unless well-shaded.

Without some shade, flowers of most rhododendrons and azaleas will fade quickly, especially if temperatures are high. Late-flowering varieties especially need partial afternoon shade to prevent sun from scalding the flowers.

The fibrous, shallow root systems of azaleas and rhododendrons make these plants particularly vulnerable to drying-out. Water plants regularly and check to be certain water is soaking into the rootball. Plants need more water during periods of bloom and fast growth than they do later in the season. Drought during this period will significantly stunt growth and retard the setting of flower buds. Winter sun dries plants. Well-watered plants are better able to survive winter. Thoroughly soak plants in late fall before soil freezes.

Apply fertilizer before mulch is renewed in spring or once a month through midseason. Iron sulfate, ammonium sulfate, and other "acid-forming" fertilizers are best. The amount of fertilizer to use depends upon the fertilizer analysis: 1/4 to 1/2 pound of a 5-10-10 (5% nitrogen, 10% phosphorus, and 10% potassium) fertilizer per mature plant should be about right. Carefully follow directions on the fertilizer package.

Most azaleas and rhododendrons are planted in spring when they are in flower, because that's the best way to choose a pleasing flower color. Spring planting is recommended for northern areas so plants can become established before severe winter weather. Fall through winter

Evergreen azalea hybrids (*Rhododendron* sp.) add dramatic color impact when in bloom.

Varieties of azaleas and rhododendrons (*Rhododendron* sp.) bloom from early spring well into summer.

Mass plantings of azaleas, such as 'Delaware Valley White' (*Rhododendron*—Glenn Dale Hybrid) brighten up shady spots in the garden.

Pruned into tree form, evergreen azaleas *(Rhododendron* sp.) take on a formal appearance.

Deciduous Knap Hill/Exbury Hybrids *(Rhododendron* sp.) add vibrant floral color in spring; warm foliage color in fall.

Pontic azalea *(Rhododendron luteum)* is a deciduous native Asian azalea. Sunny flowers are highly fragrant.

planting is preferred throughout the South and in other areas with mild winters.

Azaleas and rhododendrons are susceptible to disease if planted too deep, below the top of the rootball. Plant 1 to 2 inches above ground level so that after the plant "settles", the rootball top will be even with or slightly above natural grade.

When planting, avoid having the rootball soil surrounded by a radically different type of soil. For instance, planting a rootball of heavy clay soil in sandy soil will lead to poor water penetration and inhibited root growth.

Planting on top of the ground on mounds, bottomless boxes, or raised beds is the easy way to avoid problems created by alkaline or clay soils. Fill a raised bed that is at least 2 feet deep with a mix of equal parts coarse peat moss, ground fir bark and coarse perlite (spongerock). This mix will provide an ample supply of acidity and satisfy the need for a well-aerated soil. Water drainage is fast and water retention is fairly high.

Prune azaleas by pinching new growth in late spring or summer. This increases flower production and helps form a fuller, more compact shrub. You may cut azalea branches at any point, not just where one branch joins another. Growth buds are present all along the branches. New growth will begin behind any pruning cut.

Overgrown azaleas can be cut back to 6 to 12 inches from the ground. The best time for this "rejuvenation" pruning is just before flowering in early spring. At that time new stems and leaves will grow quickly.

Unlike azaleas, rhododendrons do not have growth buds all along their stems. Prune them during growth in spring by pinching back soft stems. This promotes branching and compact growth. Snap off flower buds when they are fading to increase bloom the following year.

The most troublesome rhododendron pest is root weevil. The larvae feed on roots, the adults on the leaves. Common azalea pests include lacebug and scale.

Azalea

Botanists have organized the genus *Rhododendron* into series and subseries and azaleas are one of the prime series. Azaleas are further categorized into the following groups of hybrids with special characteristics; each group has its own named varieties in a wide range of flower types and colors and these are listed in the charts on the following pages.

At one time azaleas were grown only in the South. Fortunately, enthusiastic nurserymen, plant breeders, and gardeners, through the years have developed azaleas that can grow in many climates of the United States and Canada.

DECIGUOUS AZALEA HYBRID GROUPS

Knap Hill and Exbury Hybrids: These large-flowered hybrids were bred in England by the Knaphill Nursery at the Rothschild's estate in Exbury. Displays clusters of squarish often fragrant flowers.

Mollis Hybrids: Bears clusters of red, orange, or yellow flowers.

Occidentale Hybrids: Flowers in clusters are colored white with a pink tinge, or yellow and red with orange markings.

Ghent Hybrids: Flowers are red, yellow, or pink, smaller than those of Mollis hybrids.

Species Azaleas: The species azaleas of America, one native to the West Coast and the others to the East from Labrador to Florida, are becoming increasingly popular garden plants. Many of the northern varieties are more hardy than indicated by their range. Several species were important in breeding the Exbury hybrids. Species native to Asia have also contributed to many modern hybrids and many are admired in their own right.

Knap Hill/Exbury Hybrid azaleas *(Rhododendron* sp.) feature large squarish flowers.

Mollis Hybrid azaleas *(Rhododendron* sp.) are the most cold-hardy azaleas.

Deciduous Azaleas

KNAP HILL/EXBURY HYBRIDS (Zones 5-8)

Name	Cold Hardiness	Flower Description	Plant Description	Bloom Season
'Aurora'	−20°F	Pale salmon-pink with an orange blotch.	Grows less than 6 ft tall.	Midseason
'Balzac'	−20°F	Star-shaped, very fragrant, red-orange with flame markings on upper petals, in trusses.	Grows less than 6 ft tall.	Late
'Brazil'	−20°F	Small, frilled, showy tangerine-red. Blooms in profusion.	Grows less than 6 ft tall.	Late
'Cecile'	−20°F	Very large, salmon-pink with a yellow blotch.	Grows less than 6 ft tall.	Late
'Fireball'	−20°F	Deep fiery-red.	Grows less than 6 ft tall.	Midseason
'Gibraltar'	−20°F	Bright orange-red with cherry coloring, in tight ball-shaped trusses.	Compact growth. Grows less than 6 ft tall.	Midseason
'Gold Dust'	−20°F	Solid gold, in ball-like trusses.	Grows less than 6 ft tall.	Midseason
'Klondyke'	−20°F	Orange-yellow bells open to flowers of solid deep tangerine-yellow.	Grows less than 6 ft tall.	Late
'Royal Lodge'	−20°F	Dark red with long stamens.	Dark, reddish-brown foliage. Grows less than 6 ft tall.	Very late
'Toucan'	−20°F	Light creamy-yellow with margins tinged pink.	Grows less than 6 ft tall.	Mid- to late season

MOLLIS HYBRIDS (Zones 5-8)

Name	Cold Hardiness	Flower Description	Plant Description	Bloom Season
'Christopher Wren'	−20°F	Large, yellow with a tangerine blotch.	Grows more than 6 ft tall.	Mid- to late season
'Directeur Moerlands'	−20°F	Sunset-gold with a darker blotch.	Grows more than 6 ft tall.	Mid- to late season
'Koster's Brilliant Red'	−20°F	Orange-red. Single.	Grows more than 6 ft tall.	Mid- to late season

OCCIDENTALE HYDRIDS (Zones 6-8)

Name	Cold Hardiness	Flower Description	Plant Description	Bloom Season
'Graciosa'	−25°F	Slightly frilled, pale yellow flushed rose.	Grows to 5-6 ft tall.	Early to midseason
'Irene Koster'	−25°F	Pure rose-pink with a small yellow blotch.	Grows to 5-6 ft tall.	Early to midseason
'Westminster'	−20°F	Clear almond-pink flowers.	Grows less than 6 ft tall.	Early

GHENT HYBRIDS (Zones 5-8)

Name	Cold Hardiness	Flower Description	Plant Description	Bloom Season
'Coccinea Speciosa'	−25°F	Brilliant orange-red with a yellowish-orange blotch.	Grows to 5-6 ft tall.	Early to midseason
'Daviesii'	−25°F	Very pale yellow fading to almost white with a showy yellow blotch, 2-1/4 in. across.	Grows more than 6 ft tall.	Late
'Narcissiflora'	−25°F	Fragrant, double yellow.	Grows more than 6 ft tall.	Late

Asian Native Azaleas

Botanical Name/ Common Name	Cold Hardiness	Origin	Flower Description	Plant Description	Bloom Season	Comments
R. japonicum Japanese Azalea	−25°F	Japan	Varies from yellow to orange to red, 2 in. across.	Dense, 2-6 ft tall. Deciduous.	Midseason	One of the parents of Mollis and Exbury hybrids.
R. luteum (R. flavum) Pontic Azalea	−25°F	Caucacus of E. Europe	Very fragrant, bright sunny yellow-orange, 2 in. across.	Grows to 2-12 ft tall. Deciduous. Fall color.	Midseason	One of parents of Ghent hybrids.
R. molle (R. mollis) Chinese Azalea	−20°F	China	Yellow to yellow-orange, spotted green, 2 in. across.	Dense, 4 ft tall. Deciduous.	Early to midseason	One of parents of Mollis and Exbury hybrids.
R. obtusum kaempferi (R. kaempferi)	−10°F	Asian	Slightly frilled, salmon-pink to salmon-orange.	Semievergreen to deciduous. Under 6 ft tall.	Mid- to late season	Prime parent of Kaempferi hybrids.
R. schlippenbachii Royal Azalea	−25°F	Manchuria, Korea, Japan	Large, fragrant, pink or rose-pink, brown-dotted throats, 2-3 in. across.	Grows to 4 ft tall or more. Dense. Deciduous. Brilliant fall foliage.	Early to mid-season, as leaves open.	Give partial shade. Beautiful but fastidious.
R. yedoense poukhanense Korean Azalea,	−5°F	Korea, Japan	Fragrant, rosy-lilac, 2 in. across.	Grows to 4-6 ft tall. Deciduous.	Early to midseason	May be semievergreen. One of the parents of Gable hybrids.

North American Native Azaleas

Botanical Name/ Common Name	Cold Hardiness	Origin	Flower Description	Plant Description	Bloom Season	Comments
R. arborescens Smooth Azalea, Sweet Azalea,	−20°F	N.Y. and Pa., south to mt. tops of Ga. and Ala.	Fragrant, pure white with pink or reddish flush and yellow blotch on upper petal, 2 in. across. Long stamens.	Reaches 6-10 ft tall. Deciduous.	Mid- to late season	A parent of Exbury hybrids.
R. atlanticum Coast Azalea	−10°F	Coastal Plains, Del. south to S. Car., Ga.	Fragrant, white or white flushed with pale red, some with yellow blotch, 1-3/4 in. long.	Low-growing shrub, 1-2 ft tall. Spreading roots. Deciduous.	Midseason	Flowers appear before leaves.
R. austrinum Florida Flame Azalea	−0°F	Fla., Ga., and Ala.	Fragrant, golden-yellow, 1-1/4 in. long.	Reaches 10-12 ft tall. Deciduous.	Very early.	Flowers appear before or with leaves.
R. bakeri Cumberland Azalea	−20°F	High elevations of W. Va., Ky., Tenn., south to Ga., Ala.	May be orange, red, or yellow with gold blotch, 1-1/2 in. across.	Varies from 1-10 ft tall. Deciduous.	Mid- to late season	Flowers appear after leaves.
R. calendulaceum Flame Azalea	−20°F	Appalachian Mts., N. Pa., Ohio, south to N. Ga.	Orange-red to clear yellow, 2-in. diameter.	Varies from 4-10 ft tall, rarely 15 ft tall. Deciduous.	Mid- to late season	Claimed as one of the most beautiful native shrubs. A parent of Exbury hybrids.
R. canadense Rhodora	−40°F	East coast of Labrador, south to N.J.	Bell-shaped with short tubes, 2 lips, 3/4 in. across. Rose-purple to white.	Grows to 3-4 ft tall. Dense. Deciduous.	Early to midseason	Flowers appear before leaves.
R. canescens Piedmont or Florida Pinxter Azalea	−0°F	N.C., Tenn., south to Tx., Ala., Ga., N. Fla.	Fragrant, varying from white to light or deep pink, 1-1/2 in. across. Long stamens.	Reaches 10-15 ft tall. Deciduous.	Early to midseason	Flowers appear before or with leaves.
R. occidentale Western Azalea	−5°F	S. Ore., south to S. Calif.	Fragrant, white to pinkish, splashed yellow or pink, often with a rosy throat. 2-1/2 in. across.	Grows to 6-10 ft tall and as wide. Deciduous.	Mid- to late season	Difficult to grow in the East. Used in development of Ghent and Exbury hybrids.
R. periclymenoides (R. nudiflorum) Pinxterbloom Azalea	−30°F	Mass., south to Ohio, N.C., Tenn., and Ga.	Sweet, fragrant, varying from white or pale pink to deep violet, 1-1/2 in. across.	Grows to 4-6 ft tall, rarely to 10 ft. Deciduous.	Early season	Used in breeding Ghent hybrids. One of the most common native azaleas.
R. prinophyllum Rose-Shell Azalea	−30°F	New England, south to mts. of Va., west to Mo.	Spicy, clove-scented, rose-pink to deep pink, 1-1/2 in. across.	Grows to 2-9 ft tall, rarely to 15 ft. Deciduous.	Midseason	Flowers appear with leaves.
R. prunifolium Plum-Leaved or Prunifolia Azalea	−0°F	S. W. Ga. and eastern Ala., along streams.	Varies from apricot to pale orange, orange-red to red, 1-1/2 in. across.	Reaches 8-15 ft tall. Deciduous.	Late to very late	Unusual candy-striped flowers buds.
R. serrulatum Hammock-Sweet Azalea	0°F	Wooded swamps of E. Ga., Fla., west to La.	Fragrance of cloves, white to creamy-white. 1-1/2 in. long. Long stamens.	Toothed leaves and red-brown twigs. Reaches 20 ft tall. Deciduous.	Very late	Flowers appear after leaves. Grows in wet soil. Valuable in South for very late bloom.
R. vaseyi Pink-Shell Azalea	−30°F	Mts. of west N. C., above 3,000 ft.	Bell-shaped, green-throated, rose-pink, with orange-red dots 1-1/2 in. across.	Reaches 12-15 ft tall. Deciduous	Early to midseason	Flowers appear before leaves.
R. viscosum Swamp Azalea	−30°F	Swamps from Maine south to Ala., Ga.	Slender, small-tubed, 2 in. long. white to creamy-white or pale pink; spicy scent.	Grows to 8 ft tall. Deciduous.	Mid- to late season	Spreads by underground runners. Grows in wet soil. Parent of Exbury hybrids.

EVERGREEN AZALEA HYBRID GROUPS

Belgian Indica: Developed for greenhouse forcing, these plants have lush foliage and produce copious quantities of large double or semidouble flowers.

Rutherfordiana: Originally developed for greenhouse forcing, these are attractive, small bushy plants with handsome foliage and abundant single, semidouble, or double blossoms of medium size.

Southern Indica: Tough, outdoor, taller-growing versions of the Belgian Indicas. They are able to take full sun. Profuse small to medium-sized single blossoms are borne in midspring.

Satsuki/Macrantha: Late blooming. Will grow in full sun. Good to extend the flowering season of azaleas.

Kurume: These familiar azaleas of Japan are compact with dense small leaves and masses of small flowers. Branches often layered in tiers. Will grow in half a day of sun.

Pericat: Developed for greenhouse forcing, these hybrids of Belgian Indicas and Kurumes greatly resemble Kurumes but have larger flowers.

Gable Hybrids: Evergreen but may drop leaves in cold climates. Cold-hardy version of Kurume hybrids.

Compact plants with heavy bloom in midspring. Many have medium-sized hose-in-hose blossom.

Glenn Dale Hybrids: Bred primarily for cold hardiness. Group includes a wide variety of flower types and sizes. May lose a few leaves in cold winters. Grows best in half-sun.

Girard Hybrids: Introduced in recent decades. Developed for cold hardiness.

Kaempferi Hybrids: Hardier than Kurumes, with a tall, upright habit and flowers including a color range of orange and red. Slightly larger than Kurumes.

Evergreen Azaleas

Name	Cold Hardiness	Flower Description	Plant Description	Bloom Season
BELGIAN INDICA (Zones 8-10)				
'Albert and Elizabeth'	20°F	White with salmon-pink edges, double, 2 in. across.	Grows less than 3 ft tall.	Midseason
'Blushing Bride'	20°F	Blush-pink, double.	Grows less than 3 ft tall.	Late season
'Chimes'	20°F	Bell-shaped, rich red, semidouble.	Grows less than 3 ft tall.	Winter through spring
'Jean Haerens'	20°F	Frilled, deep rose-pink, double.	Grows less than 3 ft tall.	Early season
'Red Poppy'	20°F	Dark red, single.	Grows 3-6 ft tall.	Midseason
RUTHERFORDIANA (Zones 8-10)				
'Alaska'	20°F	White with chartreuse blotch, single, some semi-double, 2 in. diameter.	Grows less than 3 ft tall.	Mid- to late season
'Dorothy Gish'	20°F	Frilled, single, orange-red, hose-in-hose, 2-1/2 in. across.	Grows less than 3 ft tall.	Mid- to late season
'Gloria'	20°F	Salmon-and-white variegated, hose-in-hose.	Grows 3 to 6 ft tall.	Early to midseason
'Pink Ruffles'	20°F	Shell-pink, double, 2 in. across.	Grows 3-5 ft tall.	Midseason
'Redwing'	5°F	Red, hose-in-hose, 3 in. across.	Grows less than 6 ft tall.	Midseason
SOUTHERN INDICA (Zones 8-10)				
'Brilliant'	20°F	Red, single, 2-1/4 in. across.	Dense, spreading. Grows 3-5 ft tall.	Mid- to late season
'Coccinea Major'	20°F	Orange-red, single.	Spreading, dense, less than 3 ft tall.	Late
'Duc de Rohan'	20°F	Orange-red, single, 2-1/4 in. across.	Spreading. Grows 3-5 ft tall.	Early to midseason
'Fielder's White'	20°F	Frilled, white with chartreuse blotch, single, 2-3/4 in. across.	Spreading. Grows 3-5 ft tall.	Early to midseason
'Formosa'	20°F	Lavender-magenta, single, 3-1/2 in. across.	Upright. Grows to 6 ft tall or more.	Mid- to late season
'George Lindley Taber'	20°F	White, flushed violet-red with a darker blotch, single, 3-1/2 in. across.	Grows 3-5 ft tall.	Mid- to late season
'Glory of Sunninghill'	20°F	Orange-red, single, 2 in. across.	Dense, spreading. Grows 3-5 ft tall.	Late season
'Pride of Dorking'	20°F	Brilliant orange-red, single.	Grows less than 6 ft tall.	Late season
'Pride of Mobile' ('Elegans Superba')	20°F	Deep rose-pink, single 2-1/2 in. across.	Grows to 6 ft tall or more.	Mid- to late season
'Southern Charm'	20°F	A pink sport of 'Formosa', single, 3-1/3 in. across.	Grows to 6 ft tall or more.	Midseason

'Delaware Valley White' (Glenn Dale Hybrid)

'Coral Bells' (Kurume Hybrid)

'Hershey's Red' (Kurume Hybrid)

Evergreen Azaleas (continued)

Name	Cold Hardiness	Flower Description	Plant Description	Bloom Season
GLENN DALE (Zones 7-8)				
'Copperman'	5°F	Brilliant orange-red, single with overlapping lobes, 3 in. across.	Spreading, dense. Grows 3-5 ft tall.	Late
'Delaware Valley White'	5°F	Fragrant, white, single, 3 in. across.	Grows less than 6 ft tall.	Late season
'Everest'	5°F	White with chartreuse blotch, single, 2 in. across.	Grows 3-5 ft tall.	Late midseason
'Fashion'	5°F	Orange-red with red blotch, single, hose-in-hose, 2 in. across.	Grows more than 5 ft tall.	Early to midseason
'Gaiety'	5°F	Rose-pink with a darker blotch, single, 3 in. across.	Dark green narrow leaves. Grows 3-5 ft tall.	Late midseason
'Geisha'	5°F	White, flecked and striped purple, single, 1-1/2 to 2 in. across.	Grows less than 6 ft tall.	Very early season
'Glacier'	5°F	White with a chartreuse throat, single, 2-1/2 in. across.	Upright. Grows 3-5 ft tall.	Early to midseason
'Glamour'	0°F	Rose-red, single, 2-1/2 in. across.	Dark green leaves turn bronze in fall. Grows 3-5 ft tall.	Early to midseason
'Helen Close'	5°F	White with a pale yellow blotch, single, 2-1/2 to 3 in. across.	Spreading, dense. Grows 3-5 ft tall.	Midseason
'Martha Hitchcock'	5°F	White with magenta-pink margins, single, 3-1/2 in. across.	Grows 3-5 ft tall.	Late midseason
'Treasure'	5°F	White with pink blotch, single, 4 in. across.	Dark green leaves. Grows 3-5 ft tall.	Early to midseason
KURUME (Zones 7-10)				
'Christmas Cheer'	5°F	Brilliant red, hose-in-hose, 1-1/4 in. across, in a tight truss.	Spreading. Grows 3-5 ft tall.	Early to midseason
'Coral Bells'	5°F	Shell-pink, single, hose-in-hose, tubular, 1-1/8 in. across.	Spreading. Grows less than 3 ft tall.	Early to midseason
'Eureka'	5°F	Pink, hose-in-hose.	Spreading. Grows less than 6 ft tall.	Late season
'Hershey's Red'	5°F	Bright red, double.	Grows less than 3 ft tall.	Midseason
'Hexe'	5°F	Crimson-red, hose-in-hose.	Grows 3-5 ft tall.	Mid- to late season
'H.H. Hume'	5°F	White, single, hose-in-hose, 2 in. across.	Spreading. Grows less than 6 ft tall.	Midseason
'Hino-Crimson'	5°F	Crimson-red, single.	Grows 3-5 ft tall.	Midseason
'Hinodegiri'	5°F	Violet rose-red, single, 1-1/2 in. across.	Compact. Grows 3-5 ft tall.	Early to midseason
'Orange Cup'	5°F	Reddish-orange, hose-in-hose.	Grows less than 6 ft tall.	Late season
'Pink Pearl'	5°F	Salmon-rose, hose-in-hose.	Upright. May grow to 6 ft or taller.	Midseason
'Sherwood Orchid'	5°F	Violet-red with a dark blotch, single.	Spreading. Grows 3-5 ft tall.	Midseason
'Sherwood Red'	5°F	Orange-red, single.	Grows 3-5 ft tall.	Early to midseason
'Snow'	5°F	White, hose-in-hose, 1-1/2 in. across.	Upright, spreading. Grows less than 6 ft tall.	Midseason
'Vuyk's Scarlet'	5°F	Bright scarlet, single, very large.	Grows less than 6 ft tall.	Midseason
PERICAT (Zones 7-10)				
'Sweetheart Supreme'	5°F	Frilled rose-pink with a dark blotch, semidouble, hose-in-hose, 1-3/4 in. across.	Dense and spreading. Grows 3-5 ft tall.	Mid- to late season

'Sherwood Orchid' (Kurume Hybrid)   'Rosebud' (Gable Hybrid)   'Herbert' (Kaempferi Hybrid)

Name	Cold Hardiness	Flower Description	Plant Description	Bloom Season
SATSUKI/MACRANTHA (Zones 7-10)				
'Beni-Kirishima'	5°F	Orange-red with a darker blotch, double, 2 in. across.	Grows 3-5 ft tall.	Late season
'Chinzan'	5°F	Light salmon-pink, single, large.	Compact, excellent for bonsai use with flexible branches. Grows less than 3 ft tall.	Late season
'Flame Creeper'	5°F	Orange-red, single.	Creeping plant with small leaves. Good ground cover. Grows less than 3 ft tall.	Late season
'Gumpo Pink'	5°F	Light pink, single, large.	Dense. Grows less than 3 ft tall.	Late season
'Gumpo White'	5°F	White with occasional red flakes, single, 3 in. across.	Low-growing, with small leaves. Grows less than 3 ft tall.	Late season
'Linda R.'	5°F	Soft, solid pastel-pink, single.	Dense. Grows less than 3 ft tall.	Midseason
'Salmon Macrantha'	5°F	Salmon-pink to purple, single.	Grows less than 3 ft tall.	Mid- to late season.
GABLE (Zones 6-8)				
'Campfire'	0°F	Flame-red with a darker blotch, hose-in-hose.	Dense. Grows less than 6 ft tall.	Midseason
'Caroline Gable'	0°F	Red, hose-in-hose, 1-3/4 in. across.	Grows less than 6 ft tall.	Midseason
'Kathy'	0°F	Frilled, white, single.	Grows less than 3 ft tall.	Mid- to late season
'Lorna'	0°F	Pastel-pink, double, hose-in-hose, 1-3/4 in. across.	Spreading. Grows less than 3 ft tall.	Late season
'Purple Splendor'	0°F	Ruffled, lavender with a dark blotch, hose-in-hose.	Grows less than 6 ft tall.	Midseason
'Rosebud'	0°F	Violet-red, double, hose-in-hose, 1-3/4 in. across.	Low, dense, spreading. Grows slowly up to 3 ft tall.	Late season
'Rose Greeley'	0°F	Fragrant, white with chartreuse blotch, single, hose-in-hose, 2-1/2 in. across.	Dense, spreading. Grows less than 3 ft tall.	Early to midseason
'Stewartstonian'	0°F	Bright, clear red, single.	Upright, compact, bushy. Winter foliage wine-red. Ideal for bonsai. Grows to 6-8 ft.	Late season
GIRARD (Zones 6-8)				
'Girard Crimson'	−5°F	Crimson, single.	Grows less than 6 ft tall.	Midseason
'Girard Pink'	−5°F	Pink, single.	Grows less than 3 ft tall.	Late season
'Hot Shot'	−5°F	Orange-red, double.	Grows 3-5 ft tall.	Mid- to late season
'Rene Michelle'	−5°F	Pink, single, with heavy substance.	Grows less than 3 ft tall.	Midseason
'Roberta'	−5°F	Pink, double.	Grows less than 6 ft tall.	Midseason
KAEMPFERI (Zones 6-8)				
'Alice'	−10°F	Salmon-red, fading to pale rose.	Grows to 6 ft tall or more.	Early to mid-season
'Fedora'	−10°F	Violet-red or phlox-pink, single, 2 in. across.	Upright. Grows to 6 ft tall or more.	Early season
'Herbert'	−10°F	Reddish-violet, hose-in-hose.	Spreading. Grows less than 6 ft tall.	Midseason
'Palestrina' ('Wilhelmina Vuyk')	−10°F	White with chartreuse blotch, single, 2-1/4 in. across.	Grows 3-5 ft tall.	Mid- to late season

Rhododendrons

Rhododendrons are among the most important flowering evergreen shrubs in northern gardens. Many take subzero winters in stride, then cover themselves with magnificent flowers in spring.

Most rhododendrons grow quite large and have big, bold leaves and flowers. These kinds are best planted where there is plenty of space. Choose compact or dwarf varieties for foundation plantings and small yards, where they will remain in scale.

Unlike azaleas, rhododendrons aren't broken down into hybrid groups, though most are of hybrid origin. Those called 'Ironclads' are the most cold hardy. The rhododendrons listed in the chart are the most popular according to a recent poll of 20 chapters of the American Rhododendron Society, located in many different geographic regions.

The ARS rating included in the description of each of the following plants is a measure of quality. The first number refers to flower quality and the second to shrub quality. An "ideal" rating is 5/5. Also included in each description are the minimum temperature tolerated, plant height, flower color, and time of bloom.

'Purple Gem' rhododendron

Rhododendrons

Name	Cold Hardiness	Flower Description	Plant Description	Bloom Season	Ratings & Comments
'Arthur Bedford'	−5°F	Lavender-blue with a distinctive dark blotch. Dome-shaped trusses.	Grows vigorously to 6 ft tall.	Mid- to late season	4/3. Tolerates full sun.
'America'	−20°F	Bright red flowers in tight, ball-shaped trusses.	Sprawling habit, to 5 ft tall.	Midseason	3/3. Popular ironclad.
'Anah Kruschke'	−10°F	Lavender-purple held in medium-large, tight, elongated trusses.	Bushy, to 6 ft tall. Dense, lush foliage.	Late season	4/4. Withstands full sun.
'Anna Rose Whitney'	−5°F	Large, rose-pink, in trusses of 12 flowers.	Grows to 6 ft tall. Dense foliage.	Mid- to late season	4/4. Well-shaped.
'Antoon van Welie'	−5°F	Deep pink, in big trusses.	Compact, vigorous grower reaching 6 ft tall. Broad, waxy, 6-in.-long leaves.	Mid- to late season	4/4
'Blue Ensign'	−10°F	Lilac to lavender-blue with a purplish-black blotch, frilled, held in rounded trusses.	Grows to 4 ft tall, upright and spreading with glossy dark leaves.	Midseason	4/4. Tolerates full sun.
'Blue Jay'	−5°F	Lavender-blue blotched with brown, in compact, elongated trusses.	Grows vigorously to 5 ft tall with large, bright green leaves.	Mid- to late season	3/4.
'Blue Peter'	−10°F	Light lavender-blue with a purple blotch, frilled, in elongated trusses.	Grows to 4-5 ft tall with glossy leaves.	Midseason	4/3. Popular on East Coast.
'Boule de Neige'	−25°F	Trusses of white flowers resemble snowballs.	Compact shrub grows to 5 ft tall with bright green leathery leaves.	Midseason	4/4. Tolerates heat, sun and extreme cold.
'Bow Bells'	0°F	Deep pink buds open to light pink cup-shaped flowers in loose trusses.	Rounded, spreading growth habit, eventually reaching 3 ft tall.	Early to midseason	3/4. Leaves appear after flowers, emerging shiny copper color, maturing to medium green.
'Bric-a-Brac'	5°F	Trusses display flowers that open to shades of white or pink, with chocolate-brown anthers.	Low-growing, reaching 30 in. tall.	Very early	4/3. Leaves fuzzy, round, dark green.
'Caractacus'	−25°F	Purplish-red.	Compact shrub, to 6 ft tall.	Late season	2/3. Requires partial shade.
'Carmen'	−5°F	Lavender to dark red.	Dwarf, grows slowly to 1 ft tall with round, emerald-green leaves.	Early to midseason	4/5. Handsome when not in bloom.
'Caroline'	−15°F	Fragrant, orchid-pink.	Grows to 6 ft tall. Leaves waxy with wavy margins.	Mid- to late season	3/4. Long-lasting flowers.
'Catawbiense Album'	−25°F	Pure white spotted with greenish yellow, in rounded trusses.	Compact, spreading, grows to 6 ft tall. Slightly convex dark green leaves.	Late season	3/3. Deserves to be called an ironclad.
R. carolinianum	−25°F	Pure white to pale rose, rose, lilac-rose, or commonly light purple-rose.	Compact, grows 4 ft tall.	Midseason	3/3. Native of Blue Ridge Mountains of the Carolinas and Tenn. R. carolinianum album is favored by many.
R. catawbiense	−25°F	Lilac-purple, sometimes purple-rose, spotted with green or brown-yellow. Trusses of 15 to 20 flowers.	Grows to 6 ft tall. Leaves medium-large, smooth, shiny dark green on top, pale green below.	Mid- to late season	2/2. Native to slopes and summits of southern Alleghenys, W. Va. south to Ga. and Ala. One of hardiest and best known species.

nah Kruschke' rhododendron   'Caroline' rhododendron   'Catawbiense Album' rhododendron

Name	Cold Hardiness	Flower Description	Plant Description	Bloom Season	Ratings & Comments
'Chionoides'	-15°F	Bright white, in numerous trusses.	Compact, grows to 4-6 ft tall.	Mid- to late season	3/4. Very easy to grow.
R. chryseum (R. rupicola chryseum)	-15 F	Bell-shaped, bright yellow, in clusters.	Dwarf, grows to 12 in. tall. Leaves 1/2 to 1 in. long.	Early to midseason	4/3. Many dense branches.
'Cunningham's White'	-10°F	Small, white with greenish-yellow blotch in small, upright trusses.	Semidwarf, compact, spreading to 4 ft wide with shiny, dark leaves.	Mid- to late season	2/3. Requires partial shade.
'Daphnoides'	-10°F	Bright purple, displayed in pomponlike trusses.	Grows to 4 ft tall forming dense mound.	Mid- to late season	3/4. Foliage unique, with tightly spaced, rolled glossy leaves.
'Dr. V.H. Rutgers'	-20°F	Frilled, crimson-red.	Grows to 5 ft tall.	Mid- to late season	3/3. Dense foliage with dark green leaves.
'Dora Amateis'	-15°F	Spicy-scented, 2 in. across, pure white with green spots, in clusters of up to 5.	Semidwarf, grows to 3 ft tall with dense foliage.	Early to midseason	4/4. Leaves tinged bronze when grown in full sun.
'English Roseum'	-20°F	Rose-pink, tinged lavender, in big trusses.	Grows to 6 ft tall or more.	Mid- to late season	2/4. Handsome plant, even when not in bloom. Tolerates extreme heat, cold, and humidity.
R. fastigiatum	-15 F	Lilac-purple, in small clusters that cover foliage.	Reaches 18 in. with dense, dark, shiny foliage.	Midseason	4/4. One of the hardiest of small alpine-type rhododendrons.
'Fastuosum Flore Pleno'	-10°F	Lavender-purple, double, 2 in. across, held in full trusses.	Grows vigorously to 6 ft tall with leaves dark above, light green below.	Mid- to late season	3/3. Open and rounded growth habit.
'Fragrantissimum'	20 F	Funnel-shaped, white tinged with pink, very fragrant.	Generally seen as espalier or vine to 10 ft or more. Can be kept to 5-6 ft or less with pruning.	Midseason	4/3. Flowers nutmeg-scented.
'General Eisenhower'	5°F	Large, ruffled, deep carmine-red in large clusters.	Compact, grows to 6 ft tall with large, waxy leaves.	Midseason	4/3. Strong-growing plant.
'Gomer Waterer'	-15 F	Pink flower buds open to pure white.	Grows to 5 ft tall with large, dark leaves.	Mid- to late season	3/5. Old standby tolerates full sun.
'Graf Zeppelin'	10 F	Vibrant bright pink.	Grows to 5 ft tall with dark, glossy leaves.	Mid- to late season	3/4. Vigorous and hardy.
'Herbert Parsons' ('President Lincoln')	-25 F	Lavender-pink.	Grows to 6 ft tall or more.	Mid- to late season	2/3.
'Humming Bird'	0°F	Red flowers hold their color well.	Semidwarf shrub with compact habit reaches 2-1/2 ft tall.	Early to midseason	3/4. Requires partial shade.
'Ignatius Sargent'	-20°F	Large, rose-red, slightly fragrant.	Grows to 5-6 ft tall with large leaves.	Mid- to late season	2/2. Plant has open growth habit.
R. impeditum	-15°F	Small, slightly fragrant, bright purplish-blue flowers blanket foliage.	Tight, compact, cushionlike dwarf shrub reaches 1-1/2 ft high. Tiny silvery gray-green leaves.	Midseason	4/4. Excellent for bonsai.
R. intricatum	-15°F	Attractive bluish flowers in profusion.	Low, compact, intricately branched shrub reaches 1-2 ft tall.	Early to midseason	4/3. Ideal for bonsai.

'Lee's Dark Purple' rhododendron

'Nova Zembla' rhododendron

'Roseum elegans' rhododendron

Rhododendrons (continued)

Name	Cold Hardiness	Flower Description	Plant Description	Bloom Season	Ratings & Comments
'Janet Blair'	−15°F	Frilled, light pink with a green flare on the upper petals.	Grows vigorously to 6 ft tall.	Midseason	4/3. Profuse foliage.
R. keiskei	−5°F	Lemon-yellow, bell-shaped, in clusters.	Grows to 3 ft tall. Variety *cordifolia* is dwarf, reaching only 6 in. high.	Early to midseason	4/4. Very pointed leaves.
R. keleticum	−10°F	Large, pansylike, standing erect above foliage, ranging from rose through purple with crimson flecks.	Dwarf, reaching 1 ft tall, with dense, aromatic leaves.	Midseason	4/4. Good choice for bonsai.
'Kluis Sensation'	0°F	Dark red in tight trusses.	Compact shrub to 5 ft tall.	Mid- to late season	3/4. Dark red flowers contrast with dark green leaves.
'Lee's Dark Purple'	−20°F	Dark purple, in large trusses.	Grows to 6 ft tall with dark, wavy foliage.	Mid- to late season	3/3. Ironclad. Popular old-timer.
R. maximum	−25°F	White petals, rose or pink flushed. Trusses partially hidden by current season's leaf growth.	Grows from 4-ft-tall shrub to 40-ft-tall tree, depending on climate.	Mid- to late season	2.3. Leaves resemble a bay tree.
'Moonstone'	0°F	Bell-shaped, creamy-yellow, in trusses of 3 to 5.	Grows in a tight mound, 3 ft tall, covered with smooth oval-shaped green leaves 2-1/2 in. long.	Early to midseason	4/4. Prolific bloomer.
'Mother of Pearl'	0°F	Buds open pink, fade to pearl-white. Slightly fragrant.	Grows rapidly to 6 ft tall.	Midseason	4/3. A sport of 'Pink Pearl'.
R. moupinense	−5°F	Funnel-shaped, large, fragrant, bright snowy-white with a maroon blotch.	Open, spreading growth to 30 in. wide. Bronzy-red new growth matures to shiny green leaves.	Very early season	4/3. Good choice for bonsai.
'Mrs. Charles E. Pearson'	−5°F	Large, light orchid-pink with upper petals spotted brown, in dome-shaped trusses.	Grows vigorously to 6 ft tall with lush foliage.	Midseason	4/4. Award-winning old-timer. Vigorous. Tolerates sun and heat.
'Mrs. Furnival'	−10°F	Light pink with a striking brown blotch on the upper petals, in tight, dome-shaped trusses.	Upright, spreading, reaching 4 ft tall with light green leaves.	Mid- to late season	5/4. Grows well in eastern United States.
R. mucronulatum	−15°F	Orchid-pink blossoms 1-3/4 in. across appear before leaves. 'Cornell Pink' is rose-colored.	Grows to 5-8 ft tall. Red fall color.	Very early	Decidous. Botanists consider this azalea-like shurb a rhododendron.
'Nova Zembla'	−25°F	Dark red, showy, in rounded trusses.	Grows to 5 ft tall with polished, dark green leaves.	Midseason	3/3. Grows well in difficult areas.
'Parson's Gloriosum'	−25°F	Lavender-pink in conical trusses.	Grows compact, upright, to 5 ft tall with dark green leaves.	Midseason	2/2. Very hardy. Ironclad.
R. pemakoense	0°F	Profusion of pink flowers hides leaves.	Dwarf, compact, cushionlike to 1-1/2 ft with tiny, 1-in.-long leaves.	Very early to early season	3/4. Very easy to grow.
'Pink Pearl'	−5°F	Rose-pink in large trusses.	Tall, open growth to 6 ft.	Midseason	3/3.
'P.J.M.'	−20°F	Lavender-pink in small trusses.	Compact-growing to 4 ft tall with small leaves mahogany during winter.	Early season	4/4. Will withstand full sun as well as cold and heat.

'Sappho' rhododendron

'Scintillation' rhododendron

'Vulcan' rhododendron

Name	Cold Hardiness	Flower Description	Plant Description	Bloom Season	Ratings & Comments
'Purple Gem'	−20°F	Deep purple-violet.	Compact, spreading, grows to 2 ft with bluish-green foliage.	Early to midseason	3/4. Related to 'Ramapo'.
'Purple Splendor'	−10°F	Dark purple with a black blotch; appearing almost black overall.	Shrub grows to 5 ft with deep green foliage.	Mid- to late season	4/3. The king of royal purples.
'Ramapo'	−20°F	Pale violet, small, in profusion.	Dwarf, compact, spreading, reaches 2 ft. New leaves dusty blue.	Early to midseason	4/4. Use in low borders or rock gardens. Foliage is interesting throughout all seasons.
'Roseum Elegans'	−25°F	Small, rosy-lilac, held in dome-shaped trusses.	Grows vigorously to 6 ft with abundant olive-green foliage.	Mid- to late season	2/4. Another ironclad. Also for hot climates.
'Sappho'	−10°F	Medium-size, white with a blackish blotch on upper petals, in dome-shaped trusses.	Grows vigorously with open growth to 6 ft.	Midseason	3/2. Blooms profusely.
'Scarlet Wonder'	−10°F	Ruffled, scarlet-red, in flattened trusses.	Very compact, reaching 2 ft with dense, glossy leaves.	Midseason	5/4. Awarded silver and gold medal by Dutch enthusiasts.
'Scintillation'	−10°F	Pastel-pink, with a bronze and yellow throat, in large, dome-shaped trusses.	Grows to 5 ft with deep shiny green foliage.	Midseason	4/4. Wavy leaves curl attractively.
'The Hon. Jean Marie de Montague'	0°F	Bright red, showy, in rounded trusses.	Compact shrub grows to 5 ft tall with thick, heavy emerald-green foliage.	Midseason	4/4. Standard for excellence for red flowers.
'Trilby'	−10°F	Dark, crimson-red with black markings in the center, displayed in ball-like trusses.	Compact habit, reaches 5 ft with red stems, gray-green leaves.	Mid- to late season	3/4. Handsome plant, even when not in bloom.
'Unique'	0°F	Buds open light pink, change to buttery cream-yellow flushed with peach. Displayed profusely on dome-shaped trusses.	Compact, neat, reaches 4 ft with thick, oblong clover-green leaves.	Early to midseason	4/4. Flowers completely cover plant.
'Vulcan'	−10°F	Bright fire-red.	Mound-shaped, grows to 5 ft tall.	Mid- to late season	4/4. An excellent hybrid.
'Windbeam'	−25°F	Open white, turning light pink.	Spreading, grows to 4 ft with small leaves.	Early to midseason	4/3. Aromatic foliage.
'Yaku King'	−10°F	Deep pink with light pink blotch. Up to 18 blossoms in a ball-like truss.	Semidwarf, grows less than 3 ft tall.	Mid- to late season	ARS rating not available.
'Yaku Prince'	−10°F	Pink blossom, lighter blotch with reddish-orange spots. Up to 14 blossoms in a ball-like truss.	Semidwarf, grows less than 3 ft tall.	Midseason	ARS rating not available.
'Yaku Princess'	−10°F	Apple-blossom pink with a blushed blotch, greenish spots. Up to 15 blossoms in a ball-like truss.	Semidwarf, grows less than 3 ft tall.	Midseason	ARS rating not available.
'Yaku Queen'	−10°F	Pale pink with a faint yellow blotch. Up to 16 blossoms in a ball-like truss.	Semidwarf, grows less than 3 ft tall.	Midseason	ARS rating not available.
R. yakusimanum	−15°F	Pale rose.	Semidwarf, grows less than 3 ft tall.	Midseason	5/5. Limited availability but very popular among hobbyists.

Cape grape (Rhoicissus capensis) covers lattice-work, walls, and fences with its large, shiny evergreen leaves.

Staghorn sumac (Rhus typhina) features long, featherlike leaves that turn golden-orange to scarlet in fall.

Locusts (Robinia sp.) are tough, fast-growing trees used for quick effects and light shade on difficult growing sites.

Rhoicissus capensis (Cissus capensis)
Cape Grape, Evergreen Grape
Zone: 10.
Evergreen vine.

Cape grape is a handsome vine with large, roundish to kidney-shaped leaves. Rust-colored hairs on the undersides of leaves and bronzy new growth give added visual interest. Plant form is similar to that of its relative the edible grape. Long, branched tendrils cling to fences and lattice-work to form a dense, lush green cover. The vine can reach up to 30 feet. It bears small, 1/2-inch, edible berries. Although primarily planted for their ornamental value, the glossy reddish-black fruit can be used in cooking and preserves. Flowers appear in spring but are not ornamental.

Large leaves make cape grape an excellent shade plant for patio or veranda. Provide strong support for its long branches. Drape the vine over a tall fence or send it cascading down a bank. Grows outdoors in shade.

The vine grows from large, 6- to 8-inch tubers, which do best in a rich, well-drained soil. They withstand somewhat dry conditions but flourish when kept moist and mulched. This is particularly beneficial when growing the vine in hot climates. Protect from prolonged freezing.

Cape grape is a moderate- to slow-growing vine. Young plants should be guided where you want them to grow.

Rhus typhina
Staghorn Sumac, Velvet Sumac
Zones: 3-8. To 6-30 feet.
Deciduous shrub or tree.

Staghorn sumac is the largest of the native North American sumacs, sometimes exceeding 30 feet in height with a trunk diameter in excess of 8 inches. Its featherlike leaves may exceed 2 feet in length and turn golden-orange to scarlet in the fall. Greenish flowers are borne in compact spikes at the ends of branches. Hairy fruits follow, turning scarlet in midsummer and remaining through winter. The branches of its new growth are densely covered with hair and look and feel much like the horns of deer when their antlers are in velvet, accounting for its name.

Staghorn sumac prefers a well-drained soil, and does not tolerate wet, poorly drained sites. It grows in dry, rocky soils and is well suited for planting on very dry sites such as abandoned stony pastures and fields. It tolerates air pollution and makes a good city tree.

Sumac spreads by root suckering and forms dense many-trunked stands. It can be used to quickly cover bare areas and is excellent for naturalistic plantings where it can be allowed to spread. It can, however, be confined to smaller areas by cutting the suckers back each year.

The cultivar 'Laciniata', the cut-leaf staghorn sumac, has deeply cut foliage and makes a most attractive small tree. The leaves of 'Dissecta' are even more finely textured. Its cultivar 'Laciniata' has deeply cut foliage.

Smooth sumac, *Rhus glabra*, is similar to staghorn sumac except that its new growth lacks hairs.

Robinia
Locust
Deciduous trees.

Locusts are top-rated where a fast-growing, tough, deciduous tree is needed for immediate effect. Brittle wood and invasive roots rule them out in most other situations.

Robinia x ambigua 'Idahoensis'
Idaho Locust
Zones: 5-10. To 40 feet.
Deciduous tree. Flowering.

This is the most handsome form of locust. Dense, finely divided leaves make a tight, compact head. Rosy-pink, pealike blossoms are borne in long clusters from midspring to early summer. Takes drought, poor soils, and high temperatures.

Robinia pseudoacacia
Black Locust
Zones: 3-9. To 60-75 feet.
Deciduous tree. Flowering.

Black locust has showy clusters of white fragrant flowers in spring. The tall, straight trunk has black, deeply furrowed bark. Leaves are divided and dark green. Thorny branches are covered with 4-inch beanlike pods in winter. Withstands the same tough conditions as the Idaho locust.

Rosa
Rose
Zones: 5-10.
Deciduous or semievergreen shrubs. Flowering.

Roses inspire the devotion of gardeners worldwide because their flowers are unmatched in color, fragrance, and form. For ease of identification, roses are placed in classes by similarity in flowering and shrub size. Most roses are grown as flowerbed plants for their magnificent blossoms that make excellent cut flowers. Three classes also make top-rated landscape shrubs.

Floribunda roses usually grow 2 to 4 feet tall but may reach 6 feet. They are hardy and disease-resistant. Flowers are profuse, borne in heads or clustered groups, all summer. Low and bushy shrubs, floribundas make excellent colorful barrier hedges or accent plants in a border planting. Many top-rated varieties in a range of flower colors are available.

Polyantha roses are low shrubby plants that bear masses of 2-inch-wide flowers almost continuously. Flower colors include shades of pink and orange. Use as low hedges or to line walks and driveways.

Climbing roses bring incomparable elegance and beauty to a garden. They grace building eaves, add drama to a fence or post, or create a romantic arch over an arbor or trellis. Flower color and fragrance in climbing roses is as diverse as in shrub forms.

Climbing roses do not actually twine or cling; their long branches must be trained and tied to a support. An unsupported vine can look attractive in a large landscape where it will form a sprawling, mounded shrub. Some kinds grow only to 10 feet long, others reach 50 feet.

Basically, there are 3 types of climbing roses: large-flowered climbers, climbing sports, and ramblers. Large-flowered climbers have canes that are stout, stiff, and grow from 8 to 15 feet high. Flowers are 2 to 6 inches across and borne in open clusters of up to 25 blossoms. Vines reach their bloom peak in spring but continue to flower throughout the season.

Large-flowered climbers are the best choice for cold winter areas where temperatures do not drop below −18°F. They are the most cold hardy of climbing roses and are relatively pest-free.

The second type of climbing rose is called a climbing sport. They are created by propagating exceptionally long vigorous canes that form spontaneously on normal bush roses. The prized flowers of the bush form are also produced by the climber. Although blooming less prolifically than large-flowered climbers, climbing sports offer a fine form and high quality flowers. Climbing sports are hardy to 20°F. Tipping the plant over and completely covering it in late fall with a protective mulch will help it withstand winter temperatures as low as −10°F.

Varieties of climbing sports are named for the bush rose from which they were developed, because they have the same flower and fragrance characteristics. Look for the popular shrub name preceded by the word "climbing" to select the rose variety of your choice.

Other long-caned roses suitable for climbing include the ramblers. They are hardy to −10°F, if protected. Blooms are produced in abundance on 1-year-old canes. Ramblers have supple canes growing to over 20 feet. They need a yearly pruning to remove old wood

Roses *(Rosa* sp.) are universal garden favorites prized for the exquisite fragrance, colors, and forms of their flowers. Roses trained as trees, shown above, have a formal appearance; climbing roses, such as 'Joseph's Coat' shown below, add an air of informality.

In mild climates, rosemary (Rosmarinus officinalis) is evergreen and makes an excellent ground cover for difficult sites.

Widely adapted Irish moss (Sagina subulata) forms a ground-hugging carpet of lush green foliage.

and make room for younger flowering canes. When canes are supported, ramblers make a good cover for the sides of tall fences or buildings.

These roses are hardy, tough plants that will flower and grow if their basic needs are met. Provide a sunny location, regular deep watering, and regular fertilizing. A neutral soil pH is ideal. Roses are hardy to about 18°F. Below that they need a protective layer of insulation in winter. Prune each spring to remove old and weak canes and create an open center. Reduce all branches to one-half their length. Remove faded blossoms. Roses are susceptible to aphids, scale, spider mites, and mildew.

For descriptions of hybrid tea and grandiflora roses, see page 273 in the garden flower encyclopedia.

Rosmarinus officinalis
Rosemary
Zones: 7-10. To 2-6 feet.
Evergreen shrub. Flowering.

Rosemary is a fragrant-leaved herb that is native to the Mediterranean region. It was grown in Medieval medicinal gardens and is still a favorite herb garden plant today. It is also used for hedges, especially in Southern California's inland and coastal regions. Low-growing and prostrate forms are used as ground covers on dry rocky sites. This dense-branching shrub has narrow, glossy, dark green leaves with grayish-white undersides. Small, light blue flowers appear in winter and spring.

In cold climates, grow rosemary as an annual, or plant in containers and move indoors during freezing weather. Does well in poor, dry soil in full sun. Tolerates partial shade. Prune to encourage full shape.

'Lockwood de Forest' is a creeping form 2 feet high. Foliage is lighter and brighter than the species; flowers are bluer. Use as a ground cover, in rock and herb gardens, or in planters. 'Fastigiatus' and 'Pyramidalis' are upright forms useful in hedges.

Sagina subulata
Irish Moss, Scotch Moss
Zones: 3-9. To 1-3 inches.
Evergreen ground cover.

See Arenaria verna, Irish Moss, for a description and for care and culture of this plant.

Salix
Willow, Osier
Deciduous shrubs and trees.

This genus is comprised of a large group of deciduous shrubs and trees. They range in size from creeping ground-hugging plants to large stately trees. In general, they do best in regions with defined seasons, and are fast growers in moist soils. They tolerate poor drainage. Because of their affinity for water, willow roots can be troublesome, invading drain pipes and sewers.

Foliage is small and narrow, giving plants a delicate texture. Flowers, in most cases, are very small and inconspicuous. Branches are usually slender, sometimes weeping, and on some shrubby willows are attractively colored. Bark can be rough or comparatively smooth but flaking.

Care should be taken when selecting planting sites for willows. The wood is weak, and often cracks. Willow trees should not be used near streets or houses where damage from breaking branches might create a problem. Also, willows are susceptible to a number of diseases and insect pests. Plant willows in moist soil where they will grow vigorously and be able to resist insect pest and disease problems.

Salix alba tristis
Golden Weeping Willow
Zones: 3-10. To 75-80 feet.

One of the most cold hardy Salix, golden weeping willow is a fast-growing tree. It is a particularly graceful variety with wide-spreading, arching branches. It is called golden weeping willow because the plant's one-year-old twigs are bright yellow and look attractive during the winter. Leaves are bright green to yellow-green above and paler beneath. The bark is brown to yellow-brown and has a corky appearance.

Golden weeping willow is susceptible to a number of pests. It needs to be staked until it reaches a height of 15 to 18 feet. Prune to guide upright growth and develop high branching. May be a litter producer, shedding branches and leaves.

Salix babylonica
Babylon Weeping Willow
Zones: 6-10. To 30-50 feet.
Deciduous tree.

Babylon weeping willow is a good choice when a broad-spreading tree with a graceful weeping habit is desired. The olive-green foliage is 3 to 6 inches long, and turns yellow in fall. Branches are green to brown.

Babylon weeping willow is a fast grower, and has weak wood susceptible to damage by winter ice. Needs to be staked when young.

'Crispa', ringleaf or corkscrew willow, has foliage that curls into small rings or circles. It is slightly more upright.

Salix discolor
Pussy Willow
Zones: 3-10. To 20-25 feet.
Deciduous shrub or tree.

The silky gray-white catkins, or flowers, found on male plants make pussy willow a much-loved plant. Catkins appear in early spring and measure up to 1-1/2 inches long. Catkin-laden branches can be cut and brought indoors in late winter. If put in water, the silky buds open into fuzzy yellow blossoms.

The leaves of pussy willow are oblong, 3 to 5 inches long, bright green above and silvery-white beneath. In fall their coloring becomes greenish yellow. Twigs are reddish purple to brown.

Pussy willow tolerates most average soils, but grows best if the ground is moist or wet. Prune to obtain optimum flowering by severely cutting back every 3 to 4 years.

The wide-spreading weeping branches of corkscrew willow (*Salix babylonica* 'Crispa') cast welcome shade in summer.

The fuzzy catkins of pussy willow (*Salix discolor*).

Navajo Hankow willows (Salix matsudana 'Navajo') are fast-growing shade trees adapted to dry climates.

Sweet box (Sarcococca hookerana humilis) is a good low hedge or ground cover for difficult shady spots.

California pepper trees (Schinus molle) offer fine-textured foliage and graceful branches, making an effective accent or specimen tree.

Salix matsudana
Hankow Willow, Pekin Willow
Zones: 5-10. To 35-45 feet.

This fast-growing willow is native to northern Asia. It has a pyramidal form. Selections are more commonly grown than the species. 'Tortuosa', corkscrew or contorted willow, grows to 30 feet with a 20-foot spread. Its twisted, corkscrewlike branching habit is evident after the leaves have fallen. Cut branches are handsome in flower arrangements.

'Navajo' is a large roundheaded tree to 20 feet tall, grown for its adaptation to desert climates. 'Umbraculifera', the globe willow, is about half as large as 'Navajo' and is also valued in hot climates.

Sarcococca hookerana humilis
Sweet Box
Zones: 7-10. To 15-24 inches.
Evergreen shrub. Flowering.

Sweet box is a slow-growing, handsomely formed low plant that spreads as far as 8 feet by underground runners. Glossy green, lance-shaped leaves hide the tiny, fragrant white flowers that bloom in early spring. Small, shiny black berries follow in summer. This plant tolerates deep shade and is a valuable shrub for north-facing exposures and entryways, and for greenery under tall shrubs.

Sweet box is an easy-to-grow shrub demanding little attention. Plant in a rich, well-drained soil with plenty of organic matter added. Water regularly. Watch for signs of scale. Spreading growth can be contained by cutting back underground runners. For an unrestrained, lush ground cover, do not prune.

Schinus
Pepper Tree
Evergreen trees.

Though native to South America, one species, *Schinus molle*, from Peru is so widely planted in California it is called California pepper tree.

Trees are not related to the spice pepper, but the dry fruits resemble peppercorns. The colorful winter fruit and the interesting growth habits of these trees make them top landscape plants. Pollen from male trees of both species causes an allergic reaction in some people.

Schinus molle
California Pepper Tree
Zones: 9-10. To 15-50 feet.
Evergreen tree.

Wide-spreading, heavy branches, with branchlets that hang gracefully, give a weeping willowlike appearance to this fast-growing tree. A gnarled, knobby trunk with light brown bark adds visual interest. Generally a large, spreading tree that needs plenty of growing room.

Compound leaves are 6 to 12 inches long and have 20 to 60 very narrow, light green leaflets that are 1-1/2 to 2 inches long. Yellowish-white flowers in drooping terminal clusters are not showy. Rose to red, 1/4-inch fruits add color from November to May.

Best growth is in full sun on well-drained soil. Tolerates poor drainage, heat, drought, and low fertility. Young plants should be staked.

Tends to litter, dropping fruit, twigs, and old leaves. Rapidly invasive, shallow roots can lift pavement and clog drains. Aphids can disfigure foliage.

Schinus terebinthifolius
Brazilian Pepper Tree
Zones: 9-10. To 15-30 feet.
Evergreen tree.

This moderate- to fast-growing, dense, rounded tree has spreading, horizontal branches producing an umbrella shape. Width and height are about equal. A good tree for patios or as a street tree.

Shiny, dark green compound leaves are 6 to 8 inches long and usually have 7 broad inch-long leaflets. Small whitish flowers in terminal clusters appear in late summer and are followed by showy, bright red to dull rose-red, 1/8-inch fruits that look colorful from December to March.

Brazilian pepper grows in any well-drained soil in full sun and tolerates dryness. Branches should be thinned and long ones headed back in windy areas. Surface roots form unless watered deeply and infrequently. Choose a tree with fruit on it, since fruit quantity is variable on seed-propagated plants.

Sedum
Sedum, Stonecrop
Succulent ground covers.
Flowering.

This large genus of succulent plants offers many excellent ground covers for garden use. Sedums have trailing stems with rounded, juicy leaves and clusters of colorful flowers. They are durable plants that are useful for difficult, hot dry sites. Sedums will not tolerate foot traffic, but make excellent low plants for rock walls and retaining walls, and for edging paths and patios.

Plant in spring, spacing plants 6 to 10 inches apart. They will fill in quickly, and many kinds reproduce from fallen leaves. Full sun is best in most areas; provide afternoon shade in hot climates. Soil must be well-drained; will rot in soggy soil.

Sedums *(Sedum* sp.) are quick-spreading succulent ground covers for difficult, dry sunny sites. *(Sedum x rubrotinctum),* above; *(Sedum lineare),* top right; *(S. lineare)* in bloom, lower right.

Sedum

Botanical Name	Zones	Size	Plant Description	Comments
Sedum anglicum	3-10	To 2-4 in.	Small dark green, fleshy leaves. Yellow, star-shaped flowers in spring.	Ideal for covering low mounds and small banks. Space 6-10 in. apart for ground cover.
S. brevifolium	3-10	To 2-3 in.	Slow-growing with small grayish-white leaves tinged with red. White, star-shaped flowers in summer.	Best used as small-scale ground cover. Must have good drainage. Space 6-10 in. apart for ground cover.
S. confusum	8-10	To 6-10 in.	Light green, 1-in. leaves are clustered at branch tips. Yellow flowers in dense clusters in spring.	Not for extremely hot summer climates. Good on slopes. Space 12 in. apart for ground cover.
S. dasyphyllum	8-10	To 2 in.	Small, mosslike, gray-blue leaves. Small white flowers in spring.	Good small-scale ground cover. Space 6-12 in. apart.
S. lineare (S. sarmentosum)	3-10	To 6-10 in.	Closely spaced, small light green leaves. Spreads vigorously. Masses of yellow flowers in spring.	One of the showiest sedums. Space 12 in. apart for ground cover.
S. x rubrotinctum (S. guatemalense)	8-10	To 6-8 in.	Spreads vigorously. Leaves green with reddish-brown tips, 3/4 in. and oblong. Reddish-yellow flowers in spring.	Picks up more reddish-brown color in full sun. Space 10-12 in. apart for ground cover.
S. spathulifolium	6-10	To 2-3 in.	Silvery leaves tinged red in attractive rosettes. Bright yellow flowers in late spring and early summer.	Space 6-8 in. apart for ground cover.
S. spurium	3-10	To 3-4 in.	Compact mat of bronzy-green, 1-in. leaves. Clusters of 4-5 pink flowers held above leaves in summer.	'Dragon's Blood' has rose-red flowers. Space 6-10 in. apart for ground cover.

The coast redwood *(Sequoia sempervirens),* which can reach a height of 100 feet, is a superb tree for skyline drama.

Giant sequoia *(Sequoidendron giganteum)* is the world's largest-growing tree, and must be given ample room. Use as a specimen or silhouette tree.

Sequoia sempervirens

Redwood, Coast Redwood

Zones: 7-10. To 90-100 feet.
Evergreen tree.

The tallest trees on the North American continent, some reaching over 350 feet in height, are members of this species. A redwood will probably reach 70 to 90 feet tall with a spread of 14 to 30 feet in large gardens, during the planter's lifetime.

The coast redwood is an upright, rapid-growing tree with a narrow conical or pyramidal shape when young. Initially branches grow straight out from the trunk, becoming more horizontal and spreading on older trees. Branchlets, covered with either scalelike or flat needle-like leaves, have a tendency to be drooping. Tree trunks have red-brown fibrous bark, are straight, and become massive as the tree grows older.

This geologically ancient tree formerly grew over large areas of the Northern Hemisphere. Today, natural stands of redwoods are found only in the fog belt of northern California and Oregon. Because these rapid-growing trees are so attractive and become so statuesque, many attempts have been made to grow them in other areas. However, coast redwoods rarely reach their prime outside of areas with frequent coastal fog.

Plant in groves, screens, as skyline trees, or as a specimen tree. Redwoods can also be planted close together and clipped for a fast-growing hedge. Surface roots can be a problem in lawns. Because the coast redwood is so long-lived, it should be planted to remain. Some old trees in the original forest are 2,000 to 3,000 years old.

Foliage color varies from light to dark green in seedlings and can be dense or sparse. Four varieties are top-rated. 'Aptos Blue' has dense blue-green foliage; 'Santa Cruz' has light green foliage; 'Soquel' has light-textured blue-green foliage; 'Los Altos' has deep green foliage.

Sequoiadendron giganteum

Giant Sequoia, Bigtree

Zones: 6-10. To 90-100 feet.
Evergreen tree.

This species includes the world's largest trees in volume and weight. Trunk diameters have reached up to 37 feet. These massive trees grow at a moderate rate, and after centuries may be 325 feet tall.

Giant sequoia is an isolated remnant of geologically ancient trees left over from the age of the dinosaurs. Today's natural range is a narrow belt 260 miles long on the west slopes of the Sierra Nevadas. Even in this area the trees grow only in scattered groves.

Young trees are narrowly pyramidal with dense blue-green foliage. Leaves are awl-shaped or scalelike and very different from the coast redwood. Young trees hold their branches. As the tree ages, lower branches are lost, exposing the lower trunk's attractive reddish-brown bark. On ancient trees, bark may be 20 inches, or more, thick. Slower growing than the coast redwood, it may possibly live longer.

Plant in deep, slightly acid soil with good drainage and aeration, in full sunlight. Should be watered deeply but infrequently once established.

Bigtree is easier to grow than the coast redwood but does not have as many landscape uses. Plant in large open areas as a specimen or silhouette tree, or as a conversation piece. Not suitable for small gardens since it develops too wide a spread. If planted in a lawn, roots may surface and cause problems. Trees planted in Central States and the Northeast are usually killed during severe winters. One tree, 70 feet tall, has been reported growing in Bristol, Connecticut.

Skimmia japonica

Japanese Skimmia

Zones: 6-8. To 5 feet.
Evergreen shrub. Flowering.

Japanese skimmia is a handsome plant grown for its fragrant flowers, attractive fruits, and bright green foliage. Flowers are yellowish white, fruits are bright red or bright scarlet, and leaves are 3 to 4 inches long. A dome-shaped shrub, it has a dense habit of growth.

Grows best in moist, sandy loam soils but tolerates some clay. Grows in light to full shade. Requires more shade farther south, but heavy or dense shade will cause plants to become leggy. Because male and female flowers are usually on different plants both a male and female shrub are required to ensure a set of fruit on the female plant. A number of male and female cultivars have been selected.

Skimmias are tough and will grow in urban areas. They are frequently used in foundation plantings, as specimens, in shady borders, and as container plants.

Japanese skimmia *(Skimmia japonica)* is a tough evergreen shrub with fragrant flowers, bright berries, and shiny foliage. Serves many landscape uses.

Sophora japonica
Japanese Pagoda Tree, Chinese Scholar Tree

Zones: 5-8. To 30-60 feet.
Deciduous tree. Flowering.

Valued for its late-summer flowers, Japanese pagoda tree is tolerant of heat, dryness, and city pollution. For over 1,000 years, this tree has been planted on the grounds of temples in China, Korea, and Japan. It is also top-rated as a shade and flowering tree for American gardens.

Generally a roundheaded tree as wide as tall, the tree's growth rate is moderate up to 30 feet, and slow thereafter. It has a short trunk, and the twigs and young branches are smooth and green, while older branches have a pale gray-brown bark. The fernlike, compound leaves are 6 to 10 inches long with 7 to 17 oval, dark green leaflets up to 2 inches long. Leaves drop without changing color in late fall. In late July and August, yellow-white, 1/2-inch, pea-shaped flowers in 8- to 15-inch pyramidal clusters cover the tree. Fallen flowers may stain cement. Pendulous, translucent, 3-inch green pods follow.

Tolerant of heat, dryness, and pollution, Japanese pagoda trees *(Sophora japonica)* are a good choice for large gardens in urban settings.

European mountain ash *(Sorbus aucuparia)* makes a showy lawn tree with small white flowers in spring and orange-red to red berries, shown below, in late summer or early fall.

Spanish broom *(Spartium junceum)* a tough, drought-hardy shrub is mantled with fragrant yellow blooms from mid-spring to midsummer.

Grows best in full sun and well-drained soil. Because of the low branching habit, it is not suitable as a street tree, but it grows well in cities and will tolerate drought and high temperatures. Flowering may be inconsistent in cool, cloudy summer areas. First bloom may take 10 years, but 'Regent' blooms sooner, is more erect, and faster growing.

Sorbus aucuparia
European Mountain Ash
Zones: 2-7. To 45 feet.
Deciduous tree. Flowering.

Erect when young, becoming spreading and open at maturity, European mountain ash is frequently a multistemmed tree. In spring small white flowers grow in clusters 3 to 5 inches in diameter. Large clusters of bright red to orange-red berries follow in late summer or early fall. Fruit remains until eaten by birds. Compound, pale dull-green leaves turn yellow to red in fall.

The European mountain ash is the principal species used in the United States. It has been planted since Colonial times, and has become naturalized in some areas of North America, including Alaska. Although it will grow on dry sites, best growth is made on rich, moist soils with a pH of 6.0 to 7.5. Will grow in full sun or partial shade. Does not do well in areas where there is extreme summer heat. Needs to be watered in summer.

Use as a specimen or lawn tree, also as a street tree on the Pacific Coast. Not a tree to be planted and neglected, it is subject to borers at the base of the tree, and may require sprays to control. In areas where Japanese beetles are a problem, the leaves may have to be sprayed with an insecticide to keep the adult beetles from destroying the foliage. Fireblight also can be a problem in some areas.

A number of cultivars and hybrids have been developed. 'Brilliant Yellow' has golden-yellow fruit. 'Cardinal Royal' has large clusters of bright red berries, coloring earlier than the species. 'Charming Pink' has pink fruit. 'Fastigiata' has a columnar shape. The hybrid 'Meinichii' has a pyramidal shape with larger berries than the species and larger green leaves.

The genus *Sorbus* is comprised of many ornamental trees and shrubs in addition to the European mountain ash. Several of these are excellent landscape plants but are not considered top-rated because they are not widely available in nurseries. *S. alnifolia*, Korean mountain ash, is particularly noteworthy.

The Korean mountain ash grows 25 to 35 feet tall and, unlike most other members of this genus, has simple undivided leaves and is resistant to borer attack. The foliage is a deep lustrous green and turns crimson and scarlet in fall. Small clusters of snow-white flowers are borne in spring. They are followed by bright red berries. The tree's silvery-gray bark is attractive in winter. Korean mountain ash is adapted to Zones 4 to 8.

Spartium junceum
Spanish Broom
Zones: 7-10. To 6-10 feet.
Evergreen shrub. Flowering.

One of the most drought-resistant and rugged flowering shrubs for warm climates, Spanish broom has sparse, bluish-green leaves and tough branches. It is nearly leafless but has slender, rushlike stems that remain a deep green throughout the year. Spanish broom is most noteworthy from midspring to August when golden-yellow, fragrant, pealike flowers brighten the landscape. In mass plantings, their fragrance permeates the air. Grows upright to 6 to 10 feet, spreading 6 to 8 feet wide.

Although easily controlled in the garden, this plant has naturalized itself to become a weed on open slopes in the western United States. It thrives where soils are poor and well-drained, even on hot, rocky slopes. Spanish broom is an ideal plant for low-maintenance gardens with little summer irrigation. Use as a bright accent.

Spiraea

Spiraea

Zones: 3-9. To 9 feet.
Deciduous shrubs. Flowering.

Almost 100 species of shrubs native in the Northern Hemisphere are included in this genus. Planted as ornamentals for their masses of tiny flowers in late spring or early summer, spiraeas offer a white, pink, or red floral display. The compact forms of spiraeas maintain a neat shape with very little pruning and will soon make an attractive bush with side branches arching and drooping to the ground. Spiraeas of open, airy habit grow more densely and flower more profusely if pruned. Prune spring-flowering spiraeas after they bloom; summer-flowering spiraeas in late winter.

Spiraeas thrive in many exposures and on a variety of soils but require plenty of moisture and full sunshine for best bloom. They make pretty hedges and screens along a drive or property border, and are popular specimen shrubs. Top-rated spireas are described in the chart below.

Spiraeas *(Spiraea* sp.) comprise a large genus of ornamental shrubs planted for their colorful late spring or early summer floral display. Bridal-wreath *(S. x vanhoutii),* above top; Japanese spiraea *(S. japonica),* above left; Snowmound spiraea *(S. nipponica tosaensis),* above right.

Spiraea

Botanical Name/ Common Name	Zones	Size	Flower Description	Plant Description	Comments
S. x bumalda 'Anthony Waterer' **Dwarf Pink Bridal-Wreath, Anthony Waterer Spiraea**	3-9	To 2-3 ft tall.	Summer-blooming. Rose-pink, flat clusters.	Deciduous shrub with rounded dense form. Narrow, oval leaves have maroon tinge.	Beautiful hedge or specimen plant. Trim in early spring.
S. x b. 'Froebelii' **Froebel Spiraea**	3-9	To 3-4 ft tall.	Summer-blooming. Bright pink, flat clusters.	Deciduous shrub. Rounded, dense form, with good fall color.	Excellent hedge or specimen with year-round interest.
S. x b. 'Gold Flame' **Gold Flame Spiraea**	3-9	To 3-4 ft tall.	Summer-blooming. Clusters of rosy-red blossoms.	Deciduous shrub. Rounded, dense form. New leaves bronze to orange, turn greenish yellow in summer, copper-orange in fall.	Good border, hedge, specimen, or accent plant.
S. cantoniensis (S. reevesiana) Reeves Spiraea	6-9	To 5-6 ft tall.	Summer-blooming. Double, white, dense clusters along branches.	Deciduous shrub. Graceful, upright spreading habit. Dark green leaves.	Good red fall color.
S. japonica 'Little Princess' **Little Princess Japanese Spiraea**	6-9	To 2-3 ft tall.	Summer-blooming. Flat clusters of rose-crimson blossoms.	Deciduous shrub. Wide-spreading, compact mound. Mint-green leaves.	Excellent as border in sunny sites.
S. nipponica tosaensis 'Snowmound' Tosa Spiraea, **Snowmound Spiraea**	4-9	To 2-3 ft tall.	Blooms late spring. Profuse, white, round clusters.	Deciduous shrub with rounded, dense habit. Dark blue-green leaves.	Good for borders, low hedges, or in containers.
S. prunifolia Bridal-Wreath Spiraea	5-9	To 6-9 ft tall with equal spread.	Blooms spring. Double, white, rosettelike blooms along branches.	Deciduous shrub with graceful, upright form. Dark green, finely serrated leaves.	Rich fall color in cool climates. S. p. 'Plena' bears profuse double white blooms.
S. x vanhouttei Bridal-Wreath	5-9	To 6 ft tall.	Blooms late spring to early summer. Many pure white blossoms in flat clusters along branches.	Deciduous shrub with fountainlike habit. Arching branches. Leaves are coarsely serrated, bluish on undersides.	Good informal hedge, screen or specimen plant.

Stewartia pseudocamellia
Japanese Stewartia
Zones: 6-9. To 30-60 feet.
Deciduous tree. Flowering.

Japanese stewartia is an unusual tree with white, single, camellia-type flowers in the summer, yellow, red, or purple fall color, and striking, flaking bark on distinctively arranged branches. Slow-growing, trees need moist, but well-drained, acid soil. Grows best in partial shade but can take full sun in areas with cool summer. Suitable for all but the hottest parts of Zones 6 to 9.

Japanese snowbell *(Styrax japonicus)* makes a lovely small specimen or lawn tree featuring white bell-shaped flowers in late spring; colorful foliage in fall.

Long-lived and widely grown, lilacs *(Syringa* sp.) make excellent screens or hedges. Blossoms fill the garden with fragrance in spring.

Styrax japonicus
Japanese Snowbell
Zones: 6-9. To 30 feet.
Deciduous tree. Flowering.

Japanese snowbell is an aristocrat among small flowering trees that, while often overlooked, deserves to be planted more often. Pendulous, white bell-shaped flowers line the undersides of the horizontal branches in late spring or early summer, while leaves angle upwards. Foliage turns yellow or reddish color in fall. Forms a flat-topped tree with attractive bark. Needs partial shade or full sun and acid, well-drained soil with ample organic matter. Smaller plants are most easily transplanted. Use as a specimen or lawn tree, next to patios, or in wooded areas.

Syringa
Lilac
Deciduous shrubs or trees. Flowering.

This genus contains about 30 species of deciduous shrubs or small trees originally from East Asia, the Himalayas, and southeastern Europe that are grown as ornamentals for their usually fragrant flowers. Most old-fashioned gardens in the Northeast had at least one lilac bush, and spring would not have seemed like spring without the fragrance of lilac in the garden. Long-lived, a lilac bush is often the only remaining sign of where a farmhouse once stood.

Although they grow in most soils, lilacs do best in a neutral to alkaline soil that is fertile and moist. If a site tends to be acid, limestone should be added. Over-fertilization should be avoided because rank growth can result. Plants growing in full sunlight produce the largest flowers in greatest quantities, but the farther south lilacs are planted, the more they adapt to light shade.

A dozen species and over 500 horticultural selections have been grown in the United States. Many of the various cultivars are difficult to distinguish from one another.

Scale, lilac borer, and mildew can be problems. Control measures for these pests should be initiated as soon as they first show up.

Syringa x chinensis
Chinese Lilac
Zones: 4-7. To 15 feet.
Deciduous shrub. Flowering.

This is the first hybrid lilac, recorded about 1777. Fragrant flowers are violet. Densely branched, spreading to 8 feet, Chinese lilac makes an excellent screen.

Syringa vulgaris
Common Lilac
Zones: 3-8. To 20 feet.
Deciduous shrub. Flowering.

The most widely grown lilac, with a spread to 15 feet. Hundreds of cultivars with fragrant purple, lavender, blue, white, pink, and red flowers are available.

Tamarix aphylla
Athel Tree
Zones: 7-10. To 20-30 feet.
Evergreen-appearing. Flowering.

Athel tree is top-rated in the desert climates of Arizona and California, where its fast growth and ability to tolerate extremes of heat, drought, wind, and alkaline soils make it the first line of defense against the desert climate. It is widely planted as rooted cuttings for windbreaks, shelterbelts, and soil stabilization. It can also be used near the coast. Other species of *Tamarix*, such as *T.*

hispida, are similarly valuable plants for eastern coastal conditions but are not as commonplace or as indispensable there as the athel tree is in the desert.

Leaves of the athel tree are very small and scale-like but the branches are green, giving the tree an evergreen appearance. White to pinkish flowers open primarily in late summer. When buying container-grown athel trees, select small plants, because these trees become rootbound very quickly in containers.

Taxodium distichum
Bald Cypress, Swamp Cypress
Zones: 5-10. To 60-100 feet.
Deciduous tree.

In the native swampy areas of the Southeastern United States where bald cypress thrives, it can reach a height of 100 feet. Shape at maturity is somewhat broad, but in its early years it is pyramidal with a strong central trunk. Foliage is yellow-green, feathery, and has a light delicate texture. Leaves turn an attractive orange-brown before dropping in the fall. The trunk base is often strongly buttressed in the manner of the dawn redwood. Trunk bark is fibrous and reddish brown to gray.

Bald cypress is known for its unusual root system which enables it to grow in very wet clay, silt, or mucky soils. The shallow roots produce "knees", which grow above the soil surface, giving them contact with air. Support is provided by a descending portion of the root system. In a wet site it is beneficial to plant bald cypress on a small mound.

Although best adapted to moist swampy areas, bald cypress can grow in a wide range of conditions as long as the soil is not alkaline. It can withstand fairly dry soils, cold winters, and is relatively pest free. It makes an excellent shade tree and is ideal for large lawn areas where its fine textured needles sift easily into the grass and do not require raking in fall.

Its tolerance of heat, drought, wind, and alkaline soils makes athel tree *(Tamarix aphylla)* a valuable shade tree for desert climates.

Bald cypress *(Taxodium distichum)* has delicately textured yellow-green foliage that turns russet before dropping in autumn. Grows well in wet soils.

Taxus
Yew

Zones: 5-9. To 65 feet.
Evergreen shrubs and trees.

This genus contains 8 species of slow-growing, dense-foliaged evergreens native to the Northern Hemisphere. The use of yews as ornamental plants dates back to Roman times when they were used in formal hedges and topiary work. They come in all shapes and sizes, and are commonly grown as trees or shrubs for foundation plantings, hedges, and as shrubby ornamentals. Planted as screens, they can ensure privacy or hide unpleasant features in the landscape. Tall yews planted behind flowering trees provide landscape contrast.

Inconspicuous male and female flowers are borne on separate plants. Soft red berries add interest to female plants for the short time in fall when they are ripe.

Yews will grow on most types of soil. They will not tolerate poor drainage or water standing around their roots. Excessively windy sites can be damaging to most yews. Sunlight or shade is acceptable.

Most yews root easily from cuttings. More than one form of plant can often be propagated from the mother plant. Botanists use the term *cultivarient* to indicate a plant that is a different form produced by taking cuttings from different parts of the stock plant. Leader cuttings will produce plants that develop a leader. Side cuttings from the ends of branches produce spreading plants that keep growing like a branch.

Yews can withstand heavy pruning or shearing, often necessary to keep a plant symmetrical or within bounds. Use shrubs for hedges, foundation and border plants, and trees as screens, windbreaks, and specimen plants.

Dwarf Japanese yew *(Taxus cuspidata 'Nana')* is an extremely popular shrub for hedges and foundation plantings.

Taxus

Botanical Name/Common Name	Zones	Size	Plant Description	Comments
Taxus baccata English Yew	6-9	To 30-40 ft tall.	Evergreen tree. Broad crown with spreading branches. Dark green foliage.	Dwarf cultivars most commonly grown.
T. b. 'Repandens' Spreading English Yew	6-9	To 2-3 ft tall.	Evergreen shrub. Low-spreading with dense, horizontal branches. Will grow in shade.	Excellent ground cover, low hedge, container plant.
Taxus cuspidata Japanese Yew	5-9	To 50 ft tall.	Evergreen tree. Upright, pyramidal form but often kept low and spreading. Dark green foliage, lighter beneath.	Valuable in cold climates. Cultivars most useful in the landscape.
T. cuspidata 'Capitata' Upright Japanese Yew	5-9	To 45-65 ft tall.	Evergreen shrub or tree. Forms a dense, broad pyramid.	Good as specimen or formal accent tree. Control height by pinching or by trimming new growth.
T. c. 'Nana' (Often sold as **T. brevifolia**) Dwarf Japanese Yew	5-9	Usually 2-3 ft tall. Can reach 8 ft.	Evergreen shrub. Slow-growing with horizontal branches. Dark green foliage.	Excellent low hedge or container plant.
T. x media 'Brownii' Brown's Yew	5-9	To 6 ft tall.	Evergreen shrub. Erect, conical, fine-textured.	Good dense, low hedge. Can be pruned to maintain formal globe shape.
T. x m. 'Chadwick' Chadwick Yew	5-9	To 3 ft tall.	Evergreen shrub. Wide-spreading, fine-textured. Bright green foliage.	Good container plant.
T. x m. 'Densiformis' (**T. cuspidata 'Densiformis'**) Dense Yew	5-9	To 4-6 ft tall. Spreads to 9 ft.	Evergreen shrub. Slow-growing. Dark green foliage.	Dense branching makes this cultivar an excellent hedge plant.
T. x m. 'Hatfieldii' Hatfield Yew	5-9	To 8-10 ft tall. Spreads to 6 ft.	Evergreen shrub. Forms broad, upright pyramid. Dark green foliage.	Excellent hedge. More compact than *T. x m.* 'Hicksii'.
T. x m. 'Hicksii' Hicks' Yew	5-9	To 10-12 ft tall.	Evergreen shrub with narrow upright habit. Dark green foliage.	Very common. Excellent hedge.
T. x m. 'Stovekenii' (**T. cuspidata 'Stovekenii'**) Stoveken Yew	5-9	To 12 ft tall. Spreads to 4 ft.	Evergreen shrub with upright columnar form. Dark green foliage.	Tall accent or formal row plant. More compact than *T. x m.* 'Hicksii'.
T. x m. 'Wardii' Wards Yew	5-9	To 3-5 ft tall. Spreads 10-15 ft.	Evergreen shrub. Slow-growing, compact. Dark green foliage.	Easily trained by shearing. Useful trimmed hedge or foundation plant.

Japanese yew *(Taxus cuspidata)* normally grows into a stately tree, which can be pruned to reveal multiple trunks; dwarf forms are good shrubs.

Cape honeysuckle *(Tecomaria capensis)* is a robust evergreen vine that can quickly cover a fence, bare bank, or trellis. Its brilliant flowers make a splashy show in late summer and early fall.

Ternstroemia *(Ternstroemia gymnanthera)* is an attractive foliage plant that complements flowering shrubs that also need acid soil.

Tecomaria capensis
Cape Honeysuckle
Zones: 9-10.
Evergreen vine. Flowering.

Cape honeysuckle is a vigorous, rambling, shrubby vine that is widely grown in areas with mild winter climates from Southern California to Florida. Brilliant red flowers make a striking show in the landscape. It is often planted on hot, dry banks where it forms an effective ground cover, spreading 8 to 10 feet, or used against exposed rock walls. Supported on a fence, cape honeysuckle takes the shape of a dense shrubby vine and will create a finely textured, deep green screen. Long, flexible stems can be tied to a support for an espalier or trellis cover.

The long, slender branches of cape honeysuckle bear shiny, dark green leaves that are divided into small leaflets, creating a delicate lacy effect. Borne 5 to 9 on a stem, leaflets are oval with toothed margins. Flowers appear in late summer and blooming continues through fall. Fiery orange-red flowers are held out from the foliage in upright, terminal clusters. Funnel-shaped blossoms are 2 inches long, with red protruding stamens. For yellow flowers plant the variety 'Aurea'. Its growth is less vigorous and it is not as cold-tolerant as the red-flowered form.

Cape honeysuckle is a tough plant. It thrives in hot sun and tolerates windy, coastal conditions. Grows in partial shade but will produce fewer flowers. Recovers from light frosts. In cold inland valleys protective measures will extend its range.

Flowers are borne on new growth. For best results cut back stems in late fall and winter after blossoming. Can be pruned successfully throughout the year to shape and control growth. Thin branches if they become too dense.

Ternstroemia gymnanthera
Ternstroemia
Zones: 7-10. To 3-4 feet.
Evergreen shrub.

Ternstroemia has glossy, oval-shaped foliage and is particularly attractive when grouped with rhododendron, gardenia, ferns, and other plants needing acid soil. This shrub's bronzy-red new leaves remain colored in sunny exposures, turn a greener color in shady spots. Reddish-brown stems complement the foliage color. Ternstroemia's subtle fragrance comes from inconspicuous summer flowers. They are followed by orange-red berries.

Ternstroemia makes an attractive foliage plant for entryways. When grown in containers tip-prune branches for compact growth.

Sun tolerant in cool climates, ternstroemia needs a shaded location elsewhere. To create the acid, well-drained, moist soil it demands, add peat moss when planting.

Arborvitae

Evergreen trees and shrubs.

Arborvitae belong to two very similar genera. Until recently all arborvitae were included in the genus *Thuja*. Now they are separated into the genera *Thuja* and *Platycladus*. Here they are grouped together for easier selection and comparison.

There are 6 species in the genus *Thuja*. They are small to medium-sized trees native to North America and eastern Asia. Usually dense pyramidal trees with varied foliage color. Crowns of older trees can become thin. Juvenile leaves are needlelike. Mature foliage is scalelike. Used extensively in landscape plantings because of their slow, compact growth. The top-rated species, *Thuja occidentalis,* is normally a large conical tree growing up to 60 feet in height.

The genus *Platycladus* has only one species, *Platycladus orientalis,* the Oriental arborvitae. It is normally a large rounded shrub or small conical tree and frequently is multistemmed. Many cultivars are available including dwarf and yellow-foliaged forms, giving Oriental arborvitae a broad range of landscape uses.

Best growth is made in full sunlight, although light shade is acceptable and preferred in very hot climates. Dense or heavy shade produces leggy plants with loose open foliage. Arborvitae do best on fertile, moist but well-drained soils. Pruning should be done in the spring before new growth begins.

Arborvitae are commonly used in foundation plantings, as windbreaks, tall hedges or screens, and as accent plants. Many dwarf cultivars have been developed.

Woodward arborvitae *(Thuja occidentalis* 'Woodwardii') is a dense evergreen shrub that maintains its neat form with very little pruning.

Thuja and Platycladus

Botanical Name/Common Name	Zones	Size	Plant Description	Comments
Platycladus orientalis 'Aureus Nanus' *(T. orientalis* 'Aureus Nanus') Golden Berckman Arborvitae	6-10	To 5-8 ft tall. Spread to 4-7 ft wide.	Evergreen shrub. Dwarf, globe. Branches of soft green foliage are tipped with bright golden-yellow.	*P. o.* 'Raffles' — similar, denser, brighter foliage.
P. o. 'Bakeri' *(T. o.* 'Bakeri') Baker's Arborvitae	5-10	To 10-25 ft tall.	Evergreen tree. Compact, pyramid. Bright green foliage.	Hardier than other Oriental arborvitae selections. Adaptable to hot, dry landscape sites.
P. o. 'Blue Cone' *(T. o.* 'Blue Cone') Blue Cone Arborvitae	5-10	To 10-25 ft tall.	Evergreen tree. Fine pyramidal habit. Attractive blue-green foliage.	
P. o. 'Fruitlandii' *(T. o.* 'Fruitlandii') Fruitland Arborvitae	6-10	To 10-25 ft tall.	Evergreen tree. Compact, upright cone. Rich green foliage.	
P. o. 'Westmont' *(T. o.* 'Westmont') Westmont Arborvitae	6-10	To 3 ft tall, with 2 ft spread.	Evergreen shrub. Compact, slow-growing globe. Rich dark green foliage attractively tipped with bright yellow.	Excellent choice for entryways.
Thuja occidentalis 'Hetz's Midget' Hetz's Midget Arborvitae	3-9	To 2-4 ft tall.	Evergreen shrub. Excellent compact, slow-growing globe. Dark blue-green foliage.	'Little Gem', 'Pumila', and 'Nana' are similar forms.
T. o. 'Nigra' Dark Green Arborvitae	3-9	To 10-25 ft tall.	Evergreen tree. Pyramid. Retains dark green foliage color during cold winters.	Best in cool, moist site. Good windbreak.
T. o. 'Pyramidalis' Pyramidal Arborvitae	3-9	To 25-30 ft tall.	Evergreen tree. Pyramid. Foliage light green.	Foliage may brown when used in a cold region and planted in an unprotected site.
T. o. 'Reingold' (improved *T. o.* 'Ellangeriana Aurea') Reingold Arborvitae	3-9	To 3-4 ft tall.	Evergreen shrub. Dense globe. Unique foliage color. Golden to orangish-yellow with rose-tinted tips.	Striking accent in the landscape, for containers.
T. o. 'Techny' Techny Arborvitae	3-9	To 10-25 ft tall.	Evergreen tree. Pyramid. Best arborvitae for retaining its dark green foliage color throughout the winter months.	Excellent hedge, screen, or windbreak. Tolerates seashore conditions.
T. o. 'Woodwardii' Woodward Arborvitae	3-9	To 4-6 ft tall.	Evergreen shrub. Dense, compact, globe. Dark green foliage.	Maintains globe form with little or no pruning. Good for containers.

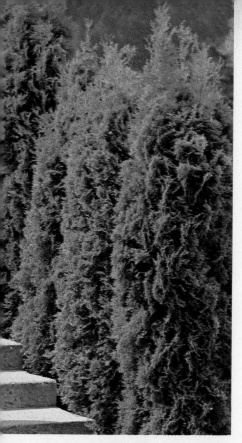

Pyramidal arborvitae *(Thuja occidentalis* 'Pyramidalis') forms an effective screen, hedge, or windbreak. Adapted to a wide climate range.

Above left: Creeping thyme *(Thymus praecox arcticus)* is a very cold-hardy ground cover that spreads over wide areas by underground runners. Above right: Woolly thyme *(Thymus pseudolanuginosus)* has very small leaves covered with gray down, giving ground cover plantings a soft, fuzzy appearance.

Golden Berckman arborvitae *(Platycladus orientalis* 'Aureus Nanus') is soft-textured. Foliage is tipped with yellow in summer.

Thymus

Thyme

Evergreen ground covers.
Flowering.

Several species of thyme with tiny fragrant leaves make excellent creeping ground covers. Their stems root along the ground and they tolerate light foot traffic. Plant between stepping stones in an herb or flower garden path, along a rock wall, or any sunny small-scale spot. Thyme, with its creeping habit, will gently cascade over the edges of a small container creating a handsome centerpiece for patio tables.

These tough plants do well in poor, dry soil in full sun. Tolerate partial shade. Water regularly until established; once established tolerates drought. Weed until a thick cover forms. Clip back stem tips to promote compact growth and prune severly in spring if plants are overgrown or have sparse centers.

Thymus praecox arcticus
Creeping Thyme
Zones: 3-10. To 2-6 inches.
Evergreen ground cover.

Forms a fine-textured carpet of 1/4-inch-long dark green leaves on low somewhat woody stems. Spreads by underground runners. Heads of small pink flowers bloom from spring to fall and attract bees. Leaves and sprigs of tender growth are useful as a cooking herb. This plant was once named *T. serphyllum.*

Thymus pseudolanuginosus
Wooly Thyme
Zones: 3-10. To 3 inches.
Evergreen ground cover.

The tiny leaves of this thyme are covered with dense gray hairs, giving it an appealing fuzzy appearance. It spreads in a dense, low mat with an undulating surface. White to rose flowers, which aren't very conspicuous, bloom in summer. Sometimes labelled *T. lanicaulis.*

Tilia
Linden, Basswood
Zones: 4-8. To 90 feet.
Deciduous tree. Flowering.

Lindens have been grown for many years on city streets of Europe and the eastern United States. Lindens bear fragrant white flowers that are a favorite of bees and honey lovers. Flowers are followed by clusters of small pea-sized fruits on winged stalks. Leaves are heart-shaped and toothed. Trees have a formal dense oval shape.

Lindens adapt to a wide range of soils and tolerate heat, drought, and urban conditions. Their fine form and foliage has consistantly ranked them high in the Secrest Arboretum Shade Tree Evalution in Wooster, Ohio. Trees are sometimes bothered by aphids.

Top-rated lindens are described in the chart below.

Little-leaf linden *(Tilia cordata)* has a formal shape well-suited for tidy landscapes.

American linden *(Tilia americana)* is a native American tree suitable for lawn or shade.

Tilia

Botanical Name/Common Name	Zones	Size	Plant Description	Comments
Tilia americana **American Linden, Basswood, Whitewood**	4-8	To 70-90 ft tall.	Deciduous tree. Grows quickly. Dense, upright, narrow crown. Large dark green, heart-shaped leaves, 4-6 in. long.	Small fragrant flowers in loose clusters.
T. cordata **Little-Leaf Linden, Small-Leaved European Linden**	4-8	To 50 ft tall.	Deciduous tree with moderate growth rate. Dense, rounded, pyramidal crown. Small leaves, dark green above, pale green below.	Small fragrant flowers attract bees. Can be sheared as hedge.
T. c. 'Chancellor' **Chancellor Little-Leaf European Linden**	4-8	To 35-40 ft tall.	Deciduous tree with narrow, upright, pyramidal habit. Symmetrical branching, dense foliage.	Listed in the top 20 of the Secrest Arboretum Shade Tree Evaluation.
T. c. 'Glenleven' **Glenleven Little-Leaf European Linden**	4-8	To 40 ft tall.	Similar to species but with more pyramidal shape.	
T. c. 'Greenspire' **Greenspire Little-Leaf European Linden**	4-8	To 30-40 ft tall.	Deciduous tree grows rapidly into well-formed pyramidal form. Symmetrical branching. Small, leathery leaves.	Listed in top 20 of the Secrest Arboretum Shade Tree Evaluation. Flowers have spicy fragrance.
T. c. 'Junebride' **Junebride Little-Leaf European Linden**	4-8	To 30 ft tall.	Similar to other cultivars. Leaves small and glossy green.	Flowers 3-4 times more abundant than species.
T. c. 'Olympic' **Olympic Little-Leaf European Linden**	4-8	To 30 ft tall.	Similar to other cultivars. Symmetrical habit with pyramidal crown. Small glossy leaves.	
T. x euchlora **Crimean Linden**	5-8	To 40 ft tall.	Deciduous tree with broad oval crown, pendulous branches. Clean-looking, dark green leaves that are larger than little-leaf European linden.	Less dense than most lindens. Exceptionally fragrant flowers.
T. x e. 'Redmont' **Redmont Crimean Linden**	5-8	To 30 ft tall.	Deciduous tree. Denser and more pyramidal than species. Large, dark green, leathery leaves.	Leaves not as glossy as species.
T. tomentosa **Silver Linden**	5-8	To 40-60 ft tall.	Deciduous tree. Pyramidal when young, becoming roundheaded. Leaves dark green above, white beneath. Turn yellow in fall.	Excellent shade tree. Leaves shimmer in the slightest breeze.

Trachelospermum
Star Jasmine

Evergreen vines. Flowering.

The sweet fragrance of their flowers and the clean, neat appearance of their foliage make star jasmines top-rated vines for the landscape. Two- to three-inch star-shaped flowers cover the plants from late April to July and contrast nicely against the glossy, dark green foliage. Supple branches criss-cross and twine to form a vine, ground cover, or sprawling shrub.

Star jasmines are versatile evergreen plants that can satisfy a variety of garden needs. They are excellent choices for trellis-work along a narrow walkway. In sun or shade, the dense foliage will create an effective, all-season screen. Supported over a small patio or entryway, their enchanting scent can be enjoyed for months. As a ground cover, star jasmines become a thick green carpet suitable on banks, near walkways, and under tall shrubs. They also make lovely cascading shrubs for raised planters.

Although slow to start, star jasmines become moderately fast-growing vines. Upright, they will reach over 15 feet. As a ground cover, growth will be more restrained, spreading 4 to 5 feet with a height of 1-1/2 to 2 feet.

Water star jasmines regularly through spring and summer months. Plant in light shade in the hottest climates, otherwise full sun is necessary.

Maintenance of these vines is easy. When buying new plants to be grown as upright vines, select plants with long branches. Tie branches to a sturdy support for early training. Prune long branches during any season to help the vine hold its shape. Shear vines covering fences in early spring or fall to keep them neat and trim. Mature vines should be pruned annually to encourage new branches and to eliminate older, woody branches. Star jasmines are relatively pest-free but can be bothered by aphids, mealybugs, red spider mites, or scale.

Trachelospermum asiaticum
Yellow Star Jasmine
Zones: 7-10.
Evergreen vine. Flowering.

Yellow star jasmine is a handsome plant native to Japan. It is less vigorous than the white-flowered star jasmine, but is a good choice for the colder climate of Zones 7 and 8.

Light yellow fragrant flowers are borne in slender terminal clusters with their wavy petals held erect. They are showy from April through June. Leaves differ from its white-flowered counterpart. They are darker in color, broader, with a dull surface. New growth is colored bronze.

This plant makes a handsome, restrained ground cover, fence screen, or plant for hanging baskets, indoors or out.

Trachelospermum jasminoides
Star Jasmine, Confederate Jasmine
Zones: 8-10.
Evergreen vine. Flowering.

Although white-flowered star jasmine is native to China, it is one of the most commonly grown vines in the United States. It has been grown for so long in the southern United States it has been given the common name of confederate jasmine. It grows more vigorously than yellow star jasmine, reaching 20 feet when supported.

Star jasmine's dark green leaves are very attractive, with a glossy surface and simple oval shape. Lacy, star-shaped flowers have twisted petals on short tubes. The fragrant blossoms open in early May, lasting until midsummer. Its sweet flowers are filled with nectar, attracting bees to the garden.

Use to cover arbors, patios, or as a screen for small gardens. Drape over walls and raised planters for a trailing effect. To establish as a ground cover, space plants 2 to 3 feet apart for dense coverage. Cut back long branches to encourage denser growth.

The leaves of 'Variegatum' have green and white variegations, often tinged with red. It is hardier than its parent.

Lindens (Tilia sp.) bear curious-looking small pea-sized fruits on winged stalks.

A popular vine in the South, star jasmine (Trachelospermum jasminoides) can be planted as a ground cover or a twining vine.

Canadian hemlocks *(Tsuga canadensis)* can be pruned to form an evergreen screen or hedge; have graceful weeping outer branches.

A fast-growing tree with feathery branches, western hemlock *(Tsuga heterophylla)* prefers moist growing conditions in western states.

Tsuga
Hemlock
Evergreen trees.

Hemlocks are large, graceful trees with fine-textured needles and a nodding leader. They grow in sun or shade.

All the top-rated species are native to the United States and Canada, growing in areas with acid soil, where the air and soil remain moist and relatively cool all year. Root systems are shallow, so hemlocks should not be used in exposed areas.

Hemlocks are normally very large forest trees and, unless controlled by pruning, easily outgrow the typical home landscape. However, unlike most conifers, sprouts will develop when trees are trimmed heavily. They naturally tend to produce multiple leaders. If you desire an ideal specimen form, young trees will require pruning of side leaders to maintain a single central trunk. Excellent as trimmed hedges, screens, specimen trees, and windbreaks.

Red spider mites are the principle pest of all species and are troublesome on dry sites.

Tsuga canadensis
Canadian Hemlock
Zones: 5-9. To 60-90 feet.
Evergreen tree.

Dense, broad, pyramidal trees with horizontal branches and drooping outer branchlets, Canadian hemlock is native from Nova Scotia to Wisconsin and south along the Appalachian Mountains to Georgia. Grows at a moderate rate, becoming 30 feet tall in 20 years. Dark, lustrous green needles, arranged in two rows on the twigs, are 1/2 to 3/4 inch long with two broad white bands underneath. Small brown cones are 1/2 to 3/4 inch long.

Over 50 varieties with different growth habits and foliage colors have been named. Most are dwarf forms. Weeping forms make graceful small trees. 'Pendula', sargent weeping hemlock, is a stunning specimen plant for rock gardens, entryways, and shrub borders. Reaches 3 feet tall and 6 feet wide.

Tsuga caroliniana
Carolina Hemlock
Zones: 5-7. To 40-70 feet.
Evergreen tree.

Carolina hemlock is a slimmer, shorter, less symmetrical tree than the Canadian hemlock. It has sparser grass-green needles that are 3/4 inch long, and arranged all around the stem instead of in opposite rows. This whorled needle arrangement gives Carolina hemlock a much softer landscape texture. Brown cones are 1 to 1-1/2 inches long. More tolerant of air pollution than the Canadian hemlock. Native to the mountains from southwestern Virginia to Georgia.

Tsuga heterophylla
Western Hemlock
Zones: 5-9. To 100-200 feet.
Evergreen tree.

This fast-growing pyramidal tree has horizontal branches with drooping branchlets and a long hanging leader, giving it a resemblance to the deodar cedar. Can be 50 to 65 feet tall in 20 years.

Feathery branches have fine-textured dark to yellowish-green needles that are 1/4 to 3/4 inch long and arranged in two rows. Many small, 1-inch-long, light brown cones hang at the branch tips.

This giant of the hemlock clan grows well only in moist regions from Alaska to northern California and in the mountains of northern Idaho and western Montana. It can be grown in dry areas but will need regular and plentiful watering. Only selections from Idaho or Montana are hardy in Zones 5 to 6.

Ulmus
Elm
Deciduous trees.

The American elm, *Ulmus americana,* was the classic street tree of Eastern, Midwestern, and even some Western cities and towns until two diseases, Dutch elm and phloem necrosis, killed most of them. For this reason many state and city ordinances prohibit planting elms.

No other tree can match the American elm for its tall graceful vase-shape and wide-spreading arching branches. One elm, *Ulmus parvifolia*, is top-rated because of its resistance to Dutch elm disease. However, even this elm is not allowed to be planted in many areas because of state or city ordinances. Another elm, *Ulmus pumila*, is top-rated in difficult climates.

Ulmus parvifolia
Chinese Elm, Evergreen Elm
Zones: 5-9. To 40-60 feet.
Deciduous tree.

Chinese elm, native to China, Korea, and Japan, is resistant to Dutch elm disease but doesn't have the traditional vase shape of the American elm. It develops a broad, low head, which is quite open. Grows at an average to fast rate. Branches are sometimes pendulous. Mottled flaking bark is attractive throughout the year.

The glossy, dark green leaves are 1 to 2 inches long, leathery, and smooth. Fall color develops late and is yellow in warm regions and red or purplish in colder areas. Chinese elm is an excellent shade tree. The cultivar 'Sempervirens' retains green leaves in warm areas until new leaves develop.

Japanese beetles don't eat the foliage as readily as that of other elms. Limb breakage may occur in windy areas.

Ulmus pumila
Siberian Elm
Zones: 5-9. To 50 feet.
Deciduous tree.

Siberian elm is an open, round-headed tree with dark green leaves. It is fast-growing and widely adapted but only recommended for the harshest climates of the Great Plains, Rocky Mountains, and desert areas where other shade trees cannot grow. Although tolerant of drought, heat, cold, and poor soils, its limbs are weak and break easily and it has very invasive roots. These factors rule it out in most landscape situations.

Its broad, low head makes Chinese elm *(Ulmus parvifolia)* an excellent shade tree. Fall color is yellow to purple.

Siberian elm *(Ulmus pumila)* is a problem-solver tree recommended for the harshest climates of the West and Midwest.

Viburnum

Viburnum
Viburnum

Zones: 2-10. To 20 feet.
Evergreen and deciduous shrubs.
Flowering.

Viburnums are a diverse group of plants. They can be evergreen or deciduous, grow low or tall, and be cold hardy or tender. Some are grown for their foliage, others for their flowers, and still others for their colorful fruit. Many species have more than one outstanding feature.

Most viburnums tolerate both alkaline and acid soils. They grow well in wet, heavy, fertile soils and some also tolerate drought. They grow in sun or shade, although evergreen species look better with some shade in hot, dry climates. Watch for aphids.

Bodnant viburnum *(Viburnum x bodnantense* 'Pink Dawn')

Fragrant snowball *(Viburnum x carlcephalum)*

Burkwood viburnum *(Viburnum x burkwoodii)*

David viburnum *(Viburnum davidii)*

Viburnum

Botanical Name/ Common Name	Zones	Size	Flower Description	Plant Description	Comments
Viburnum x bodnantense 'Pink Dawn' Bodnant Viburnum	6-10	To 10 ft tall.	Fragrant, deep rose-colored buds open nearly white. Three-in. clusters, late fall to early winter.	Deciduous shrub. Oval leaves, 4 in. long. Red leaves in late fall and winter. Red berries.	
V. x burkwoodii Burkwood Viburnum	5-10	To 6-12 ft tall. Spreads 4-5 ft wide.	Very fragrant, pinkish white in dense 4-in. clusters. Midspring.	Deciduous; evergreen in mild climates. Upright, spreading shrub. Glossy, dark green leaves. Berries not showy.	Excellent as screen, hedge, specimen or background planting.
V. x carlcephalum Fragrant Snowball	5-10	To 8-10 ft tall. Spreads to 4-5 ft wide.	Fragrant. Large white snowball clusters to 6 in. across in late spring.	Deciduous shrub with rounded, open form. Glossy, dark green leaves. No berries.	One of the best viburnums. Brilliant red full foliage.
V. carlesii Korean Spice Viburnum	5-10	To 4-8 ft tall. Spreads to 4-5 ft wide.	Very fragrant. Pinkish-red in bud, turn white. In 2-3-in. clusters. Early spring.	Deciduous shrub with rounded, open, loose form. Blue-black berries.	Flowers appear before foliage.
V. davidii David Viburnum	7-10	To 1-3 ft tall. Spreads to 4-5 ft wide.	Light pink buds. Dull white flowers. Early summer.	Evergreen shrub with rounded, compact form. Glossy, dark green leaves with prominent veins. Unique metallic-blue fruit.	Combines well with azaleas and ferns in shady, acid-soil areas. Best fruit set with more than one plant in landscape.
V. dentatum Arrowwood, Southern Arrowwood	3-8	To 10-15 ft tall.	White, in 2 to 4-in. clusters. Early summer.	Deciduous shrub with dense, spreading upright growth. Blue-black berries.	Adapts to many soils, moist and dry sites. Excellent hedge or screen.
V. dilatatum Linden Viburnum	5-8	To 8-10 ft tall.	Creamy-white in 5-in. clusters. Late spring to early summer.	Deciduous shrub with dense, rounded, upright habit. Broad oval leaves turn reddish in fall. Profuse red berries.	Good hedge, screen; or train as small tree. 'Xanthocarpum' has yellow berries.
V. japonicum Japanese Viburnum	7-10	To 10-20 ft tall.	Fragrant, white, 4-in. clusters. Spring.	Evergreen shrub or tree. Vigorous, upright growth. Large, glossy, dark green leaves. Showy, oval red berries.	Use for background plantings.
V. macrocephalum (*V. macrocephalum* 'Sterile') Chinese Snowball	6-10	To 10-20 ft tall.	Large, striking, white, snowball-like blossoms. Late spring to early summer.	Semideciduous shrub with broad, rounded form. Glossy, dark green leaves, 2-4 in. long.	Profuse blooms. Good for espalier. No berries.
V. odoratissimum Sweet Viburnum	7-10	To 10-20 ft tall.	Large, fragrant, white conical clusters, 3-6 in. Late spring.	Evergreen shrub. Long, glossy, bright green leaves may turn purple in cool winter climate. Red berries ripen to black.	Good large hedge, screen, or specimen.
V. opulus European Cranberry Bush, Cranberry Bush	3-10	To 10-20 ft tall.	Large, white clusters, 2-4 in. Late spring.	Deciduous shrub with rounded, dense habit. Maplelike, lobed leaves turn red in fall. Large glossy red berries.	Good border, specimen, or hedge in large landscapes. Aphid control needed. 'Xanthocarpum' has creamy-yellow berries.

Of all the viburnums, linden viburnum *(Viburnum dilatatum)* has about the best show of berries.

Double-file viburnum *(Viburnum plicatum tomentosum)* makes an excellent screen or hedge.

David viburnum *(Viburnum davidii)* is an evergreen shrub that's attractive year-round.

Botanical Name/ Common Name	Zones	Size	Flower Description	Plant Description	Comments
V. o. 'Compactum' Compact European Cranberry Bush	3-10	To 4-5 ft tall.	White, flat clusters. Late spring.	Deciduous shrub of compact, round habit. Dark green leaves; reddish purple in fall.	Good fall color. Showy red berries.
V. o. 'Nanum' Dwarf European Cranberry Bush	3-10	To 2 ft tall.	Flowers not showy.	Deciduous shrub. Compact, rounded dwarf. Formal habit. Does not set fruit.	Adaptable to many soil types. Low maintenance, requires no pruning. Good low hedge.
V. 'Roseum' (*V. o.* 'Sterile') Snowball, Snowball Bush, European Snowball	3-10	To 10-15 ft tall.	White snowball-like clusters. Late spring to early summer.	Deciduous shrub. Rounded form. Does not set fruit.	Some control of aphids is necessary.
V. plicatum tomentosum Japanese Snowball, Double-File Viburnum	4-9	To 12-15 ft tall. Spreads 10-15 ft wide.	White, flat clusters. Late spring.	Deciduous shrub with distinctive horizontal branching. Colorful red berries turn black.	Superb hedge or screen. *V. p. t.* 'Mariesii' has larger flowers.
V. prunifolium Black Haw	3-9	To 10-15 ft tall.	Creamy-white, flat clusters. 2-6 in. Early summer.	Deciduous shrub with upright, rounded form. Bright red-purple fall color. Blue to black edible berries.	Good specimen, screen or interesting small tree, with training.
V. rhytidophyllum Leatherleaf Viburnum	5-10	To 8-15 ft tall.	White, flat clusters, 4-8 in. Late spring.	Evergreen shrub with upright habit. Deeply veined oblong leaves, shiny dark green above, fuzzy and yellow beneath.	Adds coarse-textured interest in landscape. Protect from winter winds. Tolerates shade.
V. rufidulum Southern Black Haw	5-10	To 15-25 ft tall.	Pure white, flat clusters 5 in. Late spring.	Deciduous shrub. Large, can be trained as small tree. Finely toothed, glossy, dark green leaves. Dark blue edible fruit.	Eye-catching deep red fall color.
V. sargentii Sargent's Cranberry	6-10	To 12 ft tall.	Striking, creamy-white, flat clusters to 4 in. Late spring.	Deciduous shrub with thick, lobed leaves. Vivid crimson fall color. Scarlet berries.	*V. s.* 'Onondaga' has dark maroon new foliage. 'Flavum' has yellow berries.
V. suspensum Sandankwa Viburnum	9-10	To 8-10 ft tall with equal spread.	Rose-scented white clusters, 2-4 in. Early spring.	Evergreen shrub with dense branching habit. Shiny green oval leaves. Red to black fruit.	Often pruned into a dense hedge or screen.
V. tinus 'Compactum' Dwarf Laurustinus	7-10	To 3-5 ft tall with equal spread.	Dramatic clusters of pinkish buds open to white. Blooms from late fall to early spring.	Evergreen shrub. Compact, upright habit. Dark green oblong leaves. Shiny deep blue berries.	Good dense hedge. May develop mildew.
V. t. 'Robustum' Round-Leaf Viburnum, Robust Viburnum	7-10	To 4-10 ft tall.	Tight clusters of light pink buds open to white.	Evergreen shrub of upright habit. Deep green leaves cover dense branches. Blue berries.	Good hedge, screen, or fine, small, narrow tree. Mildew resistant.
V. t. 'Spring Bouquet'	7-10	To 6 ft tall.	Similar to other *V. tinus* cultivars.	Evergreen shrub with compact, upright habit. Blue berries.	Good hedge. Tolerates seashore conditions. May develop mildew.
V. trilobum Cranberry Bush, Highbush Cranberry	2-9	To 10-15 ft tall.	White, 4-in. flat clusters. Late spring.	Deciduous shrub with open, upright habit. Lobed leaves. Attractive, edible, persistent scarlet berries.	Good hedge or specimen *V. t.* 'Compactum' grows 5-6 ft tall; profuse berries.

Periwinkle *(Vinca minor)* is a low-maintenance ground cover outstanding for carpeting large shady areas.

Variegated forms of greater periwinkle *(Vinca major)* brighten up shady spots under trees. Spreads rapidly to form a thick knee-high ground cover.

Vinca

Periwinkle, Myrtle, Vinca

Herbaceous ground covers. Flowering.

Periwinkle is probably the all-time favorite ground cover. Dark glossy green leaves on trailing stems and bright blue pinwheel-shaped flowers in spring are the outstanding features of this genus.

Vinca major
Greater Periwinkle
Zones: 8-10. To 18-30 inches.

Lush and vigorous, this periwinkle forms a knee-high thicket of glossy leaves and 2-inch flowers. Useful naturalized in shady spots under trees, also grows in full sun. Space plants 12 inches apart; spreads rapidly and may become invasive. Needs little water or fertilizer. Cut back every year or two in early spring to keep growth dense.

Vinca minor
Periwinkle, Myrtle
Zones: 5-10. To 6 inches.

Long, trailing stems spread this tidy-looking plant quickly. The evergreen foliage forms a dense carpet highlighted with 1-inch bright blue flowrs in spring. 'Alba' has white flowers and rounder leaves. 'Bowlesii' has larger flowers. 'Miss Jekyll' has white flowers and grows to 4 inches high.

Does best in light shade in moist, rich soil. Growth is rapid, but plants aren't invasive. Excellent under trees and shrubs, or as edging to border a walk or driveway.

Vitis

Grape

Deciduous vines.

Grape vines are all-season performers. They are top-rated because of their abundant fruit production, lush foliage, colorful fall leaves, and interesting bare branches. Some varieties are grown purely for their foliage and ornamental effect. Others not only decorate the landscape, but are highly valued for their fruit, which is used for raisins, wine, juice, and eating fresh.

Native American grape vines, such as *V. labrusca* and *V. riparia* species, are the most cold hardy. American varieties have splendid fall color; their fruit has a delicious flavor.

Varieties of the European grape, *V. vinifera*, are generally used in areas with a long, warm growing season. They are hardy to 10°F and used in Zones 7 to 10. European grapes are grown in California for table grapes and wine production.

Many hybrids between American and European grape varieties exist that have intermediate climate adaptation. They are called French hybrids and include many useful varieties such as 'Aurora', 'Baco #1', and 'Seyve Villard 12-375'.

Grape vines grow with great vigor, putting out several feet of new growth in a season. They are excellent plants to grow on a lattice over a patio. Long, compact clusters of colorful fruit hang below the foliage. If fruit is not harvested, a cleanup will be needed. Grape leaves are quite large, up to 12 inches across, and make a good shady cover or interesting espalier against a wall.

Vines require training and attachment to supports. Branches can be held on a trellis of heavy wire or laid flat over the top of an arbor. Once established, grape plants have deep roots. They prefer well-drained soils that are slightly alkaline but adapt to other conditions. Fertilizing will encourage leaf and stem growth but does not increase fruit production. Grape clusters will be larger and leaves healthier if plants are given ample water.

Some varieties have high heat requirements, and plants should be grown in full sun. Planting against a warm south- or west-facing wall will help in cooler climates.

There are two basic types of grape vine pruning. Spur pruning is most often used on the fruiting European vines to encourage grape production. Canes are cut back in winter to 2 or 3 buds. These buds will produce fruiting canes. Some thinning of branches can be done for ornamental purposes. Height is achieved by increasing the point at which canes branch.

Cane pruning is primarily used on American varieties. Canes are cut back to 6 to 18 buds, and trained to a trellis or lead wire. Pruning is done in fall.

Mildew is a common problem of grape vines; dust with sulphur during the growing season to control.

When selecting vines for the garden, consult local references to determine the best variety for your area. Many varieties are suited to specific localities and extend the range in which grapes can be grown. Consider cold hardiness, heat requirement, time needed to ripen fruit, fruit size and quality when selecting a variety for your garden.

Vitis labrusca
Fox Grape, American Grape
Zones: 6-10.
Deciduous vine.

These are slip-skin grapes used for table and juice. Vines are cold-tolerant to 0°F and are a good choice where the growing season is short and cool. The fruits have a strong flavor, typified by Concord grapes. Popular American grape varieties include 'Catawba', 'Delaware', 'Fredonia', 'Himrod', 'Niagara', 'Seneca', and 'Steuben'.

Vitis rotundifolia
Muscadine Grape, Scuppernong
Zones: 8-10.
Deciduous vine.

This grape grows wild in the southern United States. It thrives in hot, humid weather. Small fruits have a strong musky aroma. Vines are vigorous. Many varieties have been chosen that have localized adaptation to different parts of the South. Check with your local nurseryman for adaptation of varieties such as 'Bountiful', 'Carlos', 'Higgins', 'Hunt', and 'Southland'.

Vitis vinifera
European Grape
Zones: 7-10.
Deciduous vine.

The fruits are tight-skinned and mild-flavored, making high quality grapes for wine and table. They are most commonly grown in California because they require a long, frost-free period with warm temperatures. European grapes are also grown in the Pacific Northwest and sometimes in Arizona. These vines are hardy to 10°F. 'Ribier', 'Thompson Seedless', and 'Muscat' are familiar table grapes good for the home garden. Popular wine grape varieties include: 'Cabernet Sauvignon', 'Chardonnay', 'Chenin Blanc', and 'Zinfandel'.

Weigela
Weigela
Zones: 4-9. To 2-7 feet.
Deciduous shrub. Flowering.

Weigela blooms in late spring and its arching branches are covered with funnel-shaped flowers. They are a favorite of hummingbirds. 'Bristol Ruby' bears ruby-red flowers in spring and again in summer. 'Candida' has pure white flowers. 'Eva Supreme' grows to 4 feet high and has pure red flowers. Plant in full sun in a moist soil.

A rapid grower, weigela is excellent as a hedge, specimen shrub, or in a shrubbery border.

Wisteria
Wisteria
Deciduous vines. Flowering.

Abundant blossoms on gracefully cascading stems make wisteria one of the most prized vines for the landscape. Old vines are especially appreciated for their grand size and woody, twisting trunks. A vigorous grower suitable for a broad range of climate zones, wisteria can grow from the cold North and Midwest to the warmest western states.

Grape vines (*Vitis* sp.) can produce delicious fruit while at the same time shading a patio.

'Bristol Ruby' weigela (*Weigela* 'Bristol Ruby'), a showy hedge or specimen plant, bears bright red blossoms in spring and again in summer.

The trunks of wisteria vines (Wisteria sp.) become thick, twisted, and picturesque with age; require a sturdy support to twine around.

Japanese wisteria (Wisteria floribunda) offers floral beauty and fragrance.

Large compound leaves look delicate and have small, oval leaflets, 7 to 9 on a stem. Their light green color is bright and appealing when draped over a patio. Dramatic clusters of pealike blossoms are borne in early spring. Color varies from a clear white to pink and shades of violet. Flowers hang in long pendulous clusters measuring from 6 inches to 3 feet. Velvety seed pods, 3 to 6 inches long, follow.

Wisteria makes an attractive garden specimen or handsome twining cover for a fence, arbor, pergola, or patio. It's best not to grow wisteria against a wooden house because the strong vines can damage shingles. The beauty of its flowers and delicate tracery of its leaves add a sense of elegance to any garden. Japanese landscapes have traditionally placed wisteria to reflect in a pool of water.

Wisteria will need a sturdy frame to support its heavy, twining branches. If trained for a small area, the woody branches can eventually support their own weight. A small, graceful tree form can be attained if the woody stem is trained to a single trunk at an early age.

To ensure prolific flowering, choose selected varieties. Plants grown from seed can take up to 15 years to bloom and will vary in flower color. Pruning wisteria after flowering, or in the winter, will reduce vegetative growth and encourage spring bloom. Prune with care when the branches are bare. Shorten long branches to within 3 to 5 buds. Pruning can also be done after blossoming in early summer to limit the number of vigorous stems and create an attractive framework.

A loamy, moist soil is ideal for wisteria. It will perform well under a wide range of conditions with adequate drainage and ample water during the growing season. Iron chlorosis may develop in alkaline soils. To encourage blossoming, fertilize in early spring with superphosphate fertilizer before bud break.

Vines listed below are two of nine recognized wisteria species. They are from East Asia and have gained the widest use in the landscape.

Wisteria floribunda
Japanese Wisteria
Zones: 5-9.
Deciduous vine. Flowering.

The blossoms of Japanese wisteria open sequentially from the top of its cluster to the bottom. Although the length of its blooming period is longer than that of Chinese wisteria, Japanese wisteria does not burst into bloom with the dramatic impact of its Chinese relative. The flower clusters measure from 8 to 48 inches in length. All varieties are pleasantly fragrant with flowers in shades of white, pink, and violet. Japanese wisteria is the hardier of the two species. Plant in full sun.

The following are a few of the more than 40 recognized varieties: 'Alba', white flowers on 1-1/2- to 2-foot stems; 'Issai', 12-inch blue-violet clusters; 'Violacea Plena', a purple, double-flowered form; 'Rosea', fragrant pink flowers; 'Macrobotrys', purple-blue flowers on stalks up to 3 feet long; 'Longissima', with the longest flower clusters reaching 4 feet under ideal conditions.

Wisteria sinensis
Chinese Wisteria
Zones: 5-9.
Deciduous vine. Flowering.

This is the wisteria most often seen in American gardens. Its blue-violet flowers open simultaneously in dense clusters 6 to 12 inches long.

Slightly fragrant blossoms appear from April to May, just before the leaves emerge. The number and size of leaflets help distinguish this species from *W. floribunda*, the Japanese wisteria. Leaves of Chinese wisteria have 7 to 13 leaflets that are 2 to 3 inches long. Japanese wisteria has 13 to 19 shorter leaflets.

Three varieties are available. 'Alba' has fragrant white flowers. 'Purpurea' is the familiar violet-colored variety. 'Plena' has double flowers.

Other species of wisteria with horticultural value include: *W. x formosa*, a fragrant hybrid of Chinese and Japanese wisteria; flowers open simultaneously. *W. macrostachya*, Kentucky wisteria, is the showiest of

North American species. *W. venusta*, silky wisteria, is characterized by velvety surfaced leaves and fragrant white flowers. Its variety 'Violacea' has violet flowers.

Xylosma congestum (X. senticosum)
Shiny Xylosma
Zones: 8-10. To 4-30 feet.
Evergreen shrub or tree.

One of the most attractive, easy-to-grow plants for foliage and structural effects, shiny xylosma is native to Japan, Korea, and China.

Uses for this plant are varied, depending on the pruning and cultural practices. Can be used as a single- or multistemmed tree, spreading shrub, ground cover (if the upright stems are cut out), espalier on a wall or fence, a tightly trimmed or natural hedge, or grown in containers 18 inches or larger. Also used for barrier and bank stabilization planting along freeways.

When left alone, an open, graceful, wide-spreading shrub 8 to 10 feet tall will develop. The variety 'Compactum' is slower-growing and matures at about half that size.

Leaves are 1-1/2 to 2 inches long with rounded bases and long tapering points. They are a beautiful shiny yellowish-green when mature; bronzy-red when new. Many old leaves drop in April when new growth starts.

Inconspicuous yellow flowers bloom August to September. Black fruits are less than 1/4 inch in diameter and ripen November to December. Some plants have thorns.

Xylosma grows on most soils and is heat-tolerant. Several experiments have shown that it also has outstanding drought tolerance. Little water or fertilizer is required to keep the plant alive. Better growth and appearance result with some watering and fertilizing. Grows best in full sun or light shade. Brief exposure to temperatures down to 10°F in midwinter will not kill the plant, but partial or total defoliation will follow.

Spraying is sometimes necessary to control red spider mites and scale. Chlorosis, leaf yellowing, may be a problem. Use iron sulfate or iron chelates to correct it.

Zelkova serrata
Japanese Zelkova, Saw-Leaf Zelkova
Zones: 5-9. To 75-100 feet.
Deciduous tree.

Japanese zelkova was introduced to the Western world from Japan in 1860. It is now the most commonly grown zelkova in the United States. This tree is an elm relative and somewhat resembles the American elm. It is being promoted as a substitute for the American elm because it is highly resistant to Dutch elm disease, which has killed the American elm. Its leaves are oval with toothed edges and turn yellow or russet red in fall. Some zelkovas have the wine-glass shape of the American elm; others develop rounded heads. Trunk bark on older trees resembles the exfoliating bark of Chinese elm.

Japanese zelkova has been planted in the United States as a shade tree, on lawns, along residental streets, and in large open areas. Prefers a deep moist soil and is not too fussy if the soil is acid or alkaline. Best development is in full sunshine.

Trees often develop narrow V-shaped crotches which have a tendency to split and become infected in the splits. Heavy accumulations of snow or ice can cause them to break.

Japanese zelkovas are from several seed sources, which causes undesirable variability in plants. Trees may leaf out at different times in spring, an undesirable quality for street tree plantings, and tree shape can vary. For this reason, named varieties are recommended.

'Village Green' is a widely used cultivar. It is reputed to be hardier and faster-growing than the species, although very little difference has been apparent in Midwestern arboretums. Fall color is rust-red while the leaves of the species may vary yellow to red. 'Village Green' is the best choice for street plantings.

Shiny xylosma *(Xylosma congestum)* makes an excellent clipped hedge; has a wide range of other landscape uses.

Japanese zelkova *(Zelkova serrata)* is an excellent, disease-resistant shade tree. Foliage turns bright shades of yellow or russet before dropping in fall.

Top-Rated Garden Flowers

The annuals, perennials, and bulbs described in this section were chosen because of their dependable flower display in the climate zones to which they are adapted. Each is widely available through mail-order catalogs or garden centers. Some are plants that have enlivened American gardens for centuries. Others are recent hybrids that offer new plant forms or new flower colors and shapes.

Encyclopedia entries: Plant descriptions are arranged aphabetically by botanical names. The most widely used common names are shown in bold type just below the genus name. Many annuals, perennials, and bulbs are familiar only by their common names. If you know only a plant's common name, refer to the index. Genera with many species and varieties are listed in charts to make comparison and selection easier.

Each entry includes the climate zones where the plant will give a top-rated performance, its potential height, and whether it's an annual, perennial, or bulb. Growth habit, flower colors and description, season of bloom, and foliage textures are discussed. Pertinent information on propagation by seed, division, or transplant is included and specifics on planting, preferred planting sites, long-term care, and any problems are given for each plant.

Climate Zones Note: Plants adapted to Zone 10 are also adapted to *new* Zone 11. Plants shown adapted to Zone 11 only, are recommended specifically for Zone 11.

At left: By planning carefully you can enjoy a long season of brilliant color in your annual flower beds and borders.

Tulips *(Tulipa sp.)*

Calendula *(Calendula officinalis)*

Oriental poppy *(Papaver orientale)*

Peony *(Paeonia hybrid)*

Fern-leaf yarrow (Achillea filipendulina)

(Achillea ageratifolia), a low-growing yarrow.

Achillea
Yarrow

Zones: 3-10. To 10 inches to 5 feet. Perennial.

Several species of this large genus are top-rated garden plants. All are admired for their flat clusters of long-lasting flowers and their aromatic, finely divided foliage. Cultivated varieties have more refined qualities than wild forms, which escaped from Colonial herb gardens and have naturalized in many parts of the country.

Yarrows are ideal for planting in dry, sunny gardens. Plants tolerate exposed sites, sandy soils, and thrive under average garden conditions. Use in dry gardens, borders, as a background filler, or in an herb garden. Dwarf varieties make a low-maintenance ground cover. Flowers are very popular for dried or fresh arrangements and have enduring color and form. (To dry, suspend freshly cut flowers upside down.)

You can purchase container-grown plants or start from seed. Sow seed directly in the garden or start plants indoors early, seeding over a light sandy mix. Germinates in 5 to 7 days at 65° to 70°F. Purchased seed will flower true to color but self-sown plants may vary from their parent. Propagating plants by division is most dependable.

Once established, yarrows are long-lived, and nearly pest-free. Water and feed sparingly or growth will become rank, and fewer flowers will be produced. Masses are easily divided every 3 to 6 years. Watch for powdery mildew and stem rot under moist conditions.

Achillea

Botanical Name/ Common Name	Zone	Plant Description	Flower Description	Comments
Achillea ageratifolia	3-10	Forms low mat. Silverish leaves have serrated or semi-smooth edges.	White clusters to 1 inch across on 4- to 10-inch stalks.	Foliage color adds interesting contrast to garden.
Achillea filipendulina Fern-leaf Yarrow	3-10	Erect-growing, 2-1/2 to 5 feet. Leaves gray-green, finely cut, up to 10 inches long.	Varied shades of yellow; blooms June to August.	Overall effect is fine textured. Excellent in groups. Good for cut flowers. Aromatic foliage.
A.f. 'Coronation Gold'		Strong stems, 3 feet.	3-inch gold clusters.	One of the best, most prolific bloomers.
A.f. 'Gold Plate'		4-5 feet tall.	Yellow flower heads are 6 inches across.	Yarrow on a grand scale. Use as background color.
A.f. 'Moonshine'		Silvery leaves on modest plants to 1-1/2 to 2 feet tall.	Clear, bright yellow flowers.	Premium foliage with long-lasting blossoms.
Achillea millefolium Common Yarrow	3-10	Fine, feathery foliage, gray or green, from a basal rosette. Grows to 3 feet, spreads by rhizomes. Aromatic.	White flowers bloom June to October.	Ideal for hot, dry sites. Wild forms seed extensively; have whitish flowers. Medicinal value.
A.m. 'Cerise Queen'		Grows to 18 inches.	Bright, cherry-red.	Fine foliage adds soft texture to garden.
A.m. 'Fire King'		Extra-fine, silvery foliage. Grows to about 2 feet.	Rosy-red flowers in 2- to 3-inch clusters.	Good with yellows, other pink flowers.
Achillea ptarmica Sneezeweed	3-10	Lance-shaped leaves, 1-4 inches, with serrated edges. Plants stay low to 2 feet. Branching.	White flowers bloom July to September.	Plants spread by rhizomes. Keep within bounds by cutting out new growth.
A.p. 'Angel's Breath'		Vigorous grower.	Abundant, double white blooms.	Control spreading growth. Use as cut flowers.
A.p. 'The Pearl'		Double flowers on 15-inch plant.	An improved variety; white, open clusters.	Most popular for front border. Good for cut flowers.
Achillea tomentosa Woolly Yarrow	3-10	Mat-forming, dwarf yarrow, extra-fine, gray-green foliage. Grows to 10 inches, spreads wider.	Cream to bright yellow flowers bloom May to July.	Excellent drought-tolerant ground cover for small areas; mowable. Perfect in rock garden or edging. Needs good drainage.
A.t. 'Aurea'			Dark yellow on 6- to 8-inch stalks.	
A.t. 'King Edward'			Palest yellow on 8-inch stems.	Low mat, good quality.
A.t. 'Moonlight'			Light yellow.	

Agapanthus
Lily-of-the-Nile
Tubers.

Handsome, strap-like evergreen leaves and long stems topped with showy clusters of blue or white flowers make this the star of many mild-climate gardens. Lily-of-the-Nile can be grown in cold climates, if tubers are dug and stored over winter or planters are taken indoors. Flaring, funnel-shaped flowers provide color throughout summer, and masses of leaves are lustrous dark green.

Landscape uses are many: It is often used as a lush container plant, mass planting, or in a mixed border. Large forms are useful for background or small forms for mid- or foreground plantings.

Few plants are so undemanding, yet so responsive to proper care. Except in hottest areas, full sun is best. Elsewhere, provide light shade during midday and early afternoon. Plant tubers 1 inch deep. Good soil and regular fertilizing produce splendid plants, though lily-of-the-Nile survives complete neglect. Regular watering is worth the effort; however, fleshy tubers will sometimes survive for months out of the ground. Clipping spent stems and dividing clumps every 4 or 5 years, in spring, keep plants looking their best.

Agapanthus orientalis
Lily-of-the-Nile
Zones: 9-10. To 48 inches.

Often sold as *A. africanus*, a smaller species, this large species of lily-of-the-Nile has blue flowers. Variety 'Albidus' has white flowers.

Agapanthus x 'Peter Pan'
Peter Pan Lily-of-the-Nile
Zones: 9-10. To 15 inches.

This dwarf variety has clusters of blue flowers held above 10-inch-tall foliage. It lends itself to many uses, particularly in small-space gardens. Dwarf white varieties are sometimes available.

Ageratum houstonianum
Flossflower, Ageratum
Zones: 2-10. To 5-10 inches.
Annual.

No annual is valued more for an edging than flossflower. Its dense clusters of fuzzy white, soft blue, or lavender-blue flowers cover compact, mounding plants all summer. Low-growing varieties make a perfect edging and taller varieties are good in the midground.

Plant seeds or seedlings outdoors after the last frost. If using seeds, it is better to sow indoors 6 to 8 weeks before your last frost date. Do not cover. Germination begins in about 5 days. Flossflower prefers full, or nearly full, sun but benefits from light shade in the hottest areas. Regular watering and a rich, fast-draining soil produce the best flowers. Overhead watering can damage flowers. Remove old flowers to keep plants blooming.

Top-rated blues are 'Blue Blazer' (6 to 7 inches) and 'Blue Mink' (10 inches). Whites are 'Summer Snow' (5 inches) and 'Spindrift' (6 to 7 inches). Occasionally you may find a pink variety.

Alcea rosea (Althaea rosea)
Hollyhock
Zones: 3-10. To 2-8 feet.
Biennial.

This stately old-fashioned favorite looks at home near a fence or wall in the back of a border. A dense clump of foliage develops first, eventually producing a tall flowering stalk. The showy single or double flowers, up to 6 inches wide, open in sequence starting from the bottom. Flowers may be single or double in a wide color range. Bloom time is midsummer until early fall. Hollyhock reseeds so freely that for practical purposes it might be considered a perennial, though most individual plants die after their second year.

Plant nursery seedlings, or sow seeds outdoors after the last spring frost, or sow indoors 6 to 8 weeks

Lily-of-the-Nile (Agapanthus orientalis) holds its striking flower clusters on slender stems rising from handsome strap-like foliage.

Flossflower *(Ageratum* sp.), a popular edging annual, produces masses of fluffy flowers all summer.

Double-flowered hollyhocks *(Alcea rosea)* feature large carnationlike blossoms that open sequentially upward.

Ornamental onion bulbs (*Allium* sp.) produce balls of tiny blossoms atop smooth slender stems in spring or summer.

The slim stems of round-headed garlic (*Allium sphaerocephalum*) are crowned with showy balls of petite flowers during summer.

earlier, under a very light sprinkling of soil. Germination takes about 10 days. Plant 2 to 3 feet apart in full sun and in rich or ordinary garden soil. Provide average watering. Hollyhock may bloom the first year but probably not until the second.

Stake taller varieties and shelter from wind. Snails, slugs, and spider mites may be problems. If rust appears on the undersides of leaves, you should remove and destroy leaves immediately.

Top-rated strains are Chater's Double (6 to 8 feet; pink, rose, red, copper, yellow, scarlet, maroon, violet, purple, and white), Powderpuffs (4 to 5 feet; apricot, pink, rose, red), and smaller Majorette (to 2 feet; same color range as Chater's Double).

Allium
Ornamental Onion
Bulbs.

Although diverse in flower color, size, and overall appearance, ornamental onions all bear a distinct resemblance to their plain relative, the garden onion. They produce roundish clusters of blossoms atop smooth vertical stems. Some have wonderfully fragrant blossoms, though if bruised, foliage has an unmistakable smell of onions. Ornamental onions make choice cut flowers, and dry nicely. They have a long bloom season, in spring or summer. Most are very hardy.

Ornamental onions prefer full sun, fast-draining sandy loam, and watering during their growing period. Plant them in fall beneath a layer of soil about three times the height of the bulb. Leaves usually die to the ground after flowering.

Allium giganteum
Giant Allium
Zones: 6-10. To 4-5 feet.

This largest of the top-rated alliums is one of the most striking—dense, bright blue-violet flower clusters, 4 inches or larger in diameter, top 4- to 6-foot-tall stems in summer. Handsome used to backdrop companion plants in borders. Flowers are excellent for fresh or dried arrangements. Plant several bulbs together, 8 to 10 inches apart.

Allium moly
Lily Leek
Zones: 4-10. To 12-18 inches.

Yellow-to-golden-flowered, this summer-blooming species has flower clusters 3 inches in diameter. Bulbs multiply rapidly and lily leek naturalizes easily to form drifts in rock gardens or borders. It is especially effective with delphinium and other bedding plants with blue flowers, or planted in ground covers such as periwinkle.

Allium neapolitanum
Daffodil Garlic, Flowering Onion
Zones: 6-10. To 12 inches.

This is the earliest-blooming allium—fragrant, white, starlike flowers in loose 3-inch clusters appear in late spring and last for a month or more. Leaves are flat and inconspicuous. Slightly less cold hardy than most other alliums, with mulching it usually survives in Zone 5. Unlike other species, daffodil garlic adapts easily to constantly moist, but not soggy, soil.

Allium ostrowskianum
Ostrowsky Onion
Zones: 4-10. To 6-12 inches.

A late-spring bloomer, this species has 4-inch spheres of striking pinkish-purple flowers. It looks especially at home in rock gardens or other informal settings. Variety 'Zwanenburg' has pink or red flowers.

Allium sphaerocephalum
Round-headed Garlic
Zones: 6-10. To 24 inches.

In mid- to late summer this species bears 1-1/2-inch clusters of purple to orchid flowers. Foliage is grasslike. Rounded-headed garlic is excellent for use in both fresh or dried floral arrangements.

Amaryllis belladonna

Belladonna Lily, Cape Belladonna, Naked-Lady Lily

Zones: 7-10. To 2-3 feet.
Bulb.

Abruptly, almost overnight, the tall flowering stalks of belladonna lily appear out of the bare ground in late summer, heralding cooler weather. A cluster of up to 10 or 12 lilylike, fragrant flowers tops each stem. Flowers are typically rose-pink but can range from white to wine. An old established clump may produce dozens of stems from its huge bulbs. In fall, after flowers die, foliage appears and endures until spring.

Belladonna lily can be planted beneath low-growing perennials or annuals that fill in around its bare stems—and it is dramatic alone, in a sheltered, sun-baked southern exposure near a wall or fence.

Any soil that is not wet is acceptable. Bulbs can be planted near the surface, but, if planted a foot deep, they endure drought, extreme heat, as well as cold beyond the normal climate range (often to Zone 6 if heavily mulched). Plant during or immediately after blooming to prevent interruption of blooming cycle. Dry soil in summer is best. No special care is needed.

Juices of this plant are poisonous if eaten.

Anemone

Anemone, Lily-of-the-Field, Windflower

Tubers and perennials.

Three species of this beautiful genus are top-rated. Two make brilliant displays in spring or early summer, and the third blooms more sedately in late summer and fall.

Anemone blanda
Grecian Windflower

Zones: 7-10. To 2-10 inches.
Tuber.

Soon after the first crocuses fade, when hyacinths, early tulips, and daffodils bloom, Grecian windflower joins the chorus. It produces masses of 2-inch, yellow-centered, silken-petaled flowers, in white or shades of pink, blue, or mauve, above attractively cut foliage. Mixed in beds with early bulbs, planted among shrubs or in rock gardens, grown in containers, or naturalized under deciduous trees, it makes a solid mass of color for as long as 6 weeks.

Grecian windflower prefers brightness but needs light shade in hot-summer areas. Moisture just prior to and during budding and blooming is important, but afterward dry soil is acceptable. Before planting, dry tubers should be soaked in water for a few hours. Plant 2 to 3 inches deep and 4 inches apart in rich, sandy loam. In the North, plant in spring; dig and store tubers in a cool, dry place over winter. In Zones 7 to 10, plant in early spring or fall.

Anemone coronaria
Poppy-flowered Windflower

Zones: 8-10. To 18 inches.
Tuber.

This brightest, showiest anemone produces single or semidouble pink, red, blue, or white flowers with black centers, to 2-1/2 inches wide, in spring. This is the spectacular anemone sold as a cut flower.

Within its hardiness range, plant in fall—or plant tubers in early spring, staggering planting times to prolong bloom season. Out of its hardiness zone, plant tubers in spring, dig in fall, dust them, and store in a cool, dry place over winter. Plant tubers 2 to 3 inches deep and 8 inches apart, in rich, moist, well-drained humus. Use lime if necessary to prevent soil from becoming too acid. It prefers light shade.

In pots and borders poppy-flowered windflower is dazzling. The de Caen group offers brilliant singles. The St. Brigid group, semidouble, offers softer colors. The St. Bavo group (actually *A. x fulgens* but usually sold as a form of *A. coronaria*) has semidouble or double flowers in a wide color range.

The large flowers of belladonna lily *(Amaryllis belladonna)* appear unexpectedly in late summer, their tall stems bursting up from the bare soil to produce a dramatic show.

Poppy-flowered windflower *(Anemone coronaria)* is an early bloomer and is a favorite florist's flower.

Golden marguerite *(Anthemis tinctoria)* provides reliable color from midsummer into fall even under difficult growing conditions.

Snapdragons *(Antirrhinum sp.)* make excellent vertical accents in garden and vase.

Anemone x hybrida (A. japonica)
Japanese Anemone
Zones: 6-9. To 30 inches.
Perennial.

This fibrous-rooted cousin of Grecian and poppy-flowered anemones is quite a different plant. From late summer through autumn, just when the garden needs a boost, it bears 2- or 3-inch, single or semi-double flowers on wiry stems above clumps of deep-lobed, neat foliage. Yellow-centered flowers are white, soft pink, or dusky rose.

Plant Japanese anemone in tall mixed borders, in front of high evergreen shrubs, around bases of trees, next to pools—in any situation where its mildly invasive tendency is acceptable. Rich, moist, well-drained soil and light shade are best. Clumps flower best if left undivided.

Closely related and similar *A. vitifolia* 'Robustissima,' occasionally available, has pale pink flowers and bolder foliage, and is hardy to Zone 4.

Anthemis tinctoria
Golden Marguerite, Ox-Eye Chamomile
Zones: 3-9. To 1-1/2-3 feet.
Perennial.

This attractive, bushy perennial for dry, sunny gardens has fine-textured aromatic foliage that creates a dense mat, above which arise tall flower stalks. Leaves are green above, woolly beneath. Flowering begins in July, blanketing the plant with golden-yellow daisies. Large-centered, 2-inch blossoms are ideal for cut flowers. Cutting encourages more blooming and extends flowering into fall.

Golden marguerite is a problem solver tolerating exposed sites, poor soils, and dry conditions. Simply provide a fast-draining soil for easy culture. Avoid overwatering and overfertilizing.

Begins to decline after the second year, when bare spots appear in the center of the clumps. Rejuvenate by dividing clumps in spring, spacing new plants 12 to 18 inches apart. Stem cuttings taken in summer root easily.

Seeds may be broadcast after last frost in spring. Golden marguerite self-sows readily, but seedlings are not true to the parent hybrid and should be weeded out.

There are several top-rated varieties with large flowers in bright colors. 'Beauty of Grallagh' is considered the best, with compact growth topped by large golden flowers. 'Kelwayi' has finest cut leaves. 'E. C. Buxton' and 'Moonlight' have clear yellow flowers.

Antirrhinum majus
Snapdragon
Perennial in Zones 8-10. Annual elsewhere. To 6-36 inches.

Ranging in size from 6-inch pygmies to 3-foot giants, colorful snapdragon hybrids have a place in every garden. You can use the smallest as edging, slightly taller ones as foreground, and midsize to large ones in mid- and background.

When pinched gently, the "snap" types of snapdragon flowers open, resembling a dragon's jaws. Many new hybrids have wide-open "butterfly" flowers, some frilled elaborately. All colors except blue are available.

In most climates, snapdragons brighten the garden from late spring to fall. In warm-winter areas, where it is a perennial, blooming starts in winter or early spring.

Set out nursery seedlings in spring or plant seeds outdoors after soil has warmed. In warm-winter areas, plant seeds or seedlings in fall. In areas with cold winters, plant seeds indoors 6 to 8 weeks before the last spring frost. Place seeds in freezer overnight before sowing. Do not cover seeds with soil. Takes at least 10 days for germination. Set seedlings out 6 to 8 inches apart in full sun and fast-draining, sandy loam. When plants have several sets of leaves, pinch out tips to cause branching. Stake tall plants. Remove fading flower stalks to encourage more flowering.

Rust fungus is sometimes a problem, though modern hybrids resist it. Avoid overhead watering, which spreads the disease.

Numerous strains of various sizes are available. Top-rated strains in the 6- to 8-inch range are Floral Carpet (snap-flowered) and Pixie (open-flowered). In the 12-inch range are Little Darling (open-flowered) and Sweetheart (double). Bright Butterflies (open-flowered) are 18 to 24 inches. In the 24- to 30-inch range are Madame Butterfly (double-flowered) and Super Tetra (open-flowered). Rockets (snap-flowered) are 24 to 30 inches tall.

Aquilegia x hybrida
Columbine

Zones: 3-9. To 1-1/2-3 feet. Perennial.

Columbine is unparalleled for flower form. Blossoms are cup-shaped, framed by colored sepals with backswept spurs that are often long and curved. All varieties flower freely in shades of pink, yellow, lavender, red, purple, blue, orange, and white. Many are bicolored. Blossoms appear from May through June, nodding on top of slender stems. Delicate foliage adds to columbine's visual charm. Leaves are bluish green, and delicately cut into rounded lobes resembling maidenhair fern.

Plants grow from thick rootstocks to form 18- to 36-inch-wide masses. Columbine is equally effective in refined, formal gardens, woodland settings, and shaded rock gardens. Flowers make exquisite bouquets.

Plant in filtered shade in warm climates, sunny locations in cool climates. Needs a rich loamy soil and excellent drainage. Amend heavy soils with organic matter.

Set out nursery seedlings or container plants in spring or fall. Seeds sown in late summer bloom the following spring. Chilling and light are both required for germination, so seeds should not be covered. Divide established plants by separating the clumps carefully. Space new plants 12 to 24 inches apart. Volunteer seedlings do not exhibit varietal colors.

Keep columbine free of weeds, apply mulch in winter, water deeply, and keep spent flowers cut. Insect pests such as leaf miner, aphids, and borers may be troublesome.

'McKana's Giant' is the most widely available hybrid. It is very prolific, bearing large long-spurred flowers in a wide range of colors. Many native species also are available, all worthy of attention for the specialty garden.

Arctotis grandis
African Daisy

Perennial in Zones 9-10. Annual elsewhere. To 10-12 inches.

Several groups of flowers are called "African daisies," but brilliant *Arctotis* hybrids are the most colorful and most widely available. Three- or 4-inch daisylike flowers are white, red, bronze, cream, apricot, pink, yellow, or orange; centers are often dark, occasionally ringed. Flowers are held, one per stem, above dense tufts of toothed or deeply cut leaves with whitish, woolly undersides. Flowers are good as cut flowers, however they close at night and in dark indoor spots.

Use in summer beds or borders, or as a summer-through-fall ground cover on slopes. African daisy is an excellent seaside flower.

Sow seeds outdoors after last spring frost, or indoors in a warm place 6 to 8 weeks earlier. Plant seedlings a foot apart in sandy loam. Good drainage and full sun are imperative. Once established, plants tolerate drought. African daisy overwinters in mild-winter climates but flowers best its first season.

Columbine *(Aquilegia x hybrida)*, a charming and widely adapted perennial, adds delicate beauty to many garden situations.

The brilliant flowers of African daisy *(Arctotis* hybrids) add a blaze of color to summer gardens. Excellent for seaside plantings.

Sea pink *(Armeria maritima),* a tidy rock garden plant, forms tufts of neat evergreen foliage and blooms from April through July.

Asters *(Aster* sp.) are valued for their sparkling color in late summer and fall.

Armeria maritima
Sea Pink, Thrift
Zones: 3-9. To 12 inches.
Evergreen perennial.

Sea pink has narrow, grasslike leaves that stay neat and green year-round, forming low-growing tufted mats. Clumps eventually spread to 1-1/2 feet. Blossoms are densely packed globes of tiny white, pink, or deep red flowers held on slender stems that rise 6 to 12 inches above the foliage. Blooms from April through July.

Sea pink creates an outstanding permanent edging along paths or flower borders, or mass in small areas as a ground cover. Its neat, hardy form fits perfectly in rock gardens, and it grows well in containers. Cut flowers are excellent for dried and fresh arrangements.

Sea pink's coastal origin suggests cool, sandy conditions for optimum growth, but this plant adapts to most garden sites, except overly rich, heavy soils that drain poorly. Plant in full sun in cool regions, partial shade where climate is hot and dry. Do not overfeed and overwater sea pink. Plants like somewhat infertile conditions and will tolerate brief dry periods.

Soak seeds overnight before sowing in the garden in a sandy bed. Seedlings will vary in color. Planting divisions and nursery-grown seedlings are preferred propagation methods. Space plants 6 to 12 inches apart.

Divide clumps about every 3 years, or when centers begin to die. Watch for cottony masses of mealybugs at leaf bases.

Top-rated varieties are 'Alba', pure white; 'Royal Rose', bright pink; and 'Rubra', dark red. *A. laucheana* has deep rose flowers, grows 6 inches tall.

Aster
Aster, Michaelmas Daisy
Zones: 4-10. To 6 inches-6 feet.
Perennial.

This large group of hardy perennials is prized for its late-season blooms. Clusters of fuzzy or daisy-like blossoms range from deep purples and blues to pinks, reds, and whites, all with bright yellow centers. They are showy from mid-summer to frost adding invaluable color to borders, containers, and flower arrangements. Stems are leafy and slender with linear foliage, and plants range from spreading dwarfs to tall vase-shaped clumps.

Garden asters are generally from hybrid crosses and are best grown by nursery transplants or divisions. Plant in spring or fall, spacing 12 to 24 inches apart in full sun and an evenly moist, well-drained soil of moderate fertility.

Asters require regular care. Avoid excessive fertilizer and splashing water. Fungal problems such as powdery mildew may require fungicide applications, especially in climates with warm, humid summers.

These vigorous growers look their best when divided every 2 or 3 years. Retain shoots from the outer portion of the clump. Pinch growing tips to encourage well-branched, compact growth. Tall varieties may need support.

Most asters are hybrids between two American wildflowers. New England aster, *A. novae-angliae,* a native of moist areas of North America, has hairy leaves and grows 2 to 6 feet tall with many-flowered clusters of rosy to deep purple blossoms. *A. novi-belgii,* New York aster, is coastal in origin, variable in height, and has smooth 7-inch leaves. These two species are the source of many hybrids known as hardy asters or Michaelmas daisies.

Astilbe x arendsii
Astilbe, False Spiraea, Perennial Spiraea
Zones: 4-9. To 18-30 inches.
Perennial.

A delight when in bloom, astilbe offers tall plumes of tiny white or pastel pink to deep red flowers, blooming from early to midsummer. The feathery stalks are held

1 to 2 feet above the handsome deeply cut foliage. Bronzy or a lustrous dark green, the leaves form dense, spreading clumps that last many years.

Astilbe is well-loved for planting in shaded gardens under tall trees or mixed with woodland shrubs and herbs. Excellent companion plants for shady sites include bergenia, lilies, and columbine. Mass plantings in drifts and borders are also effective. Plant groups in naturalized settings or near water. Astilbe is short-lived in hot, dry climates or when exposed to hot sun. Enjoy indoors as fresh or dried cut flowers. (Pick just before buds open for dried arrangements.)

Astilbe grows well in containers, and potted plants may be forced to provide early indoor color. Plant healthy root cuttings in sandy potting mix in late fall. Keep in a cool spot—30° to 40°F—for about 10 weeks, then induce growth by increasing to 65°F. After blooms are spent, plant outdoors.

Transplants or divisions are the preferred methods of propagation. Seed-grown plants take 2 years to bear flowers, and flower colors are uncertain.

Astilbe appreciates evenly moist, but not overly wet, rich soil. Prepare a well-drained planting site, adding generous amounts of compost or peat to clay or poor soils. Space plants 15 to 24 inches apart. Set dwarf varieties closer together. Mulch to protect shallow roots and to keep them cool and moist, and fertilize generously with a balanced formula. Cut back spent flower stalks. Plants need dividing every 3 to 4 years. Watch for common insect pests such as mites, slugs, and Japanese beetles.

Extensive breeding has produced high quality varieties. Top-rated are: white-flowered 'Avalanche'; 'Betsy Cuperus' in light pink; 'Deutschland', a compact vigorous plant with 2-foot white plumes; 'Europa', early bloomer with clear pink blossoms, 'Fanal', with bronze foliage and carmine flowers; 'Peach Blossom', with rosy-pink blooms; and 'Red Sentenial' with reddish leaves, scarlet flowers.

Aurinia saxatilis
Basket-of-Gold, Goldentuft Madwort, Goldentuft Alyssum
Zones: 3-10. To 8-12 inches. Perennial.

Basket-of-gold aptly describes this perennial that is laden with gilded flowers in early spring. The silvery gray-green foliage adds a bright touch of contrast throughout the growing season, forming a dense mat that spreads 12 to 15 inches.

Drought tolerance makes this plant a desirable choice for a sunny rock garden, between stones, or draped over dry walls. Take full advantage of its silvery foliage as an accent color in perennial borders.

For best growth and maximum flowering, give basket-of-gold a sunny, warm exposure. Growth tends to be compact under dry conditions, luxuriant and open where moist, though fewer flowers are produced. Most garden soils are suitable, even poor, infertile types. However, good drainage is essential. Basket-of-gold may be planted by broadcasting seeds over exposed soil in early spring or fall. Mix seed with sand or soil before sowing for spreading ease and to provide a light seed cover. Seedlings will appear in 7 to 14 days and should be carefully thinned after true leaves have developed. Divisions or seedlings transplant easily and should be spaced 6 to 12 inches apart. Mulch in winter where temperatures drop below 32°F.

Avoid overwatering or overfertilizing to keep plants compact and flowering vigorously. Prolong the blooming season by cutting spent flowers before they set seed. Although plants are short-lived, they may be rejuvenated by dividing every 3 or 4 years.

Aurinia cultivars, all profuse bloomers, vary by shade of yellow or size of plant. 'Citrina' is popular with pale, sulphur-yellow blossoms. 'Lutea' and 'Sulphurea' are similarly colored. Double-flowered 'Plenum' is literally blanketed with intense yellow flowers. 'Compacta', 'Nana', and 'Silver Queen' are compact forms.

False spiraea *(Astilbe x arendsii)*, a handsome perennial for semi-shady spots, bears graceful feathery flowers in early summer in white or shades of pink, red, and peach.

Drought-tolerant and a rampant grower, basket-of-gold *(Aurinia saxatilis)* is loved for its abundant golden blossoms that bloom from April through May.

Wax begonia *(Begonia x sem - perflorens-cultorum)*

Hybrid tuberous begonia *(Begonia x tuber - hybrida)*

Hybrid tuberous begonia *(Begonia x tuberhybrida)*

Begonia

Series or Variety	Height	Foliage	Flowers
WAX BEGONIA			
Cocktail series:			
'Brandy'	6-8 in.	Bronze.	Light pink.
'Gin'	6-8 in.	Bronze-green.	Rose.
'Vodka'	6-8 in.	Bronze.	Deep scarlet.
'Whisky'	6-8 in.	Bronze.	White.
'Gladiator'	12-18 in.	Bronze-tinted green.	Red.
Glamour Series	8-10 in.	Green.	Pink, red, rose, white, and white edged with rose. Large.
'Indian Maid'	6-8 in.	Bronze.	Scarlet.
'Linda'	6-8 in.	Green.	Deep rose.
'Othello'	6-8 in.	Dark bronze.	Scarlet-orange.
'Scarletta'	6-8 in.	Green.	Large, scarlet.
'Snowbank'	8-10 in.	Green.	White.
Thousand Wonders (Tausendschon) Series	6-8 in.	Green.	Scarlet, white.
'Viva'	6-8 in.	Green.	White.

HYBRID TUBEROUS			
Series, Variety, or Type	Form	Colors	Comments
Camellia	Upright.	White, pink, red, yellow, orange, scarlet, salmon, deep red, apricot.	Large, ruffled double flowers resemble camellias.
Carnation	Upright.	Deep red, pink, white, orange, yellow.	Large, ruffled, frilly flowers resemble carnations.
Crispa Marginata	Upright.	Bicolors: yellow edged with crimson, white edged with crimson.	Large, frilled single flowers.
Multiflora Maxima	Upright.	Orange, yellow, red, white, pink.	Multitudes of 2-in. single or double flowers on sun-tolerant plants; excellent for beds or pots.
Nonstop	Upright.	Yellow, red, orange, pink, rose, apricot, salmon.	Double, semidouble, and a few single flowers on same plants. Compact growth habit. Very free-flowering.
Picotee Double	Upright.	Bicolors: white edged with pink, red, or apricot. 'Flamenco' speckled red and white. 'Sunburst' yellow edged with red.	Flowers are large and ruffled.
Rose Form	Upright.	Apricot, pink, yellow, white, red, salmon.	Edges of petals smooth, center petals furled like center of rose.
Ruffled Double (Ballerina)	Upright.	Apricot, yellow, white, pink, scarlet.	Flowers heavily ruffled, 6 to 8 inches wide.
Hanging Basket	Pendulous.	Pink, red, yellow, orange, apricot; picotee types: assorted pastel colors with red or pink edge.	Many Belgian hybrids have slender leaves and wide-open flowers with attractively slender petals. American hybrids have rounder petals. Various Hanging Basket begonias sometimes marketed as Lloydii or Lloydii Pendula begonias.
Happy End	Pendulous.	Red, orange, salmon, white.	This series of pendulous begonias has a mixture of single and double flowers.
Sensations	Pendulous.	Red, yellow, copper, white, pink.	This series of pendulous begonias has large double flowers.

Begonia
Begonia
Annual and tuber.

Two appealing groups of garden flowers belong to this diverse genus —wax begonia and tuberous begonia. They make valuable plants for cool shady spots where other plants are finicky.

Begonia x semperflorens-cultorum
Wax Begonia, Bedding Begonia
Perennial in Zones 9-10. Annual elsewhere. To 4-18 inches.

Since the Victorian era wax begonia has been a favorite for beds, edging, and containers. It is sometimes grown as a houseplant, and many gardeners keep easily rooted cuttings as houseplants.

Dense lustrous round leaves may be green, bronze, or purple. Clusters of small crystalline-textured flowers cover plants from late spring until fall frost. Most flowers are about 3/4 inch wide, but some are 2 inches or more wide.

Plant nursery seedlings after last spring frost, or sow seeds indoors, uncovered, in a warm, bright spot 12 to 16 weeks before transplanting time. Germination takes 14 to 21 days. Plant 8 to 10 inches apart in rich, moist, well-drained soil allowed to dry between waterings. Fertilize frequently. Plants live over winter in mild climates but seldom look attractive after the first year.

Light afternoon shade is best; in cool-summer climates accepts full sun. Grows well anywhere in light to moderate all-day shade. Bronze-leaved types tolerate high temperatures and sun better than green-leaved varieties.

Begonia x tuberhybrida
Hybrid Tuberous Begonia
Hardy in Zones 9-10. Tender elsewhere. To 12-18 inches, or pendulous to 18-20 inches.
Tuber.

Spectacular flowers measure up to 8 inches wide and span all colors except green and blue. Most are double, some are fringed or ruffled. Attractive leaves are large and dark, tapering to a point. Uprights are used for beds or containers, as are

Multifloras; use pendulous varieties for hanging baskets.

If your growing season is brief, buy full-grown plants. Elsewhere, you can also buy tubers or seedlings. Or you can plant seed, uncovered, indoors in winter, if humidity is high and temperature is kept at 65° to 75°F. Seeds take 15 to 20 days to germinate. Plant barely covered tubers or seedlings in fast-draining, organic soil, 3 per hanging basket, 1 per 8-inch pot, or 8 to 18 inches apart in beds.

Cool, moist climates are ideal, but with shade, humidity, and wind protection, tuberous begonia can be grown nearly everywhere. Water regularly, but don't wet foliage as mildew can be a problem. Fertilize frequently. Protect from slugs and snails. In fall, dig and store tubers, dusted with fungicide, in a cool, dry place, or leave in dry pots.

Vast numbers of strains and varieties are sold, often under ambiguous names. Top-rated begonias are listed in the chart, under their most common commercial names.

Bellis perennis
English Daisy
Zones: 3-10. To 4-6 inches.
Perennial sometimes grown as an annual.

This cheerful daisy blooms early with spring bulbs, pansies, and primulas. Blossoms with single or double petals are available in shades of soft pink, rose, red, white, and purple. They appear from April to June; longer in cool climates. English daisies are native to Europe and have naturalized in lawns and fields in the United States. Leaves are slightly fleshy and spatula-shaped, forming a low-growing rosette or tufted mass. In Zones 8 to 10 English daisy is treated as a winter-blooming annual. In the coldest regions of Zone 3 it may need seeding each spring. Elsewhere grows as a hardy perennial.

Place English daisy where it can be viewed close-up, as a border for flower beds, or on the patio in pots. Mix with bulbs for early garden color, tuck among rocks, or mass as foreground color.

Purchase nursery-grown plants or sow seeds. Seeds grown indoors

Wax begonias *(Begonia x semperflorens-cultorum)*, are covered with sprightly flowers held above bronze or green foliage.

English daisies *(Bellis perennis)* form neat clumps of perky blossoms during cool weather in spring and summer

Heartleaf bergenia *(Bergenia cordifolia)* is prized for the year-round beauty of its lush foliage and its clusters of bell-shaped flowers in spring.

Browallia *(Browallia* sp.), a plant for shady sites, creates a mass of cool-colored flowers backdropped by handsome foliage. 'Blue Bells Improved' browallia is shown below.

germinate within 10-15 days at 70°F. Start 6-8 weeks before setting outdoors. You can depend on English daisy to reseed itself but flower colors will vary.

English daisy tolerates full sun—light shade is preferable in hot, dry climates. Provide a moist, fertile soil rich in organic matter for optimum growth. Plants benefit from light fertilizing periodically during the growing season. Flowering may be prolonged in cool areas if seed heads are removed. Cover with a mulch for winter protection in cold climates. Divide every 2 to 3 years after flowering, spacing 4 to 6 inches apart.

Among the cultivated varieties, 'Monstrosa' is the giant with dark red, double-petaled flowers. 'Tuberosa' is rose tinged, 'Snowball' has pure white blossoms, and 'Prolifera' forms clumps and has many-flowered stems.

Bergenia cordifolia
Heartleaf Bergenia
Zones: 2-10. To 12-18 inches.
Evergreen perennial.

Heartleaf bergenia is admired both for its lush foliage and its early spring flowers. Clusters of rose, pink, white, or lilac bell-shaped blossoms are held on stout red stems. Flowers usually appear from April to May, earlier in mild regions or sparingly where spring frosts come late. Large rounded leaves are thick and glossy with undulating edges, and their green summer color becomes suffused with red in winter. Forms low dense mats slowly spreading by rhizomes on or near the soil surface.

Heartleaf bergenia is useful in a variety of garden settings. Shade-tolerant, it makes a choice evergreen ground cover under trees. Plants work equally well used in rock gardens, along streambanks, or in poolside settings. Used as edging or planted in clusters, it creates bold textural patterns.

Heartleaf bergenia tolerates full sun to partial shade, dry or wet soils. A deep, well-drained soil of average fertility is ideal. Growth becomes dense in dry, sunny spots, more

open as shade and moisture increase. Once established, plants require only occasional water, light feeding, and winter mulch in coldest regions. Remains in the garden for years without needing dividing. Pest-free, but leaves provide cover for snails.

Seeds may be sown directly in the garden in fall or spring, however flower colors may vary. New plantings are easily established with nursery plants or divisions taken in early spring. Space 12 to 18 inches apart.

Other species have similar fine qualities. *Bergenia ciliata* grows to about 12 inches tall. Has handsome leaves with coarse hairs, and slightly fragrant, reddish-purple, white, or pink flowers held in loose clusters. *Bergenia crassifolia* has spoon-shaped leaves tinted red, with purple or rose flowers in dense clusters. Of the hybrid forms, 'Abendglut' and 'Evening Glow' are top-rated. Leaves turn maroon in winter, and flowers are a deep purple-pink. 'Silverlight' and 'Silberlicht' are white.

Browallia speciosa
Browallia, Bush Violet, Sapphire Flower
Perennial in Zones 9-10. Annual elsewhere. To 8-14 inches.

Browallia is a dependable, showy flower for use in shaded gardens or hanging baskets. Its star-shaped amethyst, blue, or white flowers form brilliant masses against emerald-green leaves and harmonize with other shade-tolerant annuals. In fall, planters can be taken indoors for winter color.

Buy nursery seedlings or mature plants, or plant seeds indoors 6 to 8 weeks before last spring frost. Leave seeds uncovered and keep temperature around 75°F. Germination takes 12 to 20 days. Pinch plants when they reach 6 inches to encourage branching. Set seedlings 8 to 15 inches apart in beds, 6 to 8 inches in planters, in rich, moist, well-drained soil. Browallia thrives in cool to moderate summer climates in light to medium shade.

'Major' is the most widely grown variety, with 2-inch blue or white flowers. Other popular varieties are: 'Blue Bells Improved' (amethyst-blue), 'Silver Bells' (white), 'Sky Bells' (deep indigo-blue). A 'Bells' mixture is sold as 'Jingle Bells'. Compact (8 to 10 inches) are 'Blue Troll' and 'White Troll'.

Fancy-leaved Caladium
Caladium x hortulanum

Hardy in Zone 11. Tender elsewhere. To 12-24 inches or taller. Tuber.

Bold, colorful heart-shaped leaves distinguish this tropical beauty. Leaves are veined, blotched, and bordered in white, greens, reds, pinks, and bronzes. Most varieties have 2 or 3 colors, sharply contrasting or shading into each other. Fancy-leaved caladium can overwinter in cold areas as a houseplant, or tubers can be dug and stored.

A long-time favorite potted plant, fancy-leaved caladium flourishes in well-drained containers. It is also particularly effective massed and can brighten a lightly shaded area.

Plant tubers 1 to 3 inches deep and 12 inches apart. For healthy growth and best color, provide bright light but no direct sun. Ample water, rich loam, and frequent fertilizing are ideal. Protect from wind, and watch for snails and slugs. You can have color for a long season if you start tubers indoors in late winter or early spring.

Calendula, Pot Marigold
Calendula officinalis

Zones: 2-10. To 12-18 inches. Annual.

Pot marigold has a long history of garden adornment and practical use (both in the cooking pot and as an herbalist's remedy for toothache or low spirits). Today it's valued as an ornamental for its 4- to 5-inch, double-daisylike flowers, which range from cream through yellow to vibrant orange and apricot. They brighten sunny beds and planters during cool months, from early spring to summer in most areas, well into summer in cool-summer areas, and late fall to spring in mild-winter areas.

Sow seeds outdoors in spring, or indoors 6 to 8 weeks before seedlings are to be transplanted in spring, summer, or fall. Cover seeds completely and maintain temperatures around 60° to 70°F. Germination takes 7 to 14 days. Plant seedlings about 12 inches apart in rich, moist, well-drained soil, in full sun where air circulation is good. Overhead watering encourages mildew.

Two top-rated strains are dwarf Fiesta Gitana (Gypsy Festival), to 12 inches tall, and Pacific Beauty, 18 to 24 inches tall, heat-resistant.

China Aster
Callistephus chinensis

Zones: 2-10. To 8-36 inches. Annual.

Unlike most annuals, China asters do not bloom all summer—they are showy for only 4 weeks, but come in early, mid- and late season varieties, which can be planted for a succession of bloom. The white, pink, peach, rose, mauve, scarlet, violet, and purple flowers are shaggy single or double 'daisies'.

Heights and growth habits vary widely. The tallest forms have long stems and are perfect for borders or cutting beds. (Once cut back, plants seldom produce more flowers).

Sow seeds outdoors after the last spring frost or indoors 6 to 8 weeks earlier. Germination takes 7 to 14 days at around 70°F. Many gardeners plant directly outdoors, because seedlings may be difficult to transplant. Space 6 to 15 inches apart, in full sun and rich, sandy soil kept moist but not overwatered.

A virus transmitted by leafhoppers and wilt caused by a soil fungus are troublesome diseases. To lessen chances of disease, do not plant in the same spot 2 years in a row. Pull out any stunted yellowing plants and control insects. Most new strains are disease-resistant.

Top-rated varieties are: Long-stemmed Super Giants (36 inches tall, with 5-inch shaggy flowers); Massagno Cactus mixture (24 inches tall, with 4-inch, needle-petaled flowers); Powderpuff mixture (18 to 24 inches tall, with very double 3- to 3-1/2-inch flowers); Burpee's Pompon mixture (15 inches tall, with dense 1-3/4- to 2-inch pompon flowers); and Dwarf Queen mixture (double, 3-inch flowers borne profusely on 10- to 12-inch mounds.

Fancy-leaved caladiums *(Caladium x hortulanum)* are grown for their richly variegated, heart-shaped leaves, which add color and textural interest to shady spots.

Calendula *(Calendula sp.)* provides a bold show of striking, golden-toned flowers during cool months when garden color may be most needed.

The flowers of China asters *(Callistephus chinensis)* are shaggy heads of cool blue, lavender, pink, or white petals.

Campanula

Botanical Name/ Common Name	Zones	Plant Description	Flower Description	Comments
Campanula carpatica **Tussock Bluebell, Carpathian Harebell**	3-8	Compact, clump-forming tufted plant 6-12 in. tall. Bright green 2- to 3-inch leaves. Well-formed, neat growth habit. Perennial.	Abundant, open bell-shaped flowers to 1-1/2 in. wide on erect single stem. Bright blue, purple, white, or lavender. Blooms in summer.	Likes moist soil and sun; light shade where hot. Good naturalized, or in rock gardens, beds, or mass display. Transplant or divide spring or fall. Seeds of varietals do not breed true.
C.c. 'Alba'			White.	
C.c. 'Blue Carpet'			Blue.	Very compact.
C.c. 'China Doll'			Large, open lavender-blue flowers.	
C.c. 'Cobalt'			Deep blue.	
C.c. 'White Star'			Extremely large white flowers in profusion.	
Campanula glomerata **Clustered Bellflower**	3-8	Mound-shaped, 1-1/2 to 2-1/2 ft high. Long, coarse-textured leaves on upright stems. Perennial.	Dense upright clusters of funnel-shaped blue, violet, purple, or white flowers on 15- to 20-inch-long stems, spring to midsummer.	Most robust in partial shade, fertile moist soil. Use as color accent in borders. Good as cut flowers. Plants spread by rhizomes.
C.g. 'Crown of Snow'		18- to 20-in. mound, larger leaves.	Large white flowers.	
C.g. 'Joan Elliot'			Early-blooming, deep violet.	
C.g. 'Superba'		24-in. mound.	Large clusters of intense violet-blue flowers on 2-foot stems.	Tends to spread.
C.g. acaulis	3-8	Dwarf form to 8 in.	Violet-blue.	Good for edging, in rock gardens.
C.g. dahurica	3-8	Low-growing to 12-18 in.	Large, broad deep purple or rosy-pink flowers in clusters.	
C. isophylla **Italian Bellflower**	8	Heart-shaped leaves on 2-foot-long stems. Sprawling habit. Perennial.	Profuse open bell-shaped flowers in lilac, light blue, or white. Blooms from summer into early fall.	Takes sun or light shade. Tender plants need mulching in winter. Excellent for containers, hanging baskets, over banks, on slopes, in rock gardens. Propagate by cuttings, transplants, or divisions in spring.
C.i. 'Alba'			White.	
C. medium **Canterbury-Bells**	3-8	Biennial. Grows rosette of rough, hairy, 6- to 12-inch-long leaves the first year; forms leafy 4-foot-tall flower stalks the second year.	1- to 2-inch-wide bell-shaped flowers are lavender, pink, white, mauve, or blue. Blooms spring to midsummer.	Takes partial shade; full sun in cool summer areas. Use in groups as background border. Good cut flower. Sow seeds or set out transplants in spring or early fall. Space 12 in. apart.
C.m. 'Calycanthemum'		Grows 2-3 feet tall.	Unusual double flower in mixed colors.	Easily grown from seed. Sow 1/4 to 1/2 inches deep and water regularly.
C.m. 'Cup-and-Saucer'			Petals form a deep cup, 4 inches across; sepals form the saucer.	
C.m. 'Canterbury Bells'			Flowers in clusters.	
C. persicifolia **Peach-leaved Bellflower**	3-8	Clump-forming with upright slender stems to 3 feet tall. Basal leaves to 8 inches long; narrow, 4-inch-long stem leaves. Perennial.	Perky upright cup-shaped blossoms in blue shades, white, or lavender. Blooms in summer.	Easy-to-grow in sun or partial shade. Use as color accent or massed in borders. Sow seed in early spring, thin to 12-18 in. Divide every 3-4 years. Watch for aphids.
C.p. 'Alba'			White.	
C.p. 'Blue Gardenia'			Deep blue double flowers.	
C.p. 'Moerheimii'			Semi-double white flowers.	
C.p. 'Telham Beauty'			Bright blue large flowers 2 to 3 inches across.	
C. poscharyskyana **Serbian Bellflower**	3-8	Vigorous plants form 3-foot clumps, 4 to 8 inches tall. Somewhat trailing stems have coarsely toothed, heart-shaped leaves. Perennial.	Narrow-petaled, open, starlike lavender-blue flowers borne mid-summer to fall.	Tolerates sun (partial shade where hot), dry sandy sites. Good as ground cover, draped over walls, or on banks. Easy to propagate by divisions or seeds.
C. rotundifolia **Bluebell, Harebell, Blue Bells of Scotland**	3-8	Low-growing to 18 inches, with many upright stems forming neat shape. Leaves rounded to narrow. Perennial.	Abundant 1-inch bells in shades of blue, purple, or white, in pendulous clusters. Very dainty in appearance.	Takes sun or partial shade. Easy-to-grow by seed, transplants, or divisions in spring. Use in borders or rock gardens.

Campanula
Bellflower

Zones: 3-8.
Biennials and perennials.

Bellflowers have been cultivated for centuries and they continue to be garden favorites today. This large genus offers several popular species that are much admired for their dainty bell- and star-shaped blossoms in soft shades of blue, pink, lavender, purple, and white. All have good-looking foliage that blends well in mixed plantings. Bellflowers are traditionally used in rock gardens, against stone walls, and in perennial borders. They are also effective in hanging baskets, grown in containers, or used in naturalized plantings.

Campanula tolerates full sun in cool climates, grows best with partial shade in most areas. Plants are easy to grow, and thrive in well-drained, evenly moist soil. Most varieties prefer a fertile soil high in calcium. Add gypsum or lime to acid sites.

Purchase container-grown plants or seedlings. May be started by seed sown in the garden in spring or early fall. Divide perennial clumps in August every 3 to 4 years.

Where temperatures reach freezing, mulch for winter protection. Foliage is attractive to snails and slugs. Watch for signs of leaf damage and take appropriate action.

The chart on page 232 lists those bellflowers considered top-rated.

Catharanthus roseus (Vinca rosea)
Madagascar Periwinkle

Perennial in Zones 9-10. Annual elsewhere. To 3-18 inches.

A more care-free beauty would be hard to find for summer gardens in the desert and hot cities. Blooming commences with the arrival of hot weather and lasts until mid- or late fall. Plants bear dark green glossy leaves and 1-1/2-inch, phloxlike white, pink, or rose flowers, some with red or rose eyes. Low, spreading varieties make a thick seasonal ground cover and are pretty in hanging baskets. Upright plants are useful for bedding.

You can sow seeds indoors 12 weeks before garden soil is warm, covering seeds completely and maintaining 70° to 75°F temperatures. Germination takes 15 to 20 days. Or you may prefer to buy seedlings or blooming plants. Plant in any warm, well-drained soil. In mild-summer climates, Madagascar periwinkle thrives in full sun but in hotter areas needs some shade. Once established, it tolerates drought but is lusher with regular watering. It self-sows in all climates and is perennial in Zones 9 and 10.

There are top-rated varieties in three sizes and growth habits. Spreading varieties are 'Pink Carousel', 3 to 4 inches tall and spreading to 24 inches, with rose-pink flowers; and 'Polka Dot', 4 to 6 inches tall and spreading to 24 inches, with red-eyed white flowers. Mounding to 10 inches high are 'Little Linda' (violet-rose), 'Little Blanche' (white), 'Little Pinkie' (rose-pink), 'Little Bright Eye' (red-eyed white), and 'Little Delicata' (rose-eyed pink). The Bush Periwinkle series (rose, pink, and white) reaches 18 inches.

Celosia cristata
Cockscomb, Woolflower

Zones: 2-10. To 4-36 inches.
Annual.

Both types of cockscombs—feather cockscomb and crested cockscomb—offer blazing color, long-lasting flowers, and heat resistance. Crested varieties have curious-looking convoluted flower heads that resemble giant velvety combs of roosters. Plumed varieties have soft-textured, silky flower heads. Both come in fiery and purplish-reds, and rose-pink, apricot, gold, and yellow. They are classics for low-maintenance gardens, blooming from early summer into fall. Good for fresh or dried cut flowers.

Sow seeds outdoors when soil is warm, or indoors, barely covered, 4 weeks before planting time. Germination takes 10 to 20 days. Set 6 to 18 inches apart, depending on

Bellflowers *(Campanula* sp.) create a fetching display when mass-planted in naturalistic settings in semi-shade or sun.

A durable plant even in desert climates, Madagascar periwinkle *(Catharanthus roseus)* produces glossy dark green foliage and a continuous floral display.

Cockscomb *(Celosia* sp.) offers feathery plumes in vivid colors and a blooming season that lasts from early summer into fall.

The mounds of lacy silvery-gray foliage of dusty-miller *(Centaurea cineraria)* create striking color contrast against dark green foliage.

Cool-colored flowers and fine-textured foliage have made bachelor's-button *(Centaurea cyanus)* a longtime favorite for cutting or display.

Wallflowers *(Cheiranthus* sp.) scent the garden in spring and early summer with their delightful fragrance.

eventual size. Cockscomb needs full sun. Tolerates poor soil but grows best in rich, moist soil. Planting out too early can stunt plants.

Some top-rated plumed cockscombs are: 'Apricot Brandy' (apricot-orange, 16 to 18 inches tall), 'Crusader' (crimson, 16 to 18 inches), Fairy Fountains mixture (12 to 14 inches), 'Forest Fire' (scarlet, 30 inches), 'Golden Truimph' (golden yellow, 24 inches), 'Red Fox' (bronzy orange-red turning carmine, 18 to 24 inches), and Pampas Plume mixture (36 inches).

Top-rated crested cockscombs are: 'Fireglow' (cardinal-red, 18 to 24 inches), Jewel Box mixture (4 to 6 inches), 'Toreador' (crimson, 18 inches), and Tall mixture (mainly crimson, 36 inches.)

Centaurea
Dusty-Miller and Cornflower
Perennial and annual.

Two very dissimilar *Centaureas* are appealing garden plants. One is grown for its dainty pastel-colored flowers, and the other for its silvery-white foliage.

Centaurea cineraria
Dusty-Miller
Zones: 5-10. To 12-18 inches.
Perennial, used as an annual.

Dense mounds of long, deeply lobed whitish leaves make dusty-miller a favorite for providing contrast for flowers and green foliage. It's especially effective with blue and purple flowers. During summer small flowers may appear, but are best removed.

Buy seedlings or larger plants in spring, or sow seeds indoors about 4 weeks before time for late-spring transplanting. Plant in full sun and well-drained soil. (Sow dusty-miller indoors 8 to 10 weeks before last frost; germination takes 10 to 15 days.) Plants do not grow well in areas with abundant summer rain unless soil is very sandy.

Several plants, including the popular *Senecio cineraria,* are quite similar to *Centaurea cineraria* and for all practical purposes are the same; *S.c.* 'Diamond' grows to 10 inches, and *S.c.* 'Silver Dust' to 8 inches.

Centaurea cyanus
Cornflower, Bachelor's-Button, Bluebottle
Zones: 2-10. To 12-36 inches.
Annual.

This old-fashioned flower reseeds so freely that in some areas it has become established as a pretty roadside weed. Round, tufted, 1- to 1-1/2-inch flowers are white, and shades of blue, cool red, purple. Upright plants have narrow grayish leaves. Cornflower adds fine-texture and cool color to summer gardens and is an excellent cut flower.

You can plant seeds or nursery seedlings outdoors, in mid- to late spring. Some gardeners prefer seeds, which germinate dependably. Cover seeds completely. Germination takes 7 to 14 days. Full sun and rich, well-drained soil are best. Plants bloom for a few weeks; stagger seeding for a long show.

Some top-rated bachelor's-buttons are: 'Blue Boy' (36 inches), Monarch Giant Ball Strain (24 inches, mixed colors), Polka Dot mixture (16 inches, mixed colors), and 'Jubilee Gem' (12 inches, bright blue).

Cheiranthus cheiri
Wallflower
Zones: 2-10. To 12-18 inches.
Perennial usually grown as biennial or annual.

This old-fashioned, wonderfully fragrant beauty is perfect for rock garden, bed, or border. Clusters of 1/2-inch flowers develop in rounded heads atop bushy plants with slender leaves. They bloom in spring and early summer or winter and early spring in mild-winter areas. Colors are red, mahogany, purplish brown, gold, yellow, and ivory. Wallflower grows best and sometimes endures as a perennial in cool, moist climates.

Purchase plants or sow seeds. Sow outdoors in early spring, or in a cool spot indoors, covering seeds lightly for blooming usually the next year. Germination takes 5 to 7 days. Set out seedlings 12 inches apart. Fast-draining soil is essential. Full sun is best in mild-summer areas, partial shade elsewhere.

Often sold as *C. allionii* is closely related summer- and fall-blooming *Erysimum hieraciifolium* (Siberian Wallflower). Variety 'Apricot Delight' is spring-blooming.

Chionodoxa luciliae
Glory-of-the-Snow
Zones: 3-8. To 6 inches.
Bulb.

This hardy little bulb naturalizes in areas where it is well adapted to make carpets of blue for a month in early spring. Each plant has 2 or more ribbonlike leaves and bears a cluster of 5 to 10 white-centered, 3/4-inch, intense blue flowers. 'Gigantea' has large flowers. Variety 'Rosea' has white-centered pink flowers.

Since plants are small and naturalize freely by seeding, consider planting broad drifts, perhaps around forsythia, deciduous magnolia, and other early-blooming plants. Glory-of-the-snow mixes effectively with Siberian squill. It makes an excellent rock garden plant. In grassy areas unmowed until bulbs' foliage dies back, it makes an early-spring meadow of blossoms.

Plant bulbs 3 inches deep and at least an inch apart in fall. In cool-summer areas plant in full sun or partial shade, elsewhere in partial shade. Keep moist during spring. Soil should be rich and well-drained.

Chrysanthemum
Chrysanthemum
Perennials.

This large and greatly varied group of plants includes some of the most well-loved fall- and summer-flowering perennials as well as useful herbs and florist's plants. Four different species are top-rated.

Chrysanthemum coccineum
(Pyrethrum hybridum)
Pyrethrum, Painted Daisy
Zones: 2-10. To 2-3 feet.

All-around hardiness, fine-textured foliage, and showy daisylike flowers make pyrethrum highly useful in the sunny border garden. Plants grow in an open, sprawling habit with pink, red, or white blossoms on slender stems blooming from April to July. Blooms again in late summer if cut back after the first bloom.

Pyrethrum is somewhat drought- and heat-tolerant though performs best if given regular water and fertile, well-drained soil. Heavy, wet soil causes stem rot.

Container-grown plants rather than seeding is preferred. Plant in spring, 12 to 18 inches apart. Divide in late summer after 3 to 4 years. Few pests are troublesome, though aphids may appear in spring.

Chrysanthemum frutescens
Marguerite Daisy
Perennial in Zones 8-10. Annual elsewhere. To 3-4 feet.

This is the daisy florists grow for cut flowers. In mild climates it's a reliable, shrubby plant that remains evergreen and blooms nearly year-round. Elsewhere, it is grown as an annual. Plants form a full, rounded mass of finely cut foliage and are covered in white, lemon-yellow, or pink daisies nearly year-round. Use in shrubby borders, as a colorful filler, or in large patio containers.

Marguerite is a low-maintenance addition to the dry, sunny garden, tolerating heat and most garden soils. It is short-lived and needs replacement every 3 to 4 years. Plant container-grown nursery plants. Trim foliage in early spring and midseason to keep plants tidy and foliage dense.

Chrysanthemum maximum
Shasta Daisy
Zones: 6-9. To 2-4 feet.

Shasta daisy is prized for its massive flower display from early spring to frost. Large snow-white daisies and handsome dark green foliage complement any garden setting. Plants grow from a basal clump, and have many leafy, upright sturdy stems that are topped by 2- to 4-inch flowers.

In early spring the intense blue blossoms of glory-of-the-snow *(Chionodoxa luciliae)* add sparkling color to both sunny and shady garden sites.

In mild climates, the foliage of marguerites *(Chrysanthemum frutescens)* forms a fine-textured rounded mass, brightened with colorful daisies nearly year-round.

'Alaska' shasta daisy *(Chrysanthemum maximum* 'Alaska') is a durable perennial bearing an abundance of large single flowers on sturdy stems.

Chrysanthemums *(Chrysanthemum x morifolium)* have myriad flower forms and colors, adding dramatic impact to the garden in fall.

Feverfew *(Chrysanthemum parthenium)* creates a long-lasting show of white or yellow blooms during summer.

Durable and versatile, shasta daisy is excellent for use in mass displays, or simply placed in a convenient spot for easy cutting. Cut flowers are long-lasting.

Plant container-grown plants in fall or spring, setting them 12 to 15 inches apart, or begin with seed sown in the garden in early spring. Plant in full sun or partial shade. Plants thrive on regular watering and feeding. Clip old blossoms to keep plants tidy and to extend the flowering season. Plants are long-lived, vigorous, and free-flowering if divided every 2 to 3 years. Plants are evergreen in mild climates, but in coldest areas protect with a winter mulch.

Overwatering can result in stem rot. Watch for aphids on new growth and remove plants showing symptoms of viral disease, or verticillium wilt (yellow, limp foliage on one side.)

'Alaska' is a long-time favorite, bearing large, single flowers all season on vigorous plants. 'Polaris' has massive 7-inch blossoms. 'Wirral Pride' has well-formed double flowers on 2-foot stems. 'Little Miss Muffet' is dwarf (12 to 15 inches) with semidouble flowers.

Chrysanthemum x morifolium
Chrysanthemum, Mum
Zones: 5-10. To 5-24 inches.

Mums are unexcelled for late summer and fall garden color, producing vibrant masses of showy flowers. Plant size, form, and hardiness, and flower shape and color vary greatly and many kinds are suitable only for greenhouse growing. The most popular garden plants are cushion mums, which form masses of double blossoms on 10- to 12-inch-high mounds, and pompoms, which grow 2 feet tall and bear clusters of double blooms. Both types offer a range of rich colors.

Perhaps no other flower, save the rose, is enjoyed for so many reasons. Chrysanthemums make spectacular bedding plants for mass display, and are beautiful as late-season accents in the border. Cut flowers are long-lasting, and potted plants permit versatile flower displays indoors and out.

Purchase container-grown plants in fall or spring, or purchase rooted cuttings in spring. Be sure plants are "hardy mums" not florist varieties. Plant in full sun; morning sun in hot climates. Needs rich, well-drained soil. Add organic matter and fertilizer to soil 1 to 2 weeks before planting. Soggy soil in winter or summer causes stem rot. Good air circulation and cool temperatures help prevent diseases and prolong the life of flowers.

Mums are shallow-rooted and therefore need regular watering and fertilizing. Morning watering with spray directed at soil level protects buds and prevents disease problems. Though cold hardy, the shallow roots may be damaged by alternate freezing and thawing of soil in winter; apply a thick mulch of salt hay, pine boughs, or leaves after soil freezes in fall, remove in early spring. Tall-growing varieties may need staking—most conveniently done when plants are young.

When mums are 6 to 8 inches tall in spring, the tips should be pinched. Continue pinching tips after each 6-inch spurt of growth until mid-July. This produces the sturdiest plants with the most flowers. For largest flowers, pinch off all but one flower bud per stem while buds are still quite small.

Mums should be dug up and divided early each spring to keep them vigorous, or they may be renewed with stem cuttings and the original plant discarded. Lift garden plants early in spring when new growth appears. Separate rooted young shoots from sides, discarding the old plant. Set directly in the garden or place in pots temporarily for later transplant. Plants getting an early start grow the tallest.

Tip cuttings can be made by taking 2 to 3 inches of new spring growth. Stick cutting in perlite or other light mix and keep moist, not wet; enclose in a plastic bag to keep humidity high. Plants will root in 3 to 4 weeks. Set out in the garden when 6 inches tall. Space 1-1/2 to 2-1/2 feet apart.

Chrysanthemum parthenium
Feverfew, Matricaria
Zones: 4-9. To 1-3 feet.
Perennial.

Feverfew was once used as a remedy to lower fevers; today it is a beautiful garden flower. For 6 or more weeks in summer, the highly aromatic foliage is topped by a massive display of small white or yellow button-like or daisylike flowers. A prolific seeder, feverfew has naturalized in many of our country's open areas.

Use feverfew for informal, low-maintenance gardens. Plants are short-lived but will reseed. Start by seed or container-grown plants. Trim periodically to keep neat and prevent seeds from forming, and thin-out unwanted plants.

Cleome hasslerana
Spider Flower, Spider Plant
Zones: 2-10. To 3-6 feet.
Annual.

Beautiful and imposing, this large-scale annual deserves to be grown far more widely. From early or mid-summer into fall it is crowned by airy spikes of long-stamened, rose-pink to white flowers, which open from bottom to top as the stalk grows. As lower flowers fade, they are replaced by attractive slender pods on delicate stems. Large, handsome compound leaves cover the base of the plant and graduate upward to smaller, simple leaves. Fast-growing plants serve as a background.

Sow outdoors after last spring frost, or indoors 4 to 6 weeks before last frost, in a warm spot. Germination takes 10 to 14 days. Set plants at least 2 to 3 feet apart in full sun. Withstands heat and drought, reseeds freely. Stake clumps loosely to protect from wind. Seeds are sold as a mix.

Clivia miniata
Kaffir Lily
Hardy in Zone 10. Tender elsewhere. To 24 inches.
Tuber.

A shaded entryway, a bed around the base of a tree, or a planter on a shaded patio can be transformed by Kaffir lily into one of your garden's brightest assets. Dense clusters of up to 20 flame-colored, lilylike flowers are borne above unusually handsome dark-green, straplike leaves. Blooming season, winter through spring, may start a bit later where Kaffir lily is grown as an indoor/outdoor container plant. Decorative crimson berries form after blooms wither. Occasionally salmon-, yellow- and even white-flowered forms are available. Particularly showy orange-red Kaffir lilies are sometimes marketed as Belgian hybrids.

Fairly deep shade is acceptable to Kaffir lily though it blooms best in light shade. It requires rich, well-drained soil kept moist all year, except for several weeks before buds appear. Plant with the top of the root mass just at the soil's surface, and don't move or divide unnecessarily. Feed potted specimens frequently with diluted fertilizer.

Colchicum autumnale
Autumn Crocus, Fall Crocus, Meadow Saffron
Zones: 5-10. To 6 inches.
Corm.

After foot-long leaves have appeared in spring and withered in summer, 4-inch-wide flowers appear directly out of the ground in late summer, sometimes early fall, 1 to 4 per corm. Color varies from white to purple. 'The Giant', the most popular variety, is lavender and single. 'Waterlily' has double lavender-pink flowers.

Autumn crocus is best when grouped informally in the garden. It is attractive in lightly shaded woodland areas, around azaleas and rhododendrons, or in sunnier spots with alyssum, thyme, or other low-growing plants that help hide its withered foliage.

Light shade is preferable in hot climates. Keep soil moist until leaves wither. Average-to-rich soil is best. Plant corms 3 or 4 inches apart in early August.

Corms are poisonous if eaten.

Spider flower *(Cleome* sp.) grows quickly from seed to an impressive size and produces showy clusters of delicate flowers.

Kaffir lily *(Clivia miniata)* provides handsome foliage and striking flowers for shady sites in temperate climates.

The demure blossoms of autumn crocus *(Colchicum autumnale)* burst from the bare ground in late summer or early fall, adding touches of color to informal settings.

A mass planting of a single variety of coleus (Coleus hybrids) has a pleasing visual impact.

A choice perennial for dry sites, big-flowered coreopsis (Coreopsis grandiflora) offers an abundance of golden blossoms for garden and vase.

A dwarf form of coreopsis (Coreopsis sp.) makes a showy edging plant all summer long.

Coleus x hybridus
Coleus, Flame Nettle, Painted Leaves
Zones: 2-10. To 6-12 inches.
Annual.

The colorful foliage of coleus is a bright addition to many shady gardens. Leaves are roundish to slender, 1 to 6 inches long, and most often gaily variegated with combinations of bronze, gold, white, chartreuse, green, copper, red, and pink. Colors are splashed, marbled, or striped. Some leaves are neatly bi- or tricolored. Edges may be smooth, toothed, frilly, or undulating.

Use coleus in planters and hanging baskets, in borders and beds, and as a bright edging. But combine patterns and colors carefully because too many varieties of coleus together become gaudy.

Buy seedlings or sow seeds uncovered in a warm spot indoors 6 to 8 weeks before last spring frost. Germination takes 10 to 15 days. Plant 10 to 16 inches apart in rich, moist, well-drained soil. In mild-summer climates accepts full sun; elsewhere needs moderate shade. (Too much shade or sun, however, washes out colors.) Pinch tips to encourage branching. Spikes of insignificant flowers appear in summer; to keep foliage lush, pinch flower buds when they appear. Fertilize regularly.

Coleus are available in many colors. Multicolor Rainbow series, about 15 inches tall, has striped or splashed leaves. Saber series, to only 8 inches tall, has narrow ribbonlike leaves. Fiji Mixture, 8 to 10 inches tall, has frilled leaves. Wizard series, 10 to 12 inches tall and very bushy, has toothed foliage. Seven Dwarfs mixture, to 8 inches tall, has small fringed or ruffled leaves.

Coreopsis
Coreopsis, Tickseed
Perennials.

Coreopsis is a large genus containing several favorite garden perennials, though some species are annuals.

They feature golden daisylike flowers with notched petals over a long blooming season in summer. Coreopsis will add a splash of vibrant color to both formal or naturalistic settings. Single-blossomed stems make excellent cut flowers.

Plants are easy to grow, tolerate benign neglect, and thrive with minimum attention. Accepts a wide range of soils and watering regimes, but needs full sun.

Purchase container-grown plants or start by seed in early spring for first-season flowers, August for color the following year. Transplants and divisions can be set out during either planting season, spaced 12 to 15 inches apart. Maximize performance with annual feeding and by removing spent flowers to extend the blooming season. Three species are considered top-rated for home garden use.

Coreopsis grandiflora
Big-Flowered Coreopsis
Zones: 5-10. To 3 feet.

This is the most widely-grown coreopsis, producing golden flowers on leafy stems. Deep green leaves are lance-shaped and divided. Well-adapted to dry sandy sites, this coreopsis is a perfect candidate for naturalizing in meadows; also good in flower borders. Plants may be short-lived, but reseed readily.

'Sunburst' has semidouble flowers. 'Goldfink' grows low, and is attractive close-up. Award-winning 'Sunray' is double-flowered, and very cold hardy.

Coreopsis lanceolata
Lance-leaf Coreopsis
Zones: 3-10. To 2 feet.

Foliage forms a mounded tuft and is good-looking all season. Grass-green leaves are somewhat lobed and sparse along the long, wiry flowering stems. Golden flowers have wide, notched petals and are perfect for cutting.

An excellent choice for borders. Plants are easily divided, and reseed freely without being weedy.

'Flore-pleno' is double-flowered.

Coreopsis verticillata
Thread-leaf Coreopsis
Zones: 7-10. To 3 feet.

A choice long-lived filler, thread-leaf coreopsis has a full and bushy form with narrow leaves that create a soft, fine texture. Foliage is attractive all season. Small golden blossoms are borne in profusion during midsummer. Space plants about 3 feet apart when setting out, and divide clumps every 2 years to maintain best form. Thread-leaf coreopsis is tolerant of, and performs best in, the driest locations.

Cosmos
Cosmos
Zones: 2-10. To 12-48 inches.
Annuals.

Cosmos offers airy foliage and silky, daisylike flowers that are showy from midsummer until fall frost. It makes a useful and handsome mid- to late-season annual. Larger varieties are striking in tall borders and smaller types are choice for fore- and midground.

Plant seeds in the garden after the last spring frost, or sow indoors 5 to 7 weeks before time to transplant into the garden. Maintain 70° to 85°F for germination in 5 to 10 days. Space seedlings 8 to 24 inches apart in full sun and well-drained, sandy soil. Rich soil reduces blooming. Once established, dry soil is best. Stake loosely.

Cosmos bipinnatus
Cosmos
To 4 feet.

The top-rated Sensation mixture, which grows to 4 feet high and has 4- to 6-inch white, pink, rose, or crimson flowers, is the most widely grown variety of cosmos. Foliage is feathery, dill-like, and an attractive bright green.

Cosmos sulphureus
Yellow Cosmos
To 12-36 inches.

Yellow cosmos has deeply-divided medium-textured leaves. The Klondyke strain is 24 to 36 inches tall and is top-rated. It has many-petaled 2-inch flowers of gold, orange, yellow, or red. This strain includes 'Diablo' (bright red) and Bright Lights mixture. An excellent dwarf is 'Sunny Gold', 12 to 14 inches high with 1-1/2-inch flowers.

Crocus
Crocus
Zones: 3-10. To 5 in.
Corm.

Crocuses are well-loved as harbingers of spring, sometimes even poking their way up through the snow. Less well-known, but equally beautiful, are those that bloom in fall. Flower size varies, but all have flaring, tubelike blossoms and grasslike, sometimes white-ribbed, foliage.

Plant crocuses in groups of 5 or more bulbs in a rock garden, beneath shrubs, or by a path or walk. They are especially beautiful when massed in a lawn. (Do not mow grass until crocus leaves begin to yellow.)

Crocuses grow best and spread readily in cold-winter areas. They prefer quick-draining soil and full sun. Soil need not be moist when plants are dormant. Plant corms in early fall 2 or 3 inches deep and at least 2 inches apart. Dig up and separate corms in fall if they begin crowding and pushing above the soil surface. Crocuses may be forced into bloom indoors in winter.

Top-rated species are: *Crocus chrysanthus*, available in a rainbow of named color forms, *C. ancyrensis* with named forms in yellow and cream, and *C. sieberi* with golden flowers marked with blue or purple, all blooming in late winter.

Dutch crocuses are a huge group of large-flowered hybrids of *C. vernus*, blooming in late winter or early spring. They are often sold as mixed colors. Occasionally 'Early Perfection' (blue-violet and orange), 'Pickwick' (silver-lilac striped and feathered deep lilac), 'Little Dorrit' (silvery amethyst), and 'Mammoth Yellow' ('Dutch Yellow Mammoth') are available.

With feathery bright green foliage and large flowers on tall slender stems, cosmos *(Cosmos bipinnatus)*, is striking planted in masses in borders or meadows.

Crocuses *(Crocus* sp.) are one of the earliest-blooming bulbs and are excellent for forcing indoors in containers.

Cyclamen *(Cyclamen* sp.) blossoms often have a contrasting colored eye and are borne singly atop slender stems rising from the heart-shaped leaves.

Chinese forget-me-not *(Cynoglossum amabile)* has a long bloom season in cool-summer regions; is lovely in rock gardens or massed in beds.

Fall-flowering crocuses, which should not be confused with autumn crocuses in the genus *Colchicum*, bloom in late summer to late fall, depending on the species. Foliage appears briefly in spring, and the chalice-shaped blossoms appear, leafless, in fall. Top-rated are: *C. kotschyanus (C. zonatus)*, a late-summer species, rose-lilac marked orange; *C. speciosus,* early-autumn blooming, variable but usually lavender-blue; *C.s.* 'Albus', white; and *C. sativus* (saffron crocus), lilac to white, but variable in bloom time.

Cyclamen
Cyclamen, Persian Violet
Tubers.

Cyclamens feature exotic-looking flowers with backswept petals borne one to a stem. Heart-shaped leaves, often patterned in contrasting green tones, are beautiful in their own right. Hardy types are choice rock-garden flowers, and florist's cyclamen can be enjoyed indoors in cold climates.

Cyclamen persicum
Florist's Cyclamen
Zones: 9-10. To 12 inches.

Fragrant white, purple, red, pink, salmon, or bicolored flowers adorn this large-scale cyclamen for 3 months or longer. Blooming begins in late winter and lasts until hot weather. Grow indoors in cold climates.

Plant tubers halfway out of the soil and 6 to 8 inches apart. A rich, fast-draining soil is necessary. Soil should dry somewhat between thorough waterings, but should not dry completely except during dormancy. Feed lightly every 2 or 3 weeks with a complete fertilizer. Withhold fertilizer and water in midsummer as leaves begin to die back for a brief dormancy. It flowers best at 50° to 60° F. Locate in full sun in cool areas, otherwise partial shade.

Cyclamen species
Hardy Cyclamen
Zones: 5-10. To 2-5 inches.

Several species of hardy cyclamen are top-rated: *C. cilicium*, Sicily cyclamen (Zones 7-10); *C. hederifolium* (formerly *C. neapolitanum*), baby cyclamen (Zones 5-10); *C. purpurascens* (formerly *C. europaeum*), European cyclamen (Zones 5-10); and *C. repandum*, spring cyclamen (Zones 6-10). Species may be sold as a mix.

All hardy species are diminutive plants perfect for the rock garden, for drifts among shrubs, or at the edge of a grove. They grow well in planters. Flowers bloom in spring and are shades of rose, pink, and crimson. Leaves appear during or after flowering, then wither during summer. May naturalize.

Plant tubers in midsummer 1 to 2 inches deep and 6 inches apart in rich, well-drained soil and partial shade. Culture is similar to florist's cyclamen.

Cynoglossum amabile
Chinese Forget-Me-Not,
Zones: 7-10. To 18-24 inches.
Biennial often used as an annual.

Chinese forget-me-not resembles true forget-me-not *(Myosotis)*, but it is a larger plant and its bright blue flowers lack a contrasting eye. It begins blooming in spring, fades with hot weather; in cool-summer climates it often continues blooming until fall frost. It makes pretty clumps in beds and rock gardens or at the sunny edge of a woodland.

Cynoglossum blooms quickly from seed sown directly outdoors; perpetuates itself readily by self-sowing. Sow seeds outdoors in spring as soon as ground is workable. Thin seedlings 9 to 12 inches apart. Provide full sun or partial shade, except in hottest areas, where some afternoon shade is needed. It grows in wet or dry soil.

'Firmament', with brilliant blue flowers, is compact and bushy. Pink and white varieties are sometimes available.

Dahlia hybrids
Dahlia

Hardy in Zones 9-10. Tender elsewhere. To 10 inches - 5 feet or taller. Tuber and perennial used as an annual.

Dahlias are dazzling and enormously varied in size, color, and form. Blooming spans midsummer to fall, when gardens most need color. Foliage is neat and dark green all season. Tall bushy types—the show dahlias—are grown from tender tubers and are dramatic as garden backgrounds or in exhibition beds. Dwarf types, which make beautiful bedding plants, are grown from seeds and are treated like annuals.

Set out tubers after the last frost in spring. Plant on their sides in depressions so that 6 inches of soil will eventually cover them. Initially cover with 2 inches of soil; gradually fill in as shoots grow. Space 1-3 feet apart, depending upon size. Sink tall, sturdy stakes beside the tubers.

Sow seeds of dwarf bedding dahlias outdoors after last spring frost, or indoors 4 to 6 weeks earlier at 60° to 86°F. Germinates in 5 to 10 days.

Before planting, enrich soil with organic matter or manure; provide drainage in heavy soil with a layer of gravel 15 inches below soil surface. Plant in full sun with some afternoon shade in hot areas. Water and fertilize regularly. Mulch soil. Pinch tips to encourage branching. For show-quality dahlias, prune to a single stem, thin buds and remove dead flowers.

Tubers may be left in the ground in Zones 9 and 10; elsewhere, cut off stalks and dig and divide tubers before first fall frost. Wipe off dirt, dust with pesticide, and store in barely moist peat moss in cool dry place until spring.

Insect-transmitted viruses may cause deformed growth or spotted flowers. Dig and discard infected plants. Bedding dahlias in too much shade may mildew. If soil dries out, dahlias may cease blooming.

The chart classifies dahlias according to flower form, a system devised by the American Dahlia Society.

Dahlias (*Dahlia* hybrids) offer gardeners everywhere an array of showy blossoms in a wide range of colors and forms for a long blooming season from midsummer until fall frost.

Dahlia

Group	Description and Comments	Top-Rated Strains and Varieties
Single	All have single, open-centered flowers. All top-rated strains and varieties are dwarf bedding plants.	Dahl Face mixture (3- to 4-in. flowers, mixed colors; 10 in. tall); Mignon Dahlias (3- to 4-in. flowers, mixed colors; 15 in. tall); and these 18-in.-tall varieties with 3-1/2 to 4-1/2-inch flowers: 'Murillo' (bright pink), 'Nelly Geerlings' (bright red), 'Snow White' (pure white).
Anemone-flowered (Pincushion)	A central tuft ("pincushion") of tiny, upright petals is ringed by larger, flat petals. Many flowers are bicolored. Most are about 18-20 in. tall, with 2-1/2 to 3-in. flowers, and are used for bedding.	Pincushion mixture; anemone-flowered mixture; and these varieties: 'Bridesmaid' (white with lemon tuft), 'Granato' (orange-scarlet), 'Guinea' (yellow), 'Honey' (apricot with lemon tuft).
Collerette (Collarette)	Flowers have open center surrounded by "collar" of shredded slender petals, surrounded in turn by outer ring of larger, flat petals. Many are bicolored. Similar in size to anemone-flowered.	'Alstergruss' (orange with yellow collar), 'La Gioconda' (red with cream collar), 'Violetta' (violet with white collar).
Decorative	Flowers are double with broad, bluntly pointed flat petals, arranged regularly ("Formal" varieties) or irregularly ("Informal" varieties). This is a huge and diverse group, including many of the popular dwarf bedding dahlias and the giant "dinnerplate" doubles.	Dwarf Border mixture, Dwarf Bedding mixture (15-24 in.); Unwin's Dwarf Hybrids (12 in.); Early Bird mixture (15 in.); Redskin mixture (15 in.); Rigoletto mixture (15 in.); Sunburst mixture (24 in.); Large-flowered Double mixture (around 5 ft); and this sampling of top-rated varieties: 'Drummer Boy' (3 ft, dark red 8- to 10-in. flowers), 'Alabaster White' (5 ft, white 10-in. flowers), 'Mary Elizabeth' (4 ft, cherry 12- to 14-in. flowers), 'Duet' (3 ft, 6- to 8-in. red flowers tipped white), 'Evelyn Rumbold' (4-1/2 ft, 10- to 12-in. rose-purple flowers).
Ball and Pompon	Fully double, ball-shaped or slightly flattened flowers. Pompons are more than 2 in. wide, Balls more than 3-1/2 in. wide. Plants 2-1/2 to 3 ft tall.	Balls sometimes sold by color: 'Red Ball', 'Pink Ball', 'Yellow Ball', 'Purple Ball'. Pompons often sold as Pompon mixture. 'Betty Ann' is excellent pink Pompon, 'Albino' pure white, 'Nero' purple-red, 'Bronze Beauty' bronze-orange.
Cactus	Fully double; most petals curled to be almost tubular, pointed at tips. Varieties with wider petals often classified "Semi-cactus." Plants, with some exceptions, 4-5 ft tall and flowers 4-12 in. wide. This is a large, popular group.	Cactus-flowered mixture; 'Juanita' (6-in. red flowers), 'Orfeo' (7-in. reddish-purple flowers), 'Sam Hearst' (10- to 12-in. yellow flowers), 'Pari Tahi Sunrise' (5-in. yellow flowers tipped red), 'Nikki's Burgundy' (5-in. deep red flowers on 2-1/2-ft plant), 'Park Princess' (4-in. bright pink flowers on 18-in. mounding plant).

Delphinium elatum
Delphinium
Zones: 2-10. To 4-8 feet.
Perennial.

Delphinium is the pride of discerning gardeners. Plants demand special attention, but reward you with spectacular tall flowering spires that can reach 8 feet under ideal conditions. Individual blossoms are 2 to 3 inches across, 5-petaled with a single spur, in rich tones of blue, deep violet, purple-pink, and white. Bicolored varieties have a 'bee' of dark or light petals clustered in the centers. Flowering begins in June and lasts until midsummer. A second flush may occur in fall. Palm-shaped leaves are bold-textured.

Delphiniums are unsurpassed for background color. The vertical spires are elegant in groups or planted against a fence. Makes beautiful cut flowers.

The conditions found in the Pacific Northwest are ideal—mild temperatures, even moisture, with only moderately hot sun. Soils must be neutral, well-drained and extra rich. Prepare soil with generous additions of organic matter. Use lime if soil is acid.

Delphiniums are usually treated as short-lived perennials, sometimes even as annuals. Plant nursery seedlings for guaranteed colors. Seeds sown in the garden in February or March will bloom that season. To get an early start, sow indoors 6 to 8 weeks before last spring frost. Germinates in 2 weeks at 60°F. (Fall-sown seeds will bloom in spring. Mulch young plants during winter.) Divisions can be taken from 3- to 4-year-old clumps. Treat roots with fungicide before planting and set crowns at, or slightly above, soil surface to prevent rot. Space plants 18 to 36 inches apart.

Apply a balanced fertilizer in spring and water regularly throughout the growing season. Avoid wetting plants or the weight may topple them. Staking is necessary. Use short individual stakes and add taller ones as stalks grow, tying even in between the flowers. After blossoms have faded, cut stalks just below the bottom blooms and fertilize again. New growth grows from the base; when it is 6 inches high,

remove old stems and enjoy a second flush of flowers. Watch for mildew, crown rot, sucking insects such as mites, snails, and bacterial leaf spot, and treat promptly.

Top-rated varieties include the tall, sturdy, and extra showy Pacific Hybrid series; dwarf varieties grow to 24 inches, standards to over 4 feet. Names to look for are: 'Blue Bird', a brilliant blue, with a white 'bee'; 'Blue Jay', deep blue, 'Summer Skies', soft blue with a white 'bee'; 'Galahad', pure white, 'King Arthur' the deepest purple, 'Elaine'; rosy pink, and the dwarf 'Blue Fountains' in mixed shades.

Delphinium x belladona is bushy with 3- to 4-foot multiple flower stalks. This species will outlive Pacific Hybrids. Fine selections include white-flowered 'Casa Blanca', dark blue 'Bellamosum' and 'Cliveden Beauty' in rich blue. A densely branched form, 'Connecticut Yankee', has distinct open flower clusters; plants reach 2-1/2 feet, mixed colors are available.

Dianthus species and hybrids
Carnation, Pink, Sweet William
Zones: 2-10. To 3-22 inches.
Annuals, biennials, and perennials.

Included in this diverse group of flowers are some old garden favorites—sweet William, pinks (petals of some are "pinked"), and carnations. Many *Dianthus* have an intense, spicy fragrance and most are perfect for beds, borders, planters, and cutting beds. Annual pinks and some perennials are excellent for keeping bright color in the garden from late spring into fall. Low-growing perennial pinks are choice rock garden flowers with dense, bluish, miniature grasslike foliage that's handsome year-round.

All *Dianthus* like rapidly draining, gritty, neutral to slightly alkaline soil, full sun, and cool weather. Newer hybrids tolerate more heat. Overwatering can be harmful. Clip dead flowers immediately to spur repeat blooming. Biennials and perennials benefit from heavy mulching in cold-winter climates. Some types are susceptible to rust and occasionally require fungicide.

Under ideal growing conditions, the flower spires of delphinium *(Delphinium elatum)* may grow 8 feet tall, making an elegant background for large gardens. Blossoms shown below.

Dianthus (*Dianthus* sp. and hybrids) offers a wide choice of flower colors and forms suitable for many garden uses from borders to cutting beds. Many are fragrant, most offer a long blooming season. Sweet William *(D. barbatus)* above left; pinks, above center and above right.

Dianthus

Series or Variety	Zones	Height	Flower Description	Comments
SWEET WILLIAMS *(D. barbatus)*				
Double mix	All*	18 in.	Doubles and singles; white, pink, red, red-purple, some bicolors.	From mid- or late spring into summer these old-fashioned *Dianthus* produce stems of densely clustered flowers suitable for planters, edging, and bedding. Seeded in fall, most bloom the next spring, but Summer Beauty and Wee Willie strains bloom same season from seeds planted outdoors after last frost or indoors 6-8 weeks earlier at about 70°F, for germination in 5-10 days. Most are biennials but some are grown as annuals. All can be planted as nursery seedlings.
Indian Carpet	All*	5-8 in.	Singles; scarlet, crimson, pink, white, bicolors.	
'Newport Pink'	All*	18 in.	Single; shades of salmon-pink.	
Summer Beauty	All*	12 in.	Singles; wide color range and many bicolors.	
Wee Willie	All*	3-4 in.	Singles; full range of white, pinks, reds.	
ANNUAL and BIENNIAL PINKS *(D. chinensis)*				
Charms	All*	6 in.	Singles; white and pink-to-scarlet tones.	Through summer into fall, especially if dead flowers are clipped, these profusely blooming *Dianthus* make bright displays for beds, borders, and planters. Plant nursery seedlings, or plant seeds as for Sweet William, above.
'China Doll'	All*	12-15 in.	Double clusters; crimson, red, salmon, bicolor.	
Magic Charms	All*	7 in.	Singles; scarlet, salmon-pink, white, coral, speckled.	
'Queen of Hearts'	All*	8-12 in.	Single; deep scarlet-red.	
Queen's Court	All*	8-9 in.	Singles; scarlet, crimson, orchid, pink, rose, salmon.	
'Snowfire'	All*	6-8 in.	Single, serrated; white with cherry center.	
'Snowflake'	All*	6-8 in.	Single, serrated; white, very large (2 in.)	
PERENNIAL PINKS				
D. x allwoodii 'Rainbow Loveliness'	3-8	12 in.	Lacy stars; pink, lavender, rose, white, and many combinations.	This is a huge group of *Dianthus* derived from several species, ranging from prostrate mats to large, upright types. Most bloom through summer and fall. Use, depending upon form, for rock gardens, beds and borders, edging, container plants, and cut flowers. Sow outdoors up to 2 months before first frost, for establishing in fall. Or sow indoors at about 70°F, for germination in 14-21 days. Most can be purchased as established plants. Listed are a few top-rated perennial *Dianthus* representative of various types.
D. deltoides 'Zing Rose'	3-8	6 in.	Single; bright rose-red.	
'Essex Witch'	3-7	5 in.	Single, heavily fringed; rose-pink.	
Lace	3-9	12 in.	Finely fringed; crimson, white, orchid.	
D. plumarius 'Spring Beauty'	3-8	12-14 in.	Doubles; pink, rose, salmon, white.	
'Tiny Rubies'	3-8	4-6 in.	Spring blooming. Double; ruby-red.	
CARNATIONS *(D. caryophyllus)*				
Chabaud Giants	All.*	18-20 in.	Heavily fringed; red, white, pink, scarlet, salmon, yellow, bicolors.	These florist favorites can also be grown in your garden. Double-flowered forms come in several sizes. English Giants and Dwarf Grenadin are quite hardy but others, though perennial, are best grown as annuals in most areas, or as perennials in containers wintered over indoors. They bloom during late spring and summer. Sow indoors as for perennial pinks. Stake taller types as necessary.
Dwarf Grenadin	4-9	15-18 in.	Copper-red, salmon-rose, scarlet, rose, pink, white.	
English Giants	4-9	20 in.	Large; red, rose, pink, white, speckled.	
'Juliet'	All.*	10-12 in.	Large; scarlet-red.	
Knight Series	All.*	12 in.	Crimson, scarlet, orange, white, yellow.	
'Scarlet Luminette'	All.*	16-22 in.	Large; brilliant scarlet.	

*Used as an annual in Zones 2-10

The beguiling flowers of bleeding heart (*Dicentra spectabilis*) appear on gracefully arching stems from spring until midsummer.

The regal flowering spires of foxglove (*Digitalis purpurea*) add dramatic vertical accents to shaded gardens from late spring to midsummer.

Cape marigold (*Dimorphotheca* sp.) flowers freely for a long season; provides vibrant garden color for hot and dry problem sites.

Dicentra spectabilis
Bleeding-Heart
Zones: 4-8. To 1-1/2-3 feet.
Perennial.

Bleeding-heart aptly describes the charming, rosy-pink flowers that dangle gracefully from long arching, horizontal stems. During May through June, plants appear to be wearing necklaces of colorful hearts. Bluish-green lush leaves are deeply cut into broad leaflets that are highly ornamental, but begin to die back in midsummer. Plants may reach 3 feet tall, spreading as wide.

Bleeding-heart combines well with other shade-loving plants. It adds a lovely touch to woodland gardens, is a fine border accent, or may be featured as a specimen plant. Plant where other plants will fill in when foliage dies back.

Plants are short-lived in Zones 8 to 10, but long-lived elsewhere if given a cool, moist, lightly shaded spot with well-drained soil rich in organic matter. Soggy soil and hot, dry sun are not tolerated. Full sun is acceptable if site is not too hot. Prepare the soil with compost and plant nursery plants or root-cuttings 18 to 24 inches apart. May sow seeds directly in the garden in fall, which will give them the required winter chilling. Keep area mulched, evenly moist, and fertilize each year as new growth begins. Cut back foliage at season's end.

The white-flowered variety 'Alba' is sometimes available. Fringed bleeding-heart, *Dicentra eximia*, is an American wildflower with upright stalks of dusty rose, fringed hearts that bloom from spring through summer.

Digitalis purpurea
Foxglove
Zones: 4-10. To 2-5 feet.
Biennial.

The elegant beauty of foxglove's flowering spires adds beautiful vertical accents to formal borders in early summer. Tubular bells, 2 to 3 inches long, open sequentially from the base of the spire upwards over a period of many weeks. Blossoms line one side of the stalk and hang gracefully on short stems. Flower colors may be soft purple, white, pink, or yellow, all with throats spotted deep purple. Plants reach 2 to 5 feet tall.

Most foxgloves are biennials, forming a rosette of large, lance-shaped, hairy leaves the first year, sending up a tall flowering spike the second year, and then dying. Plants often perpetuate themselves by re-seeding. To assure renewal, sow seeds in May or August for blooms the following season. Tiny seeds can be mixed with sand and lightly broadcast over a prepared garden seedbed, or you can set out nursery plants after last spring frost. Space seedlings 15 to 24 inches apart.

Foxglove does well in full sun or light shade in most areas, needs shade in hot areas. Even moisture, and a rich, well-drained soil high in organic matter are preferred. Water in summer and mulch lightly to keep soil cool and moist. Fertilize in early spring. Remove stalks after seeds have fallen. A second flowering often can be induced by removing spent flower stalks before seeds set. Watch for powdery mildew, aphids, mealybugs, and snails, especially on young plants.

'Excelsior Hybrids' are top-rated; feature horizontally held flowers encircling a 4- to 5-foot stalk. Flower colors range from pink, mauve, and white to lavender.

Dimorphotheca sinuata
Cape Marigold
Zones: 2-10. To 6-12 inches.
Annual.

Cape marigold, like *Arctotis*, is often called "African daisy"—and in appearance, cultural requirements, and garden uses is almost identical. Dark-centered daisylike flowers, 1-1/2 to 3-1/2 inches wide, range from white to yellow, orange, apricot, and salmon, with lavender undersides. In Zone 10 cape marigold can be planted for winter and spring color. Native to the South African veldt, it provides garden color in hot, dry areas (though use isn't limited to such areas).

Provide full sun and well-drained soil. Only during active

growth does it need regular watering. It grows easily from seed and reseeds freely. If you want to start it indoors for early garden bloom, sow 4 to 5 weeks before planting time. Germination takes 10 to 15 days at around 70°F.

Dimorphotheca is sold as a mix of several colors.

Echinacea purpurea
Purple Coneflower
Zones: 3-9. To 3-5 feet.
Perennial.

Purple coneflower has a prominent bristly domed center, almost metallic in appearance, surrounded by pink, rose, or white petals. Plants form open clumps of many upright 3- to 5-foot-tall stems and bloom from midsummer to fall. Flowers dry into seedheads that are often used in dried arrangements. Muted green leaves are clustered at the base.

Purple coneflower is a rugged plant for dry, exposed sites where flowers will add bright color all summer long. Also useful in borders and meadow gardens.

Nurseries offer transplants in popular colors, or you can sow seed of selected varieties in fall or early spring for first-year flowers. Plants will reseed but do not retain varietal colors. Divide plants every 3 or 4 years in spring.

Although durable under adverse conditions, keep plants in top form with an occasional watering and spring feeding with a balanced fertilizer. A sandy loam is best. For larger flowers, and a longer blooming season, cut spent flower stems before seeds set. Damaged leaves may indicate Japanese beetles. Also watch for aphids.

Several top-rated varieties are available. 'Bright Star' is richly colored rosy-red; cones are luminous maroon; plants stay neat. 'The King' has purple flowers. 'White Lustre' bears white flowers with copper-brown cones.

Endymion sp.
Bluebell
(See *Scilla*)

Eranthis hyemalis
Winter Aconite
Zones: 4-8. To 4 inches.
Tuber.

Winter aconite is one of the earliest-blooming bulbs, flowering in mid- to late winter, often surrounded by melting snow. One of its less-known names, in fact, is New Year's gift.

The golden-yellow blossoms last about 10 days, but the foliage remains, creating a lovely ground cover, until early summer. Mix with other bulbs in a rock garden or woodland setting, or use as a ground cover under shrubs and trees. It spreads rapidly.

In early fall, plant the plump tubers horizontally, 2 inches deep and 3 inches apart, in moist, fast-draining loam, where they will be undisturbed. If tubers are shrivelled, soak them in water overnight before planting. Winter aconite accepts full sun in cool-summer climates but elsewhere prefers some shade. Water dormant plants during dry summers to keep tubers from drying out.

Euphorbia marginata
Snow-on-the-Mountain
Zones: 2-10. To 12-18 inches.
Annual.

Snow-on-the-mountain makes a refreshing display of colored petal-like bracts. The predominantly white bracts are held above white-rimmed green leaves—the effect is striking and cool-looking through the hot summer months. Used to cover dry banks and other difficult areas, mixed into beds or borders, snow-on-the-mountain quickly proves its worth. It also makes an unusual cut flower if cut ends are seared immediately with flame.

Not the least of its virtues are toughness and self-sufficiency. It adapts to rich or poor, moist or dry soil in baking sun or light shade and requires no care. It reseeds so freely that it may become a handsome garden weed. Avoid getting its milky sap on skin or in eyes, since sap can cause a rash.

Sow seeds outdoors after last spring frost or indoors 6 to 8 weeks earlier, for germination in 10 to 15 days at 70° to 75°F. Or plant nursery-grown seedlings.

Purple coneflower *(Echinacea purpurea)* is a rugged, widely adapted plant that brings bright flowers to dry or difficult garden areas during late summer and fall.

The golden-yellow blossoms of winter aconite *(Eranthis hyemalis)* decorate the ground often before the snow has melted, a prelude to spring.

Snow-on-the-mountain *(Euphorbia marginata)* reseeds freely, quickly covering difficult sites with white-rimmed green foliage topped through summer with showy white bracts.

An evergreen perennial for warm climates, blue marguerite (Felicia amelloides) forms a shrublike plant graced with deep blue daisy flowers held on sturdy slim stems.

Freesia (Freesia x hybrida) flowers come in a range of sparkling colors and have a memorable fragrance. Grown in containers, they provide radiant color indoors or out.

The nodding blossoms of checkered lily (Fritillaria meleagris) appear in midspring to add visual excitement to informal garden settings.

Felicia amelloides

Blue Marguerite, Blue Daisy

Evergreen perennial in Zones 8-10. Annual elsewhere. To 1-1/2-3 feet.

Blue marguerite is a sun-loving perennial from southern Africa where summers are hot and dry, and winters mild. The Southwest, Pacific Coast, and Southeast Seaboard have climatic conditions suitable for growing blue marguerite. Elsewhere it is used as an annual.

Plants form low mats of arching stems, spreading to 4 feet from a central base. Small, oval, grassy-green evergreen leaves cover the stems. Deep, sky-blue, yellow-centered flowers are held above the foliage on strong stems from mid-spring into summer. Keeping faded blooms clipped extends blooming.

Blue marguerite is stunning in warm, sunny gardens. Use as an evergreen edging, rock garden plant, or in containers and hanging baskets. Take advantage of its spreading habit by planting among terraced stones or to soften the edge of a raised planter.

Blue marguerite performs best with average care, and is not fussy about soil if adequate drainage is provided. Fertilize in early spring. Establish plantings with nursery seedlings, spaced 12 to 24 inches apart. Pinch stems periodically to maintain a dense mat. Cut back up to three-quarters of the foliage in fall to rejuvenate plants; divide every 3 or 4 years.

Freesia x hybrida

Freesia

Hardy in Zones 9-10. Tender elsewhere. To 18 inches.
Corm.

This elegant plant produces fragrant single or double flowers that open a few at a time along an arching stem. Flowers are usually 2 inches wide and come in every color of the rainbow. White, cream, and yellow ones are generally most fragrant. Telecote and Dutch hybrids have the largest flowers.

Freesia is winter-hardy only in mild climates, where it blooms over a long season in early spring. Elsewhere, dig the corms in fall, store over winter, and replant in spring for summer bloom.

In fall, plant corms 3 inches deep, pointed side up, and 2 to 3 inches apart, in fast-draining loam. Provide full sun or light shade. Keep moist when in growth. Groups of 5 or more corms are effective in a rock garden or flower border.

Freesia may be grown indoors. For continuous bloom, plant pots at 2-week intervals, from August to January. Flowers appear 10 to 12 weeks after planting. Keep moist and locate in a cool, bright spot until roots develop. Then move to full sun. Fertilize every 2 weeks. Support spikes if necessary. Dry out soil after blooming.

Fritillaria

Fritillary

Bulbs.

This group of Old and New World lily relatives includes several curious-looking plants that do best in areas with cold winters.

Fritillaria imperialis
Crown-Imperial
Zones: 5-8. To 2-4 feet.

Crown-imperial is a bizarre-looking plant—atop its tall, purple-speckled stem is a cluster of 2- to 4-inch bell-like orange, red, or yellow flowers crowned with a tuft of foliage. Everything is intriguing about this plant except its scent, which may be unpleasant.

Crown-imperial blooms in early spring along with midseason daffodils. It prefers full sun and good soil and should be kept moist when in bloom and on the dry side afterward. Plant bulbs 6 inches deep and 12 inches apart. Use in the background, behind lower plants.

Fritillaria meleagris
Checkered Lily
Zones: 4-8. To 15 inches.

Checkered lily is also called snake's-head and Guinea-hen tulip. All names refer to its flowers, which are checked in a pattern resembling snakeskin. The flowers are nodding and about 2 inches long, borne 2 or 3 atop a slender stem. Checked flowers come in purple or white. Occasionally blossoms are pure yellow or white.

Checkered lily blooms in April and the delicate foliage soon disappears. Plant bulbs in groups, 3 or 4 inches deep and as far apart, in a woodland or rock-garden setting. Provide deep rich soil, partial shade, and even moisture.

Gaillardia x grandiflora
Blanket Flower, Gaillardia

Zones: 3-10. To 1-3 feet.
Perennial.

This superb hybrid is the result of crossing two species native to the United States: *G. aristata* and *G. pulchella*. It features 4-inch daisy-shaped blossoms with toothed petals colored scarlet-red, maroon, bronze, and yellow, often banded with yellow. The flower centers are large brown, yellow, purple, or red domes. Blanket flower forms a 1- to 3-foot plant with upright or sprawling stems that originate from a mass of basal foliage. Long, hairy leaves are a soft muted green. Blooms from June until fall frost.

The warm colors work well in combination with red salvia, yellow coreopsis, and shasta daisy. Dwarf varieties make good border accents. Cut flowers are striking in bouquets.

To propagate, plant root cuttings, divisions, or seed of a known variety. (Garden seed may not breed true.) Broadcast seeds in a prepared bed after last spring frost. Seeds germinate in 10 to 14 days and flower their first season. To stimulate growth, and to provide divisions for transplanting, drive a spade into the soil surrounding 2- to 3-year-old plants, breaking roots as if transplanting. New shoots will grow on rhizomes to use for transplanting later.

Blanket flower is tolerant of heat and full sun. A well-drained soil is essential. Watch for and promptly control whiteflies, aphids, and mildew. Should leaf spot or aster yellows virus be a problem, diseased plants should be removed.

Top-rated varieties are: 'Golden Goblin', 'Sun Gold', 'Yellow Queen', 'Monarch', 'Dazzler', and 'Burgundy'. 'Goblin' is a dwarf.

Annual blanket flower, *G. pulchella*, has similar flowers, grows to 2 feet. Leaves are softer and 5 to 6 inches long.

Galanthus
Snowdrop
Bulbs.

Snowdrops flower for a month in late winter or earliest spring, creating a welcome display. They spread readily, quickly forming clumps of slender leaves and nodding white flowers. Flowers have 6 petals. The outer 3 petals are larger and pure white, the inner ones are tipped with a green dot.

Snowdrops make excellent informal mass plantings under deciduous trees and shrubs, in rock gardens, and in lawns. (Do not mow until summer.) Plant bulbs in fall in groups 3 to 4 inches deep, 2 to 4 inches apart. Snowdrops prefer moist, well-drained soil and full sun. Since foliage withers in late spring, they can be planted where deciduous trees cast summer shade.

Galanthus elwesii
Giant Snowdrop
Zones: 4-9. To 4-12 inches.

Giant snowdrops form substantial clumps of 1-1/2-inch-long flowers and 3/4-inch-wide leaves. They grow farther south than *G. nivalis* but are slightly less cold hardy.

Galanthus nivalis
Commom Snowdrop
Zones: 3-8. To 4-12 inches.

This dainty spring favorite has flowers 3/4 to 1 inch long and leaves 1/4 inch wide. 'Flore Pleno', a double form, has 3 long outer petals and a tight cluster of green-marked or tinted inner petals.

Blanket flower *(Gaillardia x grandiflora)* takes heat and full sun in stride, providing bright garden color from June until frost.

The gracefully nodding white blossoms of common snowdrop *(Galanthus nivalis)* appear for a month in early spring.

Transvaal daisy *(Gerbera jamesonii)* is a handsome sun-loving perennial for mild climates; grows as an annual in cold regions.

The stately spires of gladiolus *(Gladiolus x hortulanus)* add dramatic vertical accents.

Gerbera jamesonii
Transvaal Daisy, Gerbera Daisy

Evergreen perennial in Zones 8-10. Annual elsewhere. To 18 inches.

Transvaal daisies produce giant colorful daisylike blossoms on tall leafless stalks that arise from a basal clump of foliage. The single or double row of long petals radiates from a broad, tufted yellow center.

New shapes and forms in rainbow colors are continuously being developed by hybridizers. Colors currently available include pure red, orange, yellow, and pink as well as many pastels. Blooms in summer and fall.

Transvaal daisy is sometimes difficult to use effectively in the garden because of the long, bare flowering stalks. Arrange plants in rows in a cutting garden, or in clusters in the midground of a bed. Transvaal daisy is an excellent plant for growing in containers. In northern climates grow as an annual, in the greenhouse, or indoors. Makes a superb cut flower, though stems tend to bend toward the light.

Transvaal daisy is deep-rooted and must have excellent drainage. Sandy soil or planting mixes provide best growing conditions. Soggy soil is not acceptable. Loves sun, but should have partial shade in hot, dry climates. Slugs and snails may sometimes require control measures.

Success with seed depends upon using fresh seed. Buying one-gallon nursery stock in flower is more reliable and assures your getting the colors you want. Space plants 12 to 18 inches apart, setting crowns slightly above soil level. Divide plants every 3 or 4 years in early spring. Both container- and garden-grown plants enjoy regular feeding and deep watering during growth. Allow to partially dry out between waterings when dormant in winter. Mulch plants heavily to protect from freezing in winter and move containers indoors to a cool spot before fall frost.

Gladiolus x hortulanus
Corn Flag, Gladiolus, Sword Lily

Zones: 9-10. To 30 inches to 5 feet. Corm.

When planted in large or small clumps of a single color, gladioluses make a dramatic vertical effect. Flowers open from bottom to top on tall spikes, over several weeks. The full spectrum of colors, except blue, is available and the 'Butterfly' varieties offer bicolored and ruffled blossoms.

Spikes of some varieties reach 5 feet tall, but types such as the Tiny Tot series, called "miniatures", reach only 3 feet.

Gladioluses like full sun, and rich, moist, well-drained soil. As spikes grow, stake and tie them to prevent toppling by wind or rain. Plant corms as soon as danger of frost is past and as late as early or midsummer. Plant at 2-week intervals for continuous blooming. Set tiny corms about 2 inches deep and large ones 3 to 6 inches deep, 4 inches apart, in fertilized soil.

Unless you live in Zones 9 or 10 or have a sheltered, heavily mulched garden in Zones 7 or 8, dig corms after first frost in fall and store over winter. If thrips are a problem, dust stored bulbs with an insecticide and also treat soil.

Gomphrena globosa
Globe Amaranth

Zones: 2-10. To 6-24 inches. Annual.

Globe amaranth gives more enduring pleasure for less effort than nearly any other garden flower. In almost any soil, poor and dry or moist and rich, *Gomphrena* produces lush foliage and colorful 3/4- to 1-1/2 inch cloverlike flowers, summer through fall. Flowers are everlasting (dry on the stalks) and are favorites for dried arrangements. Numerous rose, purple, lavender, white, orange, or pink blooms sit atop stems clothed in large, pointed leaves. Taller types are useful in beds and borders, and dwarfs make colorful edging.

Purchase seedlings or sow seeds. Sow outdoors after last spring frost, or indoors 6 to 8 weeks before planting time, at about 70° to 75°F. Seeds germinate in 10 to 20 days. Plant in full sun and well-drained soil, 8 to 15 inches apart. Water until seedlings are established after which regular watering is optional.

Globosa mix, 18 to 24 inches tall, has reddish-purple, white, pink, rose, or lavender flowers. Dwarf 'Buddy' has full-size purple flowers on 6- to 8-inch plants. Orange globe amaranth (*G. haageana*), 20 inches tall, has bright orange flower heads. A purple variety grows to 24 inches.

Helianthus annuus

Sunflower

Zones: 2-10. To 15 inches - 12 feet. Annual.

Whether you choose 12-foot sunflowers with 20-inch, seed-laden flower heads, or any of the various smaller sunflowers, they will reward you in late summer and fall with showy flowers that turn throughout the day to follow the sun. The giant common sunflower, native to the Great Plains, and its slightly smaller hybrids have tall sturdy stalks and large flower heads with brownish-purple centers and golden petals. Purely ornamental sunflowers are hybrids ranging in size from 15 inches to 5 feet. Flowers may have traditional colors or combinations of white, mahogany, golden-brown, orange, and even rosy-lavender.

Largest sunflowers make bold accents against a wall or fence, or in a sunny corner, and can provide screening. Smaller types are useful in borders and beds.

Sow seeds outdoors, in place, after last spring frost. Growth is so rapid that early indoor sowing is unnecessary. Space all but dwarfs at least 18 or 20 inches apart. The large types prefer rich, well-drained, moist soil, but purely ornamental types adapt to nearly any soil and tolerate drought. All are heat tolerant and need full sun. Support with sturdy stakes. Wrap ripening heads with net to protect seeds from birds and squirrels.

'Mammoth' and 'Gray Stripe' are excellent for seed. Top-rated for ornament and seed are 'Sunbird' and 'Sunburst', to 6-feet tall. For ornament are: 'Sungold', a 5-foot yellow double; 'Teddy Bear', a 2-foot golden-yellow double; 'Italian White', 4 feet tall with 4-inch cream or white flowers; 'Piccolo', with 4-inch single yellow flowers on 4-foot plants; and Dwarf Sungold mix, 15 inches tall, with double yellow flowers.

Helichrysum bracteatum

Strawflower, Everlasting, Immortelle

Zones: 2-10. To 12-36 inches. Annual.

Strawflower is an everlasting that does double duty as a colorful garden flower and as a cut flower, fresh or dried. The many-petaled, double, daisylike 1-3/4- to 2-1/2-inch flowers gradually open wide enough to reveal button centers. Colors include crimson, red, rose, pink, salmon, bronze, gold, and white. Strawflower blooms midsummer to frost.

Tall strawflowers sometimes look ungainly in beds but are good in a cutting garden. Shorter types are beautiful in gardens and are useful for mass planting in difficult dry, sunny sites.

Sow outdoors, uncovered, after the last spring frost or indoors 4 to 6 weeks earlier, maintaining 70°F for germination in 7 to 10 days. (Purchasing seedlings or starting indoors is better because strawflower needs a long growing season to bloom.) Set seedlings 10 to 15 inches apart in fast-draining soil and full sun. To dry flowers, cut before centers open and hang upside down.

Larger strawflowers (24 to 36 inches tall) are sold as mixes. Top-rated are: Tall Mixed Colors, Monstrosum Mixed, and Roggli Mixed Original. Smaller: Bikini strain (12 to 14 inches), including Bright Bikinis mixture; and Dwarf Mixed Colors, to 18 inches.

Globe amaranth (*Gomphrena globosa*) produces colorful, everlasting flowers from summer to fall.

Sunflowers (*Helianthus* sp.) range in size from 15- inch- to 12-foot-tall plants.

Strawflower (*Helichrysum bracteatum*) adds vibrant color to the garden from midsummer until fall frost. Used in fresh or dried bouquets.

Daylilies *(Hemerocallis* hybrids) make beautiful mass plantings and provide weeks of color in flower borders and naturalistic settings.

The low tufted mounds of foliage of coralbells *(Heuchera sanguinea)* are adorned with airy clusters of bell-like blossoms from June to September.

Hemerocallis hybrids
Daylily
Zones: 3-10. To 1-7 feet.
Perennial

This is one of the most valuable and beautiful plants for low-maintenance gardens. Daylilies thrive in almost any conditions and require very little care. Plants form clumps of arching leaves and spread by fleshy roots. Although each large trumpet-shaped flower lasts only one day, flowers are produced in quantity for about a month. Typically blooming in midsummer, daylilies that flower anywhere from May to October are available, making it possible to enjoy a long blooming season.

Blossoms open atop branching stems in open or closely held clusters. The flowers are 3 to 8 inches across with recurved petals, some with ruffled or frilled edges, in shades of yellow, orange, pink, peach, rusty-red, or maroon, and a few varieties are fragrant or bicolored.

Plant daylilies in any garden situation or naturalize along a fence or in a shady spot. Daylilies also may be planted on slopes to help control erosion. The possibilities for their use are endless.

Daylilies tolerate garden extremes and thrive under average conditions. Avoid overly rich soil and fertilize poor soil only lightly or plants will form coarse leaves and few flowers. Water during drought conditions. Blossoms tend to last longest in partial shade, although plants tolerate sun.

Daylilies endure for years. Clumps should be divided when flower production diminishes, or leaves become overcrowded. To propagate, cut sections of clumps, with both roots and leaves attached, in early spring. Plant 2 feet apart.

Hundreds of varieties are available in many sizes, forms, and bloom seasons, and have been extensively hybridized from the common roadside orange daylily. Evergreen kinds are available for warm climate zones.

Heuchera sanguinea
Coralbells
Zones: 3-10. To 10-24 inches.
Perennial.

Coralbells add a delicate grace to any flower garden with their airy spikes of tiny flowers on tall slender stems. Flowering begins in June and extends to September if faded flowers are trimmed. Deep coral-pink is the traditional color, with hybrids in white, light pink, and red.

Leaves are rounded, 2 to 4 inches long and have wavy, scalloped edges. They are densely packed and the leaf mass expands slowly from shallow woody roots to form tufted mounds that are attractive year-round. Some varieties have silver- or bronze-marbled leaves. Foliage reddens with cold weather.

All *Heuchera* species are native to North America. *H. sanguinea* is from the Southwest. Use in naturalistic plantings along stream beds or in rock gardens or formal borders.

Almost any garden soil is suitable as long as it is well-drained. Add organic matter to particularly poor and heavy soils. The dappled, cool light of overhead trees provides a perfect setting. Plants tolerate full sun if temperatures are not too high and they are watered regularly.

Coralbells should be planted in spring so that roots are well established before winter. Divisions or transplants give first-season color. Plant crowns one inch below soil surface and space 12 inches apart. Seeds need light to germinate, do not cover with soil. Seedlings should be thinned to 12 inches apart.

Once established, plants are undemanding. Short dry periods are tolerated but average watering is best. Fertilize with a balanced formula, and provide a winter mulch where soil freezes. Check plants early in spring for heaving damage, and press any elevated plants back into the soil.

'White Cloud' and 'June Bride' are top-rated white-flowering varieties. 'Chatterbox' has generous rose-pink blossoms; 'Martin Bells' coral-red; 'Pluie de Feu' bright cherry. 'Rosamundi' is an all-time favorite coral. 'Chartreuse' is unusual with yellow-green flowers. 'Bressingham Hybrids' have extra-long stems.

Hibiscus moscheutos
Rose Mallow, Swamp Rose Mallow, Wild Cotton
Zones: 6-10. To 5-8 feet.
Perennial.

Robust growth, to 8 feet tall and 3 feet wide under ideal conditions, qualifies rose mallow as one of the tallest perennials. Oval, pointed leaves with whitish undersides are 8 inches long, and showy flowers are 8 to 12 inches across—in perfect proportion to the plant's grand scale.

Typical hibiscus-shaped flowers bloom at branch ends from mid-July to first fall frost. Flower colors include rose, pink, white, and red, usually spotted with crimson.

Plant size dictates a background garden position, and the dense foliage makes rose mallow an excellent filler along a fence or used to add summer color in a new shrub border.

Rose mallows are native to the marshes of the eastern United States. Plants adapt well to most garden conditions, but growth will be most lush in rich organic soils kept evenly wet. Shorter though equally fine plants develop under less desirable conditions. Fertilize periodically throughout the growing season and water deeply on a regular basis. Plants should be protected from dry winds and reflected heat.

Plant nursery stock or divisions in spring. Bury top of crown 4 inches below soil level. Seeds germinate quickly and produce blossoms their first season. Nick seed coats, or soak seeds until they no longer float, before planting directly in the garden. Thin seedlings 2 to 3 feet apart. Second-generation seeds do not retain parent variety qualities.

Varietal names of top-rated forms are delightfully descriptive of their large flowers: 'Cotton Candy';

'Frisbee', a dwarf variety; 'Super Clown'; and 'Giant Raspberry Rose'. Select 'Southern Belle' for its compact, 3- to 4-foot stature, and 10-inch flowers in mixed colors.

Hyacinthus orientalis hybrids
Hyacinth, Dutch Hyacinth, Garden Hyacinth
Zones: 7-10. To 8-15 inches.
Bulb.

With its heady fragrance and pristine beauty, Dutch hyacinth has few rivals in springtime gardens. Each bulb sends up a sturdy, symmetrical spike of bell-shaped flowers. Colors are white, pink, salmon, red, yellow, blue, purple, or amethyst and some varieties have double flowers.

Hyacinths look best when planted in masses in formal rows, not scattered plantings or meager clumps. Plantings of a single color or a simple, harmonious combination are highly effective.

Space hyacinths carefully at a uniform depth. They should be planted 6 to 7 inches deep and 6 to 8 inches apart in early fall. Deep, fast-draining, sandy humus and full sun are best. Water regularly in fall and in spring until foliage dies.

Flower spikes are tightly packed with blossoms their first year, but are less dense in following years. Though less showy, the sparser spikes are more graceful and just as fragrant.

Hyacinths are one of the prettiest and easiest bulbs for forcing indoors. One hyacinth in a hyacinth glass or several in a large pot can delight the nose and eye almost as satisfactorily as a field of them.

Top-rated hyacinth varieties are 'Bismarck' (bright blue), 'City of Haarlem' (yellow), 'Pink Pearl', 'Jan Bos' (red), 'L'Innocence' (white), and 'Lady Derby' (apricot-pink). Occasionally you may find Roman hyacinth (*H. orientalis albulus*, usually sold as *H. romanus*), white to light blue, more open and earlier blooming than Dutch hyacinth. Other bulbs sold as hyacinths belong to other genera.

A statuesque background plant, rose mallow (*Hibiscus moscheutos*) is a robust grower with lush foliage; bears huge flowers from midsummer until fall.

Hyacinth bulbs (*Hyacinthus orientalis* hybrids) produce flowers with a heady fragrance, shown above and below, widely used for indoor or outdoor display.

Edging candytuft *(Iberis sempervirens)* is a superb perennial for rock gardens; its deep green foliage is frosted with snowy blossoms, shown below, for a long season.

Iberis

Candytuft

Perennial and annual.

Candytufts are low-growing garden plants that are ideal for rock gardens, as edging for flower borders, or for planting in front of shrubs. Flat clusters of four-petaled flowers obscure the foliage for weeks in spring, making a perfect accompaniment for late-flowering bulbs.

Iberis sempervirens

Edging Candytuft

Zones: 4-10. To 4-12 inches.
Perennial.

No neater, more pristine flower graces any garden than edging candytuft. Pure white flowers eclipse the dark green narrow leaves for several weeks in late spring. Plants spread to 8 to 24 inches and make a superlative edging, small-area ground cover, or border plant, but candytuft's graceful habit is perhaps best displayed in a rock garden.

In hot climates provide partial shade, elsewhere full sun or light shade. Fast-draining soil is necessary and moderate dryness is acceptable. In cold areas where snow cover is slight, lay evergreen branches over the plant to protect the foliage in winter. It may rebloom in summer or fall if faded flowers are clipped.

Plant nursery seedlings or sow seeds outdoors in early spring. Or sow seed indoors at 55° to 60°F for germination in 8 to 20 days in late winter. Plant seedlings 8 to 10 inches apart. Cuttings may be taken in midsummer.

Popular varieties are 'Snowflake', 10 to 12 inches tall, spreading to 24 inches, and 'Little Gem', the best for edging, 4 inches tall, spreading to 8 inches.

A similar perennial, often sold as *I. jucunda*, is *Aethionema cordifolium* (Lebanon cress), evergreen and pink-flowered, blooming in May and June, hardy to Zone 5. Culture is the same as for *I. sempervirens*, except that full sun and slightly alkaline soil are best.

Iberis umbellata
Globe Candytuft

Zones: 2-10. To 8-15 inches.
Annual.

This candytuft makes an attractive companion for late-blooming spring bulbs. Flower colors include pink, rose, carmine, crimson, lavender, and white.

This cool-season annual blooms from early spring into summer; the longest blooming occurs in mild-summer climates, where staggered sowing prolongs the bloom season. Sow seeds outdoors in late fall for early spring bloom in Zones 3-7; in fall for late winter bloom in Zones 8-10. Or purchase seedlings.

Fairy strain, 8 inches high and in mixed colors, is a good edging and rock garden plant.

Impatiens wallerana
Impatiens, Busy Lizzy

Zones: 2-10. To 8-20 inches.
Annual.

Impatiens is a special delight to most gardeners and a godsend to those with very shady gardens. Most varieties are compact and mounding, with many-branched, bright green or reddish stems and neat, pointed leaves. In beds and borders, pots, and hanging baskets, its masses of luminous 1- to 2-inch, flat flowers are colorful from late spring or early summer until fall frost. Colors are white or shades of pink, orange, red, and burgundy. Some are bicolored, and one series has double, bicolored flowers.

Plant nursery seedlings, or sow seeds outdoors after last frost or indoors 6 to 8 weeks before planting time. Germination takes 10 to 18 days at around 70°F. Plant seedlings 12 to 18 inches apart (closer in planters) in rich, well-drained soil, in light or medium shade. *Impatiens* tolerates more sun in coastal climates. Warmth, infrequent light feeding with a balanced fertilizer, and drying out slightly between waterings encourage compact growth and good flowering.

Impatiens (Impatiens wallerana) is a choice plant for creating a sparkling display of vibrant color in shady garden areas. Blossoms blanket plants all during the summer season.

Impatiens

Series or Variety	Colors	Comments
DWARF (8-10 in.)		
Super Elfin	Fuchsia, orange, orchid, rose, pink, hot pink, scarlet, salmon, red, white, bicolors.	Profuse flowering, good branching at base of plants, and very compact habit make this series especially suitable for hanging baskets and pots as well as beds. 'Blush' is delicate pink with red eye; 'Lipstick', deep rose with white eye. Others are named for colors. Super Elfin varieties are also sold as a mix.
INTERMEDIATE (10-12 in.)		
Futura	Burgundy, coral, orange, orchid, pink, red, rose-pink, scarlet, white, pale rose.	The all-time favorite series, useful for hanging baskets, planters, and beds. Growth habit is compact and mounding. Varieties are named for colors; often sold as a mix. 'Wild Rose' is especially iridescent.
Novette	Bright orange, deep orange ('Scarlet'), orange, deep rose, pink, red, salmon, violet, white, bicolor.	Same growth habit and uses as Futura series. 'Rose & White Star' is bicolored. 'Bright Orange' has bronze leaves.
Twinkles	White-star pattern on fuchsia, red, rose, scarlet.	Same growth habit and uses as Futura and Novette series. Sold by color names or as a mix.
TALL (12-16 in.)		
'Blitz'	Intense scarlet.	Other impatiens have 1- to 2-in. flowers, but 'Blitz' has 2-1/2-in. ones. Bronze foliage. Excellent in beds and hanging baskets. An award winner.
Duet	White with red, scarlet, and deep rose.	Double and semidouble bicolored flowers on large, relatively upright plants. Useful for beds and large containers. Sold as a mix. Can grow taller than other tall impatiens—to 18-20 in.
Grandé	Coral, orange, orchid, purple, red, rose, white.	Large flowers on plants suitable for all uses. Sold by color names or as a mix.
'Tangeglow'	Very bright orange.	Suitable for all uses.
Zigzag	White with scarlet, orange, pink, rose, salmon, or purple.	Striking bicolors sold as a mix. Suitable for all uses.

Morning-glory *(Ipomoea purpurea)* clambers quickly up fence, trellis, or bank. Ephemeral flowers bloom in early morning from midsummer until fall.

Siberian iris *(Iris sibirica)* is elegant grown by stream or pool; adds grace to any garden site.

Ipomoea purpurea
Morning-Glory
Zones: 2-10. To 8-20 feet.
Annual.

While most flowers mark the seasons, morning-glory also marks the freshest time of day, its funnel-shaped flowers unfurling at dawn and closing with the midday heat. Heart-shaped leaves and slender buds decorate the vines during the rest of the day. Modern varieties remain open longer, often all day during cloudy weather. *Ipomoea* blooms early summer until frost.

The vigorous vines need support to display flowers and foliage most effectively, and the twining stems waste no time in climbing. Plant at the base of a fence or trellis, or use to cover a wall or a bank. (Provide something for it to wrap around.)

It's best to sow seeds directly outdoors after the last spring frost since seedlings are difficult to transplant. Nick the hard surface of each seed, or soak in warm water for 24 hours before sowing. Needs full sun and light, well-drained sandy soil. Soil that is too fertile produces foliage and few flowers. Water ocassionally

Many top-rated varieties are widely available. 'Heavenly Blue Improved' and 'Early Heavenly Blue' have 4- to 5-inch, sky-blue flowers with pale centers. 'Pearly Gates' has 4-1/2-inch pure white flowers. 'Scarlett O'Hara' has 4- to 5-inch crimson-carmine flowers. Japanese Imperial Giant mixture has white, pink, rose, red, purple, and blue flowers to 6 inches wide, many of them bicolored. The Early Call series, flowers 4 inches wide, are sold by color—'Blue', 'Rose', and as a mixture including pink, lavender-pink, and violet.

Iris
Flag, Iris, Fleur-de-Lis
Zones: 3-10. To 3-48 inches.
Rhizomes and bulbs.

These elegant plants offer diversity of form, color, texture, and size for every garden, container, and vase. Most have delicately fragrant, exquisitely shaped flowers. Depending upon the species or hybrid group, irises can be found to bloom during much of the gardening year, from the very early reticulata irises to the Japanese, Siberian, and late bearded irises far into summer. Hybridizers are refining already-developed bearded irises that bloom a second time, in fall.

Every iris has the same perfectly symmetrical blossom structure: 3 *standards*, the upright petals of most irises; and 3 *falls*, the outer, usually pendulous petals. Many falls, even some standards, are blotched, shaded, feathered, or veined. Blossoms are often bi- or tricolored. Colors include almost the whole spectrum, lacking only true red. Petals of some irises are substantial and waxy, others gossamer-delicate and, on close inspection, sparkling and crystalline.

Leaves as well as flowers are strikingly attractive. Foliage is grasslike or boldly swordlike—always creating, on small or large scale, a distinctive texture in the garden.

Landscape uses of irises are many and diverse. Crested iris can create a spring and early-summer ground cover, and it makes a brilliant feature in a small planter. Reticulata irises provide exquisite early-spring detailing in the rock garden, or in large drifts of mixed early bulbs. Tall bearded irises, with their strongly vertical habit and massive display of color, are effective in large formal beds, or in clumps in mixed borders. Siberian irises' stateliness is well displayed next to a garden pool—and pots of Japanese iris can be submerged, during growth and bloom, so that they become dramatic, willowy aquatic plants.

If situated properly, most irises are virtually care-free, though iris borer can sometimes be serious.

The chart lists top-rated types and a few of their best varieties. Other types are occasionally sold, but those listed are widely available and easily grown over much of the continent. The system used in the chart to classify bearded irises is from the American Iris Society.

Iris *(Iris)* offers a broad range of plant types and flower forms, so that one type or another can be enjoyed in nearly every garden situation. Dutch iris, above left; bearded iris, above center; Japanese iris, above right.

Iris

	Zones	Height	Flower Description	Comments
BEARDED IRIS				
Miniature Dwarf	4-9	to 8 in.	Fuzzy "beard" on each fall, often of brilliantly contrasting color. Flowers often bicolored, ruffled, frilled; colors include all but true red and green. Some ("picatas") have pale falls edged with color. Flowers of Standard Talls (the most available) often to 6 in. wide.	Bearded iris bloom just after late tulips, on into early summer. Some smaller types start earlier. All require full sun and drainage and grow best in rich soil; regular watering through bloom season is best. Plant rhizomes flat, beneath 1 in. or less of soil, 12-18 in. apart, in late summer or early fall. Divide every 3 or 4 years, about 6 weeks after blooming. Varieties of Standard Talls are usually sold as "Bearded Irises." A few top-rated varieties are 'Lemon Brocade' (yellow, ruffled, midseason), 'Esther Fay' (pink with red beard, ruffled), 'Stepping Out' (white edged with violet, midseason to late), 'Study in Black' (red-black, early midseason), and 'Margarita' (white standards and beard, blue-purple falls, midseason to late).
Standard Dwarf	4-9	9-15 in.		
Intermediate	4-9	15-27 in.		
Miniature Tall	4-9	15-27 in.		
Border	4-9	15-27 in.		
Standard Tall	4-9	27-48 in.		
CRESTED IRIS				
Iris cristata **Dwarf Crested Iris**	6-10	3-6 in.	Lilac-blue, 2-1/2 in. wide, with yellow crest at base of falls. White variety, 'Alba', sometimes available.	Best in partial shade, forming colonies and creating ground cover as rhizomes creep along surface. Leaves die early spring to midsummer. Blooms late spring. Needs drainage and some moisture. Perfect for rock garden or woodland. Plant close to surface, in fall. East Coast native.
BEARDLESS IRIS				
Iris kaempferi **Japanese Iris**	5-9	2-3 ft	Huge single or double flowers (6-9 in.), flat, crepe-textured, intricately veined. White, blues, purples, lavenders, roses.	Requires heavy watering while growing; during spring and early summer can be grown in ponds in slightly submerged containers; but well-watered garden soil suffices. Likes less water in other seasons. Needs acid soil, full sun (light shade in hottest areas). Plant 3 in. deep, spring or early fall. Late blooming. Higo strain, to 2 ft tall, widely sold.
Iris sibirica **Siberian Iris and Hybrids**	3-9	2-4 ft	Elegant 2- to 4-in. flowers, 2 or 3 per stem, white or shades of blue, mauve, violet, purple, often marked or veined.	Needs slightly acid soil, sun or light shade. Water amply during growth. Plant 2 in. deep, 12-15 in. apart, in fall. Can grow near pond or stream but thrives under ordinary garden conditions. Blooms late.
BULBOUS IRIS				
Dutch Irises	6-9	18-36 in.	Waxy, often fragrant, 5-in. flowers range from white to yellow, gold, bronze, purple, orange, and bicolors.	These hybrids bloom from early spring (all-time favorite 'Wedgwood', blue with yellow blotch) to midseason or late. Plant 3 or 4 in. deep, 4 in. apart, in full sun. Keep soil moist during growth and blooming, rather dry in summer. Mass plant among tall perennials, or force like crocus.
Reticulata Irises	5-9	3-8 in.	Smaller (2-3 in.) but otherwise like flowers of Dutch hybrids, these are yellow, purple, light and and dark blue, and white, all with yellow, white, or brown blotches.	Often sold as "Dutch miniatures" or "early-blooming miniatures," this group comprises several closely related species—*I. reticulata*, *I. bakerana*, *I. danfordiae*, and *I. histrioides*—and hybrids between them, such as 'Cantab' (pale blue, blotched gold and white), 'Harmony' (deep blue, blotched gold), and 'Violet Beauty' (violet-purple, blotched orange). Excellent in rock garden, among other early bulbs, or in pots. In fall plant in sheltered, sunny, well-drained spot, 4 in. deep and apart. Moist soil in spring, fairly dry soil in summer.

A cool-season flower, annual sweet pea *(Lathyrus odoratus),* shown above and below, covers fences or trellises in dazzling color; scents the garden with its sweet fragrance.

Giant snowflake *(Leucojum aestivum),* a choice bulb for naturalized plantings, bears graceful nodding bell-like flowers from mid- to late spring.

Lathyrus
Sweet Pea
Perennial and annual.

Large, pastel-hued flowers with a heavenly fragrance characterize sweet peas. They are old-fashioned favorites for nosegays and spring bouquets. Though sweet peas usually do best in cool climates, modern hybrids offer heat-resistance.

Culture for the annual and perennial species is similar. Both should be started from seed in well-drained, moist, slightly alkaline soil. Prepare soil in fall for spring planting by turning over to a depth of at least 18 inches and working in plenty of organic matter and complete fertilizer or well-aged manure. Soak seeds for 24 hours in warm water or scratch with a file before planting. Plant 2 inches deep in full sun. Mulch to keep soil cool and water regularly.

Lathyrus latifolius
Perennial Pea, Everlasting Pea
Zones: 4-10. To 6-9 feet.
Perennial.

This vigorous vine has bluish-green compound leaves, and it produces large clusters of 1-1/2-inch flowers in white and soft shades of pink, rose, red, purple, and blue throughout summer. Given adequate support, perennial pea makes an effective screen.

In Zones 8 to 10, sow outdoors in early fall, elsewhere early spring. You can sow seeds indoors 6 to 8 weeks before planting outside. Germination takes 20 to 30 days at 55° to 65°F.

Lathyrus odoratus
Sweet Pea
Zones: 2-10. To 9 inches - 6 feet.
Annual.

In addition to traditional vining sweet peas, bush types have been developed to serve as edging, border, and container plants. Supports such as a fence, trellis, string, and net are suitable for vines.

In northern areas where summer heat arrives suddenly and calls an end to blooming, start seeds indoors in late winter. Seeds germinate in 10 to 14 days. When soil can be worked, plant outside. Use a different location every year. In Zones 8 to 10, plant in fall for early bloom.

Top-rated bush sweet peas, all early-blooming, are: Burpee's Bijou mixture (15 inches high), Burpee's Patio mixture (9 inches), Knee-Hi All Color mixture (30 inches), and Little Elf mixture (24 inches). An early-blooming vine is Early Multiflora Gigantea (Early Spencer), to about 6 feet. Spring-blooming vines are: Cuthbertson's Floribunda and Royal Family mixtures. Heat-resistant summer-flowering vines are: Burpee's Galaxy mixture and Giant Late Heat-Resistant mixture.

Leucojum
Snowflake
Bulbs.

Snowflakes are often confused with snowdrops *(Galanthus)* because their names and appearances are similar. Snowflake is the larger of the two plants. The white flowers are 3/4 inch long and are distinguished from snowdrops because the 6 petals are of equal length and are reflexed at their tips.

Snowflakes naturalize freely and are suitable around shrubs, in the rock garden, or massed informally under deciduous trees and in low ground covers.

Snowflake does best in light shade (or full sun in mild-summer climates) and fast-draining soil with plenty of water. Plants are long-lived and naturalize best in areas with cold winters. Planting and culture are the same as for snowdrop.

Leucojum aestivum
Giant Snowflake,
Summer Snowflake
Zones: 5-10. To 12-18 in.

Neither giant nor summer-blooming (it blooms mid- to late spring), giant snowflake has 2 to 8 nodding flowers per stem.

Leucojum vernum
Spring Snowflake
Zones: 5-8. To 9-12 in.

In late winter or early spring a single snowy flower nods at the tip of each plant stem. This somewhat shorter species is particularly well suited to the scale of most rock gardens.

Liatris spicata
Gay-Feather, Blazing-Star

Zones: 3-10. To 2-5 feet.
Perennial.

Gay-feather bears tall spikes of fuzzy flowers in late summer that have the unusual habit of opening from the top of the spike downward. A summer bloomer, gay-feather is a bright spectacle from July to September. Flower colors feature purple tones—lavender, pink, magenta—and occasionally white. Long, 4- to 16-inch, linear leaves cover the lower stems.

This American native grows in the marshes and wet spots of the eastern United States. A setting near a stream or in low spots is ideal. Include with naturalized plantings.

Purchase container-grown plants for guaranteed variety color. Set out in early spring, spacing about 15 inches apart. Seeds can be sown in the garden up to 2 months before fall frost. Plants will reseed freely but colors vary.

While gay-feather tolerates a range of conditions from poor to peaty wet or dry soils, good drainage is best. Once established, it needs little attention, and plants last for years. Tall-flowered varieties may need staking. Water freely during dry periods. Divide when overcrowded.

Top-rated are: 'Kobald', compact to 24 inches, flowers a deep rose-lavender; 'Floristan White', long-lasting flowers. Flowers of *Liatris scariosa* open simultaneously, making it especially good as a cut flower; 'September Glory' grows to 5 feet, has rich purple spikes.

Lilium
Lily

Zones: 4-10. To 1-7 feet.
Bulbs.

An astonishing array of hybrid lily groups, strains, and varieties is available, developed from the numerous European, Asian, and North American species and various groups of hybrids descended from them.

All lily blossoms have six petals. Forms vary widely, from trumpet to bowl, star, flat-faced, and turban shapes, and blossoms may be upright, outfacing, or pendant. Flowers, often in clusters of 10 or 12—or in many dozens on some varieties—bloom on vertical spikes and may be up to a foot wide. Colors range through the spectrum, except blue. Petals are often dappled, mottled, veined, or shaded. Bloom time varies from the end of spring to early fall. Heights vary from 1 to 8 feet.

Lilies are suitable for beds and borders, planters, and woodland and rock gardens. They grow especially well among shallow-rooted plants that shade the ground.

Ideal time for planting most bulbs is October to mid-November. Many of the most successful lily growers, however, plant in spring; late-bloomers such as Oriental hybrids are perhaps best planted in spring. In mildest climates, bulbs can be planted in winter as well. Lily bulbs never go completely dormant, so they should be selected for plumpness, planted immediately, and never allowed to dry out. Plant at least 12 inches apart, beneath 4 inches of soil. Bulbs in pots may be grown indoors for a season. Keep pots in a cool spot, and water and feed regularly.

Nearly all lilies like shade around their bases but some sun on their tops. In hottest areas, some midday shade is best. Deep, rich, gritty, perfectly drained moist soil is mandatory. Once planted, they should remain undisturbed by cultivating or digging. Mulching is desirable to maintain moisture and avoid temperature extremes. Wind protection is important, and staking and tying are necessary.

Top-rated lilies fall into several of the officially designated divisions created by the North American Lily Society and the Royal Horticultural Society. (See chart on next page.)

Low-growing forms of gay-feather (*Liatris spicata*) are an unusual choice for the midground of a flower border; offer fine-textured foliage and fluffy flower spikes from late summer to fall.

Lilies (*Lilium* hybrids) are available in a rich variety of forms. Most are statuesque plants with dramatic blossoms.

Easter lily *(Lilium longiflorum)* bears pristine white trumpet-shaped flowers in the early part of summer.

Oriental hybrid lilies *(Lilium* hybrids) are highly fragrant; bear 8- to 10-inch-wide flowers in vivid colors.

Lilium

Divisions	Zones	Height	Flower Description	Comments
DIVISION 1: Asiatic Hybrids	4-10	1-1/2-4 ft	Most are 4-6 in. wide. *Upright flowers:* 'Enchantment' (orange-red), 'Firecracker' (cherry-red), 'Pirate' (tangerine-red), 'Scarlet Emperor' (scarlet), and 'True Grit' (bright orange). *Pendant flowers:* 'Hornback's Gold' (dark-spotted lemon-yellow). *Outward-facing flowers:* 'Ming Yellow' (bright yellow).	Early-summer blooming. Division includes Mid-Century Hybrids and Harlequin Hybrids. A few top-rated varieties are listed under "Flower Description." Members of this Division are ideal for potting because of their compact growth.
DIVISION 6: Aurelian Hybrids	4-10	3-6 ft	Most are 6-10 in. wide. Most widely available top-rated members are trumpet types: Black Dragon strain (pure white inside, purple-brown outside), Golden Splendor strain (deep gold, striped outside), and Pink Perfection strain (fuchsia-pink, often dark shading to light).	Mid- to late-summer blooming. Division includes Olympic Hybrids. Some members of this Division are called Trumpet Lilies because of their flower shape. Other members have bowl-shaped, star-shaped, and flat-faced flowers that may be upright, outward facing, or pendant.
DIVISION 7: Oriental Hybrids	4-10	4-7 ft	Most are 8-10 in. wide, flat with recurved petals. Widely available top-rated lilies are members of the Imperial strains: Imperial Crimson, Imperial Gold, Imperial Pink, and Imperial Silver strains.	Late-summer blooming. Besides the listed flat-flowered lilies, other Oriental Hybrids may also have flat, or bowl-shaped, flowers. All are very fragrant.
DIVISION 9: Species				
Lilium candidum **Madonna Lily**	4-10	3-6 ft	Pure satiny-white, trumpet-shaped flowers, strongly scented, early to midsummer.	Listed species are the most available and dependable old-fashioned garden lilies, some having been cultivated for 2,000 years. *L. candidum* is the only top-rated lily whose bulb roots at its base rather than on the stem just above the bulb. It should be planted with only 2 in. of soil over the bulb in late summer. Accepts some alkalinity, unlike other lilies, and likes full sun.
L. lancifolium (L. tigrinum) **Tiger Lily**	4-10	4-6 ft	Orange, spotted purple-black, turban-shaped flowers, pendulous, late summer.	
L. longiflorum **Trumpet Lily, Easter Lily**	4-10	2-3 ft	Pure white, trumpet-shaped flowers, early to midsummer.	
L. regale **Regal Lily**	4-10	3-6 ft	White with carmine outside, trumpet-shaped flowers, very fragrant, midsummer.	
***L. speciosum* 'Rubrum'** **Showy Japanese Lily**	4-10	3-5 ft	Large, crimson, turban-shaped flowers, late summer.	

Lobelia

Lobelia

Perennial and annual.

Of the many lobelias, two very different ones, a tall perennial and a low annual, have become special garden favorites. Culture is easy, and both provide a long season of spectacular bloom.

Lobelia erinus
Edging Lobelia
Zones: 2-10. To 4-6 inches, or pendulous to 8-10 inches.
Annual.

This tidy plant produces masses of small irregular-shaped flowers in white, rose, or shades of blue, including a blue so electric that it is unmatched by any other plant. Edging lobelia is frequently planted as a low, colorful edging for beds and borders. Trailing types are excellent in planters and window boxes. It blooms from late spring to fall frost.

Plant nursery seedlings, or sow indoors 10 to 12 weeks before last frost, for germination in 8 to 20 days at around 70°F. Set 4 to 6 inches apart in moist, rich soil and feed regularly with a balanced fertilizer. Does best in cool areas in full sun; in hot areas needs light shade. Too much shade makes plants leggy and flowers sparse. Clip dead flowers.

Cascading types: 'Blue Cascade' (light blue), 'Red Cascade' (magenta), and 'Sapphire' (vibrant blue with white eyes) trail to 8 to 10 inches below planter edge. More upright are: 'Crystal Palace' (especially vibrant dark blue, with bronze foliage), 'Cambridge Blue' (light blue), 'Mrs. Clibran' (dark blue with white eyes), 'White Lady' (pure white), and 'Rosamond' (rosy red with white eyes).

Lobelia splendens (L. fulgens)
Cardinal Flower
Zones: 4-10. To 24-48 inches.
Perennial.

This late-summer-blooming plant from Mexico produces tall spikes of 1-1/2-inch flowers that are an incomparably brilliant scarlet. Foliage

and stems are bronzy-purple and add handsome color contrast to the garden all season.

Buy container-grown plants or sow seeds. Sow outdoors in late fall for spring germination or sow indoors in spring. Germination takes 15 to 20 days at about 70°F. Space 16 to 18 inches apart in rich loam. Keep moist to very moist. Partial shade is best though full sun is acceptable where summers are cool.

Another perennial lobelia, *L. cardinalis*, an American wildflower, is almost identical in culture and appearance except it has green foliage. It is also called cardinal flower.

Lobularia maritima
Sweet Alyssum
Zones: 2-10: To 3-4 inches.
Perennial used as annual in most areas.

Sweet alyssum blooms heavily over a long season and reseeds generously. Besides the traditional white, rosy-purple varieties are available. Flowering begins 6 weeks after seeding and, with occasional shearing, mounding carpets of fragrant flower heads continue until the first hard freeze. In mild climates also blooms in winter.

Sweet alyssum is a favorite for edging flower borders and for mass planting in beds. Use as a seasonal ground cover or filler.

Seedlings are available, but growth from seeds is easy. Sow uncovered as soon as ground thaws or indoors 4 to 6 weeks before last frost. Seeds germinate in 8 to 15 days at 65° to 70°F. Plant 4 inches apart in sun or light shade in ordinary, well-drained soil. Growth is lush with regular watering, but *Lobularia* tolerates drought and heat.

'Carpet of Snow', 'New Carpet of Snow', and 'Snowcloth' (all to 4 inches tall) are top-rated whites. 'Tiny Tim' is a slightly smaller white. 'Midnight' (3 inches) is deep purple; 'Royal Carpet' (3 inches), violet-purple; 'Oriental Night' (4 inches), lavender-rose; and 'Wonderland' (4 inches), rosy red. Mixes are Pastel Carpet and Color Carpet.

Rapid growth, a tidy form, and masses of brightly hued flowers make edging lobelia (*Lobelia erinus*) invaluable as a border for beds, paths, and rock gardens.

Cardinal flower (*Lobelia splendens*) prefers moist sites and produces brilliant scarlet blossoms on tall spikes.

Sweet alyssum (*Lobularia maritima*) creates lush mounds of sparkling white flowers with a sweet fragrance.

Available in a rainbow of colors, Russell lupine *(Lupinus 'Russell hybrids')* flourishes in cool areas.

German catchfly *(Lychnis viscaria)* is durable in northern climates.

Bee balm *(Monarda didyma)* entices bees and hummingbirds to the garden.

Lupinus 'Russell Hybrids'
Russell Lupines
Zones: 3-9. To 2-5 feet.
Perennial.

Russell lupines are a superior strain of hybrid lupines. Of all the lupines available, no others offer such exceptional beauty and durability. Available in a range of colors including white, pinks, blues, purples, and yellows, this strain offers large pea-like blossoms whorled tightly around 1- to 2-foot-tall pointed spires. Many are bicolored and sweetly scented. Several flower spikes bloom on each plant in early summer.

Lupines show to best advantage if set in groups of at least 3 to 5 plants. Plant solid colors together or mix colors for a rainbow effect. The mounds of foliage are elegant until the end of the season in most climates.

Lupine performs best in cool, moist, mild climates similar to the Pacific Northwest. In other areas situate plants out of direct sun, provide good drainage, and water regularly. Mulch to help keep roots cool and soil moist. In warm regions may die back after flowering.

Select nursery-grown plants for fall and spring planting. Carefully set in place without disturbing the roots, spacing 18 to 24 inches apart. Seeds can be sown directly in the garden or in peat pots indoors. Pretreat seeds by soaking 24 hours in water or filing a nick in the seed coat. Germination takes 8 to 10 weeks. Volunteer plants will not have hybrid colors.

Depending on growing conditions, lupine may need replacing every 2 to 3 years. Longer-lived clumps need dividing when plants become overcrowded; separate clumps carefully in spring before growth begins.

Cut spent flower stalks to prevent seeding. Protect basal growth with a mulch in winter. Aphids can be a nuisance on flower buds. Wash off with a hose or use pesticide. Leaf damage caused by powdery mildew and cyclamen mite needs prompt treatment.

'Lulu' and 'Marinette' are smaller forms growing to 18 inches tall; useful in the foreground.

Lychnis chalcedonica
Maltese-Cross, Campion
Zones: 3-9. To 1-1/2-3 feet.
Perennial.

The brilliant flowers of maltese-cross are clustered in flattened domes atop leafy stems and make a vivid display in summer. Plants form stands of upright 1- to 3-foot flowering stems that grow from a dense basal clump. Varieties are available in orange-red, rose, crimson, and occasionally white.

Plant in full sun among shasta daisy, coreopsis, salvia and gaillardia for a colorful show. Plants self-sow in naturalized settings. Trim spent flower stems to encourage a second bloom in August, and help keep seed-drop to a minimum in formal gardens.

While maltese-cross plants are short-lived, they are easily renewed by divisions or self-seeding. For a new planting, sow seed over a prepared bed and do not cover because light is required for germination. Thin plants to 15 inches. Divisions or nursery plants can be set out in spring or fall, about 15 inches apart.

Maltese-cross prefers rich, organic soil, and must have perfect drainage. Soggy conditions kill plants during dormancy. Plants may suffer from fungal diseases: leaf spot, rust, and root rot.

Three other *Lychnis* species are top-rated. Rose campion, *Lychnis coronaria*, is a biennial with magenta flowers held in loose clusters and woolly white leaves; reseeds freely. *Lychnis x haageana*, haage campion, has brownish-red leaves and scarlet-orange flowers on 12-inch stems held in loose clusters. Most cold hardy is *Lychnis viscaria*, whose sticky leaves account for its common name, German catchfly. Grows to 18 inches tall and has reddish-purple double flowers held in clusters.

Monarda didyma
Bee Balm, Bergamot, Oswego Tea
Zones: 4-10. To 2-3 feet.
Perennial.

A native American wildflower with red blossoms, bee balm attracts bees and hummingbirds to its fragrant spidery flowers, which bloom from mid- to late summer. Garden varieties of bee balm also come in purple, pink, or white. The foliage, which is used for tea, resembles that of mint and has a pronounced minty fragrance. Plants grow quickly, forming a lush, bushy mass.

Bee balm is excellent in naturalized settings and is effective in perennial borders. Flowers are long-lasting when cut, and picking prolongs blooming.

Needs moist, fertile soil and tolerates wet spots. Plant in sun or light shade. Plants spread easily by shallow rhizomes; locate where can be easily contained. Divide every 3 to 4 years when crowding causes lanky growth. Start new stands with divisions or with seeds broadcast in fall or spring.

Water regularly, but do not fertilize except in the poorest soils. Good air circulation helps prevent mildew on leaves as does thinning of dense clumps.

Cold-hardy 'Craftway Pink' blooms prolifically; has rosy-pink flowers. 'Granite Pink' has clear pink blossoms; 'Violet Queen' lavender; and 'Blue Stocking' pale purple. Darker shades of red are found in 'Mahogany', 'Cambridge Scarlet', and 'Adam'.

Muscari
Grape Hyacinth
Bulbs.

Carpets of these fragrant blue-, purple-, or sometimes white-flowered beauties, with their dense clusters of grapelike or fringed flowers, are one of the joys of the earliest bloom season. Grape hyacinths are often interplanted with other early bulbs, as well as early annuals. Clumps are pretty by walks or low walls.

All forms prefer well-drained soil, sun, or, especially in hot dry areas, light shade, and moisture during the growing season. Plant 3 inches deep and 4 inches apart, in late summer or early fall.

Muscari armeniacum
Armenian Grape Hyacinth
Zones: 3-10. To 8-12 inches.

Each 9-inch spike of this early-blooming, most popular species has

20 to 40 tightly clustered blue flowers. Leaves appear in fall and last through the winter, dying in spring. Outstanding forms are 'Blue Spike' (bright blue, double), 'Early Giant' (light blue, very fragrant), and 'Cantab' (light blue, small, later blooming).

Muscari botryoides
Common Grape Hyacinth
Zones: 3-10. To 6 inches.

Earliest blooming of the grape hyacinths, this species has pale blue flowers. Flower stalks are shorter than the leaves, 6 to 8 inches tall. 'Pearls of Spain' is a white-flowered variety.

Muscari comosum 'Plumosum'
Feather Hyacinth
Zones: 3-10. To 12 inches.

Reddish-purple, shredded flowers and tall size (to 12 to 18 inches) distinguish this from other grape hyacinths. It blooms in late spring.

Myosotis sylvatica
Forget-Me-Not
Zones: 2-10. To 6-12 inches.
Annual or biennial.

These charming plants with dainty blue flowers and perky yellow eyes are one of the garden's earliest delights. They keep on blooming from early spring until summer's heat arrives. Use as a companion plant with spring bulbs, as a woodland ground cover, as a garden edging, or in bog gardens. It readily self-sows to become a permanent garden feature.

Plant nursery seedlings, or sow seed outdoors in fall or as soon as the ground is workable in spring. Sow in early summer for fall bloom. Seeds must be covered with soil in order to germinate. Thin plants 8 to 12 inches apart in rich, moist soil, in partial shade. Forget-me-nots accept wet soil and grow best where summers are cool.

Pink and white varieties are sometimes available. 'Blue Bird' (12 inches tall) blooms more quickly than most. 'Indigo Dwarf' (7 inches) is useful for underplanting bulbs or planting with pansies. 'Victoria Blue' (6 to 8 inches) has azure flowers. Less available *M. scorpioides* (12 inches) bears bright blue flowers from spring through summer.

Grape hyacinths *(Muscari* sp.) produce clusters of grapelike flowers early in spring.

Forget-me-not *(Myosotis* sp.) blooms in cool weather in spring and summer, making a bright blue edging or small-area ground cover.

One of the easiest spring-flowering bulbs to care for, *Narcissus* naturalize freely except in coldest climates. Hundreds of varieties are available, such as 'King Alfred', shown above, and 'Scarlet Gem', shown below.

Narcissus
Daffodil, Jonquil, Narcissus

Zones: 5-10. To 5-20 inches.
Bulbs.

When the earliest daffodil breaks through snow or blooms in a bright window, winter's days are numbered. When the last one blooms, spring is giving way to summer.

Daffodils are splendid, by whatever name—and their names are confusing. The Latin name for all of this large group is *Narcissus*. In common usage, however, the name "narcissus" identifies those with small clustered flowers. "Daffodil," in everyday language, is usually applied to large-trumpet-flowered types. The name jonquil is generally used synonymously with daffodil, though it properly refers to just one species and its hybrids.

Predominantly yellow or white and borne singly or in clusters, daffodil flowers have a unique structure: 6 petals surround a long, flared trumpet or a shorter cup. Trumpets or cups of most double flowers have been replaced by furled petals. Foliage is usually straplike and dark green. It withers by midsummer.

Daffodils are most pleasing planted in drifts, or at least large clumps. They are classic planted beneath deciduous trees and in rock gardens and may be easily forced indoors.

Daffodils are far less demanding than tulips and many other bulbs. Planted in well-drained soil and full sun or partial shade, they persist and many types naturalize. An ideally situated planting may last for centuries without being touched. In your garden, however, more and larger flowers will result if you dig, separate, and thin bulbs every 2 or 3 years after foliage has ripened. You can replant these bulbs immediately, or store until late summer or early fall if the planting area is to be heavily watered for summer plants. Watering is desirable after planting to encourage root growth.

Plant large bulbs 5 or 6 inches beneath soil, small ones 2 to 4 inches. Deep plantings are more durable, especially in hot-summer areas. Daffodils planted 8, even 10, inches apart need digging only every 3 or 4 years to maintain strong flowering.

Rodents and other animals avoid bitter daffodil bulbs, foliage, and flowers, but maggots of bulb fly occasionally infest a few bulbs. If basal rot, a fungus, attacks, soak bulbs in a fungicide solution.

The Royal Horticultural Society has classified the hundreds of varieties according to flower form or ancestry. The chart is organized according to the 11 divisions of this system.

Narcissus

Division Name	Zones	Height	Flower Description	Comments
Trumpet Narcissus	5-10	15-20 in.	One per stem, trumpet as long as, or longer than, petals, usually about 2 in. Most varieties cream, white, yellow, or bicolored.	Hybrids of *N. pseudonarcissus*, these are the most planted division. They naturalize freely, grow vigorously, and force easily. Full sun or light shade is best. Most bloom early to midseason. Some top-rated varieties: 'King Alfred' (golden-yellow with deeply frilled trumpet), 'Music Hall', (yellow-tinted white petals, deep-golden trumpet), 'Mount Hood' (pure white with wide, ruffled trumpet), and 'Spellbinder' (large yellow flowers with shading toward paler tone at base of trumpet and petals).
Large-Cupped Narcissus	5-10	15-20 in.	One per stem, trumpet one-third the length of petals, or longer. Many are boldly contrasting bicolors—the most colorful division of *Narcissus*.	Hybrids of *N. x incomparabilis*, they are popular for bedding and cutting. Produce lush foliage. Flowers keep color longest in light shade. Sometimes called "weatherproofs" for their strong, long-lasting flowers. Usually bloom midseason. Some top-rated varieties: 'Binkie' (opening pale yellow with pale cup, fading to ivory with yellow edging), 'Mrs. R.O. Backhouse' (ivory petals, apricot-pink cup shell-pink at ruffled edge), 'Ice Follies' (white petals, flaring cup opening yellow, changing to creamy white), and 'Professor Einstein' (white petals, bright red-orange cup).

Division Name	Zones	Height	Flower Description	Comments
Small-Cupped Narcissus	5-10	15-20 in.	Cup less than one-third the length of petals, making daintier-looking flowers than those of large-cupped narcissus. Most are fragrant.	Like large-cupped daffodils, they are hybrids of *N. x incomparabilis* and have the same exposure preference and bloom time (though 'Frigid' and a few others are late). Most naturalize easily. Some top-rated varieties: 'Apricot Distinction' (petals soft amber with ochre overtones, cup deep red-amber), 'Chunking' (yellow petals, vivid deep red cup), 'Limerick' (white petals, cup red-rimmed, bright green toward base), 'Frigid' (small, pure white flowers).
Double Narcissus	5-10	variable	Large or small double blossoms resemble small roses; one or several blossoms per stem, thinly or very densely petaled. Flowers of this division reflect diversity of ancestry.	No common ancestor; distinguished by double flowers. Many are fragrant. Nearly all have very long-lasting flowers. Some top-rated varieties: 'Golden Ducat' (large, deep golden-yellow flowers), 'Tahiti' (soft-yellow outer petals, center petals marked orange; large), 'Bridal Crown' (3 to 5 blossoms per stem, white with traces of lemon-yellow between overlapping petals), and 'White Lion' (large, waxy white outer petals, soft apricot-yellow center petals).
Triandrus Narcissus	5-10	8-18 in.	Gracefully curved-back petals and bell-shaped cup. One to several nodding blossoms per stem. Most white or soft yellow.	All resemble ancestor *N. triandrus*. Many have grasslike foliage; most are short. Prefer full sun and light, well-drained soil. Excellent for rock garden or container culture. Most bloom late. Some top-rated varieties: 'Thalia' (2 or 3 pure white flowers per stem), 'Silver Chimes' (at least 6 small, creamy white flowers with pale yellow cups, heavily scented), 'Liberty Bells' (2 or 3 golden-yellow flowers per stem), and 'Hawera' (short, with 4 to 6 clear, lemon-yellow flowers per stem).
Cyclamineus Narcissus	5-10	5-18 in.	Petals of most varieties are folded back at tighter angle than those of Triandrus Narcissus, resembling cyclamen petals.	All resemble ancestor *N. cyclamineus*. Most are miniatures, suited to full sun, well-drained soil, and sheltered spots in the rock garden, or to container culture. Most are very early. Some top-rated varieties: 'February Gold' (1 or 2 pale yellow flowers; especially suitable for forcing), 'February Silver' milky petals; trumpet opening lemon-yellow, turning ivory), 'Tête-à-Tête' (1 or 2 pure yellow flowers per stem), and 'Dove Wings' (creamy white petals, pale yellow trumpet).
Jonquilla Narcissus	5-10	10-22 in.	Saucer-shaped flowers in clusters of 2 to 6. Many are partially or entirely rich yellow.	All resemble *N. jonquilla*. Leaves are hollow, sedge-like. They prefer full sun and grow well in hot climates. This is the most fragrant division of narcissus. Most bloom late. Top-rated varieties: 'Trevithian' (rich to pale yellow), 'Suzy' (bright yellow petals, orange cup).
Tazetta Narcissus	8-10	8-18 in.	Small, heavily scented flowers in clusters of up to 10.	All resemble *N. tazetta* in its various wild forms. Among Tazetta Narcissus are the Poetaz varieties. Tazettas are excellent for forcing or for clumping in the garden. Most bloom early. Rich moist soil is best. Some top-rated varieties are 'Paper White' (pure white, the favorite for forcing), 'Soleil d'Or' (rich yellow), 'Silver Chimes' (white with orange cup), and 'Minnow' (white with bright yellow, flat cup). 'Geranium' is white with orange-red cup.
Poeticus Narcissus	5-10	8-18 in.	All are white with a small, shallow cup edged orange or red.	All resemble the Poeticus group, their ancestors from the wilds, and are called, collectively, Poet's Narcissus or Pheasant's-Eye Narcissus. Most are fragrant. They naturalize readily with good drainage and some light shade. All bloom late. The widely available variety is 'Actaea' (largest flower, about 3 inches wide, yellow cup rimmed with red).
Species and Wild Hybrid Narcissus	5-10	variable	Most have small, unshowy but exquisite flowers best seen at close range.	Most are easily and attractively grown in pots or rock garden. Most are sold by common rather than Latin names. *N. bulbocodium* (hoop-petticoat daffodil) prefers moist places, grows to 6 inches or more, has widely flaring yellow trumpet and tiny petals. *N. tazetta orientalis* (Chinese sacred lily) sometimes sold as *N. canaliculatus orientalis*, is a yellow to dark yellow variety, to 18 inches high, similar to the Tazetta Narcissus hybrids. *N. jonquilla* (Jonquil), often sold as yellow jonquil, reaches 12 to 18 inches, bears 2 to 6 flowers per stem, and resembles its larger-flowered hybrids. *N. triandrus albus*, to 12 inches, white form of angel's tears, resembles its hybrids, described above.
Miscellaneous Narcissus	5-10	variable	Butterfly daffodils have large, showy flowers with wide-spreading, split cups, with stripes of yellow, orange, or red radiating from center. Some cups are so large that they obscure the petals.	This division is a catchall for types that don't fit into other divisions. Many new hybrids belong here. Notable are recently developed butterfly daffodils, 18 to 20 inches tall, blooming midseason to late.

Available in a wide range of heights and flower colors, nicotiana *(Nicotiana alata)* serves many useful garden functions. Foliage is handsome, flowers dramatic.

A petite plant for beds, borders, rock gardens, or edging, dwarf cupflower *(Nierembergia hippomanica)* has fernlike foliage; bears small purplish blossoms during summer.

The lovely flower forms and sweet fragrance of peony *(Paeonia* hybrids) make it a prized garden flower for growing en masse, as a seasonal hedge, or as a specimen plant.

Nicotiana alata
Flowering Tobacco, Nicotiana,
Perennial in Zones 9-10. Annual elsewhere. To 16-32 inches.

This beautiful cousin of tobacco and petunia features tall spikes of flaring, star-shaped, 2-inch tubular flowers ranging from intense crimson to rose, wine, purple, yellow, white and even chartreuse. The fragrant blossoms are fully open only during the evening and during cloudy days but are always attractive. The flowers of many hybrids stay open during the day. Use in beds, borders, and containers.

Plant nursery seedlings, or sow seeds outdoors after last spring frost, or indoors 6 to 8 weeks earlier, at 65° to 85°F for germination in 10 to 20 days. Do not cover seeds. Set seedlings 10 to 12 inches apart in full sun or light or medium shade. Rich, evenly moist, well-drained soil is best.

Flowers of the Nicki series (18 to 24 inches tall) stay fully open throughout the day; 'Nicki Red' is one of the most intense crimsons in the garden. Dwarf Potpourri mixture reaches only 12 inches. At the other extreme in size, Sensation mixture reaches 30 inches, and highly scented, pure white 'Affinis' reaches 32 inches.

Nierembergia hippomanica
Cupflower
Perennial in Zones 7-10. Annual elsewhere. To 6 inches.

Cupflower is one of the prettiest and most dependable blue summer flowers. Its low mounds of needled foliage make a perfect edging or foreground. Chalice-shaped bluish-purple or bluish-violet flowers, an inch wide, bloom all summer.

Sow indoors 10 to 12 weeks before the last spring frost, for germination in 15 to 20 days at 70° to 75°F. To grow as a perennial in Zones 7–10, sow outdoors up to 2 months before first fall frost. Space 3 to 4 inches apart. In hot areas, plant in light shade and keep moist, elsewhere in light shade or full sun. Well-drained, rich soil is best. Clip for continuous bloom.

'Purple Robe' is the most widely available variety, and an excellent one. *N. repens*, whitecup, is a creeping 4-inch-high perennial with creamy flowers, recommended for Zones 7-9.

Paeonia hybrids
Peony
Zones: 5-9. To 2-4 feet.
Perennial.

Peony's virtues include a long life (20 years is not unusual), easy culture, and a generous supply of incredibly beautiful flowers that are prized for arrangements. Peonies can be grouped to form shrubby masses, creating a colorful, seasonal hedge, used in a flower border, or as specimen plants. They are bold-textured and dramatic.

Peonies have tuberous roots that support rapid, lush growth. In early spring, reddish shoots poke through the soil and grow quickly into a bushy mass of glossy green, deeply lobed leaves. The foliage remains green and lush all season, turning red in fall.

Showy, fragrant blossoms open slowly from rounded buds in midspring. Colors range from softest pastels to deep reds and purples. Blossom size varies from 4 to 8 inches across and flower types are classified by petal number and form. *Single* and *Chinese* forms have one row of petals and centers packed with yellow stamens. *Japanese* and *Anemone* types have tufted centers of small petallike stamens. Fully petaled *semidoubles* and *doubles* are most common.

Peonies should be planted in full sun or light shade away from wind and reflected heat. Pale-colored flowers last better in shade. Need deep, well-drained soil, generously amended with compost; keep soil evenly moist and apply mulch in late fall. Best in cold-winter climates.

Plant divisions or nursery stock in early fall. Divisions should have 3 to 5 red-colored buds per section; plant 1 inch below soil surface, spacing 2 to 3 feet apart. Unless roots are near the soil surface, peonies will not flower. Poor flowering also can be caused by too much shade, poor drainage, premature cutting back of stems, or late spring frost damage.

Peonies grow well with very little care. Water generously when establishing new plants. Feed annually with a balanced fertilizer and keep roots well mulched. Double-flowered forms need staking to prevent blossoms from bending to the ground. Remove spent flowers.

For the largest, single-stemmed flowers, pinch developing side buds, leaving only the top bud. For longest-lasting cut flowers, cut when flowers are half open. Pick long-stemmed flowers (with more than two leaves) sparingly until plants have grown for 3 or 4 years.

Anthracnose, botrytis, and phytophthora, three troublesome fungal diseases, can be prevented by periodic fungicide sprays.

Papaver
Poppy
Perennials.

Two members of the colorful poppy family are top-rated. Both bloom in the cool months of spring, putting on an alluring display of silky-textured blossoms. Flowers can be cut for indoor enjoyment—for long-lasting cut flowers, cut when buds are beginning to open and sear the cut end immediately in a flame.

Papaver nudicaule
Iceland Poppy
Perennial or biennial in Zones 2-8. Annual elsewhere. To 1-2 feet.

The silky, pastel-colored flowers of Iceland poppy have a delicate, ethereal beauty. They open from nodding hairy buds that top wiry 1- to 2-foot-tall stems. Slightly fragrant, 2 to 4 inches across, and with a single or double row of petals surrounding showy yellow stamens, blooms are pink, rose, yellow, peach, orange or bi-colored. Blue-green leaves are deeply cut into rounded lobes and form a basal tuft.

Iceland poppies bloom during spring and summer until warm weather arrives. Plants die to the ground in heat. Use in mass plantings or smaller, clustered groups in garden borders. Poppies may be replaced after flowering with annuals or fall-bloomers such as chrysanthemum.

They are easily propagated by seed, making it practical to grow them as annuals for short-season color. Sow seed directly in the garden in early spring in Zones 2-8, in late summer in Zones 9-10. Thin to 10 inches apart. In mild-winter areas, nurseries offer seedlings in spring and fall to plant along with other hardy perennials.

Flowering is best if planted in full sun. Iceland poppy thrives with cool air and a rich fertile soil. Provide good drainage to prevent root rot but keep evenly moist throughout the growing season. Several flowering stems arise from each plant and cutting faded blossoms prolongs blooming. If grown as a perennial, cover with an airy, lightweight winter mulch. Foliage needs protection from snails.

Look for 'Champagne Bubbles', a robust, popular variety to 15 inches tall with huge blossoms and lush foliage. 'Summer Promise' is available in solid or two-toned colors and has flower stems to 2 feet.

Papaver orientale
Oriental Poppy
Zones: 3-10. to 2-4 feet.
Perennial sometimes grown as an annual.

Oriental poppies bear lavish flowers in early summer that begin as nodding, balloonlike, hairy buds on sinuous stems, then open wide to 6 to 12 inches across. Their large petals have a silky sheen and form a loosely held cup around a large cluster of black stamens. While flame-orange is the original color, a large selection of hybrids offers pink, maroon, peach, and white, many varieties with dark spots at the petal bases. A distinctive nobbed seedpod is left when flowers fade.

Grayish-green, coarse-textured, sharply toothed leaves create a basal clump of foliage. The leaves fade after flowering, but new growth appears by fall.

Oriental poppies flower for a short but spectacular period, so use for accent rather than mass planting. Plant where other plants will hide the space left by fading leaves.

Iceland poppy *(Papaver nudicaule)* has showy yellow stamens; bears huge colorful blossoms in spring.

Oriental poppy *(Papaver orientale)* produces spectacular flowers in vivid colors during early summer. Prefers cool, moderate climates.

Painted with dark blotches and veins, the flowers of Martha Washington geranium (Pelargonium x domesticum) form showy clusters during cool weather.

Geraniums (Pelargonium x hortorum) are old-fashioned, low-maintenance garden favorites with a wide range of uses.

Blooms best in cool, moderate climates, ideal growing conditions for these long-lived plants. Where summers are hot, plants fade earlier and often die. In such areas, use as an early spring annual. Plant in full sun or partial shade in well-drained soil. Tolerates some dryness, but not wetness.

To establish new plantings, purchase plants or take divisions in August. Set 18 inches apart, burying crown 3 inches below soil surface. Once in place avoid disturbing roots, except to divide every 4 or 5 years. Seeds require light for germination, and may be sown in spring or early fall.

Provide a winter mulch for young plants. Avoid disease problems such as mildew and bacterial blight, by watering only in early morning and providing good air circulation. Watch for aphids in spring.

Pelargonium
Geranium
Perennials in Zones 9-10. Annuals elsewhere.

Geraniums bring some of the sparkle of a sunny Mediterranean day to window boxes and planters. Four closely related groups of geraniums are popular garden and houseplants. All are perennials grown in most climates as annuals, and cultural requirements overlap considerably.

Most geraniums can be purchased in 2- to 6-inch pots. Zonal geranium takes 5 months to bloom from seed. Sow indoors 12 to 16 weeks before last frost, at about 75°F for germination in 5 to 15 days. Scented geraniums should be started indoors 12 weeks before last frost. Germination takes 20 to 50 days at 68° to 86°F. Cuttings of all geraniums root easily, and all can be grown as houseplants.

Pelargonium x domesticum
Lady Washington Geranium, Martha Washington Geranium
To 10-36 inches.

Clusters of vibrant flowers, marked with contrasting blotches, and pleated leaves characterize this showy group of geraniums. It prefers moister (but well-drained), richer soil and cooler summers than zonal geranium and tolerates less sun in hot climates. It needs a cold period to stimulate flowering, so houseplants will not bloom unless chilled first. Seeds are not sold; purchase cold-treated plants.

Pelargonium x hortorum
Zonal Geranium, Bedding Geranium
To 10-36 inches.

The downy, rounded, and scalloped-edged, 3- to 5-inch leaves are often "zoned" or ringed with bronze, pink, white, or light green. Flowers, usually single but sometimes double, are held in tight clusters to 5 inches wide, and are white or shades of red, pink, or salmon, sometimes bicolored.

In most climates full sun is best, but some light shade is needed in hot areas and tolerated elsewhere. Well-drained, sandy loam allowed to dry somewhat between waterings and frequent fertilizing keeps plants blooming.

Pelargonium peltatum
Ivy Geranium
To 36 inches.

Three-pointed, ivy-shaped, waxy leaves and long-stemmed clusters of flowers decorate the trailing stems of ivy geranium. It makes an exceptional hanging basket plant or ground cover. Needs partial shade in hot climates.

Pelargonium species
Scented Geraniums
To 10-36 inches

There is a wide variety of scented geraniums, their foliage smelling of rose, coconut, apple, lemon, lime, peppermint, or eucalyptus. Foliage varies from ruffled to very deeply cut and is usually fuzzy. Flowers are pretty but unshowy compared to their hybrid cousins. Many are upright, a few trailing. You may find plants sold as herbs at the nursery.

Geraniums *(Pelargonium x hortorum)* make a bright, colorful ground cover for small spaces.

Geraniums *(Pelargonium x hortorum)* make excellent container plants and are widely used in window boxes and in pots for gay summer color.

Ivy geranium *(Pelargonium peltatum)* is a festive plant for hanging baskets or containers.

Pelargonium

ZONAL GERANIUM *(P. x hortorum)*

Variety or Series	Height	Flowers	Comments
'Bright Eyes'	16 in.	Scarlet with white centers.	Deep green, lightly zoned leaves. The most distinct bicolor.
'Cherry Glow'	16 in.	Cherry-red.	Bright green foliage.
Marathon	14-16 in.	Red, rose, scarlet.	Double flowers in 4-inch heads are long-lasting. Deep green foliage. Seed sold by varieties.
'Merlin'	15 in.	Iridescent crimson-rose with orange-scarlet eye.	Lightly zoned foliage, very compact habit.
'Orange Cascade'	pendulous, to 24 in.	Salmon-orange to scarlet.	Created for hanging baskets. Cross with *P. peltatum*.
Orbit	14 in.	Red, coral, scarlet, apple-blossom pink, salmon, white, cherry.	Beautifully dark-zoned foliage in most varieties, visible zoning in white variety. Compact, base-branching habit. Seed sold by varieties and as mixture. Early.
Playboy	10 in.	White, pink, salmon, scarlet, red.	A true dwarf, with medium-size flower heads and darker green foliage than most. Seed sold as mixture.
'Red Elite'	15 in.	Fire-engine red.	Dense 4-in. clusters of large flowers. Early.
Ringo	15 in.	Reds ('Rouge', 'Scarlet'), medium pink ('Rose'), white ('Ice Queen'), salmon with white center ('Dolly').	Distinct zoning in most varieties. Dense flower heads, 3-5 in. wide. Seed sold by varieties.
Smash Hit	15 in.	Red, salmon, rose, pink.	Dense, mounding habit. Seed sold by varieties.
Sprinter	15-18 in.	White ('Snow White'), scarlet, salmon-pink ('Cherie'), bright rose-pink ('Showgirl'), deep red ('Vulcan'), salmon ('Debutante').	Vigorous, bushy, self-branching. Big (4-in.) flower heads. Seed sold by varieties and as mixture. Very early.

OTHER GERANIUMS

Type	Height	Species or Varieties
Ivy Geranium *(P. peltatum)*	pendulous to 12-36 in.	'L'Elegante' has bluish-pink flowers and variegated leaves; 'Galilee', double, bright rose-pink; 'La France', double, mauve; 'Mexican Beauty', claret red; 'The Pearl', semidouble, light pink.
Lady Washington *(P. x domesticum)*	18-24 in.	'Applause' has pale pink, frilly flowers; 'Aztec', white with crimson blotch; 'Cézanne', purple and lavender, bicolored; 'Flame', brilliant red, 'Grand Slam', rose-red shading into crimson.
Scented Geranium	variable	'Apple' *(P. odoratissimum)* has moss-green leaves and pink flowers. 'Bode's Peppermint' (variety of *P. tomentosum)* has small white flowers splotched with red. 'Coconut' *(P. grossularioides)* is a hanging basket plant with deep rose-purple flowers. 'Fair Ellen', variety of *P. quercifolium,* is eucalyptus scented and has pink flowers and bicolored foliage; variety 'Prostratum', a trailing form, has pink flowers with purple veins.

Perennial garden penstemon (*Penstemon gloxinioides*) makes a showy floral display in early summer.

Cascading types of petunias (*Petunia x hybrida*) create a sparkling display in window boxes or hanging baskets.

Petunias (*Petunia x hybrida*) fill the garden with alluring masses of vibrant flowers over an extended season.

Penstemon gloxinioides

Garden Penstemon, Beard-Tongue

Zones: 8-10. To 1-1/2-2 feet. Perennial, sometimes grown as an annual.

Garden penstemon, a vigorous, bushy plant with a handsome form and luxurious flowers, is actually a hybrid of two American wildflowers, *P. hartwegii* and *P. cobaea*. Upright stems, with a fairly dense covering of linear, horizontally-held leaves, grow from a basal clump of foliage. One-inch-long tubular flowers flare into two lips—the upper lip with two lobes and the lower one with three—and are arranged in loose spikes. They are richly colored in reds, purples, and pinks with fuzzy white throats.

Penstemon blooms in early summer. It mixes well in flower borders, and semiformal plantings and shows to best advantage when planted in groups or masses.

Purchase plants or sow seeds in the garden during late summer for flowers the following year. Start seed indoors, 8 weeks before last spring frost for early spring planting. Germination takes 30 days. Space plants 10 to 18 inches apart in porous, slightly acid soil with average fertility and moisture. Provide

full sun in cooler areas, partial shade in hot areas.

If faded flowers are trimmed, plants may rebloom in late summer. Heavily mulched plants may survive in Zone 7. Clumps need dividing every 2 to 4 years. Do not overwater or fertilize excessively.

Petunia x hybrida

Petunia

Perennial in Zone 10. Annual elsewhere. To 12-14 inches.

Modern petunias represent the state of the hybridizer's art. Once gangly, homely cousins of the potato, petunias have been transformed into robust, compact plants with astonishingly showy flowers. Downy-leaved, slightly sticky mounding or cascading plants produce flaring trumpet-shaped flowers in colors encompassing white, purples, violets, reds, near-blues, pinks, roses, salmons, corals—and recently, soft yellows—together with many bicolors. Single and double flowers may be fringed, frilled, or smooth-edged.

The list of choices is nearly endless, as is the list of available strains and varieties. Most popular are the Single Grandifloras, a large group of foot-high petunias with flowers 3

to 6 inches wide; extravagant Double Grandifloras are of comparable size. Single and Double Multifloras are 1 foot high and have equally impressive colors, patterns, and forms; flowers are smaller (2 to 2-1/2 inches), but are more profuse than Grandifloras. Single petunias are generally more vigorous plants than those producing double flowers. They bloom all summer until fall frost.

Petunias are excellent in beds, window boxes, and planters. Cascading types are especially useful for hanging baskets.

Buy seedlings, or sow seeds indoors 10 to 12 weeks before the last spring frost, and maintain 70° to 75°F for germination in 10 days. Some varieties, including all doubles, need 80°F for germination. Do not cover seeds with soil. Plant seedlings 12 inches apart in rich, well-drained soil. In most areas petunia needs all-day or half a day of full sun, but requires light shade in hottest climates.

When seedlings reach 6 inches, pinch tips to induce branching, and pinch again after first flush of blooming. Remove spent flowers faithfully. Feed monthly with a balanced fertilizer. Midway to late in the season, clip gangly plants back to encourage fresh growth.

Petunia

Variety or Series	Flowers	Comments
SINGLE GRANDIFLORA		
'Appleblossom'	Soft salmon-pink, fringed, slightly variegated.	Compact, weather tolerant. An award winner.
'Blue Picotee'	Deep blue-violet with fringed white edges.	Free flowering.
'Burgundy'	Velvety wine-red, dark-veined throat.	Early, compact.
'California Girl'	Deepest of the yellows.	Beautiful. Best yellow color.
'Candy Apple'	Vivid scarlet.	More rain-resistant than other reds.
Cloud	White ('Snow Cloud'); deep blue, bright red, deep rose, deep salmon; especially large (4-5 in.).	Good in hanging baskets. Sold by varieties and as mixture.
Color Parade	Fringed and frilled, wide color range.	Sold as mixture.
'Fiesta'	Candy-striped bright rose and white.	Very early.
'Flamenco'	Vibrant, deep rose-red.	Early and compact.
Frost	Deep cherry-red with white outer edge ('Cherry Frost'), or deep violet-blue edged white ('Blue Frost').	Compact, spreading. Sold by varieties.
'Glacier'	Pure white.	Smog tolerant.
Magic	Deep violet-blue ('Black Magic'); medium violet-blue ('Blue Magic'); silvery light blue with light throat ('Sky Magic'); yellow, white, pink, red, light pink ('Chiffon Magic'); salmon-pink ('Coral Magic'); ruby-red ('Ruby Magic').	Compact, good for bedding. Sold by varieties and as mixture.
'Malibu'	Medium blue, fading blue-violet.	Free flowering.
'Mariner'	Rich deep blue.	Rain-resistant, dwarf.
Razzle Dazzle	Bicolors: white-starred scarlet, deep rose, deep blue, crimson.	Sold as mixture.
'Red Picotee'	Bright red with broad white edge.	Compact plant. An award winner.
'Starburst'	Rose starred with white.	Beautiful planted with pure whites.
Ultra	Rose-pink ('Ultra Pink'), red, soft salmon-pink ('Ultra Salmon'), white.	Compact and spreading. Sold by varieties.
DOUBLE GRANDIFLORA		
'Blue Danube'	Lavender-blue with deep blue veining, very lacy.	Widely considered the outstanding blue double.
'Blushing Maid'	Soft salmon-pink with deeper center.	Compact, free flowering. An award winner.
Bouquet	Deep violet-blue ('Blue Bouquet'); white ('Bridal Bouquet'); orchid-lavender, veined ('Orchid Bouquet'); rose-pink ('Pink Bouquet'); scarlet ('Red Bouquet'); light salmon-pink ('Salmon Bouquet'); all fringed.	Compact, early. Sold by varieties.
'Circus'	Salmon-red and white bicolor.	Early, profuse bloomer. Compact, with basal branching. An award winner.
Double mix	Variable.	Most seed companies and growers sell a mixture.
'Sonata'	Pure white, large.	Tall, to 14 inches—may need pinching.
'Valentine'	Vivid red, large.	Compact, branching habit.
SINGLE MULTIFLORA		
'Comanche'	Scarlet-crimson.	Very free flowering.
Joy	Bright scarlet ('Red Joy'); violet-blue ('Blue Joy'); rose-pink ('Rose Joy'); soft, light blue ('Sky Joy'); rose with white star ('Star Joy'); rich blue with white star ('Starlight Joy'); white, medium salmon-pink ('Pink Joy'); deep violet-purple ('Purple Joy').	Early and compact. Flowers large (to 3 in.). Sold by varieties and as mixture.
'Paleface'	White with creamy throat.	Excellent for every kind of planter.
Plum	Light blue, dark veins ('Plum Blue'); light purple, dark veins ('Plum Purple'); rose-pink, dark veins ('Plum Pink'); bright orchid, wine veins ('Sugar Plum').	The most resistant petunias to weather damage. Sold by varieties and as mixture (Plum Pudding) which includes 'Summer Sun'.
'Summer Sun'	Yellow.	Compact habit. Very weather tolerant.
DOUBLE MULTIFLORA		
Delight	Rose-lavender, dark veins ('Lavender Delight'); light rose-pink, dark pink veins ('Pink Delight'); scarlet-and-white ('Red and White Delight'); light salmon-pink ('Salmon Delight'); white.	Compact, weather tolerant. Sold by varieties and as mixture.
Tart	Coral-red ('Apple Tart'); rose-pink and white ('Cherry Tart'); soft pink veined rose-pink ('Peppermint Tart'); orchid veined wine-red ('Plum Tart'); white ('Snowberry Tart').	Compact, weather tolerant. Sold by varieties and as mixture (Sweet Tarts).

Mixed varieties of phlox *(Phlox drummondii)* create a mass of lively color in the midground of a flower bed.

Summer phlox *(Phlox paniculata)*, in foreground, is a mainstay of traditional perennial borders and flowers profusely during July and August.

Phlox

Botanical Name/ Common Name	Zones	Plant Description	Flower Description	Comments
Phlox carolina Thick-leaf Phlox	3-9	Upright to 4 feet with 5-inch, lance-shaped glossy leaves. Perennial.	Clustered flat-faced flowers with long tubes. Fragrant. Purple, pink, occasionally white. Blooms in midspring.	Full sun. Less disease-prone than other phlox. Propagate by division in spring.
P.c. 'Miss Lingard'		3 feet tall.	Pure white.	Popular variety.
P.c. 'Gloriosa'			Salmon-pink.	
Phlox divaricata Blue Phlox, Wild Sweet William	3-9	Spreading by underground shoots, reaches 1 to 1-1/2 feet tall. Foliage oval, 1 to 2 inches long. Perennial.	Violet-blue, pink, lavender, white. Blooms in midspring. Flowers lightly scented, 1-1/2-inch blossoms blanket plant. Held in loose clusters 10-15 inches above foliage.	Plants prefer light shade, average water, rich slightly acid soil. Take root-stem cuttings or divisions in spring, space 12 inches. Divide every 2-3 years in late summer.
P. d. 'Laphamii'			Deep blue large flowers.	Sun hardy.
Phlox drummondii Annual Phlox	2-10	Plants with upright leafy stems, to 1-1/2 feet. Leaves 3 inches long. Annual.	Rose, red, pink, purple, white. Blooms in summer.	Full sun to light shade where hot. Propagate by seed in spring. Dwarf varieties available. Excellent for flower border.
Phlox nivalis Trailing Phlox	8-10	Low growing, trailing to 6 inches. Leaves linear, 1/2 inch long. Perennial.	Similar to moss pink. Flowers 1 in. across on 3- to 6-inch stems. Purple, pink, white. Blooms in spring.	Plant in sun, partial shade. Tolerates some dryness. Colorful, low cover for edging and rock garden.
P. n. 'Azurea'			Pale blue.	
P. n. 'Cemla'			Salmon-pink.	
P. n. 'Sylvestris'			Rose-pink.	
Phlox paniculata Garden Phlox, Summer Phlox	3-9	Clump-forming plants with many upright stems, 2-6 feet tall. High-quality foliage. Dense, 3- to 5-inch lance-shaped leaves. Perennial.	Soft, rich colors, enchanting fragrance. Flowers in large, densely packed domes, 10 to 14 inches across, 12 to 15 inches tall. White, wine, rose, magenta, crimson, lilac, salmon, pink, some with contrasting eye. Blooms in summer.	Sun to part shade. Divide taking most vigorous shoots, every 3 years. Space 1-1/2 to 2-1/2 feet apart. Thin old growth annually. Seeds take 3 years to flower. One of the best cut flowers, and border plants. Foliage may get mildew.
P. p. 'B. Symon-Jeune'			Rose-pink, red eye.	
P. p. 'Dresden China'			Soft pink.	
P. p. 'Progress'			Purple.	
P. p. 'Star Free'			Brilliant red.	
P. p. 'White Admiral'			White.	
Phlox stolonifera Creeping Phlox	3-9	Low growing; forms spreading mat. Hairy leaves, 3 to 4 inches. Perennial.	Flowers large, 1 inch across, held in loose clusters 6 to 12 inches high. Purple, violet, white. Blooms from spring to summer.	Treat as with other low-growing phlox. Rock gardens, low, colorful covers.
P. s. alba			White.	
P. s. 'Blue Ridge'			Pale blue.	
P. s. 'Rosea'			Pink.	
Phlox subulata Moss Pink	3-9	Low-growing mat, spreading to 2 feet, 6-8 inches high. Small leaves sharply pointed, fully covering stems, evergreen. Perennial.	Vivid colors: pink, red, magenta, lavender, white. Blooms in spring. Plants carpeted in color, small flowers on 1/2- to 3/4-inch stems.	Full sun. Plants root along stems, easy propagation by layering or division in spring or fall. Tolerates dry conditions and poor soil. Excellent for low ground cover, dry rock gardens.
P. s. 'Brilliant'			Magenta.	
P. s. 'Emerald Cushion'			Pink.	
P. s. 'Scarlet Flame'			Red.	

Phlox
Phlox

Zones: 2-10. To 6 inches-4 feet.
Annuals and perennials.

Phlox are loved for their unfailing lavish clusters of funnel-shaped flowers that flare into five wide lobes. Low-growing species make ideal rock garden, border, or edging plants. Taller varieties are favorites in perennial gardens.

Most tall species thrive with a regular care routine. Plant in moist, fertile soil and feed with a balanced formula once or twice during the growing season. Keep evenly moist and water only early in the day to discourage mildew.

Trailing varieties tolerate sandy, drier conditions. They are low-maintenance plants once established. Shear lightly after flowering to stimulate new growth.

Balloon Flower
Platycodon grandiflorus

Zones: 3-9. To 1-1/2 to 2-1/2 feet.
Perennial.

The cheerful balloons promised by balloon flower's common name are inflated flower buds that open into five-pointed bowl-shaped blossoms. Blossoms are broad, 2 to 3 inches across, colored in richest blues, lilac, pink, and white. Darker-colored veins streak the open flower bowl. Flowers resemble those of *Campanula*, a close relative. Balloon flowers bloom from June to September if spent flowers are removed.

These attractive plants have leathery, glossy foliage that stays good-looking all season. Stems grow upright and make well-formed clumps, effective as accent groups in the fore- or midground of a bed or border. For long-lasting cut flowers, sear cut end of stem.

Balloon flowers grow under a variety of conditions. A sandy soil of average fertility is best, and good drainage is a must for plants to survive wet winters. Locate in full sun or partial shade; pinks and whites do best in light shade. Plant nursery plants or take divisions from thick crowns by carefully cutting several roots and buds from around the edges of established plants in spring. Seeds may be sown directly in the garden, but plants will take 2 years to flower.

Removing spent flowers and an occasional fertilizing are all the care balloon flower needs. Plants are slow to start growth in spring, and care should be taken not to injure dormant crowns and roots. Plants rarely need division, spread very slowly, and are pest-free.

Top-rated varieties are: 'Shell Pink', a soft creamy pink, or 'Mariesii', a double-flowered compact form, to 18 inches, with bright blue, white, and rosy-lilac variations.

Portulaca, Rose Moss, Sun Plant
Portulaca grandiflora

Zones: 2-10. To 2-7 inches.
Annual.

Quick to bloom from seed, utterly care-free, and never so happy as in a hot, dry place, portulaca is a colorful solution to many gardening problems. Sprawling or compact plants with needlelike, succulent leaves produce 2-1/2-inch, semidouble or roselike double flowers in white, orange, gold, yellow, cream, pink, rose, rose-purple, orchid, and scarlet. Blooms appear from early summer to frost, closing in the evening and when cloudy.

Portulaca makes an excellent seasonal ground and dry bank cover; and is perfect for hanging baskets, seldom-watered beds and borders, and rock gardens. It brings sparkle to any sunbaked, dry spot—growing even in pavement cracks and between stones. It reseeds freely.

Plant nursery seedlings in late spring; or sow outdoors after the last spring frost, or indoors at 68° to 86°F for germination in 10 to 14 days. Plant 8 to 18 inches apart, depending upon ultimate size. Poor, sandy soil is best. Water infrequently, and give full sun.

Sunglo Hybrid mixture grows to 7 inches, and double flowers stay fairly open on dark days. Afternoon Delight mixture is dwarf with full-size double flowers that close late in the day. Sunnyside mixture, 6 inches tall, has large double flowers in many colors, including variegated rose. The most compact mixture, Minilaca, has semidouble flowers, 2-inch plants.

Dwarf forms of annual phlox *(Phlox drummondii)* bring bright summer color to many garden sites.

The puffed up flower buds of balloon flower *(Platycodon grandiflorus)* open into long-lasting, starlike blossoms.

Rose moss *(Portulaca grandiflora)* is a fast-growing annual that requires minimal care and provides masses of colorful blooms in dry, hot sites.

Flowers of polyanthus primrose *(Primula x polyantha)* come in clear vibrant colors with contrasting yellow eyes.

Deliciously fragrant and delicately showy, auricula primrose *(Primula auriculata)* makes an appealing addition to shady settings in early spring.

Primula
Primrose
Zones: 2-10. To 4-12 inches.
Annuals and perennials.

Primroses are beautiful additions to woodland plantings, formal flower beds, or used as a companion for spring bulbs. They generally have a rosette or basal clump of foliage. Flowers may be tightly clustered, whorled or tiered like a candelabra.

The cool, moist, and partly shaded growing conditions of a woodland setting are ideal for these spring-bloomers. Soil should be well-drained, fertile, and neutral. Plants tolerate full sun, but the flowers fade rapidly.

It's best to purchase plants or use divisions. Set out in early spring or late fall. Water deeply periodically and feed each spring. Mulch in summer to help retain soil moisture. Plants need winter mulch in cold climates. Divide established plants every 3 or 4 years.

Primula

Botanical Name/ Common Name	Zones	Plant Description	Flower Description	Comments
Primula auricula **Auricula Primrose**	4-8	Large leathery leaves, 8 in. long, have mealy coating.	Yellow, rose, purple, with white or yellow eye. Blooms in early spring.	Flowers fragrant, held on 6- to 8-inch stems. Needs excellent drainage away from crown. Various forms used in alpine rock gardens, pots, bedding.
Primula denticulata **Himalayan Primrose**	5-8	Plant grows to 12 inches, leaves 6 to 8 inches.	Flowers appear early before leaves fully out, held in rounded cluster on 12-inch stem. Lilac, red, white, mauve. Early spring.	Hardy and easy to grow.
Primula japonica **Japanese Primrose**	5-8	Leaves large, lush, 10 inches long. Plant grows 2 to 3 ft tall.	Flowers in candelabra form on 2- to 3-foot stem. White, pink, magenta, crimson. Spring blooming.	Plants grow in moist to boggy soils, demand rich conditions.
Primula malacoides **Fairy Primrose**	8-10	Plant low-growing, delicate looking. Leaves rounded, thin, hairy.	Flowers on slender stems in whorls, airy, delicate appearance. Pastel lavender, pink, white, red. Early-spring blooming.	Plants grown as annual with early-flowering bulbs. Good with ferns, in shady gardens, under tall shrubs, in pots. Propagate by seed or transplants.
Primula x polyantha **Polyanthus Primrose**	5-9	Basal rosette of 4- to 6-in. tongue-shaped leaves with rich green crinkled texture. Plants attractive all season. 6 to 12 inches tall.	Flowers 1 to 2 in. across in large clusters, on thick erect stems. Pure red, purple, yellow, pink, bronze, apricot, maroon. All with yellow eye, some gold-edged, or double. Blooms in spring.	A most popular, colorful bedding or pot plant, often used as an annual. Plants short-lived but divide easily every 2-3 years. Plants die back, resprout in early spring. May self-sow.
P. x p. **'Pacific Giants'**			Full color range.	Large flowers, productive.
P. x p. **'Colossea Hybrids'**			Yellow, pink, copper, red.	Large flowers.
P. x p. **'Blue Beauties'**			Violet, blue, with gold eye.	
Primula sieboldii **Siebold Primrose**	5-9	Leaves scalloped-edged, crinkled texture.	White, pink, rose, lilac or bi-colored. Blooms in late spring. Flowers on long slender stems.	Leaves die back in summer heat. Shallow rhizomes. Propagate by division or root cuttings.
Primula vulgaris **English Primrose**	5-8	Rosette of 6- to 10-in. leaves.	Butter-yellow, white, blue, red, purple. Early spring. Flowers fragrant, single-stemmed, 1 inch across.	Traditional garden primrose. Long-lived, and evergreen in mild climates. Divide every 3 years.

Ranunculus asiaticus
Persian Ranunculus, Persian Buttercup

Hardy in Zones 8-10. To 12-18 inches.

Tender tuber.

You can enjoy the camellialike, 3- to 5-inch flowers of this exotic buttercup in all climate zones if you dig and store the tubers during winter; in the South, they can remain in place year-round. In late spring or summer, white, red, pink, rose, orange, yellow, gold, or salmon flowers made up of numerous tightly wound petals bloom 1 to 4 per stem. Established plants produce several stems each.

Use ranunculus massed in beds or mixed with other flowers. They are unexcelled as cut flowers.

In Zones 8 to 10, plant in late fall. Elsewhere, plant in spring when the soil is warm. Soak tubers in tepid water for several hours, then plant, claws down, 2 to 3 inches deep and 4 to 6 inches apart. *Ranunculus* needs rich, moist soil with rapid drainage. You can start tubers indoors in moist sand 8 weeks before the last frost; do not overwater sprouting tubers. Regular water and fertilizer and a cool environment are best. Dig tubers in autumn, after foliage begins to die.

Persian ranunculus is often sold simply by color or as a mixture. Telecote Giants are sold in shades of various colors—for example, Telecote Giants Rose has shades that range from light rose to rose-red. Telecote Giants Picotee Mixture has multicolored flowers.

Rosa
Rose

Zones: 5-10. To 3-10 feet.

Deciduous or semievergreen woody perennial.

Two types of roses, hybrid teas and grandifloras, are grown almost exclusively for their flowers rather than as landscape shrubs.

Hybrid teas are the classic long-stemmed flower that comes to mind whenever roses are mentioned. Hundreds of varieties are available with every color except blue represented. A wide range of bicolored flowers is also available. Many hybrid teas are intensely fragrant. All are excellent cut flowers. Plants vary in height, but most varieties grow between 3 and 5 feet high. They are often trained as small trees. Flowers are borne singly or in clusters of 2 or 3.

Grandifloras are taller than hybrid teas, often reaching 8 to 10 feet high. They are vigorous bloomers, producing large clusters of flowers. Blossoms are similar to hybrid teas but slightly smaller. All colors except blue and green are represented. Many varieties are very fragrant.

Hybrid tea and grandiflora roses bloom primarily in spring and again in fall. However, many varieties repeat bloom throughout summer. Hybrid teas are excellent container or accent plants and are particularly exciting combined with annuals lining a walk or entryway. Grandifloras are colorful backgrounds for perennial borders.

Annual pruning is very important to keep hybrid tea and grandiflora roses looking their best. In winter, remove all but 3 to 6 of the the strongest canes. The remaining canes should be evenly spaced around the plant crown. Cut the selected canes back to 10 to 18 inches above the ground. The number of canes left should depend on the vigor of the plant. Strong-growing plants that are several years old can support the most canes. Older grandifloras can support up to 8 canes.

For more information on growing roses, see page 193.

Rudbeckia hirta
Black-eyed Susan, Gloriosa Daisy

Zones: 4-10. To 3 feet.

Annual, biennial, or short-lived perennial

Black-eyed Susan creates glowing swatches of bright color from spring until fall frost when planted en masse. The 3- to 6-inch daisies are

Available in a full color spectrum, the frilly double flowers of Persian ranunculus *(Ranunculus asiaticus),* are dazzling in spring gardens.

Roses *(Rosa* sp.) are universally loved garden flowers treasured for their memorable fragrance and attractive blooms.

Black-eyed Susan *(Rudbeckia hirta)* is bright and dramatic in large-scale plantings and low-maintenance gardens.

Tolerating dry or moist conditions, gloriosa daisy *(Rudbeckia hirta 'Gloriosa Daisy')* is a choice plant for difficult situations.

An annual with extravagantly beautiful flowers, painted-tongue *(Salpiglossis sinuata)* makes a lavish display massed in beds or used in large drifts in borders.

orange-yellow, maroon, or mahogany with big, dark brown domes forming the eye. Bicolored varieties are banded dramatically with contrasting colors. Flowering stems grow upright to several feet tall from a basal clump of foliage and are perfect for cutting. The leaves are rough and hairy, somewhat gray-green in color.

Use black-eyed Susan to create bold, mass plantings in wildflower and meadow gardens. Plant in smaller groups as a color accent in flower beds and borders. An excellent choice for low-maintenance gardens.

Extremely adaptable, black-eyed Susan tolerates both hot, dry conditions and partially shady moist sites. Average garden conditions are best. This short-lived perennial is not invasive and volunteer seedlings are thinned easily. Cutting flowers regularly prolongs blooming.

To establish new beds, set out nursery plants or divisions in spring or early fall, spacing 12 to 24 inches apart. Seed can be sown directly in the garden in spring if preferred and plants will usually bloom that summer. Avoid mildew by watering only in morning and providing good air circulation.

Top-rated varieties include 'Gloriosa Daisy' in mixed colors, with banded or solid flowers.

R. fulgida sullivantii is a longer-lived perennial with slightly drooping golden-yellow petals surrounding large-coned centers. Foliage is attractive, on well-branched stems to 2-1/2 feet tall. Look for 'Goldsturm', a particularly fine variation.

Salpiglossis sinuata
Painted-Tongue, Salpiglossis
Zones: 2-10. To 15-30 inches.
Annual.

This elegant beauty looks like a psychedelic petunia—funnel-shaped velvety blossoms are intricately netted, veined, and shaded. Colors are vivid, including purple, mahogany, yellow, scarlet, magenta, and many bicolors. Plants are willowy or bushy, depending upon the variety. *Salpiglossis* blooms from midsummer to frost. Mass in beds or make drifts in borders for a dazzling display. It makes a superlative cut flower.

Success with salpiglossis depends largely upon planting seedlings immediately after last spring frost, well before summer heat. (Cool summer climate is ideal but not mandatory.) Purchase seedlings or sow indoors, at 70° to 80°F, 8 weeks before the last spring frost, for germination in 15 to 20 days. Do not cover seeds with soil, but keep dark with a black plastic cover. Plant seedlings 8 inches apart in full sun in rich, moist, fast-draining soil. Don't overwater or overfertilize, and don't allow soil to get too dry.

Top-rated taller salpiglossis are Bolero and Splash mixtures, to 30 inches tall. Friendship mixture grows to 15 inches.

Salvia
Sage
Zones: 2-10. To 2-5 feet.
Annuals and perennials.

Several species of sage make excellent plants for flower beds and borders. They offer a long season of colorful slender flower spikes in blues, purples, reds, and white. Plants generally grow upright, forming a tidy clump of well-branched stems cloaked with soft, hairy bright green or grayish leaves.

The tall flower spikes look striking in mass plantings or placed in groups for a vertical accent.

Plant all species in full sun. Many varieties thrive in the warmest garden sites and are tolerant of dry conditions. Nearly all garden soils are suitable.

Start new plantings by seed or nursery transplants. Half-hardy perennials and annuals can be started indoors 10 to 12 weeks before last spring frost. Plants bloom the first season. Plant hardy perennials in early fall or spring. Perennials should be divided every 3 to 4 years.

Keep soil moderately moist and feed in early spring. Pinching back tips during growing season will create a denser, bushier plant. Cut stems back after hard frost in fall and provide a mulch for winter protection in coldest areas.

The clarion color of scarlet sage *(Salvia splendens)* makes it a brilliant addition to flower beds; blooms profusely from summer to fall.

Most members of the sage family *(Salvia* sp.) produce graceful spikes of blue flowers that enhance a variety of garden situations during a long blooming season.

Salvia

Botanical Name/ Common Name	Zones	Plant Description	Flower Description	Comments
Salvia azurea **Azure Sage**	Perennial in 6-10.	Gray-green leaves form a dense mass. Plants reach 4 to 6 feet.	Brilliant blue flowers bloom summer into fall.	Hardy perennial, takes heat and full sun. Plants may tolerate colder zones if adequately mulched.
S. a. grandiflora		Plants 3 to 5 feet tall have lance-shaped leaves 1-1/2 to 4 inches long.	Clear, deep blue flowers.	Abundant, large flowers. Good for cutting.
Salvia farinacea **Mealy-cup Sage**	Perennial in 8-10, annual elsewhere.	Bushy with fernlike gray-green, linear leaves to 4 inches. Plants reach 3 feet.	Violet-blue flowers bloom early summer to frost.	Half-hardy perennial, annual in coldest zones. Popular ornamental for its long bloom season, fine flowers. Use as edging, border color. Good cut flowers.
S. f. 'Blue Bedder'		Compact, to 2 feet.	Blue flowers.	
S. f. 'Victoria'		Dwarf, to 18 inches.	Violet-blue.	Prolific bloomer; intense color.
Salvia patens **Gentian sage**	Perennial in 8-10, annual elsewhere.	Compact, leafy form 1-1/2 to 3 feet tall. Leaves triangular in shape, green, downy beneath. Tuberous rooted.	Flowers white, dark or light blue. Bloom in early summer.	Annual or half-hardy perennial. Chosen for its large flowers, handsome foliage. Treated as annual where temperatures freeze. Roots may be stored over winter, with partial success, grows readily by seed. Does best in mild climates.
S. p. 'Alba'			White.	
S. p. 'Cambridge Blue'			Light blue.	
Salvia pratensis **Meadow Clary**	Perennial in 4-10.	Many flowering stems, 3-1/2 feet tall, from basal rosette. Plants well formed, sturdy. Leaves wrinkled, 2 to 6 in. long, broad lance-shaped.	Blue shades, bloom early to mid-summer.	Short-lived perennial. Valued for its abundant blossoms, long flower stems.
Salvia splendens **Scarlet Sage**	Perennial in 9-10, annual elsewhere.	Broad heart-shaped leaves, 2 to 3 in. long, have fine deep green color. Leafy, upright stems 2 to 3 ft tall.	Vivid reds, large blossoms. Pink, white, purple varieties available. Blooms summer to fall.	One of the most popular annuals for bedding plant color. Dwarf 1-foot plants good as edging, in pots.
Salvia x superba	Perennial in 6-10.	2-1/2- to 3-foot plants with dwarf forms available. Leaves gray-green, aromatic. Plants uniform.	Violet-purple. Blooms June to August.	Perennial hybrid of high quality with tall, long-lasting flower spikes. Effective massed. Flowers good cut fresh or in dried arrangements. Cut back stems in fall.
S. x s. 'May Night'		1-1/2 to 2 feet.	Violet-blue.	
S. x s. 'East Friesland'		Compact to 18 inches.	Vivid violet-blue.	

Graceful arching straplike foliage and lush spikes of nodding flowers make Spanish bluebells *(Scilla hispanica)* a choice bulb for woodland settings.

A tender bulb ideal for container-growing in cold climates or for garden use in mild climates, Peruvian jacinth *(Scilla peruviana)* offers large domelike heads of tiny flowers from mid- to late spring.

Durable and long-lived, showy stonecrop *(Sedum spectabile)* has distinctive succulent foliage and bears large flat-topped clusters of tiny flowers in August.

Scilla
Scilla, Squill
Bulbs.

Formerly a large group of plants, *Scilla* has been diminished since botanists renamed the popular bluebells or wood hyacinths *Endymion*. They are still usually sold under the name *Scilla* however. Scillas naturalize in sunny or lightly shaded spots. Blue, pink, and white forms of each are sold.

Scilla hispanica (S. campanulata)
Spanish Bluebell
Zones: 4-10. To 20 inches.

Recently renamed *Endymion hispanicus*, Spanish bluebell is a favorite for adding beautiful blue color to gardens in late spring. Tall stalks bearing as many as 30 bell-like flowers rise above a basal cluster of strap-shaped leaves. Pink and white varieties are available. It grows in full sun or deep shade and naturalizes well in woodland settings. Plant bulbs in fall 6 to 8 inches apart, 2 to 3 inches deep.

Scilla peruviana
Cuban Lily, Hyacinth-of-Peru, Peruvian Jacinth
Zones: 9-10. To 12-18 inches.

This tender bulb is prized in mild climates for its large, lush, informal clumps in the garden. Elsewhere, it can be forced indoors. In mid- or late spring, masses of small, deep blue flowers form 6-inch domelike heads atop bare 1-1/2-foot-tall stems. White and pink forms are available. Light green, foot-long, strap-shaped leaves arch gracefully and form attractive, dense masses at the base of the flower stalks.

Cuban lily does best in light shade in rich, fast-draining soil. Plant bulbs in fall, 3 inches deep.

Scilla siberica
Siberian Scilla, Siberian Squill
Zones: 3-8. To 6 inches.

Among early-spring bulbs, Siberian scilla is one of the daintiest. Nodding, frilly blue flowers are borne 1 to 6 in a cluster, on gracefully tapering 6-inch-tall stems, above small, narrow leaves. Colors are white and several shades of blue. Naturalize in masses beneath deciduous trees or around flowering shrubs or use in rock gardens or as edging. Use it alone or combine with other early-blooming bulbs. Plant 3 inches deep and 3 inches apart, in sun or partial shade. Bulbs quickly form clumps. Siberian squill does not adapt well in Zones 9 and 10.

Sedum spectabile
Showy Stonecrop
Zones: 3-10. To 1-1/2 to 2 feet. Perennial.

This stunning succulent offers late-season color and an interesting form. The fleshy leaves are light gray-green and are arranged in whorls on upright stems that spread from the plant base, forming a neat 2-foot mound. Big, flat flower clusters top each stem in August, opening white, pink, carmen, or rose and aging to bronze. Spent flowers are attractive until frost.

Showy stonecrop is an outstanding plant for sunny spots and is highly effective massed among rockery in dry gardens. Plants tolerate partial shade where summer temperatures are high. Plants aren't fussy about soil, although extra-rich or poorly drained soils are not recommended. Standing water near plant crown causes rotting. Once established, this sedum is durable and long-lived.

Plant rooted stem cuttings or nursery plants in spring. Space approximately 18 inches apart. Seed may be sown at the same time but flower color is often unpredictable. Plants seldom need dividing and are not bothered by pests or diseases

'Autumn Joy' has large flower heads opening pink, aging to salmon, then rusty red. 'Star Dust' has white flowers and blue-green leaves. 'Carmen' is deep rose, 'Meteor' wine-red, and 'Brilliant' carmine.

Solidago hybrids
Goldenrod
Zones: 3-10. To 1-1/2 to 3-1/2 feet. Perennial.

Garden varieties of goldenrod reflect the finest features of our native species, which are mistakenly blamed for causing hayfever. Lavish late-summer bloom, an exceptionally care-free nature, and a sturdy form make goldenrod top-rated. Plants form clumps of upright stems covered with long lance-shaped leaves. In August, tiny golden blossoms are borne in plumelike clusters.

Plant in small groups in the midground of a flower bed where its bold color will create dramatic accents, or naturalize in a meadow. Cut flowers make handsome bouquets.

Undemanding, goldenrod thrives in nearly any garden. Full sun assures maximum flowering. Tolerates wet or dry soil. Set out nursery plants in spring, about 12 inches apart. Plants are pest-free, long-lived, and stay within bounds. Divide every 4 years.

Top-rated varieties offer many shades of yellow. Select colors that complement your garden's color scheme. 'Cloth of Gold' is soft yellow; good with other pastels; growth is compact to 18 inches. 'Golden Mosa' reaches 3 feet with huge lemon-yellow plumes. 'Leraft' is golden. 'Peter Pan' bushy and clear yellow. Choose 'Golden Dwarf' for border edges.

Sparaxis
Wandflower, Harlequin Flower
Zone: 10. To 12-18 inches.
Corm.

Spikes of blossoms up to 3 inches wide, in shades of orange, red, yellow, white, or purple and marked with yellow throats and black splotches, distinguish wandflower. The graceful spring-blooming spikes and the narrow, grasslike foliage resemble that of relatives freesia, iris, and gladiolus.

In Zone 10 wandflower often naturalizes in rock gardens or borders. Elsewhere it must be grown in planters that can be moved indoors during winter.

Planter culture also enables you to meet two of its special needs: complete dryness during summer dormancy (foliage dies back in summer and regrows in fall) and excellent drainage. Full sun and regular watering are important during growth and blooming. Any fast-draining soil is suitable. Plant corms 1 to 2 inches deep and 2 to 3 inches apart in fall.

Wandflower is usually sold in mixtures. Telecote Mixture has especially large flowers.

Tagetes hybrids
Marigold
Zones: 2-10. To 8-40 inches.
Annual.

Modern garden marigolds originated from two roadside Mexican wildflowers. Extensive breeding turned them into brilliant, sturdy flowers—today's most popular sun-loving annuals. Flowers may be single, crested (with large outer petals and tighter, more upright center petals), or double (a tight, carnationlike ball of petals).

Colors are cheery shades of yellow, gold, orange, mahogany and, recently developed, an almost-pure white. Many varieties are bicolored. Plants are erect and often very bushy. Bright green, toothed, ferny foliage has a distinctive scent. Marigolds bloom profusely from summer until frost.

Small marigolds are excellent in beds and borders and as edging, and they make dependable showy container plants. Tall types can be planted to form a dense, background. All are superb cut flowers.

Smaller types bloom rapidly from seed sown outdoors. Taller ones should be started indoors 4 to 6 weeks before last frost, at 70° to 75°F, for germination in 5 to 7 days. All types are widely available as nursery seedlings. Plant 6 to 18 inches apart, depending upon ultimate size, in full sun or very light shade, in well-drained, ordinary soil. Plant taller types out of the wind, and stake if necessary. Marigolds look best with occasional watering and light, infrequent feeding. Remove spent flowers to stimulate blooming. (See chart on next page.)

All during August clusters of tiny yellow flowers cover the tops of the upright stems of goldenrod (*Solidago* hybrids).

The colorful blossoms of wandflower (*Sparaxis* sp.) appear in spring.

Low-growing forms of marigolds (*Tagetes* hybrids) are colorful until fall frost.

Marigolds *(Tagetes* hybrids) offer a wide choice of flower forms, from small crested blossoms, above left, to large pompons, above right, in a range of warm, rich colors and in various sizes. Use tall varieties in the background and lower ones as edging.

Tagetes

Series or Variety	Height	Flower Type	Color and Comments
Aztec	10 in.	Semidouble, flat-crested.	Gold, orange, yellow, sold by color-named variety, or as mixture. Flowers 3-1/4 in. wide.
Boy	8-10 in.	Crested double.	Golden-yellow ('Golden Boy'), maroon-and-deep-orange ('Harmony Boy'), orange ('Orange Boy', award winner), maroon-and-yellow ('Spry Boy'), yellow ('Yellow Boy'). Sold by variety or as Boy O' Boy mixture. Flowers to 2 in. wide.
Burpee's Nugget	10 in.	Double.	Golden-yellow ('Gold Nugget'), orange ('Orange Nugget'), gold overlaid with scarlet ('Red Nugget'), yellow ('Yellow Nugget'), sold by variety or as mixture. Flowers 2 inches wide.
Janie	8 in.	Crested double.	Yellow ('Janie Yellow'), bright golden-yellow ('Janie Gold', award winner), yellow-orange ('Janie Golden Orange') red-and-gold bicolor ('Janie Flame'). Sold by variety or as mixture. Flowers 1-1/2 to 1-3/4 in. wide.
'Lemondrop'	9 in.	Crested double.	Canary-yellow. Flowers 2 in. wide.
Petite	8 in.	Crested double.	Yellow, orange, gold. 'Petite Yellow' sold separately or as mixture. Flowers 1-1/2 to 2 in. wide.
'Bolero'	10-12 in.	Double.	Maroon petals, gold center. Flowers 2 in. wide. Award winner.
Dolly (Guys and Dolls)	10-12 in.	Double.	Lemon, gold, orange ('Dolly'), gold ('Papaya Crush'), yellow ('Pineapple Crush'), deep orange ('Pumpkin Crush'). Sold by variety. Flowers 3-1/2-4 in. wide.
'Matador'	10-12 in.	Double.	Red petals, gold center. Flowers 2 in. wide.
Queen	10-12 in.	Double.	Gold marked with red ('Queen Beatrix'), golden-bronze and russet ('Queen Sophia', award winner), deep scarlet ('Scarlet Sophia'). Sold by variety or as mixture. Flowers 2 in. wide.
'Red Cherry'	10-12 in.	Crested double.	Scarlet-mahogany-and-gold. Flowers 2 to 2-1/2 in. wide.
'Showboat'	10-15 in.	Double.	Bright yellow. Flowers 2 to 2-1/2 in. wide. Award winner.
'Copper Canyon'	12-16 in.	Double.	Orange. Flowers 2-1/2 in. wide.
'Dainty Marietta'	12-16 in.	Single.	Golden-yellow. Flowers 2 in. wide.
Galore	16-18 in.	Double.	Gold ('Gold Galore') and yellow ('Yellow Galore'). Sold separately. Flowers to 3-3/4 in. wide. Award winners.
Inca	14-16 in.	Double.	Yellow and orange, sold by color. Huge flowers—4-5 in. wide.
Lady	15-18 in.	Double.	Yellow ('First Lady', award winner), gold ('Gold Lady'), orange ('Orange Lady'), primrose ('Primrose Lady', award winner). Sold by variety or as Gay Ladies mixture. Flowers 3-1/2 in. wide.
'Naughty Marietta'	12 in.	Single.	Bicolored, golden-yellow marked with scarlet. Flowers 2-1/2 in. wide. Award winner.
'Red Seven Star'	12-16 in.	Double.	Scarlet tinged with gold. Flowers 2-1/2 to 2-3/4 in. wide.
Space Age	14-16 in.	Double.	Golden-orange ('Apollo'), yellow ('Moonshot'), gold ('Viking'). Sold by variety or as mixture. Flowers 3 in. wide.
'Sparky Improved'	12 in.	Double.	Orange, red, yellow. Flowers 2-1/2 in. wide.
'Snowbird'	18 in.	Double.	White, to 2-1/2 in. 3 in. wide. The first named white variety.
Climax	30-36 in.	Double.	Deep orange ('Toreador', award winner), lemon ('Primrose Climax'), golden-yellow ('Golden Climax Improved'), bright yellow ('Yellow Climax'). Sold by variety or as mixture. Flowers to 5 in. wide.
Crackerjack	30-40 in.	Double.	Primrose, yellow, orange, gold. Sold as mixture.
'Happy Face'	24 in.	Double.	Yellow, to 5 in. wide. Award winner.
Jubilee	24-30 in.	Double.	Yellow ('Diamond Jubilee Improved'), gold ('Golden Jubilee', award winner), orange ('Orange Jubilee'). Sold by variety or as mixture. Flowers to 3 in. wide.
'Mellow Yellow'	24-36 in.	Double.	Yellow, to 4 in wide.

Tropaeolum majus
Nasturtium, Indian Cress

Perennial in Zones 9-10. Annual elsewhere. To 12 inches, or trailing to 6 feet.

Nasturtium is a charming plant with dusty-green parasol-shaped leaves and perky irregular-shaped blossoms often with spurs. Flowers are shades of orange, yellow, and red, and modern hybrids hold their blooms well above the foliage. Some varieties are dwarf and mounding and others clamber up trellises or fences and cascade over garden walls.

Nasturtium is best sown outdoors. Covered seeds germinate in 7 to 12 days at around 65°F. Full sun to light shade, ordinary-to-poor, well-drained soil, and average-to-scant watering produce best blooming. Richness and wetness make for lush foliage and few flowers. Nasturtium is at its best in cool-summer areas but grows nearly anywhere. Aphids can be an occasional problem.

Top-rated 1-foot-high dwarfs are: Dwarf Single mixture, Whirlybird mixture (with upward-facing flowers), Jewel mixture (sometimes sold also by colors), and 'Cherry Rose' (with double bright rose flowers). Medium-size and perfect for hanging baskets and training on string is the Gleam mixture (24 inches, with double and semidouble flowers, sometimes sold by colors). Fordhook Favorites and Park's Fragrant Giant mixtures have single flowers and trail to 6 feet.

Tulipa
Tulip

Zones: 5-9. To 8-30 inches.
Bulbs.

By far the most popular garden bulb, tulip makes a dazzling spring floral display. You can plant a range of types for a very long blooming season—up to nearly 3 months. Bloom season spans early spring to late May. Some tulips can be forced for winter blooming indoors.

Tulips are spectacular in formal bedding displays, and add grace to less formal plantings in borders, beds, and containers. Parrot and most species tulips are used to best advantage as specimens or accent clumps. Some small types such as *T. kaufmanniana* are perfect rock-garden plants.

There are two distinct approaches to growing tulips. One is to plant them 10 to 12 inches deep and give them the "rock-garden" conditions of the Near and Middle East—dry summers and baking soil. Deep planting makes them less vulnerable to rodents and to diseases. This method increases longevity and helps them naturalize.

The second approach produces a uniform plant size and lends itself more to formal than naturalistic plantings. Bulbs are planted beneath 4 to 6 inches of rich, sandy loam and spaced 5 to 10 inches apart. They are dug and divided every year and graded by size, then replanted in fall all at the same depth. (Bedding tulips tend to decline in vigor after their first blooming and require digging and replacing every 2 or 3 years anyway.) The shallower planting depth of this system is also an asset wherever deeper soil is wet, because tulip bulbs rot in poorly drained soil.

Direct sun is necessary for vigorous growth and strong, straight stems. Some filtered sun in the hottest hours, however, prolongs blossom life and prevents fading.

If bulbs are to be dug up, wait until foliage has withered. Dust with pesticide and store in a cool, dry place. Plant them (and new bulbs) from October to mid-November; late November to late December in hot-autumn areas. Mix bone meal into the soil beneath bulbs as you plant them, and in early fall work bone meal into the soil above bulbs not dug up.

New bulbs from reputable suppliers have had necessary winter chilling. But in southern areas, dug bulbs should be chilled yearly at 40° to 50°F in the vegetable drawer of the refrigerator for a month immediately before replanting.

Gophers and field mice often eat tulip bulbs, so you may need to plant bulbs in wire-mesh cages. Another troublesome pests is aphids.

The chart on pages 280 and 281 lists principal classes of tulips and some top-rated varieties within these classes in order of bloom. Zone numbers refer to areas of easy adaptability in the garden.

Nasturtium *(Tropaeolum majus)*, a vigorous trailing plant bearing brightly colored flowers, cascades over slopes, walls, or containers with equal grace.

Lush, colorful, and expansive, nasturtium *(Tropaeolum majus)* gives its best performance with sparse water and not-too-rich garden soil.

Late-season tulips *(Tulipa sp)* mix well with *Scilla* and other late-season bulbs.

Tulips (*Tulipa* sp.) offer flowers from early to late spring, depending upon the variety. Single early tulips, above left, begin the early season; *T. fosterana* 'Red Emperor', above center, blooms in early midseason; and Darwin hybrids, above right, bloom in late midseason.

Tulipa

Class Name	Zones	Height	Flower Description	Comments
EARLY				
Single Early	5-8	10 to 16 in.	Small flowers borne on straight, sturdy stems. Colors are red, yellow, gold, pink, and white.	Favorites for indoor forcing and for early color in garden. Short stems make them suitable for window boxes. 'White Hawk' and 'Yellow Prince' are good choices. 'General De Wet' (orange-red) and 'Keiserskroon' (red-and-yellow) have larger flowers than the rest.
Double Early (Early Peony-Flowered)	5-8	6 to 12 in.	Flowers often 4 to 6 in. wide when fully open, resemble peonies, last longer than singles. Same color range as singles.	Short, sturdy stems support the large blossoms. Plant with low companions like early pansies and violas, or use in containers. Weather sometimes damages larger flowers, 'Murillo' (pale pink) and 'Peach Blossom' (pink) are favorites.
MIDSEASON				
Mendel	5-8	18 to 20 in., sometimes taller	Cup-shaped flowers are red, apricot, pink, rose, yellow, and white.	Useful for keeping color in garden between early types and Darwin Hybrids. Good for containers and beds. 'Apricot Beauty' (apricot-rose tinged with red) and 'Athleet' (white) are among best.
Triumph	5-8	18 to 20 in.	Wide color range, but no yellows.	A bit stronger-stemmed and more vigorous than Mendels. Created by crossing Single Early Tulips and various late bloomers. Excellent bedders. Favorites are 'Bruno Walter' (gold-and-purple), 'Johanna' (salmon), and 'Red Matador'.
Darwin Hybrid	5-8	24 to 30 in.	Huge (to 7 inches), roundish, brilliant flowers, in scarlet-to-yellow range.	Created recently by crossing Darwins with *Tulipa fosterana;* becoming immensely popular. Long stems and outstanding flowers make them suitable for beds or cutting. Among best are 'General Eisenhower' (red), 'Apeldoorn' (red-orange), 'Gudoshnik' (cream flecked and veined with red), 'Parade' (orange), 'Dawn Glow' (red shading into gold), and 'Jewel of Spring' (yellow edged with red).
LATE				
Darwin	5-8	24 to 30 in.	Very large (to 5-6 inches) cup-shaped flowers in unusual array of colors including near-black purples and maroons.	Straight stems make this most popular group choice for vase or bed. 'The Bishop' (plum-purple), 'Duke of Wellington' (white), 'Queen of the Night' (deep purple), and 'Landseadel's Supreme' (cherry-and-yellow) are among many favorites. 'Clara Butt' (rose) persists in gardens for years.
Lily-Flowered	5-8	22 to 26 in.	Pointed, reflexed long petals form elegant flowers. Long lasting. Wide color range, some varieties with contrasting edges.	Large plants lend themselves to formal beds or informal drifts and provide good cut flowers. Among favorites are 'Red Shine' (deep red), 'West Point' (yellow), 'White Triumphator', 'Mariette' (salmon), and 'Queen of Sheba' (mahogany edged in yellow).

Tulips (*Tulipa* sp.) are suitable for a variety of garden situations, depending upon the variety. Darwin hybrids, above left, are stately and formal in mass plantings. Species tulips, above right, are excellent in naturalistic rock gardens.

Class Name	Zones	Height	Flower Description	Comments
Cottage (Single Late)	5-8	25 to 30 in.	Single flowers egg-shaped, some with pointed petals. Wide color range, including outstanding yellows like 'Asta Nielsen'.	Old class, notable for easy naturalizing and tall gracefulness. Unsurpassed for bedding and cutting. Two of best are 'Maureen' (white) and 'Rosy Wings' (apricot-pink).
Rembrandt	5-8	20 to 30 in.	Like many tulips in old Dutch paintings, these are "broken"—bicolored with streaked and feathered variegation. Other classes of "broken" tulips, aside from some Parrots, are Bizarre and Bybloems (Bijloemens) Tulips.	Are actually Darwins with variegation caused by a benign virus—so plant them and other "broken" tulips apart from solid colors to keep them solid. They make striking bed or planter displays. Often sold unnamed in mix.
Parrot	5-8	18 to 24 in.	Flowers sometimes "broken," usually interestingly twisted and fringed.	Twisted, weak stems make them better in arrangements or containers than formal beds. Isolate "broken" ones from solid-color tulips. Some top-rated ones are 'Black Parrot' (purple-black), 'Blue Parrot' (heliotrope), 'Fantasy' (rose-and-green), 'Orange Favorite' (orange-and-green), and 'Texas Gold' (golden-yellow).
Double Late Late Peony-Flowered	5-8	To 24 in.	Quite similar to Early Doubles in peony shape and color range.	Rigid stems make these good for cutting as well as bedding—but plant out of wind, as flowers are heavy. Most tolerate light shade. Some outstanding varieties are 'Mount Tacoma' (white), 'Symphonia' (cherry), and 'May Wonder' (pink).
SPECIES (BOTANICALS) AND SPECIES HYBRIDS				
Tulipa kaufmanniana Water-lily Tulip and Kaufmanniana Hybrids	5-8	3 to 12 in.	Large, open flower resembles waterlily. Species varies from white to cream or yellow, often streaked red or pink on outside of petals. Hybrids vary in color.	This low grower blooms with early daffodils and hyacinths, naturalizes freely, and persists in garden. Excellent for rock garden, container, border. 'Johann Strauss' has mottled leaves, petals yellow-and-red edged cream outside, pure white inside. 'Shakespeare' is brilliant apricot, red, and cream.
Tulipa fosterana and Fosterana Hybrids	5-8	16 to 18 in.	Largest flower of any species—opens to 6 inches. Most hybrids shades of red, gold, or orange with black base.	Blooms early. Popular 'Red Emperor' ('Mme. Lefeber'), usually sold as a hybrid, is a form of the species. Various other 'Emperors' are named by colors. 'Princeps', similar to species, and 'White Emperor' bloom a week later than others. Use in borders and containers.
Tulipa greigii and Greigii Hybrids	5-8	8 to 24 in.	Species orange-red with blotched base. In hybrids yellows, oranges, and reds predominate. Many flowers marked. Flowers unusually large, petal tips curved back.	Blooms early. Some like 'Red Riding Hood' (scarlet with black center) have handsomely patterned purple-and-green leaves. Another favorite is 'Oriental Splendor' (yellow-and-red). Use in containers, as foreground of beds, and—especially the small forms—in rock garden.
Tulipa clusiana Lady Tulip	5-9	12 to 18 in.	Closed flower is 2 inches long, slender and pointed, white alternating with crimson; open flower, white with black-purple center.	Blooms midseason. Accepts warm-winter climates better than most tulips. Naturalizes freely. Excellent for container, rock garden, or border.

Verbena (Verbena x hybrida) is a rapid-growing and trouble-free plant for dry, sunny sites. Use as an annual in cold climates, as a perennial in warm climates. Blossoms shown below.

A widely adapted summer-blooming perennial, speedwell (Veronica hybrids) blooms in July and August.

Verbena x hybrida
Verbena, Vervain, Garden Verbena
Perennial in Zones 9-10. Annual elsewhere. To 6-12 inches.

Verbena is a beautiful problem solver that maintains a steady blaze of color from summer to frost under difficult growing conditions, even in desert areas. Rounded clusters of tiny bright red, pink, purple, blue, yellow, orange, wine-red, violet, rose, or white flowers, usually with small white eyes, provide a mass display of vibrant color. Plants branch at the base to form spreading mats of stems clothed by lance-shaped, toothed leaves.

Verbena is a superb ground or bank cover in sunny, hot, sandy areas, and it is excellent for growing in planters. A care-free plant, it is a wise choice for use in seldom-watered beds and borders. And it makes a splendid cut flower for long-lasting arrangements.

It's best to purchase seedlings, because germination is slow and unpredictable. If you use seed, sow indoors 12 to 14 weeks before last spring frost, at 70° to 75°F for germination in 20 to 25 days. Cover the seed flat with black plastic. Set seedlings at least 12 inches apart in fast-draining soil, in full sun. Growth rate is fast. Once plants are established, let soil dry out between waterings. Mildew can be a problem, so never wet the foliage. Good air circulation will also help prevent mildew. Clip spent flower heads to encourage blooming.

Top-rated mixtures with a wide color range are: Ideal Florist mixture, 8 to 12 inches high, many flowers with white eyes; Showtime mixture, 10 to 12 inches with especially vivid colors; Springtime mixture, 10 to 12 inches with softer shades than Showtime; Sparkle mixture 8 to 10 inches; Rainbow mixture, 8 to 10 inches and the most upright in growth habit. 'Blaze' (6 to 8 inches), perhaps the most popular verbena variety, has brilliant, solid red flowers on a compact, spreading plant. 'Sangria' (10 to 12 inches) has wine-red flowers with white eyes.

Veronica hybrids
Speedwell, Veronica
Zones: 4-10. To 12-30 inches. Perennials.

Veronica offers a collection of dependable summer-blooming perennials valued for their blue flowers. Most are hybrids bred for durability and fine form. Some are low-growing, reaching only 12 inches tall. Others grow into medium-sized, 2-1/2-foot plants. Narrow flower spikes are borne at the ends of the leafy stems from July through August. Colors are usually blue or violet, sometimes pink and white. The spikes are 12 to 18 inches tall and blossoms open sequentially from the bottom to the top.

Veronicas make highly attractive perennials for vertical accents in formal and informal gardens. They combine well with yellow and white flowers, such as shasta daisies, coreopsis, and garden phlox. The flowers are excellent for cutting.

Purchase nursery transplants or divide mature clumps to establish new plantings in spring or fall. Stem cuttings may be taken in late spring and rooted in porous mix; the plants should be set out in the garden the following spring. Space plants 12 to 18 inches apart.

Plant in full sun in cooler climates, partial shade in warm climates. Avoid low or poorly drained sites, and fertilize moderately. Divide established clumps every 4 years. Water only in morning to avoid fungal diseases

There are many top-rated veronica hybrids and species. 'Blue Charm', a hardy and lush grower with brilliant blue flowers, reaches 18 inches. 'Icicle' has white flowers, gray-green leaves. *Veronica incana*, woolly speedwell, grows to 12 inches with white leaves, vivid blue flowers; 'Barcarolle' has rose flowers. *Veronica latifolia* 'Crater Lake Blue' grows to 3 feet; has violet-blue long-lasting flowers. *Veronica longifolia* grows low; has pale blue, rose, or white blossoms. *Veronica spicata*, spike speedwell, reaches 18 inches tall; has silver-gray leaves and pink or white flowers.

Viola
Pansy, Viola, Sweet Violet

Perennials and annuals.

The genus *Viola* contains some of the most beloved garden flowers, cherished for their fragrance and old-fashioned good looks.

Viola cornuta
Viola

Zones: 2-10. To 6-8 inches.
Perennial grown as annual
or biennial.

A smaller-flowered (2-inch) faceless pansy with or without a spur, viola has solid or bicolored flowers in white and tones of yellow, apricot, red, purple, and blue. It grows like pansy, except it tolerates more sun in warm areas.

Every grower and seed company has a mixture, nearly all by different names, or just Viola Mixture. Popular named varieties include: bright maroon, dark centered 'Arkwright Ruby'; medium blue 'Blue Perfection'; apricot 'Chantreyland'; violet-blue 'Jersey Gem'; golden-yellow 'Scottish Yellow'; and 'White Perfection'.

Viola odorata
Violet, Sweet Violet

Zones: 6-10. To 5-8 inches.
Perennial.

This woodland beauty produces small, fragrant blue, white, purple, red-violet, or pink flowers from among heart-shaped leaves in spring and sometimes again in fall. Violets are beautiful planted beneath shrubs and trees, in the rock garden, or in any other naturalistic planting. They spread by runners to form clumps. Buy plants, or sow seeds outdoors anytime from spring through fall. Or start indoors like pansies and violas. Grow in loose, sandy, moist soil and partial shade.

Flowers are generally 3/4 to 1 inch wide. Widely grown are: Single pink 'Rosina'; purple 'Royal Robe'; red-violet 'Red Giant' and 'Semperflorens'; plain white 'White Crystal'; white with penciled center 'White Czar'.

Confederate violet (*V. sororia*, formerly *V. princeana*) is white with creamy centers heavily penciled with purple. It naturalizes by seeding rather than runners. Usually sold as 'Princeana'.

Viola tricolor
Johnny-Jump-Up

Zones: 2-10. To 6-12 inches.
Annual.

Old-fashioned Johnny-jump-up resembles a miniature pansy with dainty painted faces in blue, yellow, and white. Grow in gardens where it can sprawl and reseed freely, rather than in formal plantings. Same care requirements as viola.

Johnny-jump-up naturalizes freely under ideal growing conditions. The typical kind has small, 3/4 to 1 inch, yellow-and-purple flowers and is sometimes sold as 'Helen Mount'. Deep violet to light blue forms are sold as 'Blue Elf' and 'King Henry'.

Viola x wittrockiana
Pansy

Zones: 2-10. To 6-8 inches.
Perennial grown as annual
or biennial.

Pansies, with flowers in solid colors or painted with several colors like a face, are by far the most widely grown *Violas*. They bear a profusion of 2- to 4-inch, 5-petaled flowers. Colors are white and shades of blue, purple, apricot, yellow, gold, bronze, pink, red, and lavender. Blooming starts in late winter or early spring and in cool-summer areas continues through summer. Heat-tolerant varieties bloom longer. Pansies are often the earliest annuals to be set out since they are able to tolerate light frost.

Purchase seedlings in early spring or sow seeds in flats during summer and keep through winter in a cold frame. Or sow indoors in midwinter. Before sowing, refrigerate seeds in a moist medium for several days. In darkness and at 70°F, seeds germinate in 10 to 20 days. Plant outside in spring 5 to 6 inches apart in rich, moist, cool, fast-draining soil. In cool-summer areas, pansies accept full sun but need some shade elsewhere. Feed with balanced fertilizer. Pinch old flowers to encourage blooming. If leggy, clip back.

Sweet violets *(Viola odorata)* form a lush carpet of colorful blossoms in spring, and are most at home naturalized in woodland settings.

Johnny-jump-ups *(Viola tricolor)* reseed freely to form informal clumps blessed with an abundance of charming small flowers throughout spring.

Pansies *(Viola x wittrockiana)* often have fanciful 'faces' or mottled flowers and are mainstays during cool seasons.

Top-rated pansies that are heat tolerant include: The Imperial series with flowers to 2-1/2 inches wide; 'Imperial Blue' is light lavender-blue shading to violet at the center with a small yellow eye; 'Orange Prince' is bright orange with a brown-black center. Majestic Giants and Mammoth Giants have flowers to 4 inches wide, and include a wide color range, many with faces. Universal series includes striking bi-colored, plain and blotched flowers, to 3 inches wide. Vikings come in blue, purple, rose, scarlet, white, and yellow, with faces.

Pansies for cool climates or early growing include: Color Festival in a broad color range of 4-inch flowers, all with large blotches. 'Lake of Thun', mid-blue with a blotch, flowers to 3-1/2 inches wide. 'Pay Dirt' with dark-lined yellow flowers, to 3-1/2 inches wide. Roggli Giant Elite and Steele's Jumbo both come in many shades. Flowers have faces and grow to 4 inches wide.

Zantedeschia
Calla, Calla Lily
Rhizomes.

Besides the best-known, large white form, there are smaller white, yellow, pink, and rose forms of calla lily. Each flower is an elegantly furled, flaring, matte-textured sheath tapering out to a point and surrounding a golden rod. Arrow-shaped leaves are rich green, on tall stalks, and may be attractively flecked.

All may easily be grown in any climate area, if in cold climates dormant rhizomes are dug and stored in slightly moist sand during winter, then started indoors in March. All look best when grown in rich soil and given abundant moisture during growth.

Zantedeschia aethiopica
Arum Lily, Florist's Calla, Garden Calla
Zones: 8-10. To 3-4 feet.

This largest, best-known calla has flowers to 10 inches long and leaves to 18 inches long. In Zones 8 to 10 it naturalizes in moist or wet soil and tolerates fairly dry soil—a beautiful

The clean lines of calla lily *(Zantedeschia sp.)* add elegance to many garden settings. Pink calla *(Z. rehmannii),* shown above; golden calla *(Z. elliottiana),* shown below.

solution for a poorly drained spot in the garden. It grows in full sun to medium shade. Plant rhizomes beneath 2 to 4 inches of soil. A large clump is effective near a garden pond. Dwarf forms are available.

Zantedeschia elliottiana
Golden Calla, Yellow Calla
Zones: 8-10. To 30 inches.

Flowers, to 6 inches long, are green shading upwards to yellow or gold. Leaves have translucent flecks or dots. Unlike florist's calla, golden calla needs well-drained soil.

Zantedeschia rehmannii
Pink Calla, Red Calla
Zones: 8-10. To 12 inches.

Flower color varies, as the common names indicate. Leaves are narrow and speckled with translucent white. It needs well-drained soil.

Zinnia hybrids
Zinnia
Zones: 2-10. To 4-36 inches.
Annuals.

As with marigold, hybridizers have transformed a tough, homely Mexican wildflower into a brilliant, sturdy garden favorite. Zinnia comes in myriad colors and several forms and sizes. Colors include all hues but blue, even bright green and bicolors. Most are semidouble or double, and typical forms are large or small pompons, dahlia-, cactus-, and carnationlike shapes.

From early summer until frost zinnias bloom profusely on upright, often bushy, plants with oval leaves. Side branches produce flowers after first flowers wither or are cut. Zinnias are excellent for borders and beds, and cutting.

Plant nursery seedlings, or sow seed outdoors after last spring frost, when soil is warm, or indoors 4 weeks earlier. Germination takes 5 to 7 days at 70° to 75°F. Plant in a hot spot with full sun and rich, well-drained soil. Avoid overhead watering and water early in the day, because wet foliage and nighttime moisture encourage zinnia's only big problem, mildew. Regular watering produces the best flowers, but zinnia tolerates dryness.

Zinnias (*Zinnia* hybrids) blaze with color from early summer until frost. The long-lasting flowers come in a wide selection of forms and colors, and plants range from low clumps ideal for edging to tall-stemmed beauties perfect for cutting.

Zinnia

Series or Variety	Height	Flower Description	Comments
Short Stuff	8-12 in.	Coral-pink; light pink; orange; scarlet ('Short Stuff Red'); white; golden-yellow ('Short Stuff Yellow'). Flowers 4 in. wide, double.	Dwarf plants with Peter Pan-size flowers. Sold by color-named varieties or as mixture.
Thumbelina	4-6 in.	Salmon ('Mini-Salmon'); pink ('Mini Pink') sold by variety. Mixture also includes gold, scarlet, yellow, orange, red, lavender. Flowers 1-1/4 to 2 in. wide, semidouble.	Compact, dome-shaped plants start blooming when 3 in. tall. Award-winning series.
Buttons	12 in.	Cherry, pink, red, yellow. Flowers 1-1/2 in. wide pompons.	Sold by color-named varieties or as mixture sometimes labeled Button Box.
Peter Pan	12 in.	Cream; red ('Flame'); gold; orange; coral-pink ('Pink'); rose-plum ('Plum'); scarlet; pink ('Princess'). Flowers 3 in. wide, double.	Plants start blooming when 6-8 in. tall. Award-winning series. Sold by varieties or as mixture.
Burpeeana Giants	24 in.	White ('Big Snowman'); purple ('Purple Giant'); deep scarlet ('Red Man', award winner); golden-yellow ('Sun God'). Cactus-flowered doubles, 5 to 5-1/2 in. wide.	Sold by varieties or as mixture. This is one of many available giant cactus-flowered mixtures.
Liliput	18 in.	Full color range, sold as mixture. Pomponlike flowers 1-1/2 to 2 in. wide, double or semidouble pompons.	Bushy, branching. Sold as mixture.
'Old Mexico'	16 in.	Bicolored deep red with yellow petal tips, 2-1/2 in. wide, double.	Compact, mounding. Award winner.
Whirligig	20-24 in.	Bicolors: carmine, rose, and scarlet petals contrast with white, gold, pink, or buff tips. Flowers 3 to 4-1/2 in. wide, double and semidouble.	Sold as mixture.
'Envy'	24-30 in.	Apple-green, 3 to 4 in. wide, dahlia-type double.	Especially good for cutting.
Fruit Bowl	24-30 in.	Rose-pink ('Nectarine'); deep orange ('Tangerine'); 2-toned cerise ('Wild Cherry', award winner); deep scarlet ('Winesap'). Flowers 2 to 2-1/2 in. wide, cactus-flowered doubles.	Sold as mixture or by varieties.
Ruffles	26 in.	Soft cherry-red ('Cherry Ruffles', award winner); salmon-pink ('Pink Ruffles'); deep scarlet ('Scarlet Ruffles', award winner); golden-yellow ('Yellow Ruffles', award winner). Flowers 2-1/2 to 3-1/2 in. wide, ruffled, double.	Sold by varieties or as mixture.
Sun	25 in.	Golden-yellow ('Gold Sun'), reddish-scarlet shading lighter toward center ('Red Sun'), 3-1/2 to 4-1/2 in. dahlia-type doubles.	Award-winning series. Sold separately.
'Carved Ivory'	30-36 in.	Cream double, very regularly shaped, 5 in. wide.	Award winner.
Giants of California	30 in.	Wide color range of double and semidouble flowers.	Sold as mixture. There are other mixtures, some taller, with similar names.
State Fair	30-36 in.	Complete color range; 5- to 6-in. broad-petaled doubles.	Thick leaves, stocky growth. Resistant to mildew.
Zenith	30 in.	Golden-orange ('Bonanza', award winner); red ('Firecracker', award winner); salmon-cerise ('Goddess'); cherry-crimson ('Lipstick'); rose-pink ('Rosy Future,' award winner); bright orange ('Torch', award winner); yellow ('Yellow Zenith', award winner). Flowers 5-1/2 to 6 in. wide, cactus-flowered doubles.	Vigorous, mildew resistant.

Planting and Care

Getting new plants off to a good start by locating them where sun exposure and soil conditions are appropriate, planting them properly, and providing correct initial care is essential to their long-term health and happiness. Choosing plants that grow well in the soil and light conditions the site has to offer—or choosing a site that offers the soil and light conditions the plant needs—is the key to success.

This is true whether you are planting a tree to shade your front window, a flowering shrub as an accent in a foundation planting, or a bed of flowering annuals, perennials, or bulbs for seasonal color.

This chapter tells you everything you need to know to care for your landscape plants and garden flowers.

SOIL TEXTURE

Soil may be either loamy, sandy, or clayey, or somewhere in between. Most landscape plants do best in a loamy soil—one that is fertile, holds water well, and is loose enough so that it doesn't compact. Not all gardens offer the ideal soil, so it's important either to improve your soil or to choose plants that will tolerate the soil you have.

Sandy soil has a very loose texture and drains too quickly. It is low in organic matter, which provides fertility and moisture-holding capacity. Clay soil is too heavy and it compacts, excluding air, which is necessary for root growth. It drains poorly and may stay wet too long, encouraging root-rot diseases.

Both sandy and clay soil can be improved by adding organic matter. This breaks up clay so that the resulting soil is more crumbly, holding more air and allowing water to drain more quickly. Sandy soil is made denser and more water retentive.

At left: Lily-of-the-valley shrub *(Pieris japonica)* is a widely adapted ornamental evergreen that blooms profusely in very early spring.

'Vulcan' rhododendron

Oleander *(Nerium oleander)*

Kaffirboom coral tree *(Erythrina sp.)*

Rocky mountain juniper *(Juniperus sp.)*

Clay soil has a smooth texture and retains moisture.

Sandy soil is gritty, loose, and fast-draining.

Loam soil combines the best features of clay and sandy soils.

Both of these soil types need generous quantities of organic matter such as peat moss, leaf mold, compost, or composted ground bark. In addition, perlite can also be added to soil that has a very high clay content to improve aeration. Spread 3 to 6 inches of organic matter on top of the soil, and spade it in to a depth of 1-1/2 to 2 feet, depending upon how much the soil needs to be improved.

For a large planting area, you can use a power tiller to work the entire planting bed. For just a few shrubs, add organic matter in a 2- to 3-foot radius of where the shrub's trunk will be. (See planting instructions on page 289.)

WET SPOTS

Even where soil texture provides for good drainage, waterlogging may be a problem in some low spots in your garden where water collects after a rain. Such waterlogged soil is certain death for most plants. Only plants that do well specifically in wet soil will grow well there.

You can improve drainage problems by digging out and replacing pockets of clay soil with fast-draining soil, or by regrading. An easier solution is to plant on top of the poor soil in raised beds of improved soil.

SOIL pH

The acidity or alkalinity of a soil is measured on the pH scale. The scale ranges from 0 to 14, with the lower numbers being most acidic and the higher numbers most alkaline. The midpoint, 7, is neutral. The pH of the soil determines the chemical forms of the soil nutrients.

Most plants prefer a slightly acid pH of 6.5, but are not too fussy unless soil conditions are extreme. Acid-loving plants need a soil with a pH of 4.0 to 5.5; in more alkaline soil, they cannot take up iron and magnesium. Other plants can tolerate alkaline conditions offering a pH of 7.5 or 8.

Soil pH varies throughout the continent, ranging from acidic on the East and Northwest Coasts to alkaline in arid regions of the Midwest and West. In areas where rainfall is high, pH tends to be acidic, because the rain washes the alkaline elements calcium and magnesium from the soil. Where soils are high in organic matter, this also contributes to soil acidity.

SOIL pH

RAISING pH	Amount of lime per 100 sq ft (9 sq m)		
Change in pH	Sandy	Loamy	Clay
6.0 ⟶ 6.5	2 lb (1 kg)	4 lb (2 kg)	5 lb (2.5 kg)
5.6 ⟶ 5.9	3 lb (1.5 kg)	4½ lb (2.25 kg)	5 lb (2.5 kg)
5.1 ⟶ 5.6	6 lb (3 kg)	9 lb (4.5 kg)	10 lb (5 kg)
4.6 ⟶ 5	12 lb (16 kg)	16 lb (8 kg)	20 lb (10 kg)

LOWERING pH	Amount of sulfur per 100 sq ft (9 sq m)		
Change in pH	Sandy	Loamy	Clay
8.5 ⟶ 6.5	4 lb (2 kg)	5 lb (2.5 kg)	6 lb (3 kg)
7.5 ⟶ 6.5	1 lb (.5 kg)	1½ lb (.75 kg)	2 lb (1 kg)
7.5 ⟶ 5.5	2 lb (1 kg)	3 lb (1.5 kg)	4 lb (2 kg)
6.5 ⟶ 5.5	1 lb (.5 kg)	1½ lb (.75 kg)	2 lb (1 kg)

You can determine the pH of your garden's soil by using a test kit available at most garden centers. Test several areas of your property, since the pH can vary from place to place in your garden. The soil along your house foundation may be more alkaline because lime in the cement foundation leaches into the surrounding soil.

You can lower you soil's pH by adding ground agricultural-grade powdered sulfur. To raise the pH, add dolomitic lime. The table on page 288 shows rates for different pH's and soil types. Yearly applications may be needed, because the soil will slowly revert to its original pH.

SUN EXPOSURE

For a plant to thrive, providing it with the proper light exposure is essential. In full sun, a plant requiring shade will lose its foliage or at least its healthy color, and flowers will dry and burn quickly. A plant needing full sun will grow weak and lanky and eventually succumb if given dense shade.

In this book, plants are described as needing full sun, light shade, partial shade, and full shade. All of these kinds of sun exposures can be found on most properties.

Full sun means 6 or more hours of direct sunlight a day. A foundation planting on the south side of your house will be in full sun unless it is shaded by trees. A southeastern or southwestern exposure may also provide full sun. Other areas of your yard may be in full sun if they are not in the shadow of taller plants and buildings.

Light shade is created by the shadows of high, overhead tree branches. Dappled sun filters to the ground and the shadows are constantly shifting. It is acceptable for some direct sun to strike the area only during the early morning or late afternoon, not around noon.

Partial shade means half a day of sun and half a day of shade. Both the eastern and the western side of your house receive partial shade if they are not shaded by trees or other buildings. Some plants that prefer light shade will also grow in partial shade, but they prefer the cooler morning sun of an eastern exposure over the hotter afternoon sun of a western exposure.

Full shade is denser than light shade. It is found on the north side of your house where the house's shadow keeps the ground dark and in the shade cast by thick-foliaged or low-branched trees. Some northern exposures that are open to the sky may be fairly bright due to reflected light and can pass as light shade.

When you are trying to determine the sun exposures of various areas of your property, there are several things to keep in mind. The angle of the sun changes during the year, changing the length of the shadows cast by your house and by trees. Evergreen trees provide year-round shade, but deciduous trees drop their leaves and let the sun shine through.

Growing Landscape Plants

PLANT SELECTION

Trees, shrubs, vines, and many ground covers are available at the nursery as either container-grown, balled-and-burlapped, or bareroot plants. Ground covers such as pachysandra are often sold in flats. Planting techniques are basically similar, though they vary slightly.

Plants in metal, plastic, or fiber containers were grown in those containers and their entire root system is intact. Balled-and-burlapped plants were grown in the ground and recently dug up. Their ball of roots and soil is wrapped up in protective burlap. Because they were dug from the field, they have lost some roots and are more fragile than container-grown plants. Bareroot plants were dug from the growing field while still dormant and shipped with little or no soil around their roots. They must be planted immediately, and care should be taken to keep their roots from drying out or being injured.

After you bring a new plant home, keep it in a cool shaded spot until planting time. If left in the sun, dark containers can heat up quickly to root-damaging temperatures and burlapped rootballs will quickly dry out. Balled-and-burlapped shrubs should be planted as soon as possible so transplanting shock is minimized. Container plants can be kept for several weeks as long as they are watered regularly and kept cool. Bareroot plants should have their roots wrapped in wet newspaper until they are planted.

Sturdy well-branched plants that have thick foliage are the healthiest. Choose the largest plants that fit in your budget, but don't be fooled by mere size. A plant's top growth should be in proportion to its roots. The root system of an overly large container-grown plant is crowded and coiled and transplants poorly. A balled-and-burlapped plant with a large top and a small rootball has lost too many roots and cannot supply the top growth adequately with water.

WHEN TO PLANT

Both spring and fall are usually good times to plant. Most people prefer to plant in spring, because that's when their minds turn to gardening. Spring is the best time where winters are cold, because it allows the new plant time to become established before cold weather. In areas where the soil does not freeze at all, or only for short periods, summer heat is more strenuous to new plants than winter cold, so fall planting is recommended. In any climate, summer planting is stressful to new plants, but can be safely done if plants are kept well-watered and given extra attention.

THE PLANTING HOLE

Whether you're planting a container-grown, balled-and-burlapped, or a bareroot plant, you start with a similar planting hole. A planting hole dug much bigger than the rootball and filled back in

Planting

1. Combine organic amendment with garden soil to make backfill mix.

2. Add backfill to planting hole if it is deeper than the rootball.

3. Add water to planting hole to moisten and settle backfill.

4. Loosen roots that the container has forced to coil or circle, and set rootball in planting hole.

5. Add backfill around rootball, firming with your hands as you go.

6. Be sure the original rootball receives ample water the first year after planting.

with improved soil will give a plant the best start. This will provide the roots with soil that is a gradual transition between the soil it was grown in and your garden's soil. Roots will be able to penetrate the soil easily and plants will become established more quickly.

A hole about 1-1/2 times as deep and as wide as the rootball is usually recommended. Dig out the soil and place it on a tarpaulin or sheet of plastic. Mix in organic matter such as moist peat moss or compost. If your soil is very sandy or very heavy clay, you may have to take more drastic measures. (See page 287.) Use this amended soil as backfill to refill the hole.

First refill the bottom of the hole with backfill (build a cone of soil in the center of the hole to support the roots of a bareroot plant) so the plant will be sitting at the proper level—with its rootball slightly above ground level to allow for soil settling. Fill the planting hole part way with water to settle the backfill. Allow the water to drain, then position the plant in the hole with the most attractive side facing forward.

A container-grown shrub can be removed from its plastic can by turning the can on its side and rolling it, pressing hard, then grasping its trunk and gently twisting and pulling. The rootball should come out all in one piece if it is properly

moist. Metal cans should be cut with a can cutter.

The burlap surrounding a balled-and-burlapped rootball can be planted along with the plant. Unfasten the burlap and fold it back laying it along the bottom of the planting hole after the plant is in position. The burlap will eventually rot. Do not remove it before planting, or the soil will probably fall away from the roots.

Sometimes when a plant is dug from the field its rootball is encased in heavy clay to keep it from drying out. This is particularly true if the plant is being shipped a long distance. If you put such a rootball into desirably crumbly, well-draining soil, water and fertilizer will flow past the rootball but won't be absorbed. Remove all or most of the clay with a hose and then plant immediately.

After the plant is positioned, fill around the rootball with backfill, firming with your hands as you go. Be sure the rootball is slightly above soil level—if too deep the surface roots may suffocate. Water the plant in after planting is finished—this will wash soil particles into any harmful air spaces. A water basin made of a ring of firmed soil directly over the rootball will help catch water, allowing it to soak into the rootball.

STAKING

Some trees and tall shrubs may need staking after planting to keep them from falling over and to encourage straight growth. Drive three stakes into solid ground beyond the planting hole. Attach them by looping rope around the trunk about 2 or 3 feet above soil level. Protect the trunk by encasing the rope in a piece of garden hose where it rubs against the bark.

A tree will become stronger and support itself sooner if allowed to sway somewhat in the wind. Remove the stakes as soon as possible; one season is usually enough.

SPACING PLANTS

Ideally, shrubs and trees should be spaced so that they will not be crowded at maturity. When full grown, shrubs' branch tips should touch or intermingle slightly if planted in a foundation planting or in a shrub border. When calculating spacing distances, allow for the growth of all plants that are near each other. For instance, two shrubs that will each grow 5 feet wide should be planted with a space of 5 feet between their trunks. But a 5-foot-wide plant only needs to be 2-1/2 feet from a building or fence. Plants to be used as hedges should be planted twice as close as otherwise recommended.

Most people tend to plant closer than this, since new shrubs planted

so far apart look skimpy. But if planted too close, the shrubs quickly will become crowded and jumbled looking. One way to avoid the problem is to space small plants about 2-1/2 feet apart and after they begin to look crowded in 3 or 4 years, transplant every other shrub to another spot in the garden.

Ground Covers

Although ground covers are usually problem solvers, turning the most difficult spots into pleasing, low-maintenance seas of green, this is only true once the plants are established. Planting a large area in ground cover can be a task, and the first 2 or 3 years after planting, ground covers require relatively high maintenance. Plants must be watered regularly, whether or not they are drought-tolerant, and weeds must be controlled.

PLANTING GROUND COVERS

If you are planting a ground cover to replace a lawn, you will have to get rid of the grass completely. This means digging up the turf and removing all clods and roots. (If you use a power tiller, you will chop up grass roots, which will come back to haunt you as weeds.) Turn over the soil, incorporating generous quantities of organic matter if soil is heavy or sandy.

Many ground covers, including gazanias, English ivy, and hypericum, are sold in flats as rooted cuttings. They should be separated carefully into individual plants by cutting or gently pulling them apart. Plant them as you would annuals and perennials. Shrubby ground covers are usually sold in one-gallon containers. Plant them as you would any other shrub.

The ground cover descriptions in the encyclopedia include recommended planting distances. Close spacing will result in a faster cover but if you plant too close, shrubby ground covers may look crowded at maturity.

Pruning Ground Covers

Many low-growing ground covers can be rejuvenated by mowing in spring. Set mower blade at highest setting.

A hand-held weed eater is an efficient tool for use in mowing ground covers in large plantings.

Ground covers in small areas can be trimmed by cutting back with hand shears.

PREVENTING WEEDS

If weeds are allowed to grow between ground cover plants, they will compete with them for nutrients and water, slow their growth, and lengthen the time it takes the ground cover to spread over the ground. A thick layer of organic mulch is one of the best ways to control weeds between shrubby ground covers. Covering the area with black plastic before applying the mulch is even more effective.

Watering practices also influence weed growth. If you apply water directly to the plants, with drip irrigation for example, areas between plants will remain drier and produce fewer weeds.

WATERING AND FERTILIZING

Even the most drought-tolerant plant needs regular watering until its roots are firmly established in the surrounding soil. This usually takes at least 2 years. Decide how you will water before you plant. Drip irrigation is most efficient but the equipment required can be expensive on large sites and is impractical with ground covers that are planted close together. Overhead sprinklers are also effective but can encourage weed growth. Mulches are a very good method of conserving moisture.

Regular fertilizing speeds the establishment of many ground covers, however, some plants grow better in infertile soil. Check the encyclopedia descriptions for specific recommendations.

MOWING GROUND COVERS

Many herbaceous ground covers look better if they are routinely cut back every year or two. This process forces clean-looking new growth and is referred to as mowing even though many lawn mowers cannot be set high enough to do the job properly. In early spring cut back ground covers such as hypericum, English ivy, and pachysandra to 4 to 6 inches above the ground. Handheld weed-eaters are the easiest tool to use. Hedge shears are good on small areas.

Routine Care

When grown under proper light and soil conditions in an amenable climate, most landscape plants need only routine watering, mulching, and fertilizing.

WATERING

Newly transplanted plants are particularly vulnerable to drying out because their roots are shallow. During the first growing season, water plants slowly and thoroughly, keeping the soil moist but not soggy. Check to be sure the water is soaking into the rootball.

When in bloom and during growth in spring, most plants need plenty of water. Drought during blooming results in short-lived flowers. If water is lacking during spring and early summer, new growth will be stunted and flower buds for the next season's bloom will be sparse.

During periods of summer drought, water shrubs, vines, and ground covers weekly. Trees have deeper roots and are usually unharmed by short dry spells. Water can be tapered off in late summer, since this encourages dormancy and preparation for winter. However, shrubs should not go into winter lacking water because once soil freezes, roots cannot take up water and cold wind and winter sun dehydrate plants. If autumn rains do not provide adequate water, give plants a thorough watering after the first fall frost.

MULCHING

A mulch, a layer of organic or inorganic material placed over the soil, is one of the best things you can do for your garden. It conserves moisture, keeps the ground cool, shades out weeds, all while dressing up the garden.

The most common organic mulches are shredded bark, shredded leaves, sawdust, pine needles, and compost. Inorganic mulches such as gravel and rocks or pebbles are decorative in desert-style landscapes.

Spread the mulch over the soil in a planting bed, beneath and somewhat beyond the spread of the branches, to a depth of about 2 inches. Renew mulch in spring and fall as needed.

FERTILIZING

Most garden soils provide plants with the necessary nutrients, but light fertilizing usually makes for best growth. Commonly used general purpose garden fertilizers are 5-10-10 (5% nitrogen, 10% phosphorus and 10% potassium) and 10-10-10. Both provide a balance of nutrients and a good supply of nitrogen, the element most frequently lacking in garden soils. Acid-loving plants need a fertilizer designed especially for them.

Apply granular-type fertilizer at the rate recommended on the package by raking back the mulch, if any, and sprinkling the fertilizer on top of the soil under the branch spread of each plant. Foliar fertilizing by spraying foliage with diluted liquid fertilizer is a method that delivers fertilizer to plants quickly. Carefully follow the label directions as to the amount of fertilizer to use. Apply fertilizer once in spring, or more lightly once a month until midsummer. Fertilizer applied after midsummer will stimulate undesirable tender growth that may be injured by frost in fall. Some gardeners apply a fertilizer containing no nitrogen (0-10-10) in late summer or fall—this won't stimulate growth but may increase cold tolerance.

Plants grown in containers need regular fertilizer. Slow-release kinds mixed in the soil are effective over long periods. Light applications of liquid fertilizers applied with weekly waterings from spring through summer are also good.

Pruning

Plants are pruned for many reasons. They are first of all pruned while young to guide their growth. Later pruning may be needed to maintain an attractive shape or to encourage flowering. If a plant wasn't given enough growing space,

Watering

Drip watering systems are efficient. They apply water directly over roots at a rate soil can absorb.

A basin of firmed soil directs water to roots, however periodic repair is required.

Many types of sprinkler heads are available to use with your garden hose. Easy to move where needed.

Mulching

Bark mulch is available in many sizes. Use uniform-size particles to give plantings a neat appearance.

Rock mulch does not wash away and lasts indefinitely, but does not add humus to soil.

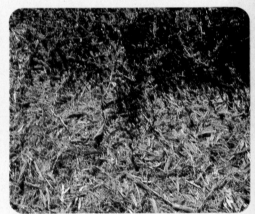

Irregular particls of low-cost shredded bark bind together to form a mulch that will hold well on slopes.

Fertilizing

Spray leaves with foliar fertilizer for fastest results.

Time-release fertilizer pellets provide required nutrients for 1 to 5 years, depending on the manufacturer. Read package directions.

Granular fertilizer applied on surface can promote good growth. Do not apply directly over rootball.

Pruning Deciduous Trees

Bareroot tree at planting: (left) If poorly branched, cut off all limbs, forcing new growth; (right) If well-branched, thin and head back 1/2 of growth.

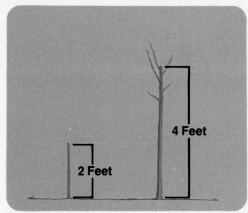

Heading bareroot tree at planting: (left) Low heading; (right) high heading.

Headed trees after 1 year: (left) Low heading forces new shoots, some low; (right) high-headed trees tend to lean in wind and trunks may sun-scald.

Thin to reduce development of new shoots and direct growth: (left) Thinning cut made; (right) resulting growth.

Head to increase the number of new shoots and stiffen branches: (left) Heading cuts made; (right) resulting growth.

To remove heavy limb (left): 1) undercut, 2) cut through limb, 3) remove stub. To remove dead stub (right): Cut flush with healthy growth, not trunk.

it may need regular pruning to keep it within bounds. And overgrown plants can be rejuvenated with drastic pruning measures.

PRUNING DECIDUOUS TREES

The first 2 or 3 years after planting are the most important in developing the framework of a young tree. Most trees should have only one main trunk or leader. At planting, remove any competing leaders unless it is a multi-trunked tree.

The second or third year after planting is the time to shape the tree. Keep in mind that as a tree grows, the position of its branches remains the same distance from the ground. Select 2 to 4 primary scaffold branches at the height you wish to have permanent branches. Ones with a 60° to 90° angle are strongest. Prune off all those remaining below this height.

For a fuller, dense tree, prune off the tips of the scaffold branches to promote interior branching. For a more open look and lighter shade, do not prune off the tips.

PRUNING EVERGREEN TREES

Broad-leaved evergreen trees can be pruned in a manner similar to the way you would prune deciduous trees. Conifers however require special pruning.

Many conifers, such as spruce and fir, have tall symmetrical shapes with whorls of branches radiating from the main trunk. They look best with branches all the way down to the ground and should not be pruned except to remove a competing leader. To encourage denser growth, you may shear the new spring growth lightly with two-handed hedge shears.

Conifers with open random branching patterns, such as yew and hemlock, can have branches removed to create a more open shape, though it is seldom necessary. Light shearing will encourage denser growth. Lower branches can be removed without harming the tree's appearance.

Pruning Evergreens

Clip back random-growing needled evergreens once or twice during spring or summer to control size.

To control size and encourage dense growth, clip or pinch back candles of pines when they enlarge in spring.

Pinch back growth of broad-leaved evergreens in spring to control size and promote denser branching.

Pruning Shrubs

An overgrown shrub will lose vigor and bloom less if it becomes too dense.

Rejuvenate by cutting out oldest stems at ground level, after blooming in spring.

Remove faded flowers to improve vigor and appearance.

PRUNING DECIDUOUS SHRUBS

Timing: If a shrub flowers in spring, prune after flowering. Spring-flowering shrubs, such as lilac, develop flowers on growth that occurred the previous summer. Pruning after flowers fade stimulates rapid regrowth that will bear flowers the next spring. Pruning in late summer or winter will remove the following spring's flower buds.

Some flowering shrubs, such as pyracantha, flower in spring on wood two or more years old. These shrubs are usually pruned in late winter before growth begins. Pruning after flowering will not damage the plant, but many berries, which add important color in fall and winter, are lost. Also, pruning in the late dormant season stimulates more growth and, eventually, more flowers.

Shrubs that flower in summer or fall are best pruned in late winter or early spring before growth begins. Summer-flowering crape myrtle is an example. Its flowers develop on new growth that begins in spring. If you prune crape myrtle during growth and before flowers appear, you are pruning potential flowers away.

Pruning for shape: To shape a plant that is growing too large for its allotted space, you can cut into the shrub and prune out carefully chosen branches to thin the shrub. Use one-handed clippers and cut off the branches where they emerge from larger branches. Then to reduce size, clip back the ends of the remaining long branches. For a graceful natural shape, let the branching pattern tell you where to make the cuts.

For formal-looking shrubs, you can clip them in spring with hedge shears. Be sure not to prune off flower buds.

Pruning for renewal: Many deciduous shrubs are continually renewing themselves by sending up new stems directly from the ground. You can encourage this renewal process and improved flowering by cutting out

Pruning Hedges

A hedge with a wide top (left) loses lower branches from shading. If correctly pruned, branches remain (right).

For an informal shape, thinning branches at their origins with a hand clipper results in looser, more open growth.

For a formal shape, shearing off outer growth with two-handed hedge shears results in dense foliage.

the oldest stems, the thickest darkest colored ones, at ground level in spring if shrubs look overgrown. You can cut back all the stems of severely overgrown shrubs to a foot above the ground in early spring before growth begins.

PRUNING NEEDLE-LEAVED SHRUBS

Evergreens, such as juniper, yew, hemlock, and podocarpus, grow slowly and steadily throughout the growing season, rather than in a short spurt. Prune them anytime from spring to midsummer, as needed. Avoid pruning in fall—pruning stimulates new growth that might not mature and harden before winter.

Conifers that have random growth can be sheared with two-handed hedge clippers. This creates a formal-looking plant with square or rounded contours. Shearing promotes a dense outer layer of foliage, but leaves the inside of the shrub bare.

For a more natural and informal look, prune with a one-handed pruning tool. Reach inside the shrub and cut out selected long branches, taking care to maintain the natural shape of the shrub. This thins the interior of the plant and promotes thick foliage. Shorten the tips of the remaining branches.

Some evergreens, such as pine, spruce, and fir, make a major growth push once a year, in spring. New growth is produced in long, symmetrical shoots known as "candles". Snapping off or cutting candles back one-half to two-thirds their length before needles enlarge, will encourage denser growth.

PRUNING BROAD-LEAVED EVERGREEN SHRUBS

Broad-leaved evergreens with small leaves, such as Japanese holly, boxwood, and privet, can be sheared or pruned in the manner described for random-growing conifers. Large-leaved kinds must have selected branches thinned and shortened.

Be sure not to cut through the foliage of coarse-leaved shrubs, as this will result in a ragged look.

PRUNING HEDGES

Deciduous and evergreen plants used for hedges can tolerate heavy shearing so begin shaping your hedge right away. Plants used for informal hedges, such as cotoneaster, are pruned, not sheared. To lessen their density, remove larger, interior branches. To make an informal hedge more dense, pinch tips of new growth.

Formal hedges require frequent shaping with hedge shears. Proper taper is the most important aspect of formal hedge pruning. The hedge base must always be wider than the top. If not, lower branches are shaded and gradually die.

Growing Annuals, Perennials, and Bulbs

ANNUALS

A wide choice of annual seedlings, often already in bloom, is available in spring and early summer at garden centers everywhere. And these plants promise a garden of instant color. However, many gardeners wish to start annuals themselves, either sowing the seed indoors in late winter, or sowing directly outdoors once the weather has warmed. Some take the trouble to start from seed because they enjoy nurturing the seedlings along, others do it because then they have an even wider choice of varieties, and still others do it because buying seeds is less expensive than buying seedlings.

Hardy annuals and cool-season annuals, such as pansies and sweet peas, can tolerate cold and even light frost. They can be planted outdoors several weeks before the last frost date in spring, or in fall in mild winter climates, where they will provide winter flowers. Tender annuals need more warmth and are harmed by frost.

Annuals and Perennials — Seeding and Transplanting

Where the growing season is short, annuals and perennials may be started indoors from seed in flats of fine-textured potting soil.

In regions with long growing seasons, flower seeds may be successfully sown directly in the garden.

Transplant seedlings into prepared garden soil preferably either late in the afternoon or on an overcast day.

Nursery-grown seedlings: If you purchase plants, choose sturdy ones with good green foliage color and compact growth. Avoid flats of seedlings that have many roots growing through the drainage holes—this indicates plants are root-bound and may not transplant well. Try to plant seedlings as soon as possible. If you must delay planting for a day or so, put the flats or containers in a bright place sheltered from wind and burning sun and keep them moist—they will dry out quickly, so check often.

It's usually a good idea to prepare the soil in your flower bed a few weeks before planting. Spread an inch or two of moist peat moss or shredded compost over the top of the soil, sprinkle on complete dry fertilizer such as 5-10-5, higher in phosphorus (the second number) than nitrogen (the first number), and with garden fork or power tiller, work into the top 6 inches of the bed. Where annuals are planted in small patches between shrubs or perennials, use a trowel to loosen soil and work in organic matter.

Plant seedlings in a hole dug twice the size of the rootball and filled back in with soil that's been mixed with peat. It's easy to remove seedlings from the cell pack or flat by pushing up and squeezing from the bottom—do not pull on the stem. Spread the outer roots slightly without removing soil from the inner ones and bury the rootball just below soil level. Firm the soil gently, then water. Plants fare best if set out in the evening or on an overcast day.

Sowing seeds outdoors: Annuals can be sown directly outdoors in areas with long growing seasons, where plants will have plenty of time to germinate and mature and still have a long blooming season. Where the season is short, annuals may not flower until well into summer, so it is probably better to buy seedlings or sow seeds indoors.

Prepare the planting bed as described above and rake smooth. Sow seeds as instructed on the seed package or as described in the plant description in the encyclopedia section of this book. Seeds of cold hardy annuals may be sown in fall (for winter bloom in warm climates and spring bloom in cold climates) or in early spring as soon as the ground is workable. Tender annuals should not be sown until all danger of frost is past and the soil has warmed up.

Keep seeds and seedlings moist until they begin to mature by watering with a gentle spray from a sprinkler. After seedlings have sprouted, thin to proper spacing when they have grown their first set of true leaves.

Starting annuals indoors: You can get a jump on the growing season by sowing seeds indoors in late winter so you'll have young plants to transplant into the garden come spring. Many gardeners fail however to grow satisfactory seedlings, because they cannot provide proper growing conditions indoors—not providing bright enough light is the most common cause of failure.

The most suitable germinating medium is a commerical sterilized seed-starting mix composed of fine peat and vermiculite. Spread this medium about 3 inches deep in seed flats or trays with ample drainage holes. Moisten well the day before planting. Sow seeds according to individual needs. The encyclopedia gives germination requirements for each annual. Notice that seeds of some must be covered by soil (and some by black plastic for total darkness), whereas others should be pressed gently into the soil but left uncovered for exposure to light (but not direct sun).

Cover the tray with plastic, such as that from a dry-cleaning bag, that has some holes poked in it for ventilation. Keep covered until seedlings break through the soil, then gradually remove the covering over the following week. Without disturbing

Annuals and Perennials — Early Care

To encourage vigorous growth and bushiness, pinch off buds from seedlings when transplanting.

Water transplanted seedlings immediately to settle soil and eliminate air pockets.

If transplanting in hot weather, provide shade until plants become well established.

the seedlings, keep the soil moist but not wet; watering from the bottom works well.

Most seeds germinate best at a particular soil temperature range. You should provide this as best you can by locating trays in warm spots out of drafts, or better, with thermo-statically-controlled soil heating cables. Germination temperatures given in the encyclopedia refer to soil, not to surrounding air, which is a few degrees cooler.

For most annuals, a source of bright light, usually unshaded south-facing windows or two or three fluorescent tubes positioned several inches above flats, is absolutely necessary to produce strong plants. Turn the fluorescent lights on 24 hours a day until germination, then 12 to 14 hours a day, and raise them as the seedlings grow so lights are about 6 inches above the tops of the plants.

When seedlings have their first true set of leaves and are beginning to be crowded, transplant them into peat pots or other containers filled with a packaged potting soil. Keep in bright light and fertilize them frequently but lightly.

A few weeks before your last frost date (or the time you intend to transplant to the garden) begin to harden-off the seedlings. This is a process that aids the seedlings in surviving their move to the great outdoors. Begin by setting the plants outdoors in bright light for gradually increasing periods of time each day. Bring indoors the first few nights if the air is very chilly. You can safely transplant to the garden after a week or two of acclimation.

Caring for annuals: Once your annuals are in the ground, they will need regular tending to keep them blooming. Watering, fertilizing, pinching, pruning, staking, and maybe even pesticide applications will be called for.

If you pinch the tips off young plants, they will grow bushier and have more flowers in the long run, though it will delay flowering by about 10 days. Once blooming commences, you'll need to continually remove faded flowers to keep the plants attractive and to encourage them to keep on making more flowers. After weeks of blooming, if plants become leggy and flowers are sparse, they can often be renewed by pruning them halfway back and fertilizing.

Most annuals need monthly fertilizing with a fertilizer higher in phosphorus than nitrogen. Applying time-release fertilizer when you plant usually suffices for the season. A few annuals prefer no fertilizing. Most annuals need constant moisture (but not wetness). Water during early morning hours.

PERENNIALS

Perennials are usually bought as mature plants in 4-inch or 1-gallon cans. Such plants usually bloom their first year in your garden and are often purchased already in bud or bloom. Certain fast-growing perennials, such as coneflower, are sold in flats similar to the way annuals are sold and they will bloom their first year too. Choose sturdy healthy green plants that are not outgrowing their containers. Spring and fall planting are best; summer planting requires careful shading and watering until plants become established.

Roots of dormant perennials may also be ordered from mail-order suppliers. They are usually shipped wrapped in moist sphagnum and plastic at their proper planting time.

A more economical approach is to grow perennials from seeds. Some plants will not bloom for several years however. Seeds of many perennials are available and are grown the same way described for annuals. If you sow seeds in flats outdoors during the summer for fall planting, place the flats on shaded benches or tables to lessen chances of damage by sun and pests.

Planting perennials: Planting is generally the same as for annuals, but because perennials remain in place for years deep and thorough soil preparation is important. If the soil is poor, use composted organic amendments generously.

Prepare new beds many weeks in advance of summer for fall planting, and in fall for spring planting. See the encyclopedia for recommended spacing, especially important for these permanent plants.

Caring for perennials: Most perennials require regular watering, especially in hot or windy weather. Water thoroughly enough to wet the deepest roots. Mulching retains moisture, keeps roots cool, discourages weeds, and improves soil, as well as giving a finished look to the garden and keeping soil from splashing onto flowers and foliage.

Fertilize in spring with a complete fertilizer such as 5-10-5. You may be able to force reblooming by pruning plants after blooming ends and fertilizing again, but do not fertilize late in summer.

Many perennials, and some annuals, require staking to protect them from breaking during summer thunderstorms. Tall single-stemmed plants such as foxglove can be staked by gently tying individual stalks to separate stakes. Clumps of plants, such as coreopsis or shasta daisy, benefit from a loose support created by making a circle of stakes and string around the outside of the clump.

After foliage and stems wither in fall, clip plants back, making sure to remove all dead branches and fallen leaves and flowers, which can harbor insect pests and diseases. In cold climates, you can protect perennials by laying a mulch, several inches thick, over the flower bed after the soil freezes. Use pine boughs, salt hay, or leaves—be sure to remove in early spring before tender shoots appear.

Dividing perennials: Perennials live for many years in your garden and their clumps increase in size. Plants will lose vigor if they get too crowded, and most perennials are best divided every three or four years. A bonus you get from dividing the clumps is more plants. The best time to divide is usually early spring just as growth is beginning. Dig up the clump with a sharp spade, being sure to dig deeply. Using the spade or a sharp knife, cut the clump into separate plants (these are usually apparent upon close inspection) and plant the divisions as you would new plants. The divisions can be planted about a foot and a half apart to create a large drift, or used elsewhere in your garden.

BULBS

Bulbs include not only plants with true bulbs (underground clusters of fleshy storage leaves) but also rhizomes (thick, horizontal stems close to the surface), tubers (swollen storage roots), and corms (enlarged underground stem bases).

Planting bulbs: Nearly all bulbs are best planted while dormant and free of foliage, but early enough in fall to grow roots before the ground freezes. See the chart for planting times, depths, and spacing, and read about individual needs in the encyclopedia. *Planting depths recommended in the chart refer to depth of soil above the top of the bulb.* Suggested spacing allows bulbs to create a mass effect, yet have room to multiply for at least 2 or 3 years before they need to be divided.

Bulbs in light, fluffy soil may be planted deeper, and bulbs in heavy soil shallower, than the depths recommended. In very hot and very cold climates, deep planting provides protective insulation.

Formal plantings call for precise spacing (and depth) between each bulb, whereas informal plantings look most natural with variations in spacing. Use a trowel or bulb planter to plant bulbs individually, or dig and prepare the entire planting area, removing the top layer of soil, spacing out bulbs, then replacing the layer of soil. This is especially helpful in formal beds.

Before you plant, prepare the soil as for annuals and perennials so that it drains well and contains generous amounts of organic matter deeper than bulbs' roots will penetrate. Mix bone meal or superphosphate into the soil beneath the bulbs. Water thoroughly after planting, and whenever the weather is dry, until after blooming.

Caring for bulbs: Routine care is simple—and essential. Remove dead flowers before seeds begin to develop, but let foliage remain until it begins to wither or bulbs will be unable to gather and store energy for next season's blooming. Fertilize every spring with bone meal scratched into the soil surface. Keep soil moist during the blooming period.

Planting and Storing Bulbs

When planting bulbs for a formal effect spacing and depth should be uniform; variations in spacing look more naturalized.

Dig tender bulbs at the end of the growing season, separate, and allow to dry before storing.

To store tender bulbs over winter, sprinkle with bulb dust or fungicide, place in a dry medium, and keep in a cool, well-ventilated spot.

When bulbs have multiplied until they are crowded, blooming often declines. Soon after foliage dies, you can dig crowded bulbs carefully with a spading fork. Break bulbs apart and allow them to dry for a few days. (Lilies and evergreen bulbs must not be dried; see the encyclopedia entries for methods of handling.) Replant them within a few days, after dusting all cuts and breaks with fungicide.

Tender bulbs, those that must be lifted and stored to survive winters in your area, should be dug during dormancy, soon after foliage dies. (Evergreen bulb plants such as *Clivia* must overwinter indoors as houseplants in most climates.) Remove soil, dry bulbs for a few days, divide as necessary, use bulb dust or fungicide, and store in vermiculite or another sterile, dry medium, in a cool, dry, ventilated place until the ground thaws. (Some bulbs, such as tulips, require refrigeration in southern climate zones.) Replant them as you would new bulbs.

Forcing bulbs: You can enjoy the beauty of spring flowers during cold winter months by forcing bulbs to bloom indoors in containers. This is easily done—the trick lies in knowing how. Bulbs purchased for planting outdoors in fall already contain a preformed flower bud, however, winter's chill is needed to break the dormancy. Unless you purchase specially treated bulbs, you'll have to provide that cold to trick the bulbs into blooming indoors in the middle of winter.

Almost any bulbs can be forced—favorite ones are narcissus, tulip, hyacinth, crocus, and scilla. Planting groups of five bulbs in a container gives a good show.

Plant in any decorative somewhat shallow container. Use lightweight soil mix (vermiculite also works well). Add a layer to the bottom of the container. Set the bulbs on top of the soil, placing so they nearly touch. Loosely fill the area around the bulbs with soil, leaving peaks of the bulbs even with the top of the container. The bulbs generally used for forcing all require a cooling period at around 45°F for 10 to 12 weeks for best performance. (Tulips need about 15 weeks.) During the cooling period, the bulbs develop the roots that will support later top growth.

To provide the needed cold, place the containers of bulbs outdoors in a trench or raised bed and cover with at least 6 to 8 inches of loose soil, sand, fir bark, or peat moss. An unheated cellar may also work. In Zones 8-10, the outdoors may not be cold enough, and you can chill bulbs in a refrigerator.

Keep soil moist. Check the bulbs often as the cooling period nears its end. Look for roots coming out the bottom of the container, or gently tip the container over and partially remove the rootball for inspection. When the whitish tips of plant sprouts appear and the root system is well established, move containers indoors to a cool, bright spot. Keep moist, and let nature provide you with a show of brilliant spring blossoms.

If you wish to later plant the bulbs outdoors, you should fertilize lightly and keep the foliage in bright light after flowers fade. Plant in the garden in spring. Bulbs should only be forced one time.

BULB PLANTING CHART

Botanical Name	Planting Depth	Spacing	When to Plant
Agapanthus sp.	1 in.	12-18 in.	any season
Allium sp.	3 times height of bulb	4-12 in.	fall
Amaryllis belladonna	2-12 in.	12-18 in.	immediately after blooming
Anemone blanda	2-3 in.	4 in.	fall, early spring
A. coronaria	2-3 in.	8 in.	fall, early spring
Caladium x hortulanum	1-3 in.	12 in.	spring
Canna x generalis	3-5 in.	18-24 in.	spring
Chionodoxa luciliae	3 in.	1 in.	fall
Clivia miniata	slightly exposed	6 in.	any season
Colchicum autumnale	3 in.	3-4 in.	early August
Crocus sp.	2-3 in.	2-4 in.	fall
Eranthis hyemalis	2 in.	3 in.	late summer-early fall
Freesia x hybrida	3 in.	2-3 in.	fall
Fritillaria imperialis	6 in.	12 in.	early fall
F. meleagris	3-4 in.	3-4 in.	early fall
Galanthus sp.	3-4 in.	2-4 in.	fall
Gladiolus x hortulanus	2-6 in.	4 in.	spring, early fall
Hyacinthus orientalis hybrids	6-7 in. (cover gradually)	6-8 in.	early fall
Iris, Bearded	barely covered	12-18 in.	late summer-early fall
Iris cristata	1 in. or less	3 in.	early fall
Iris, Dutch	3-4 in	4 in.	fall
Iris kaempferi	2 in.	12-15 in.	spring, early fall
Iris, Louisiana	3 in.	12-48 in.	early fall
Iris, Reticulata	4 in.	4 in.	fall
Iris sibirica	2 in.	12-15 in.	fall
Leucojum sp.	3-4 in.	2-4 in.	fall
Lilium sp.	4 in.	12 in.	fall, early spring
Muscari sp.	3 in.	4 in.	late summer-early fall
Narcissus sp.	2-6 in.	8-10 in.	fall
Scilla peruviana	3 in.	8 in.	immediately after flowering
S. siberica	3 in.	3 in.	fall
Tulbaghia sp.	1 in.	8-12 in.	any season
Tulipa sp.	4-6 in.	5-10 in.	fall
Zantedeschia sp.	2-4 in.	12-24 in.	spring, fall
Zephyranthes sp.	2-3 in.	3-6 in.	early fall

Forcing Bulbs

Set bulbs on top of lightweight soil so they are nearly touching; fill in around bulbs with soil, leaving peaks even with top of container. Water well.

To provide the needed cold, bury containers of bulbs after placing in a trench or raised bed outdoors; keep soil moist.

When bulbs have established a good root system and whitish plant sprouts appear, move containers indoors to a cool, well-lit area and keep moist.

Pest Problems and Solutions

Insects, mites, snails and slugs, and diseases are responsible for many, but not all, problems you might have in your garden. Pale, weak growth or skimpy flowering can be caused by poor cultural practices such as improper planting technique, over- or underwatering, overfertilizing, untimely frosts, or air pollution.

Organic controls: When insects and diseases strike, it's not always necessary to resort to chemical warfare. Small infestations can often be controlled by an insecticidal soap or by hosing insects off with a strong stream of water. You can also get rid of some pests, such as caterpillars, weevils, and slugs, by collecting them and dropping them into a jar of rubbing alcohol. Beneficial insects such as ladybug beetles, lacewing flies, praying mantis, and parastic wasps, if not killed off by insecticides, can be helpful in keeping pesty insects under control.

Chemical controls: The many chemical *pesticides* that gardeners can use come in several categories. *Insecticides* kill insects—creatures with 6 legs—such as aphids, beetles, and mealybugs. *Miticides* control spiderlike pests with 8 legs such as spider mites. A *fungicide* is needed for fungus diseases and *bactericides* help keep bacterial infections in check. *Herbicides* kill weeds—they can also harm desirable plants if used incorrectly. And finally, if you're troubled by snails and slugs, you can use a *molluscicide*. *Botanicals* are made from toxic plants; they are considered environmentally safe, but may still harm people and pets. *Systemics* are absorbed by the plant, turning it into a toxic meal.

Safe use: All pesticides are toxic to some degree to pets and people. Read the label thoroughly before use to determine how to use it safely. Chemicals available for home use are rated according to toxicity. "Caution" on the label means it is the safest thing available. However, avoid getting it on your skin or breathing its vapors. "Warning" indicates that the material is fatal if swallowed. Minimal contact with skin or eyes can cause irritation. The most toxic chemicals are labelled "Danger". Swallowing, inhaling, or touching the material can be bad for your health. Wear gloves, a respirator, and goggles when using dangerous chemicals; wash yourself and your clothes afterwards.

Apply pesticides only on windless days. Be sure children and pets are indoors. Measure chemicals with spoons and cups set aside only for their use. Always wash sprayers thoroughly after use and never spray plants with a sprayer that has contained herbicide—any residue may kill your ornamental plants.

Insect Pests

APHIDS

Aphids are small soft-bodied insects, often colored pale green, that damage many kinds of plants by sucking out the plant juices from tender stems, leaves, and flowers. They cause stunted, distorted growth and curled leaves. Aphids secrete honeydew, the medium of growth of sooty mold fungus, which disfigures plants. Honeydew can also drip from infested trees and damage car paint and pavement. These pests reproduce very rapidly and hundreds of them are often seen smothering shoots in spring.

Control: Aphids have many natural enemies, including ladybug beetles and lacewing flies. Rely upon these and other beneficial insects first. Frequent forceful spraying with water dislodges aphids and helps keep their numbers down. Washing plants with insecticidal soap or ordinary dishsoap (1 teaspoon liquid dishsoap per gallon) is even more effective.

Heavy infestations call for insecticides such as nicotine sulfate, malathion, diazinon, Metasystox-R, or dimethoate. In northern areas aphids survive winter in their egg stage. If aphids are an annual springtime problem, spray horticultural-grade oil in late winter to reduce the number of aphid eggs.

BLACK VINE WEEVIL

This serious pest of rhododendrons sometimes troubles azaleas and is serious on other plants including yew and hemlock. The blackish-brown beetle measures 3/8 of an inch long and has a hard shell and no wings. Beetles live in the soil at the bases of the plants and emerge at night to feed on the leaves, chewing characteristic semi-circular notches along the leaf margins.

The worst damage is done however by the larvae, which feed on the roots. These small white, curved grubs destroy the fine root hairs and may also strip the stem of bark. Damage from the larvae causes the plant to wilt even when the soil is moist. If you pull the soil away from the plant's crown, you may be able to observe the root damage.

Larvae feed on roots in early spring, then pupate and emerge as beetles in early summer. Adult beetles feed on leaves for about a month, then lay eggs that soon hatch into larvae. Larvae feed before hibernating for the winter.

Control: Control beetles with three applications of Orthene® or Ficam® spaced about one month apart. Spray when beetle damage is first observed and then in 3 or 4 weeks to kill later-emerging beetles. Follow up with another spraying a month later. Spray both the ground and the area around and under the plant and the lower leaves and branches.

You may also try to control beetles without insecticides. Lay boards on the soil beneath the plant at night. The beetles feed on the leaves while it is dark and will hide under the boards when it is light. Turn over the boards each morning and collect the beetles and any larvae.

BORERS

Borers damage plants by tunneling under the bark, causing structural damage, but more importantly, by destroying water and food-conducting tissues. Twigs, branches, and sometimes the entire plant can be killed, depending upon where the borer tunnels.

Some borers are caterpillars, the larvae of moths, and some are grubs, the larvae of beetles. Most are attracted to plants of low vigor. Wounds such as ragged branch stubs, gouges in tree trunks, or bruises from lawn mowers are common points of entry. The best protective strategy is to keep plants healthy and vigorous.

Dogwood borer: This pest attacks landscape dogwoods, rarely naturalized trees. Wounds and branch crotches are points of entry. Curled wilted leaves in summer and sloughing of loose bark are early symptoms; die-back plus root and trunk suckers are advanced symptoms.

Lesser peach tree borer: Colonizes primarily peach, cherry, and almond in upper parts of tree, crotches, or old wounds. Wilted branches and suckers on trunk or from roots are symptoms.

Lilac borer: Areas of damaged bark are favored sites for egg laying. Sawdustlike material accumulates around exit holes. Wilting even though soil is moist is a common symptom. Branches are structurally weakened and break easily.

Pacific flathead borer: Common west of Rocky Mountains and one of the most significant pests of young trees. Flat-headed apple tree borer is a similar eastern species and also frequently attacks young trees. The strong sap flow of a healthy and vigorously growing tree kills tunneling larvae.

Peach tree borer: Very common. Attacks plants of *Prunus* genus, including flowering peach, cherry, and plum. Lays eggs near ground.

Roundheaded apple tree borer: A significant problem in the northeastern United States. Hosted by mountain ash, shadbush, crab apple, and hawthorn. Eggs laid on trunk near ground.

Control: Protect young and recently transplanted trees by painting the trunks with white latex (never oil-base) paint, or by wrapping trunks with commercially available tree wrap. These steps prevent sunburn, which commonly damages bark and invites borers. Water and fertilize adequately to maintain vigorous growth. Maintain mulched basin around trees to reduce weed and grass competition, improve soil, and reduce probability of bumping trunk with lawn mower. Spray lindane, chlorpyrifos, or carbaryl in early spring—the specific product will include timing and other instructions for specific pests.

CATERPILLARS

Caterpillars are the larvae, an immature feeding stage, of moths and butterflies. Length at maturity varies between 1/2 and 3 inches, and colors may be any imaginable. Some are smooth and others hairy, and many are decorated with tufts of hair or spines. Many caterpillars feed on foliage and are notable pests.

Often a caterpillar's name indicates its habit: leaf rollers, webworms, gypsy moth, catalpa sphinx moth, forest tent caterpillar, inchworm, bagworm, and so on.

Control: Birds and many kinds of parasitic wasps normally keep caterpillar populations in check. Occasionally—gypsy moth is a good example—they get out of control and trees are defoliated if not killed outright.

Many caterpillars, including gypsy moths, can be controlled by spraying a bacteria called *Bacillus thuringiensis*. The bacteria is harmless to people and animals, but infects and quickly kills caterpillars. This biological control is favored by many people over chemical sprays. Effective chemicals are acephate, carbaryl, diazinon, malathion, and methoxychlor.

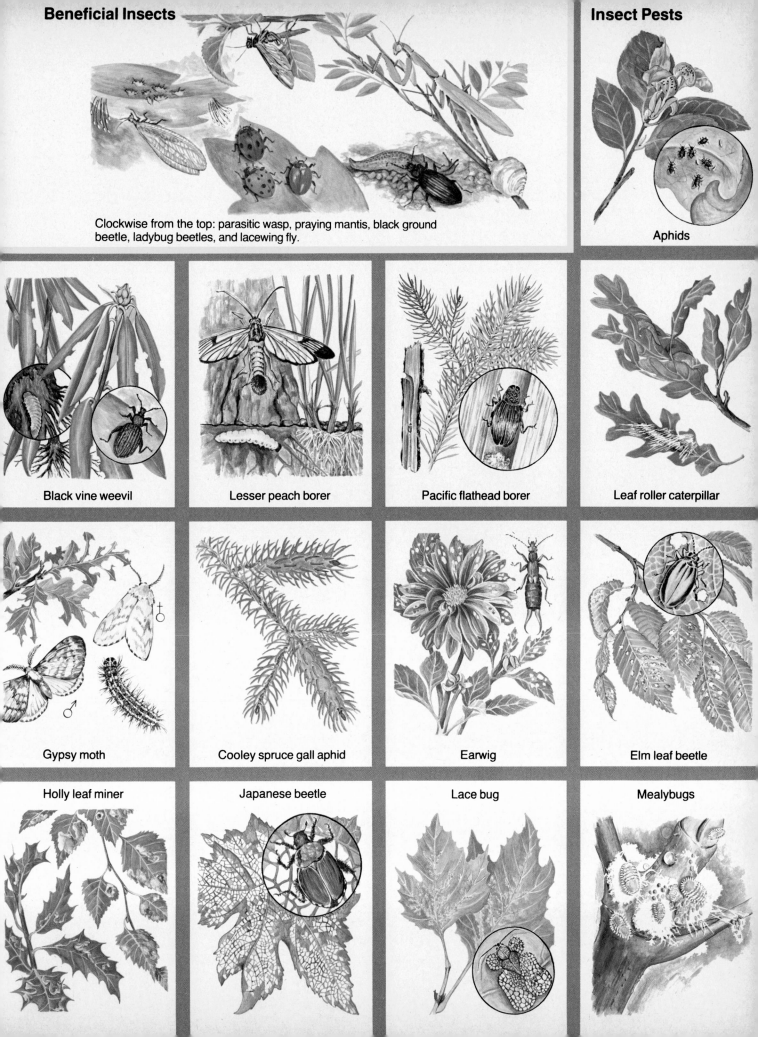

Beneficial Insects

Insect Pests

Clockwise from the top: parasitic wasp, praying mantis, black ground beetle, ladybug beetles, and lacewing fly.

Aphids

Black vine weevil

Lesser peach borer

Pacific flathead borer

Leaf roller caterpillar

Gypsy moth

Cooley spruce gall aphid

Earwig

Elm leaf beetle

Holly leaf miner

Japanese beetle

Lace bug

Mealybugs

COOLEY SPRUCE GALL APHID

Cooley spruce gall aphid can seriously disfigure spruce and Douglas fir, but does not usually damage the health of the trees. Though similar to aphids in many ways, this pest is not a true aphid. Its life cycle is many times more complex than an aphid's, often taking 2 years and requiring two separate kinds of plant for completion.

Immature females overwinter on spruce, mature in early spring, and lay eggs near branch tips. Eggs hatch and "nymphs" begin feeding on new spring growth. Their feeding causes the tree to develop a tumorlike gall that resembles a pineapple to grow around and over them. About midsummer they become winged females and fly to Douglas fir or another spruce to renew the cycle. Eggs laid on Douglas fir hatch into a generation of "woolly aphids" which do not form galls.

Control: Control by spraying bark crevices and bud bases of terminal shoots with a horticultural-grade oil in mid- to late April. Be sure to use a high-grade oil. Oil sprays will wash the blue color from needles of Colorado blue spruce for a short time. Avoid planting spruce and Douglas fir together. Cut out galls before they hatch in midsummer.

EARWIGS

Earwigs, commonly called pincherbugs by many people, have prominent pinchers at the end of their body. They feed primarily on decaying organic matter, and compost piles are one of their favorite homes. However, they also love young, tender foliage and opening blossoms of annuals and perennials. Irregular holes in leaves and flowers are characteristic signs of earwigs. Earwigs are most active at night. They hide in cool, sheltered spots such as under boards or debris during the day.

Control: If you place a rolled-up newspaper in the garden at night, many earwigs will hide in it the next morning and you can dispose of them easily, or use commerical earwig baits that contain baygon, for control.

ELM LEAF BEETLE

This serious pest of many kinds of elm and of Japanese zelkova can completely defoliate trees by midsummer, leaving behind only leaf skeletons of stems and veins. It is a serious pest in towns and cities, since the beetles like to spend the winter in warm dry places such as basements and cellars.

Beetles emerge from their winter hiding places in spring and begin eating small holes in tree leaves. Soon after, they lay clusters of yellow eggs on the leaf undersides. These hatch in about a week into dark yellow larvae striped and spotted with black. The larvae do the worst damage, eating the soft tissue between the veins.

The larvae feed for several weeks, then fall to the ground and pupate, emerging as beetles in a week or two to begin another generation of feeding larvae. Depending upon the region, several generations can reproduce in one growing season, so damage is most severe in mild climates.

Control: Where beetles are a problem, keep adults from overwintering by weatherstripping your house and collecting beetles in fall from your basement. Spray with methoxychlor, acephate, carbaryl, or rotenone when leaves are partially expanded and again in midsummer if neighbors' trees are infested.

HOLLY LEAF MINER

American, English, and Japanese holly, as well as yaupon, are disfigured by leaf miners. The insects responsible are five species of tiny black flies. The flies emerge in spring when new leaves are expanded and feed on them, making tiny pinpricks in the undersides of the foliage. Eggs are laid in the leaves and these hatch into larvae which tunnel into the leaves, causing unsightly brown blotches.

Control: Spray foliage with diazinon or dimethoate when adult flies are active, or spray with Metasystox-R or dimethoate in summer to kill larvae.

JAPANESE BEETLE

This very destructive beetle was imported from Japan to New Jersey about 1912 and it is now one of the most damaging and annoying pests in the Atlantic Coast States. Some 200 to 300 plants are damaged by Japanese beetles. Among its most favored plants are little-leaf linden, Boston ivy, Virginia creeper, and roses.

Japanese beetles spend winter as soil grubs below the frost line. In spring, they feed on grass roots, and shortly thereafter pupate near the soil surface. Adults emerge from the soil in early summer—about late May in North Carolina and early July in New Hampshire. Adults feed during daylight, preferring warm days and sunny locations.

They live for 1 to 1-1/2 months so are most abundant during the months of July and August. After mating they deposit eggs several inches deep in the soil. Tiny grubs hatch after 2 weeks and feed on grass roots until cold weather forces them deeper into the soil.

Control: The natural microbial insecticide *Bacillus popilliae*, milky spore disease, has been available for many years. If applied to soils community-wide and given a season or two to become established, it will significantly lower Japanese beetle populations. Do not use chemical soil insecticides after applying milky spore disease.

Traps that contain an attractant and effectively lure and capture adult beetles are very useful. Locate traps as far as possible from host plants so that beetles are not drawn to the plants.

Recommended insecticides include carbaryl, methoxychlor, and diazinon. Soil applications of diazinon or trichlorfon from mid-July through August will reduce the number of grubs.

Oyster scale

San Jose scale

Spider mites

Thrips

Plant Diseases

Whiteflies

Azalea petal blight

Botrytis

Cedar-apple rust

Chlorosis

Damping-off

Fireblight

Mildew

Rhododendron root rot

Scab

Soil rot

Verticillium wilt

LACE BUG

These pests can be especially severe on azaleas and rhododendrons. Tiny nymphs (immature insects) and mature fly-like insects, which are 1/8 inch long with lacy wings, feed on the undersides of the leaves, sucking the sap. The damage is unsightly and the plant's vigor is reduced by heavy infestations.

Damage first appears in spring as white specks or blotches on the tops of the leaves. The undersides have rusty-colored varnish-like spots. Several generations of lace bugs can be produced during each growing season, developing into a serious problem as the season progresses.

Control: Lace bugs are most troublesome in the East and South and on plants grown in full sun. Providing shade will reduce infestations. Sprays of carbaryl, malathion, Ficam®, or Metasystox-R® will control insects. Apply as soon as symptoms are noticed; repeat in several weeks. Be sure to wet leaf undersides.

MEALYBUGS

Mealybugs are soft-bodied and covered with a cottony fluff. They make visible white clusters in branch crotches, leaf undersides, or similar protected locations and damage many kinds of plants by sucking their sap. Mealybugs also secrete honeydew, which can encourage black sooty mold fungus. (See Aphids.)

Control: Mealybugs are subject to many predators and parasites. *Cryptolaemus* beetle, a kind of ladybug beetle, and lacewing larvae are two excellent predators. Both are available commercially. Insecticidal soap is also effective. Use insecticides acephate, malathion, diazinon, or nicotine sulfate to bring a severe outbreak under control.

SCALE

Scale are small insects protected by a soft or hard shell; they attach themselves in clusters to stems and leaves. They damage many kinds of plants by sucking their juices. Scales move only during the *crawler* stage in spring. Once crawlers are established, they form a shell under which they feed and reproduce.

There are many kinds of scale and two main types, *soft* and *armored*. Shells of soft scale are an integral part of the pest, like a turtle's shell. Only soft scale secretes honeydew (see Aphids) that encourages sooty mold and attracts ants.

Control: Sprays of horticultural-grade oil in spring are most effective. Be sure to check the label for plants damaged by oil sprays, timing, and proper rates. Crawlers, which are active in late spring, are susceptible to sprays of diazinon, dimethoate, and acephate.

SLUGS AND SNAILS

These common garden pests hide in cool, moist locations during the day and do most of their feeding at night. Both damage plants by eating leaves. They chew both leaf edges and centers. They are most serious in rainy seasons or moist climates.

Control: Keep snails and slugs under control by using one or all of the following methods.

Eliminate as many of their hiding places—bricks, boards, containers, and rocks—as possible. Walk through the garden at night with a flashlight, or during the day after a rain, and look for slugs and snails to pick up and dispose of.

Manufactured traps that attract slugs and snails are available. Poison baits are most useful in spring and fall when the numbers of slugs and snails are greatest. Scatter baits containing metaldehyde or Mesurol® as label directs. Be sure to spread bait along migration borders, such as between ground cover and lawn.

SPIDER MITES

Spider mites are tiny pests that damage plants by sucking plant juices. You'll need a magnifying glass to see them clearly though sometimes they spin tiny, visible webs. They live and work on leaf undersides and produce a yellow, stippled effect on leaf topsides.

Spruce, fir, pine, arborvitae, juniper, hypericum, holly, citrus, and pyracantha are often colonized by spider mites as are many other plants growing in hot, dry locations.

Control: Dusty leaves encourage mites (or discourage their predators), so keeping plants clean by frequent hosing helps. Predators of mites include lacewing larvae and predatory mites, both available from commercial insectaries.

Horticultural oil, Kelthane®, and insecticidal soaps are the recommended sprays. Dusting sulfur also effectively controls mites.

THRIPS

Thrips are significant pests of citrus, Indian laurel fig (*Ficus retusa*), and privet. They cause leaves to curl, which hides the thrips from sight and sprays. Citrus thrips make a circular-to-spiral-shaped scar around the fruits and may even cause young fruits to drop. Leaves of Indian laurel fig drop prematurely. Privet leaves are puckered and gray. (Note: Indian laurel figs—especially those in containers—also drop leaves as a response to environmental shock, usually too much or too little water.)

Thrips can also be troublesome on many annuals, perennials, and bulbs (especially gladiolus). Look for silvery flecks or mottling on leaves and flowers that gradually turn brown. If the infection is severe, flower buds can become distorted. Thrips will also infect dormant bulbs, roughing up their surface and turning them sticky and brown. Avoid planting infected bulbs and dust gladiolus with malathion before storing.

Control: Systemic insecticides are the most effective remedy. Apply granular disulfoton to soil, or liquid sprays of dimethoate, acephate, or Metasystox-R® to foliage. If you plan to harvest citrus fruit, do not use a systemic insecticide. Instead, use diazinon immediately after blossoms drop.

Insecticides and Miticides

Chemical Name	Trade Name	Use
acephate	Orthene®	Aphids, bagworms, gypsy moth, lace bugs, scales, whiteflies, tent caterpillars, root weevil.
Bacillus popilliae	Doom®, Japidemic®	Non-toxic, microbial. Affects only Japanese beetle grubs.
Bacillus thuringiensis	Dipel®, Thuricide®, Biotrol®	Non-toxic, microbial. Affects only caterpillars.
carbaryl	Sevin®	Bagworm, birch leaf miners, elm leaf beetles, lace bugs.
chlorpyrifos	Dursban®	Aphids, cutworms, thrips, lilac borers.
diazinon	Spectracide®	Whiteflies, bagworms, many other pests.
dicofol	Kelthane®	Spider mites.
dimethoate	Cygon®	Systemic. Leaf miners, aphids, pine needle scale, whiteflies.
disulfoton	Di-Syston®	Systemic. Aphids, birch leaf miner, pine needle scale.
lindane	Lindane®	Borers.
malathion	Cythion®	Aphids, bagworms, leaf miners, whiteflies.
methiocarb	Mesurol®	Slugs and snails.
metaldehyde	rnany	Slugs and snails.
methoxychlor	Marlate®	Cankerworms, whiteflies, gypsy moths, elm leaf beetles.
nicotine sulfate	Black Leaf 40®	Botanical. Aphids, thrips, leafhoppers.
oil	Horticultural Oil, Superior Oil	Aphids, mites, mealybugs, soft and some armored scales.
oxydemeton methyl	Metasystox-R®	Systemic. Aphids, birch leaf miners, mites, whiteflies, pine needle scale.
pyrethrins	many	Botanical. Whiteflies.
resmethrin	Chryson®, Sythrin®	Synthetic. Whiteflies.
soap	Insecticidal soap	Non-toxic. Aphids, whiteflies, mites.
trichlorfon	Pylox®	Gypsy moths, Japanese beetle grubs.

Fungicides and Bactericides

Chemical Name	Trade Name	Use
benomyl	Benlate®	Systemic. Powdery mildew, botrytis, damping off, and other soil rots.
captan	Orthocide®	Apple scab, damping off, botrytis, and other soil rots.
ferbam	Carbamate®	Apple rust and scab.
"fixed" copper	Cuprocide®	Powdery mildew. (Injures apple leaves.)
folpet	Phaltan®	Apple scab.
lime sulfur	Dormant Disease Control	Mildew, apple scab.
PCNB	Terrachlor®	Controls several root, stem, and crown rot diseases
streptomycin	Agri-Strep®, Agrimycin®	Fireblight of apple and pear.
sulfur	Flotox® garden sulfur	Powdery mildew, rust, apple scab.
thiram	Arasan®	Apple scab, rust, dampening off
turban	many, including Turban®	Azalea petal blight and root rot.
triforine	Funginex®	Mildew.
zineb	Dithane Z-78®	Azalea petal blight.

WHITEFLY

Whiteflies damage many trees, shrubs, vines, and flowers, including fuchsia, hibiscus, lantana, azalea, and citrus. Adults are pure white, about 1/8 inch long and cluster on leaf undersides. They swarm into the air when disturbed, then return. Immature whiteflies do the most damage, sucking plant juices and causing leaves to yellow and sometimes die.

Control: Effective control of whiteflies has eluded more than one careful gardener. Doing absolutely nothing—allowing nature's predators and parasites to do their job—is often the best approach. It is now possible to supplement nature by buying eggs of the whitefly parasite *Encarsia formosa*. This is an excellent control in enclosed areas such as greenhouses.

Horticultural-grade oils are an important phase in whitefly control. Applied during the growing season as a curative, it can be highly effective. However, be sure any plant you spray is listed on the product label as tolerant of oil sprays.

Insecticidal soaps and even ordinary liquid dish soap (1 teaspoon per gallon) provide some relief. The botanical insecticide pyrethrin or its synthetic analog, resmethrin, are safe and effective. Acephate, methoxychlor, and dimethoate are standard, proven controls.

Plant Diseases

AZALEA/RHODODENDRON PETAL BLIGHT

This devastating disease can wipe out azalea flowers seemingly overnight. (Rhododendrons may also be infected.) The fungus starts as tiny white pin-pricks on the petals (brown spots on white flowers), and by the next day the blossoms are reduced to a slimy mass. The blight is serious in the South and occurs in other eastern areas where high humidity and warm days encourage the fungus.

Control: Petal blight is spread by rain splashing the fungus spores from the soil onto the plants. Cleaning up any blighted petals and not allowing them to drop to the ground will help control the disease. In areas where the blight is severe, it is necessary to drench the soil with Terrachlor® or Turban® before blooming and to spray the flowers with thiram or zineb. Use a fine spray mist. Apply the fungicide three times a week beginning when the buds show color. The blight is worse on mid- and late season azaleas, since spores are not active when early azaleas bloom.

BOTRYTIS (Gray Mold)

This is another fungus disease that is particularly troublesome in warm, humid weather. It attacks annuals, perennials, and bulbs, usually infecting spent flowers and old foliage. It begins with yellowish-orange to red or brown circular spots that gradually develop a slimy grayish fuzz. If it infects stems, it usually causes a portion of the plant to collapse.

Control: Fungicides such as benomyl and captan will help control botrytis. Also, avoid planting bulbs that show characteristic lesions, don't overhead water, and remove diseased plants or plant parts promptly.

CEDAR-APPLE RUST

This fungus disease causes bizarre-looking bright orange growths on eastern and western red cedars and other members of the genus *Juniperus,* and it can cause poor fruit quality and premature leaf drop on apples, native crab apples (Asian species are not affected), and hawthorns. The fungus needs both cedar and apple to complete its life cycle.

Control: One method of control is to keep the two kinds of plants separated by several hundred yards. In some states, it is unlawful to plant cedars within a mile of commercial apple orchards. Galls may be picked from cedars before they mature. Spray apples and crab apples with ferbam or zineb immediately after flowers fade.

CHLOROSIS

Chlorosis is a deficiency disease caused by an inadequate supply of iron or manganese in leaves. Diseased plants can't make the green pigment chlorophyll and leaves become yellow with green veins. Chlorosis is common to "acid-loving" flowering shrubs such as azalea, rhododendron, citrus, gardenia, and camellia. Bottlebrush and acacia occasionally suffer from chlorosis, as do yew and arborvitae.

Soil that is unusually cold in spring or waterlogged prevents optimum root activity and often causes chlorosis. Some evergreens are chlorotic in early spring, then green-up as weather and soil warm.

Roots of rhododendrons and azaleas are especially poor extractors of iron from soil. Soil that is very acid (see page 288) eases iron extraction, one reason these plants require acid soil.

Solution: Iron (or manganese) in chelate form most effectively corrects iron chlorosis. You will find chelated iron at your garden center with trade names Sequestrene 330 FE and Versenol FL among others.

Apply chelated iron to soil and spray on foliage in spring just before growth starts, then perhaps two more times through midsummer or as leaf color dictates. Correct soil acidity.

DAMPING-OFF

Several soil micro-organisms cause a disease called damping-off, which affects young seedlings. The common symptom is that seedlings rot near the soil surface, wilt, and fall over. However, the fungus can also affect seedlings before they emerge from the ground.

Control: To help avoid damping-off, drench your germination medium with a fungicide such as benomyl and avoid overwatering.

FIREBLIGHT

This bacterial disease destroys many plants in the rose family, including apple, cotoneaster, crab apple, hawthorn, pear, pyracantha, and quince. The bacteria overwinters in sunken cankers on twigs and branches and is spread to flowers in spring by rain or insects. It quickly works its way into the flowers and twigs, clogging the conducting vessels and causing the blossoms and twigs to wilt. Wilted leaves and twigs die, looking scorched and turning brown to black, and hang onto the branches.

Control: Diseased twigs and branches should be pruned away as soon as they are noticed. The bacteria usually spreads into live wood, so cut 4 to 7 inches beyond the blackened area. With each cut, dip pruning shears into a coffee can of bleach to sterilize the tool and prevent spreading the disease. Rinse shears with water when the job is done to prevent corrosion.

To prevent infection of flowers, spray with agricultural-grade streptomycin or fixed copper every 4 or 5 days throughout the flowering season.

MILDEW

This fungus disease covers leaves of many plants, such as lilac, euonymus, crape myrtle, many annuals and perennials, and grape, with a white coating. Unlike many fungus diseases, mildew doesn't need a film of water to begin growth. High humidity is enough. In arid regions where cool nights follow warm days, humidity soars at night and mildew can be a common problem. In other areas, cool springs and crisp falls, as well as crowded or shaded areas where air circulation is bad, encourage mildew.

Control: Sulfur dust and lime-sulfur sprays are traditional cures. Benlate® is effective, and triforine is useful only for plants noted on the label.

RHODODENDRON OR AZALEA ROOT ROT

Rhododendrons and azaleas can suffer from root rot, caused by the widespread fungus *Phytophthora cinnamomi,* during warm wet summers if they are grown in slowly draining soil. Roots and then stems rot. The first observable symptom is wilted yellowing leaves that hang onto the plant. The plant may die soon after wilting is first noticed. If you cut into the stem of a plant with root rot, you will notice reddish streaks under the bark caused by the fungus.

Control: Root rot is difficult to cure because once symptoms are noticed it's too late to apply fungicide. The best prevention is to plant shrubs in well-aerated, fast-draining soil. If rhododendrons and azaleas die of root rot, do not replant in the same spot without first improving soil drainage.

SCAB

Scab is a serious leaf and fruit fungus of crab apple, pear, hawthorn, and mountain ash. Favored by wet and cool weather, the disease can ruin the fruit and progress to defoliating the tree. In dry climates the disease is rarely a problem.

Symptoms begin in spring as new leaves expand. Circular spots on leaves are dark green at first, eventually turning black. Developing fruit show similar symptoms at first, then become rough and "scabby".

Control: Plant disease-resistant varieties. During the dormant season, just before growth begins, spray with lime sulfur. Spray at 10-day intervals with wettable sulfur or captan beginning when flower buds show color and ending approximately one month after petal fall.

SOIL ROTS

Warm weather, frequent rainfall or overwatering, and poorly drained soils promote soil rots that affect many plants. This is a particularly troublesome problem in the Deep South. Many bulbs, such as gladiolus, that can be left in the ground year-round in dry climates, must be dug and stored in warm, humid areas or they may rot. Signs of soil rot include yellowish, stunted foliage growth, and mushy or dry areas on underground bulbs. Many perennials and annuals are also affected, showing similar yellowish, unhealthy looking growth. Affected plants will eventually die.

Control: The best way to prevent such rots is to plant in quick-draining, well aerated soil, with ample organic matter, and avoid overwatering. Dust bulbs with a fungicide such as captan before planting, then dig and store them properly after flowering.

TEXAS ROOT ROT (COTTON ROOT ROT)

Pear, eucalyptus, and oleander are just a few of the plants susceptible to this devastating root-rotting disease. Many fruits, vegetables, and ornamental trees and shrubs—as well as cotton—are attacked.

Texas root rot occurs in southwestern United States in the summer and is severe in heavy, alkaline soil. During hot summer months the fungus grows quickly through the soil and penetrates roots of susceptible plants. Within one summer season, roots are invaded and decayed by the fungus. Bark of dead roots is brownish, and woolly strands of light brown fungus are evident on the root surface. Extensive root death causes leaves to wilt and infected plants die fast.

Control: There is no sure way to stop the disease's progress once established. The best defense is to plant resistant trees.

A soil acidifying treatment developed by University of Arizona pathologist Robert Streets can stop the fungus. Spread ammonium sulfate fertilizer at a rate of 1 pound for every 10 square feet over the root zone, extending slightly beyond the drip line. Water it into the soil to a depth of 3 feet. Also remove about 25 percent of all branches with wilted leaves. For these treatments to be successful, early diagnosis is essential.

VERTICILLIUM (MAPLE) WILT

This common fungus disease attacks many different kinds of plants. Silver maple (*Acer saccharinum*) is perhaps most notably susceptible. Sugar maple (*A. saccharum*), red maple (*A. rubrum*), elms (*Ulmus* species), ash (*Fraxinus* species), beech (*Fagus* species), camphor (*Cinnamomum camphora*), magnolia (*Magnolia* species), and tulip tree (*Liriodendron tulipifera*) are also affected.

The disease is caused by *Verticillium dahliae*, a long-lived, soil-borne fungus. The typical symptom in maple is sudden, midsummer wilt of a large branch or one section of the tree. If you peel the bark of a wilted branch, greenish streaks beneath the bark indicate the problem is verticillium wilt. On elms symptoms are difficult to distinguish from Dutch elm disease.

Control: Maples sometimes may be saved by removing the infected branch. Tools should be disinfected by dipping into bleach. It is often wiser to remove and replace the tree with a non-susceptible species.

If verticillium wilt is a problem in your area, plant resistant trees and shrubs. Yews (*Taxus* species) and other conifers are immune. Birch (*Betula* species), hawthorn (*Crataegus* species), ginkgo (*Ginkgo biloba*), crab apple (*Malus* species), and sycamore (*Platanus* species) show some resistance.

WHITE PINE BLISTER RUST

This fungus disease can destroy most of the pines known as the "white" pines—those pines with 5 needles to each cluster. Specific white pines susceptible to blister rust include Japanese white pine (*Pinus parviflora*) and eastern white pine (*Pinus strobus*).

The fungus needs two different plant hosts to complete its life cycle: a susceptible pine and a shrub in the genus *Ribes*, usually currant or gooseberry. Spores from pine can only infect *Ribes* and vice versa.

The common early symptom is a branch with dead red-brown needles that was killed by a girdling canker. Sap flows from around the canker. Gradually the infection spreads until a canker surrounds the main trunk; needles throughout the tree fade to a pale yellow-green and the tree dies.

Control: Effective disease control comes with removal of all black currants (red currants are less susceptible) and gooseberries within a 900-foot radius of the susceptible tree. This interrupts the fungus life cycle and prevents it from infecting trees. If the disease is prevalent in an area, plant only resistant pines.

Infected trees can sometimes be saved by removing branches with cankers as soon as possible. Cut small cankers out of the main trunk, removing 1 inch of bark beyond the canker margin. Remove the tree if a canker extends more than halfway around the main trunk.

Index

Plants are indexed both by their common and their Latin, or botanical, names. Page numbers in bold type indicate the main entry for a plant; page numbers in italics refer to photographs. Along with page numbers, every common name entry also includes the Latin name of the plant.